P9-BYB-666

EUROPE

NORTHERN EUROPE
120

THE LOW COUNTRIES
100

UNITED KINGDOM AND IRELAND
88

WESTERN CENTRAL EUROPE
104

EASTERN EUROPE
116

FRANCE
96

SOUTHEASTERN EUROPE
112

SPAIN AND PORTUGAL
92

ITALY
108

RUSSIA
126

EUROPE
92
(see inset)

CENTRAL ASIA
132

WESTERN ASIA
130

EASTERN ASIA
148

JAPAN
152

THE MIDDLE EAST
136

Ryukyu Islands
153

THE PACIFIC OCEAN
26

NORTHERN AFRICA
158

SOUTHERN ASIA
140

Mariana Islands
172

Micronesia
172

Marshall Islands
172

Maldives
141

SOUTHEAST ASIA
144

THE PACIFIC ISLANDS
172

SOUTHERN AFRICA
162

THE INDIAN OCEAN
30

AUSTRALIA AND PAPUA NEW GUINEA
168

NEW ZEALAND
172

ANTARCTICA
32

The Children's
World
Atlas

Copyright © 2004 by Weldon Owen Inc.

This 2007 revised and expanded edition published by
Barnes & Noble Publishing, Inc.,
by arrangement with Weldon Owen Inc.

All rights reserved. No part of this book
may be used or reproduced in any manner
whatsoever without the written permission
of the Publisher.

Barnes & Noble Publishing, Inc.
122 Fifth Avenue
New York, NY 10011

ISBN-13: 978-0-7607-9309-1
ISBN-10: 0-7607-9309-3

Printed and bound in Singapore

 04 05 06 07 08 MCH 10 9 8 7 6 5 4 3 2 1

Library of Congress Cataloging-in-Publication Data available upon request.

The Children's
World
Atlas

BARNES & NOBLE

NEW YORK

Contents

How to use this atlas

Map Pages

Illustrations
Illustrations and captions show and describe places, people, wildlife and activities in the area.

Grid reference
The letters and numbers on the border are the key to finding places listed in the gazetteer.

Gazetteer
The gazetteer, starting on page 184, lists a letter and number for each place.

Location map

Continent

Map area

Flag and facts
The flag, population and capital city of each country on the map are shown here. The countries are listed by the size of their population.

Inset map
This is a place linked to the main map but outside the map area.

United States of America

UNITED STATES OF AMERICA
POPULATION 299,398,000 · CAPITAL WASHINGTON D.C.

Frontier wagon trail
People set off on the long trail from the east to the far west for a number of reasons. Economic collapse and rising unemployment in the east, religious freedom, or the lure of California gold encouraged many to head west.

Abraham Lincoln's House
Abraham Lincoln, 16th President of the USA, lived with his family in this house in Springfield, Illinois. Built in 1844, the house was enlarged with a second story in 1856 to accommodate the Lincoln's growing family of four sons.

Liberty Bell
The bell was cast in London and arrived in Philadelphia in 1752. The most famous occasion it rang was to celebrate the Declaration of Independence on July 4, 1776.

Native Americans
Tribes of Native Americans lived in all parts of North America. The landscape determined how they lived. Coastal tribes ate mainly fish. Tribes around the Great Lakes cleared the forest to plant corn and tobacco, while tribes on the plains hunted buffalo.

Plains Indians
The Plains Indians followed the buffalo herds and were often on the move. They trained wild horses and were expert horsemen. Children as young as five years old rode their own horses.

Statue of Liberty
The Statue of Liberty was presented to the people of the USA by the French in 1886. It took nine years to make the statue, which is an international symbol of refuge and democracy.

Bald eagle

American football
American football started in schools and colleges in the 1800s. It is now America's favorite winter game.

American alligator

Inside this starburst is a world record held by the area covered by the map, or an important fact about the area.

Regional map
This physical map shows landscape features, cities, towns and roads.

Scale bar
The scale bar makes it possible to calculate distances on the map.

Compass
The compass shows the way the map is facing.

THEMATIC MAP

Life zones

CONTINENT OPENER

Europe

CONTINENT COLORS

North America

South America

Europe

Asia

Africa

Oceania

MAP SYMBOLS

Capital city	■ **PARIS**
State capital	● **DES MOINES**
Major city	● **San Francisco**
Town	● Grand Rapids
Point of interest	★ *Grand Canyon*
▲ Mountain	Major border
▲ Sea mountain	State border
■ Arctic base	Disputed border
+ Pole	Line of control
Lake	Metropolis
River	Highway
	Main road

Fact File Pages

Fact File Pages

Quirky fact
This is a snippet of surprising or unusual information about the region.

Categories
The information in the fact file is divided into five categories, marked by blue banners.

Illustrations
Illustrations and photographs support the text entries.

Feature panel
Selected topics of interest are treated in more depth in colored feature panels.

History panel
This provides a timeline of events or a snapshot of a region's history.

Location finder
- Continent
- Map area

Land use image
This provides further information about how the land is used.

Inset map
This is an area linked to the region but outside the area of the main map.

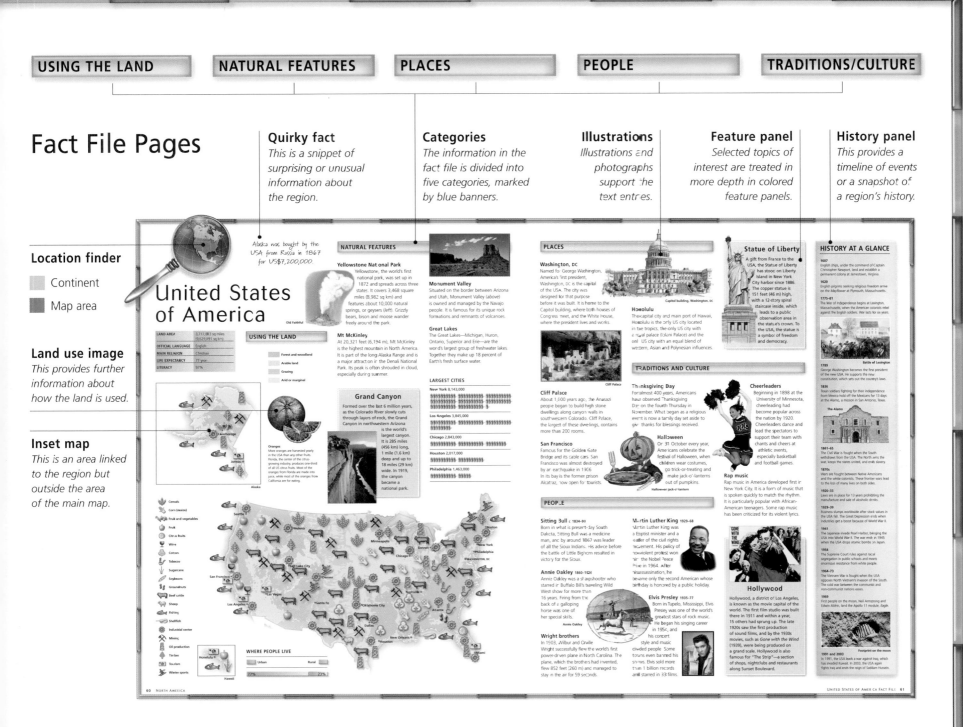

LAND USE

The colors of the map depict the different types of land in the region.

- Forest and woodland
- Arable land
- Grazing
- Arid or marginal

MAP ICONS

These symbols show how the land is used. They include farming, industry, mining and tourism.

- Cereals
- Rice
- Wheat
- Barley
- Corn (maize)
- Flax
- Jute
- Potatoes
- Fruit and vegetables
- Fruit
- Vegetables
- Citrus fruits
- Bananas
- Wine
- Cotton
- Coffee
- Tea
- Cocoa
- Tobacco
- Sugarcane
- Sugar beet
- Flowers
- Coconuts
- Groundnuts
- Dates
- Palm oil
- Olives
- Rubber
- Oilseed rape
- Beef cattle
- Dairy cattle
- Sheep
- Poultry
- Pigs
- Goats
- Reindeer
- Fishing
- Whaling
- Shellfish
- Industrial center
- Mining
- Oil production
- Gas production
- Timber
- Tourism
- Winter sports

FACT FILE STATISTICS

LAND AREA	3,717,813 sq miles (9,629,091 sq km)
OFFICIAL LANGUAGE	English
MAIN RELIGION	Christian
LIFE EXPECTANCY	77 years
LITERACY	97%

This panel contains statistics about the country or region. If the fact file is about a region, the statistics of the countries in the region are combined.

POPULATION

LARGEST CITIES

New York 8,143,000

These diagrams show the population of the main cities in the region. Each figure represents 100,000 people.

URBAN AND RURAL

WHERE PEOPLE LIVE

- Urban
- Rural

75% 25%

This graph shows the percentage of people who live in urban and rural areas. If there are more than six countries in the region, the graphs show the countries with the highest and lowest percentages in the area and the regional average.

RIVERS AND MOUNTAINS

LONGEST RIVERS

Loire 634 miles (1,020 km)

HIGHEST MOUNTAINS

Mt Logan 19,551 feet (5,959 m)
Mt St Elias 18,009 feet (5,489 m)
Mt Lucania 17,146 feet (5,226 m)
King Peak 16,972 feet (5,173 m)

Where we live

Earth's 6 billion people are not spread evenly around the planet. Most live where resources are plentiful or can easily be obtained by trading. Therefore, few people live in deserts or polar regions, but many live in fertile areas close to energy sources, and near coasts and rivers. As the lights in the photograph below show, the continents of Europe and North America, and parts of Asia, are densely populated. Australia, Africa and South America are less densely populated, and most of their people live along the coast. The River Nile can be seen in Egypt. The image was made by combining information gathered by satellites over a period of nine months.

US–Mexico border
When seen from space, our planet looks very different. This satellite image, which has been artificially colored, clearly shows the contrast between developed and less-developed farmland. At the top, in red, are the gridded and irrigated fields of California's Imperial Valley in the USA, north of the border with Mexico. Below, in blue, are Mexico's less-developed farmlands. The border town of Mexicali-Caliexico is in the center of the photo.

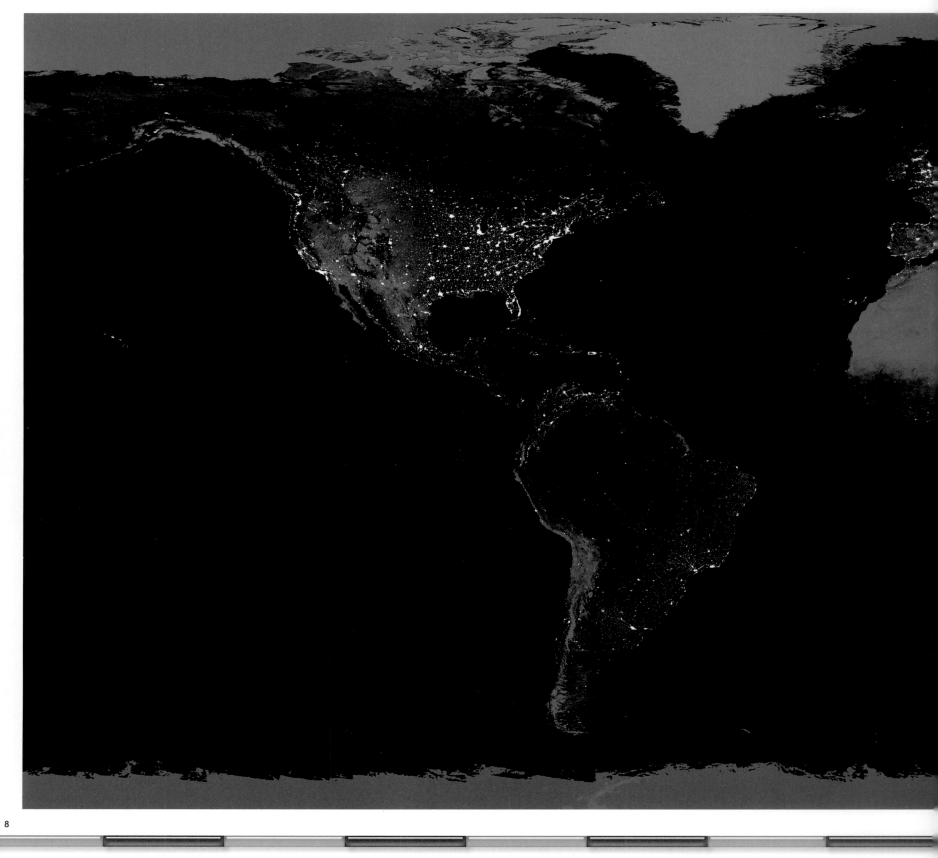

Istanbul, Turkey

In this view of Istanbul (*left*), city areas are blue-green and vegetation is red. Dividing the city is the busy shipping channel of the Bosporus, spanned by two bridges. The image also shows water depth—colder water is a deeper shade of blue.

Tokyo, Japan

Tokyo, with its surrounds, is the largest city in the world. In this view (*right*), the buildings (in blue) spread over a huge distance. The vegetation is colored red. Three rivers can be seen, as well as Tokyo's port area. The block-shaped islands are reclaimed land.

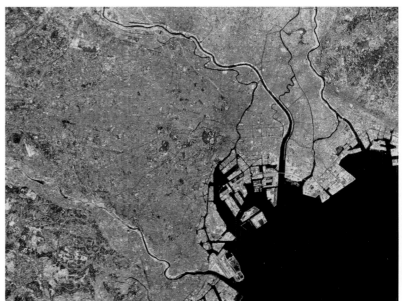

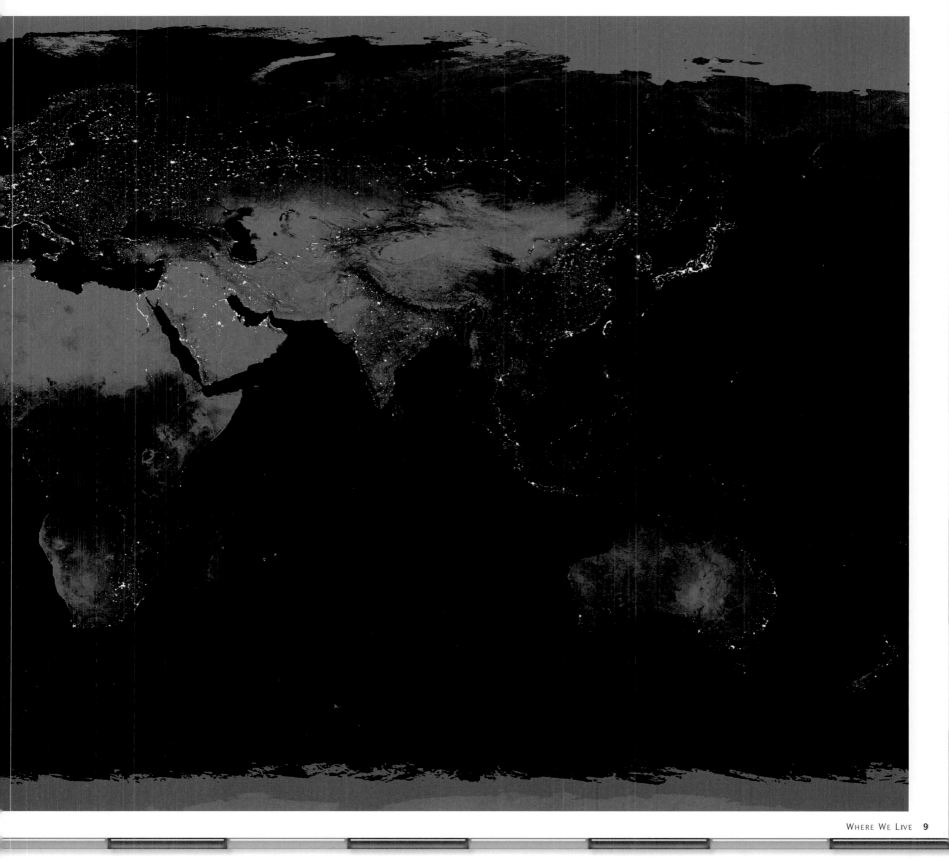

World weather

Since 1960, satellites orbiting high in the sky have sent back to Earth images of land and ocean, clouds and storms. Scientists now rely on these images to monitor the weather and predict how it will change. In the image below, taken from satellites 440 miles (700 km) above Earth, clouds swirl over the landmasses. The tropical region, around the Equator, is less cloudy than the areas to the north and south. The Sahara Desert in northern Africa and the dry lands of the Middle East can be seen, as well as the forests of South America. Greenland is the large white shape at the top. The light blue areas are seas and lakes.

Hurricanes

Hurricanes—also known as cyclones and typhoons—are powerful storms that produce winds of up to 150 miles an hour (250 km/h). These winds, and the heavy rain that follows, can cause enormous damage. Satellite images show hurricanes forming, and scientists can track their progress as they move toward land. This enables them to warn people of the coming danger. This image shows Hurricane Fran as it nears the east coast of the USA in 1996.

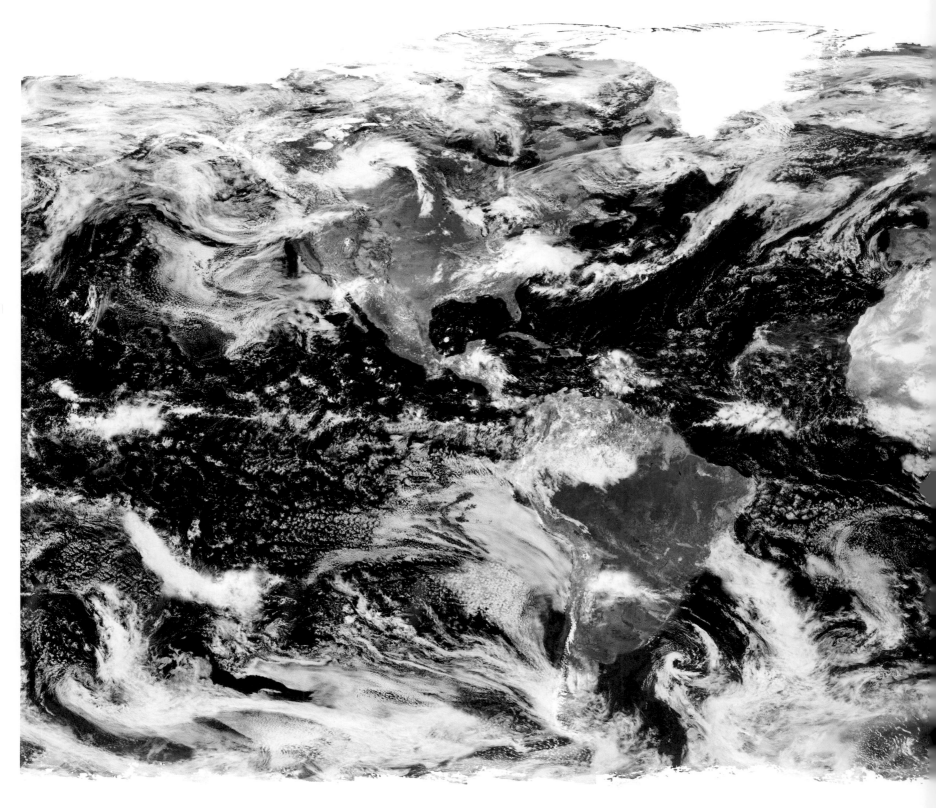

El Niño

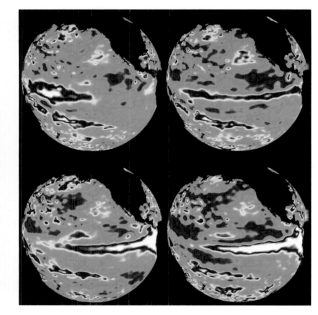

El Niño is an ocean current that develops off the coast of Peru every year. In some years, it flows much farther south than usual. This changes the temperature of the ocean, and produces extreme weather, such as droughts and flooding rains, over a wide area. These satellite images show El Niño developing in the Pacific Ocean over a six-month period. Landmasses are black and El Niño is the red and white tongue moving westward along the Equator.

1985

1990

Ozone ho e

Antarctica

A "hole" in the sky

Ozone is a gas high in the atmosphere that absorbs most of the harmful rays from the Sun, and prevents heat from being lost from Earth. Since the 1980s, the amount of ozone over Antarctica has declined. The dark shades of blue show the growth of the ozone hole since 1985. The 2000 hole was the largest ever recorded—about three times the size of the USA.

2000

Earth's patterns

Photographs from space show things that cannot be seen on land. Many satellite images are artificially colored to make them clearer. They provide a large-scale view of natural events, such as volcanic eruptions, wildfires, dust storms, droughts and floods. They show how our cities are growing, and how our forests are disappearing. Using radar, satellites can "see" below the Sahara Desert to the rocks beneath. The view from space is now a vital tool in agricultural planning and weather forecasting. Satellite images help scientists understand how Earth's climate has changed over millions of years. And, as these pages show, they make interesting patterns.

Coastline, Guinea-Bissau
In this view of the coastline of Guinea-Bissau, in western Africa (*left*), the blue ribbons are rivers. The light blue areas are silt that has been deposited into the Atlantic Ocean at the bottom of the image.

Reservoir, Brazil
The Represa Três Marias winds across southeastern Brazil (*below*). This reservoir was built in 1960 to generate hydroelectric power for the state of Minas Gerais.

Grand Canyon, USA
Snow lies on the north and south rims of the Grand Canyon, Arizona (*above*). The canyon, the largest in the world, was carved out by the Colorado River. The image shows the lack of vegetation around this dramatic landform. The canyon's south rim, on the left of the photograph, is 1 mile (1.6 km) above its floor.

Comet scarring, Sahara
A comet slammed into the Sahara Desert millions of years ago and left the circular scars seen in this image (*left*).

Rain forest, Brazil
Brazil's remaining forest appears as bright red, while dark areas are cleared land, and black and gray patches are recently burned areas (*right*).

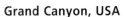

Mississippi River, USA
The Mississippi River (*left*) enters the Gulf of Mexico and dumps a load of silt that it has carried on its long journey through the Great Plains. The silt forms a delta at the river's mouth.

Fjords, Norway
Several of Norway's fjords—steep, narrow inlets from the sea—can be seen in this view of the southern part of the country (*right*).

Volcano, New Zealand
The snow-capped peak of volcanic Mt Taranaki (*below*) towers over the surrounding forest. It last erupted in 1755.

Malaspina Glacier, USA
The Malaspina Glacier, shown in light blue, fans out between Icy Bay and Yakutat Bay in Alaska (*right*). The red ridged area is a moraine, or deposit of rocks, that has built up as the glacier moved toward the sea. The moraine prevents the glacier from reaching the ocean, shown as a dark blue area at the bottom of the image.

Planet Earth

Earth is a giant ball of rock, just one of the many bodies that travel around the Sun. It was born about 4.6 billion years ago, when a swirling cloud of gas and dust gradually turned into the solar system. Inside the young Earth, radioactive materials began to decay and heat up. Rocks started to melt, with heavier metals sinking to the center, leaving lighter minerals on top. Eventually, Earth settled into four main layers—a thin rocky crust on the surface; a partly molten layer of rock called the mantle beneath the crust; an outer core of liquid iron and nickel; and an inner core of solid iron and nickel. Reaching temperatures of 5,400°F (3,000°C), the core is still extremely hot. This intense heat drives movements of the surface rocks and forms many of Earth's features.

Birth of a solar system

About 4.6 billion years ago, a cloud of gas and dust was drifting through space. Perhaps triggered by a nearby exploding star, the cloud began to collapse in on itself and rotate. The densest part of the cloud formed a core that grew hotter and larger as its gravity attracted more material. Eventually, this core became the young Sun. Around the Sun, some of the cloud formed a broad disk, called the solar nebula. Particles in the disk collided and stuck together, gradually growing bigger until they became the planets of the solar system.

1. Spinning disk
A cloud of dust and gas starts collapsing in on itself, forming a disk with a hot core. The core eventually becomes the Sun.

Our place in space

In the immensity of space, our planet is a mere speck. Earth orbits the Sun, one of the billions of stars in the Milky Way galaxy. The Milky Way and its companions in the Local Group are just a handful of the universe's 50 billion galaxies.

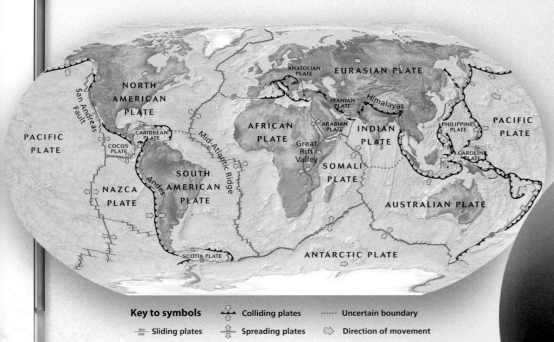

Key to symbols
- ⚯ Sliding plates
- ⚯ Colliding plates
- ⚯ Spreading plates
- ⋯⋯ Uncertain boundary
- ⇨ Direction of movement

The Local Group
Our little corner of the universe is occupied by the Local Group, a cluster of about 30 galaxies.

Tectonic puzzle

Earth's rocky crust and the upper part of the mantle form a layer called the lithosphere. The lithosphere is broken up into several tectonic plates, like a giant jigsaw puzzle (above). These plates float on molten rock in the mantle, moving toward, away from, and past each other.

Crust: 3–43 miles (5–69 km) thick

Mantle: 1,800 miles (2,880 km) thick

Outer core: 1,400 miles (2,240 km) thick

Inner core: 750 miles (1,200 km) thick

Moving plates

As the hot rocks in Earth's mantle circulate, the tectonic plates above them gradually shift, moving about as fast as fingernails grow. On the surface, we see the results of these movements—valleys and mountains are formed, volcanoes erupt, and the ground rattles in earthquakes.

The Andes
South America's Andes Mountains formed when a plate carrying thin ocean crust slid under a plate of thicker continental crust. This movement pushed up the mountain range and formed volcanoes.

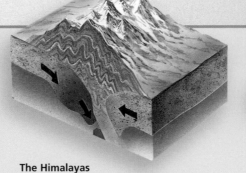

The Himalayas
The collision of two continental plates created the massive Himalayas mountain range in Asia. Because the plates were about as thick as each other, the crusts buckled and folded to form the peaks.

The San Andreas Fault
California's San Andreas Fault is the line where two plates—the Pacific and the North American—are sliding past each other. The friction between the two plates often jolts the ground in earthquakes.

2. Colliding particles
Particles in the disk smash into each other and stick together, gradually forming larger bodies.

3. The nine planets
The clumps in the disk keep colliding and building up until they form the nine planets. The solar system has been born.

Sun
Mercury
Venus
Earth
Mars
Jupiter
Saturn
Uranus
Neptune
Pluto

Sizing up the planets

Shown here to scale, all nine planets are dwarfed by the Sun. About 1,400 Earths would fit inside Jupiter, while 900 Jupiters could fit inside the Sun.

The Milky Way
Our galaxy, the Milky Way, is a giant spiral measuring about 100,000 light-years across.

The Great Rift Valley
In East Africa, two continental plates are slowly moving apart and have formed a wide valley known as the Great Rift Valley. Eventually, Africa will split, water will flood in, and a new ocean will form.

The Mid-Atlantic Ridge
The Mid-Atlantic Ridge marks where two ocean plates are separating. Molten rock from the mantle rises through the gap between the plates. When the rock cools, it adds to the underwater ridge.

The solar system
Earth is the third of the nine planets that orbit the Sun. The Sun itself is just one of the Milky Way's 200 billion stars.

Life zones

From steamy tropical rain forests to icy polar regions, Earth is home to a remarkable range of environments. Distinct weather patterns have helped to create this variety. Earth is unevenly heated by the Sun. Areas around the Equator receive intense sunlight all year long, polar regions receive weak sunlight, and the areas in between receive varying amounts of sunlight throughout the year. The circulation of Earth's air and ocean waters around the globe bring wind and rain to particular areas at different times.

The long-term pattern of weather in a region is known as its climate and influences the kind of lifeforms that can survive there. An arid climate, for example, is always hot and dry, creating a desert where only tough, scrubby plants and cacti can grow. Desert animals must be especially hardy.

Earth's environments shelter a staggering number of different plants and animals. So far, scientists have identified almost 2 million species, but they estimate that there are about 14 million in all. Of this total, nearly 8 million are thought to be insects, while fewer than 5,000 are mammals. Together, the land, oceans and atmosphere occupied by living things are called the biosphere.

Greatest temperature change in a day:
100°F (56°C), from 44°F (6.7°C) to −56°F (−49°C), at Browning, Montana, USA, 1916

Strongest measured wind gust:
231 mph (372 km/h) on Mt Washington, New Hampshire, USA, 1934

Most snow in one year:
1,224 inches (31,102 mm) on Mt Rainier, Washington, USA, 1971–72

NORTH AMERICA

SOUTH AMERICA

Driest place:
0.02 inches (0.5 mm) per year in Quillagua, Atacama Desert, Chile, 1964–2001

Arctic Circle

Antarctic Circle

Underwater life

While the lifeforms on Earth's land show great variety, many of the world's species are found in water, either in freshwater habitats such as lakes, ponds and rivers, or in the salt water of the oceans. Life in the oceans ranges from microscopic plankton to giant squid. Oceans can be divided into four life zones by water depth.

Sunlight zone
The sunlight zone contains most of the ocean's life, including microscopic plankton; small and large fishes; sharks and rays; and mammals such as seals, dolphins and whales.

Twilight zone
Some sunlight filters through to the twilight zone, but not enough for plants to survive. Many of the fishes contain light-producing bacteria and glow in the dark.

Midnight zone
Sunlight does not reach the midnight zone, a vast mass of dark, cold, slow-moving water. There are fewer lifeforms here than in the waters above.

Abyssal zone
The ocean's bottom layer is near freezing and pitch black. In some places, black smokers spew out hot mineral-rich water, which helps mussels, clams and tubeworms to make their own food.

0

650 ft (198 m)

3,250 ft (990 m)

9,850 ft (3,000 m)

Mountain Mountain zones are colder, wetter and windier than nearby low-lying areas. Mountain goats move down the slopes when winter comes.

Polar Polar zones are extremely cold and dry all year. They are covered in either low-growing tundra plants or ice. The arctic fox's thick coat keeps it warm.

Season to season

Earth takes about 365 days, or one year, to complete one orbit around the Sun. Because Earth is slightly tilted, most regions receive varying amounts of sunlight during the year, which produce seasons. Europe and North America, for example, experience winter when the Northern Hemisphere is tilted away from the Sun, and summer when it is tilted toward the Sun.

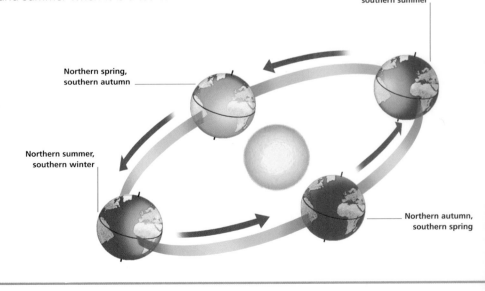

Northern winter, southern summer

Northern spring, southern autumn

Northern summer, southern winter

Northern autumn, southern spring

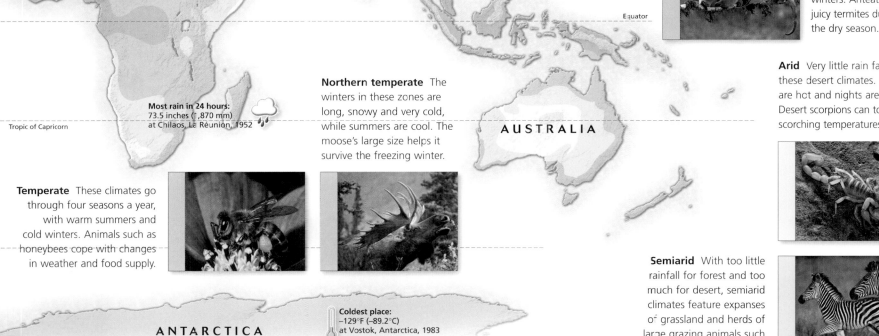

Hot and cold, wet and dry

This map shows eight climate zones, which range from being hot and wet near the Equator, to cold and dry near the poles. The photos show plants and animals that have adapted to the weather conditions in each zone.

EUROPE

ASIA

Hottest place:
136°F (57.3°C)
at El Azizia, Libya, 1922

Most rain in one year:
1,042 inches (26,461 mm)
at Cherrapunji, India, 1860–61

Tropic of Cancer

AFRICA

Equator

Tropic of Capricorn

Most rain in 24 hours:
73.5 inches (1,870 mm)
at Chilaos, La Réunion, 1952

Northern temperate The winters in these zones are long, snowy and very cold, while summers are cool. The moose's large size helps it survive the freezing winter.

AUSTRALIA

Temperate These climates go through four seasons a year, with warm summers and cold winters. Animals such as honeybees cope with changes in weather and food supply.

Coldest place:
−129°F (−89.2°C)
at Vostok, Antarctica, 1983

ANTARCTICA

Tropical Hot and wet all year round, tropical climates feature dense, lush rain forests with abundant animal life, including amphibians such as tree frogs.

Subtropical These climates are hot and wet through summer, but have drier, cooler winters. Anteaters eat juicy termites during the dry season.

Arid Very little rain falls in these desert climates. Days are hot and nights are cold. Desert scorpions can tolerate scorching temperatures.

Semiarid With too little rainfall for forest and too much for desert, semiarid climates feature expanses of grassland and herds of large grazing animals such as kangaroos and zebras.

The circulating atmosphere

The Sun strikes Earth more directly near the Equator than at the poles. Because warm air rises and cold air sinks, this uneven heating makes air circulate around the globe. Warm air near the Equator rises and moves toward the colder polar regions, sinking as it cools and then traveling back toward the Equator. These patterns of air movement also produce Earth's major wind systems.

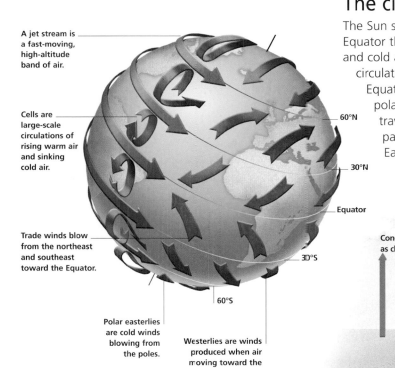

A jet stream is a fast-moving, high-altitude band of air.

Cells are large-scale circulations of rising warm air and sinking cold air.

Trade winds blow from the northeast and southeast toward the Equator.

Polar easterlies are cold winds blowing from the poles.

Westerlies are winds produced when air moving toward the poles is redirected by Earth's rotation.

60°N
30°N
Equator
30°S
60°S

The water cycle

Much of our weather is generated by the water cycle, the endless movement of moisture between oceans, land, plants and clouds. Moisture enters the atmosphere when water in oceans, rivers and lakes is heated by the Sun and evaporates, and when plants release water as part of photosynthesis. It condenses as clouds and returns to Earth's surface when it falls as rain, hail or snow.

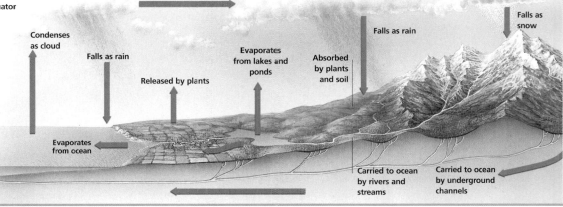

Condenses as cloud

Falls as rain

Released by plants

Evaporates from lakes and ponds

Absorbed by plants and soil

Falls as rain

Falls as snow

Evaporates from ocean

Carried to ocean by rivers and streams

Carried to ocean by underground channels

The world's people

More than 6 billion people live on our planet, and another 1 million are born every five days. There are now more than 10 times as many people as there were 400 years ago. This incredible population explosion happened because living standards and medical care have improved, allowing people to live longer than ever before. At the same time, birth rates—the number of babies born in each family—stayed high in many parts of the world. Until birth rates fall significantly, the world population will continue to grow, and may reach 10 billion by 2200.

Most of today's increase in population is in developing countries—ones with limited industry and technology. These include most of Asia and Africa, and parts of Central and South America. Many developing countries are finding it difficult to feed and care for their enormous populations. Countries with large industries and advanced technology are known as developed countries. They include Japan, Australia, and much of Europe and North America. Most of their populations have stopped growing, and some are shrinking.

Rich and poor

The gap between the world's rich and poor is growing. Developing countries are home to 75 percent of the world's people, but share just 20 percent of the world's wealth. On average, people in developing countries can expect to have less money, food, medical care, education and access to technology than people in developed countries. These graphs compare living standards in five countries, ranging from one of the world's wealthiest countries, Europe's Norway, to one of the poorest, Africa's Sierra Leone.

Many languages

About 6,000 different languages are spoken today, but more than half the people in the world have one of the 12 languages shown on this chart as their first language. English has fewer than half as many first-language speakers as Mandarin Chinese, but it is spoken by many more people as a second language and is becoming the main world language.

NUMBER OF NATIVE SPEAKERS

Mandarin Chinese	874,000,000	
Hindi	366,000,000	
English	341,000,000	
Spanish	340,000,000	
Bengali	207,000,000	
Portuguese	176,000,000	
Russian	167,000,000	
Arabic	150,000,000	
Japanese	125,000,000	
German	100,000,000	
Korean	78,000,000	
French	77,000,000	

Many languages are now endangered. The language of Japan's indigenous people, the Ainu (left), is virtually extinct, with just a handful of elderly speakers remaining. On average, one language is lost every 10 days, and half of the world's 6,000 languages are likely to disappear by 2100.

POPULATION DENSITY

Persons per sq mile	Persons per sq km
Uninhabited	Uninhabited
Less than 2.6	Less than 1
2.6	1
26	10
65	25
130	50
260	100
520	200
1040	400
2080	800
More than 2080	More than 800

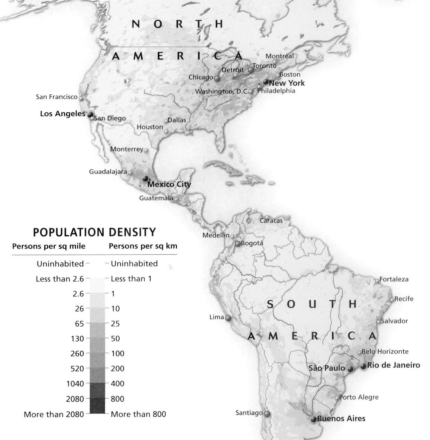

World religions

The earliest signs of religious belief date back 60,000 years, and virtually every culture since has followed some kind of religion. There are now hundreds of different religious traditions in the world, but Hinduism, Buddhism, Judaism, Christianity and Islam have had the broadest influence. Hinduism and Buddhism both developed in Asia, while Judaism, Christianity and Islam started in the Middle East.

Islamic mosque

Stained glass window from Christian church

Ganesh, the Hindu god of wisdom

HOW THE WORLD WORSHIPS

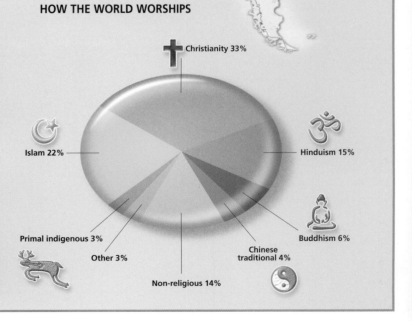

Christianity 33%
Islam 22%
Hinduism 15%
Buddhism 6%
Chinese traditional 4%
Non-religious 14%
Other 3%
Primal indigenous 3%

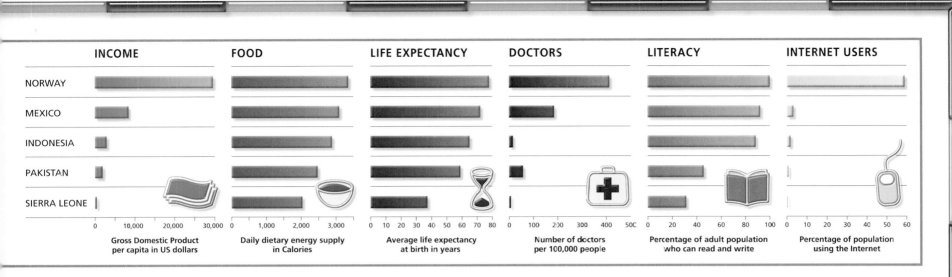

	INCOME	FOOD	LIFE EXPECTANCY	DOCTORS	LITERACY	INTERNET USERS
NORWAY						
MEXICO						
INDONESIA						
PAKISTAN						
SIERRA LEONE						

INCOME	FOOD	LIFE EXPECTANCY	DOCTORS	LITERACY	INTERNET USERS
0 10,000 20,000 30,000	0 1,000 2,000 3,000	0 10 20 30 40 50 60 70 80	0 100 200 300 400 500	0 20 40 60 80 100	0 10 20 30 40 50 60
Gross Domestic Product per capita in US dollars	Daily dietary energy supply in Calories	Average life expectancy at birth in years	Number of doctors per 100,000 people	Percentage of adult population who can read and write	Percentage of population using the Internet

Where people live

The 6 billion people on Earth are spread very unevenly over its landmasses, with China, India and Europe the most crowded areas. People have tended to settle near rivers or the coast. About half of all people now live in cities.

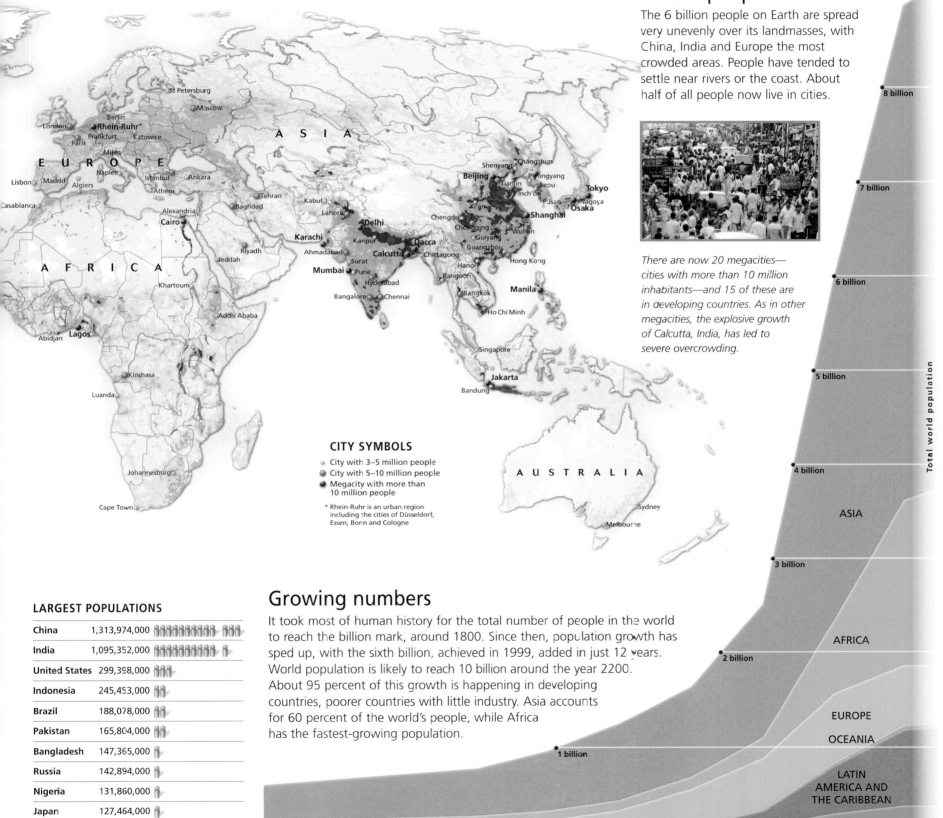

There are now 20 megacities— cities with more than 10 million inhabitants—and 15 of these are in developing countries. As in other megacities, the explosive growth of Calcutta, India, has led to severe overcrowding.

CITY SYMBOLS

- City with 3–5 million people
- City with 5–10 million people
- Megacity with more than 10 million people

* Rhein-Ruhr is an urban region including the cities of Düsseldorf, Essen, Bonn and Cologne

LARGEST POPULATIONS

China	1,313,974,000
India	1,095,352,000
United States	299,398,000
Indonesia	245,453,000
Brazil	188,078,000
Pakistan	165,804,000
Bangladesh	147,365,000
Russia	142,894,000
Nigeria	131,860,000
Japan	127,464,000
Mexico	107,450,000
Philippines	89,469,000

Growing numbers

It took most of human history for the total number of people in the world to reach the billion mark, around 1800. Since then, population growth has sped up, with the sixth billion, achieved in 1999, added in just 12 years. World population is likely to reach 10 billion around the year 2200. About 95 percent of this growth is happening in developing countries, poorer countries with little industry. Asia accounts for 60 percent of the world's people, while Africa has the fastest-growing population.

Geographic comparisons

Largest Islands

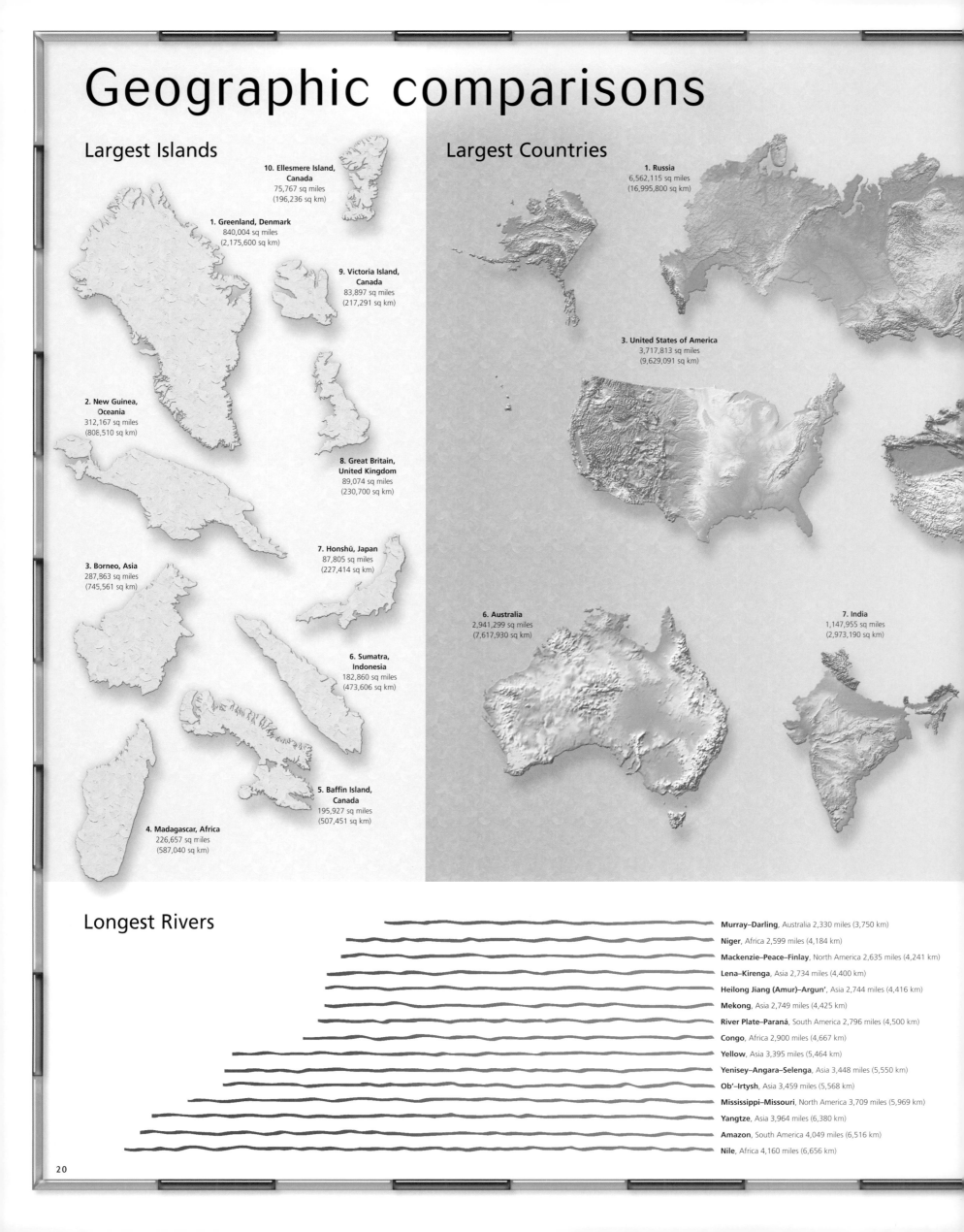

10. Ellesmere Island, Canada
75,767 sq miles
(196,236 sq km)

1. Greenland, Denmark
840,004 sq miles
(2,175,600 sq km)

9. Victoria Island, Canada
83,897 sq miles
(217,291 sq km)

2. New Guinea, Oceania
312,167 sq miles
(808,510 sq km)

8. Great Britain, United Kingdom
89,074 sq miles
(230,700 sq km)

7. Honshū, Japan
87,805 sq miles
(227,414 sq km)

3. Borneo, Asia
287,863 sq miles
(745,561 sq km)

6. Sumatra, Indonesia
182,860 sq miles
(473,606 sq km)

5. Baffin Island, Canada
195,927 sq miles
(507,451 sq km)

4. Madagascar, Africa
226,657 sq miles
(587,040 sq km)

Largest Countries

1. Russia
6,562,115 sq miles
(16,995,800 sq km)

3. United States of America
3,717,813 sq miles
(9,629,091 sq km)

6. Australia
2,941,299 sq miles
(7,617,930 sq km)

7. India
1,147,955 sq miles
(2,973,190 sq km)

Longest Rivers

Murray–Darling, Australia 2,330 miles (3,750 km)

Niger, Africa 2,599 miles (4,184 km)

Mackenzie–Peace–Finlay, North America 2,635 miles (4,241 km)

Lena–Kirenga, Asia 2,734 miles (4,400 km)

Heilong Jiang (Amur)–Argun', Asia 2,744 miles (4,416 km)

Mekong, Asia 2,749 miles (4,425 km)

River Plate–Paraná, South America 2,796 miles (4,500 km)

Congo, Africa 2,900 miles (4,667 km)

Yellow, Asia 3,395 miles (5,464 km)

Yenisey–Angara–Selenga, Asia 3,448 miles (5,550 km)

Ob'–Irtysh, Asia 3,459 miles (5,568 km)

Mississippi–Missouri, North America 3,709 miles (5,969 km)

Yangtze, Asia 3,964 miles (6,380 km)

Amazon, South America 4,049 miles (6,516 km)

Nile, Africa 4,160 miles (6,656 km)

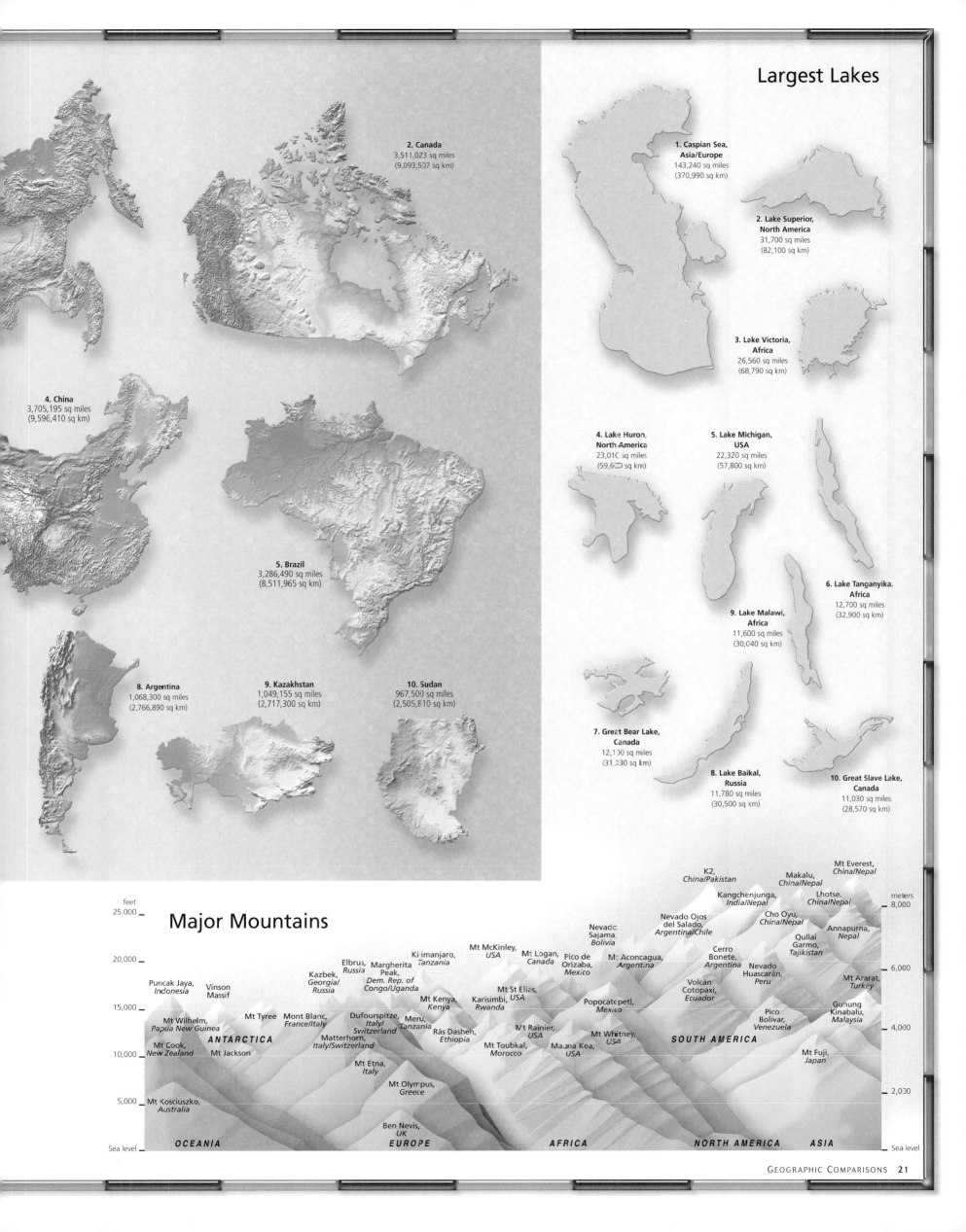

2. Canada
3,511,023 sq miles
(9,093,507 sq km)

4. China
3,705,195 sq miles
(9,596,410 sq km)

5. Brazil
3,286,490 sq miles
(8,511,965 sq km)

8. Argentina
1,068,300 sq miles
(2,766,890 sq km)

9. Kazakhstan
1,049,155 sq miles
(2,717,300 sq km)

10. Sudan
967,500 sq miles
(2,505,810 sq km)

Largest Lakes

1. Caspian Sea, Asia/Europe
143,240 sq miles
(370,990 sq km)

2. Lake Superior, North America
31,700 sq miles
(82,100 sq km)

3. Lake Victoria, Africa
26,560 sq miles
(68,790 sq km)

4. Lake Huron, North America
23,010 sq miles
(59,600 sq km)

5. Lake Michigan, USA
22,320 sq miles
(57,800 sq km)

6. Lake Tanganyika, Africa
12,700 sq miles
(32,900 sq km)

9. Lake Malawi, Africa
11,600 sq miles
(30,040 sq km)

7. Great Bear Lake, Canada
12,100 sq miles
(31,330 sq km)

8. Lake Baikal, Russia
11,780 sq miles
(30,500 sq km)

10. Great Slave Lake, Canada
11,030 sq miles
(28,570 sq km)

Major Mountains

feet
25,000

20,000

15,000

10,000

5,000

Sea level

meters
8,000

6,000

4,000

2,000

Sea level

Mt Everest, *China/Nepal*
K2, *China/Pakistan*
Makalu, *China/Nepal*
Kangchenjunga, *India/Nepal*
Lhotse, *China/Nepal*
Nevado Ojos del Salado, *Argentina/Chile*
Cho Oyu, *China/Nepal*
Nevado Sajama, *Bolivia*
Annapurna, *Nepal*
Cerro Bonete, *Argentina*
Qullai Garmo, *Tajikistan*
Mt McKinley, *USA*
Mt Logan, *Canada*
Pico de Orizaba, *Mexico*
Mt Aconcagua, *Argentina*
Nevado Huascarán, *Peru*
Kilimanjaro, *Tanzania*
Elbrus, *Russia*
Margherita Peak, *Dem. Rep. of Congo/Uganda*
Volcán Cotopaxi, *Ecuador*
Mt Ararat, *Turkey*
Kazbek, *Georgia/Russia*
Popocatepetl, *Mexico*
Gunung Kinabalu, *Malaysia*
Puncak Jaya, *Indonesia*
Vinson Massif
Mt St Elias, *USA*
Karisimbi, *Rwanda*
Pico Bolívar, *Venezuela*
Mt Wilhelm, *Papua New Guinea*
Mt Tyree
Mt Kenya, *Kenya*
Mont Blanc, *France/Italy*
Dufourspitze, *Italy/Switzerland*
Meru, *Tanzania*
Ras Dashen, *Ethiopia*
Mt Rainier, *USA*
Mt Whitney, *USA*
Mauna Kea, *USA*
Mt Fuji, *Japan*
Mt Cook, *New Zealand*
Mt Jackson
Matterhorn, *Italy/Switzerland*
Mt Toubkal, *Morocco*
ANTARCTICA
SOUTH AMERICA
Mt Etna, *Italy*
Mt Kosciuszko, *Australia*
Mt Olympus, *Greece*
OCEANIA
Ben Nevis, *UK*
EUROPE
AFRICA
NORTH AMERICA
ASIA

The physical world

CIRCUMFERENCE OF EARTH AROUND THE EQUATOR
24,902 miles (40,067 km)

AREA OF SEA
139 782,000 square miles (362,033,000 sq km)

AREA OF LAND ABOVE SEA LEVEL
57,´51,000 square miles (148,021,000 sq km)

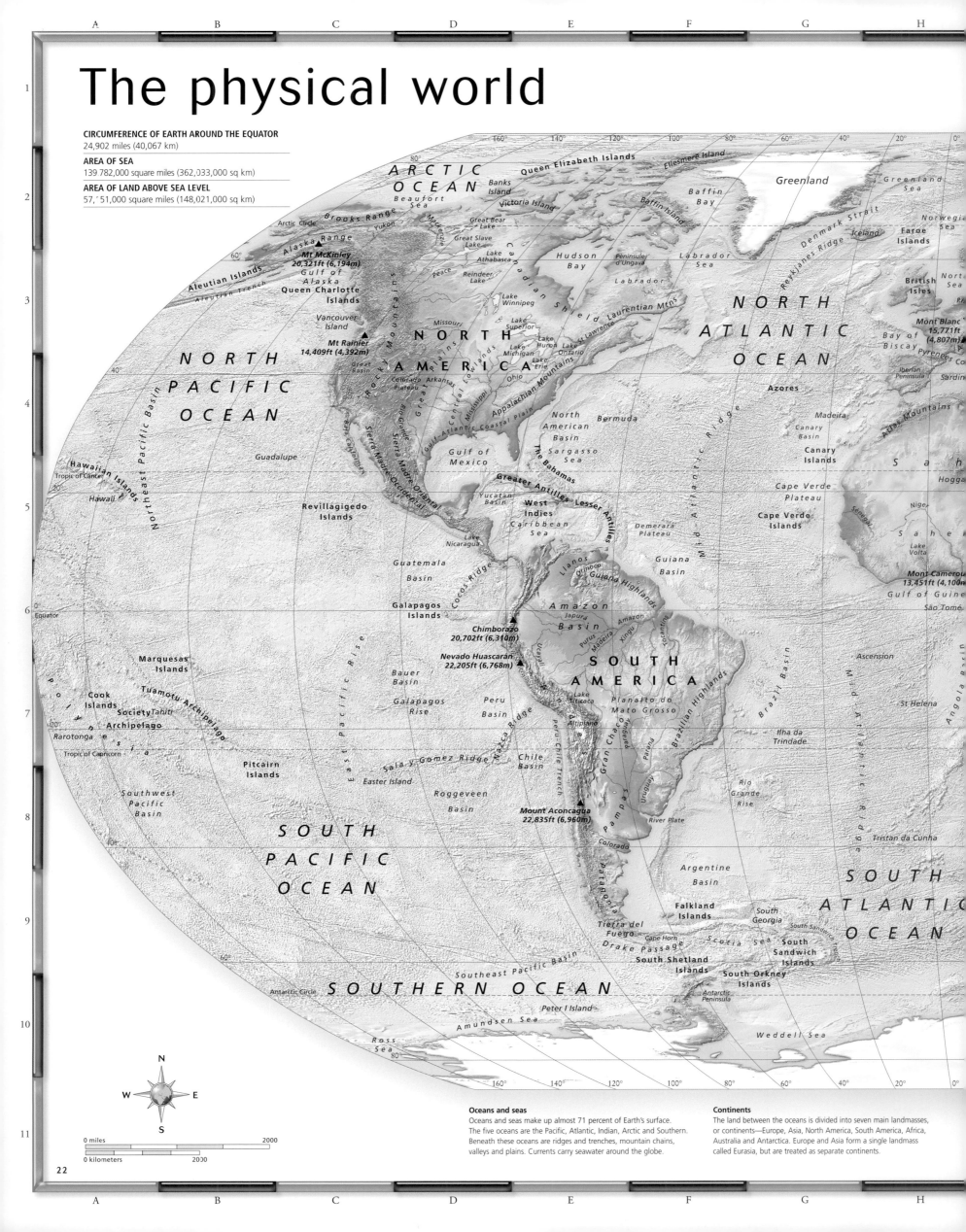

Oceans and seas
Oceans and seas make up almost 71 percent of Earth's surface.
The five oceans are the Pacific, Atlantic, Indian, Arctic and Southern.
Beneath these oceans are ridges and trenches, mountain chains,
valleys and plains. Currents carry seawater around the globe.

Continents
The land between the oceans is divided into seven main landmasses,
or continents—Europe, Asia, North America, South America, Africa,
Australia and Antarctica. Europe and Asia form a single landmass
called Eurasia, but are treated as separate continents.

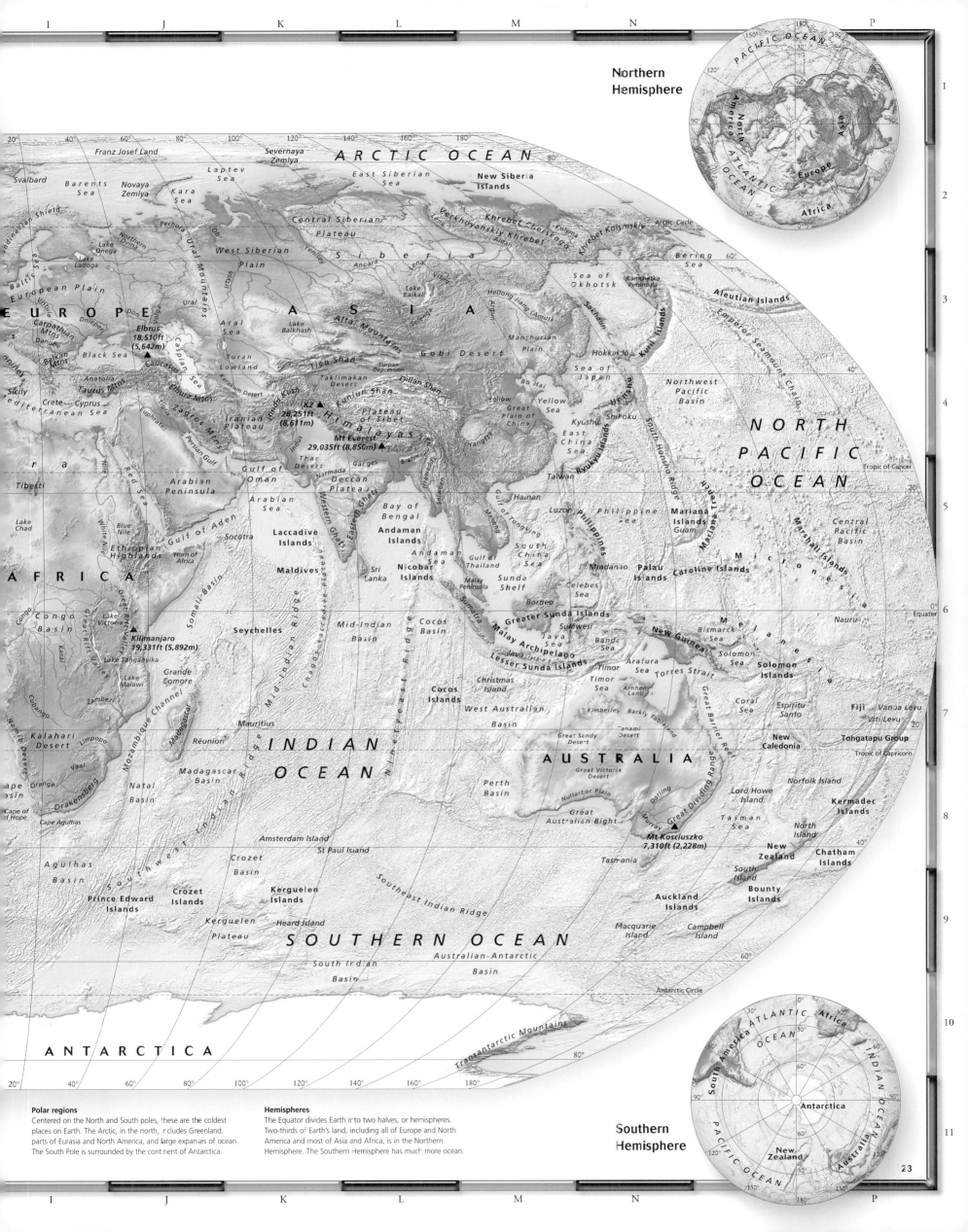

Polar regions
Centered on the North and South poles, these are the coldest places on Earth. The Arctic, in the north, includes Greenland, parts of Eurasia and North America, and large expanses of ocean. The South Pole is surrounded by the continent of Antarctica.

Hemispheres
The Equator divides Earth into two halves, or hemispheres. Two-thirds of Earth's land, including all of Europe and North America and most of Asia and Africa, is in the Northern Hemisphere. The Southern Hemisphere has much more ocean.

Northern Hemisphere

Southern Hemisphere

23

Countries of the world

NUMBER OF COUNTRIES	193
NUMBER OF TERRITORIES	65
LONGEST BORDER	USA–Canada 3,987 miles (6,379 km)
LARGEST POPULATION	China 1,313,974,000

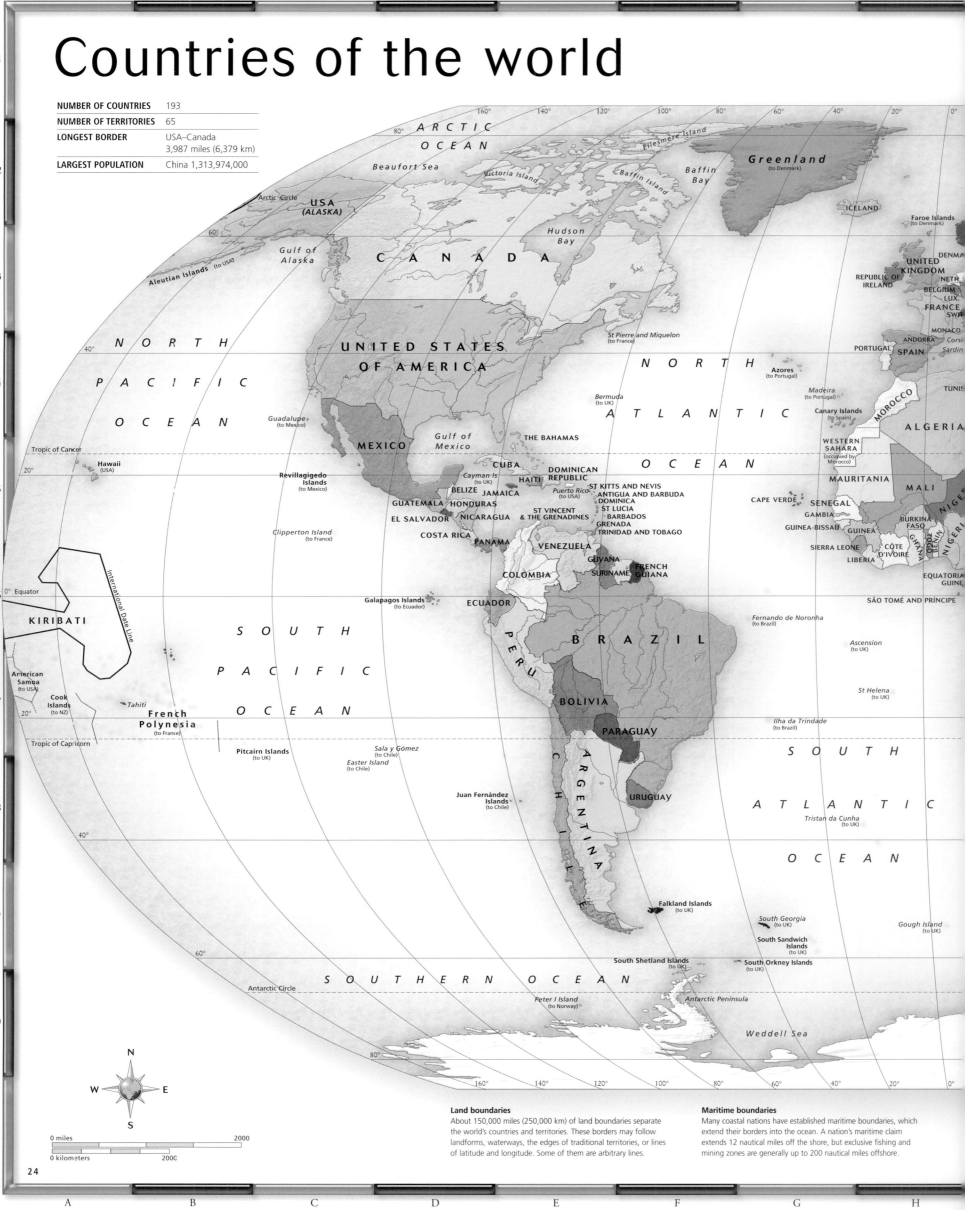

Land boundaries
About 150,000 miles (250,000 km) of land boundaries separate the world's countries and territories. These boundaries may follow landforms, waterways, the edges of traditional territories, or lines of latitude and longitude. Some of them are arbitrary lines.

Maritime boundaries
Many coastal nations have established maritime boundaries, which extend their borders into the ocean. A nation's maritime claim extends 12 nautical miles off the shore, but exclusive fishing and mining zones are generally up to 200 nautical miles offshore.

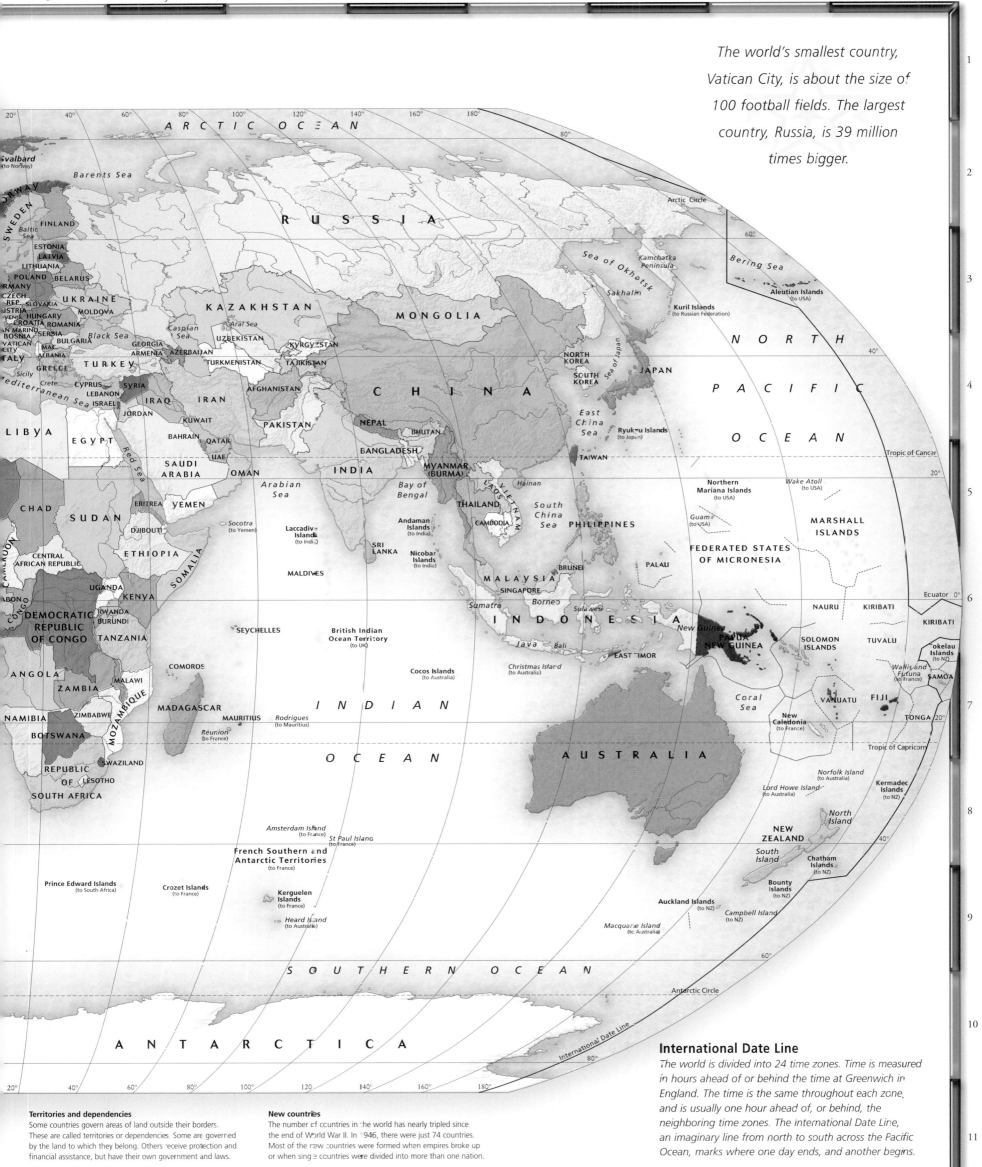

The world's smallest country, Vatican City, is about the size of 100 football fields. The largest country, Russia, is 39 million times bigger.

International Date Line

The world is divided into 24 time zones. Time is measured in hours ahead of or behind the time at Greenwich in England. The time is the same throughout each zone, and is usually one hour ahead of, or behind, the neighboring time zones. The international Date Line, an imaginary line from north to south across the Pacific Ocean, marks where one day ends, and another begins.

Territories and dependencies

Some countries govern areas of land outside their borders. These are called territories or dependencies. Some are governed by the land to which they belong. Others receive protection and financial assistance, but have their own government and laws.

New countries

The number of countries in the world has nearly tripled since the end of World War II. In 1946, there were just 74 countries. Most of the new countries were formed when empires broke up or when single countries were divided into more than one nation.

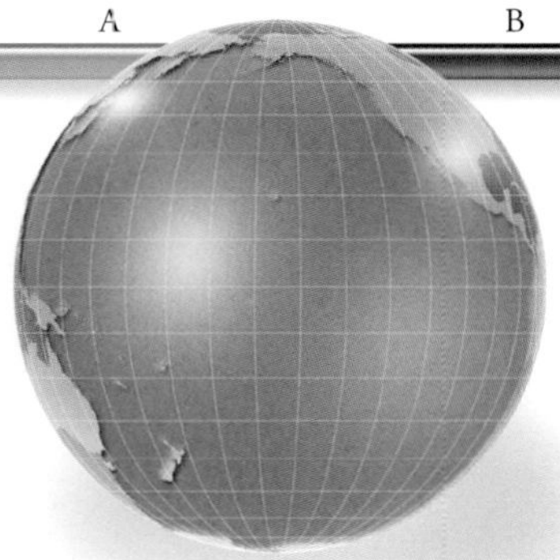

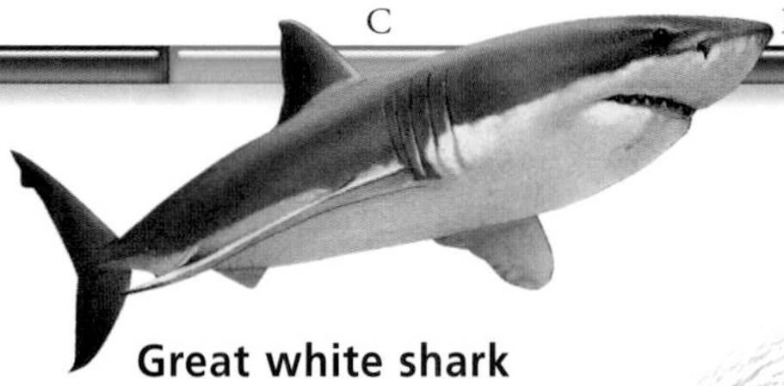

Great white shark
The great white shark constantly prowls coastal waters. It eats seals, small whales and other sharks.

The Pacific Ocean

Sunfish
When its long back fin breaks the ocean surface, the sunfish can be mistaken for a shark. It is more usual to see the fish lying on its side, warming its flat, almost circular, body with heat from the Sun. The sunfish measures up to 12 feet (3.5 m) long and weighs up to 2 tons (2 t). It eats crustaceans and jellyfishes, and is harmless to humans.

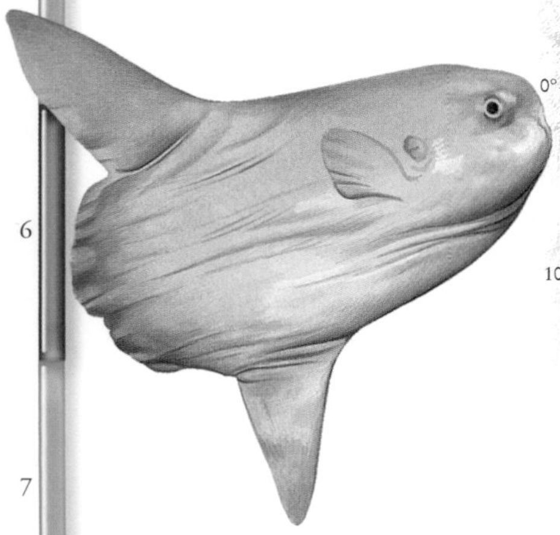

Double canoe
The great ocean voyages of the ancient Polynesians were probably made in double canoes. These canoes were light, fast and stable, and were steered by a long oar used as a rudder. Large double canoes could carry up to 100 people.

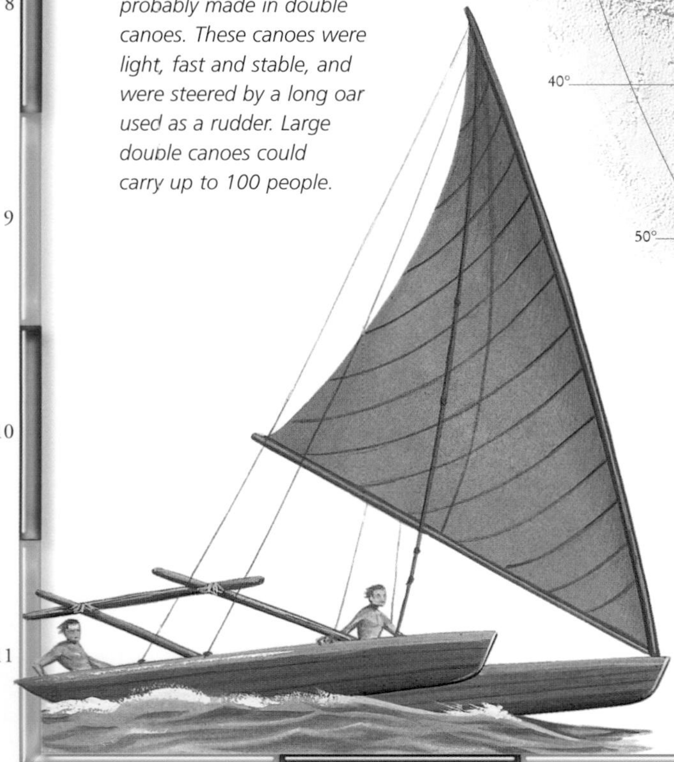

Bering Sea
Aleutian Basin
Aleutian Islands
Aleutian Trench
Kamchatka Peninsula
Sea of Okhotsk
Kuril Islands
Kuril Trench
Emperor Seamount Chain
Emperor Trough
Chinook Trough
Mendocin
Sea of Japan
Northwest Pacific Basin
Japan Trench
Shikoku Trench
Kyushu Ridge
Izu Trench
East China Sea
ASIA
Makarov Seamount
Midway Islands
Hawaiian Islands
Hawaiian Ridge
Muff
Tropic of Cancer
Taiwan
Ryukyu Trench
Luzon Strait
Central Basin
Mariana Islands
South Mariana Trench
East Mariana Basin
Mid-Pacific Mountains
Johnston Atoll
Christmas Ridge
Luzon
Philippines Trench
Philippine Sea
Guam
Mariana Trench
MICRONESIA
Marshall Islands
Central Pacific Basin
Kingman Reef
South China Sea
Philippine Basin
Challenger Deep 35,826 ft (10,920m)
West Caroline Basin
East Caroline Basin
Melanesian Basin
Howland Island
Palmyra Atoll
Sunda Shelf
Palawan Trough
Palau Islands
Caroline Islands
Baker Island
Jarvis Island
Celebes Sea
Palau Trench
Nauru
Borneo
Makassar Strait
Sulawesi
Equator
Greater Sunda Islands
Bismarck Sea
MELANESIA
PACIFIC
Java Sea
Banda Sea
New Guinea
Solomon Islands
Phoenix Islands
Sumatra
Java
Arafura Sea
Torres Strait
Coral Sea Basin
Wallis and Futuna Islands
Timor Sea
Gulf of Carpentaria
Great Barrier Reef
Coral Sea
Espiritu Santo
North Fiji Basin
Fiji
Samoa
Cook Islands
Tropic of Capricorn
AUSTRALIA
New Caledonia
New Caledonia Trough
Lord Howe Rise
Tonga
Tongatapu Group
Horizon Deep
Tonga Trench
South Fiji Basin
Niue
Rarotong
Ozbourn Seamount
Louisville Ridge
Norfolk Island
Kermadec Islands
Kermadec Trench
Lord Howe Island
North Island
Southwes
Tasman Sea
Challenger Plateau
Chatham Rise
Bass Strait
New Zealand
Chatham Islands
Tasmania
Tasman Basin
South Island
Bounty Trough
South Tasman Rise
Campbell Plateau
Bounty Islands
Macquarie Ridge
Antipodes Islands
Macquarie Island
SOUTHERN OCEAN
Pacific-Antarcti
Balleny Islands
Antarctic Circle
Cape Adare
Iselin Seamount
Ross Sea

Longitude markers: 160° 180° 170° 140° 150° 160° 170° 180° 60° 30° 40° 120° 130° 110° 100° 20° 10° 0° 10° 20° 30° 40° 50° 60° 70° 80°
100° 110° 120° 130° 140° 150° 160° 170° 180° 170° 160°

Compass: N E S W

0 miles 1500
0 kilometers 1500

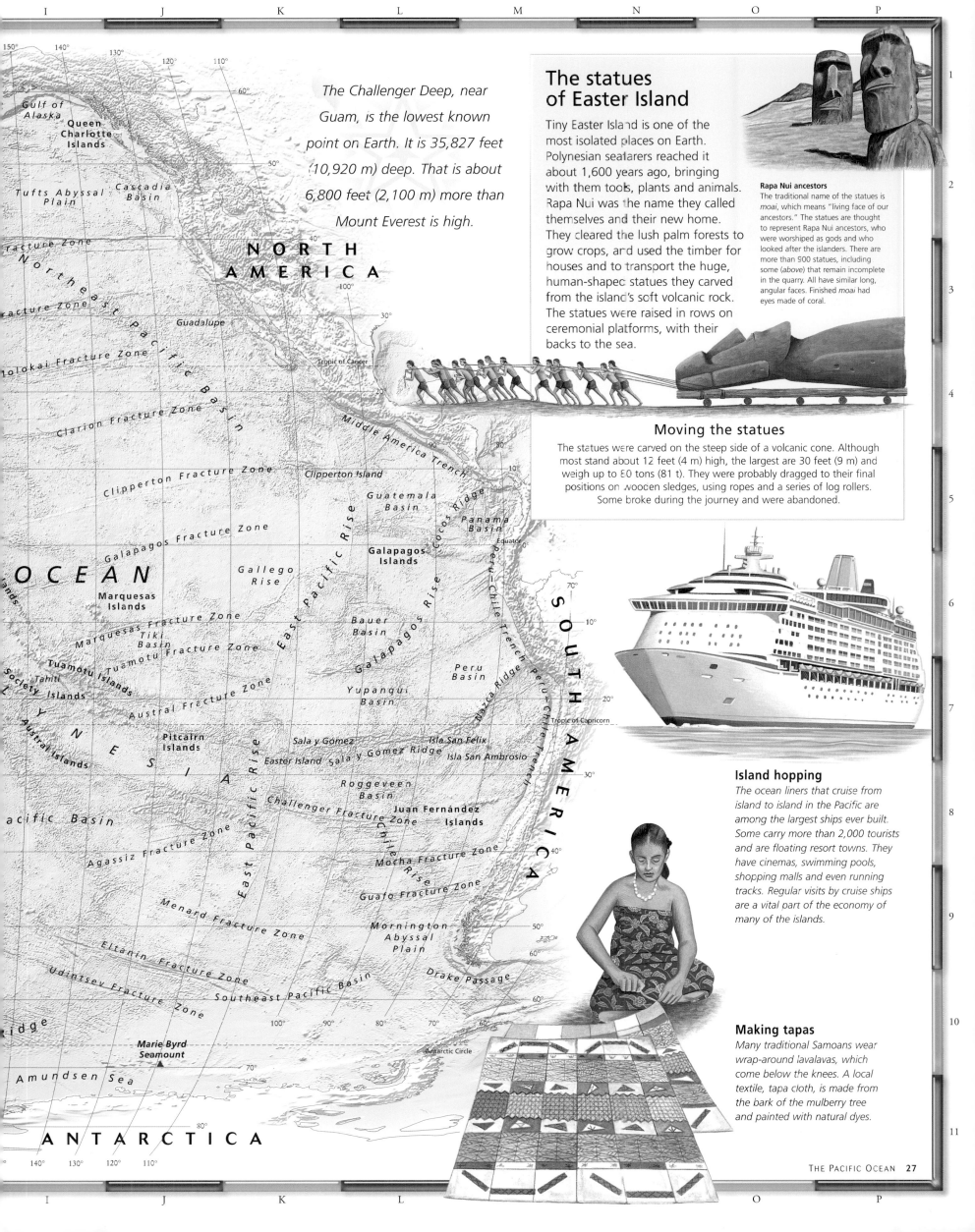

The Challenger Deep, near Guam, is the lowest known point on Earth. It is 35,827 feet (10,920 m) deep. That is about 6,800 feet (2,100 m) more than Mount Everest is high.

The statues of Easter Island

Tiny Easter Island is one of the most isolated places on Earth. Polynesian seafarers reached it about 1,600 years ago, bringing with them tools, plants and animals. Rapa Nui was the name they called themselves and their new home. They cleared the lush palm forests to grow crops, and used the timber for houses and to transport the huge, human-shaped statues they carved from the island's soft volcanic rock. The statues were raised in rows on ceremonial platforms, with their backs to the sea.

Rapa Nui ancestors
The traditional name of the statues is *moai*, which means "living face of our ancestors." The statues are thought to represent Rapa Nui ancestors, who were worshiped as gods and who looked after the islanders. There are more than 900 statues, including some (*above*) that remain incomplete in the quarry. All have similar long, angular faces. Finished *moai* had eyes made of coral.

Moving the statues
The statues were carved on the steep side of a volcanic cone. Although most stand about 12 feet (4 m) high, the largest are 30 feet (9 m) and weigh up to 80 tons (81 t). They were probably dragged to their final positions on wooden sledges, using ropes and a series of log rollers. Some broke during the journey and were abandoned.

Island hopping
The ocean liners that cruise from island to island in the Pacific are among the largest ships ever built. Some carry more than 2,000 tourists and are floating resort towns. They have cinemas, swimming pools, shopping malls and even running tracks. Regular visits by cruise ships are a vital part of the economy of many of the islands.

Making tapas
Many traditional Samoans wear wrap-around lavalavas, which come below the knees. A local textile, tapa cloth, is made from the bark of the mulberry tree and painted with natural dyes.

The Atlantic Ocean

The Titanic
In 1912, on its first voyage, the luxury liner Titanic struck an iceberg and sank. More than 1,400 passengers and crew perished in the icy Atlantic. The ship still lies in water 2½ miles (4 km) deep.

Giant squid
The giant squid lives in the depths of the ocean, and has never been seen alive by humans. It can grow as long as a bus and has eyes as big as basketballs. The two longest tentacles catch food and bring it to the squid's mouth.

Flying fish

Water spouts
Water spouts are funnels of whirling spray that form between the surface of the sea and the clouds above. They are common in late summer, when cool air moving over warm water produces strong updrafts.

CAPE VERDE POPULATION 421,000 ∗ CAPITAL PRAIA

Map labels

EUROPE
AFRICA
NORTH AMERICA
SOUTH AMERICA
ATLANTIC OCEAN

Greenland
Denmark Strait
Iceland
Shetland Islands
North Sea
British Isles
Faroe-Shetland Trough
Rockall Bank
Rockall Trough
Hatton Ridge
Irminger Basin
Reykjanes Basin
Reykjanes Ridge
Eirik Ridge
Iceland Basin
Rockall Basin
Goban Spur
Celtic Shelf
Bay of Biscay
Biscay Abyssal Plain
Galicia Bank
Tagus Abyssal Plain
Madeira
Monaco Basin
Corsica
Sardinia
Sicily
Mediterranean Sea
Azores
Azores-Biscay Rise
Charlie-Gibbs Fracture Zone
Mid-Atlantic Ridge
Northwest Atlantic Mid-Ocean Channel
Flemish Cap
Newfoundland Basin
Newfoundland Ridge
Grand Banks of Newfoundland
Hamilton Bank
Cape Sable
Cape Cod
New England Seamounts
Sohm Abyssal Plain
Bermuda Rise
Bermuda
North American Basin
Hatteras Abyssal Plain
Cape Hatteras
Blake-Bahama Ridge
Nares Abyssal Plain
Puerto Rico Trench
Greater Antilles
Lesser Antilles
Jamaica
Caribbean Sea
Colombian Basin
Venezuelan Basin
Sargasso Sea
Kane Fracture Zone
Atlantis Fracture Zone
Oceanographer Fracture Zone
Great Meteor Tablemount
Cape Verde Plateau
Canary Islands
Canary Basin
Cape Verde Islands
Cape Vert
Gambia Basin
Sierra Leone Basin
Gambia Abyssal Plain
Gulf of Guinea
São Tomé
Congo Cone
Angola Basin
Guinea Basin
St. Helena
Ascension
Bode Verde Fracture Zone
Pernambuco Plain
Fernando de Noronha
Pernambuco Abyssal Plain
Ceará Abyssal Plain
Amazon Cone
Demerara Plateau
Demerara Abyssal Plain
Do drums Fracture Zone
Four North Fracture Zone
Saint Paul Fracture Zone
Vema Fracture Zone
Barracuda Fracture Zone
Ilha da Trindade
Vitória
Trindade
Ilhas Martin Vaz
Hotspur Seamount
Saint Helena Fracture Zone

50°, 60°, 70°, 80°, 90°
Tropic of Cancer
Equator 0°
Tropic of Capricorn

Cape Verde inset

CAPE VERDE

ATLANTIC OCEAN

Santo Antão
Porto Novo
Mindelo
São Vicente
Vila do Tarrafal
Vila Nova Sintra
Brava
São Nicolau
Ribeira Brava
Vila da Brava
São Filipe
Fogo
Sal
Santa Maria
Maio
Vila do Maio
Boa Vista
Vila da Sal Rei
Porto Inglês
São Tiago
PRAIA

Cape Verde

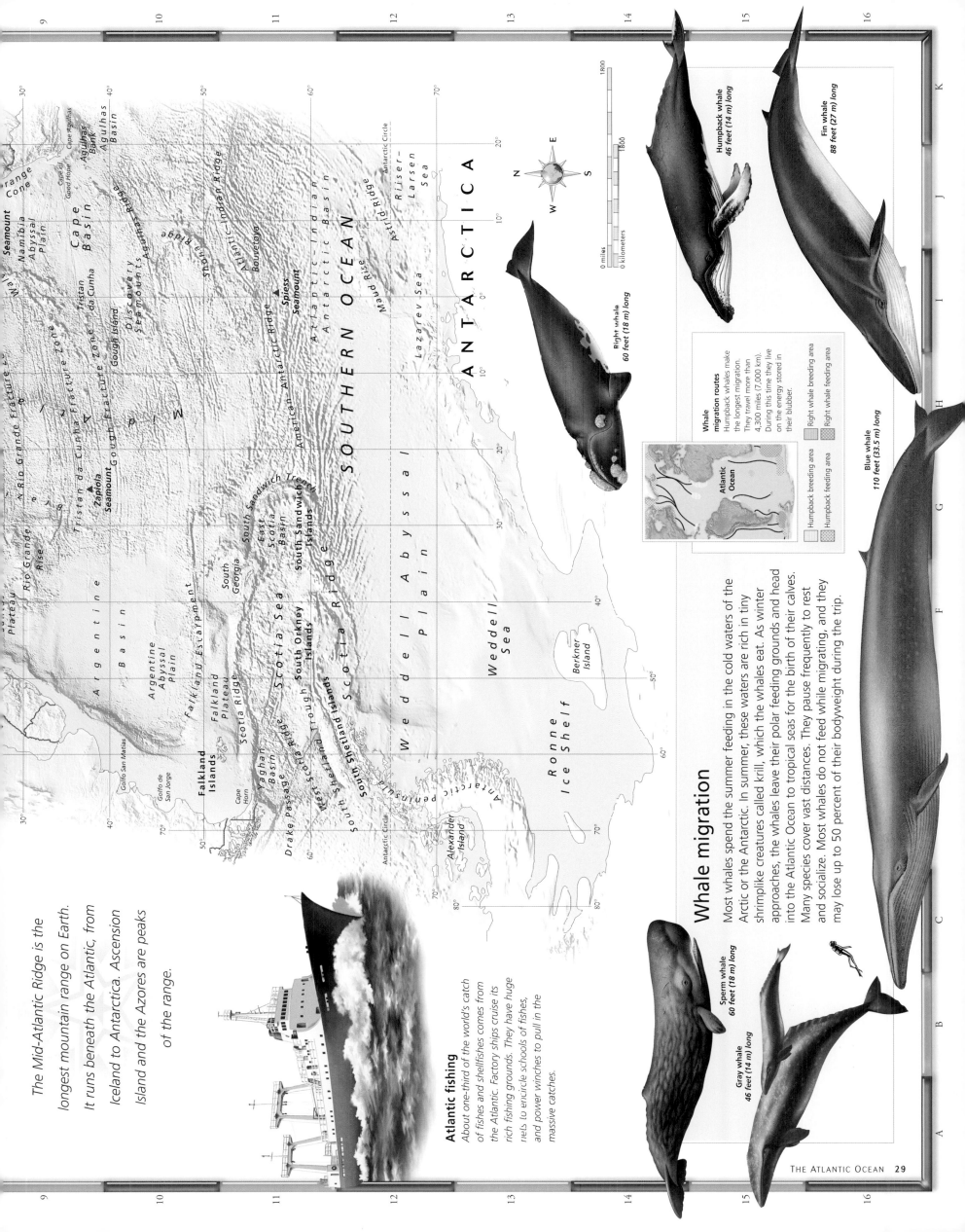

The Mid-Atlantic Ridge is the longest mountain range on Earth. It runs beneath the Atlantic, from Iceland to Antarctica. Ascension Island and the Azores are peaks of the range.

Atlantic fishing

About one-third of the world's catch of fishes and shellfishes comes from the Atlantic. Factory ships cruise its rich fishing grounds. They have huge nets to encircle schools of fishes, and power winches to pull in the massive catches.

Whale migration

Most whales spend the summer feeding in the cold waters of the Arctic or the Antarctic. In summer, these waters are rich in tiny shrimplike creatures called krill, which the whales eat. As winter approaches, the whales leave their polar feeding grounds and head into the Atlantic Ocean to tropical seas for the birth of their calves. Many species cover vast distances. They pause frequently to rest and socialize. Most whales do not feed while migrating, and they may lose up to 50 percent of their bodyweight during the trip.

Whale migration routes
Humpback whales make the longest migration. They travel more than 4,300 miles (7,000 km). During this time they live on the energy stored in their blubber.

Atlantic Ocean

Humpback breeding area
Humpback feeding area
Right whale breeding area
Right whale feeding area

Humpback whale
46 feet (14 m) long

Fin whale
88 feet (27 m) long

Right whale
60 feet (18 m) long

Blue whale
110 feet (33.5 m) long

Sperm whale
60 feet (18 m) long

Gray whale
46 feet (14 m) long

SOUTHERN OCEAN

ANTARCTICA

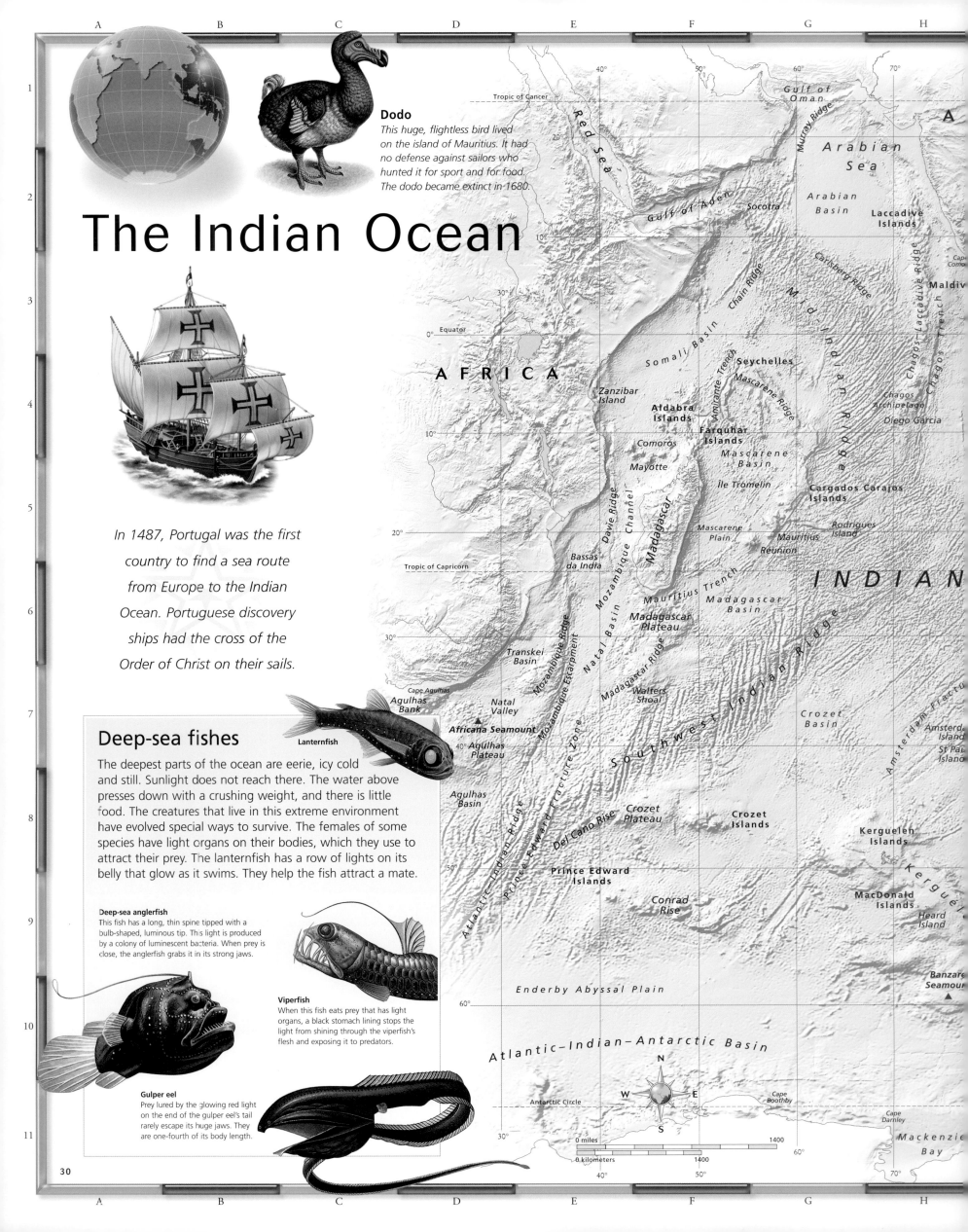

Dodo
This huge, flightless bird lived on the island of Mauritius. It had no defense against sailors who hunted it for sport and for food. The dodo became extinct in 1680.

The Indian Ocean

In 1487, Portugal was the first country to find a sea route from Europe to the Indian Ocean. Portuguese discovery ships had the cross of the Order of Christ on their sails.

Deep-sea fishes

Lanternfish

The deepest parts of the ocean are eerie, icy cold and still. Sunlight does not reach there. The water above presses down with a crushing weight, and there is little food. The creatures that live in this extreme environment have evolved special ways to survive. The females of some species have light organs on their bodies, which they use to attract their prey. The lanternfish has a row of lights on its belly that glow as it swims. They help the fish attract a mate.

Deep-sea anglerfish
This fish has a long, thin spine tipped with a bulb-shaped, luminous tip. This light is produced by a colony of luminescent bacteria. When prey is close, the anglerfish grabs it in its strong jaws.

Viperfish
When this fish eats prey that has light organs, a black stomach lining stops the light from shining through the viperfish's flesh and exposing it to predators.

Gulper eel
Prey lured by the glowing red light on the end of the gulper eel's tail rarely escape its huge jaws. They are one-fourth of its body length.

Map labels

Tropic of Cancer
Gulf of Oman
Murray Ridge
Red Sea
Arabian Sea
Gulf of Aden
Socotra
Arabian Basin
Laccadive Islands
Carlsberg Ridge
Chain Ridge
Maldives
Maldiv
Cape Como
Mid-Indian Ridge
Equator
Somali Basin
Chagos-Laccadive Ridge
Chagos Trench
AFRICA
Zanzibar Island
Seychelles
Aldabra Islands
Mascarene Ridge
Antante Trench
Farquhar Islands
Comoros
Mascarene Basin
Chagos Archipelago
Diego Garcia
Mayotte
Île Tromelin
Cargados Carajos Islands
Davie Ridge
Madagascar
Mascarene Plain
Rodrigues Island
Mauritius
Réunion
Bassas da India
INDIAN
Tropic of Capricorn
Mozambique Channel
Mauritius Trench
Madagascar Basin
Madagascar Plateau
Natal Basin
Mozambique Ridge
Mozambique Escarpment
Transkei Basin
Walters Shoal
Madagascar Ridge
Cape Agulhas
Agulhas Bank
Natal Valley
Southwest Indian Ridge
Crozet Basin
Amsterdam Fractu
Amsterdam Island
St Pai Island
Africana Seamount
Agulhas Plateau
Prince Edward Fracture Zone
Agulhas Basin
Atlantic-Indian Ridge
Del Cano Rise
Crozet Plateau
Crozet Islands
Kerguelen Islands
Prince Edward Islands
Conrad Rise
MacDonald Islands
Heard Island
Kerguel
Enderby Abyssal Plain
Banzare Seamou
Atlantic-Indian-Antarctic Basin
N
W E
S
Antarctic Circle
Cape Boothby
Cape Darnley
0 miles 1400
0 kilometers 1400
Mackenzie Bay

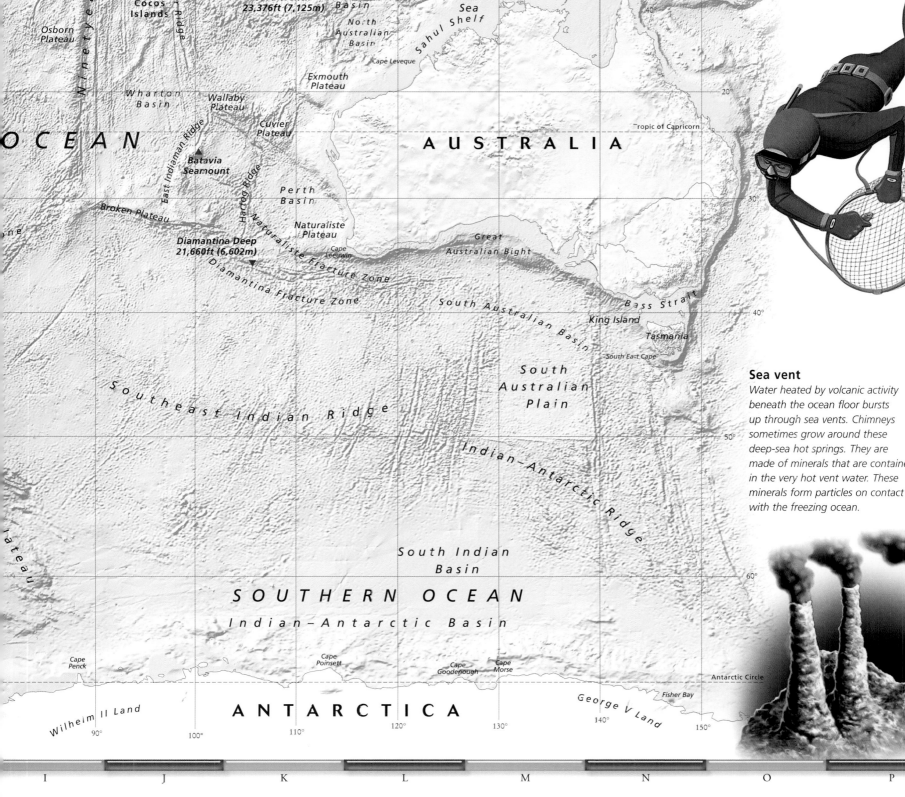

Manta ray

Rays are related to sharks. The manta ray grows to 23 feet (7 m) across and is the largest ray in the world. It feeds on plankton, small crustaceans and fishes. Manta rays are harmless to humans.

Pearl diver

Pearls form inside living mollusks in tropical waters. This process occurs naturally but, today, most pearls are specially farmed. A bead is inserted in the pearl oyster shell, and a pearl grows around it. Divers tend the oysters until the pearls are ready to be harvested.

Sea vent

Water heated by volcanic activity beneath the ocean floor bursts up through sea vents. Chimneys sometimes grow around these deep-sea hot springs. They are made of minerals that are contained in the very hot vent water. These minerals form particles on contact with the freezing ocean.

Tropic of Cancer

A

Ganges
Cone

Bay of
Bengal

Andaman
Sea

Andaman
Islands

Andaman
Basin

Sri
nka

Nicobar
Islands

Ceylon
Plain

Mid-
Indian
Basin

Ninetyeast Ridge

Cocos
Basin

Sumatra

Investigator Ridge

Java Ridge

Java

Bali

Sumbawa

Timor

Christmas
Island

Java Trench
23,376ft (7,125m)

Lombok
Basin

North
Australian
Basin

Timor
Sea

Sahul Shelf

Cape Leveque

Cocos
Islands

Osborn
Plateau

Wharton
Basin

Wallaby
Plateau

Cuvier
Plateau

Exmouth
Plateau

AUSTRALIA

Tropic of Capricorn

OCEAN

East Indianan Ridge

Batavia
Seamount

Hartog Ridge

Perth
Basin

Broken Plateau

ne

Naturaliste Ridge

Naturaliste
Plateau

Cape
Leeuwin

Great
Australian Bight

Bass Strait

King Island

Tasmania

South East Cape

Diamantina Deep
21,660ft (6,602m)

Diamantina Fracture Zone

Diamantina Fracture Zone

South Australian Basin

Southeast Indian Ridge

South
Australian
Plain

Indian–Antarctic Ridge

South Indian
Basin

SOUTHERN OCEAN

Indian–Antarctic Basin

lateau

Cape
Penck

Cape
Poinsett

Cape
Goodenough

Cape
Morse

Antarctic Circle

Fisher Bay

George V Land

Wilhelm II Land

ANTARCTICA

Equator

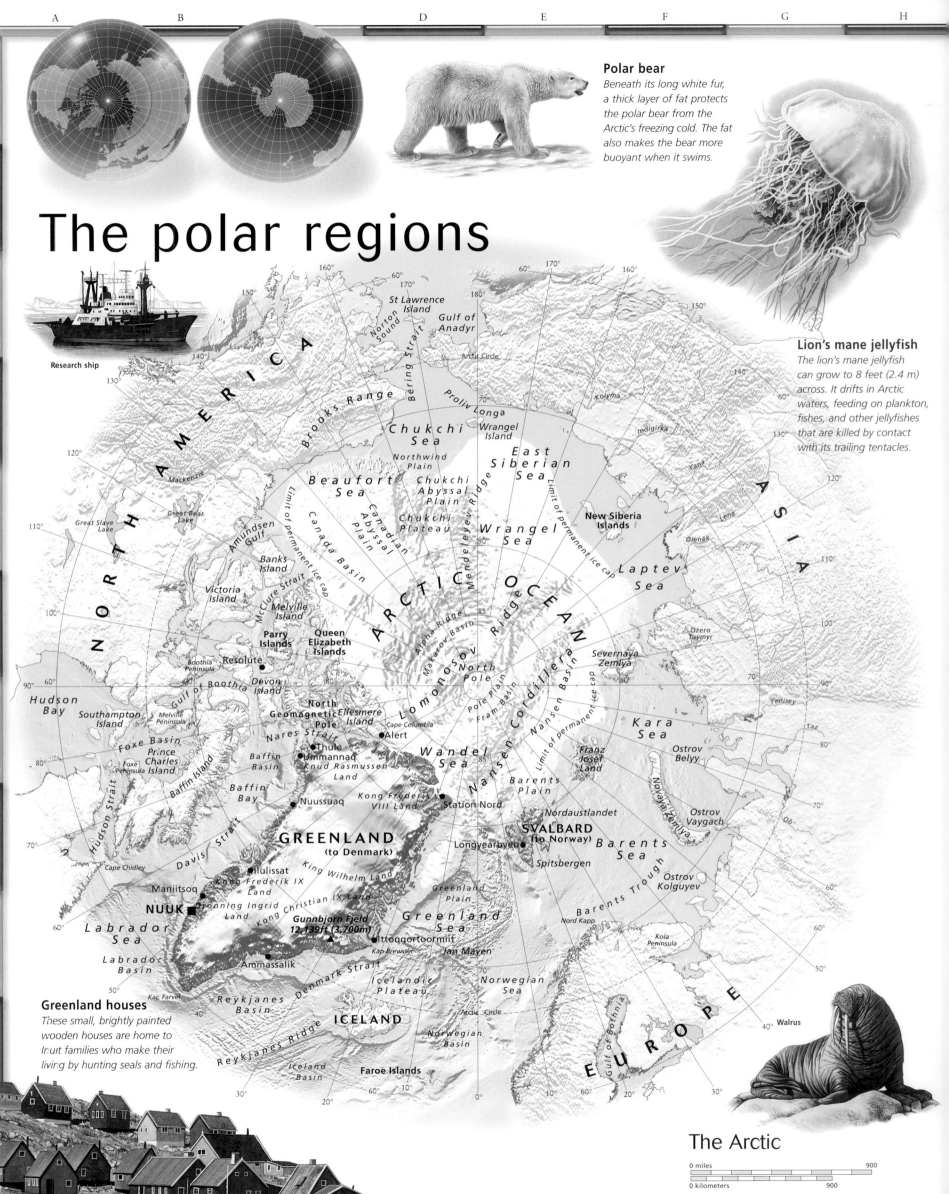

The polar regions

Polar bear
Beneath its long white fur, a thick layer of fat protects the polar bear from the Arctic's freezing cold. The fat also makes the bear more buoyant when it swims.

Research ship

Lion's mane jellyfish
The lion's mane jellyfish can grow to 8 feet (2.4 m) across. It drifts in Arctic waters, feeding on plankton, fishes, and other jellyfishes that are killed by contact with its trailing tentacles.

Greenland houses
These small, brightly painted wooden houses are home to Inuit families who make their living by hunting seals and fishing.

The Arctic

0 miles   900
0 kilometers   900

Walrus

NORTH AMERICA
ASIA
EUROPE

Arctic Circle

St Lawrence Island
Gulf of Anadyr
Norton Sound
Bering Strait
Proliv Longa
Kolyma
Indigirka
Yana

Chukchi Sea
Wrangel Island
East Siberian Sea
Northwind Plain
Beaufort Sea
Chukchi Abyssal Plain
Chukchi Plateau
Wrangel Sea
New Siberia Islands
Lena
Laptev Sea
Olenëk

Brooks Range
Mackenzie
Great Bear Lake
Great Slave Lake
Amundsen Gulf
Canada Basin
Canadian Abyssal Plain
Mendeleyev Ridge
Limit of permanent ice cap
Limit of permanent ice cap
Ozero Taymyr

Banks Island
Victoria Island
McClure Strait
Melville Island
Alpha Ridge
Makarov Basin
Lomonosov Ridge
North Pole
Pole Plain
Fram Basin
ARCTIC OCEAN
Severnaya Zemlya

Parry Islands
Queen Elizabeth Islands
Boothia Peninsula
Resolute
Devon Island
Nansen Cordillera
Nansen Basin
Limit of permanent ice cap
Franz Josef Land
Kara Sea
Ostrov Belyy
Yenisey
Taz

Hudson Bay
Southampton Island
Melville Peninsula
Gulf of Boothia
North Geomagnetic Pole
Ellesmere Island
Cape Columbia
Alert
Wandel Sea
Barents Plain
Novaya Zemlya
Ostrov Vaygach
Ob'

Foxe Basin
Prince Charles Island
Nares Strait
Baffin Basin
Thule
Ummannaq
Knud Rasmussen Land
Station Nord
Nordaustlandet
SVALBARD (to Norway)
Barents Sea
Ostrov Kolguyev

Hudson Strait
Foxe Peninsula
Baffin Island
Baffin Bay
Nuussuaq
Kong Frederik VIII Land
Longyearbyen
Spitsbergen
Barents Trough
Nord Kapp

Davis Strait
GREENLAND (to Denmark)
King Wilhelm Land
Greenland Plain

Cape Chidley
Illulissat
Kong Frederik IX Land
Dronning Ingrid Land
Kong Christian IX Land
Greenland Sea
Kola Peninsula

Maniitsoq
NUUK
Gunnbjorn Field 12,139ft (3,700m)
Ittoqqortoormiit
Kap Brewster
Jan Mayen

Labrador Sea
Ammassalik
Denmark Strait
Norwegian Sea
Norwegian Basin

Labrador Basin
Icelandic Plateau
Gulf of Bothnia

Kap Farvel
Reykjanes Basin
ICELAND
Arctic Circle

Reykjanes Ridge
Norwegian Basin
Faroe Islands
Iceland Basin

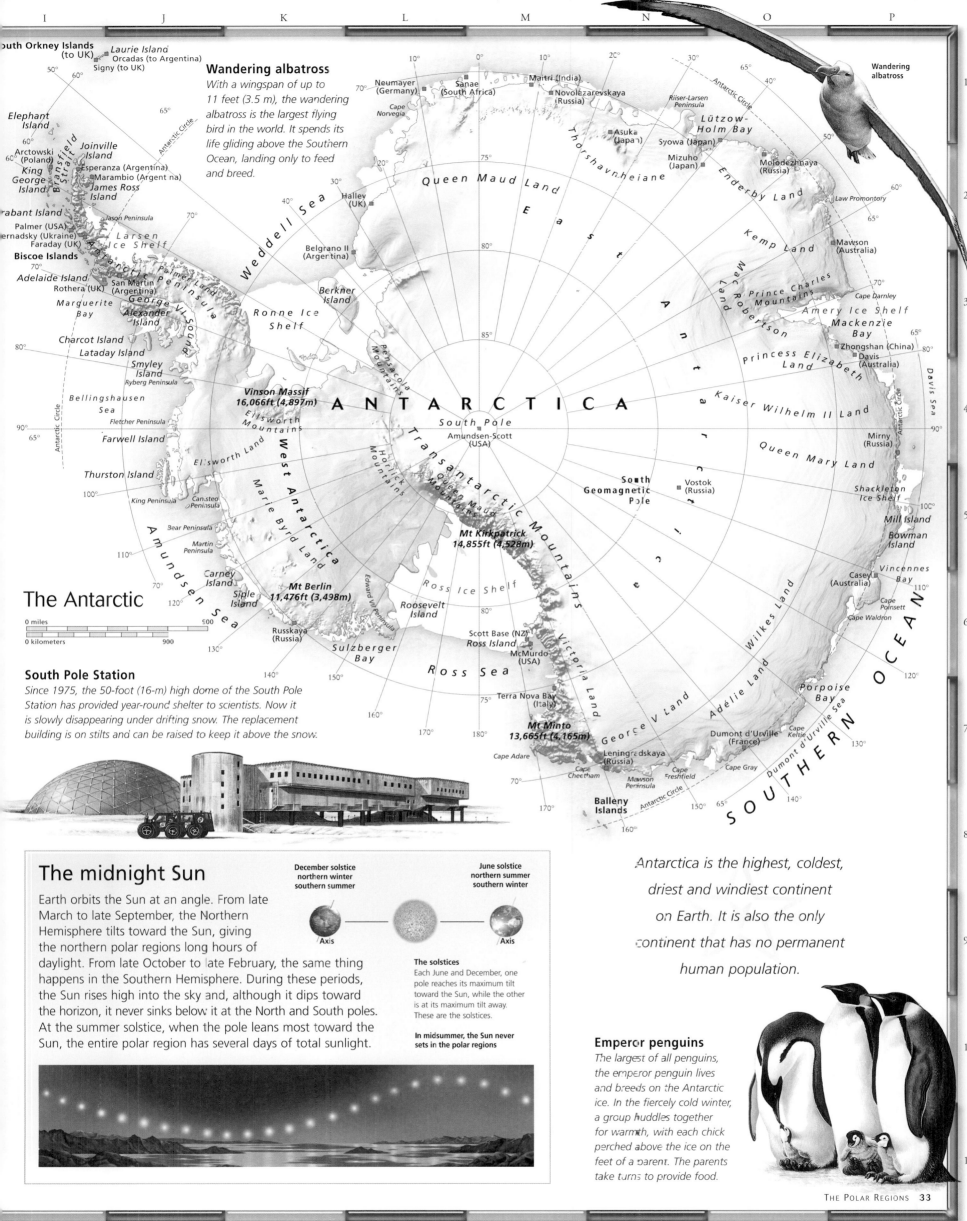

Wandering albatross

With a wingspan of up to 11 feet (3.5 m), the wandering albatross is the largest flying bird in the world. It spends its life gliding above the Southern Ocean, landing only to feed and breed.

Wandering albatross

The Antarctic

0 miles 900
0 kilometers 900

South Pole Station

Since 1975, the 50-foot (16-m) high dome of the South Pole Station has provided year-round shelter to scientists. Now it is slowly disappearing under drifting snow. The replacement building is on stilts and can be raised to keep it above the snow.

Map labels

South Orkney Islands (to UK)
Laurie Island
Orcadas (to Argentina)
Signy (to UK)
Elephant Island
Arctowski (Poland)
Joinville Island
King George Island
Esperanza (Argentina)
Marambio (Argentna)
James Ross Island
Brabant Island
Palmer (USA)
Vernadsky (Ukraine)
Faraday (UK)
Biscoe Islands
Adelaide Island
Rothera (UK)
San Martin (Argentina)
Marguerite Bay
George VI Sound
Alexander Island
Charcot Island
Lataday Island
Smyley Island
Ryberg Peninsula
Bellingshausen Sea
Fletcher Peninsula
Farwell Island
Ellsworth Land
Thurston Island
King Peninsula
Canisteo Peninsula
Amundsen Sea
Bear Peninsula
Martin Peninsula
Carney Island
Siple Island
Russkaya (Russia)
Sulzberger Bay
Roosevelt Island
Ross Ice Shelf
Ross Sea
Scott Base (NZ)
Ross Island
McMurdo (USA)
Terra Nova Bay (Italy)
Cape Adare
Leningradskaya (Russia)
Mawson Peninsula
Cape Cheetham
Cape Freshfield
Cape Gray
Balleny Islands

Larsen Ice Shelf
Antarctic Peninsula
Palmer Land
Weddell Sea
Halley (UK)
Belgrano II (Argentina)
Berkner Island
Ronne Ice Shelf
Vinson Massif 16,066ft (4,897m)
Ellsworth Mountains
West Antarctica
Marie Byrd Land
Edward VII Peninsula
Mt Berlin 11,476ft (3,498m)
Pensacola Mountains
Horlick Mountains
Queen Maud Mountains
Transantarctic Mountains
Mt Kirkpatrick 14,855ft (4,528m)
South Pole
Amundsen-Scott (USA)
ANTARCTICA
Victoria Land
Mt Minto 13,665ft (4,165m)
George V Land

Neumayer (Germany)
Sanae (South Africa)
Cape Norvegia
Maitri (India)
Novolazarevskaya (Russia)
Asuka (Japan)
Thorshavnheiane
Queen Maud Land
East Antarctica
Riiser-Larsen Peninsula
Lützow-Holm Bay
Syowa (Japan)
Mizuho (Japan)
Enderby Land
Molodezhnaya (Russia)
Law Promontory
Kemp Land
Mac Robertson Land
Mawson (Australia)
Prince Charles Mountains
Cape Darnley
Amery Ice Shelf
Mackenzie Bay
Princess Elizabeth Land
Zhongshan (China)
Davis (Australia)
Davis Sea
Kaiser Wilhelm II Land
South Geomagnetic Pole
Vostok (Russia)
Mirny (Russia)
Queen Mary Land
Shackleton Ice Shelf
Mill Island
Bowman Island
Wilkes Land
Vincennes Bay
Casey (Australia)
Cape Poinsett
Cape Waldron
Adélie Land
Porpoise Bay
Dumont d'Urville (France)
Dumont d'Urville Sea
Cape Keltie

SOUTHERN OCEAN
Antarctic Circle

The midnight Sun

Earth orbits the Sun at an angle. From late March to late September, the Northern Hemisphere tilts toward the Sun, giving the northern polar regions long hours of daylight. From late October to late February, the same thing happens in the Southern Hemisphere. During these periods, the Sun rises high into the sky and, although it dips toward the horizon, it never sinks below it at the North and South poles. At the summer solstice, when the pole leans most toward the Sun, the entire polar region has several days of total sunlight.

December solstice
northern winter
southern summer

June solstice
northern summer
southern winter

Axis

Axis

The solstices

Each June and December, one pole reaches its maximum tilt toward the Sun, while the other is at its maximum tilt away. These are the solstices.

In midsummer, the Sun never sets in the polar regions

Antarctica is the highest, coldest, driest and windiest continent on Earth. It is also the only continent that has no permanent human population.

Emperor penguins

The largest of all penguins, the emperor penguin lives and breeds on the Antarctic ice. In the fiercely cold winter, a group huddles together for warmth, with each chick perched above the ice on the feet of a parent. The parents take turns to provide food.

ARCTIC OCEAN

Queen Elizabeth Islands

Axe
Heibe
Islar

Parry Islands

Chukchi
Sea

Beaufort
Sea

Banks
Island

Melville Island

Bathurst
Island

Prince of
Wales Island

Bering Strait

Brooks Range

Victoria Island

Bering
Sea

Mt McKinley
20,321ft (6,194m)

Great Bear
Lake

Alaska ▲ Range

Aleutian Islands

Aleutian Range

Mackenzie Mountains

Great Slave
Lake

Yukon

Gulf of
Alaska

Coast Mountains

Lake Athabasca

Reindeer
Lake

Mackenzie

Peace

R   O   C   K   Y

Saskatchewan

Lake
Manitoba

Mt Rainier
14,409ft (4,392m) ▲

M   o   u   n   t   a   i   n   s

G
r
e
a
t

Columbia

Coast Ranges

Cascade Range

Snake

PACIFIC OCEAN

Sierra Nevada

Great Salt
Lake

G   r   e   a   t

B   a   s   i   n

Mt Whitney
14,495ft (4,418m) ▲

Colorado

▲ Mt Elbert
14,432ft (4,399m)

Colorado

Death Valley
282ft (–86m) ▲

Grand
Canyon

Plateau

Mojave
Desert

Sonoran
Desert

Baja California

Gulf of California

Sierra Madre Occidental

Sierra Madre Oriental

Volcan Popocatépe
17,837ft (5,452m

Sierra Madre

PACIFIC OCEAN

North America

Ellesmere Island

Devon Island

merset and

oth ia insula

Greenland

Baffin Bay

Baffin Island

Melville Peninsula

Davis Strait

Foxe Basin

Hudson Strait

Péninsule d'Ungava

Labrador Sea

Labrador

Hudson Bay

Canadian Shield

ake Winnipeg

Reservoir Manicouagan

Laurentian Mountains

Newfoundland

Lake Nipigon

Lake Superior

Great Lakes

Lake Huron

Nova Scotia

Lake Michigan

Lake Ontario

ATLANTIC OCEAN

Central Lowlands

Lake Erie

Missouri

Ohio

Appalachian Mountains

Plains

Arkansas

Mississippi

Gulf-Atlantic Coastal Plain

Mississippi Delta

Gulf of Mexico

The Bahamas

West Indies

Cuba

Greater Antilles

Leeward Islands

Yucatan Peninsula

Pico de Orizaba
18,405ft (5,610m)

Caribbean Sea

Lesser Antilles

Sur

Lake Nicaragua

of Panama

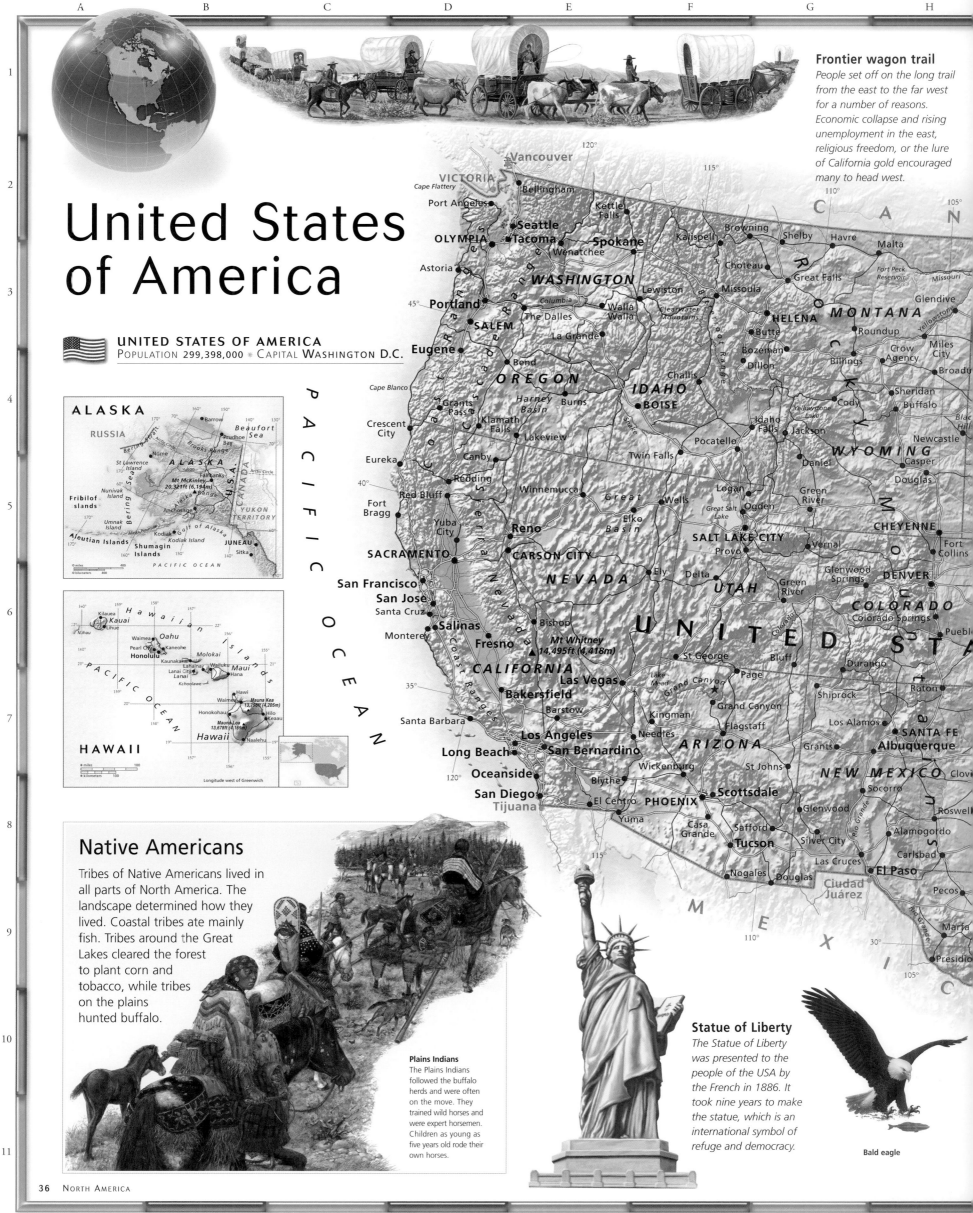

Frontier wagon trail
People set off on the long trail from the east to the far west for a number of reasons. Economic collapse and rising unemployment in the east, religious freedom, or the lure of California gold encouraged many to head west.

United States of America

UNITED STATES OF AMERICA
POPULATION 299,398,000 ＊ CAPITAL WASHINGTON D.C.

ALASKA

RUSSIA
Barrow
Beaufort Sea
Prudhoe Bay
Brooks Range
Nome
Bering Strait
Arctic Circle
St Lawrence Island
ALASKA
Fairbanks
CANADA
USA
Nunivak Island
Mt McKinley 20,321ft (6,194m)
Alaska Range
YUKON TERRITORY
Pribilof Islands
Anchorage
Umnak Island
Kodiak
Gulf of Alaska
Kodiak Island
JUNEAU
Sitka
Aleutian Islands
Shumagin Islands
PACIFIC OCEAN

HAWAII

Hawaiian Islands
Kilauea
Kauai
Niihau
Lihue
Oahu
Waimea
Honolulu
Pearl City Kaneohe
Kaunakakai
Lahaina
Molokai
Lanai City
Lanai
Wailuku
Maui
Hana
Kahoolawe
Waimea
Mauna Kea 13,796ft (4,205m)
Hilo
Keaau
Honokohau
Mauna Loa 13,678ft (4,169m)
Hawaii
Naalehu
PACIFIC OCEAN
Longitude west of Greenwich

PACIFIC OCEAN

Vancouver
VICTORIA
Cape Flattery
Bellingham
Port Angeles
Seattle
OLYMPIA Tacoma
Kettle Falls
Spokane
Astoria
Wenatchee
Kalispell
Browning
Shelby
Havre
Malta
CANADA
WASHINGTON
Choteau
Great Falls
Fort Peck Reservoir
Missouri
Portland
Columbia
The Dalles
Lewiston
Walla Walla
Clearwater Mountains
Missoula
Helena
MONTANA
Glendive
SALEM
La Grande
HELENA
Butte
Roundup
Crow Agency
Miles City
Broadu
Eugene
Bend
Bitter Root Range
Bozeman
Dillon
Billings
Cape Blanco
OREGON
Harney Basin
Burns
IDAHO
BOISE
Yellowstone Lake
Sheridan
Buffalo
Cody
Grants Pass
Klamath Falls
Lakeview
Idaho Falls
Jackson
WYOMING
Newcastle
Crescent City
Canby
Twin Falls
Pocatello
Casper
Eureka
Redding
Winnemucca
Wells
Logan
Green River
Daniel
Douglas
Red Bluff
Great Basin
Elko
Great Salt Lake
Ogden
Fort Collins
Fort Bragg
Yuba City
Reno
CARSON CITY
SALT LAKE CITY
Provo
Vernal
CHEYENNE
SACRAMENTO
NEVADA
Ely
Delta
UTAH
Glenwood Springs
DENVER
San Francisco
San Jose
Santa Cruz
Bishop
Green River
COLORADO
Colorado Springs
Pueblo
UNITED STA
Salinas
Fresno
Mt Whitney 14,495ft (4,418m)
St George
Bluff
Durango
Raton
Monterey
CALIFORNIA
Las Vegas
Lake Mead
Grand Canyon
Page
Shiprock
Bakersfield
Barstow
Grand Canyon
Flagstaff
Los Alamos
SANTA FE
Santa Barbara
Kingman
Needles
Grants
Albuquerque
Los Angeles
San Bernardino
Wickenburg
ARIZONA
NEW MEXICO
Clov
Long Beach
St Johns
Oceanside
Blythe
St George
Socorro
Roswell
San Diego
Tijuana
El Centro
PHOENIX
Scottsdale
Glenwood
Yuma
Casa Grande
Safford
Silver City
Alamogordo
Tucson
Carlsbad
Nogales
Douglas
Las Cruces
Ciudad Juárez
El Paso
Pecos
MEXICO
Marfa
Presidio

Native Americans

Tribes of Native Americans lived in all parts of North America. The landscape determined how they lived. Coastal tribes ate mainly fish. Tribes around the Great Lakes cleared the forest to plant corn and tobacco, while tribes on the plains hunted buffalo.

Plains Indians
The Plains Indians followed the buffalo herds and were often on the move. They trained wild horses and were expert horsemen. Children as young as five years old rode their own horses.

Statue of Liberty
The Statue of Liberty was presented to the people of the USA by the French in 1886. It took nine years to make the statue, which is an international symbol of refuge and democracy.

Bald eagle

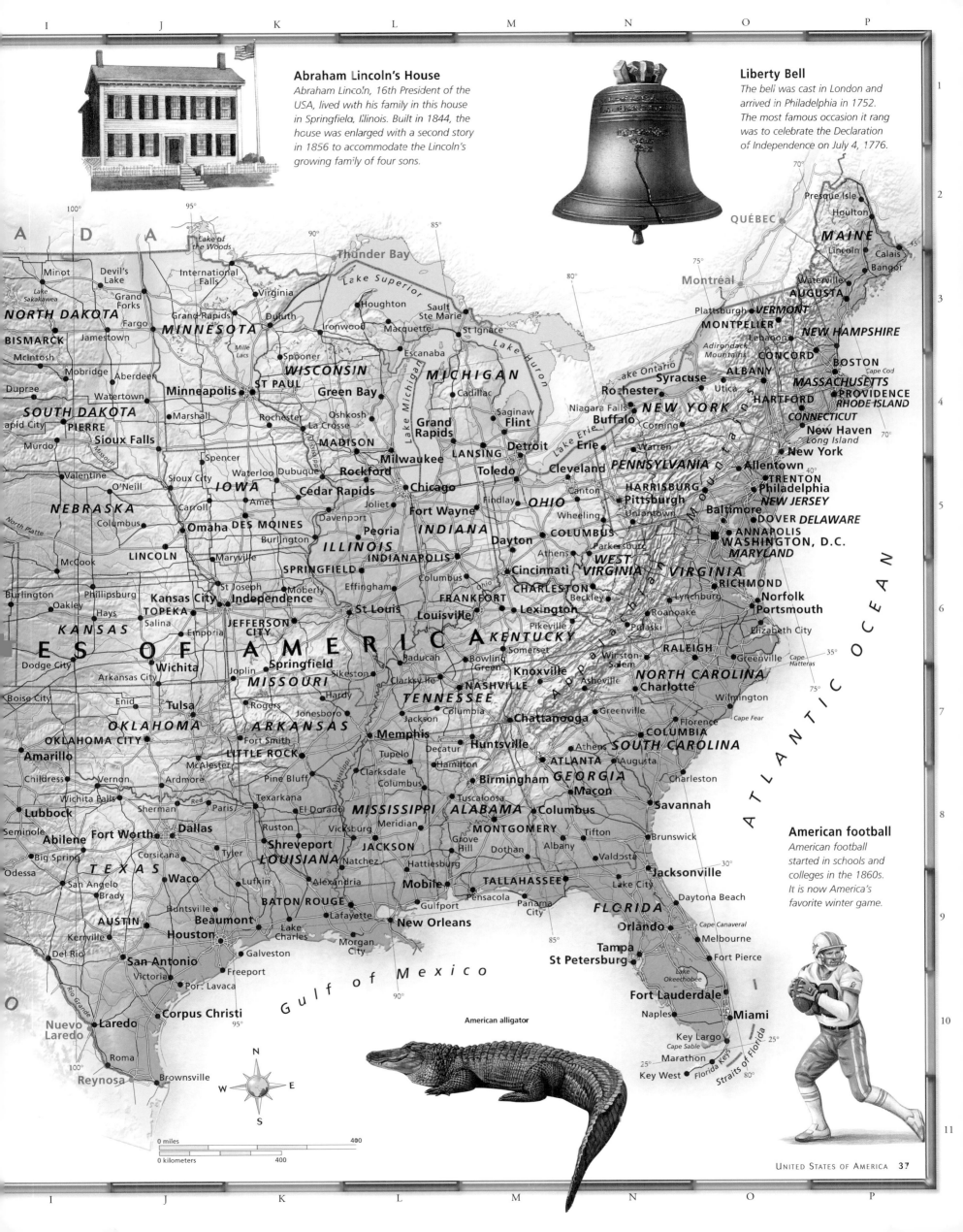

Abraham Lincoln's House
Abraham Lincoln, 16th President of the USA, lived with his family in this house in Springfield, Illinois. Built in 1844, the house was enlarged with a second story in 1856 to accommodate the Lincoln's growing family of four sons.

Liberty Bell
The bell was cast in London and arrived in Philadelphia in 1752. The most famous occasion it rang was to celebrate the Declaration of Independence on July 4, 1776.

American football
American football started in schools and colleges in the 1860s. It is now America's favorite winter game.

American alligator

0 miles 400

0 kilometers 400

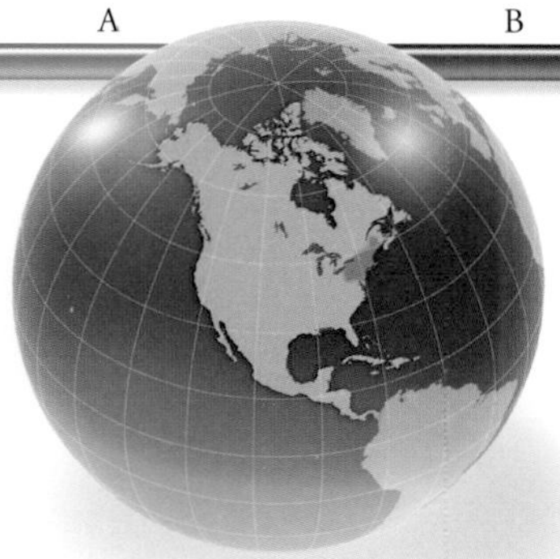

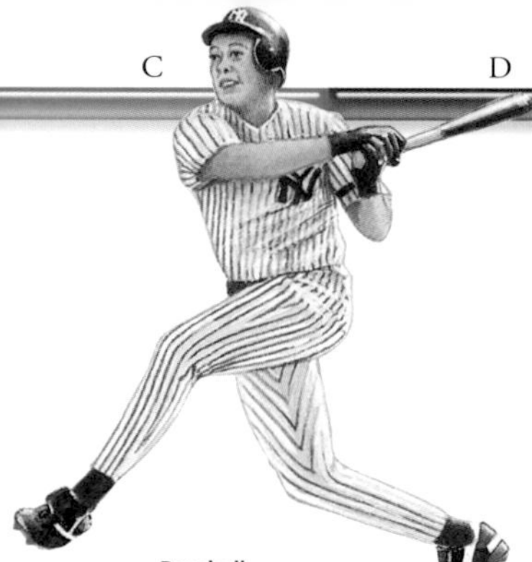

Baseball

Northeastern USA

NEW YORK
POPULATION 19,306,000 * CAPITAL ALBANY

PENNSYLVANIA
POPULATION 12,441,000 * CAPITAL HARRISBURG

NEW JERSEY
POPULATION 8,725,000 * CAPITAL TRENTON

MASSACHUSETTS
POPULATION 6,437,000 * CAPITAL BOSTON

CONNECTICUT
POPULATION 3,505,000 * CAPITAL HARTFORD

MAINE
POPULATION 1,322,000 * CAPITAL AUGUSTA

NEW HAMPSHIRE
POPULATION 1,315,000 * CAPITAL CONCORD

RHODE ISLAND
POPULATION 1,068,000 * CAPITAL PROVIDENCE

VERMONT
POPULATION 624,000 * CAPITAL MONTPELIER

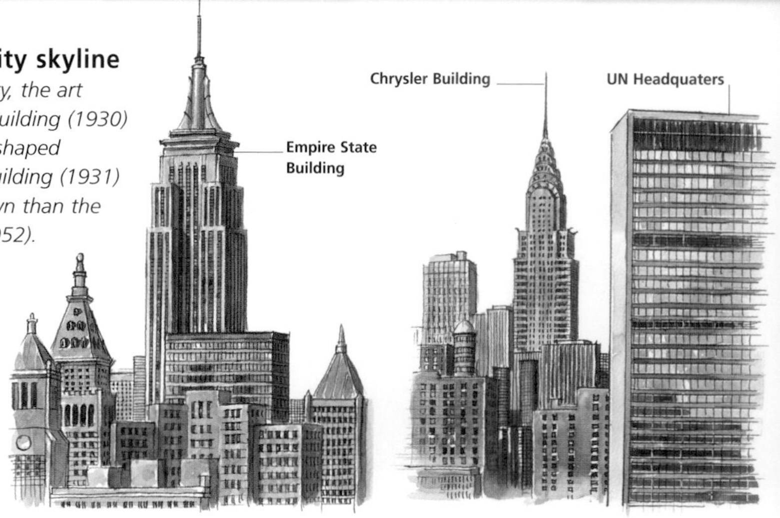

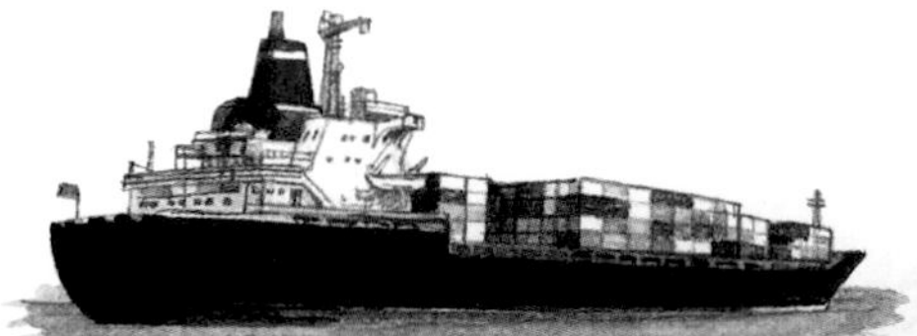

Chrysler Building
UN Headquaters
Empire State Building

New York City skyline
In New York City, the art deco Chrysler Building (1930) and the pencil-shaped Empire State Building (1931) are better known than the UN Building (1952).

Container ship
The USA is the world's major market. Container ships carry exports to, and bring imports from, the rest of the world.

Amish people, Pennsylvania
During the 19th century, many Amish farmers from Germany settled in Pennsylvania. With strong religious beliefs, Amish families reject many modern conveniences such as automobiles. They believe in living a simple life on the land.

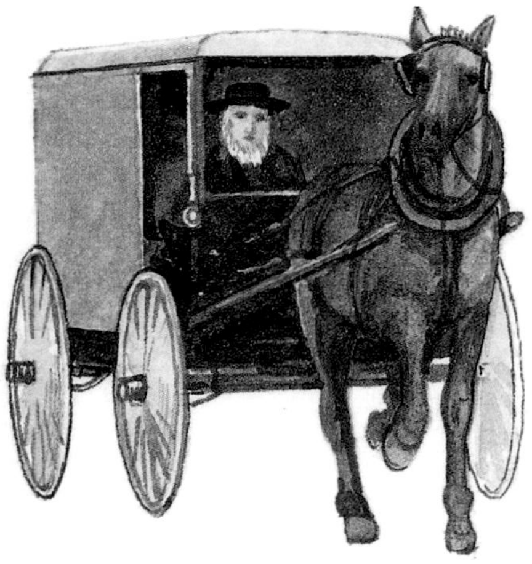

Niagara Falls
Niagara Falls creates a boundary between the USA and Canada. There are two large waterfalls and one small one. The American Falls are about 1,000 feet (300 m) long. The Horseshoe Falls on the Canadian side are twice as long.

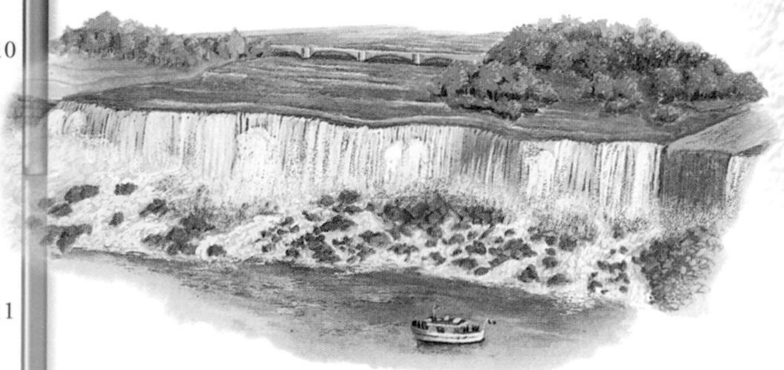

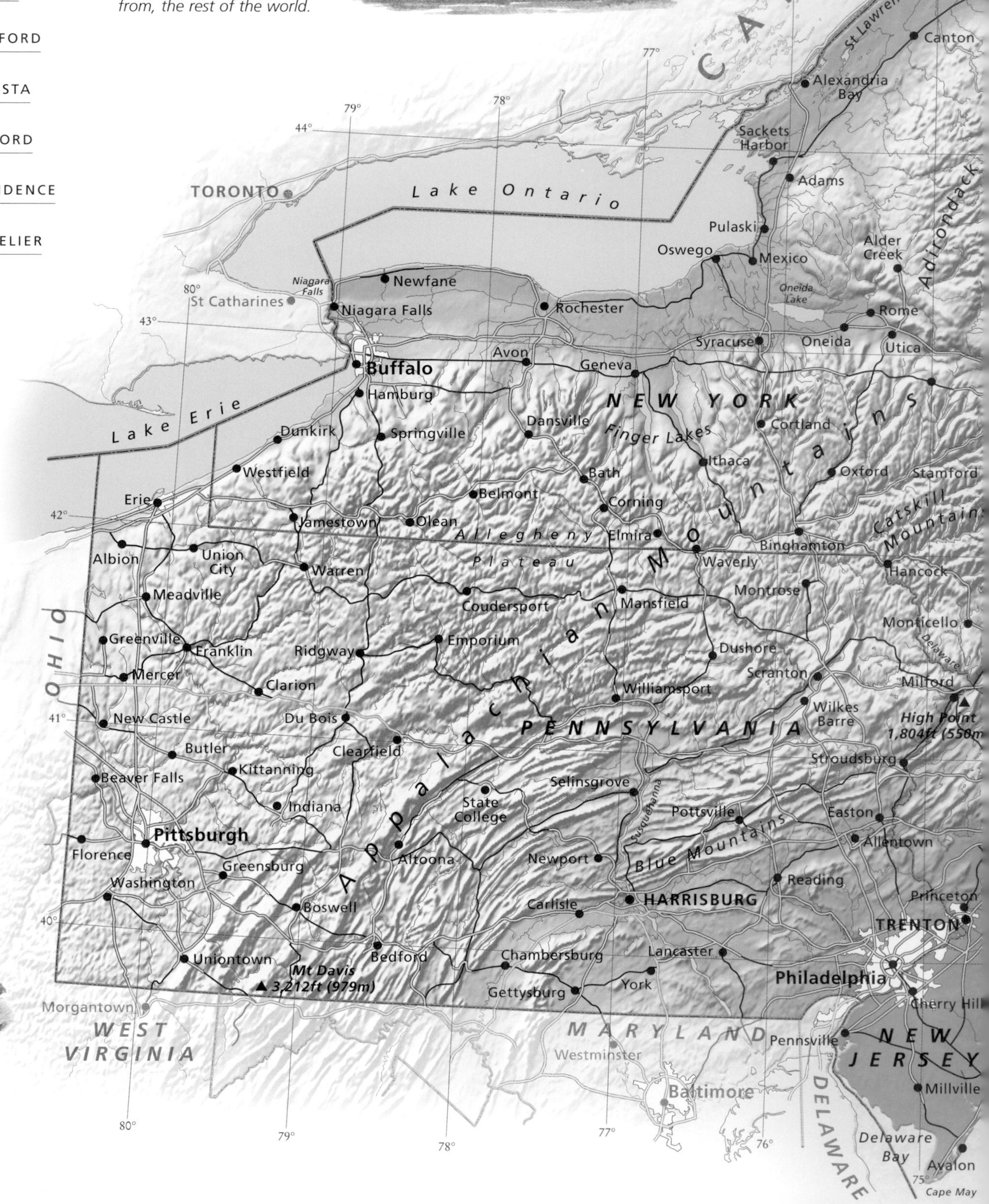

CANADA
TORONTO
Lake Ontario
Lake Erie
St Lawrence
Massena
Canton
Alexandria Bay
Sackets Harbor
Adams
Pulaski
Oswego
Mexico
Alder Creek
Oneida Lake
Adirondack
Rome
Oneida
Utica
Syracuse
Niagara Falls
St Catharines
Newfane
Niagara Falls
Rochester
Buffalo
Avon
Geneva
Hamburg
NEW YORK
Dansville
Finger Lakes
Cortland
Dunkirk
Springville
Ithaca
Oxford
Stamford
Westfield
Bath
Belmont
Corning
Catskill Mountains
Erie
Jamestown
Olean
Elmira
Binghamton
Allegheny Plateau
Waverly
Hancock
Albion
Union City
Warren
Montrose
Meadville
Coudersport
Mansfield
Monticello
OHIO
Greenville
Franklin
Emporium
Ridgway
Dushore
Delaware
Mercer
Scranton
Clarion
Williamsport
Milford
New Castle
Du Bois
Appalachian Mountains
Wilkes Barre
High Point 1,804ft (550m)
PENNSYLVANIA
Butler
Clearfield
Kittanning
Stroudsburg
Beaver Falls
Selinsgrove
Indiana
State College
Pottsville
Easton
Susquehanna
Pittsburgh
Blue Mountains
Allentown
Florence
Greensburg
Altoona
Newport
Washington
Reading
Princeton
Boswell
Carlisle
HARRISBURG
TRENTON
Bedford
Uniontown
Mt Davis 3,212ft (979m)
Chambersburg
Lancaster
Philadelphia
York
Gettysburg
Cherry Hill
Morgantown
WEST VIRGINIA
MARYLAND
Westminster
Pennsville
NEW JERSEY
Baltimore
Millville
DELAWARE
Delaware Bay
Avalon
Cape May
75°
76°
77°
78°
79°
80°
45°
44°
43°
42°
41°
40°

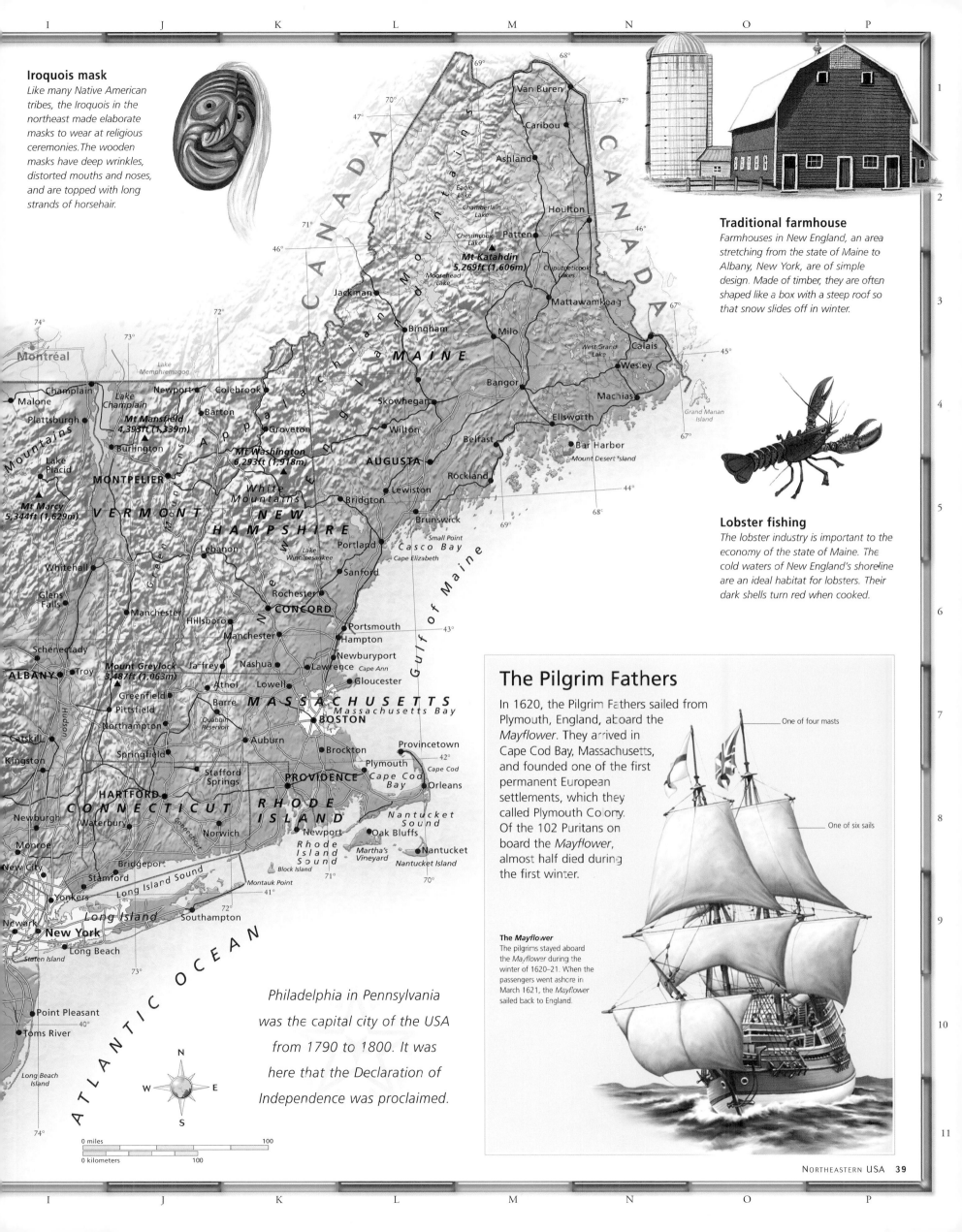

Iroquois mask

Like many Native American tribes, the Iroquois in the northeast made elaborate masks to wear at religious ceremonies. The wooden masks have deep wrinkles, distorted mouths and noses, and are topped with long strands of horsehair.

Traditional farmhouse

Farmhouses in New England, an area stretching from the state of Maine to Albany, New York, are of simple design. Made of timber, they are often shaped like a box with a steep roof so that snow slides off in winter.

Lobster fishing

The lobster industry is important to the economy of the state of Maine. The cold waters of New England's shoreline are an ideal habitat for lobsters. Their dark shells turn red when cooked.

The Pilgrim Fathers

In 1620, the Pilgrim Fathers sailed from Plymouth, England, aboard the *Mayflower*. They arrived in Cape Cod Bay, Massachusetts, and founded one of the first permanent European settlements, which they called Plymouth Colony. Of the 102 Puritans on board the *Mayflower*, almost half died during the first winter.

One of four masts

One of six sails

The *Mayflower*
The pilgrims stayed aboard the *Mayflower* during the winter of 1620–21. When the passengers went ashore in March 1621, the *Mayflower* sailed back to England.

Philadelphia in Pennsylvania was the capital city of the USA from 1790 to 1800. It was here that the Declaration of Independence was proclaimed.

Map labels

Van Buren
Caribou
Ashland
Houlton
Patten
Mt Katahdin 5,269ft (1,606m)
Eagle Lake
Chamberlain Lake
Chesuncook Lake
Moosehead Lake
Chiputneticook Lakes
Jackman
Mattawamkeag
MAINE
Bingham
Milo
West Grand Lake
Calais
Montréal
Lake Memphremagog
Newport
Colebrook
Skowhegan
Bangor
Wesley
Machias
Champlain
Malone
Barton
Lake Champlain
Groveton
Wilton
Ellsworth
Grand Manan Island
Plattsburgh
Mt Mansfield 4,393ft (1,339m)
Burlington
Mt Washington 6,293ft (1,918m)
AUGUSTA
Belfast
Bar Harbor
Mount Desert Island
Lake Placid
White Mountains
Rockland
Mt Marcy 5,344ft (1,629m)
VERMONT
NEW HAMPSHIRE
Lewiston
Bridgton
MONTPELIER
Whitehall
Brunswick
Glens Falls
Lebanon
Portland
Casco Bay
Small Point
Cape Elizabeth
Manchester
Lake Winnipesaukee
Rochester
Sanford
Gulf of Maine
Schenectady
CONCORD
Portsmouth
Troy
Hillsboro
Manchester
Hampton
ALBANY
Mount Greylock 3,487ft (1,063m)
Jaffrey
Nashua
Newburyport
Cape Ann
Gloucester
Greenfield
Athol
Lowell
Lawrence
Pittsfield
Barre
MASSACHUSETTS
Northampton
Quabbin Reservoir
Massachusetts Bay
Catskill
BOSTON
Kingston
Springfield
Auburn
Brockton
Provincetown
Stafford Springs
Plymouth
Cape Cod
HARTFORD
PROVIDENCE
Cape Cod Bay
Orleans
CONNECTICUT
RHODE ISLAND
Newburgh
Waterbury
Norwich
Newport
Oak Bluffs
Nantucket Sound
Nantucket
Monroe
Martha's Vineyard
Nantucket Island
New City
Bridgeport
Block Island
Rhode Island Sound
Stamford
Montauk Point
Newark
New York
Long Island Sound
Yonkers
Long Island
Southampton
Staten Island
Long Beach
Point Pleasant
Toms River
Long Beach Island

ATLANTIC OCEAN

CANADA

Appalachian Mountains

Green Mountains

Hudson

Connecticut

0 miles 100
0 kilometers 100

N
W E
S

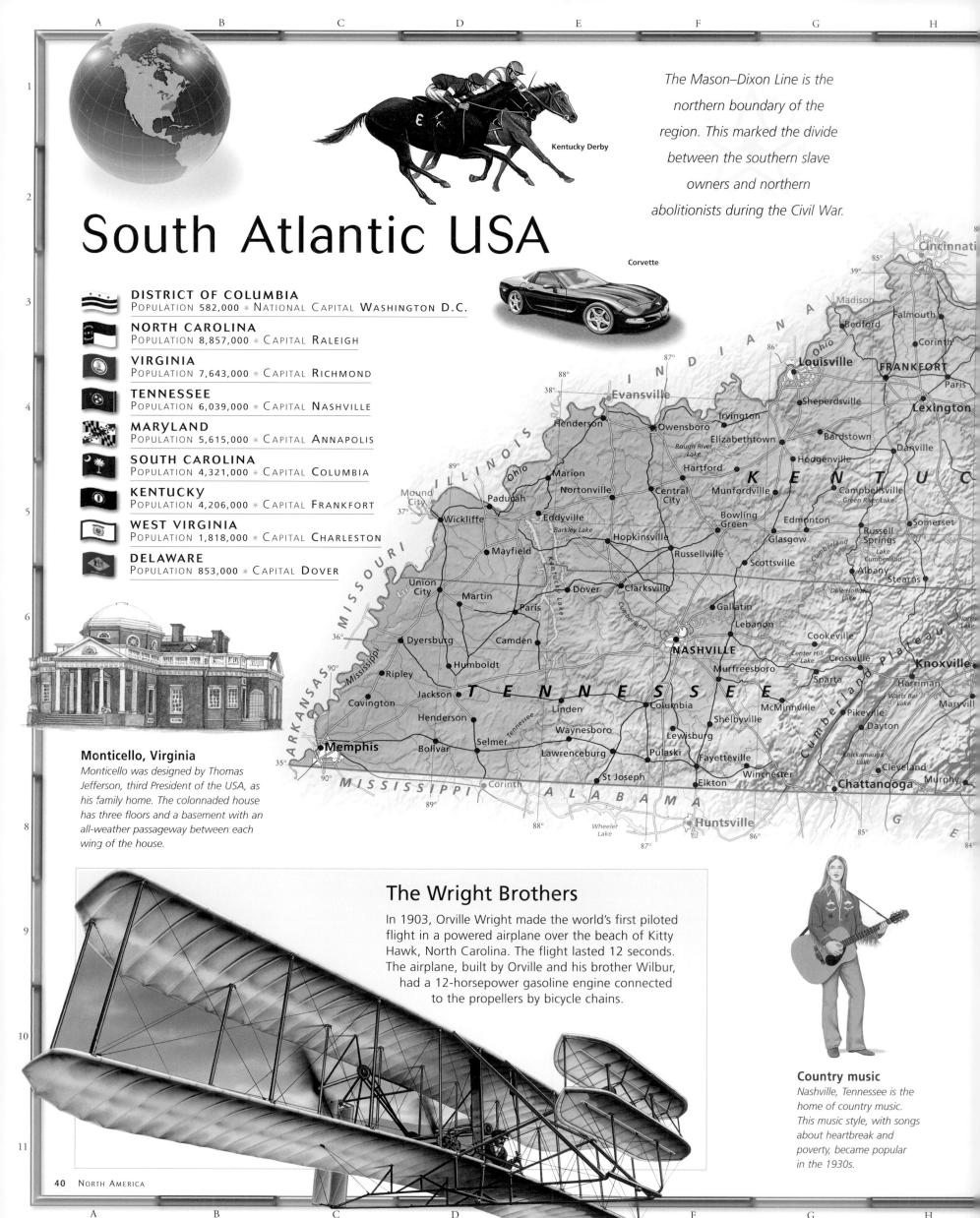

Kentucky Derby

The Mason–Dixon Line is the northern boundary of the region. This marked the divide between the southern slave owners and northern abolitionists during the Civil War.

South Atlantic USA

Corvette

DISTRICT OF COLUMBIA
POPULATION 582,000 ∗ NATIONAL CAPITAL WASHINGTON D.C.

NORTH CAROLINA
POPULATION 8,857,000 ∗ CAPITAL RALEIGH

VIRGINIA
POPULATION 7,643,000 ∗ CAPITAL RICHMOND

TENNESSEE
POPULATION 6,039,000 ∗ CAPITAL NASHVILLE

MARYLAND
POPULATION 5,615,000 ∗ CAPITAL ANNAPOLIS

SOUTH CAROLINA
POPULATION 4,321,000 ∗ CAPITAL COLUMBIA

KENTUCKY
POPULATION 4,206,000 ∗ CAPITAL FRANKFORT

WEST VIRGINIA
POPULATION 1,818,000 ∗ CAPITAL CHARLESTON

DELAWARE
POPULATION 853,000 ∗ CAPITAL DOVER

Monticello, Virginia

Monticello was designed by Thomas Jefferson, third President of the USA, as his family home. The colonnaded house has three floors and a basement with an all-weather passageway between each wing of the house.

The Wright Brothers

In 1903, Orville Wright made the world's first piloted flight in a powered airplane over the beach of Kitty Hawk, North Carolina. The flight lasted 12 seconds. The airplane, built by Orville and his brother Wilbur, had a 12-horsepower gasoline engine connected to the propellers by bicycle chains.

Country music

Nashville, Tennessee is the home of country music. This music style, with songs about heartbreak and poverty, became popular in the 1930s.

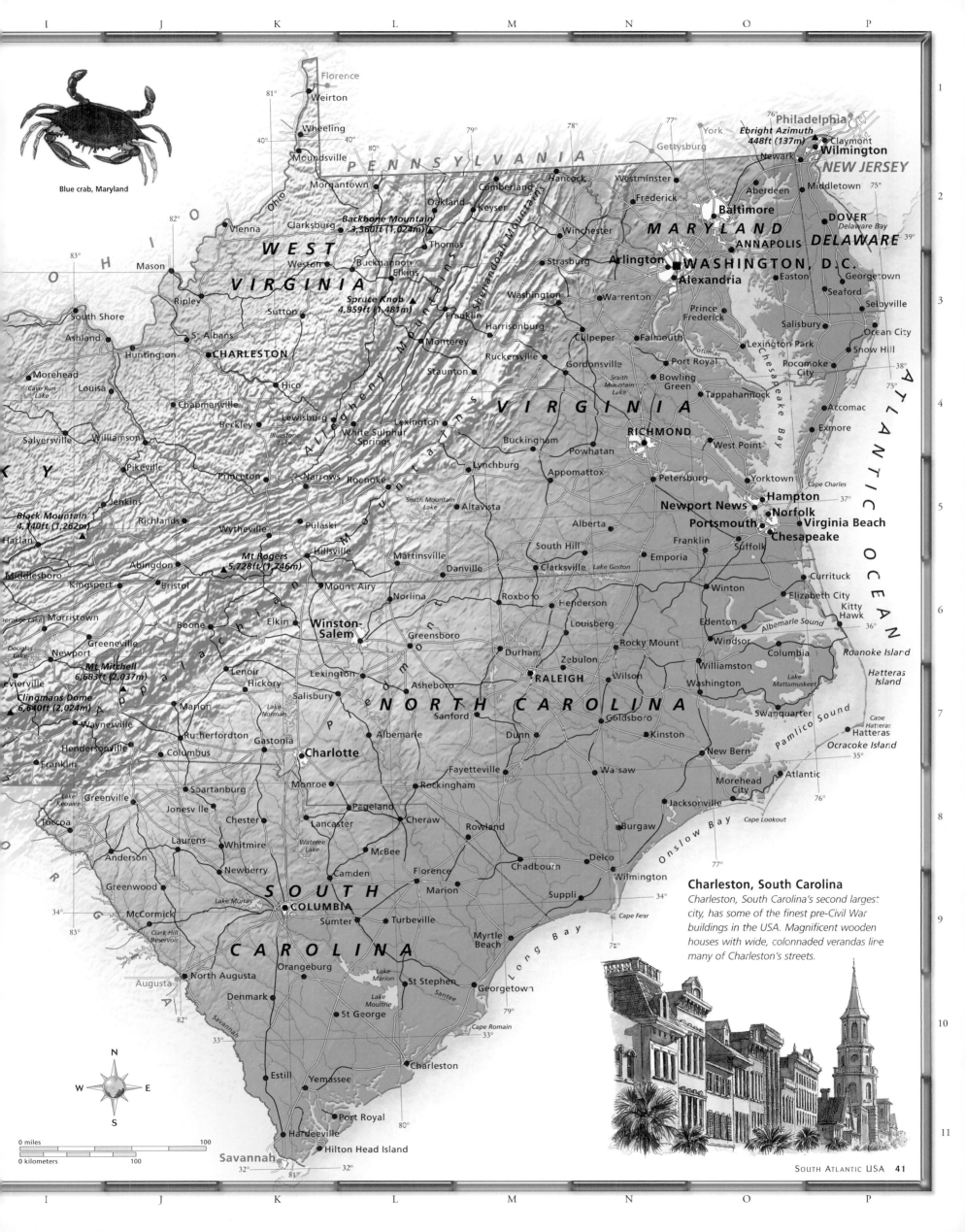

Blue crab, Maryland

Charleston, South Carolina
Charleston, South Carolina's second largest city, has some of the finest pre-Civil War buildings in the USA. Magnificent wooden houses with wide, colonnaded verandas line many of Charleston's streets.

Plantation mansion
In the early 1860s, wealthy plantation owners in the southern states built large, elegant homes inspired by classical Greek architecture. These mansions featured covered porches, pillars, sweeping staircases, and ballrooms.

Southeastern USA

FLORIDA
POPULATION 18,090,000 ✳ CAPITAL TALLAHASSEE

GEORGIA
POPULATION 9,364,000 ✳ CAPITAL ATLANTA

ALABAMA
POPULATION 4,599,000 ✳ CAPITAL MONTGOMERY

LOUISIANA
POPULATION 4,288,000 ✳ CAPITAL BATON ROUGE

MISSISSIPPI
POPULATION 2,911,000 ✳ CAPITAL JACKSON

Mississippi paddle steamer
With paddles driven by a steam engine, paddle steamers carried building materials, farm produce, and people along the Mississippi, America's longest river. Today, paddle steamers are used as tourist boats.

Hurricanes

Hurricanes begin as small thunderstorms over warm water. They often hit towns and cities on the coast of the Gulf of Mexico and the Atlantic Ocean. Satellite tracking has helped to provide early warning of approaching hurricanes.

Hurricane life cycle

Day 1: a storm cluster forms

Day 2: storm starts to spin

Day 3: spiral shape develops

Day 6: eye emerges

Day 12: begins to fade

Cross section of a hurricane
The warm water of the ocean heats the air and creates a rising current of moist air. Cool air is pulled in to replace the moist air. As the hurricane rotates, it draws in more moist air and its energy increases.

Jazz music
New Orleans was the birthplace of jazz in the late 1800s. Jazz is a combination of music styles, including blues and ragtime.

Produce of the region

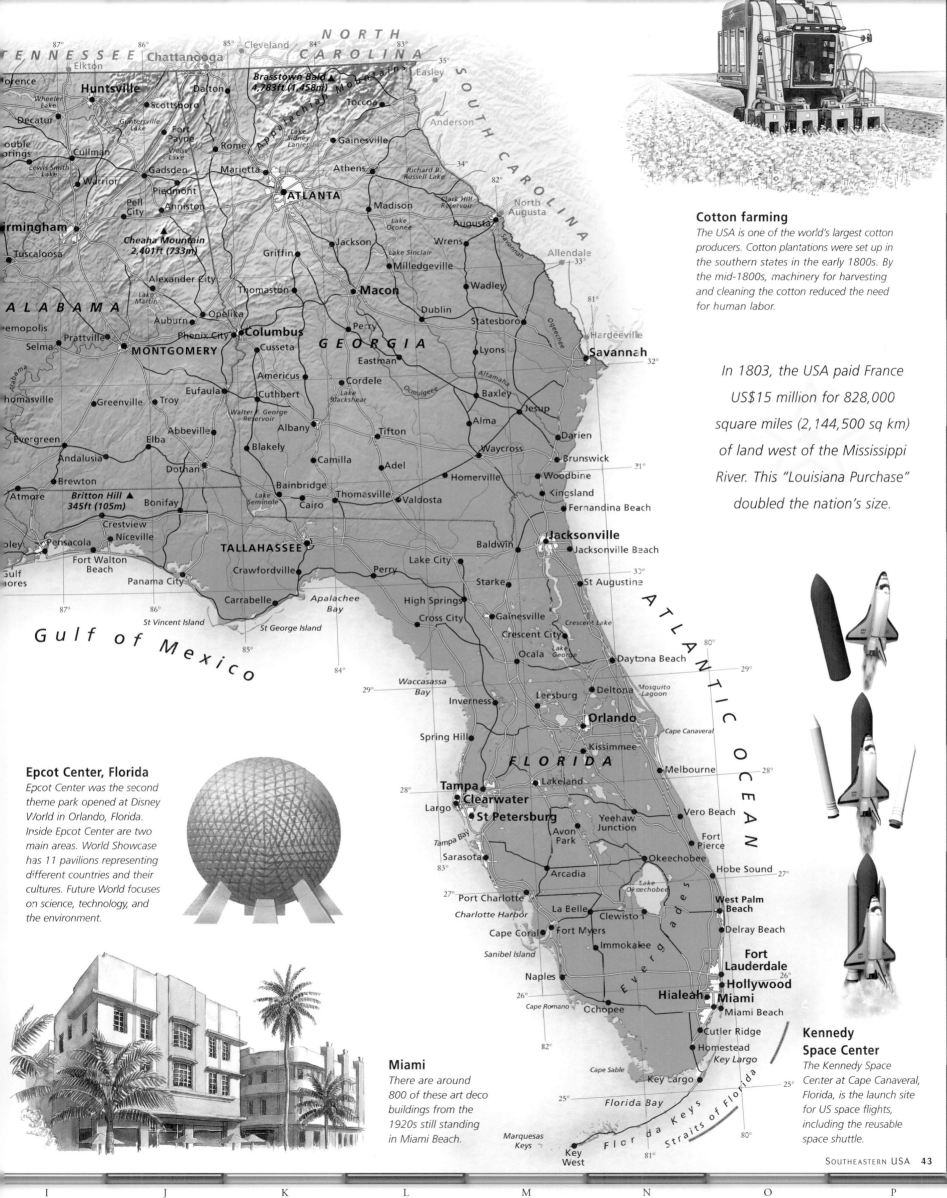

NORTH CAROLINA

Cleveland Chattanooga Easley 35°

Florence Elkton

Huntsville Dalton Brasstown Bald ▲ 4,783ft (1,458m) Toccoa

Decatur Scottsboro Anderson

Wheeler Lake Guntersville Lake Fort Payne Rome Marietta Gainesville

SOUTH CAROLINA

Double Springs Cullman Gadsden Piedmont Athens Richard B. Russell Lake 34° 82°

Lewis Smith Lake Warrior Anniston ATLANTA Madison Clark Hill Reservoir North Augusta

Birmingham Pell City Cheaha Mountain 2,401ft (733m) Jackson Lake Oconee Augusta Allendale 33°

ALABAMA Tuscaloosa Alexander City Griffin Lake Sinclair Milledgeville 81°

Auburn Thomaston Macon Wadley Statesboro Hardeeville

Emopolis Prattville Opelika Perry GEORGIA Lyons Savannah 32°

Selma Montgomery Phenix City Columbus Cusseta Eastman Baxley Jesup

Thomasville Greenville Troy Americus Cuthbert Cordele Lake Blackshear Alma Darien

Evergreen Eufaula Walter F. George Reservoir Albany Tifton Waycross Brunswick 31°

Andalusia Elba Blakely Camilla Adel Homerville Woodbine

Atmore Brewton Dothan Bainbridge Thomasville Valdosta Kingsland

Britton Hill ▲ 345ft (105m) Bonifay Lake Seminole Cairo Lake George Fernandina Beach

Boley Pensacola Crestview Niceville Baldwin Jacksonville

Gulf Shores Fort Walton Beach TALLAHASSEE Lake City Jacksonville Beach

Panama City Crawfordville Perry Starke St Augustine 32°

Carrabelle Apalachee Bay High Springs Gainesville Crescent Lake

Gulf of Mexico St Vincent Island St George Island 85° Cross City Crescent City Daytona Beach 80°

84° Ocala Lake George 29°

Waccasassa Bay Deltona Mosquito Lagoon

29° Inverness Leesburg Orlando Cape Canaveral

Spring Hill Kissimmee Melbourne 28°

FLORIDA Lakeland

28° Tampa Clearwater Yeehaw Junction Vero Beach

Largo St Petersburg Avon Park Fort Pierce

Tampa Bay Sarasota Okeechobee Hobe Sound 27°

27° Port Charlotte Arcadia Lake Okeechobee West Palm Beach

Charlotte Harbor La Belle Clewiston Delray Beach

Cape Coral Fort Myers Immokalee Fort Lauderdale

Sanibel Island Everglades Hollywood 26°

Naples Hialeah Miami

26° Cape Romano Ochopee Miami Beach 82°

Cutler Ridge

Cape Sable Homestead Key Largo

Key Largo 25°

Florida Bay 25°

Marquesas Keys Florida Keys Straits of Florida 80°

Key West 81°

Cotton farming

The USA is one of the world's largest cotton producers. Cotton plantations were set up in the southern states in the early 1800s. By the mid-1800s, machinery for harvesting and cleaning the cotton reduced the need for human labor.

In 1803, the USA paid France US$15 million for 828,000 square miles (2,144,500 sq km) of land west of the Mississippi River. This "Louisiana Purchase" doubled the nation's size.

Epcot Center, Florida

Epcot Center was the second theme park opened at Disney World in Orlando, Florida. Inside Epcot Center are two main areas. World Showcase has 11 pavilions representing different countries and their cultures. Future World focuses on science, technology, and the environment.

Miami

There are around 800 of these art deco buildings from the 1920s still standing in Miami Beach.

Kennedy Space Center

The Kennedy Space Center at Cape Canaveral, Florida, is the launch site for US space flights, including the reusable space shuttle.

Great Lakes, USA

Automobiles

The first gasoline-powered automobile was built at Kokomo, Indiana, in 1894. But a few years later, Henry Ford began producing cars in his plant in Detroit, Michigan. From 1914, Ford's use of the moving assembly line for mass production made Detroit the leading automobile manufacturing city in the USA.

Model-T Ford
First produced in 1908, at Ford's Piquette Avenue plant in Detroit, the Model-T Ford revolutionized the automobile industry. At a price of $850, the Model-T was a car that most families could afford.

Indianapolis 500
The "Indy 500" race started in 1911 and is the world's largest annual sporting event. Racing cars circle the track 200 times to complete the 500-mile (805-km) race each Memorial Day weekend.

Chicago skyline
Chicago was a bustling city of a million people when fire burnt the downtown area in 1871. When Chicago was rebuilt, it became the birthplace of skyscrapers.

Great Lakes freighter
From the early 19th century, steamboats transported farm goods and timber from the Great Lakes via river and canal to the Atlantic Ocean. Freighters on the Great Lakes today transport iron ore, coal, and grain along the same route.

ILLINOIS · POPULATION 12,832,000 ∗ CAPITAL SPRINGFIELD

OHIO · POPULATION 11,478,000 ∗ CAPITAL COLUMBUS

MICHIGAN · POPULATION 10,096,000 ∗ CAPITAL LANSING

INDIANA · POPULATION 6,314,000 ∗ CAPITAL INDIANAPOLIS

WISCONSIN · POPULATION 5,557,000 ∗ CAPITAL MADISON

Michigan has the longest shoreline of any inland state. Michigan's 3,288 miles (5,291 km) of shoreline is longer than the Atlantic coast from Maine to Florida.

Blue jay

Lumberjack

Covered bridge
Covered bridges provided protection from slippery snow and ice. Parke County, Indiana, is the covered bridge capital of the region with more than 30 covered bridges.

Serpent Mound
Native Americans built more than 10,000 burial mounds in Ohio. One of the best known is Serpent Mound outside Hillsboro, Ohio. Shaped like a giant snake, Serpent Mound is a quarter of a mile (0.4 km) long and around 2,000 years old.

Skunk

Mount Rushmore, South Dakota

Upper Midwest, USA

MINNESOTA
POPULATION 5,167,000 ∗ CAPITAL ST. PAUL

IOWA
POPULATION 2,982,000 ∗ CAPITAL DES MOINES

NEBRASKA
POPULATION 1,768,000 ∗ CAPITAL LINCOLN

SOUTH DAKOTA
POPULATION 782,000 ∗ CAPITAL PIERRE

NORTH DAKOTA
POPULATION 636,000 ∗ CAPITAL BISMARCK

Chimney Rock, Nebraska
The most famous landmark on the Oregon Trail, Chimney Rock stands 325 feet (99 m) high above the North Platte River. For pioneers, Chimney Rock, which can be seen from 30 miles (48 km) away, marked the beginning of the "West."

Capitol Building, Des Moines, Iowa
Thirty types of marble were used in the interior of the Capitol Building in Des Moines. But it is the central dome, gilded with 23-carat gold leaf, that is its most magnificent feature.

Railroads

It was only with the coming of the railroads in the 19th century that intensive settlement of the Upper Midwest was possible. The region had no access to water transportation—or the ocean. Roads were rough, rutted by wagon wheels, and very slow going. But steam trains could bring in thousands of settlers to farm— and then transport their wheat back out again.

Steam locomotive
Coal is burnt to heat water and make steam, which forces pistons along cylinders and makes the wheels of a steam locomotive turn. Eventually replaced by diesel-electric locomotives, steam locomotives are now used as tourist trains.

Fireman
The fireman shoveled coal into the firebox to keep the steam level up. He also monitored the water level in the boiler, filling the tender with water at the water tanks along the route.

Corn on the cob

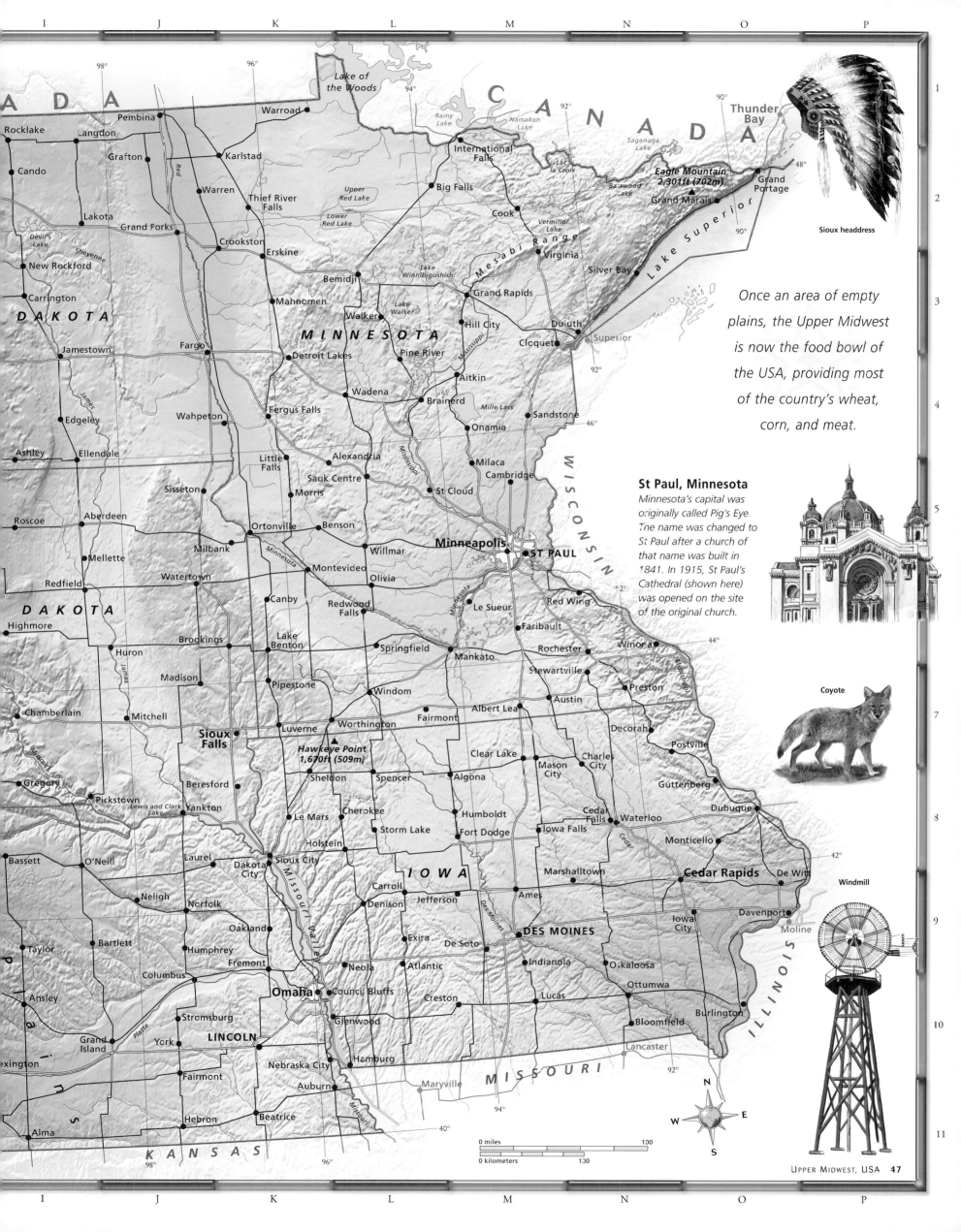

Once an area of empty plains, the Upper Midwest is now the food bowl of the USA, providing most of the country's wheat, corn, and meat.

Sioux headdress

St Paul, Minnesota

Minnesota's capital was originally called Pig's Eye. The name was changed to St Paul after a church of that name was built in 1841. In 1915, St Paul's Cathedral (shown here) was opened on the site of the original church.

Coyote

Windmill

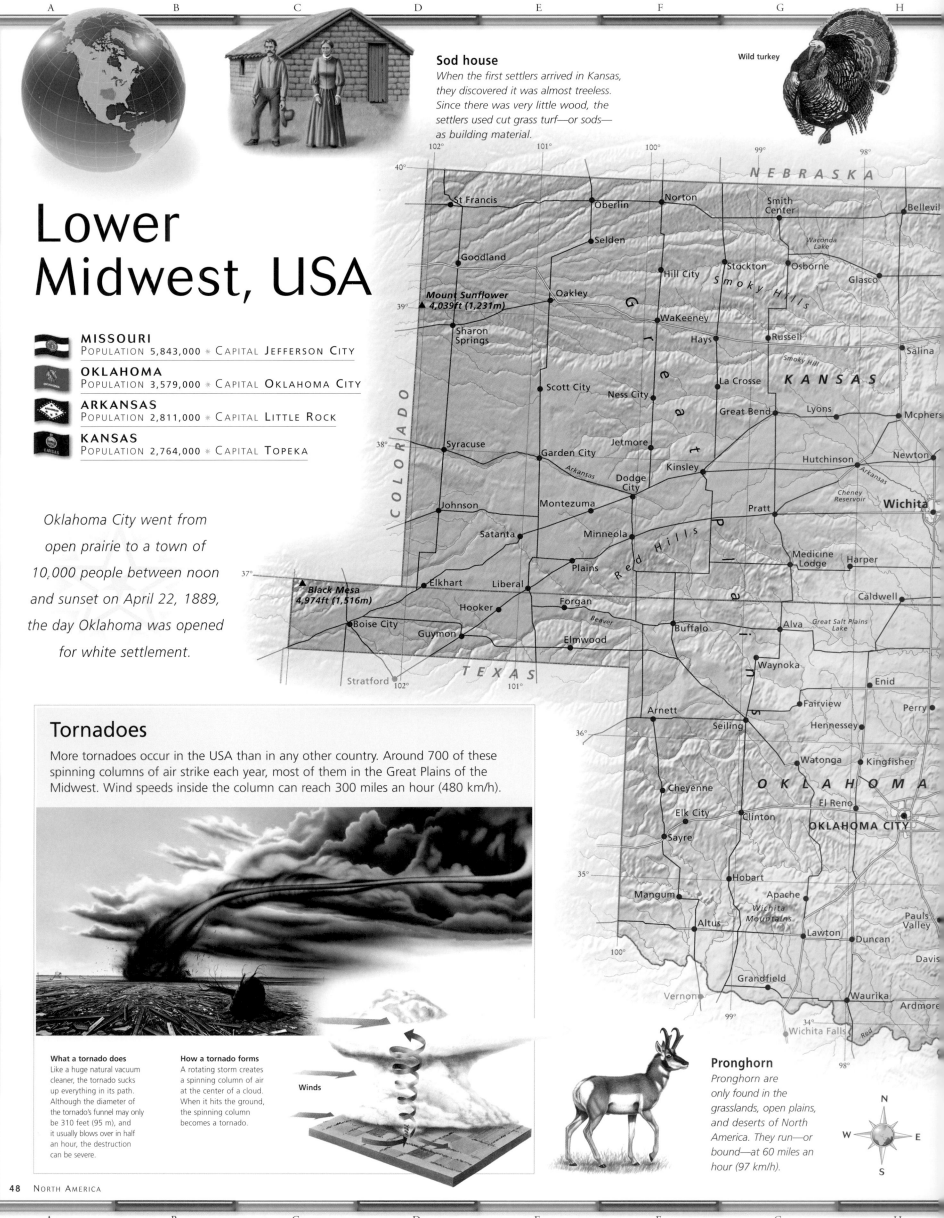

Lower Midwest, USA

Sod house
When the first settlers arrived in Kansas, they discovered it was almost treeless. Since there was very little wood, the settlers used cut grass turf—or sods— as building material.

Wild turkey

MISSOURI
POPULATION 5,843,000 * CAPITAL JEFFERSON CITY

OKLAHOMA
POPULATION 3,579,000 * CAPITAL OKLAHOMA CITY

ARKANSAS
POPULATION 2,811,000 * CAPITAL LITTLE ROCK

KANSAS
POPULATION 2,764,000 * CAPITAL TOPEKA

Oklahoma City went from open prairie to a town of 10,000 people between noon and sunset on April 22, 1889, the day Oklahoma was opened for white settlement.

Tornadoes

More tornadoes occur in the USA than in any other country. Around 700 of these spinning columns of air strike each year, most of them in the Great Plains of the Midwest. Wind speeds inside the column can reach 300 miles an hour (480 km/h).

What a tornado does
Like a huge natural vacuum cleaner, the tornado sucks up everything in its path. Although the diameter of the tornado's funnel may only be 310 feet (95 m), and it usually blows over in half an hour, the destruction can be severe.

How a tornado forms
A rotating storm creates a spinning column of air at the center of a cloud. When it hits the ground, the spinning column becomes a tornado.

Winds

Pronghorn
Pronghorn are only found in the grasslands, open plains, and deserts of North America. They run—or bound—at 60 miles an hour (97 km/h).

Gateway Arch, St Louis
The 630-foot (192-m) tall Gateway Arch commemorates the role of St Louis in the westward expansion of the USA.

Aircraft industry

The Trail of Tears
In 1838–39, 15,000 Cherokees were forced from their land east of the Mississippi River to Oklahoma—4,000 died on "the trail of tears" or shortly after arriving in Oklahoma.

Dallas skyline
The skyscrapers of Dallas, the second largest city in Texas with a population of more than one million, were built with wealth generated by oil and cattle.

Texas, USA

TEXAS
POPULATION 23,508,000 * CAPITAL AUSTIN

The Alamo, San Antonio
In 1836, war between the Mexicans, who claimed Texas, and native Texans raged. The Mexican army besieged the Alamo with 187 Texas volunteers inside. After 13 days, the Mexicans took the Alamo. All those inside, including Davy Crockett, died.

Desert cactus
Prickly pear cactus is one of more than 100 species of cacti growing in Texas. The seed pods are used in salads and jellies. The pads, with the prickles burnt off, are used as cattle food.

Oil

In 1901, the first oil gushed 200 feet (61 m) high on Spindletop Hill near Beaumont, east of Houston. The Spindletop "gusher," or oil well, produced 100,000 barrels of oil a day. Now, almost a quarter of the USA's oil comes from Texas, which has boomed because of its "black gold."

Oil pump
Many Texan oil fields are small and privately owned. A pump like this can produce a few barrels of oil a day.

How oil is formed
1. Tiny sea creatures fall to the ocean floor where, over millions of years, they are covered in mud and silt.

2. Rock layers pile up on top and, as pressure increases, the sea creatures turn into oil and gas.

3. The oil and gas rise through the rock layers until they hit an impermeable layer that they cannot pass through.

4. Oil and gas collect in a pool or reservoir under the impermeable rock layer.

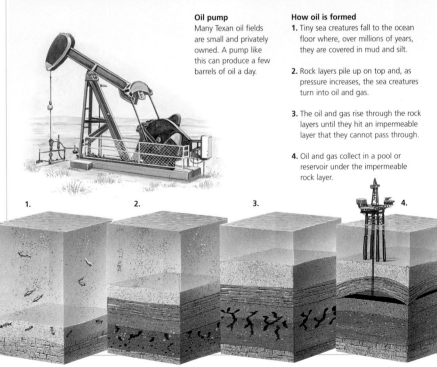

1. 2. 3. 4.

Texas has almost 300,000 miles (480,000 km) of roads and highways. The state spends more than US$800,000,000 each year on road maintenance.

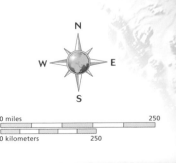

0 miles 250
0 kilometers 250

Map labels:
Guymon, Perryton, Stratford, High Plains, Dalhart, Dumas, Stinnett, Channing, Lake Meredith, Borger, Nara Visa, Pampa, Adrian, Shamrock, Amarillo, Canyon, Clarendon, Hereford, Matador, Childress, Farwell, Plainview, Littlefield, Floydada, Ralls, Guthrie, Lubbock, Brownfield, Hamlin, Hobbs, Seminole, Lamesa, Sweetwa[ter], Eunice, Ackerly, Andrews, Big Spring, Colorado City, Midland, Bronte, Anthony, Orla, Kermit, Odessa, Sterling City, El Paso, Salt Flat, Guadalupe Peak 8,749ft (2,667m), Ciudad Juárez, Monahans, San Angelo, Sierra Blanca, Pecos, Crane, McCamey, Van Horn, Kent, Fort Stockton, Eldorado, Davis Mountains, Stockton Plateau, Ozona, Glass Mountains, Marathon, Sanderson, Shafter, Presidio, Terlingua, Ojinaga, Del Rio, Ciudad Acuña, Piedras Negras, Eag[le] Pas[s], NEW MEXICO, MEXICO, Llano Estacado, Cap Rock Escarpment, Rocky Mountains, Sierra Vieja, Santiago Mountains, Edwards Plateau, Rio Grande, Pecos, Devil's Lake, Balcones

American kestrel

The American kestrel is one of the world's most colorful birds of prey and is the USA's most common falcon. Unlike other falcons, the American kestrel captures smaller birds on the ground, not in mid-air.

Johnson Space Center, Houston

NASA's Lyndon B. Johnson Space Center opened in Houston in 1961. The Center is the command post for all US-manned space flights, including the International Space Station. This giant laboratory allows astronauts from many different countries to work in space for months at a time.

Concepción Mission, San Antonio

This mission was one of six built by Spanish Franciscan monks in Texas. Dedicated in 1755, Concepción Mission has not been restored so it looks very much the same as it did when it was built. Only the geometric designs covering the walls have faded or worn away.

Nine-banded armadillo

Common dolphin

In addition to its vast open spaces and huge amount of land, Texas also has 600 miles (966 km) of coastline. The common dolphin is one of 14 species of whales and dolphins found in the Gulf of Mexico off Texas.

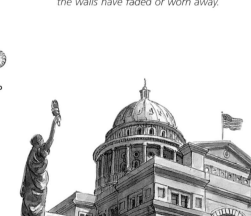

Capitol Building, Austin

Austin is not the biggest city in Texas but its Capitol Building, built of granite in 1888, is bigger than the Capitol Building in Washington D.C. or any other Capitol in the USA.

American bison grazing

Northern Rockies, USA

IDAHO
POPULATION 1,466,000 ✳ CAPITAL BOISE

MONTANA
POPULATION 945,000 ✳ CAPITAL HELENA

WYOMING
POPULATION 515,000 ✳ CAPITAL CHEYENNE

The V-shape in Idaho's otherwise straight western border is where the Snake River has carved out Hell's Canyon, the USA's deepest river gorge.

Rodeo
Rodeo events test riding and roping skills. Cody, Wyoming, named after Buffalo Bill Cody, is the rodeo capital of the world. Rodeos are held in Cody, day and night.

Blackfoot nation

The Blackfoot nation of Montana got their name because they dyed their moccasins black. The Blackfoot were largely dependent on buffalo for food, clothing, homes, and other domestic items. The mass killing of the buffalo by settlers with rifles led to near starvation for the Blackfoot. Many still live in reservations in Montana.

Smoke flaps

Tepee
Buffalo hides, tanned and smoked then decorated and sewn together, were used to build a Blackfoot tepee. The tepee could be folded up quickly and transported easily when the tribe moved on.

Painted Blackfoot symbols

Family possessions

Jurassic dinosaur, *Stegosaurus*

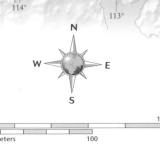

0 miles 100
0 kilometers 100

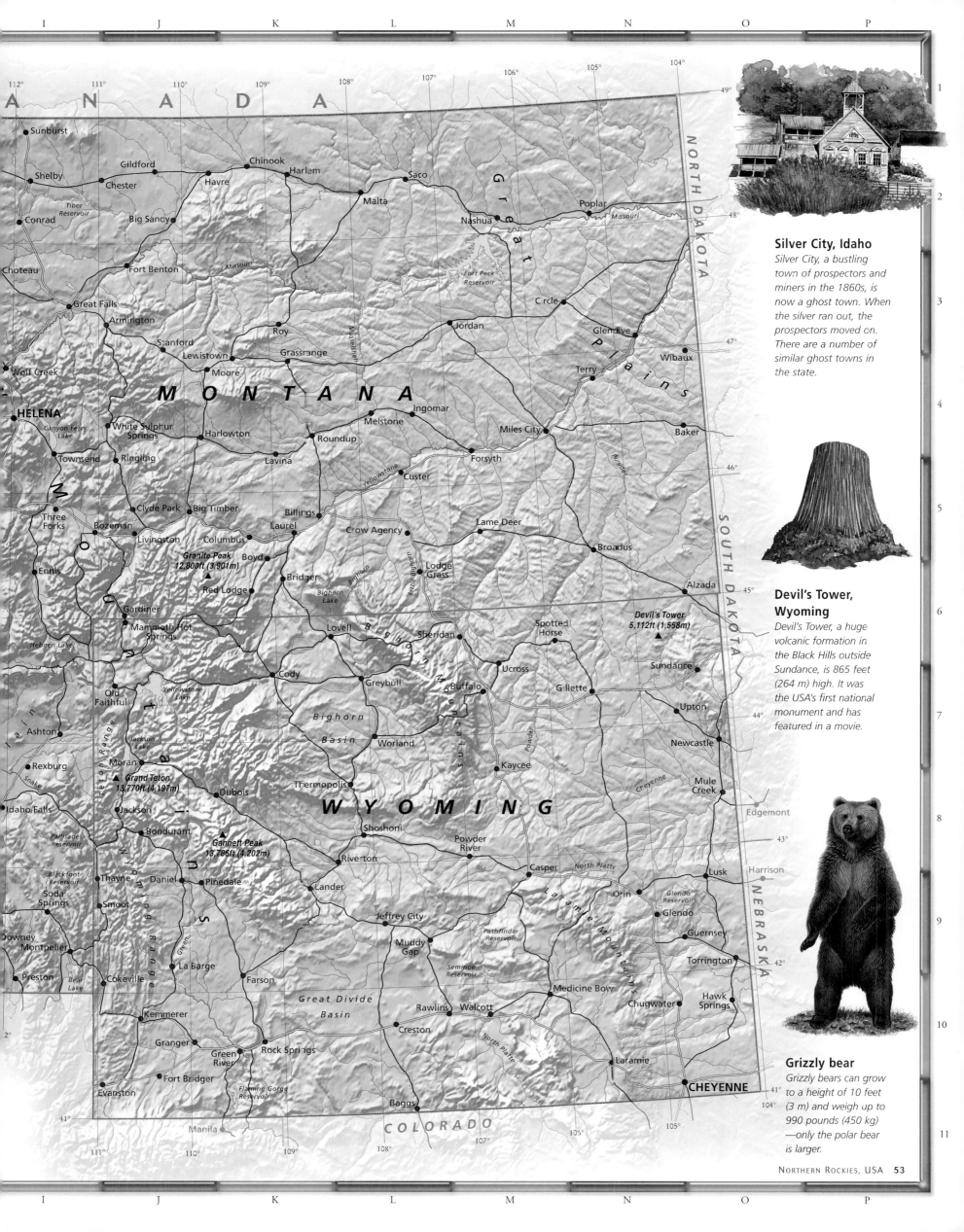

Silver City, Idaho

Silver City, a bustling town of prospectors and miners in the 1860s, is now a ghost town. When the silver ran out, the prospectors moved on. There are a number of similar ghost towns in the state.

Devil's Tower, Wyoming

Devil's Tower, a huge volcanic formation in the Black Hills outside Sundance, is 865 feet (264 m) high. It was the USA's first national monument and has featured in a movie.

Grizzly bear

Grizzly bears can grow to a height of 10 feet (3 m) and weigh up to 990 pounds (450 kg) —only the polar bear is larger.

Grand Canyon
One of the Seven Natural Wonders of the World, the Grand Canyon is 277 miles (446 km) long and more than a mile deep.

Southwestern USA

ARIZONA
POPULATION 6,166,000 ∗ CAPITAL PHOENIX

COLORADO
POPULATION 4,753,000 ∗ CAPITAL DENVER

UTAH
POPULATION 2,550,000 ∗ CAPITAL SALT LAKE CITY

NEW MEXICO
POPULATION 1,955,000 ∗ CAPITAL SANTA FE

Pueblo pottery

Gila monster

Colorado comes from the Spanish word for "colored red." The Colorado River, the biggest of the many rivers in Colorado, flows through canyons of red stone.

Carlsbad Caverns, New Mexico

The Carlsbad Caverns National Park is a spectacular maze of underground chambers covering 73 square miles (189 sq km). The caverns were carved out over thousands of years by rain seeping into limestone. The dissolved limestone was deposited by the dripping water onto floors and ceilings, slowly forming stalagmites and other elaborate shapes. A stalagmite grows from the ground up. A stalactite grows from the ceiling down. When a stalagmite and a stalactite meet, a pillar is formed.

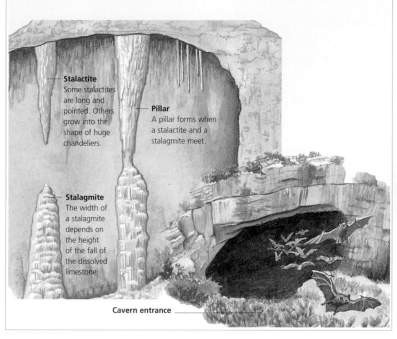

Stalactite
Some stalactites are long and pointed. Others grow into the shape of huge chandeliers.

Pillar
A pillar forms when a stalactite and a stalagmite meet.

Stalagmite
The width of a stalagmite depends on the height of the fall of the dissolved limestone.

Cavern entrance

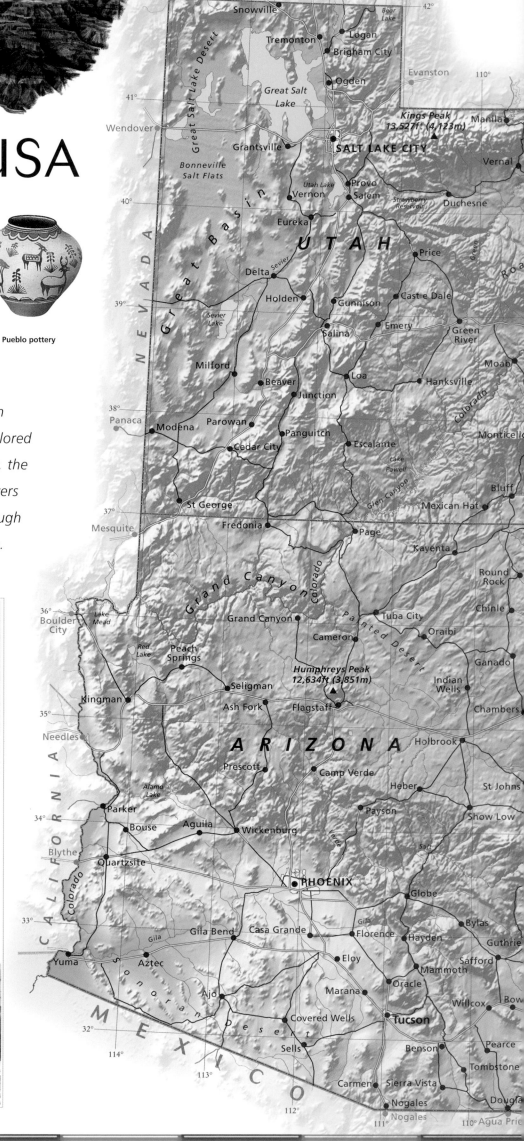

Stegosaurus

Stegosaurus, one of the largest Jurassic dinosaurs, roamed in what is now the state of Colorado, 150 million years ago. Stegosaurus is Colorados' state fossil.

Navajo weaver, Arizona

With wool from their own sheep, originally brought to the Southwest by Spanish colonists, and skills in weaving learned from their Pueblo neighbors, Navajo women wove their own colorful and distinctive clothing and blankets.

Taos Pueblo, New Mexico

The Pueblo civilization was at its peak between 950 and 1200 AD. The Taos Pueblo, which has been continuously inhabited for 1,000 years, is one of 18 self-governing pueblos or villages in New Mexico.

Satellite dishes

The Very Large Array radio telescope in the desert near Socorro, New Mexico, consists of 27 large dish antennas. They are ideally sited to capture radio waves from the universe because there is no interference from city lights or noise.

Mormon Temple, Utah

There were only 148 Mormons in the first group to settle in what was then called Great Salt Lake City, in 1847. Over the next six years, other Mormons joined them and building of the Mormon Temple began. The Temple took 40 years to complete.

0 miles 120

0 kilometers 120

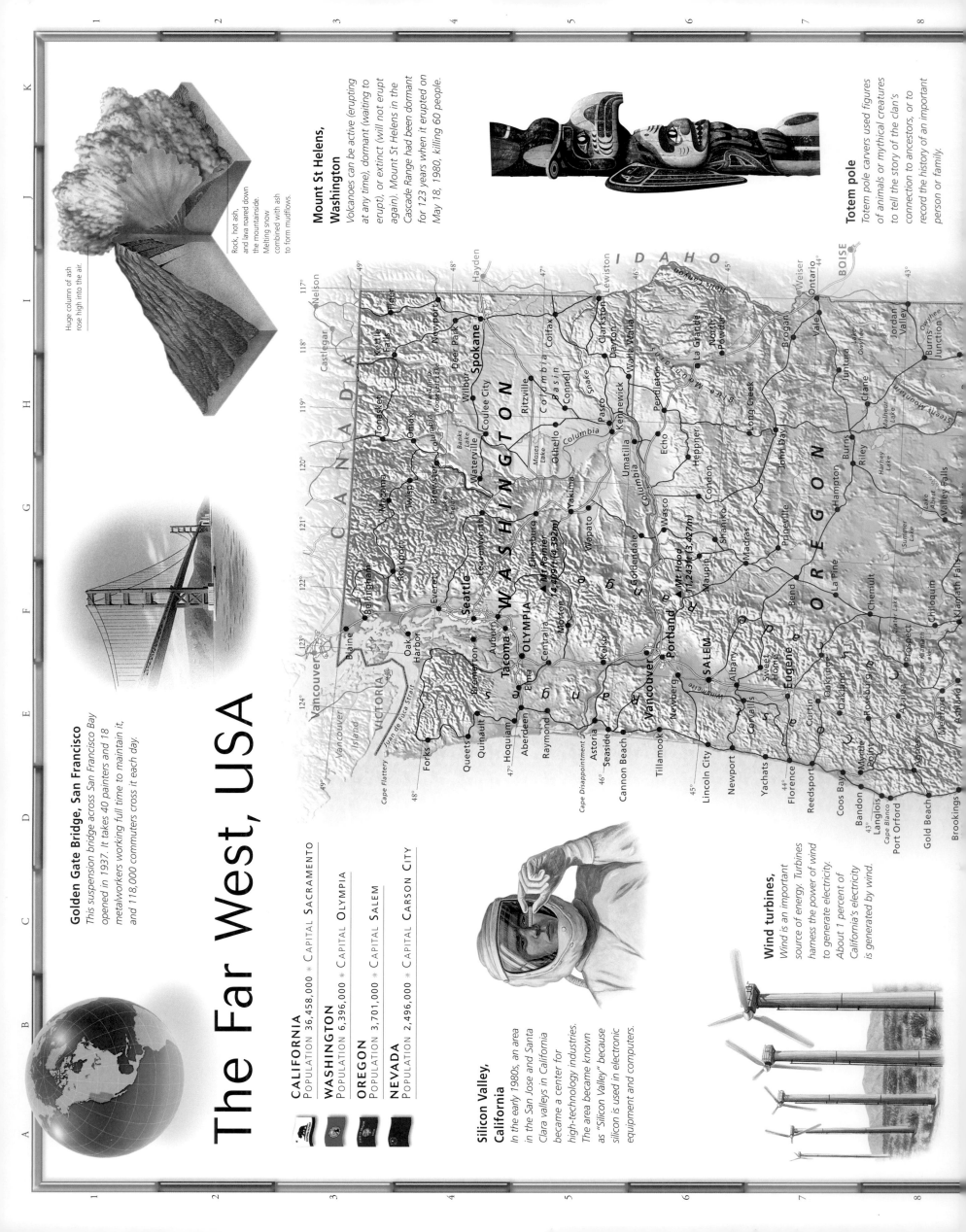

The Far West, USA

Golden Gate Bridge, San Francisco

This suspension bridge across San Francisco Bay opened in 1937. It takes 40 painters and 18 metalworkers working full time to maintain it, and 118,000 commuters cross it each day.

CALIFORNIA
POPULATION 36,458,000 ✳ CAPITAL SACRAMENTO

WASHINGTON
POPULATION 6,396,000 ✳ CAPITAL OLYMPIA

OREGON
POPULATION 3,701,000 ✳ CAPITAL SALEM

NEVADA
POPULATION 2,496,000 ✳ CAPITAL CARSON CITY

Silicon Valley, California

In the early 1980s, an area in the San Jose and Santa Clara valleys in California became a center for high-technology industries. The area became known as "Silicon Valley" because silicon is used in electronic equipment and computers.

Wind turbines,

Wind is an important source of energy. Turbines harness the power of wind to generate electricity. About 1 percent of California's electricity is generated by wind.

Huge column of ash rose high into the air.

Rock, hot ash, and lava roared down the mountainside. Melting snow combined with ash to form mudflows.

Mount St Helens, Washington

Volcanoes can be active (erupting at any time), dormant (waiting to erupt), or extinct (will not erupt again). Mount St Helens in the Cascade Range had been dormant for 123 years when it erupted on May 18, 1980, killing 60 people.

Totem pole

Totem pole carvers used figures of animals or mythical creatures to tell the story of the clan's connection to ancestors, or to record the history of an important person or family.

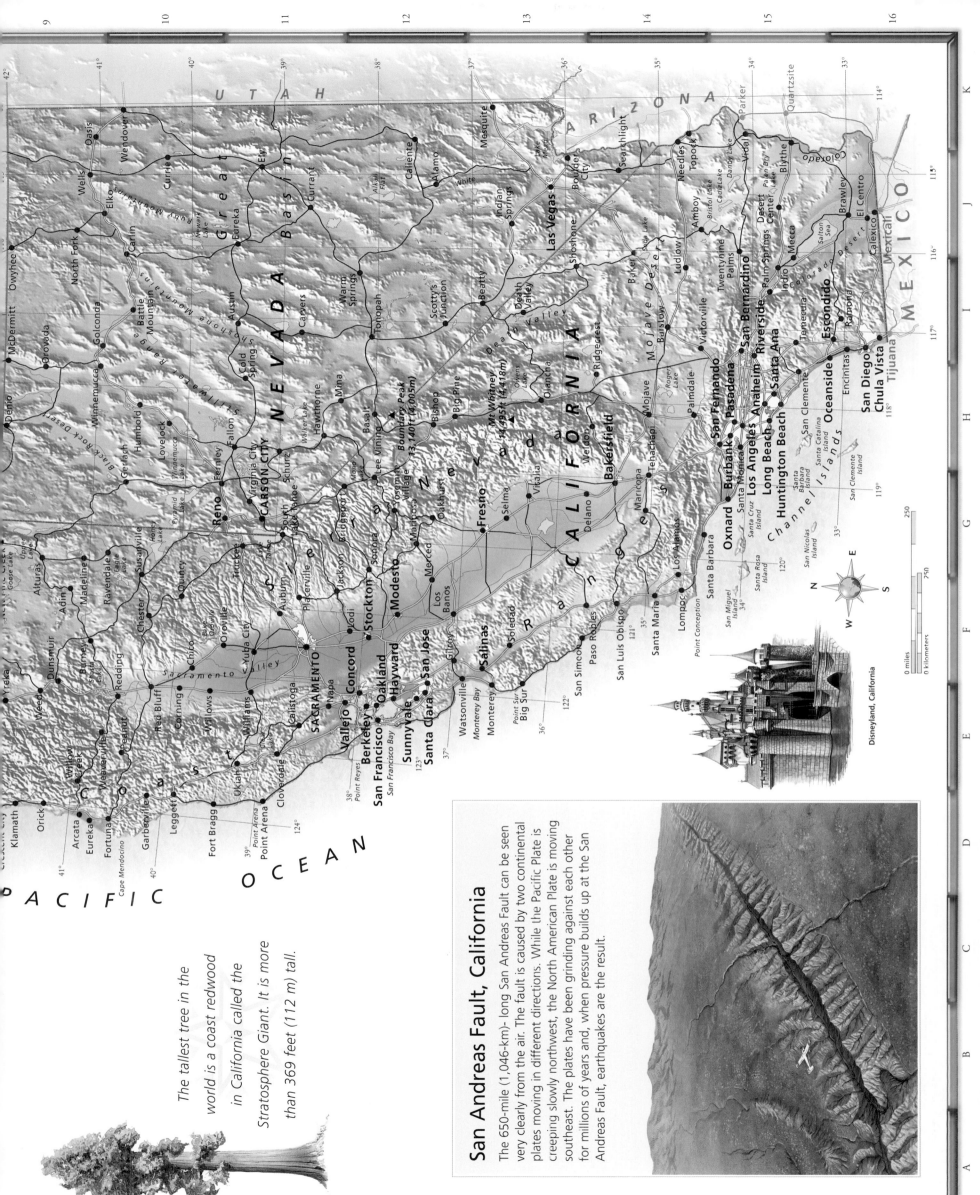

The tallest tree in the world is a coast redwood in California called the Stratosphere Giant. It is more than 369 feet (112 m) tall.

San Andreas Fault, California

The 650-mile (1,046-km)- long San Andreas Fault can be seen very clearly from the air. The fault is caused by two continental plates moving in different directions. While the Pacific Plate is creeping slowly northwest, the North American Plate is moving southeast. The plates have been grinding against each other for millions of years and, when pressure builds up at the San Andreas Fault, earthquakes are the result.

Disneyland, California

Volcanic islands

The islands of Hawaii are the peaks of underwater volcanoes in the Pacific Ocean. A new underwater volcano is now forming as, deep down, Earth's mantle melts and feeds magma upward. The volcano is still 3,000 feet (914 m) below the surface of the ocean—and growing.

Alaska and Hawaii, USA

HAWAII
POPULATION 1,285,000 ✳ CAPITAL **HONOLULU**

ALASKA
POPULATION 670,000 ✳ CAPITAL **JUNEAU**

Hawaii

Hawaii is the only US state that was once a monarchy. The last queen of Hawaii was Queen Liliuokalani, who lived in Iolani Palace but lost her throne in 1893.

Pineapple

Humpback whale

Humpback whales spend the winter months in the warm waters off Hawaii. In summer, they migrate to the Arctic waters of Alaska. It is only in these cold Arctic waters that they find their food supply— small fish and krill.

HAWAII map

Chukchi Sea

RUSSIAN FEDERATION

Wevok
Point Hope
Kotzebue Sound
Arctic Circle
Seward Peninsula
Teller
Nome
Cape Nome
Norton Sound
St Lawrence Island
Emmonak
Bering Strait
Bering Sea
Hooper Bay
St Matthew Island
Tanunak
Nunivak Island
Kipnuk
Kuskokwim Bay
Pribilof Islands
Bering

Surfer

Near Islands
Attu Island
Agattu Island
Rat Islands
Kiska Island
Segula Island
Little Sitkin Island
Rat Island
Semisopochnoi Island
Amchitka Island
Tanaga Island
Aleutian Islands
Amchitka Islands
Kanaga Island
Adak
Adak Island
Atka Island
Atka
Seguam Island
Amlia Island
Andreanof Islands
Yunaska Island
Umnak Island
Fox Islands
Unimak Island
Akutan Island
Dutch Harbor
Unalaska Island
Alaska
False Pass
Sanak Islands

PACIFIC OCEAN

HAWAII inset map labels

Kilauea
Kauai
Niihau
Lihue
Hawaiian Islands
Waimea
Oahu
Pearl City
Kaneohe
HONOLULU
Kaunakakai
Molokai
Lahaina
Wailuku
Maui
Lanai City
Lanai
Hana
Kahoolawe
Hawi
Waimea
Mauna Kea 13,798ft (4,205m)
Honokohau
Hilo
Keaau
Mauna Loa 13,678ft (4,169m)
Naalehu
Hawaii
PACIFIC OCEAN
HAWAII

0 miles 100
0 kilometers 100

Longitude west of Greenwich

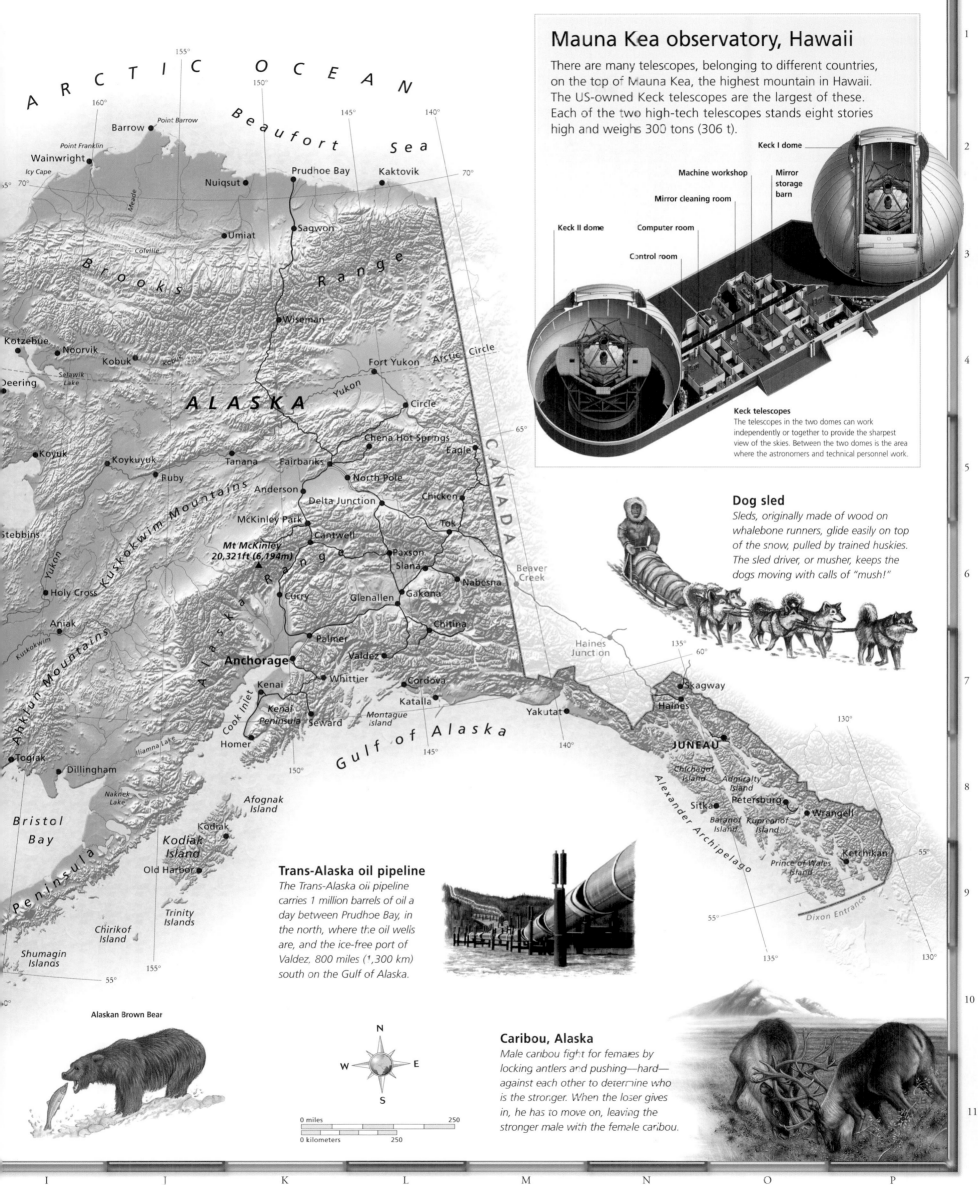

Grid coordinates (top): I J K L M N O P

Grid coordinates (right): 1 2 3 4 5 6 7 8 9 10 11

ARCTIC OCEAN

Beaufort Sea

160°
155°
150°
145°
140°

Point Barrow
Barrow
Point Franklin
Wainwright
Icy Cape
65° 70°

Prudhoe Bay
Kaktovik
70°

Nuiqsut
Sagwon
Umiat
Meade
Colville

Brooks Range

Kotzebue
Noorvik
Kobuk
Deering
Selawik Lake
Kobuk

Wiseman

Fort Yukon   Arctic Circle

ALASKA
Yukon
Circle
65°

Koyuk
Koyukuk
Ruby
Tanana
Fairbanks
Chena Hot Springs
Eagle

Stebbins
Kuskokwim Mountains
North Pole
Anderson
Delta Junction
Chicken

Holy Cross
Yukon
McKinley Park
Cantwell
Tok

Aniak
Kuskokwim
Mt McKinley
20,321ft (6,194m)
Paxson
Slana
Nabesha

CANADA

Curry
Glenallen
Gakona
Beaver Creek

Alaska Range
Chitina

Palmer
Anchorage
Valdez
Haines Junction
60°
135°

Ahklun Mountains
Togiak
Dillingham
Naknek Lake
Iliamna Lake

Kenai
Whittier
Cordova
Katalla
Yakutat
140°

Kenai Peninsula
Seward
Montague Island
Cook Inlet
Homer
150°
145°

Skagway
Haines
JUNEAU
130°

Gulf of Alaska

Bristol Bay
Afognak Island

Chichagof Island
Admiralty Island

Peninsula
Kodiak
Kodiak Island
Old Harbor

Sitka
Baranof Island
Kupreanof Island
Petersburg
Wrangell

Alexander Archipelago

Chirikof Island
Trinity Islands

Prince of Wales Island
Ketchikan
55°

Shumagin Islands
155°

55°
135°

130°
Dixon Entrance

Mauna Kea observatory, Hawaii

There are many telescopes, belonging to different countries, on the top of Mauna Kea, the highest mountain in Hawaii. The US-owned Keck telescopes are the largest of these. Each of the two high-tech telescopes stands eight stories high and weighs 300 tons (306 t).

Keck I dome

Machine workshop
Mirror storage barn
Mirror cleaning room
Computer room
Keck II dome
Control room

Keck telescopes
The telescopes in the two domes can work independently or together to provide the sharpest view of the skies. Between the two domes is the area where the astronomers and technical personnel work.

Dog sled

Sleds, originally made of wood on whalebone runners, glide easily on top of the snow, pulled by trained huskies. The sled driver, or musher, keeps the dogs moving with calls of "mush!"

Trans-Alaska oil pipeline

The Trans-Alaska oil pipeline carries 1 million barrels of oil a day between Prudhoe Bay, in the north, where the oil wells are, and the ice-free port of Valdez, 800 miles (1,300 km) south on the Gulf of Alaska.

Caribou, Alaska

Male caribou fight for females by locking antlers and pushing—hard—against each other to determine who is the stronger. When the loser gives in, he has to move on, leaving the stronger male with the female caribou.

Alaskan Brown Bear

N
W   E
S

0 miles   250
0 kilometers   250

Alaska was bought by the USA from Russia in 1867 for US$7,200,000.

United States of America

LAND AREA	3,717,813 sq miles (9,629,091 sq km)
OFFICIAL LANGUAGE	English
MAIN RELIGION	Christian
LIFE EXPECTANCY	77 years
LITERACY	97%

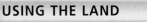
Alaska

NATURAL FEATURES

Yellowstone National Park

Yellowstone, the world's first national park, was set up in 1872 and spreads across three states. It covers 3,468 square miles (8,982 sq km) and features about 10,000 natural springs, or geysers (left). Grizzly bears, bison and moose wander freely around the park.

Old Faithful

Mt McKinley

At 20,321 feet (6,194 m), Mt McKinley is the highest mountain in North America. It is part of the long Alaska Range and is a major attraction in the Denali National Park. Its peak is often shrouded in cloud, especially during summer.

Monument Valley

Situated on the border between Arizona and Utah, Monument Valley (above) is owned and managed by the Navajo people. It is famous for its unique rock formations and remnants of volcanoes.

Great Lakes

The Great Lakes—Michigan, Huron, Ontario, Superior and Erie—are the world's largest group of freshwater lakes. Together they make up 18 percent of Earth's fresh surface water.

USING THE LAND

- Forest and woodland
- Arable land
- Grazing
- Arid or marginal

Oranges

More oranges are harvested yearly in the USA than any other fruits. Florida, the center of the citrus-growing industry, produces one-third of all US citrus fruits. Most of the oranges from Florida are made into juice, while most of the oranges from California are for eating.

Grand Canyon

Formed over the last 6 million years, as the Colorado River slowly cuts through layers of rock, the Grand Canyon in northwestern Arizona is the world's largest canyon. It is 285 miles (456 km) long, 1 mile (1.6 km) deep and up to 18 miles (29 km) wide. In 1919, the canyon became a national park.

LARGEST CITIES

New York 8,143,000

Los Angeles 3,845,000

Chicago 2,843,000

Houston 2,017,000

Philadelphia 1,463,000

Alaska

Anchorage

Juneau

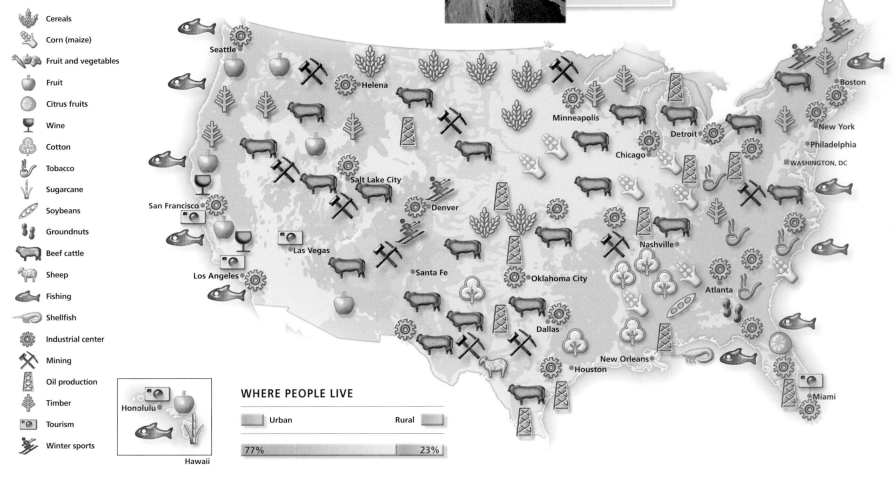

Seattle
Helena
Minneapolis
Detroit
Boston
New York
Philadelphia
Chicago
WASHINGTON, DC
Salt Lake City
San Francisco
Denver
Nashville
Las Vegas
Santa Fe
Oklahoma City
Atlanta
Los Angeles
Dallas
New Orleans
Houston
Miami

- 🌾 Cereals
- 🌽 Corn (maize)
- 🥬 Fruit and vegetables
- 🍎 Fruit
- 🍊 Citrus fruits
- 🍷 Wine
- Cotton
- Tobacco
- Sugarcane
- Soybeans
- Groundnuts
- 🐄 Beef cattle
- 🐑 Sheep
- 🐟 Fishing
- Shellfish
- ⚙️ Industrial center
- ⛏️ Mining
- Oil production
- 🌲 Timber
- 📷 Tourism
- ⛷️ Winter sports

Honolulu

Hawaii

WHERE PEOPLE LIVE

Urban	Rural
77%	23%

PLACES

Washington, DC
Named for George Washington, America's first president, Washington, DC is the capital of the USA. The city was designed for that purpose before it was built. It is home to the Capitol building, where both houses of Congress meet, and the White House, where the president lives and works.

Capitol building, Washington, DC

Honolulu
The capital city and main port of Hawaii, Honolulu is the only US city located in the tropics, the only US city with a royal palace (Iolani Palace) and the only US city with an equal blend of western, Asian and Polynesian influences.

Cliff Palace

Cliff Palace
About 1,000 years ago, the Anasazi people began to build high stone dwellings along canyon walls in southwestern Colorado. Cliff Palace, the largest of these dwellings, contains more than 200 rooms.

San Francisco
Famous for the Golden Gate Bridge and its cable cars, San Francisco was almost destroyed by an earthquake in 1906. In its bay is the former prison Alcatraz, now open for tourists.

PEOPLE

Sitting Bull c 1834–90
Born in what is present-day South Dakota, Sitting Bull was a medicine man, and by around 1867 was leader of all the Sioux Indians. His advice before the battle of Little Bighorn resulted in victory for the Sioux.

Annie Oakley 1860–1926
Annie Oakley was a sharpshooter who starred in Buffalo Bill's traveling Wild West show for more than 16 years. Firing from the back of a galloping horse was one of her special skills.

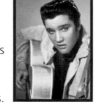
Annie Oakley

Wright brothers
In 1903, Wilbur and Orville Wright successfully flew the world's first power-driven plane in North Carolina. The plane, which the brothers had invented, flew 852 feet (260 m) and managed to stay in the air for 59 seconds.

Martin Luther King 1929–68
Martin Luther King was a Baptist minister and a leader of the civil rights movement. His policy of nonviolent protest won him the Nobel Peace Prize in 1964. After his assassination, he became only the second American whose birthday is honored by a public holiday.

Elvis Presley 1935–77
Born in Tupelo, Mississippi, Elvis Presley was one of the world's greatest stars of rock music. He began his singing career in 1954, and his concert style and music divided people. Some towns even banned his shows. Elvis sold more than 1 billion records and starred in 33 films.

Statue of Liberty
A gift from France to the USA, the Statue of Liberty has stood on Liberty Island in New York City harbor since 1886. The copper statue is 151 feet (46 m) high, with a 12-story spiral staircase inside, which leads to a public observation area in the statue's crown. To the USA, the statue is a symbol of freedom and democracy.

TRADITIONS AND CULTURE

Thanksgiving Day
For almost 400 years, Americans have observed Thanksgiving Day on the fourth Thursday in November. What began as a religious event is now a family day set aside to give thanks for blessings received.

Halloween
On 31 October every year, Americans celebrate the festival of Halloween, when children wear costumes, go trick-or-treating and make jack-o'-lanterns out of pumpkins.

Halloween jack-o'-lantern

Cheerleaders
Beginning in 1898 at the University of Minnesota, cheerleading had become popular across the nation by 1920. Cheerleaders dance and lead the spectators to support their team with chants and cheers at athletic events, especially basketball and football games.

Rap music
Rap music in America developed first in New York City. It is a form of music that is spoken quickly to match the rhythm. It is particularly popular with African-American teenagers. Some rap music has been criticized for its violent lyrics.

Hollywood
Hollywood, a district of Los Angeles, is known as the movie capital of the world. The first film studio was built there in 1911 and within a year, 15 others had sprung up. The late 1920s saw the first production of sound films, and by the 1930s movies, such as Gone with the Wind (1939), were being produced on a grand scale. Hollywood is also famous for "The Strip"—a section of shops, nightclubs and restaurants along Sunset Boulevard.

HISTORY AT A GLANCE

1607
English ships, under the command of Captain Christopher Newport, land and establish a permanent colony at Jamestown, Virginia.

1620
English pilgrims seeking religious freedom arrive on the *Mayflower* at Plymouth, Massachusetts.

1775–81
The War of Independence begins at Lexington, Massachusetts, when the American colonists rebel against the English soldiers. War lasts for six years.

Battle of Lexington

1789
George Washington becomes the first president of the new USA. He supports the new constitution, which sets out the country's laws.

1836
Texan soldiers fighting for their independence from Mexico hold off the Mexicans for 13 days at the Alamo, a mission in San Antonio, Texas.

The Alamo

1861–65
The Civil War is fought when the South withdraws from the USA. The North wins the war, keeps the states united, and ends slavery.

1870s
Wars are fought between Native Americans and the white colonists. These frontier wars lead to the loss of many lives on both sides.

1920–33
Laws are in place for 13 years prohibiting the manufacture and sale of alcoholic drinks.

1929–39
Business slumps worldwide after stock values in the USA fall. The Great Depression ends when industries get a boost because of World War II.

1941
The Japanese invade Pearl Harbor, bringing the USA into World War II. The war ends in 1945 when the USA drops atomic bombs on Japan.

1954
The Supreme Court rules against racial segregation in public schools and meets enormous resistance from white people.

1964–73
The Vietnam War is fought when the USA opposes North Vietnam's invasion of the South. The cold war between the communist and non-communist nations eases.

1969
First people on the moon, Neil Armstrong and Edwin Aldrin, land the Apollo 11 module, *Eagle*.

Footprint on the moon

1991 and 2003
In 1991, the USA leads a war against Iraq, which has invaded Kuwait. In 2003, the USA again fights Iraq and ends the reign of Saddam Hussein.

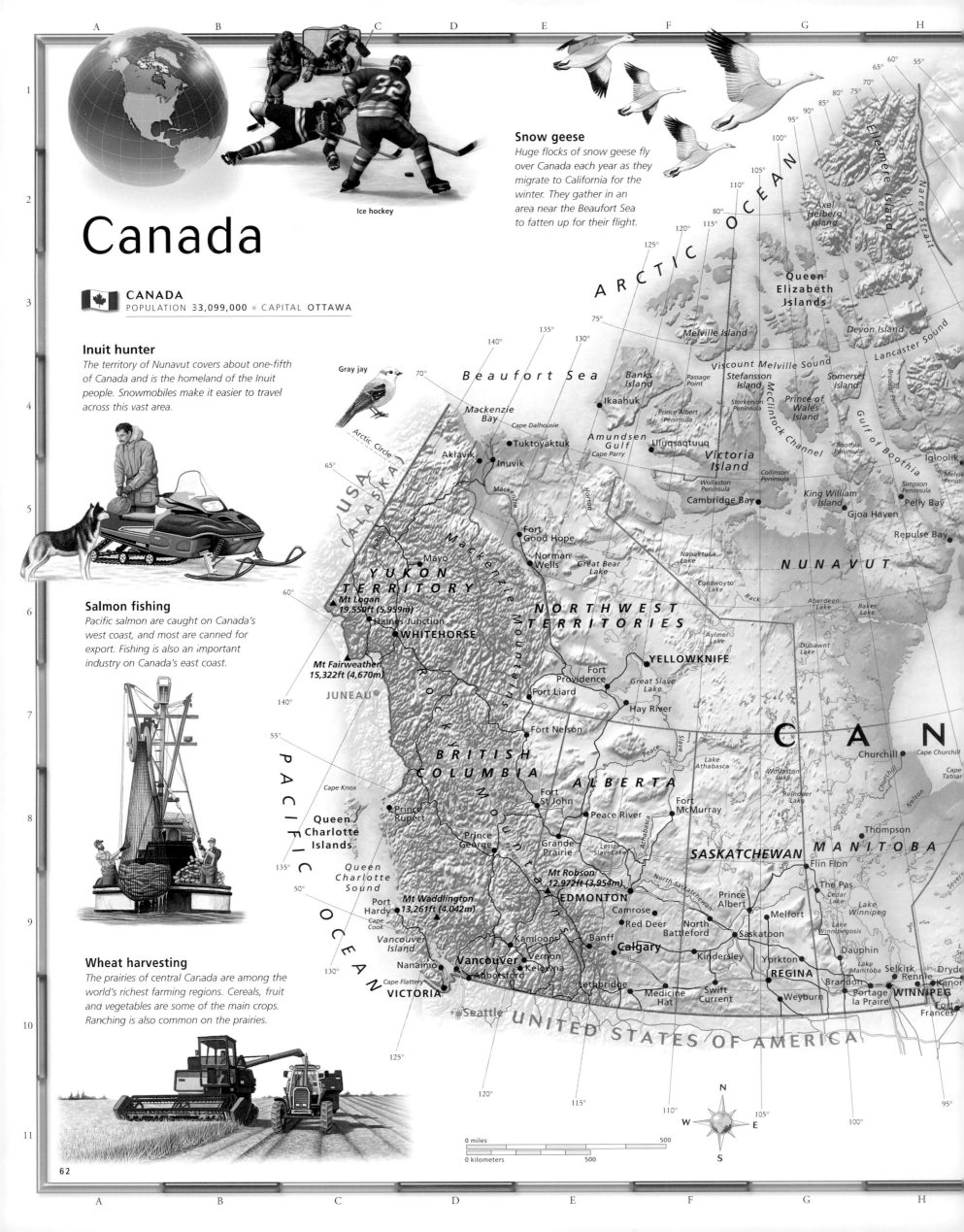

Canada

🍁 **CANADA**
POPULATION 33,099,000 ✳ CAPITAL OTTAWA

Ice hockey

Snow geese

Huge flocks of snow geese fly over Canada each year as they migrate to California for the winter. They gather in an area near the Beaufort Sea to fatten up for their flight.

Inuit hunter

The territory of Nunavut covers about one-fifth of Canada and is the homeland of the Inuit people. Snowmobiles make it easier to travel across this vast area.

Salmon fishing

Pacific salmon are caught on Canada's west coast, and most are canned for export. Fishing is also an important industry on Canada's east coast.

Wheat harvesting

The prairies of central Canada are among the world's richest farming regions. Cereals, fruit and vegetables are some of the main crops. Ranching is also common on the prairies.

Gray jay

A R C T I C   O C E A N

Ellesmere Island
Nares Strait
Queen Elizabeth Islands
Axel Heiberg Island
Melville Island
Devon Island
Viscount Melville Sound
Banks Island
Passage Point
Stefansson Island
Somerset Island
Brodeur Peninsula
Prince Albert Peninsula
Storkerson Peninsula
Prince of Wales Island
Boothia Peninsula
Gulf of Boothia
Igloolik
Melvi
Penin
Collinson Peninsula
King William Island
Simpson Peninsula
Wollaston Peninsula
Pelly Bay
Cambridge Bay
Gjoa Haven
Repulse Bay

Beaufort Sea
Mackenzie Bay
Cape Dalhousie
Ikaahuk
Amundsen Gulf
Cape Parry
Uluqsaqtuuq
Victoria Island

Arctic Circle
Aklavik
Tuktoyaktuk
Inuvik
Fort Good Hope
Napaktulik Lake
Norman Wells
Great Bear Lake
Contwoyto Lake
Aberdeen Lake
Baker Lake
N U N A V U T
Back
Dubawnt Lake

Mayo
Mackenzie

Y U K O N   T E R R I T O R Y

Mt Logan 19,550ft (5,959m)
Haines Junction
WHITEHORSE

N O R T H W E S T   T E R R I T O R I E S

Fort Providence
Fort Liard
YELLOWKNIFE
Great Slave Lake
Hay River
Aylmer Lake

Mt Fairweather 15,322ft (4,670m)

JUNEAU

Fort Nelson

B R I T I S H   C O L U M B I A

Rocky Mountains

Cape Knox

Prince Rupert

Queen Charlotte Islands

Queen Charlotte Sound

Prince George

Fort St John
Peace River
A L B E R T A
Fort McMurray
Peace
Slave
Lesser Slave Lake
Athabasca
Lake Athabasca
Wollaston Lake
Reindeer Lake
Churchill
Churchill
Cape Churchill
Cape Tatnar
Nelson
Thompson
M A N I T O B A

C A N

SASKATCHEWAN
Flin Flon
The Pas
Cedar Lake
Grande Prairie
Mt Robson 12,972ft (3,954m)
EDMONTON
Camrose
Red Deer
North Battleford
Prince Albert
Melfort
Lake Winnipeg
Dauphin
Lake Winnipegosis

Mt Waddington 13,261ft (4,042m)
Port Hardy
Cape Cook
Banff
Calgary
Saskatoon
Kindersley
Yorkton
Lake Manitoba

Kamloops
Vancouver Island
Nanaimo
Vancouver
Vernon
Kelowna
Abbotsford
Cape Flattery
VICTORIA
Lethbridge
Medicine Hat
Swift Current
REGINA
Weyburn
Brandon
Portage la Prairie
Selkirk
Rennie
Kenor
Dryde
WINNIPEG
Fort Frances

Seattle

U N I T E D   S T A T E S   O F   A M E R I C A

P A C I F I C   O C E A N

N
W E
S

0 miles 500
0 kilometers 500

Dinosaurs from Canada's past

About 75 million years ago, dinosaurs roamed along the gullies and rivers of southern Alberta. Ten million years later, the dinosaurs vanished. In 1909, a rancher reported that he had discovered dinosaur bones on his property. Today that property is part of the Dinosaur Provincial Park. Up to 250 dinosaur skeletons of 36 different species have been found there. They can be seen in more than 30 museums all round the world.

Corythosaurus

Albertosaurus
This dinosaur's name means "Alberta lizard." It grew to 26 feet (8 m) long.

Fossil foot
This fossil foot of *Albertosaurus* shows its powerful clawed toes.

Ankylosaurus
This dinosaur used its massive tail club to protect itself.

Parasaurolophus
This dinosaur probably used the long crest on its head to signal to other dinosaurs.

Triceratops
This bulky, slow-moving dinosaur was a plant eater. It grew to 30 feet (9 m) long.

Container shipping
Canada is the world's largest supplier of wood products, but its factories also produce many kinds of industrial goods. About 90 percent of Canada's exports are sent to the USA.

The Bay of Fundy, between New Brunswick and Nova Scotia, has the highest tides in the world. The difference between high and low tide can be as large as a three-story building.

Beaver

CN Tower, Toronto
The CN Tower, a telecommunications hub, rises high above the city of Toronto. When it was built in 1976, it was the world's tallest building.

GREENLAND 75° (to Denmark)

Baffin Bay

Davis Strait

Labrador Sea

Arctic Circle

65°
70°
60°
55°
50°
45°

Baffin Island
Prince Charles Island
Foxe Basin
Foxe Peninsula
Southampton Island
Coats Island
Mansel Island
Ottawa Islands
Hudson Bay
Belcher Islands

Kangeeak Point
Cape Dyer
Cumberland Peninsula
Cape Mercy
Cumberland Sound
Nettilling Lake
Amadjuak Lake
IQALUIT
Resolution Island
Cape Labrador
Hudson Strait
Cap Hopes Advance
Akpatok Island
Ungava Bay
Péninsule d'Ungava
Ivujivik
Inukjuak
Kuujjuaq
Nain
Cartwright
Cape Bauld

Rivière aux Feuilles
George
Churchill
NEWFOUNDLAND AND LABRADOR
Smallwood Reservoir
Happy Valley Goose Bay
Gander
ST JOHN'S
Newfoundland
Corner Brook

ADA
CANADA
Fort Severn
Winisk
James Bay
Akimiski Island
Attawapiskat
Albany
Moose
Moosonee
Nottaway
Harricana

QUEBEC
Lac Caniapiscau
Réservoir la Grande Deux
Réservoir la Grande Trois
Réservoir Manicouagan
Eastmain
Péribonca
Lac Mistassini
Chibougamau
Jonquière
Chicoutimi
Rivière-du-Loup
Baie-Comeau
Sept-Îles
Gaspé
Matane
Natashquan
Île d'Anticosti
Gulf of St Lawrence
Cabot Strait
ST PIERRE & MIQUELON (to France)
Cape Breton Island
Glace Bay
Sydney
PRINCE EDWARD ISLAND
Prince Edward Island
CHARLOTTETOWN
Campbellton
NEW BRUNSWICK
Moncton
New Glasgow
Truro
HALIFAX
NOVA SCOTIA
FREDERICTON
St John
Bay of Fundy
Liverpool
Yarmouth
Gulf of Maine
QUÉBEC
La Tuque
Trois-Rivières
Victoriaville
Drummondville
Sherbrooke
Sorel
Joliette
Réservoir Cabonga
Laurentian Mountains
St Lawrence
Lac Saint-Jean

ONTARIO
Lake Nipigon
Kapuskasing
Timmins
Kirkland Lake
Val-d'Or
Marathon
Nipigon
Thunder Bay
Wawa
Sudbury
North Bay
Pembroke
OTTAWA
Montreal
St Jean sur-Richelieu
Cornwall
Sault Ste Marie
Lake Superior
Lake Michigan
Lake Huron
Lake Nipissing
Owen Sound
Orillia
Peterborough
Lake Ontario
Rochester
TORONTO
Kitchener
Niagara Falls
Buffalo
St Catharines
London
Sarnia
Lake Erie
Erie
Detroit
Windsor
Cleveland
Milwaukee
Chicago
Oshawa

ATLANTIC OCEAN

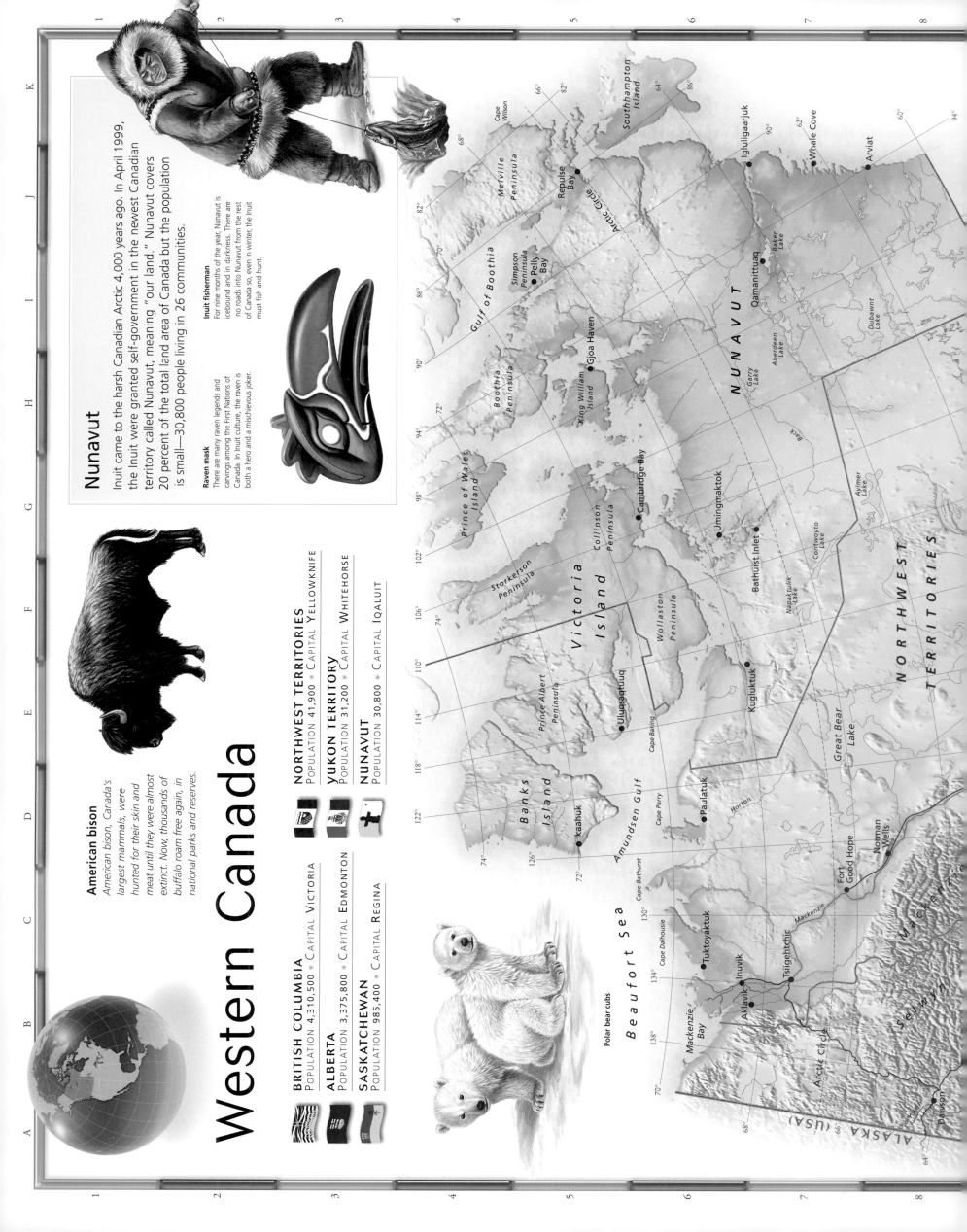

Western Canada

American bison

American bison, Canada's largest mammals, were hunted for their skin and meat until they were almost extinct. Now, thousands of buffalo roam free again, in national parks and reserves.

BRITISH COLUMBIA
POPULATION 4,310,500 ∗ CAPITAL VICTORIA

ALBERTA
POPULATION 3,375,800 ∗ CAPITAL EDMONTON

SASKATCHEWAN
POPULATION 985,400 ∗ CAPITAL REGINA

NORTHWEST TERRITORIES
POPULATION 41,900 ∗ CAPITAL YELLOWKNIFE

YUKON TERRITORY
POPULATION 31,200 ∗ CAPITAL WHITEHORSE

NUNAVUT
POPULATION 30,800 ∗ CAPITAL IQALUIT

Nunavut

Inuit came to the harsh Canadian Arctic 4,000 years ago. In April 1999, the Inuit were granted self-government in the newest Canadian territory called Nunavut, meaning "our land." Nunavut covers 20 percent of the total land area of Canada but the population is small—30,800 people living in 26 communities.

Raven mask
There are many raven legends and carvings among the First Nations of Canada. In Inuit culture, the raven is both a hero and a mischievous joker.

Inuit fisherman
For nine months of the year, Nunavut is icebound and in darkness. There are no roads into Nunavut from the rest of Canada so, even in winter, the Inuit must fish and hunt.

Polar bear cubs

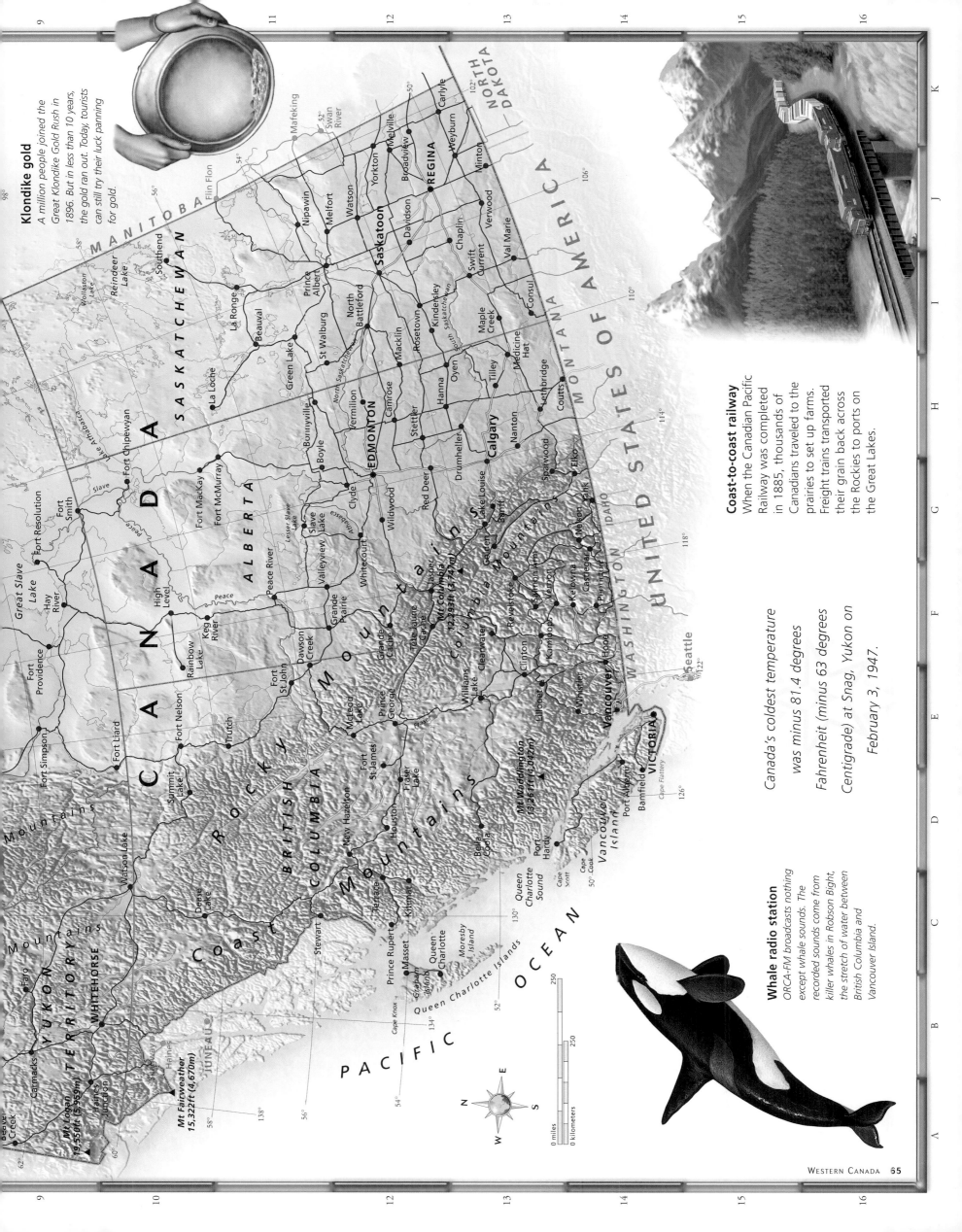

Klondike gold
A million people joined the Great Klondike Gold Rush in 1896. But in less than 10 years, the gold ran out. Today, tourists can still try their luck panning for gold.

Coast-to-coast railway
Coast-to-coast railway
When the Canadian Pacific Railway was completed in 1885, thousands of Canadians traveled to the prairies to set up farms. Freight trains transported their grain back across the Rockies to ports on the Great Lakes.

Canada's coldest temperature was minus 81.4 degrees Fahrenheit (minus 63 degrees Centigrade) at Snag, Yukon on February 3, 1947.

Whale radio station
ORCA-FM broadcasts nothing except whale sounds. The recorded sounds come from killer whales in Robson Bight, the stretch of water between British Columbia and Vancouver Island.

MANITOBA

SASKATCHEWAN

ALBERTA

CANADA

BRITISH COLUMBIA

YUKON TERRITORY

Rocky Mountains

Coast Mountains

Columbia Mountains

MONTANA

NORTH DAKOTA

UNITED STATES OF AMERICA

IDAHO

WASHINGTON

PACIFIC OCEAN

Vancouver Island

Queen Charlotte Islands

Mt Logan 19,550ft (5,959m)
Mt Fairweather 15,322ft (4,670m)
Mt Waddington 13,260ft (4,042m)
Mt Columbia 12,293ft (3,747m)

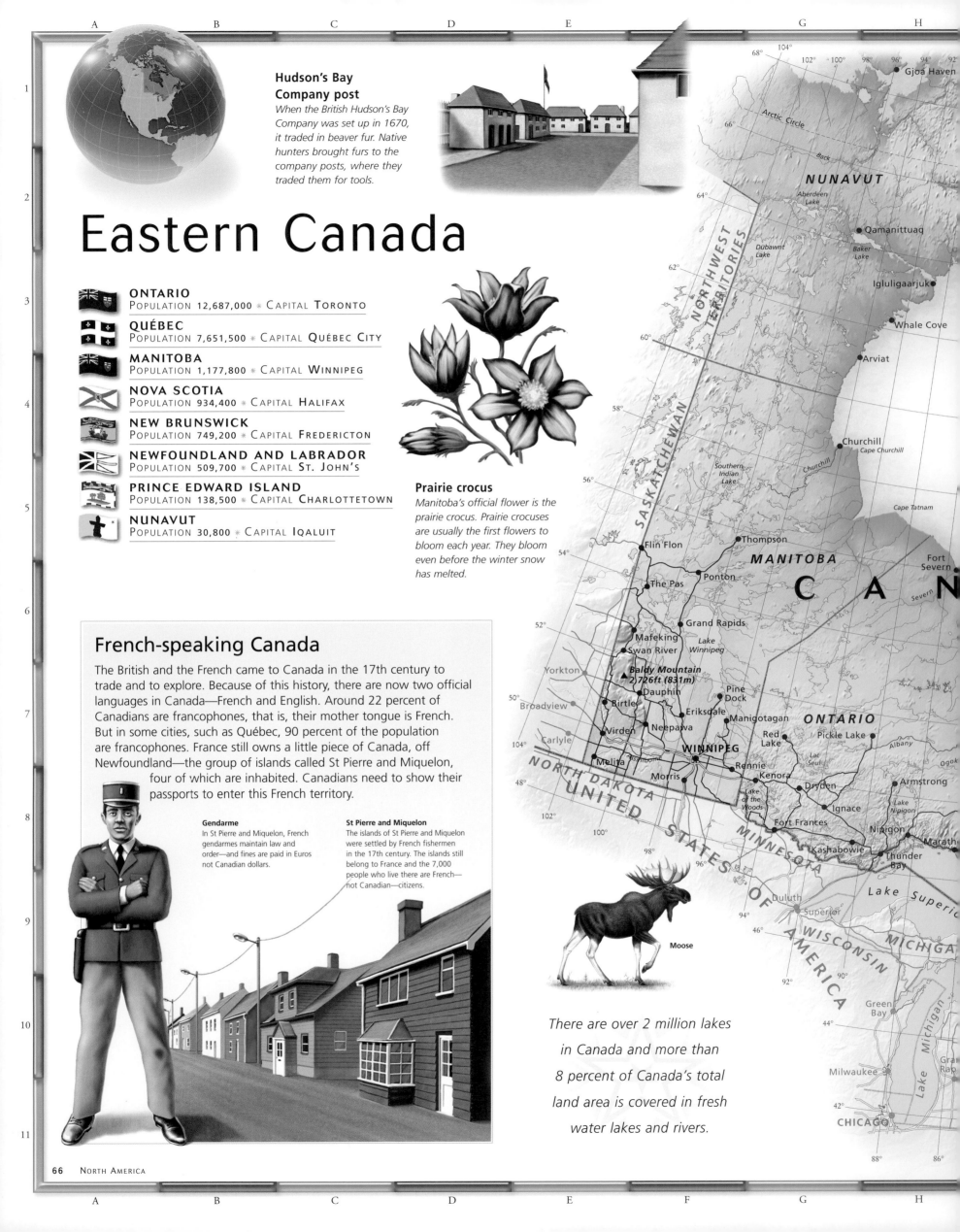

Hudson's Bay Company post

When the British Hudson's Bay Company was set up in 1670, it traded in beaver fur. Native hunters brought furs to the company posts, where they traded them for tools.

Eastern Canada

ONTARIO
POPULATION 12,687,000 ∗ CAPITAL TORONTO

QUÉBEC
POPULATION 7,651,500 ∗ CAPITAL QUÉBEC CITY

MANITOBA
POPULATION 1,177,800 ∗ CAPITAL WINNIPEG

NOVA SCOTIA
POPULATION 934,400 ∗ CAPITAL HALIFAX

NEW BRUNSWICK
POPULATION 749,200 ∗ CAPITAL FREDERICTON

NEWFOUNDLAND AND LABRADOR
POPULATION 509,700 ∗ CAPITAL ST. JOHN'S

PRINCE EDWARD ISLAND
POPULATION 138,500 ∗ CAPITAL CHARLOTTETOWN

NUNAVUT
POPULATION 30,800 ∗ CAPITAL IQALUIT

Prairie crocus

Manitoba's official flower is the prairie crocus. Prairie crocuses are usually the first flowers to bloom each year. They bloom even before the winter snow has melted.

French-speaking Canada

The British and the French came to Canada in the 17th century to trade and to explore. Because of this history, there are now two official languages in Canada—French and English. Around 22 percent of Canadians are francophones, that is, their mother tongue is French. But in some cities, such as Québec, 90 percent of the population are francophones. France still owns a little piece of Canada, off Newfoundland—the group of islands called St Pierre and Miquelon, four of which are inhabited. Canadians need to show their passports to enter this French territory.

Gendarme
In St Pierre and Miquelon, French gendarmes maintain law and order—and fines are paid in Euros not Canadian dollars.

St Pierre and Miquelon
The islands of St Pierre and Miquelon were settled by French fishermen in the 17th century. The islands still belong to France and the 7,000 people who live there are French—not Canadian—citizens.

Moose

There are over 2 million lakes in Canada and more than 8 percent of Canada's total land area is covered in fresh water lakes and rivers.

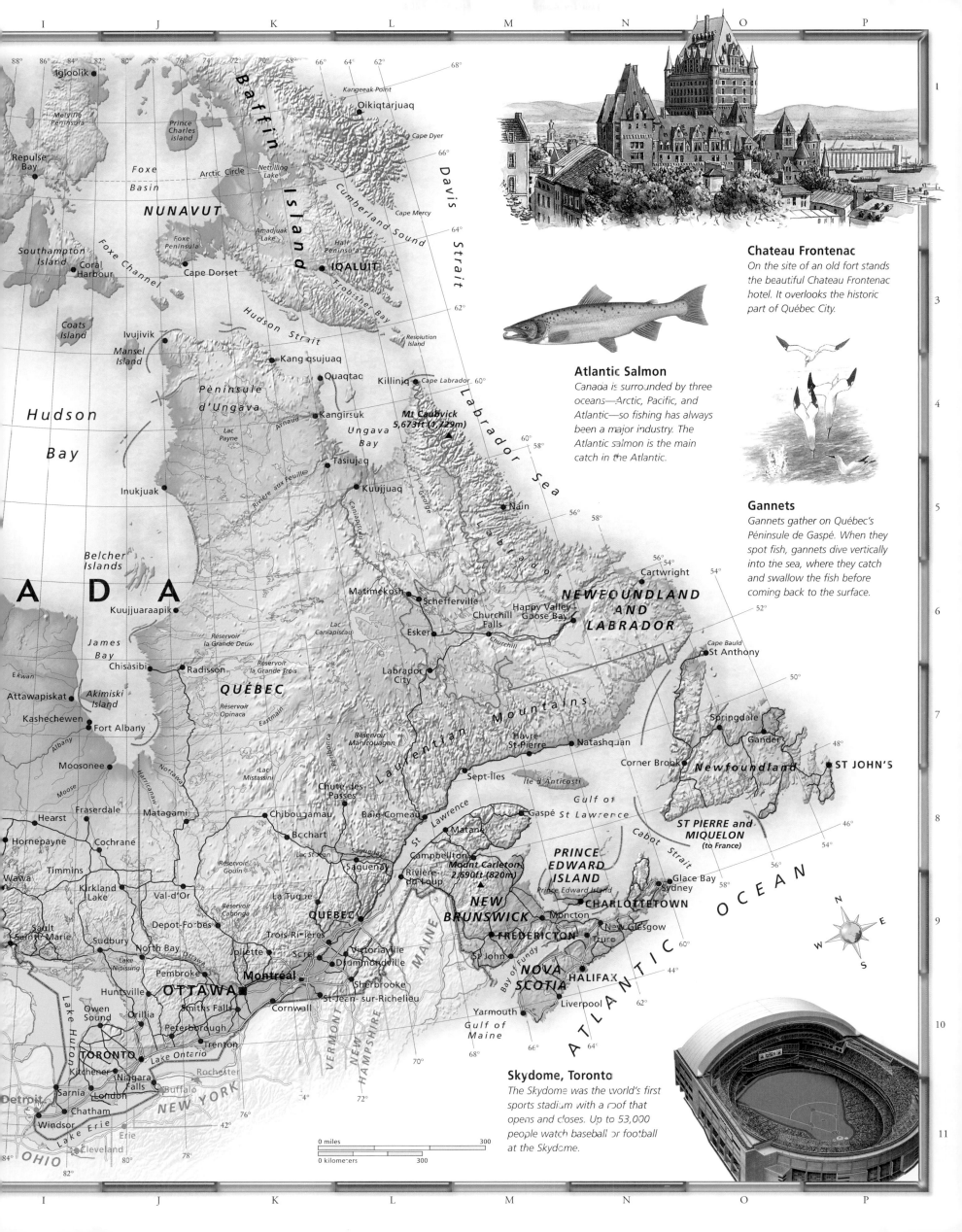

Map labels

Igloolik
88° 86° 84° 82° 80° 78° 76° 74° 72° 70° 68° 66° 64° 62° 68°

Melville Peninsula
Repulse Bay
Prince Charles Island
Kangeeak Point
Oikiqtarjuaq
Cape Dyer

Foxe Basin
Arctic Circle
Nettilling Lake
Cumberland Sound
Davis Strait

Baffin Island

NUNAVUT

Cape Mercy
66°
Amadjuak Lake
Hall Peninsula
64°
Frobisher Bay
Cape Dorset
Foxe Peninsula
IQALUIT

Southampton Island
Coral Harbour
Coats Island
62°

Foxe Channel
Hudson Strait
Resolution Island
Mansel Island
Ivujivik

Hudson Bay

Kangiqsujuaq
Quaqtaq
Killiniq Cape Labrador 60°
Kangirsuk
Mt Caubvick 5,673ft (1,729m)
Lac Payne
Arnaud
Ungava Bay
58°
Tasiujaq
60°
Rivière aux Feuilles
Kuujjuaq

Péninsule d'Ungava

Inukjuak

George
Nain
56°   58°

Belcher Islands

Caniapiscau
A D A
Kuujjuaraapik
56°   54°
Cartwright
54°

Matimekosh
Schefferville
NEWFOUNDLAND AND LABRADOR
52°

James Bay
Réservoir la Grande Deux
Lac Caniapiscau
Esker
Churchill Falls
Happy Valley-Goose Bay
Churchill

Ekwan
Chisasibi
Radisson
Réservoir la Grande Trois
Cape Bauld
St Anthony

Attawapiskat
Akimiski Island
Réservoir Opinaca
Eastmain
Labrador City
Springdale
50°

Kashechewen
Fort Albany
Reservoir Manicouagan
Gander
48°

Albany
Moose
Moosonee
Lac Mistassini
Mountains
Havre-St-Pierre
Natashquan
Corner Brook
Newfoundland
ST JOHN'S

Nottaway
Harricanaw
Sept-Îles
Île d'Anticosti
Gulf of St Lawrence
46° 54°

Fraserdale
Hearst
Matagami
Chibougamau
Baie-Comeau
Gaspé St Lawrence
ST PIERRE and MIQUELON (to France)

Hornepayne
Cochrane
Bechart
Matane
56°

Timmins
Lac St-Jean
Campbellton
Laurentian
58°
Glace Bay
Sydney

Wawa
Réservoir Gouin
Mount Carleton 2,690ft (820m)
PRINCE EDWARD ISLAND
Prince Edward Island
CHARLOTTETOWN

Kirkland Lake
Saguenay
Rivière-du-Loup
60°

Sault Sainte-Marie
Val-d'Or
La Tuque
NEW BRUNSWICK
Moncton
New Glasgow

Sudbury
Réservoir Cabonga
QUÉBEC
Trois-Rivières
FREDERICTON
Truro
44°

North Bay
Depot-Forbes
Joliette
Sorel
Victoriaville
St John
NOVA SCOTIA
HALIFAX
62°

Huntsville
Lake Nipissing
Pembroke
Drummondville
Sherbrooke
Bay of Fundy
Liverpool

OTTAWA
Montréal
St-Jean-sur-Richelieu
Yarmouth

Owen Sound
Orillia
Smiths Falls
Cornwall
VERMONT
MAINE
Gulf of Maine
64°

Peterborough
NEW HAMPSHIRE
68°

TORONTO
Trenton
Lake Ontario
70°

Kitchener
Niagara Falls
Rochester

Detroit
Sarnia
London
Buffalo
NEW YORK
76°
42°

Windsor
Chatham
Lake Erie
Erie
78°

OHIO
Cleveland
82° 80°

Side illustrations

Chateau Frontenac
On the site of an old fort stands the beautiful Chateau Frontenac hotel. It overlooks the historic part of Québec City.

Atlantic Salmon
Canada is surrounded by three oceans—Arctic, Pacific, and Atlantic—so fishing has always been a major industry. The Atlantic salmon is the main catch in the Atlantic.

Gannets
Gannets gather on Québec's Péninsule de Gaspé. When they spot fish, gannets dive vertically into the sea, where they catch and swallow the fish before coming back to the surface.

Skydome, Toronto
The Skydome was the world's first sports stadium with a roof that opens and closes. Up to 53,000 people watch baseball or football at the Skydome.

ATLANTIC OCEAN

0 miles 300
0 kilometers 300

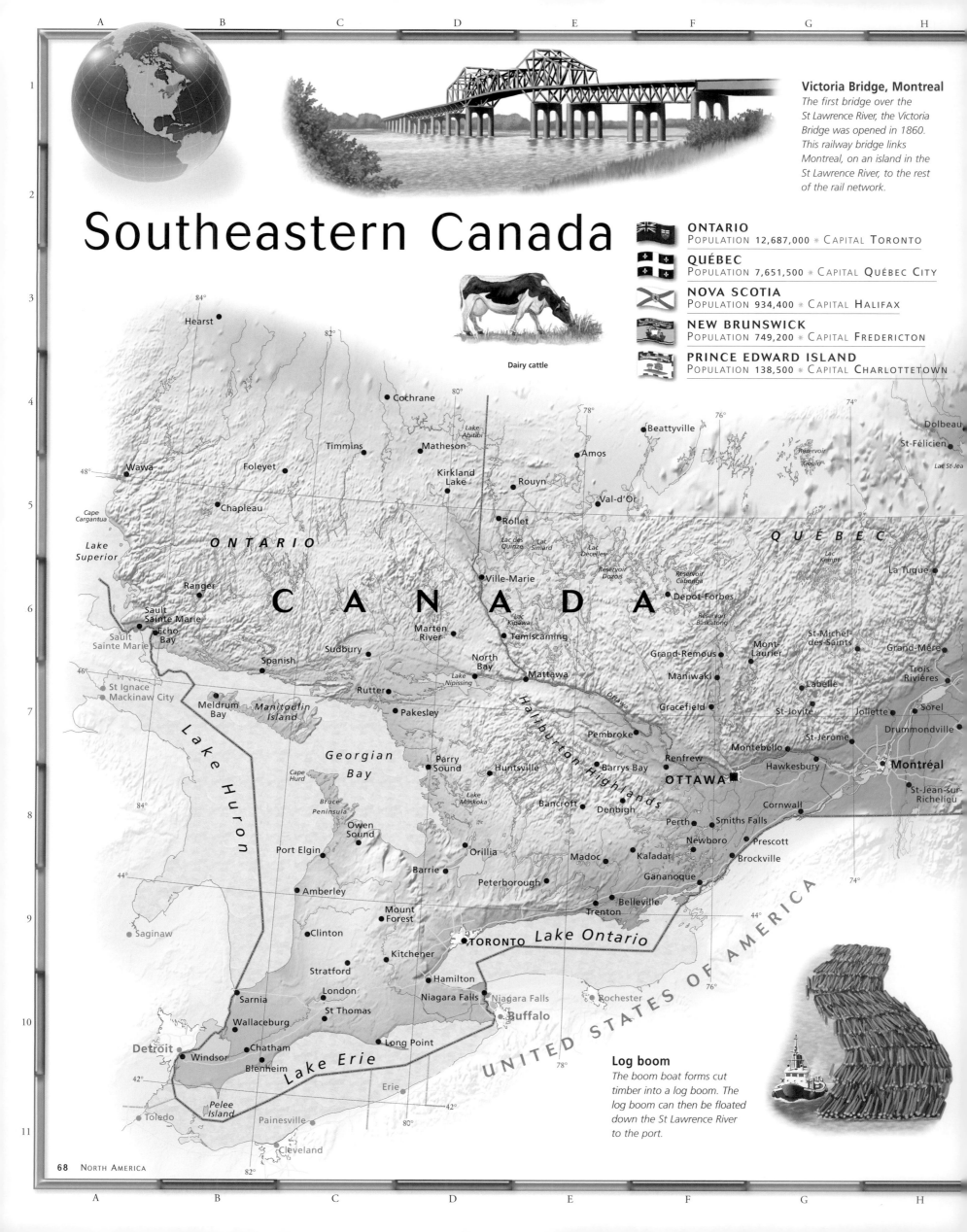

Southeastern Canada

ONTARIO
POPULATION 12,687,000 * CAPITAL TORONTO

QUÉBEC
POPULATION 7,651,500 * CAPITAL QUÉBEC CITY

NOVA SCOTIA
POPULATION 934,400 * CAPITAL HALIFAX

NEW BRUNSWICK
POPULATION 749,200 * CAPITAL FREDERICTON

PRINCE EDWARD ISLAND
POPULATION 138,500 * CAPITAL CHARLOTTETOWN

Victoria Bridge, Montreal
The first bridge over the St Lawrence River, the Victoria Bridge was opened in 1860. This railway bridge links Montreal, on an island in the St Lawrence River, to the rest of the rail network.

Dairy cattle

Log boom
The boom boat forms cut timber into a log boom. The log boom can then be floated down the St Lawrence River to the port.

84°

Hearst

82°

Cochrane

Lake Abitibi

80°

Beattyville

78°

Reservoir Gouin

76°

Dolbeau

St-Félicien

74°

Lac St-Jea

Timmins

Matheson

Amos

Wawa

48°

Foleyet

Kirkland Lake

Rouyn

Chapleau

Rollet

Val-d'Or

Cape Cargantua

Lake Superior

ONTARIO

Ville-Marie

Lac des Quinze

Lac Simard

Lac Décelles

Reservoir Dozois

Reservoir Cabonga

Lac Kempt

QUÉBEC

La Tuque

Ranger

C A N A D A

Depot-Forbes

Reservoir Baskatong

St-Michel des-Saints

Grand-Mère

Sault Sainte Marie

Echo Bay

Sault Sainte Marie

Marten River

Lac Kipawa

Temiscaming

Grand-Remous

Mont-Laurier

Trois-Rivières

Spanish

Sudbury

North Bay

Mattawa

Maniwaki

Labelle

46°

St Ignace

Mackinaw City

Rutter

Lake Nipissing

Hamilton Highlands

Gracefield

St-Jovite

Joliette

Sorel

Meldrum Bay

Manitoulin Island

Pakesley

Pembroke

Ottawa

Montebello

St-Jérôme

Drummondville

Georgian Bay

Parry Sound

Huntsville

Barrys Bay

Renfrew

Hawkesbury

Montréal

Cape Hurd

Bruce Peninsula

Lake Muskoka

Bancroft

Denbigh

Perth

Smiths Falls

Cornwall

St-Jean-sur-Richelieu

Lake Huron

Owen Sound

Orillia

Madoc

Newboro

Prescott

Kaladar

Brockville

Port Elgin

Barrie

Peterborough

Gananoque

44°

Amberley

Belleville

Trenton

44°

Mount Forest

Lake Ontario

74°

Saginaw

Clinton

TORONTO

UNITED STATES OF AMERICA

Stratford

Kitchener

Sarnia

London

Hamilton

76°

Niagara Falls

Niagara Falls

Rochester

Wallaceburg

St Thomas

Buffalo

Detroit

Chatham

Windsor

Long Point

42°

Blenheim

Lake Erie

78°

Toledo

Pelee Island

Painesville

Erie

42°

80°

Cleveland

82°

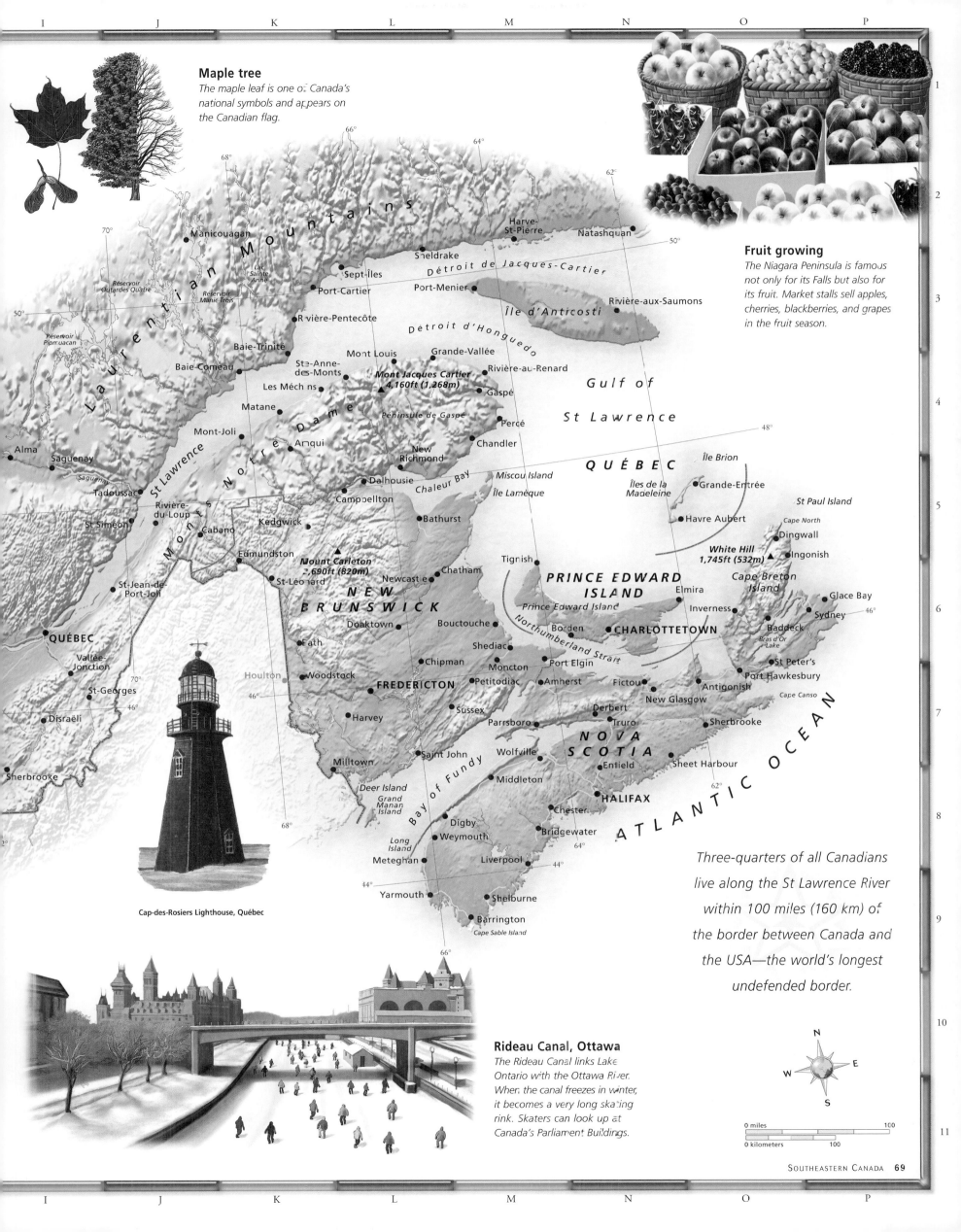

Maple tree
The maple leaf is one of Canada's national symbols and appears on the Canadian flag.

Fruit growing
The Niagara Peninsula is famous not only for its Falls but also for its fruit. Market stalls sell apples, cherries, blackberries, and grapes in the fruit season.

Laurentian Mountains

Manicouagan

Réservoir Outardes Quatre

Lac Sainte Anne

Réservoir Manic Trois

Réservoir Pipmuacan

Sheldrake

Sept-Îles

Port-Cartier

Rivière-Pentecôte

Baie-Trinité

Baie-Comeau

Ste-Anne-des-Monts

Mont Louis

Les Méchins

Matane

Mont-Joli

Amqui

Alma

Saguenay

Tadoussac

Rivière-du-Loup

St Siméon

Cabano

QUÉBEC

Vallée-Jonction

St-Georges

Disraëli

Sherbrooke

St-Jean-de-Port-Joli

Kedgwick

Edmundston

St-Léonard

St Lawrence

Monts Notre Dame

Détroit de Jacques-Cartier

Harve-St-Pierre

Natashquan

Port-Menier

Île d'Anticosti

Rivière-aux-Saumons

Détroit d'Honguedo

Grande-Vallée

Mont Jacques Cartier ▲ 4,160ft (1,268m)

Rivière-au-Renard

Gaspé

Péninsule de Gaspé

Percé

Chandler

New Richmond

Dalhousie

Chaleur Bay

Campbellton

Bathurst

Mount Carleton ▲ 2,690ft (820m)

Tignish

Miscou Island

Île Lamèque

Gulf of St Lawrence

QUÉBEC

Île Brion

Îles de la Magdeleine

Grande-Entrée

Havre Aubert

St Paul Island

Cape North

Dingwall

Ingonish

White Hill ▲ 1,745ft (532m)

PRINCE EDWARD ISLAND

Prince Edward Island

Elmira

Cape Breton Island

Glace Bay

Sydney

Inverness

Baddeck

Bras d'Or Lake

St Peter's

Port Hawkesbury

Cape Canso

Chatham

Newcastle

NEW BRUNSWICK

Doaktown

Bath

Chipman

Woodstock

Houlton

FREDERICTON

Harvey

Sussex

Milltown

Saint John

Deer Island

Grand Manan Island

Bay of Fundy

Bouctouche

Shediac

Petitcodiac

Moncton

Port Elgin

Amherst

Borden

Northumberland Strait

CHARLOTTETOWN

Pictou

Antigonish

New Glasgow

Derbert

Truro

Parrsboro

Sherbrooke

NOVA SCOTIA

Wolfville

Middleton

Enfield

Sheet Harbour

Digby

Weymouth

Long Island

Meteghan

Chester

Bridgewater

HALIFAX

Liverpool

Yarmouth

Shelburne

Barrington

Cape Sable Island

ATLANTIC OCEAN

Cap-des-Rosiers Lighthouse, Québec

Rideau Canal, Ottawa
The Rideau Canal links Lake Ontario with the Ottawa River. When the canal freezes in winter, it becomes a very long skating rink. Skaters can look up at Canada's Parliament Buildings.

Three-quarters of all Canadians live along the St Lawrence River within 100 miles (160 km) of the border between Canada and the USA—the world's longest undefended border.

0 miles 100
0 kilometers 100

N W E S

Canada

LAND AREA	3,511,023 sq miles (9,093,507 sq km)
OFFICIAL LANGUAGE	English/French
MAIN RELIGION	Christian
LIFE EXPECTANCY	80 years
LITERACY	97%

- Forest and woodland
- Arable land
- Grazing
- Arid or marginal

USING THE LAND

- Cereals
- Fruit and vegetables
- Fruit
- Beef cattle
- Fishing
- Industrial center
- Mining
- Oil production
- Gas production
- Timber
- Tourism
- Winter sports

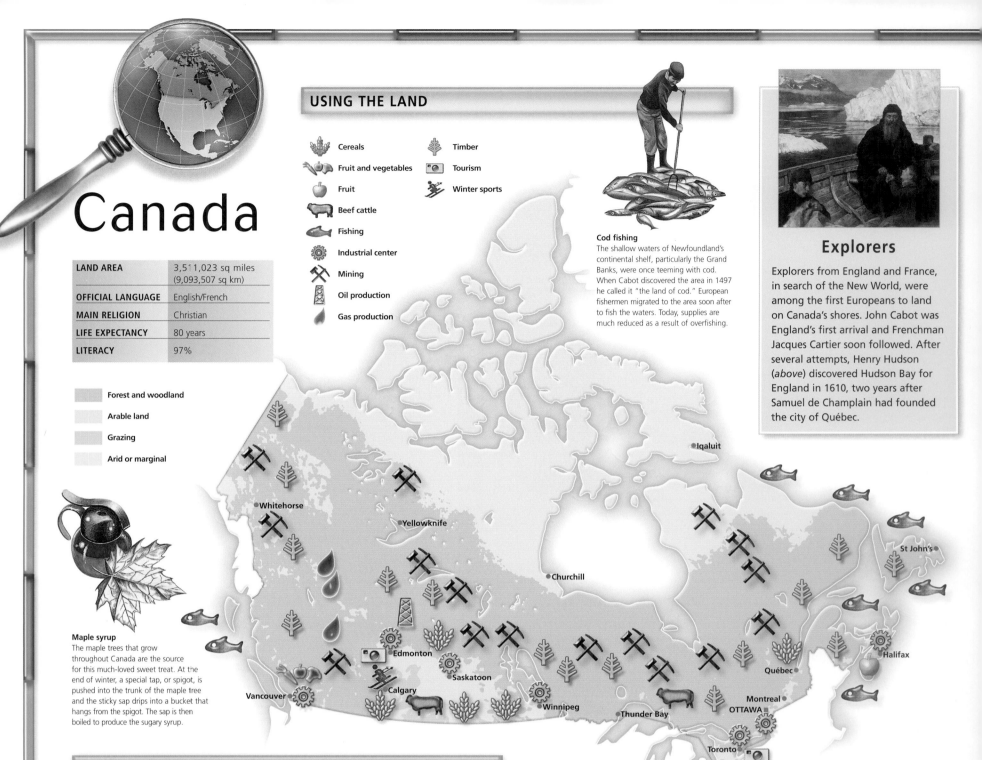

Whitehorse · Yellowknife · Iqaluit · Churchill · St John's · Edmonton · Saskatoon · Calgary · Vancouver · Winnipeg · Thunder Bay · Montreal · OTTAWA · Québec · Halifax · Toronto

Maple syrup
The maple trees that grow throughout Canada are the source for this much-loved sweet treat. At the end of winter, a special tap, or spigot, is pushed into the trunk of the maple tree and the sticky sap drips into a bucket that hangs from the spigot. The sap is then boiled to produce the sugary syrup.

Cod fishing
The shallow waters of Newfoundland's continental shelf, particularly the Grand Banks, were once teeming with cod. When Cabot discovered the area in 1497 he called it "the land of cod." European fishermen migrated to the area soon after to fish the waters. Today, supplies are much reduced as a result of overfishing.

Explorers
Explorers from England and France, in search of the New World, were among the first Europeans to land on Canada's shores. John Cabot was England's first arrival and Frenchman Jacques Cartier soon followed. After several attempts, Henry Hudson (*above*) discovered Hudson Bay for England in 1610, two years after Samuel de Champlain had founded the city of Québec.

NATURAL FEATURES

Hudson Bay
This inland sea on Canada's northern boundary is linked by channels and straits to both the Atlantic and Arctic oceans. Its coastal marshes provide a wetland habitat for an array of unique animals, notably bird species.

Nunavut
Established as Inuit territory in 1999, Nunavut (*below*), meaning "our people," is in the eastern Arctic region. The Inuit have claim to native land in this region, which includes Baffin and Ellesmere islands.

Rocky Mountains
This string of mountain ranges stretches for 3,000 miles (4,800 km) from the Yukon in Canada, down through the USA to Mexico. Banff National Park, home of the Moraine Lake, is in the Canadian Rockies.

Moraine Lake

The prairies
These flat, fertile, treeless grasslands east of the Rockies—which seem to stretch forever—now contain 75 percent of Canada's farmland, although they were once home to roaming buffalo herds.

St Lawrence River
The waters of Lake Ontario—one of the Great Lakes—flow into this river. The icy river supports a population of about 650 beluga whales.

Beluga whale

Forty percent of Toronto's population was born overseas—UNESCO voted it the world's most diverse city.

Wheat
This grain crop—Canada's largest agricultural export—is ideally suited to the natural grassland areas of the prairies. Two-thirds of Canadian wheat is grown in the Saskatchewan province. Once harvested, the grain is pooled, then stored in tall structures called silos (*above*), which dot the landscape.

WHERE PEOPLE LIVE

Urban	Rural
77%	23%

HIGHEST MOUNTAINS

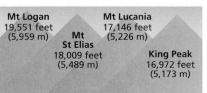

Mt Logan 19,551 feet (5,959 m)
Mt Lucania 17,146 feet (5,226 m)
Mt St Elias 18,009 feet (5,489 m)
King Peak 16,972 feet (5,173 m)

LARGEST CITIES

Toronto 4,726,000

Montreal 3,291,000

Vancouver 1,840,000

Calgary 1,014,000

Ottawa 896,000

PLACES

Québec City
Situated above the mighty St Lawrence River, this capital city of Québec province has a predominantly French lifestyle, and over 90 percent of the population speaks French. Its Old Town is filled with classic 18th- and 19th-century houses.

Château Frontenac, Québec City

Vancouver
This busy port is Canada's contact point for trade with Japan and the East. Canada Place Pavilion overlooks the harbor, and the city's coastal setting, framed by hills and mountains, is ideal for outdoor sports.

St John's
Established in 1528 after John Cabot's discovery of its harbor, this city was the first British colony outside England, and is the oldest city in North America. It is where the Trans-Canada Highway starts.

Parliament building
Ottawa's parliament building (above), built in the mid-19th century and overlooking the Ottawa River, is the seat of Canada's government.

Dawson
During the gold rush of the late 1800s, this town (below) in the Klondike region was home to 40,000 people; now only about 2,000 people live there. Buildings from the gold rush have been preserved.

Basketball was invented in 1891 by James Naismith, a Canadian teacher, to occupy his students.

TRADITIONS AND CULTURE

Curling
Curling, one of Canada's most popular winter sports, is played on ice. Team members compete to slide a smooth, round stone toward a mark, called a tee.

Totem poles
These tall cedar poles depicting totems, or storytelling symbols, of different tribes were carved by native peoples, such as the Tlingits, of North America.

Tlingit totem pole

Buffalo jump
For almost 6,000 years, the native people of the North American Plains hunted buffalo by forcing them to run over a cliff, then collecting their carcasses. At Alberta, the Head-Smashed-In Buffalo Jump, named for a boy who was crushed by the falling beasts, has been declared a World Heritage Site by UNESCO.

Calgary Stampede
Every July, this huge 10-day rodeo in Calgary attracts cowboys who compete in a range of horse- and bull-racing events. In the chuckwagon-racing event (above), introduced in 1925, cowboys sit on a wagon behind teams of four horses and race around a track.

Inuit carvings
The Inuit have carved sculptures from stone and other materials for thousands of years. Today, the carvings are sold to collectors around the world.

Dog mushing
This activity, in which people travel across snow-covered land on sleds pulled by teams of dogs, is a competitive sport in Canada and Alaska. Huskies are used as they are intelligent and adapt well to cold conditions.

Huskies

Canadian Mounties
The Royal Canadian Mounted Police, called the Mounties, was established in 1873 to maintain order between new settlers and native people in Canada's northwest. The Mounties rode horses, wore distinctive red jackets and flat-brimmed hats and, as legend goes, "always got their man." Today, they patrol in cars and ride horses only on special occasions.

PEOPLE

Laura Secord 1775–1868
In 1813, during the Battle of Beaver Dams, this courageous woman trekked through the wilds for 18 hours to inform the British that the USA intended to attack and take over Niagara Peninsula. Her news saved this territory.

Norman Bethune 1890–1939
Born in Ontario, this dedicated doctor pioneered many medical procedures, particularly in blood transfusions, that changed the lives of the sick. He worked with soldiers in China, and devised a public health system for Canada.

Joe Shuster 1914–92
This talented artist, who moved from Canada to Ohio, USA, in 1923, teamed up with writer Jerry Siegel to create *Superman*, one of the world's most successful comic strips.

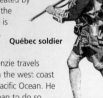

Shuster's Superman

Pierre Trudeau 1919–2000
First elected as Canada's prime minister in 1968, and in power for 16 years, this progressive politician led the country through some of its most challenging times.

Jim Carrey born 1962
This internationally renowned actor is known for his comedy antics and impersonations, as well as character acting.

Jim Carrey in *The Mask*

HISTORY AT A GLANCE

c 20,000 BC
The first inhabitants, ancestors of the Inuit, come to Alaska from Asia via the Bering Strait.

AD 1000
Led by Leif Eriksson, the Vikings start to colonize the Newfoundland coast, but not permanently.

1497
John Cabot, an Italian–British explorer, reaches and names Newfoundland, claiming it for Britain.

1534
Jacques Cartier explores the Gulf of St Lawrence, then discovers the St Lawrence River and claims Canada for France.

Jacques Cartier

1605
The first European colony is established by France at Port Royal, Nova Scotia. Samuel de Champlain founds Québec three years later.

1663
Canada, known as New France, becomes a province of France.

1670
King Charles II of England allows the Hudson Bay Company to trap animals. Trade, especially in fur, is encouraged between England and Canada.

1754
Britain and France fight in the French and Indian War. France gives up Québec to Britain.

1759
Battle of the Plains of Abraham is fought outside Québec City and France is defeated by Britain. By 1763, the whole of Canada is in Britain's hands.

Québec soldier

1793
Alexander Mackenzie travels overland to reach the west coast of Canada—the Pacific Ocean. He is the first European to do so.

1846
The Oregon Treaty confirms Canada's northwest borders with the USA. The Dominion of Canada is established 21 years later.

1885
Canadian Pacific Railway is completed, creating a link across the country.

Canadian Pacific Railway

1949
Newfoundland becomes the newest province. Canada is a founding member of NATO.

1968
The Québec Party is formed, sparking independence for the province.

1989
Britain transfers all power relating to Canada in British law back to Canada.

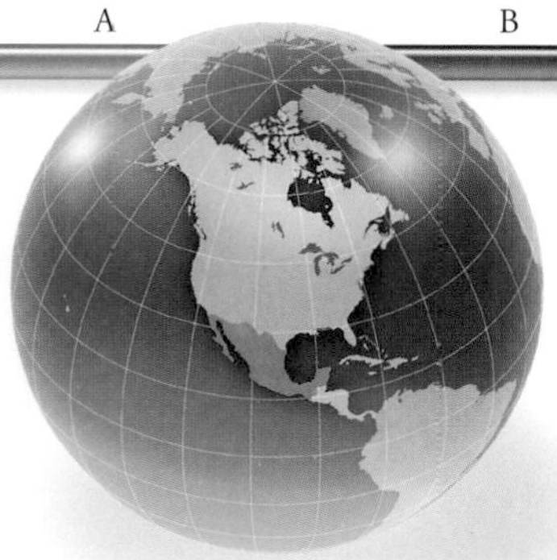

Mexico

Sombrero

Sombrero

MEXICO
POPULATION 107,450,000 ● CAPITAL **MEXICO CITY**

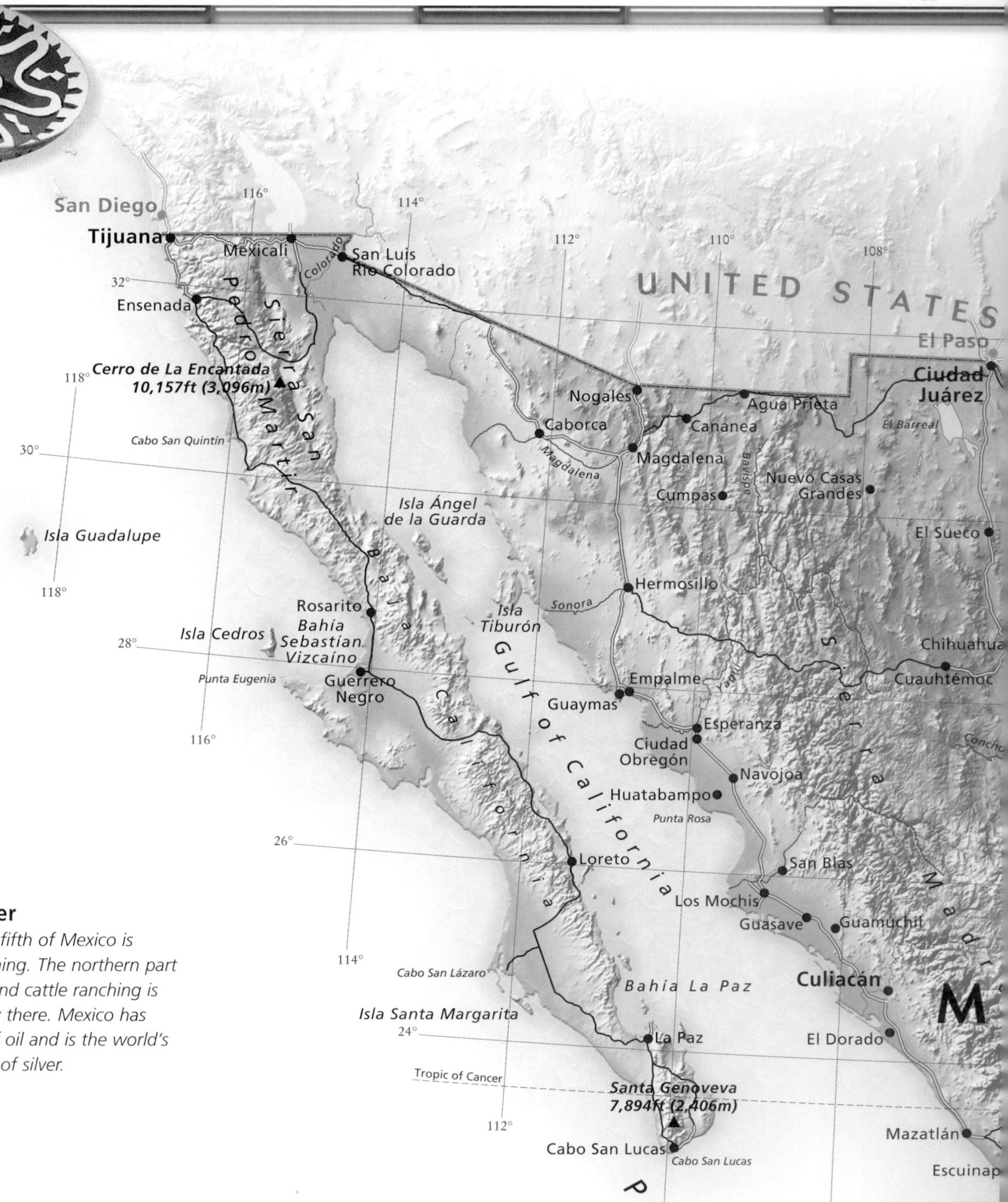

Monarch butterflies

The monarch butterfly is a long-distance traveler. Each year, tens of millions of these colorful butterflies fly up to 2,500 miles (4,000 km) from Canada and the east coast of the USA to spend the winter in Mexico.

Cattle rancher

Only about one-fifth of Mexico is suitable for farming. The northern part is hot and dry, and cattle ranching is the main activity there. Mexico has large supplies of oil and is the world's biggest supplier of silver.

Piñata

A piñata is a papier-mâché container filled with toys and sweets. At Mexican celebrations, a piñata is hung from the ceiling or a tree branch, and children take turns trying to break it open with a stick to get the treats.

Traditional dancers

Folk dances and music are popular at fiesta time. Many of the dances performed today are based on Indian dances from before the Spanish conquest of Mexico.

The cardón cactus is the world's largest cactus. It grows in the deserts of the Baja California peninsula. Some are nearly 70 feet (21 m) high. These plants can live for more than 300 years.

San Diego
Tijuana
Mexicali
San Luis
Rio Colorado
Ensenada
116°
114°
112°
110°
108°
32°
UNITED STATES
El Paso
Ciudad Juárez
Cerro de La Encantada 10,157ft (3,096m)
118°
30°
Cabo San Quintín
Nogales
Agua Prieta
Caborca
Cananea
El Barreal
Magdalena
Nuevo Casas Grandes
Cumpas
El Sueco
Isla Guadalupe
118°
28°
Isla Cedros
Rosarito
Bahía Sebastián Vizcaíno
Isla Ángel de la Guarda
Hermosillo
Sonora
Isla Tiburón
Chihuahua
Cuauhtémoc
Punta Eugenia
Guerrero Negro
Empalme
Guaymas
Esperanza
116°
Ciudad Obregón
Navojoa
Conchos
Huatabampo
Punta Rosa
26°
Loreto
San Blas
114°
Los Mochis
Guasave
Guamúchil
Cabo San Lázaro
Bahía La Paz
Culiacán
Isla Santa Margarita
24°
La Paz
El Dorado
Tropic of Cancer
Santa Genoveva 7,894ft (2,406m)
112°
Cabo San Lucas
Cabo San Lucas
Mazatlán
Escuinapa
22°
110°
108° Islas Marías
Punta de
PACIFIC OCEAN
Cabo Corrien
20°
106°
Gulf of California

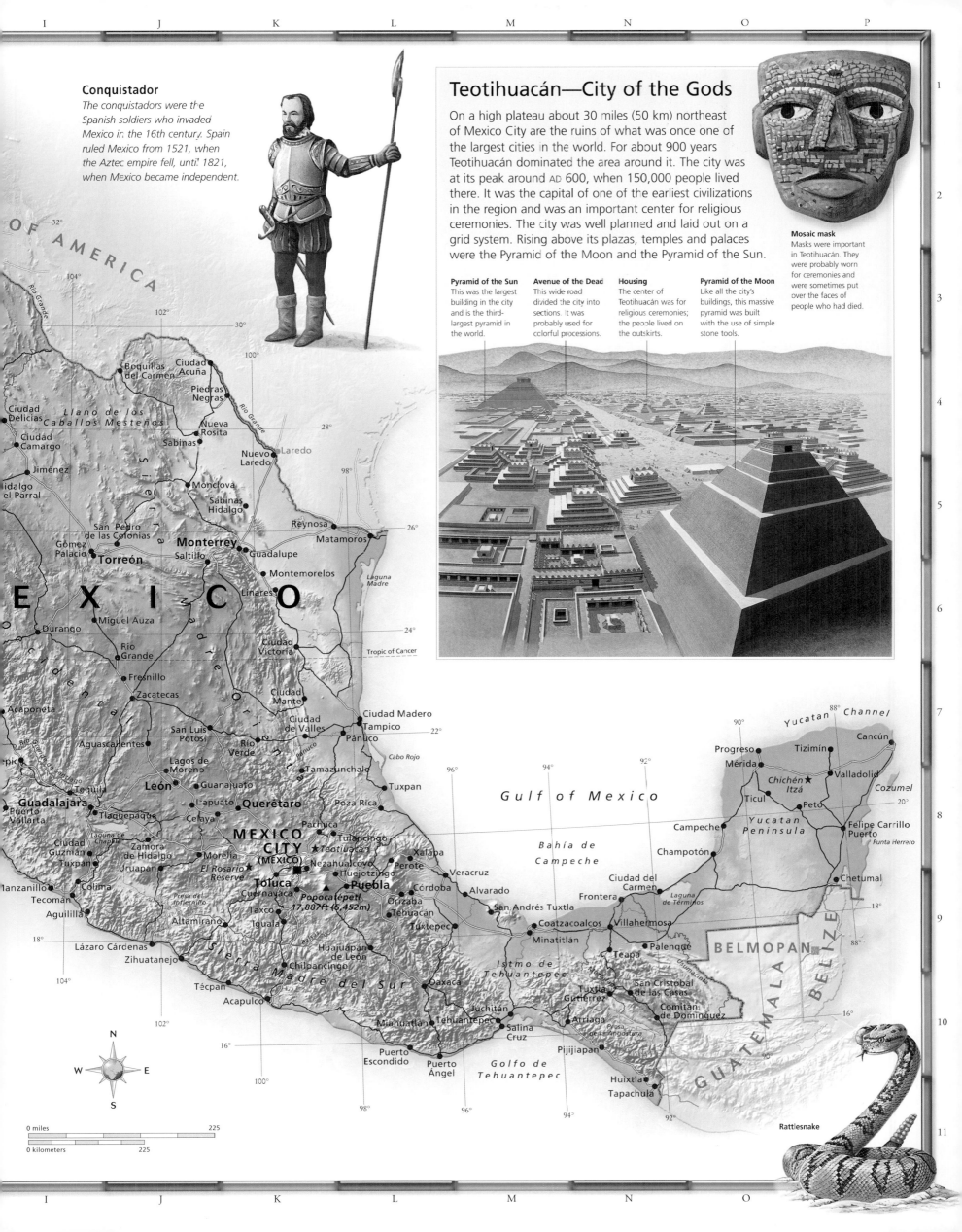

Conquistador

The conquistadors were the Spanish soldiers who invaded Mexico in the 16th century. Spain ruled Mexico from 1521, when the Aztec empire fell, until 1821, when Mexico became independent.

Teotihuacán—City of the Gods

On a high plateau about 30 miles (50 km) northeast of Mexico City are the ruins of what was once one of the largest cities in the world. For about 900 years Teotihuacán dominated the area around it. The city was at its peak around AD 600, when 150,000 people lived there. It was the capital of one of the earliest civilizations in the region and was an important center for religious ceremonies. The city was well planned and laid out on a grid system. Rising above its plazas, temples and palaces were the Pyramid of the Moon and the Pyramid of the Sun.

Mosaic mask
Masks were important in Teotihuacán. They were probably worn for ceremonies and were sometimes put over the faces of people who had died.

Pyramid of the Sun
This was the largest building in the city and is the third-largest pyramid in the world.

Avenue of the Dead
This wide road divided the city into sections. It was probably used for colorful processions.

Housing
The center of Teotihuacán was for religious ceremonies; the people lived on the outskirts.

Pyramid of the Moon
Like all the city's buildings, this massive pyramid was built with the use of simple stone tools.

Rattlesnake

Central America and the Caribbean

Spotted eagle ray

Pirate
In the 1600s, pirates set up bases in the Caribbean, attacking and robbing trading ships. Pirate Edward Teach, known as Blackbeard, was much feared during the 1700s.

GUATEMALA
POPULATION 12,294,000 ∗ CAPITAL GUATEMALA

CUBA
POPULATION 11,383,000 ∗ CAPITAL HAVANA

DOMINICAN REPUBLIC
POPULATION 9,184,000 ∗ CAPITAL SANTO DOMINGO

HAITI
POPULATION 8,309,000 ∗ CAPITAL PORT-AU-PRINCE

HONDURAS
POPULATION 7,326,000 ∗ CAPITAL TEGUCIGALPA

EL SALVADOR
POPULATION 6,822,000 ∗ CAPITAL SAN SALVADOR

NICARAGUA
POPULATION 5,570,000 ∗ CAPITAL MANAGUA

COSTA RICA
POPULATION 4,075,000 ∗ CAPITAL SAN JOSÉ

PANAMA
POPULATION 3,191,000 ∗ CAPITAL PANAMA CITY

JAMAICA
POPULATION 2,758,000 ∗ CAPITAL KINGSTON

TRINIDAD AND TOBAGO
POPULATION 1,066,000 ∗ CAPITAL PORT-OF-SPAIN

THE BAHAMAS
POPULATION 304,000 ∗ CAPITAL NASSAU

BELIZE
POPULATION 288,000 ∗ CAPITAL BELMOPAN

BARBADOS
POPULATION 280,000 ∗ CAPITAL BRIDGETOWN

ST LUCIA
POPULATION 168,000 ∗ CAPITAL CASTRIES

ST VINCENT AND THE GRENADINES
POPULATION 118,000 ∗ CAPITAL KINGSTOWN

GRENADA
POPULATION 90,000 ∗ CAPITAL ST GEORGE'S

DOMINICA
POPULATION 69,000 ∗ CAPITAL ROSEAU

ANTIGUA AND BARBUDA
POPULATION 69,000 ∗ CAPITAL ST JOHN'S

ST KITTS AND NEVIS
POPULATION 39,000 ∗ CAPITAL BASSETERRE

Cuban music
Conga, mambo, jazz cubano and rumba are among the many lively styles of Cuban music. The rumba involves drumming, dancing, and call-and-response singing, in both Spanish and African languages.

Keel-billed toucan
This toucan is the national bird of Belize. It lives in rain forests, and nests in holes in tree trunks. The toucan uses its huge bill to snip off pieces of fruit from trees and then flips back its head and gulps the food down. It also eats snakes.

Map labels

USA

Gulf of Mexico
Straits of Florida
Tropic of Cancer
HAVANA (LA HABANA)
Matanzas
CUBA
Pinar del Río
Santa Clara
Cienfuegos
Sancti Spíritus
Cabo San Antonio
Cabo Corrientes
Isla de la Juventud
Cayo Largo
Archipiélago de los Jardines de la Reina
Little Cayman
Cayman Brac
GEORGE TOWN
Grand Cayman
CAYMAN ISLANDS (to U.K.)
Angilla Cays

MEXICO
Corozal
Orange Walk
Belize City
Tikal
San Ignacio
Flores
BELMOPAN
Dangriga
BELIZE
GUATEMALA
Huehuetenango
Cobán
Quezaltenango
Puerto Barrios
Golfo de Honduras
La Ceiba
Trujillo
Islas de la Bahía
Chiquimula
San Pedro Sula
Santa Rosa de Copán
HONDURAS
Laguna Caratasca
GUATEMALA
Escuintla
Comayagua
Juticalpa
Puerto Lempira
Mosquito Coast
Cayos Miskitos
Santa Ana
San Miguel
TEGUCIGALPA
Puerto Cabezas
Nueva San Salvador
SAN SALVADOR
EL SALVADOR
NICARAGUA
Matagalpa
Isla de Providencia (to Colombia)
Grande
León
Lago de Managua
Boaco
Juigalpa
Laguna de Perlas
Isla de San Andrés (to Colombia)
Islas del Maíz
MANAGUA
Granada
Bluefields
Jinotepe
Isla de Ometepe
Rivas
Lago de Nicaragua
Punta del Mono
Cabo Santa Elena
San Juan
Liberia
COSTA RICA
Puntarenas
Alajuela
Limón
Golfo de los Mosquitos
El Porveni
SAN JOSÉ
Cartago
Bocas del Toro
Portobelo
Colón
Cerro Chirripó Grande 12,529ft (3,819m)
Cordillera Talamanca
Laguna de Chiriqui
Lago Gatún
Puerto Cortés
PANAMA CITY
PACIFIC OCEAN
David
PANAMA
Santiago
San Miguel
Golfo Dulce
Golfo de Chiriqui
Soná
Isla del Re
Las Tablas
Isla Coiba
Península de Azuero
Gulf of Panam

0 miles 300
0 kilometers 300

N W E S

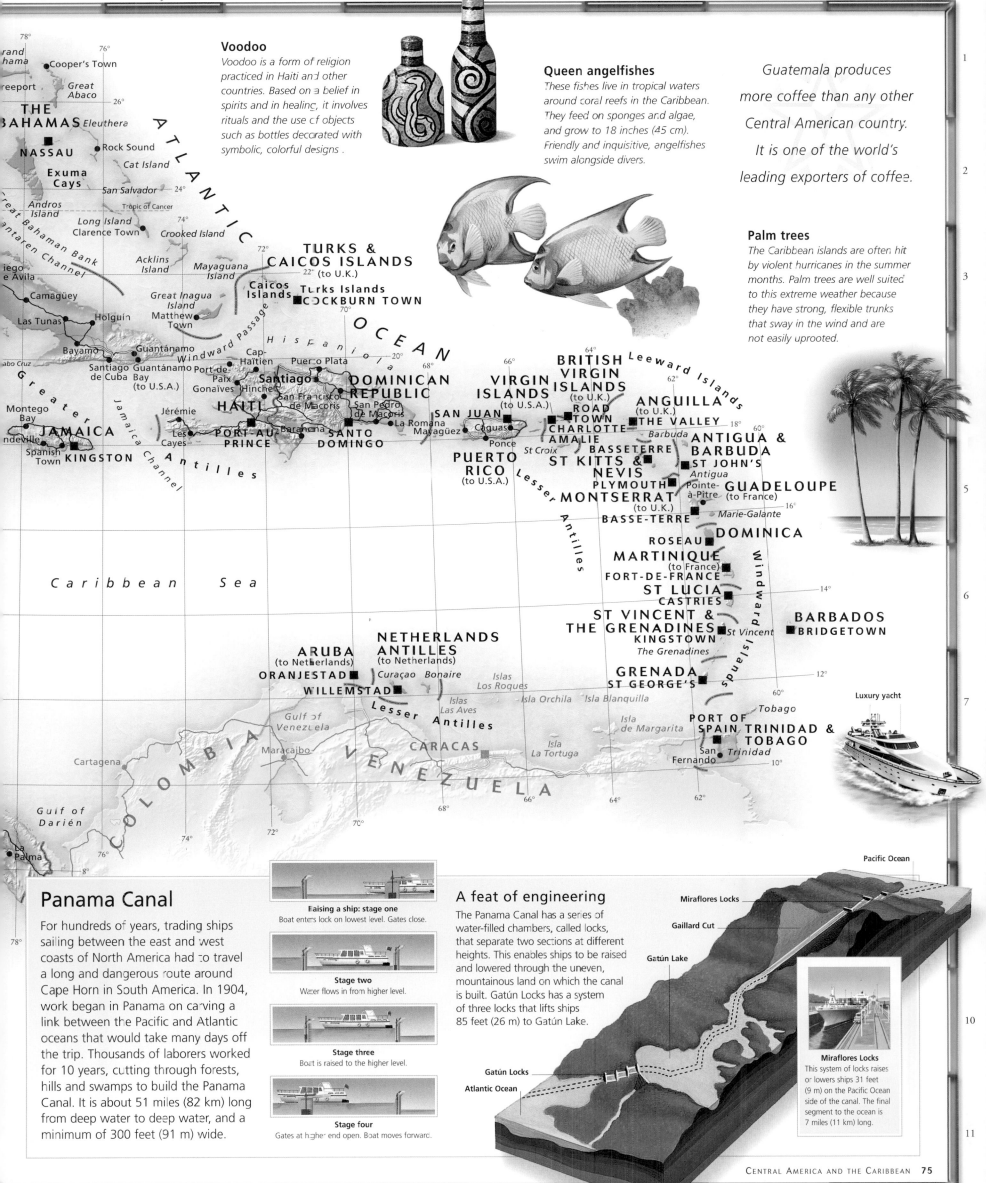

Voodoo

Voodoo is a form of religion practiced in Haiti and other countries. Based on a belief in spirits and in healing, it involves rituals and the use of objects such as bottles decorated with symbolic, colorful designs .

Queen angelfishes

These fishes live in tropical waters around coral reefs in the Caribbean. They feed on sponges and algae, and grow to 18 inches (45 cm). Friendly and inquisitive, angelfishes swim alongside divers.

Guatemala produces more coffee than any other Central American country. It is one of the world's leading exporters of coffee.

Palm trees

The Caribbean islands are often hit by violent hurricanes in the summer months. Palm trees are well suited to this extreme weather because they have strong, flexible trunks that sway in the wind and are not easily uprooted.

Map labels:

78° · 76° · Grand Bahama · Cooper's Town · Freeport · Great Abaco · 26° · THE BAHAMAS · Eleuthera · Rock Sound · NASSAU · Cat Island · Exuma Cays · San Salvador · 24° · Andros Island · Tropic of Cancer · Great Bahaman Bank · Long Island · Clarence Town · Crooked Island · 74° · Santaren Channel · Diego de Avila · Camagüey · Acklins Island · Mayaguana Island · 72° · TURKS & CAICOS ISLANDS · 22° (to U.K.) · Las Tunas · Holguín · Great Inagua Island · Matthew Town · Caicos Islands · Turks Islands · COCKBURN TOWN · Cabo Cruz · Bayamo · Guantánamo · Cap-Haïtien · Windward Passage · 70° · Santiago de Cuba · Guantánamo Bay (to U.S.A.) · Port-de-Paix · Gonaïves · Hinche · Hispaniola · 20° · Puerto Plata · San Francisco de Macoris · DOMINICAN REPUBLIC · 68° · Montego Bay · Greater Antilles · Jérémie · Santiago · HAITI · San Pedro de Macoris · VIRGIN ISLANDS · BRITISH VIRGIN ISLANDS · 64° · Leeward Islands · 62° · JAMAICA · Jamaica Channel · Les Cayes · PORT-AU-PRINCE · Barahona · La Romana · SAN JUAN · (to U.K.) · ROAD TOWN · ANGUILLA · THE VALLEY · 18° · 60° · Mandeville · Spanish Town · KINGSTON · SANTO DOMINGO · Mayagüez · Caguas · CHARLOTTE AMALIE · St Croix · BASSETERRE · Barbuda · ANTIGUA & BARBUDA · Ponce · PUERTO RICO (to U.S.A.) · Lesser Antilles · ST KITTS & NEVIS · PLYMOUTH · ST JOHN'S · Antigua · Pointe-à-Pitre · GUADELOUPE (to France) · MONTSERRAT (to U.K.) · Marie-Galante · 16° · BASSE-TERRE · DOMINICA · ROSEAU · MARTINIQUE (to France) · Windward Islands · FORT-DE-FRANCE · Caribbean Sea · ST LUCIA · CASTRIES · 14° · ST VINCENT & THE GRENADINES · BARBADOS · BRIDGETOWN · NETHERLANDS ANTILLES (to Netherlands) · St Vincent · KINGSTOWN · The Grenadines · ARUBA (to Netherlands) · Curaçao · Bonaire · Islas Los Roques · GRENADA · 12° · ORANJESTAD · ST GEORGE'S · 60° · WILLEMSTAD · Islas Las Aves · Isla Orchila · Isla Blanquilla · Tobago · Luxury yacht · Lesser Antilles · Gulf of Venezuela · Isla de Margarita · PORT OF SPAIN · TRINIDAD & TOBAGO · Cartagena · COLOMBIA · Maracaibo · CARACAS · Isla La Tortuga · San Fernando · Trinidad · 10° · Gulf of Darién · VENEZUELA · 68° · 66° · 64° · 62° · 74° · 72° · 70° · La Palma · 8° · 78°

Panama Canal

For hundreds of years, trading ships sailing between the east and west coasts of North America had to travel a long and dangerous route around Cape Horn in South America. In 1904, work began in Panama on carving a link between the Pacific and Atlantic oceans that would take many days off the trip. Thousands of laborers worked for 10 years, cutting through forests, hills and swamps to build the Panama Canal. It is about 51 miles (82 km) long from deep water to deep water, and a minimum of 300 feet (91 m) wide.

Raising a ship: stage one
Boat enters lock on lowest level. Gates close.

Stage two
Water flows in from higher level.

Stage three
Boat is raised to the higher level.

Stage four
Gates at higher end open. Boat moves forward.

A feat of engineering

The Panama Canal has a series of water-filled chambers, called locks, that separate two sections at different heights. This enables ships to be raised and lowered through the uneven, mountainous land on which the canal is built. Gatún Locks has a system of three locks that lifts ships 85 feet (26 m) to Gatún Lake.

Pacific Ocean · Miraflores Locks · Gaillard Cut · Gatún Lake · Gatún Locks · Atlantic Ocean

Miraflores Locks
This system of locks raises or lowers ships 31 feet (9 m) on the Pacific Ocean side of the canal. The final segment to the ocean is 7 miles (11 km) long.

Sapodilla, a Central American plant, produces chicle, the gum in most chewing gum.

Mexico, Central America and the Caribbean

LAND AREA	1,024,715 sq miles (2,654,000 sq km)
LARGEST COUNTRY	Mexico
SMALLEST COUNTRY	St Kitts-Nevis
MAIN RELIGION	Christian
LIFE EXPECTANCY	70 years
LITERACY	87%

NATURAL FEATURES

Soufrière Hills MONTSERRAT
In July 1995, this volcano began erupting and spitting out lava. The volcanic activity still continues, and has destroyed almost half of Montserrat.

Las Baulas COSTA RICA
This national park, which covers about 4 sq miles (10 sq km) of swamps and beaches, was founded in 1995 to protect endangered wildlife species, especially leatherback turtles, which nest there each year.

Leatherback turtle

Baja peninsula

Baja peninsula MEXICO
This is the world's longest peninsula. Its extremely arid land supports some hardy lizards, such as the gila monster and the Mexican beaded lizard. More than 120 species of cactus thrive there.

Lake Nicaragua NICARAGUA
This freshwater lake is the largest in Central America. It is home to the slow-moving bull shark, which is one of the most frequent attackers of humans.

Belize's reefs BELIZE
Parallel to the coastline, and fringed by tiny islands called cays, Belize's barrier reef is famous for its sponges, coral and fishes. Just beyond is Lighthouse Reef, with its underwater cave, the Blue Hole.

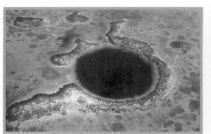

Blue Hole, Lighthouse Reef, Belize

USING THE LAND

- 🌽 Corn (maize)
- 🍎 Fruit
- 🍌 Bananas
- Cotton
- ☕ Coffee
- Sugarcane
- 🐖 Beef cattle
- 🐟 Fishing
- Shellfish
- ⚙ Industrial center
- ⛏ Mining
- 🛢 Oil production
- 📷 Tourism

Corn
Corn has been grown in Mexico for the last 7,000 years. It is one of Mexico's most important commercially grown crops, and more than half of Mexico's farmland is used for its cultivation. Tortillas, the flat bread that most Mexicans eat every day, are made from corn flour.

- Forest and woodland
- Arable land
- Grazing
- Arid or marginal

Tijuana
La Paz
Monterrey
Guadalajara
MEXICO CITY
Puebla
Acapulco
Mérida
BELMOPAN
GUATEMALA
SAN SALVADOR
TEGUCIGALPA
MANAGUA
SAN JOSÉ
PANAMA CITY
HAVANA
PORT-AU-PRINCE
KINGSTON
SANTO DOMINGO
SAN JUAN
PORT OF SPAIN

There are more Spanish speakers in Mexico than any other country.

Bananas
Bananas are especially important in Honduras, which is one of the poorest countries in the Western Hemisphere. Grown along the northern lowlands near the Caribbean Sea, they are a leading source of income.

Cigars
Cigars from Havana, Cuba, are famous as being among the finest in the world, and exporting them is one of Cuba's best sources of foreign revenue. The choicest tobacco comes from western Cuba. The highest-quality cigars are rolled by hand.

The quetzal
This beautiful jungle bird lives in the dense rain forests of Central America. The male is especially brightly colored, with a long, green, feathered tail that can add up to 3 feet (90 cm) to its length. The Aztecs believed the quetzal to be a symbol of freedom because it dies in captivity. Anyone caught killing a quetzal could be sentenced to death. Today, the quetzal is the national emblem of Guatemala, and appears on its flag and postage stamps.

Resplendent quetzal

LARGEST CITIES

Mexico City 8,659,000
🧍🧍🧍🧍🧍🧍🧍🧍🧍🧍🧍🧍🧍🧍🧍🧍🧍🧍🧍🧍

Santo Domingo 2,306,000
🧍🧍🧍🧍🧍🧍

Havana 2,164,000
🧍🧍🧍🧍🧍🧍

Guadalajara 1,632,000
🧍🧍🧍🧍

Puebla 1,442,000
🧍🧍🧍🧍

WHERE PEOPLE LIVE

Urban	Rural

REGION
| 54% | 46% |

Most urban: THE BAHAMAS
| 88% | 12% |

Most rural: ST KITTS-NEVIS
| 34% | 66% |

Blue agave
This plant is cultivated in Mexico. It produces a sweet sap, which is fermented to make a mild alcoholic drink called pulque. Pulque is then distilled and made into a stronger drink called tequila. Tequila, Mexico's national drink, is named for the town in which it was first made.

PLACES

Havana CUBA
The capital and largest city in Cuba, Havana is also its commercial and industrial center. The old colonial city includes the Spanish governor's palace and the 18th-century Havana Cathedral.

Colonial architecture, Havana

Mexico City MEXICO
Built on the ruins of Tenochtitlán in the 16th century, this city is one of the most populated urban areas in the world. It is home to Mexico's government and is its industrial and business center. Its cathedral (*below*) forms part of the main square.

Temple of the Magician MEXICO
In Uxmal lie the ruins of the Mayan Temple of the Magician (*below*), named

for the legend of a boy who built the temple in one night. The Mayans often built a new temple over an old one. This one has been built five separate times.

Antigua GUATEMALA
Built in the 16th century, Antigua, the capital of Guatemala in colonial days, was badly damaged by an earthquake in 1773. It is a city of old, historic buildings, although many of them are now preserved only as ruins.

San Juan PUERTO RICO
The second-oldest city in the Americas, San Juan is Puerto Rico's main seaport. In the early 16th century it was a walled city and the site of Spanish fortifications, many of which have been restored and are tourist attractions today.

The smallest bird in the world is the bee hummingbird, from Cuba.

PEOPLE

Montezuma 1466–1520
An Aztec emperor who extended Aztec land to include most of south-central Mexico, Montezuma was captured by Hernán Cortés in 1519. He was killed in 1520 when the Aztecs rebelled.

Hernán Cortés
Sent by the Spanish governor of Cuba in 1519 to explore the coast of Mexico, Cortés spent the next two years conquering central and southern Mexico. By 1521, Cuauhtémoc, the last Aztec emperor, had surrendered to Cortés, and the Aztec empire became a Spanish colony. When Cortés took over Tenochtitlán, the Aztec capital, he tore down all the buildings.

Frida Kahlo 1907–54
This Mexican painter is famous for her

brightly colored self-portraits, which reflected her tragic life. Kahlo taught herself to paint after she was severely injured in a traffic accident in 1925.

Fidel Castro born c 1926
Largely unchallenged as leader of Cuba since 1959, Castro has a poor relationship with the USA. However, he has improved Cuba's health and education standards.

Bob Marley 1945–81
Marley was a Jamaican musician and composer who popularized reggae music—a mix of native styles, rock and soul, with lyrics about social and political problems.

TRADITIONS AND CULTURE

Spirit dances GUATEMALA
A number of the Guatemalan folk dances re-enact old spiritual rituals and historical events. The Dance of the Conquistadores depicts the fierce battles between the Guatemalans and Hernán Cortés.

Calypso music TRINIDAD AND TOBAGO
The West Indies is the home of calypso music—a lively style of music, with lyrics

that express the mood and beliefs of the people. The Carnival in Trinidad is the most important musical event of the year. Bands and dancers fill the streets.

Day of the Dead MEXICO
In this festival, Mexicans remember their loved ones who have died. Families have feasts for the living next to the graves of the dead, and children exchange toy skeletons or dolls to honor them.

Chilies
Mexicans are very fond of chilies, and grow more than 100 varieties. Chilies range in color from green to red and black. The most common is the jalapeño chili, which is very hot.

Mayan sun calendar

Early calendars
Mayans were one of the first people to develop a reliable system of measuring the passing of time. They used two main systems for counting days which, when used together, produced a 52-year cycle called the Calendar Round. The first system was a 260-day year, and the second was a 365-day year, based on the orbit of Earth around the Sun.

HISTORY AT A GLANCE
GREAT CIVILIZATIONS

Aztec gold mask

OLMECS 1150–800 BC
The Olmecs were the first people to develop an advanced culture in Mexico. They lived near the rivers and swamps in southeast Mexico, in what are now the states of Veracruz and Tabasco. They devised their own way of writing and counting, and worked out a basic calendar. They carved huge stone heads with flat faces, wearing a type of helmet, to honor their gods, warriors and kings. An important Olmec settlement was found at La Venta, leading some historians to believe that Olmec culture began there.

Olmec head

MAYANS AD 250–900
The Mayans were the most advanced of all the Native American peoples. They settled in villages and developed agriculture in southern Mexico, Guatemala and northern Belize. They built stone cities, palaces and temple pyramids decorated with fine carvings. Religion played a large part in the life of the Mayans. Priests climbed the stairs of the pyramids and performed ceremonies in the temple at the top, offering sacrifices—animal and human—to their gods. The Mayans developed a system of picture writing, or hieroglyphics, and made paper from the bark of wild fig trees.

Mayan temple, Tikal, Guatemala

TOLTECS 900–1200
These were a warrior people who invaded central Mexico from the north, burning the city of Teotihuacán, one of the most important cultural centers in Mexico. The Toltecs were craftspeople, skilled in intricate sculptures, such as this huge carved statue of a soldier (*right*). They worshiped many gods, in particular, Quetzalcóatl, the Feathered Serpent, whose image (a snake crowned with quetzal feathers) adorns many of the buildings at Chichén Itzá and Tula.

Toltec carved stone column

AZTECS 1428–1521
The Aztecs came from the northwest and built their capital, Tenochtitlán (now Mexico City), in the Valley of Mexico. They had one of the most advanced cultures in the Americas, and created art, sculpture, poetry and music. They were deeply religious, and their religion affected every aspect of their lives. They worshiped more than 120 gods—nearly every event, day, month and city had its own special god. The Aztecs built many huge temples and elaborate sculptures to worship their gods. They especially honored Huitzilopochtli, a fierce god to whom they sacrificed thousands of people every year.

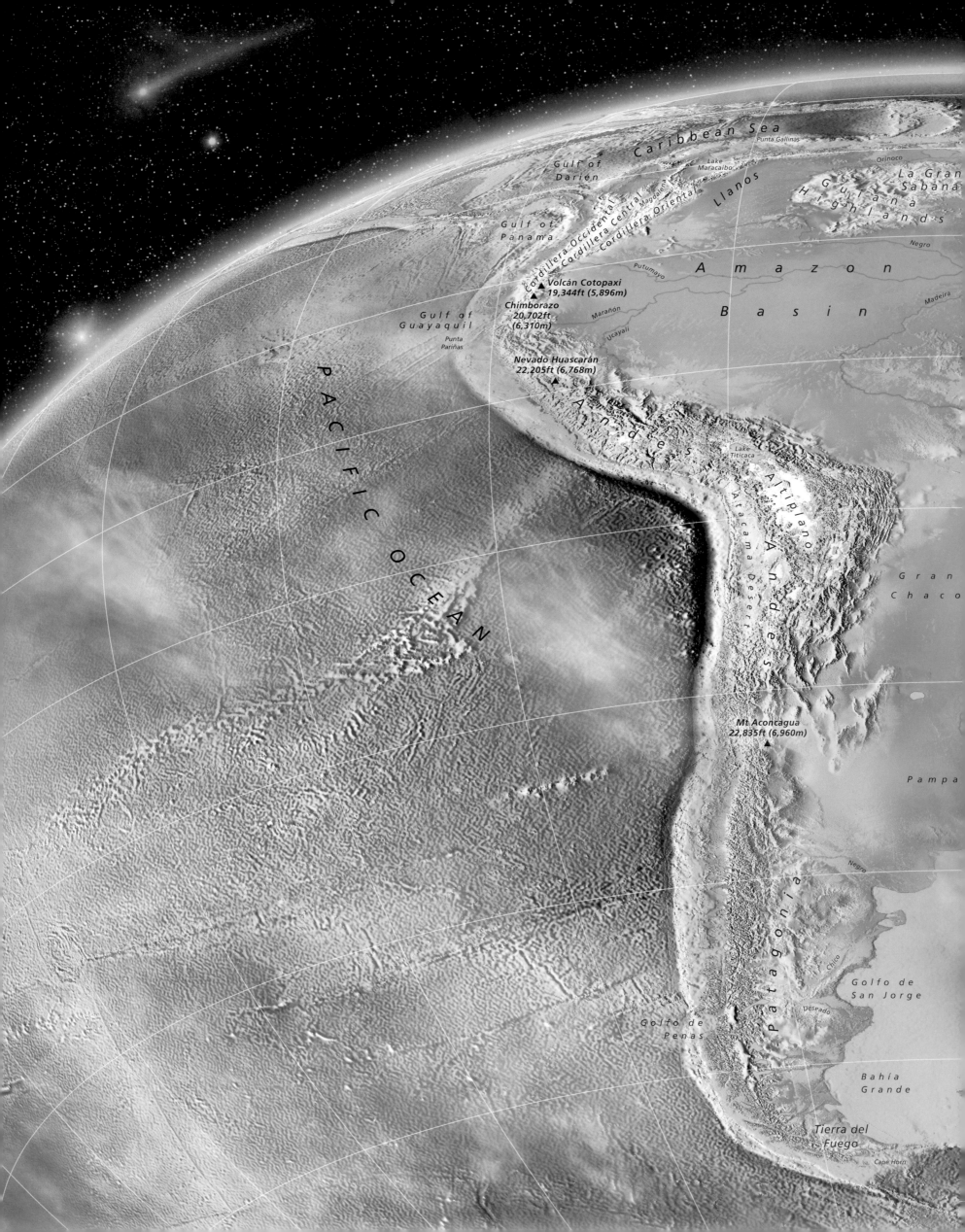

Caribbean Sea

Gulf of
Darién

Punta Gallinas

Lake
Maracaibo

Orinoco

La Gran
Sabana

Gulf of
Panamá

Llanos

Guiana
Highlands

Cordillera Occidental

Cordillera Central

Magdalena

Cordillera Oriental

Putumayo

Amazon

Negro

▲ Volcán Cotopaxi
19,344ft (5,896m)

Marañón

Basin

Madeira

Chimborazo
20,702ft
(6,310m)

Gulf of
Guayaquil

Ucayali

Punta
Pariñas

Nevado Huascarán
22,205ft (6,768m) ▲

PACIFIC OCEAN

A
n
d
e
s

Altiplano

Lake
Titicaca

A
n
d
e
s

Atacama Desert

Gran
Chaco

Mt Aconcagua
22,835ft (6,960m) ▲

Pampa

Negro

Chico

Golfo de
San Jorge

P
a
t
a
g
o
n
i
a

Deseado

Golfo de
Penas

Bahía
Grande

Tierra del
Fuego

Cape Horn

Tumuc-Humac
Mountains

Amazon

Xingu

*Planalto
do Mato
Grosso*

Araguaia

Tocantins

*Planalto da
Borborema*

Cabo de
São Roque

São Francisco

Paraguay

*B r a z i l i a n
H i g h l a n d s*

*Serra
Geral*

Paraná

Serra do Mar

Mesopotamia

Paraná

Uruguay

Lagoa dos
Patos

Lagoa Mirim

River Plate

A T L A N T I C   O C E A N

South America

Falkland
Islands

South
Georgia

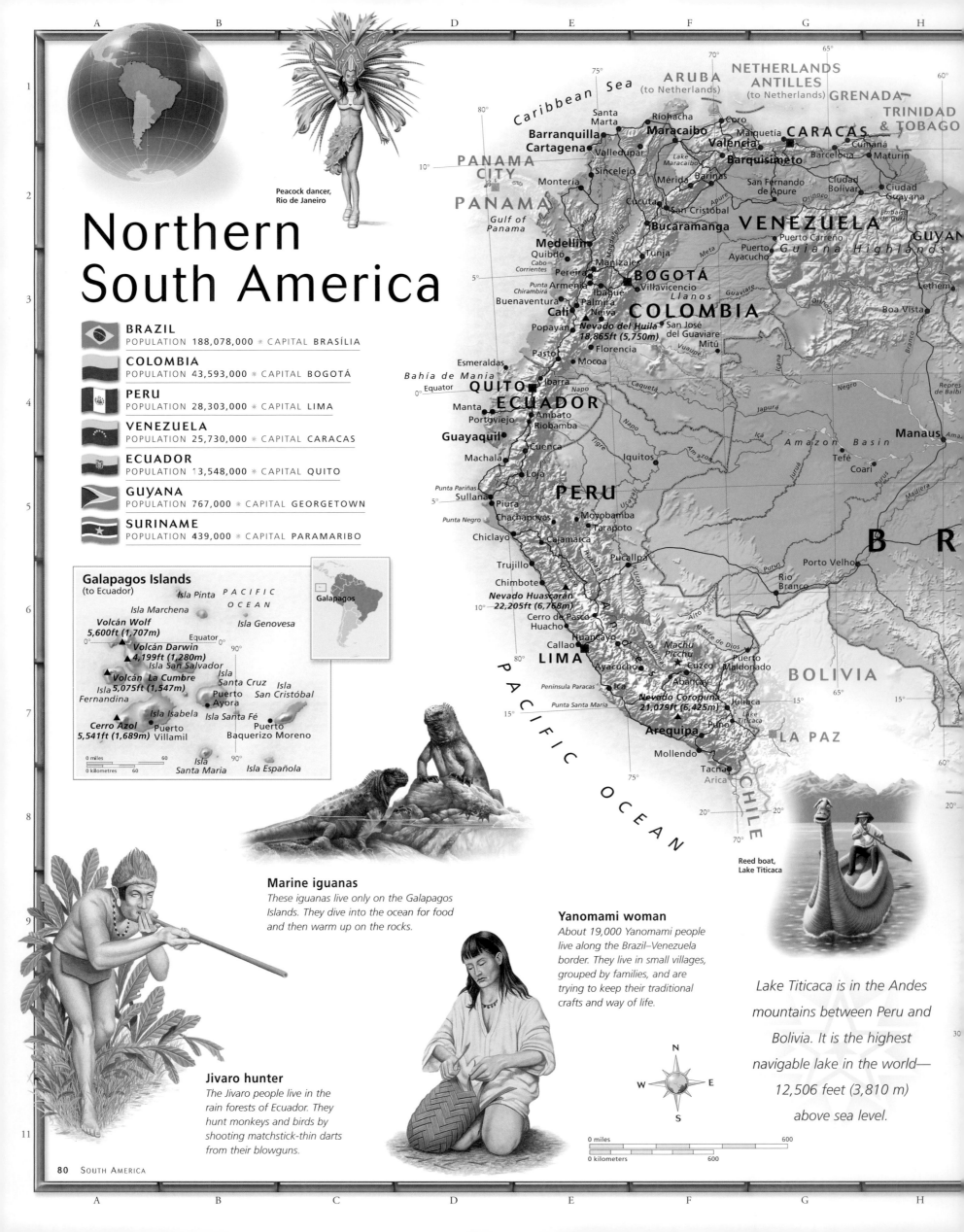

Northern South America

Galapagos

BRAZIL
POPULATION 188,078,000 ✶ CAPITAL BRASÍLIA

COLOMBIA
POPULATION 43,593,000 ✶ CAPITAL BOGOTÁ

PERU
POPULATION 28,303,000 ✶ CAPITAL LIMA

VENEZUELA
POPULATION 25,730,000 ✶ CAPITAL CARACAS

ECUADOR
POPULATION 13,548,000 ✶ CAPITAL QUITO

GUYANA
POPULATION 767,000 ✶ CAPITAL GEORGETOWN

SURINAME
POPULATION 439,000 ✶ CAPITAL PARAMARIBO

Galapagos Islands
(to Ecuador)

Isla Pinta

*PACIFIC
OCEAN*

Isla Marchena

**Volcán Wolf
5,600ft (1,707m)**

Isla Genovesa

Equator

**Volcán Darwin
4,199ft (1,280m)**
Isla San Salvador

**Volcán La Cumbre
Isla 5,075ft (1,547m)**
Fernandina

Isla
Santa Cruz
Puerto
Ayora

Isla
San Cristóbal

Isla Santa Fé

**Cerro Azol
5,541ft (1,689m)**
Puerto
Villamil

Puerto
Baquerizo Moreno

Isla
Santa Maria

Isla Española

0 miles 60
0 kilometres 60

Peacock dancer,
Rio de Janeiro

Map labels

Caribbean Sea

ARUBA
(to Netherlands)

NETHERLANDS
ANTILLES
(to Netherlands)

GRENADA
TRINIDAD
& TOBAGO

Santa
Marta

Ríohacha

Coro

Maiquetía **CARACAS**

Cumaná
Maturin

Barranquilla
Cartagena

Valledupar

Maracaibo

Valencia

Barcelona

PANAMA
CITY

Sincelejo

*Lake
Maracaibo*

Barquisimeto

Ciudad
Bolívar

Ciudad
Guayana

PANAMA

Montería

Mérida
Barinas

San Fernando
de Apure

*Gulf of
Panama*

Cúcuta
San Cristóbal

Apure

Orinoco

VENEZUELA

GUYANA

Medellín

Bucaramanga

Puerto Carreño

Guiana Highlands

Quibdó

Tunja

Puerto
Ayacucho

Meta

Lethem

Cabo
Corrientes

Pereira

Manizales

BOGOTÁ

Llanos

Guaviare

Boa
Vista

Punta
Chirambirá

Armenia

Villavicencio

San José
del Guaviare

Orinoco

Branco

Buenaventura

Ibagué

Palmira

Cali

Neiva

COLOMBIA

Mitú

Vaupés

Içana

*Represa
de Balbi*

Popayán

*Nevado del Huila
18,865ft (5,750m)*

Florencia

Vaupés

Negro

Pasto

Mocoa

Caquetá

Japurá

Esmeraldas

Bahía de Mania

Ibarra

Napo

Içá

Tefé

Manaus

0° Equator

QUITO

ECUADOR

Amazon Basin

Manta

Ambato

Portoviejo

Riobamba

Napo

Coari

Guayaquil

Tigre

Iquitos

Amazon

Jurua

Machala

Cuenca

Loja

Ucayali

PERU

Madeira

Punta Pariñas

Amazon

Sullana

Piura

Chachapoyas

Moyobamba

5°

Punta Negro

Tarapoto

Chiclayo

Cajamarca

Pucallpa

Purus

Porto Velho

Trujillo

B

Chimbote

*Nevado Huascarán
22,205ft (6,768m)*

Ucayali

Rio
Branco

Cerro de Pasco

Alto Purus

Madre de Dios

Huacho

Huancayo

Machu
Picchu

Callao

LIMA

Ayacucho

Cuzco

Puerto
Maldonado

BOLIVIA

Peninsula Paracas

Ica

Abancay

*Nevado Coropuna
21,079ft (6,425m)*

Juliaca

Punta Santa Maria

*Lake
Titicaca*

Arequipa

Puno

Mollendo

LA PAZ

PACIFIC OCEAN

Tacna

Arica

CHILE

Captions

Marine iguanas
*These iguanas live only on the Galapagos
Islands. They dive into the ocean for food
and then warm up on the rocks.*

Yanomami woman
*About 19,000 Yanomami people
live along the Brazil–Venezuela
border. They live in small villages,
grouped by families, and are
trying to keep their traditional
crafts and way of life.*

Reed boat,
Lake Titicaca

*Lake Titicaca is in the Andes
mountains between Peru and
Bolivia. It is the highest
navigable lake in the world—
12,506 feet (3,810 m)
above sea level.*

Jivaro hunter
*The Jivaro people live in the
rain forests of Ecuador. They
hunt monkeys and birds by
shooting matchstick-thin darts
from their blowguns.*

N
W — E
S

0 miles 600
0 kilometers 600

Quechua Indian

About 45 percent of Peru's people are Indians, and most of these are Quechua. Their ancestors were the Incas who once ruled Peru.

The Amazon

The mighty Amazon River flows from the highlands of Peru through Brazil to the coast near Macapá. Dense tropical rain forest surrounds the river and its many tributaries. Here, trees can grow as tall as 20-story buildings to reach sunlight. More kinds of animals live in these jungles than anywhere else on Earth. At least 1,500 kinds of birds fly above the forest and up to 3,000 kinds of fishes swim in the rivers. Lizards and snakes slither along the ground. More than 800 types of mammals—including the world's largest group of bats—and countless insects are all at home in the Amazon.

Layers of life

High above the ground is the rain-forest canopy. Its tall trees and vines are home to birds and monkeys. The middle forest is more sheltered. Many birds also live here, along with reptiles and thousands of insects. The forest floor is cool, damp and dark. Ferns, fungi and saplings grow here, providing shelter and food for animals that live on the ground.

Kinkajou

Toucan

Tamandua
The tamandua is a skilled climber in its search for ants, termites and bees.

Jaguar
A jaguar is on the watch for prey. This powerful big cat is at risk because of rain-forest clearing.

Palla's long-tongued bat
Bats of many kinds are found in the Amazon rain forest. They feed on insects, fruits and nectar.

Bushmaster snake
Snakes thrive on the rain-forest floor. The bushmaster is the largest poisonous snake in the Americas. It grows to 10 feet (3 m).

Hoatzin
The hoatzin is an unusual bird—it eats only leaves. Fifteen percent of all known bird species live in the Amazon rain forest.

Bird-eating spider
The bird-eating spider is a giant: it can be as wide as 11 inches (28 cm).

Rio de Janeiro

Rio de Janeiro—home to 7 million people—is Brazil's most famous city. It was named in January 1502 by the Portuguese explorer Gaspar de Lemos, who mistook its huge bay for a river and called it Rio de Janeiro (River of January). The mountain Corcovado rises straight up from the city and is topped by a huge statue, Christ the Redeemer.

Christ the Redeemer

Sugarloaf Mountain

Copacabana Beach

Guanabara Bay

Map labels:

GEORGETOWN
New Amsterdam
PARAMARIBO
Apoera
Moengo
Kourou
CAYENNE
SURINAME
FRENCH GUIANA (to France)
Cabo Orange
Cabo Norte
Mouths of the Amazon
Amazon ferry
Macapá
Baía de Marajó
Ilha de Marajó
Belém
Castanhal
Parintins
Santarém
Baía de São Marcos
São Luís
Parnaíba
Santa Inês
Sobral
Fortaleza
Bacabal
Teresina
Mossoró
Marabá
Imperatriz
Natal
Araguaína
Carolina
Iguatu
João Pessoa
BRAZIL
Picos
Juàzeiro do Norte
Campina Grande
Redenção
Recife
Barragem de Sobradinho
Juàzeiro
Arapiraca
Palmas
Maceió
Gurupi
São Francisco
Aracaju
Feira de Santana
Cuiabá
Camaçari
Salvador
Mato Grosso
Barragem de São Simão
Vitória da Conquista
Itabuna
Ilhéus
Rondonópolis
Anápolis
BRASÍLIA
Pantanal
Goiânia
Rio Verde
Brazilian Highlands
Montes Claros
Teófilo Otôni
Corumbá
Represa São Simão
Ponta da Baleia
Campo Grande
Represa Porto Primavera
Uberlândia
Uberaba
Represa Três Marias
Ipatinga
Colatina
Linhares
Governador Valadares
Dourados
São José do Rio Preto
Franca
Belo Horizonte
Serra
Vitória
Araçatuba
Ribeirão Preto
Poços de Caldas
Barbacena
Juiz de Fora
Cachoeiro do Itapemirim
Marília
Bauru
Limeira
Campos dos Goytacazes
Londrina
Piracicaba
Nova Iguaçu
Macaé
Maringá
Campinas
São Gonçalo
São Paulo
Rio de Janeiro
Foz do Iguaçu
Ponta Grossa
Santos
Iguaçu Falls
Tropic of Capricorn
Curitiba
Chapecó
Joinville
Uruguai
Lages
Florianópolis
Passo Fundo
Caxias do Sul
Novo Hamburgo
Santa Maria
Canoas
Porto Alegre
Bagé
Lagoa dos Patos
Pelotas
URUGUAY
Rio Grande
Lagoa Mirim
Lagoa Manguiera
PARAGUAY
ARGENTINA

ATLANTIC OCEAN

Southern South America

Andean condor

This bird is a type of vulture. It is one of two animals that appear on the national coat of arms of Chile. The Andean condor ranges from the Pacific coast to the high Andes in search of the dead animals on which it feeds. It has a wingspan of 10 feet (3 m).

ARGENTINA
POPULATION 39,922,000 ✳ CAPITAL BUENOS AIRES

CHILE
POPULATION 16,134,000 ✳ CAPITAL SANTIAGO

BOLIVIA
POPULATION 8,989,000 ✳ CAPITAL LA PAZ

PARAGUAY
POPULATION 6,506,000 ✳ CAPITAL ASCUNCIÓN

URUGUAY
POPULATION 3,432,000 ✳ CAPITAL MONTEVIDEO

Llamas

Llamas are related to the camel. They are domesticated animals and are used to carry goods in mountainous regions in Bolivia, Chile and Argentina. They are also farmed for their meat, wool and hides.

The Andes extends down western South America and is the longest continuous mountain chain in the world. It has 13 peaks more than 20,000 feet (6,100 m) high, and many active volcanoes.

Bolivian dress

The Aymara are one of the native peoples of Bolivia. They weave textiles to make colorful ponchos and shawls. The women wear bowler hats. Married women wear their hats straight, and unmarried ones tip them to one side.

Jesuit mission

Jesuits are a Roman Catholic order of religious men known for missionary and educational work. In the 1600s, Jesuits went to Bolivia and set up religious settlements called missions. The church buildings, such as the one at Concepción, were often built of rare timbers, decorated with ornate carving.

Map labels

BRAZIL

BOLIVIA

PARAGUAY

ASUNCIÓN

PERU

CHILE

PACIFIC OCEAN

San Matías
San Ignacio
Puerto Suárez
Roboré
Bahia Negro
Concepción
Magdalena
Negro
San Miguel
Santa Cruz
Montero
Trinidad
Mamoré
Camiri
Villa Montes
Yacuiba
Filadelfia
Pozo Colorado
Las Lomitas
Ibarreta
Formosa
Presidencia Roque
Resistencia
Corrientes
Pedro Juan Caballero
Paraguay
Concepción
San Lorenzo
Villarrica
San Juan Bautista
Pilar
Ensenación
Posadas
Santo Tomé
Añatuya
Frías
Santiago del Estero
San Miguel de Tucumán
Catamarca
Cafayate
Metán
San Salvador de Jujuy
Salta
La Banda
Eldorado
Foz do Iguaçu
Cascavel
San Borja
Riberalta
Beni
Rio Branco
Madre de Dios
Laguna Rogaguado
Laguna San Luis
SUCRE
LA PAZ
Cochabamba
Oruro
Huanuni
Punata
Potosí
Uyuni
Villa Martín
Tupiza
Villazón
Lake Titicaca
Nevado Sajama 21,463ft (6,542m)
Lago de Poopó
Salar de Uyuni
Salar de Atacama
Tacna
Arica
Putre
Pica
Iquique
Lagunas
Tocopilla
Calama
Chuquicamata
San Pedro de Atacama
Antofagasta
Taltal
Chañaral
Caldera
Copiapó
Vallenar
Nevado Ojos del Salado 22,664ft (6,908m)
Volcán Llullaillaco 22,057ft (6,723m)
Volcán Licancábur 19,426ft (5,921m)
Nevado de Cachi 22,047ft (6,720m)
Juliaca
Grande
Chaco

Atacama Desert

The Atacama Desert is the driest place on Earth. Rain has never been recorded in some parts. The desert extends about 600 miles (1,000 km) from northern Chile to the adjacent Peruvian Desert. It is bordered by the Pacific Ocean on one side and the Andes mountains on the other. The land is made up of salt basins, sand and lava flows, and is so rugged that it has been compared to the surface of the Moon.

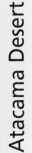

Rainfall

A passing shower may occur only a few times each century in some parts of the Atacama Desert. In general, there is so little rain that it can hardly be measured.

Fog-catcher nets
Fog catchers are used in very dry areas where there is frequent fog. As the fog passes through the nets, beads of moisture are trapped and drip down into pipes. The pipes carry this water to villages for use in homes and on farms.

Fog-catcher nets

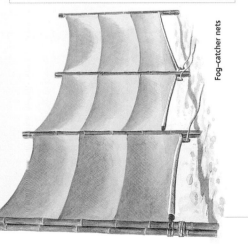

Coastal deserts

Frequent fog and cold water along the shore are common features of coastal deserts. The Pacific Ocean waters on the coast of the Atacama Desert are chilled by the cold Humboldt Current that flows north from Antarctica. Onshore winds are normally warm and moist, bringing rain, but in this region, they are cooled by the cold current. This lowers the rate of evaporation from the water's surface, reduces moisture, produces fogs, and makes the desert even drier

Low-latitude winds

High-latitude winds

Cold current

Cold water

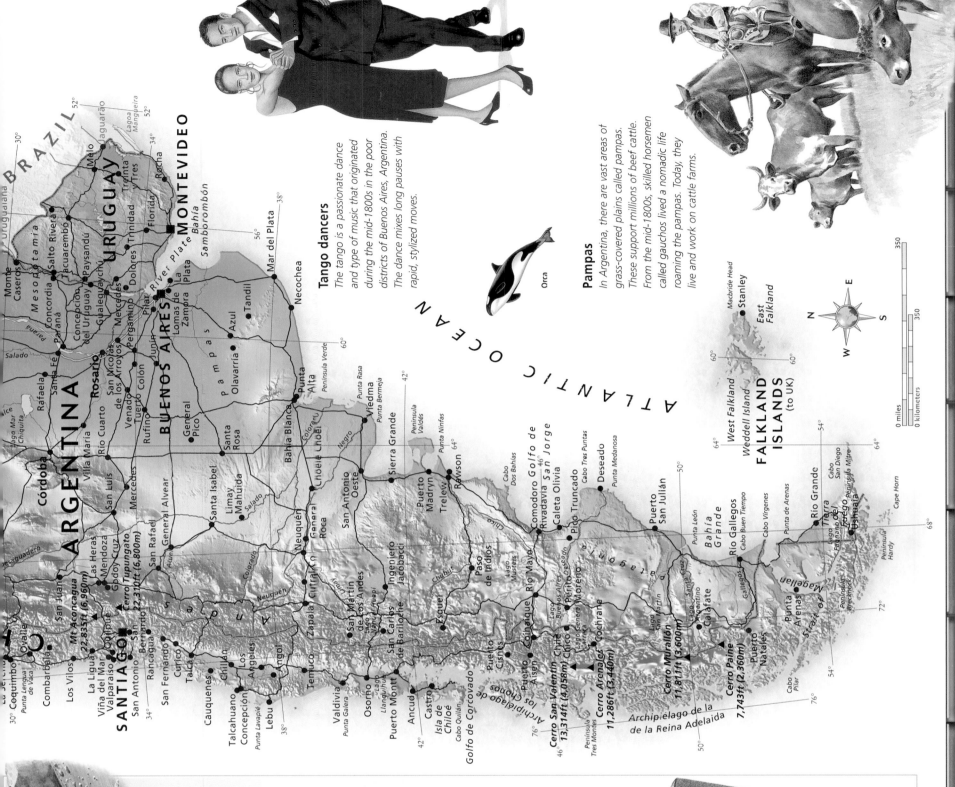

Tango dancers

The tango is a passionate dance and type of music that originated during the mid-1800s in the poor districts of Buenos Aires, Argentina. The dance mixes long pauses with rapid, stylized moves.

Orca

Pampas

In Argentina, there are vast areas of grass-covered plains called pampas. These support millions of beef cattle. From the mid-1800s, skilled horsemen called gauchos lived a nomadic life roaming the pampas. Today, they live and work on cattle farms.

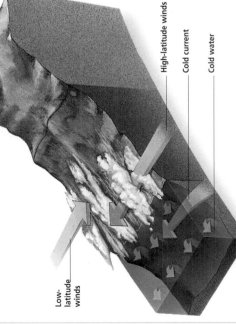

ATLANTIC OCEAN

N E S W

0 miles 350
0 kilometers 350

South America

LAND AREA	6,731,004 sq miles (17,433,220 sq km)
LARGEST COUNTRY	Brazil
SMALLEST COUNTRY	Suriname
MAIN RELIGION	Christian
LIFE EXPECTANCY	72 years
LITERACY	93%

Anchovies
Peru is one of the top five fishing countries in the world, and anchovies are the main catch. Recent supplies have been affected by overfishing, and the seasonal changes to ocean currents called the El Niño effect. Most of the anchovies are dried to produce fish meal, which is sold for livestock feed.

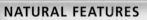

USING THE LAND

- Forest and woodland
- Arable land
- Grazing
- Arid or marginal

- Cereals
- Fruit
- Citrus fruits
- Bananas
- Wine
- Cotton
- Coffee
- Cocoa
- Sugarcane
- Soybeans
- Rubber
- Beef cattle
- Sheep
- Fishing
- Shellfish
- Industrial center
- Mining
- Oil production
- Timber
- Tourism

Silver and tin
In 1545, huge silver deposits were found at Potosí, Bolivia, and it soon became the richest source of silver in the world. After four centuries of mining, the mine was largely exhausted. Tin has since become Bolivia's most important mineral.

Tomatoes and potatoes are originally from South America.

Potatoes
Potatoes grow wild in the Chilean highlands. Sliced, dried potato, called *chuño*, which was eaten centuries ago by the Incas, is still eaten today. It can be stored for months for later use.

NATURAL FEATURES

Moreno Glacier ARGENTINA
Moreno Glacier, at the southern tip of the Andes, is 30 miles (50 km) long and 2 miles (3 km) wide. Named for the naturalist Francisco Moreno, it is the largest glacier in Patagonia and the only one not decreasing in size.

Moreno Glacier

Salar de Uyuni BOLIVIA
The Salar (salt pan) de Uyuni was once a prehistoric lake. Today, it covers 4,680 square miles (12,120 sq km) of the Bolivian altiplano, or high plains. When it rains, the salt pan fills with a layer of water and shines like a mirror.

The Pantanal BRAZIL
Covering an area of 50,000 square miles (129,500 sq km), the Pantanal in western Brazil is the world's largest wetland. It sustains huge flocks of birds, as well as anacondas, crocodiles, deer and giant river otters.

Iguaçu Falls

Iguaçu Falls ARGENTINA–BRAZIL
These spectacular falls on the Argentine border with Brazil include 275 separate waterfalls, some of which drop 262 feet (80 m). The surrounding subtropical rain forest is home to howler monkeys, jaguars and tapirs.

Torres del Paine CHILE
The Torres (towers) del Paine are three jagged granite peaks that rise more than 6,560 feet (2,000 m) above the surrounding plain in Patagonia. The earliest was formed about 12 million years ago. Glaciers flow from the peaks.

Torres del Paine

Blue-footed booby

Galapagos Islands
About 600 miles (960 km) off the coast of Ecuador, the Galapagos Islands are home to many unique plants and animals. Some species of animals and birds, such as the blue-footed booby, are found only on these islands. The Galapagos tortoise, the world's largest living tortoise, can survive for up to 200 years—longer than any other animal.

WHERE PEOPLE LIVE

Urban	Rural

REGION
73% | 27%

Most urban: URUGUAY
91% | 9%

Most rural: PARAGUAY
55% | 45%

LARGEST CITIES

Buenos Aires 11,612,000

São Paulo 10,095,000

Lima 7,980,000

Bogota 7,363,000

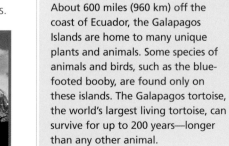

Map city labels
CARACAS, GEORGETOWN, PARAMARIBO, CAYENNE, BOGOTÁ, QUITO, Guayaquil, Macapá, Belém, Manaus, Fortaleza, Trujillo, Recife, LIMA, Arequipa, LA PAZ, SUCRE, BRASÍLIA, Salvador, São Paulo, Rio de Janeiro, ASUNCIÓN, Porto Alegre, Córdoba, SANTIAGO, BUENOS AIRES, MONTEVIDEO, Bahía Blanca, Puerto Montt, Stanley, Punta Arenas

PLACES

La Paz BOLIVIA
At an altitude of 12,500 feet (3,812 m) at its center, La Paz, the administrative capital of Bolivia, is the highest capital city in the world. This hub of Bolivian commerce lies in a valley surrounded by Altiplano (high plains).

Cartagena COLOMBIA
Founded in 1533, Cartagena was once a slave port. Although the Spanish built forts to ward off British and French attacks, they were unsuccessful—in the 17th and 18th centuries Spain built the largest defense system in South America.

Machu Picchu
The Incas built this city on a ridge 50 miles (80 km) from Cuzco, in southern Peru, in the mid-1400s. They abandoned it 100 years later, and it was not rediscovered until 1911. The site is a 2-square-mile (5-sq-km) complex of granite buildings and plazas surrounded by farm terraces. It was probably a royal estate or religious center.

National Congress, Brasília

Brasília BRAZIL
The construction of Brasília, the capital of Brazil, began on an almost barren site in 1956. The city, complete with parks and artificial lakes, was laid out to a plan that, from the air, some say resembles a bow and arrow and others say a bird in flight.

Buenos Aires ARGENTINA
Buenos Aires was founded in the 16th century and became the capital of Argentina in the 18th century. More than a third of Argentina's people live in the city and its suburbs. Buenos Aires has a large number of theaters and museums.

Paramaribo SURINAME
This city, the capital of Suriname, was settled by the French around 1640. It became a British colony in 1651 and, in a deal in 1667, Britain swapped it for present-day New York, which was then owned by the Dutch.

Dutch colonial buildings

TRADITIONS AND CULTURE

Maté tea
Maté tea is made in a gourd (below) from a herb called yerba mate, and sipped through a metal straw called a *bombilla*. Groups of people often drink the tea together, passing the gourd and straw from person to person.

Gauchos
Gauchos are cowboys of the pampas of Argentina and Chile. Centuries ago, they led a tough, independent life. Now they work on ranches and are no longer self-reliant, but they still value their strength and independence.

Gauchos

Amazon peoples
People have lived in the Amazon rain forest for at least 10,000 years. They obtain a small amount of their food by hunting and gathering, but most of their food is harvested from small agricultural plots. Their traditional way of life is today threatened by the destruction of much of the rain forest.

Apus
People in parts of Peru have combined their traditional beliefs with Christianity. They worship apus, or spirits of the mountains, by marking the apu's home, such as a hill or a stream, with a type of Christian cross.

Hallaca
This traditional Christmas dish in Venezuela consists of a corn or maize dough filled with meat and seasonings, wrapped in a banana leaf and steamed. It is eaten after mass on Christmas Eve.

Amazon animals
The anaconda (*above*), which kills its prey by squeezing until it suffocates, is found in the Amazon River. It can reach 30 feet (9 m) in length. The goliath bird-eating spider, the largest in the world, lives in rain-forested regions. It eats young birds, frogs and even bats. When threatened, it makes a loud hissing noise by rubbing its legs together. The world's heaviest rodent, the capybara, is also a rain-forest dweller. It can weigh up to 145 pounds (65 kg).

PEOPLE

Atahuallpa c 1502–33
Atahuallpa was the last ruler of the Inca. In 1532, after a five-year struggle, he was captured by the Spaniards, who asked the Incas for a huge ransom for his release. Although the ransom was paid, Atahuallpa was executed in 1533.

Bernardo O'Higgins 1776–1842
A revolutionary leader who fought to achieve Chile's independence from Spain, O'Higgins became the director of Chile in 1817. However, he was unpopular and resigned in 1823.

Simón Bolívar 1783–1830
Bolívar (*right*), born in Venezuela, was called "the Liberator" for his role in helping several South American nations to gain independence. The country of Bolivia was named in his honor.

Eva Perón 1919–52
Known also as Evita, Eva was the popular wife of Juan Perón, the president of Argentina. She gained women the right to vote in 1947 and provided financial assistance to the poor.
Eva Perón

Pelé born 1940
Brazilian-born Pelé is a world-famous soccer player and the only player to have played in four World Cup championships. In 1999, Pelé was named the athlete of the century by the National Olympics Committee.

HISTORY AT A GLANCE
GREAT CIVILIZATIONS

Moche ear ornament

NAZCA
The Nazca people lived in southern Peru from about 200 BC to AD 600. They are best known for their distinctive pottery, which was decorated with bright, multicolored images of humans and animals, and for the huge depictions of animals and shapes they made on the desert floor. No one knows why these "Nazca lines" were created.

MOCHE
Moche was the main civilization on the north coast of Peru from the 1st to the 8th century. Two well-known remnants of this civilization are the Temple of the Sun and the Temple of the Moon. In 1987, tombs filled with treasures were found near Sipán. The most famous tomb is thought to contain the Lord of Sipán, a Moche warrior-priest.

Kalasasaya temple, Tiwanaku

TIWANAKU AND HUARI
These two civilizations held power in the south-central Andes from the 1st to the 9th century. The Tiwanaku built temples and pyramids south of Lake Titicaca. The Huari people established their city in the Ayacucho Basin. Huari buildings have not survived, but remnants of their pottery have been found.

CHIMÚ AND CHINCHA
The Chimú people appeared in the 10th century in the Moche Valley and built the city of Chan Chan as their capital. They dug irrigation canals to supply water to the city and their crops. Chincha, on the south coast of Peru, was a rich desert kingdom. It was a powerful commercial center that was brought under Inca control.
Inca statue

THE INCAS
The Incas were a group of tribes that lived around Cuzco in southern Peru. By the 13th century they began to expand, and in the 15th century were well established. At its height, the Inca empire was the largest in the Americas, extending 2,500 miles (4,000 km) from Colombia and Equador south to Chile and Argentina. In 1532, the empire fell to the Spanish conquistador Francisco Pizarro, who had with him only 167 men.

Francisco Pizarro

Norwegian
Sea

Iceland

Faroe
Islands

Shetland
Islands

Outer Hebrides
Ben Nevis
4,406ft
(1,343m)

Orkney
Islands

Atlantic

ATLANTIC OCEAN

North
Sea

Skagerrak

Kattegat

Vänern Vättern

Jutland

Öland

Fyn Sjaelland

Bornholm

British Isles

Pennines

Ireland

Irish Sea

United Kingdom

Thames

Elbe

Odel

Hartz
Mountains

Ore Mountains

English Channel

Seine

Rhine

Mosel

Bohemian
Forest

Loire

Black
Forest

Danube

Jura

Vosges

Bay of
Biscay

Garonne

Massif
Central

Rhone

Mont Blanc
15,771ft
(4,807m)

A l p s

Lake
Geneva

Dolomites

Po

A p e

D i n a

Adriatic Sea

Pyrenees

Aneto
11,168ft (3,404m)

Ebro

Duero

Ligurian Sea

Corsica

Tyrrhenian Sea

Vesuvius
4,202ft (1,281m)

Iberian

Peninsula

Minorca

Sardinia

Balearic Islands

Majorca

Sierra Morena

Ibiza

Guadalquivir

Sistemas Béticos

Mediterranean Sea

Sicily

Mt Etna
10,902ft (3,323m)

Malta

Scand

Highlands

Kõle

Scand

Novaya
Zemlya

Kara
Sea

Barents
Sea

Ostrov
Kolguyev

Inarijärvi

Lappland

Kola
Peninsula

White Sea

Pechora

Ural Mountains

Gulf of Bothnia

lavian Shield

Northern Dvina

Lake
Onega

Kama

Lake
Ladoga

Åland

Gulf of Finland

Rybinsk
Reservoir

otland

Baltic Sea

Lake
Peipus

Gulf of
Riga

Kuybyshev
Reservoir

Dnieper

Valdai
Hills

Volga

Vistula

North European Plain

Central Russian Uplands

Volga Uplands

Kiev
Reservoir

Carpathian Mountains

Dnieper

Tsimlyansk
Reservoir

Great
Hungarian
Plain

Don

Danube

Transyvanian Alps

Sea of
Azov

Crimea

Elbrus
18,510ft
(5,642m)

Danube

Balkan Mountains

Caucasus

Caspian Sea

Alps

Rhodope Mountains

Black Sea

Pindus Mountains

Sea of
Marmara

Aegean Sea

Dodecanese

onian

Peloponnese

Sea

Crete

Rhodes

Europe

United Kingdom and Ireland

UNITED KINGDOM
POPULATION 60,609,000 * CAPITAL LONDON

IRELAND
POPULATION 4,062,000 * CAPITAL DUBLIN

Stonehenge

The circle of standing stones on Salisbury Plain, in southwestern England, was built between 2900 BC and 1800 BC. While the function of this monument remains unknown, one theory is that the circle formed an astronomical observatory for predicting the best times to plant and harvest.

The first stage
The first builders of Stonehenge laid out a circular bank of earth and a ditch about 380 feet (116 m) in diameter. They raised a huge stone, the Heel Stone, at the entrance.

The second stage
Around 2800 BC, an inner stone circle, the Bluestone Circle, was built. The stone used may have come from another monument.

The third stage
Stonehenge as it looks today was built around 1800 BC. It consists of a ring of 30 stones topped by stone lintels. Within this ring are taller pairs of stones set in a horseshoe shape.

The summer solstice

At sunrise on the summer solstice, which is the longest day of the year, the Sun shines straight through the Heel Stone.

Positioning the stones
Many of the stones were probably brought great distances to the site. Each one was levered into a deep pit with sloping sides, called a posthole.

Pulling the stones upright
A system of ropes was attached to each stone. Because of the immense weight, hundreds of people were needed to pull the stones upright.

Raising the lintels
Each lintel, or cross beam, was shaped to the curve of the circle. A timber scaffold was built so that the lintels could be raised to the top of the stones.

Securing the lintels
A groove carved on the base of each lintel fitted into pegs carved on the top of each stone, ensuring that the two fitted securely together.

Scottish Highland band

Bagpipers traditionally led regiments into battle. The tunes inspired the soldiers and frightened their enemies. The sound of bagpipes carries a long way. Today, military bands of pipers and drummers play on ceremonial occasions.

Loch Ness monster

Loch Ness, in the Scottish Highlands, is the largest freshwater lake in the United Kingdom. It is 788 feet (240 m) deep and about 23 miles (37 km) long. Although many people believe they have seen a monster rather like a dinosaur in the lake, there is still no proof that it exists.

Hadrian's Wall

The emperor Hadrian ordered his army to build and patrol a wall at the northernmost boundary of Roman territory, to keep out invaders. Built between AD 122 and AD 129, near what is now the Scottish border, it extended 73 miles (118 km). Parts of it remain.

North Sea

Shetland Islands
Unst
Yell
Mainland
Lerwick
Fair Isle

Orkney Islands
Sanday
Kirkwall
Mainland
Hoy
Duncansby Head
John o'Groats
Wick
Thurso

Cape Wrath
Loch Shin
Stornoway
Isle of Lewis
Harris
North Uist
South Uist
Skye
Portree
Rum
Eigg
Coll
Tiree
Mull
The Minch
Outer Hebrides
Inner Hebrides

Mallaig
Fort William
Ben Nevis 4,406 ft (1,343 m)
Oban
Firth of Lorn
Jura

North West Highlands
Inverness
Loch Ness
Moray Firth
Grampian Mountains
Aberdeen
Dee
Dundee
Perth
Firth of Forth
EDINBURGH
Falkirk
Forth
Loch Lomond
Glasgow

SCOTLAND

OCEAN

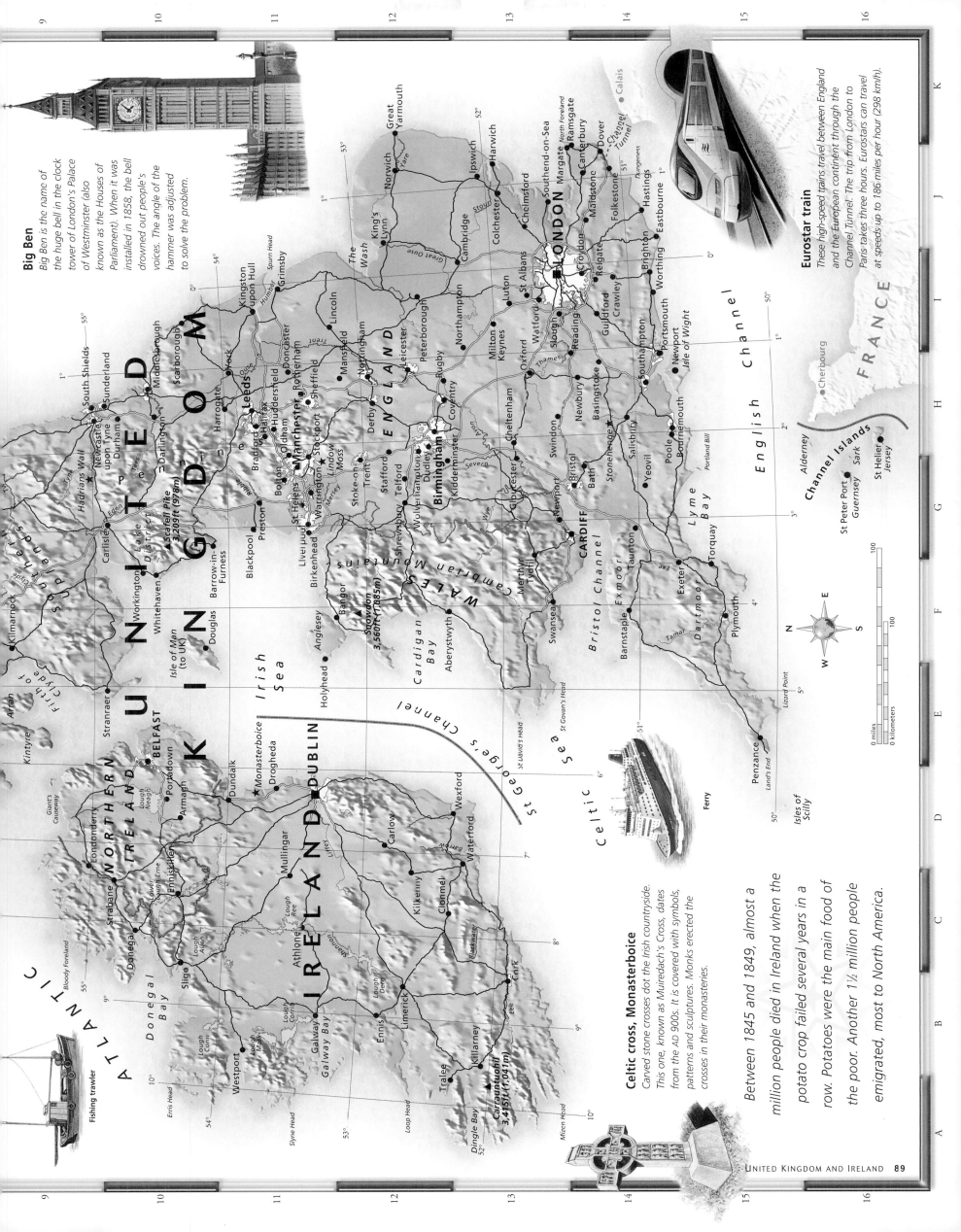

Big Ben

Big Ben is the name of the huge bell in the clock tower of London's Palace of Westminster (also known as the Houses of Parliament). When it was installed in 1858, the bell drowned out people's voices. The angle of the hammer was adjusted to solve the problem.

Eurostar train

These high-speed trains travel between England and the European continent through the Channel Tunnel. The trip from London to Paris takes three hours. Eurostars can travel at speeds up to 186 miles per hour (298 km/h).

Celtic cross, Monasterboice

Carved stone crosses dot the Irish countryside. This one, known as Muiredach's Cross, dates from the AD 900s. It is covered with symbols, patterns and sculptures. Monks erected the crosses in their monasteries.

Between 1845 and 1849, almost a million people died in Ireland when the potato crop failed several years in a row. Potatoes were the main food of the poor. Another 1½ million people emigrated, most to North America.

Fishing trawler

Ferry

ATLANTIC

UNITED KINGDOM

NORTHERN IRELAND

BELFAST

IRELAND

DUBLIN

WALES

CARDIFF

ENGLAND

LONDON

FRANCE

English Channel

Celtic Sea

Irish Sea

St George's Channel

Bristol Channel

Cardigan Bay

Lyme Bay

Channel Islands

In 1690, the remains of a mammoth were discovered near the present-day Kings Cross Station in London.

United Kingdom and Ireland

UNITED KINGDOM LAND AREA	94,525 sq miles (244,820 sq km)
OFFICIAL LANGUAGE	English
MAIN RELIGION	Christan
LIFE EXPECTANCY	78 years
LITERACY	99%

IRELAND LAND AREA	27,135 sq miles (70,280 sq km)
OFFICIAL LANGUAGE	English
MAIN RELIGION	Christan
LIFE EXPECTANCY	77 years
LITERACY	98%

WHERE PEOPLE LIVE

Urban   Rural

UNITED KINGDOM
89%   11%

IRELAND
59%   41%

LARGEST CITIES

London 7,554,000

Dublin 1,037,000

Birmingham 989,000

Glasgow 604,000

Liverpool 468,000

Black Death

In the late 1340s, the Black Death, a type of bubonic plague, swept through Europe, killing more than a third of the people. By 1348 it had arrived in England. Over the next few centuries, the plague continued to strike, and Londoners fled the city (*above*) with each outbreak. It was finally wiped out by the Great Fire of London in 1666.

NATURAL FEATURES

Lake District ENGLAND

In this beautiful national park in the northern highland area of England (*below*), ice has worn away the land to create valleys and form what are England's largest lakes. The Lake District attracts millions of visitors each year.

Lake District

Norfolk Broads ENGLAND

These shallow, inland waterways, which were caused by peat diggings in the 14th century, crisscross Norfolk. The area is popular with visitors, who hire boats to sail from town to town.

Giant's Causeway NORTHERN IRELAND

This 3-mile (5-km) stretch of basalt columns was formed when molten lava erupted from beneath the sea and cooled very quickly. Some columns are nearly 20 feet (6 m) tall.

Giant's Causeway

USING THE LAND

Forest and woodland

Arable land

Grazing

Cereals   Sheep

Potatoes   Fishing

Fruit and vegetables   Shellfish

Sugar beet   Industrial center

Oilseed rape   Mining

Beef cattle   Gas production

Dairy cattle   Timber

Tourism

Sheep
Sheep are the United Kingdom's chief livestock. Farming sheep is particularly important in areas such as Wales where the soil is too poor for raising cattle and growing crops.

Oil mining
Oil was discovered in the United Kingdom under the North Sea in the early 1970s. Extracting it proved difficult. Oil rigs were built to provide a stable surface for drilling into the seabed. By 2001, the United Kingdom had become the 12th-largest oil producer in the world.

Glasgow   Edinburgh

Newcastle upon Tyne

Belfast

Leeds

Liverpool   Manchester

DUBLIN

Birmingham

Cardiff   LONDON

Scottish Highlands SCOTLAND

The Scottish Highlands, which make up more than half of Scotland's landmass, have numerous rivers and lochs (lakes). Many native species have died out, but the shaggy-haired Highland cattle (*left*) still wander freely.

Highland cattle

The population of Ireland is 95% ethnic Irish.

TRADITIONS AND CULTURE

Wimbledon
Every year since 1877, one of the most famous tennis tournaments in the world has been held at Wimbledon, a suburb of London.

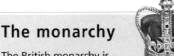

Scottish tartans
Originally hand-woven from woolen material, Scottish tartans are a symbol of Scotland. Items of clothing, especially kilts, are made from different patterns to represent different clans, or families.

Welsh choirs
Almost every town in Wales has a voice choir. There are male, female, mixed and children's choirs, many of which compete in the annual eisteddfod, a festival of music and arts.

St Patrick's Day
Celebrated on 17 March, this day began as a religious holiday to commemorate St Patrick, the patron saint of Ireland. Today, Irish people around the world gather together, wear green clothes and parade through the streets.

Arthurian legends
King Arthur, according to the legends, became king of Britain when he was 15 years old. He married Guinevere and created the knights of the round table. When he went to fight a war in Rome, he left his castle in the care of his nephew Mordred, who betrayed him.

King Arthur fighting Mordred

It's said that if you kiss the Blarney Stone in Ireland, you'll become a clever talker.

PEOPLE

William Wallace 1270–1305
William Wallace became a hero by leading Scottish resistance to English rule. In 1297, he captured Stirling Castle, but was later defeated by Edward I and executed.

Shakespeare 1564–1616
Recognized as England's greatest dramatist and poet, Shakespeare wrote more than 150 poems and 36 plays. One of his most famous plays is *Romeo and Juliet*.

William Shakespeare

Isaac Newton 1642–1727
Isaac Newton, an influential scientist of the 17th century, invented the reflecting telescope in 1668. Although it was only 6 inches (15 cm) long, it could magnify objects more than 30 times.

Florence Nightingale 1820–1910
In 1854 Florence Nightingale led a group of nurses to work in military hospitals during the Crimean War. Her patients called her the "Lady with the Lamp." After the war, she established a school for nurses in England.

Winston Churchill 1874–1965
A statesman and orator, Churchill was the prime minister of Britain during World War II. His speeches inspired the people during the difficult war years.

The Beatles 1959–70
The Beatles, comprising John Lennon, Paul McCartney, George Harrison and Ringo Starr, were a world-famous rock-and-roll group. They also produced and starred in movies.

The Beatles

Henry VIII
The son of Henry VII and Elizabeth York, Henry VIII (1491–1547) had six wives. Of these, he divorced two and had two beheaded. When the pope refused Henry permission to divorce his first wife, he broke away from the Roman Catholic Church and created the Church of England. His actions aided the Protestant movement in Europe.

The monarchy

The British monarchy is the oldest institution of government in the United Kingdom. James VI of Scotland became the first king of the United Kingdom in 1603. Until the end of the 17th century, the monarch had the right to make and pass legislation, but this is no longer the case. The British monarchy is hereditary—the crown is inherited by the next eligible family member.

Royal carriage

PLACES

London ENGLAND
The Romans chose a small town on the Thames River as their capital in the 1st century AD, and named it Londinium. After being ruled by the Saxons and the Normans, today it is England's capital.

Canterbury Cathedral

Canterbury Cathedral ENGLAND
This cathedral is the seat of the Anglican Church. Archbishop Thomas Becket was murdered there in 1170 and the cathedral is now a site for pilgrims.

Dublin IRELAND
Starting as a permanent Viking settlement in AD 841, Dublin, built on the banks of the River Liffey, is the capital of Ireland and the center of its government.

Edinburgh SCOTLAND
The capital city of Scotland, Edinburgh is a financial, legal and cultural center. Edinburgh Castle stands in the medieval Old Town, once the center of the city.

Roman baths ENGLAND
Ancient Romans spent some leisure time in baths (hot and cold swimming pools), such as those in Bath (*right*). These baths are filled with the water from three natural hot springs.

HISTORY AT A GLANCE

3000–100 BC
The Celts spread over much of Europe, gradually moving into Britain between 500 and 100 BC.

54 BC
Julius Caesar, Roman general and statesman, travels from Gaul and invades England.

AD 43–410
England and Wales become part of the Roman empire. Boudicca, Queen of the Iceni, a tribe of Britons, leads a revolt against the Roman soldiers and sets fire to London.

c AD 450
Anglo-Saxons arrive in Britain, and settle in southern and eastern England.

AD 871–899
Alfred the Great rules as king of Wessex. He prevents the Danish conquest of Britain and draws up a legal code.

The Alfred Jewel

1066
William the Conqueror, Duke of Normandy, invades England, kills King Harold at the Battle of Hastings (*below*) and becomes king.

Bayeux tapestry

1215
The Magna Carta, a charter limiting the king's power and making him responsible to English law, is signed by King John.

1509–47
Henry VIII rules England and breaks away from the Catholic Church. He eventually unites Wales and England under one system of government.

1642
Civil war breaks out in England between those loyal to King Charles I (Royalists) and supporters of the parliament against Charles (Roundheads).

1837–1901
Queen Victoria rules the United Kingdom, and the British empire expands to cover one-fourth of the world and its people.

1914–18
The United Kingdom enters World War I when Germany invades Belgium. About 750,000 of the British armed forces die, and the war leaves the United Kingdom with severe economic problems.

1922
Ireland splits into Northern Ireland, which remains in the United Kingdom, and the Irish Free State, which is a self-governing member of the empire.

World War II Spitfire aircraft

1939–45
World War II is fought. The United Kingdom and France declare war on Germany after it invades Poland. With the Allies, the United Kingdom defeats Germany and Japan, and then helps to establish the United Nations.

1949
The Irish Free State becomes the Republic of Ireland and leaves the British Commonwealth.

1997
Referendums are held in Scotland and Wales and both vote in favor of greater control over their affairs. They set up their own parliamentary governing bodies.

Spain and Portugal

Basque folk dancer

SPAIN
POPULATION 40,398,000 • CAPITAL MADRID

PORTUGAL
POPULATION 10,606,000 • CAPITAL LISBON

ANDORRA
POPULATION 71,000 • CAPITAL ANDORRA LA VELLA

The Alhambra

For almost 800 years, from AD 711 until 1492, Spain was ruled by the Islamic Moors. The Alhambra, in Granada, is one of the most beautiful and practical buildings from this period. It was built in the 1300s as a fortress against the Spanish, and was later used as a palace for the sultan and his family. It features cool, airy courtyards and pavilions, trickling fountains and wonderful gardens.

Tower of the Ladies
The oldest decorations in the Alhambra are here, with views into the valley.

Hall of the Two Sisters
This hall is in the center of a series of chambers where the sultan's family lived.

Court of the Lions
A fountain carved with lions stands in the middle of this shaded courtyard.

Mosaic
Decorative patterns of tiles and semi-precious stones are a common feature of Islamic art. The mosaics of the Alhambra are extremely complicated and beautiful.

Court of the Myrtles
This peaceful walkway leads to the throne room.

Azores
(to Portugal)

Corvo
Flores
30° 28°
Graciosa
São Jorge 26°
Nova Lajes
Horta Terceira
Faial Angra do
Pico Heroísmo
Ribeira
Grande
São Miguel 38°
Ponta
Degada
ATLANTIC OCEAN
38°
30° 28° 26°
Santa Maria

0 miles 125
0 kilometers 125

Madeira
(to Portugal)

Ilha de
Porto Santo
17°
Porto Santo
33° 33°
Ilha da
Madeira
ATLANTIC
OCEAN
Câmara
de Lobos
Machico
Funchal
17°
Deserta
Grande
Ilhas
Desertas
Bugio

0 miles 40
0 kilometers 40

Canary Islands
(to Spain)

16° 14°
Alegranza
Graciosa
18° ATLANTIC OCEAN
Lanzarote
Arrecife
Santa Cruz
de la Palma
La Palma
San Cristóbal
de la Laguna
Lobos
Puerto
del Rosario
Pico del Teide
12,198ft (3,718m)
Santa Cruz
de Tenerife
La Gomera
Tenerife
Fuerteventura
28° 28°
Las Palmas de
Gran Canaria
Gran
Canaria
Pico de las Nieves
6,394ft (1,949m)
El Hierro
18° 16° 14°

0 miles 100
0 kilometers 100

Azores
Madeira
Canary Islands

Cork trees
One-third of the world's cork oaks grow in Portugal. It takes nearly 60 years before they are mature enough for the cork bark to be harvested.

ATLANTIC OCEAN
PORTUGAL

Cabo Ortegal 8° 7° 6°
Cabo de Peña
Ferrol Luarca Avilés Gijón
9° Villaviciosa de
A Coruña Asturias
Betanzos Vilalba Oviedo Mieres
43° Lugo
Santiago del
Cabo Fisterra Compostela
Ribeira Lalín Ponferrada León
Pontevedra Ourense Astorga
Vigo Ponteareas Benavente
Cabo Silleiro
42° Zamora Toro
Viana do Ponte Duero
Castelo da Barca
Póvoa de Varzim Bragança Salamanca
Matosinhos Porto Vila Real Embalse de
Vila Nova Almendra
de Gaia
41° Ovar Béjar
Aveiro Viseu
Ciudad Almanzo
Guarda Rodrigo 8,504ft (2,592m
Figueira da Foz Coimbra
40° Covilhã Plasencia Embalse
de Valdecañas
Castelo Cáceres
Leiria Branco
Caldas da Rainha Trujillo Embalse de
Cabo Carvoeiro Torres García Sola
Novas Portalegre Herrer
Torres Vedras Santarém del Drug
39° Estremoz Elvas Badajoz Embalse
Sintra de Orellana
LISBON Barreiro Mérida Embalse
(LISBOA) Almendralejo del Zújar
Setúbal Évora Zafra
Cabo Espichel
Alcácer do Sal
38° Sines Beja Sierra
Cabo de Sines Écija
Cortegana
Seville Carmona
Algarve Huelva Osuna
37° Cabo de Ayamonte Dos Hermanas
São Vicente Lagos Andalucia
9° Faro Tavira Golfo Marismas del
Cabo de Santa María Olhão de Cádiz Guadalquivir
8° Lebrija
Sanlúcar de
Barrameda Ronda
El Puerto de Jerez de
7° Santa María la Frontera
Cádiz Marbe
San Fernando
36° Barbate Gibralt
Cabo Trafalgar Algeciras GIB
(to U.
Strait of Gibraltar Ceuta
Tanger Punta
6° Almina
MOROCCO

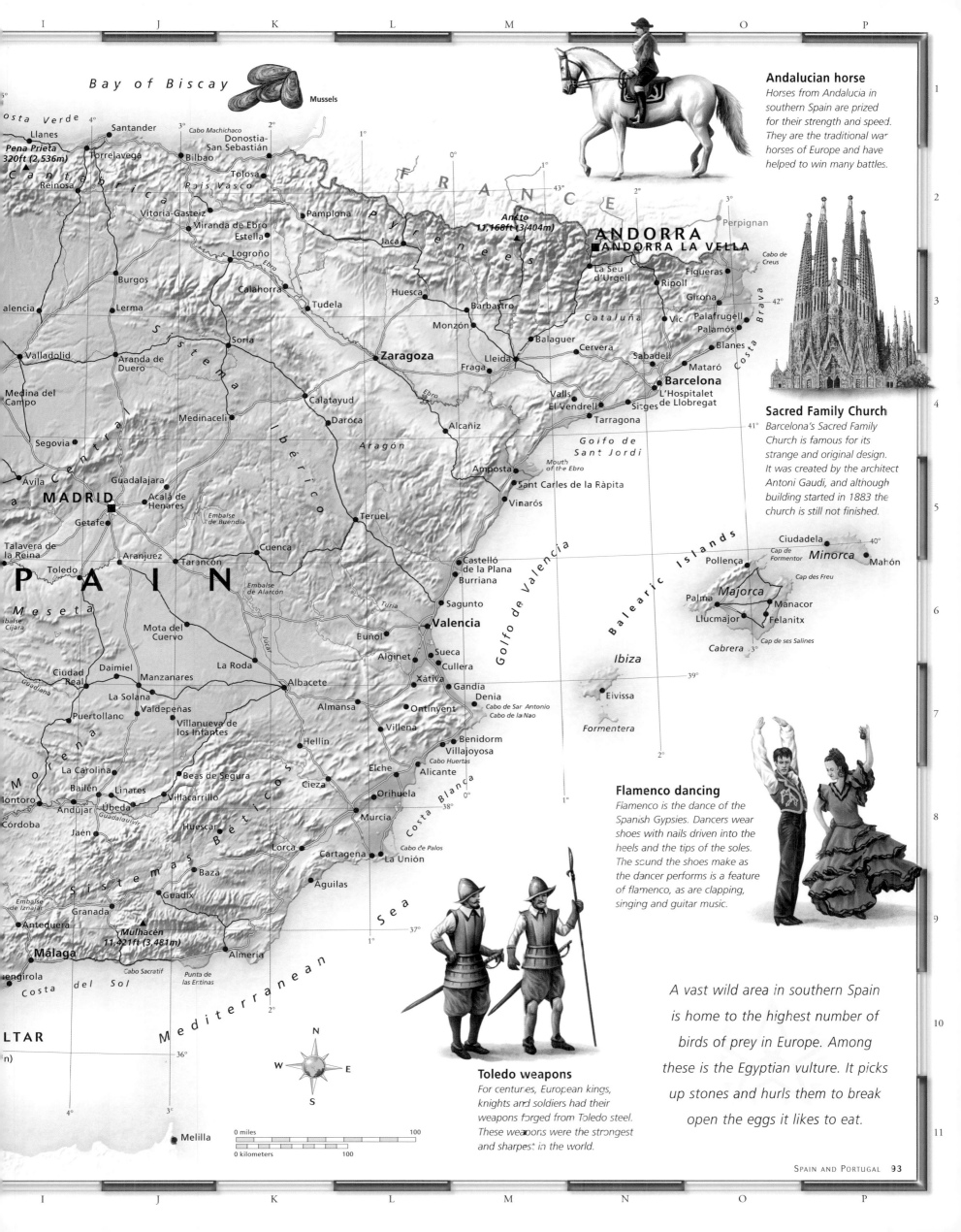

Bay of Biscay

Mussels

Andalucian horse
Horses from Andalucia in southern Spain are prized for their strength and speed. They are the traditional war horses of Europe and have helped to win many battles.

osta Verde

Costa Verde
• Llanes
Peña Prieta
320ft (2,536m)▲
• Santander
Cabo Machichaco
Donostia-
San Sebastián
• Reinosa
• Torrelavega
• Bilbao
Tolosa

Cantabrica
País Vasco
FRANCE

Vitoria-Gasteiz
Pamplona
Pyrenees
Aneto
11,168ft (3,404m)▲
Perpignan

ANDORRA
■ANDORRA LA VELLA

Miranda de Ebro
Estella•
Jaca
La Seu
d'Urgell
Figueras
Cabo de
Creus

• Logroño
Calahorra
Huesca
Barbastro
Ripoll
Girona
Palafrugell

Burgos
• Lerma
Ebro
Tudela
Monzón
Cataluña
Vic
Palamós

alencia
Soria
Balaguer
Cervera
Sabadell
Blanes

Valladolid
Aranda de
Duero
Zaragoza
Lleida
Fraga
Barcelona
L'Hospitalet
de Llobregat

Sacred Family Church
Barcelona's Sacred Family Church is famous for its strange and original design. It was created by the architect Antoni Gaudi, and although building started in 1883 the church is still not finished.

Medina del
Campo

Sistema Iberico
Calatayud
Ebro
Valls
El Vendrell
Sitges

Daroca
Alcañiz
Tarragona
41°

Segovia
Medinaceli
Aragón
Golfo de
Sant Jordi

Ávila
Guadalajara
Amposta
Mouth
of the Ebro

MADRID■
Acalá de
Henares
Sant Carles de la Ràpita

Getafe
Teruel
Vinarós

Talavera de
la Reina
Aranjuez
Tarancón
Embalse
de Buendía
Ciudadela
Cap de
Formentor
Minorca
40°

Toledo
Cuenca
Castelló
de la Plana
Balearic Islands
Pollença
Mahón

SPAIN
Embalse
de Alarcón
Burriana
Cap des Freu

Meseta
Turia
Sagunto
Palma
Majorca
Manacor

mbalse
Cijara
Mota del
Cuervo
Jucar
Valencia
Felanitx

Buñol
Cabrera
Cap de ses Salines
Llucmajor

La Roda
Alginet
Sueca
Cullera
Ibiza

Ciudad
Real
Daimiel
Manzanares
Albacete
Xàtiva
Gandía
39°

Guadiana
La Solana
Valdepeñas
Almansa
Ontinyent
Denia
Cabo de San Antonio
Cabo de la Nao
Eivissa

Puertollano
Villanueva de
los Infantes
Hellín
Villena
Benidorm
Villajoyosa
Formentera

La Carolina
Beas de Segura
Elche
Alicante
Cabo Huertas

Morena
Bailén
Linares
Villacarrillo
Cieza
Orihuela
Costa Blanca

Iontoro
Úbeda
Andújar
Guadalquivir
Huéscar
Murcia
38°

Córdoba
Jaén
Sistemas Béticos
Lorca
Cartagena
La Unión
Cabo de Palos

Baza
Aguilas

Guadix
Mediterranean Sea

Embalse
de Iznaja
Granada
Mulhacén
11,421ft (3,481m)▲
Almería
37°

iengirola
Málaga
Antequera
Cabo Sacratif
Punta de
las Entinas

Costa del Sol
N

LTAR
W ● E
36°

n)
S

Melilla

Flamenco dancing
Flamenco is the dance of the Spanish Gypsies. Dancers wear shoes with nails driven into the heels and the tips of the soles. The sound the shoes make as the dancer performs is a feature of flamenco, as are clapping, singing and guitar music.

Toledo weapons
For centuries, European kings, knights and soldiers had their weapons forged from Toledo steel. These weapons were the strongest and sharpest in the world.

A vast wild area in southern Spain is home to the highest number of birds of prey in Europe. Among these is the Egyptian vulture. It picks up stones and hurls them to break open the eggs it likes to eat.

0 miles   100
0 kilometers   100

Spain and Portugal

USING THE LAND

- 🌾 Cereals
- Citrus fruits
- 🍷 Wine
- 🐟 Fishing
- Olives
- 🐂 Beef cattle
- 🐑 Sheep
- ⚙️ Industrial center
- ⛏️ Mining
- 🌲 Timber
- 📷 Tourism
- Forest and woodland
- Arable land
- Grazing

SPAIN	
LAND AREA	194,897 sq miles (504,782 sq km)
OFFICIAL LANGUAGE	Spanish
MAIN RELIGION	Christian
LIFE EXPECTANCY	79 years
LITERACY	97%

PORTUGAL	
LAND AREA	35,672 sq miles (92,391 sq km)
OFFICIAL LANGUAGE	Portuguese
MAIN RELIGION	Christian
LIFE EXPECTANCY	76 years
LITERACY	87%

Portugal's most famous wine is called port—named after Porto, a major seaport.

Olives
More olive oil is produced in Spain than in any other country. Over 1 million tons (1.02 million t) of olives are grown each year, most of which are crushed for olive oil. Olive groves are a common sight all over Spain.

Map labels: Bilbao, ANDORRA LA VELLA, Zaragoza, Barcelona, Porto, MADRID, Valencia, LISBON, Murcia, Seville, Málaga, Cádiz

Cod fishing
Cod is a favorite fish in Portugal. The Bay of Biscay has the most plentiful supplies of cod, tuna and sardines. Supplies have been severely reduced in recent years, causing problems in the local fishing industry. Although fishing is still a way of life for many coastal people, many fishermen have turned to other jobs.

Mediterranean lynx

Saffron farming
Saffron, the aromatic spice ingredient of Spain's famous rice dish, paella, is made from the stigmas of the saffron crocus flower. It takes 250,000 flowers to make just 1 pound (500 g) of saffron.

Citrus fruits
The areas around Valencia, Spain, are part of La Huerta, which means "the orchard," because they are bursting with fresh produce. Orange and lemon groves stretch through the countryside.

NATURAL FEATURES

Azores PORTUGAL
This archipelago of nine main islands in three separate groups lies about 1,000 miles (1,600 km) west of Portugal. The islands, formed by volcanic activity and earthquakes, have a subtropical, humid climate in which plants thrive. The island of Pico has the highest point in Portugal, at 7,713 feet (2,351 m).

The Pyrenees SPAIN
Stretching 270 miles (432 km) from the Bay of Biscay to the Mediterranean Sea, this rugged mountain range forms a barrier between Spain and France. During summer, warm air masses from Africa are trapped in the high regions, and cause rainfall to the south.

Doñana SPAIN
This wetland area south of Seville is Europe's largest nature reserve. Many rare animals roam the area, including the endangered Mediterranean lynx (*above*), fewer than 50 of which exist today. During winter, Doñana is home to thousands of migratory birds. A royal hunting ground for many centuries, it was made a national park in 1969.

Meseta SPAIN
Lying in the dry center of Spain, this high, arid plateau covers about two-thirds of the country and extends into Portugal. Warm air from the Pyrenees settles here, producing long, hot summers. In winter, conditions change and icy winds whip across the wide expanse. Parts of the meseta are mountainous.

La Tomatina
Every August, at the height of the tomato season, the town of Buñol, near Valencia, hosts the biggest food fight in the world. More than 20,000 entrants from Spain and beyond converge on the main street, ready to hurl tomatoes at anyone in sight. Part of a week-long festival, the battle is short-lived—about an hour—but in that time, many truckloads of tomatoes are reduced to pulp.

WHERE PEOPLE LIVE

	Urban	Rural
SPAIN	77%	23%
PORTUGAL	63%	37%

LARGEST CITIES

Madrid 3,183,000

Barcelona 1,606,000

Valencia 815,000

Seville 705,000

Zaragoza 665,000

PLACES

Madrid SPAIN
As Spain's capital, Madrid is the focus for industry, business and leisure. It is home to the Prado, a great art museum. King Juan Carlos lives in Madrid in the Royal Palace. Madrid is one of the highest capital cities in Europe.

Guggenheim Museum

Guggenheim Museum SPAIN
This distinctive modern building (above) in Bilbao, designed by the architect Frank O. Gehry, was opened in 1997. With its curving walls clad in thin sheets of titanium, the outside of the museum looks like a huge, free-form ship.

Santiago de Compostela SPAIN
Known as the Town of the Apostle, this university town's name comes from the apostle Saint James, who is buried there. It is the final destination on a popular pilgrimage trail, and has many religious monuments. Impressive processions pass through the streets during Easter week.

PEOPLE

Trajan AD 53–117
The first Roman emperor to be born outside Italy, in what is now Spain, Trajan tried to extend the empire to the east. He improved social welfare and commissioned many new buildings.

Queen Isabella 1451–1504
In 1469, Isabella of Castile married Ferdinand of Aragón, uniting their Catholic kingdoms to form the basis of modern Spain.

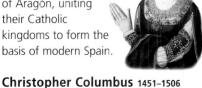

Christopher Columbus 1451–1506
This Italian-born sailor left Spain in 1492, in search of western trade routes to India. Three months later, he reached the Americas, not sure where he was. His accidental discovery made Spain a rich and powerful nation.

Vasco da Gama 1460–1524
This Portuguese navigator made three voyages to India (in 1497–99, 1502–03 and 1524), which opened up a new sea route from Europe to Asia and helped to make Portugal a world power.

Évora PORTUGAL
This city, east of Lisbon, was for many years an important military center for the Roman empire. It has also been under Moorish and Spanish control. Ruins of Roman buildings can still be seen throughout the city.

Lisbon PORTUGAL
Lisbon, Portugal's capital, is the country's main seaport. In the 8th century, it was invaded by Moors from Africa, and the city's buildings retain influences from this time. One of the greatest earthquakes ever recorded struck Lisbon in 1755, killing 30,000 people.

Alcazar, Segovia SPAIN
The Alcazar (right) takes its name from the Arabic word for castle. Isabella was crowned there in 1474. Built in the Middle Ages, it was rebuilt after being destroyed by fire in 1862.

The Alcazar at Segovia

Spanish Armada
The Armada was the name given to the Spanish navy under the rule of Phillip II in the 1500s. A flotilla of 130 ships, with 27,000 men on board, set sail to invade Britain in 1588. However, the English navy was better prepared. Using fire ships, it split the Spanish fleet apart and forced the Spaniards to return home in defeat. Spain's reputation as a maritime power was lost forever.

Pablo Picasso 1881–1973
This modern Spanish artist experimented with several different styles in his life. His Cubist period produced masterpieces such as *La Casserole Émailée* (below).

La Casa Mila

Gaudí's Barcelona
The city of Barcelona is adorned with the eye-catching architecture of Spain's most distinctive architect, Antoni Gaudí (1852–1926). Gaudí's buildings combined his love of the natural world with his knowledge of metalwork. The apartment block La Casa Mila (above) was built between 1906 and 1910 in the center of Barcelona. Its ornate roof and curved walls were inspired by the nearby ocean.

Portuguese water dogs were said to have sailed with the Spanish Armada in 1588 as messenger dogs between ships.

TRADITIONS AND CULTURE

Running of the bulls
This tradition is part of an annual festival held each July in Pamplona. As a climax to the 10 days of festivities, six bulls are released into the cobbled streets, behind crowds of young men who dodge the beasts' sharp horns.

Running of the bulls

Spanish food
Small plates of spicy food called tapas are eaten as snacks or appetizers. Rice is a favorite dish in many parts, often prepared with saffron, seafood and meat in paella. A specialty of the Andalucian region, in the south, is gazpacho—a chilled, tomato-based soup.

Jai alai
This game originated in the Basque region and is said to be the fastest ball game in the world. A player must fling the ball from a scooped basket called a cesta against a wall. The other player then catches it.

Cave painting, Altamira

15,000 BC
Prehistoric people create paintings depicting wild beasts in caves at Altamira, in northern Spain.

218 BC
Romans attack Hannibal's army and gradually move into the area. They remain until AD 409, when they are attacked by the Goths. The Goths rule until AD 711.

AD 711
Moorish Muslims invade southern Spain and Portugal from north Africa. In 1139 they lose control of Portugal and face problems in Spain.

1469
Monarchs Ferdinand and Isabella marry to form one reign, which is the start of modern Spain. By 1492, the Moors are driven out of Spain. The Jews are also expelled.

1492
Christopher Columbus discovers the Americas, and Spain begins to form its empire. The golden age of discovery and cultural activity starts 50 years later and lasts more than 100 years. In 1500, Portugal claims Brazil as a colony.

1561
The first permanent Spanish settlement in the Philippines is founded at Cebu. The Spaniards rule until independence in 1898.

1640
Portugal, a subject of Spain since 1580, gains independence. The country is ruled by kings until it becomes a republic in 1910.

1808–26
The Wars of Independence break out after Latin American countries rebel against the colonial rule imposed by Napoleonic Spain. The Spanish empire rapidly declines: Argentina becomes independent in 1816, Chile in 1817, Peru in 1824 and Bolivia in 1825. Brazil becomes independent from Portugal in 1822.

1926
The republic of Portugal is overthrown in a military coup. The dictator António Salazar is prime minister from 1932 until 1968.

1931
National elections result in overwhelming support for Spain as a republic.

Spanish Civil War

1936
The Spanish Civil War breaks out and military dictator General Franco takes power by 1939. He replaces the Spanish parliament with fascist rule: more than 100,000 are executed.

1974
After Salazar's death in 1970, the virtually bloodless Revolution of the Carnations in Portugal leads to democracy in 1974.

1975
Franco dies and King Juan Carlos I becomes ruler of Spain. He introduces democratic laws with more freedom than under Franco's rule.

France

FRANCE
POPULATION 60,876,000 * CAPITAL PARIS

MONACO
POPULATION 33,000 * CAPITAL MONACO

Boules player

Mont-St-Michel

The abbey of Mont-St-Michel was built in AD 966, and gradually changed over the next thousand years. It stands high on a rocky mound, attached to the mainland by a causeway. When tides are high, Mont-St-Michel becomes an island.

Cave art in Lascaux

Lascaux cave in the Dordogne, in southern France, was discovered in 1940 by four boys and a dog. They explored a hole in the forest and found themselves inside a beautiful painted cave system. There are 600 paintings in Lascaux, dating back 17,000 years. They depict hunting scenes, cattle, horses, deer and extinct animals. The cave is closed to visitors but a nearby replica is a tourist attraction.

1 Great Hall of the Bulls
The walls of this area of the cave seem to come alive with paintings of four aurochs (wild cattle) drawn in black outline. Some are 16 feet (5 m) tall and are the largest ice-age artworks.

2 Painted Gallery
This gallery is in a narrow passage off the Great Hall. Horses, bison and deer are crowded together on the wall.

Cave plan

Guillemots

3 Main Gallery
A second passage, to the right of the Great Hall, leads to the Main Gallery. The most impressive painting shows a row of stags swimming. The scene is almost 10 feet (3 m) above the ground. The artist must have used scaffolding.

4 Shaft of the Dead Man
Another passage leads to an area decorated with a scene of a wounded bison that has attacked and killed a man. The bird on a stick may be a spear. The artist made his paints with crushed rock and animal fat.

Bordeaux vineyard

Bordeaux, in France's southwest, is the largest wine-making region in the world. It is famous particularly for its red and sweet white wines. More than 13,000 wine growers in the area produce a third of all France's wine exports.

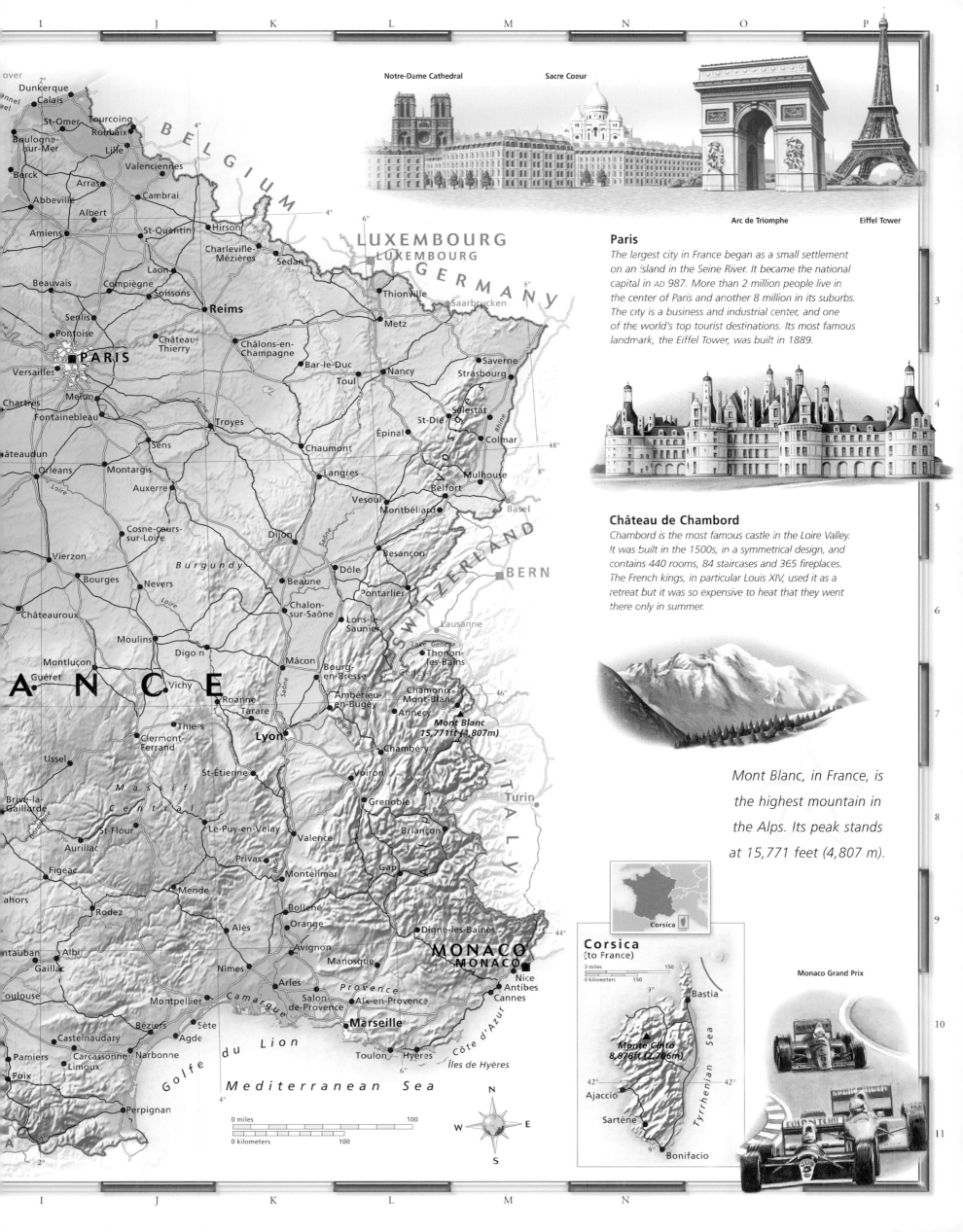

Notre-Dame Cathedral

Sacre Coeur

Arc de Triomphe

Eiffel Tower

Paris

The largest city in France began as a small settlement on an island in the Seine River. It became the national capital in AD 987. More than 2 million people live in the center of Paris and another 8 million in its suburbs. The city is a business and industrial center, and one of the world's top tourist destinations. Its most famous landmark, the Eiffel Tower, was built in 1889.

Château de Chambord

Chambord is the most famous castle in the Loire Valley. It was built in the 1500s, in a symmetrical design, and contains 440 rooms, 84 staircases and 365 fireplaces. The French kings, in particular Louis XIV, used it as a retreat but it was so expensive to heat that they went there only in summer.

Mont Blanc, in France, is the highest mountain in the Alps. Its peak stands at 15,771 feet (4,807 m).

Map labels

BELGIUM

LUXEMBOURG
LUXEMBOURG

GERMANY

SWITZERLAND

BERN

ITALY

Dover
Dunkerque
Calais
St-Omer
Tourcoing
Boulogne-sur-Mer
Roubaix
Berck
Lille
Valenciennes
Abbeville
Arras
Cambrai
Albert
Amiens
St-Quentin
Hirson
Charleville-Mézières
Laon
Sedan
Beauvais
Compiègne
Soissons
Senlis
Reims
Thionville
Saarbrücken
Pontoise
Metz
PARIS
Château-Thierry
Châlons-en-Champagne
Saverne
Versailles
Bar-le-Duc
Nancy
Strasbourg
Chartres
Melun
Toul
Sélestat
Fontainebleau
Troyes
St-Dié
Colmar
Châteaudun
Chaumont
Épinal
Orléans
Montargis
Langres
Mulhouse
Auxerre
Vesoul
Belfort
Sens
Montbéliard
Basel
Vierzon
Cosne-cours-sur-Loire
Dijon
Bourges
Nevers
Besançon
Beaune
Dôle
Châteauroux
Burgundy
Pontarlier
Moulins
Chalon-sur-Saône
Lausanne
Digoin
Mâcon
Lons-le-Saunier
Montluçon
Bourg-en-Bresse
Lake Geneva
Guéret
Thonon-les-Bains
Vichy
Geneva
Roanne
Ambérieu-en-Bugey
Chamonix-Mont-Blanc
FRANCE
Tarare
Annecy
Thiers
Lyon
Mont Blanc 15,771ft (4,807m)
Clermont-Ferrand
Chambéry
Ussel
St-Étienne
Brive-la-Gaillarde
Massif Central
Voiron
St-Flour
Le-Puy-en-Velay
Grenoble
Turin
Aurillac
Valence
Briançon
Figeac
Privas
Cahors
Mende
Montélimar
Gap
Rodez
Bollène
Albi
Alès
Orange
Montauban
Avignon
Digne-les-Bains
Gaillac
Nîmes
Manosque
MONACO
Toulouse
Arles
Salon-de-Provence
MONACO
Montpellier
Aix-en-Provence
Nice
Béziers
Provence
Antibes
Castelnaudary
Sète
Cannes
Pamiers
Agde
Camargue
Marseille
Foix
Carcassonne
Narbonne
Toulon
Hyères
Côte d'Azur
Limoux
Golfe du Lion
Îles de Hyères
Perpignan
Mediterranean Sea

Corsica inset

Corsica

Corsica
(to France)

0 miles 150
0 kilometers 150

Bastia
Monte Cinto 8,878ft (2,706m)
Tyrrhenian Sea
Ajaccio
Sartène
Bonifacio

Monaco Grand Prix

Scale

0 miles 100
0 kilometers 100

N
W E
S

France

LAND AREA	210,669 sq miles (545,630 sq km)
OFFICIAL LANGUAGE	French
MAIN RELIGION	Christian
LIFE EXPECTANCY	79 years
LITERACY	99%

Monaco has been ruled by the Grimaldi dynasty for more than 700 years.

NATURAL FEATURES

Massif Central
This vast and rugged plateau in central and southern France covers almost one-sixth of the country. The higher slopes are forested, and cattle and sheep graze on the lower grasslands.

Corsica
About one-fifth of this mountainous, rocky Mediterranean island is forested with chestnuts, pines and oak trees. The scent of its shrubby underbrush carries for miles, and has given Corsica the name "the scented isle."

Corsican landscape

Normandy beaches
Normandy's shoreline features towering chalk cliffs, golden tourist beaches and elegant resorts. The cliffs of Jobourg are the highest in Europe. Parts of the coast have very swift tides, reaching speeds of 6 miles per hour (10 km/h) in spring.

The Camargue
One of Europe's largest wetlands, this sparsely populated area is known for its free-ranging herds of cattle, horses and bulls (raised for bullfights) and for birds such as flamingoes (*left*). Rice is grown here, and salt is harvested. Nature tourism is a major industry.

USING THE LAND

Forest and woodland
Arable land
Grazing
Arid or marginal

Fishing
Fishing is still a major industry despite its decline over several years as a result of overfishing in the Atlantic Ocean. Recently there has been a move to develop fish farms to make up for the decrease in fish numbers.

Lavender
Lavender is native to the southern Alps, where different varieties grow wild. In the 16th century, the peasants of Provence extracted from it an oil that was used for medicinal purposes. Today, lavender is cultivated for perfumes, soaps and herbal essences.

Map legend:
- Cereals
- Potatoes
- Fruit and vegetables
- Wine
- Sugar beet
- Beef cattle
- Dairy cattle
- Sheep
- Fishing
- Industrial center
- Mining
- Tourism

Map labels: Lille, PARIS, Strasbourg, Rennes, Nantes, Dijon, Clermont-Ferrand, Lyon, Bordeaux, Toulouse, MONACO, Nice, Marseille, Perpignan, Ajaccio

Wheat
France is one of the world's top five wheat-growing countries. It also exports more food than any other country except the USA.

Tour de France
France's most famous sporting event, the Tour de France, is held over a period of three weeks and covers a grueling 2,200 miles (3,520 km) around the country, ending in the center of Paris. Every year, in summer, more than 150 cyclists compete in this world-famous race.

Dairy farms
Dairy products, such as yogurt and cheese, play a major part in French cuisine and exports. Camembert, a popular soft cheese, has been produced in the lush, fertile fields of Camembert, in Normandy, for more than 200 years.

Nuclear power
France is the world's largest user of nuclear power. Its 58 nuclear reactors generate more than 75 percent of the country's electricity. Nuclear power is produced from the fission, or splitting apart, of the nuclei of atoms. The fuel most widely used in this process is the metal uranium.

WHERE PEOPLE LIVE

Urban — Rural

75% — 25%

LONGEST RIVERS
Loire 634 miles (1,020 km)
Rhône 505 miles (813 km)
Seine 485 miles (780 km)
Garonne 357 miles (575 km)

LARGEST CITIES
Paris 2,144,000
Marseille 791,000
Lyon 479,000
Toulouse 445,000
Nice 337,000

Eiffel Tower

Once the tallest structure in the world, the Eiffel Tower was erected as a temporary exhibit for the Centennial Exposition in Paris in 1889 by engineer Alexandre-Gustave Eiffel. When radio was invented, the tower began its long career as an antenna. It carried the first transatlantic radio–telephone call. Each year, about 6 million people visit the tower.

PEOPLE

Joan of Arc 1412–31

Joan of Arc, France's patron saint, led French troops to victory against the English at Orléans in 1429. Captured soon after and accused of witchcraft, she was burned at the stake in 1431.

Victor Hugo 1802–85

The most famous of the French Romantic writers, Victor Hugo is best known for his novels *The Hunchback of Notre Dame* and *Les Misérables*.

Louis Pasteur 1822–95

During his brilliant scientific career, Pasteur invented pasteurization, proved that germs cause many diseases and produced a rabies vaccine. His work provided the basis for a number of branches of science and medicine.

The Water-Lily Pond, by Claude Monet

Claude Monet 1841–1946

One of the great Impressionist artists, Monet is known for his atmospheric paintings of landscapes, water-lilies (*above*) and Rouen Cathedral.

Charles de Gaulle 1890–1970

An outstanding international figure, General de Gaulle became president of the Fifth Republic in 1959, achieving independence for Algeria in 1962. He resigned from office in 1969.

PLACES

Carcassonne

The walled city of Carcassonne lies on the top of a steep bank of the Aude River. It was often besieged in the Middle Ages, and was restored in the 19th century. It has the finest remains of medieval fortifications in Europe.

Carcassonne

Lyon

The Romans founded Lyon in 43 BC, and it later became the capital of Gaul. Today, the city is a center of banking, textiles and pharmaceuticals, but most people associate it with food. It is famed for its fine cuisine, which is sourced from the fertile agricultural land and many vineyards of the region.

The Louvre was formerly the royal family's main residence.

Chartres Cathedral

Chartres Cathedral

The people of Chartres, helped by lavish contributions from the king and nobles, built this cathedral (*above*) in just over 25 years (1195–1220). With its twin west towers, rose windows and figured stained glass, it is one of the finest examples of French Gothic architecture.

Château de Versailles

This palace (*below*) was built between 1668 and 1710 by Louis XIV to display his power and wealth. Set in an immense park, it is more than a quarter of a mile (400 m) long. World War I officially ended here when the Treaty of Versailles was signed in 1919.

Versailles

TRADITIONS AND CULTURE

Perfume and fashion

The French are known for their style and elegance. French perfumes, such as those produced by Chanel, and French fashion designers, such as Pierre Cardin, are famous worldwide.

French cuisine

Good food is essential to the French way of life. The kitchen is the center of the household, and meals are an important part of French leisure activity. Almost every part of France boasts its own ham and wine, and its cheeses are famous all over the world. Nearly every meal is accompanied by bread of some sort, and breakfast often includes a buttery pastry called a croissant.

Croissants

Cafes

Cafes began in the 17th century as places to sample the popular new drinks chocolate and coffee. Le Procope, founded in 1686 in Paris, claims to be the world's oldest coffee house. Writers, artists, intellectuals and students met in cafes to talk and work.

Bastille Day parade (1880)

Bastille Day

Each year on 14 July, parades and ceremonies commemorate the 1789 destruction of the Bastille, the king's prison. At the time, it held only seven prisoners. The fall of the Bastille marks the birth of the French Republic.

Napoleon

Born in Corsica in 1769, Napoleon Bonaparte was a general and reformer of law, education and the army. His goal was the military conquest of Europe. He declared himself emperor of France in 1804, but was forced to abdicate in 1814. He died in exile in 1821 on the island of St Helena.

HISTORY AT A GLANCE

700–500 BC
The Celtic Gauls gradually arrive in France from the north and east.

58–50 BC
Julius Caesar defeats the Gauls and France becomes part of the Roman empire until AD 476, when the Romans lose control of the region to the Franks and Visigoths.

Asterix the Gaul

AD 506
The Franks unite under Clovis, convert to Christianity and grow in power. Their leader, Charlemagne, is crowned the Holy Roman Emperor by the pope in AD 800. By this time, the Franks rule most of Germany, Italy and the Low Countries.

1066
Led by William the Conqueror, the Normans from northern France conquer England, making William the most powerful ruler in France.

1337–1453
England and France fight the Hundred Years' War, an on-and-off struggle over a series of disputes, including who was the rightful king of France. After a great deal of suffering on both sides, the English are eventually driven out of France. France loses nearly a third of its population when plague breaks out in 1348.

1643
Louis XIV—the Sun King—becomes king of France at the age of five and rules until 1715. French culture appears to be at its height.

1685
Religious persecution provokes the emigration of 400,000 Protestant Huguenots.

1789
The French Revolution begins with the storming of the Bastille. Louis XVI and his Austrian queen Marie Antoinette are executed in 1793 after the people rebel against the monarchy. The reign of terror that follows sees thousands of people executed by guillotine. The young republic fights off attacks by Austria and Prussia.

Guillotine

1799
Napoleon Bonaparte comes to power and extends France's territory through much of Europe until he is defeated by England and Prussia at the Battle of Waterloo in 1815. The monarchy is restored until 1848, when another revolution brings in the Second Republic.

Battle of Waterloo

1914–18
World War I devastates France and more than 1.3 million French soldiers die. France fights on the side of the British, Russians, Americans and Italians against Germany, Austria and Turkey.

1939–44
Germany occupies France during World War II. The French resistance works underground to help the Allied powers defeat the Germans. On D-Day—6 June 1944—the largest invasion fleet in history, comprising 156,000 troops and a vast armada of ships, planes and tanks, lands at five beaches on the Normandy coast. This campaign to liberate France is successful within months.

The Low Countries

NETHERLANDS
POPULATION 16,491,000 ∗ CAPITAL AMSTERDAM

BELGIUM
POPULATION 10,379,000 ∗ CAPITAL BRUSSELS

LUXEMBOURG
POPULATION 474,000 ∗ CAPITAL LUXEMBOURG

Land below the sea

A third of the land in the Netherlands
is below sea level, including the cities
of Amsterdam and Rotterdam. Nearly
two-thirds of the population lives
below sea level. For centuries,
reclaiming land from the sea
for housing and farming, and
keeping it drained, have been
essential to the country's survival.
Dikes and canals hold back the
sea, and windmills drain the land.

The windmills at Kinderdijk
The Netherlands was once dotted
with thousands of working windmills.
Kinderdijk, near Rotterdam, has
19 windmills dating from 1740 lined
up in long rows. They are still used
to pump excess water from reclaimed
land and keep it drained.

Afsluitdijk (the barrier dyke)
This 19-mile (30-km) barrier was built
in 1932 as part of a project to reclaim
1,274 square miles (3,330 sq km) of land
from the Zuider Zee (South Sea). IJsselmeer
lake was created at the same time.

The Maaslandkering storm surge barrier
In 1997 the storm surge barrier outside
Rotterdam was completed. During a severe
storm, two massive gates can be closed to
protect the land on either side from floods.

THE LOW COUNTRIES

Dutch trade
For 200 years, starting in the early 1600s,
the Dutch had a vast and powerful trading
network in the Dutch East Indies (now named
Indonesia). Merchant ships carried cargoes of
gold to India and on to Asia, using it to buy
jade, porcelain, spices, tea, coffee, sugar
and tobacco to sell in Europe.

The canals of Amsterdam
The city of Amsterdam was founded in 1275.
A network of canals was built to criss-cross
the city because the land on which it is built
is low and at risk of flooding. Today there are
165 canals and 1,281 bridges. The best way
to get around the busy streets is by bicycle.

Clogs

GERMANY

NETHERLANDS

AMSTERDAM

THE HAGUE
('S-GRAVENHAGE)

Rotterdam

North Sea

Waddenzee

West Frisian Islands

IJsselmeer

Afsluitdijk

Mackerel

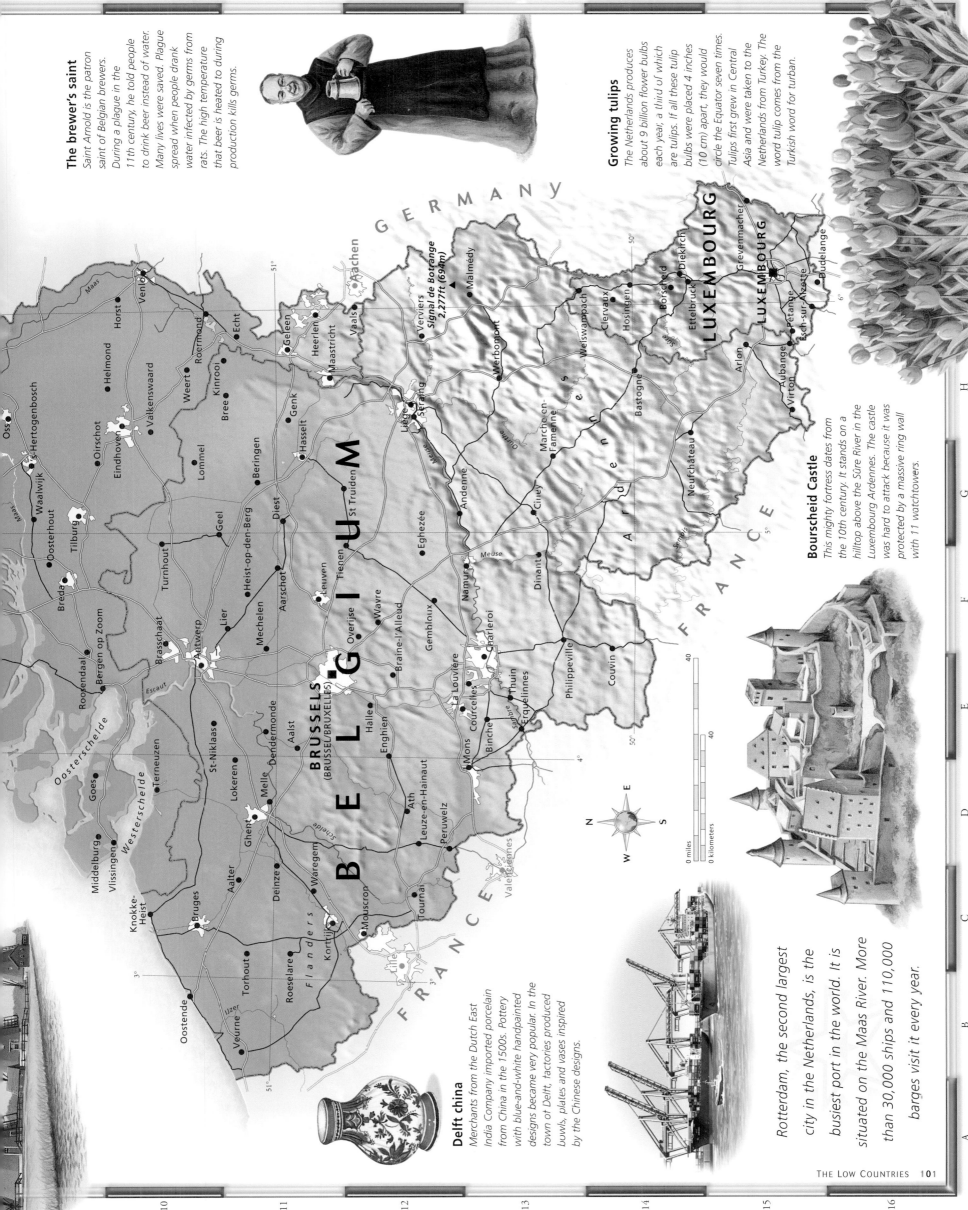

The brewer's saint

Saint Arnold is the patron saint of Belgian brewers. During a plague in the 11th century, he told people to drink beer instead of water. Many lives were saved. Plague spread when people drank water infected by germs from rats. The high temperature that beer is heated to during production kills germs.

Growing tulips

The Netherlands produces about 9 billion flower bulbs each year, a third of which are tulips. If all these tulip bulbs were placed 4 inches (10 cm) apart, they would circle the Equator seven times. Tulips first grew in Central Asia and were taken to the Netherlands from Turkey. The word tulip comes from the Turkish word for turban.

Bourscheid Castle

This mighty fortress dates from the 10th century. It stands on a hilltop above the Sûre River in the Luxembourg Ardennes. The castle was hard to attack because it was protected by a massive ring wall with 11 watchtowers.

Delft china

Merchants from the Dutch East India Company imported porcelain from China in the 1500s. Pottery with blue-and-white handpainted designs became very popular. In the town of Delft, factories produced bowls, plates and vases inspired by the Chinese designs.

Rotterdam, the second largest city in the Netherlands, is the busiest port in the world. It is situated on the Maas River. More than 30,000 ships and 110,000 barges visit it every year.

Map labels

GERMANY

FRANCE

BELGIUM

LUXEMBOURG

LUXEMBOURG

BRUSSELS
(BRUSSEL/BRUXELLES)

Signal de Botrange
2,277ft (694m)

Flanders

Ardennes

Maas

Meuse

Oosterschelde

Westerschelde

Escaut

Schelde

Ijzer

Ourthe

Semois

Our

Sûre

Oss
's-Hertogenbosch
Oosterhout
Tilburg
Waalwijk
Breda
Roosendaal
Bergen op Zoom
Brasschaat
Antwerp
Middelburg
Goes
Vlissingen
Terneuzen
St-Niklaas
Lokeren
Dendermonde
Aalst
Ghent
Aalter
Deinze
Waregem
Kortrijk
Mouscron
Tournai
Roeselare
Torhout
Oostende
Knokke-Heist
Bruges
Veurne
Helmond
Horst
Venlo
Echt
Roermond
Weert
Valkenswaard
Kinrooi
Bree
Lommel
Eindhoven
Oirschot
Geel
Turnhout
Heist-op-den-Berg
Lier
Aarschot
Mechelen
Leuven
Overijse
Wavre
Braine-l'Alleud
Halle
Enghien
Ath
Leuze-en-Hainaut
Peruwelz
Lille
Valenciennes
Mons
Binche
La Louvière
Courcelles
Charleroi
Thuin
Erquelinnes
Philippeville
Couvin
Dinant
Ciney
Namur
Gembloux
Eghezée
St Truiden
Tienen
Diest
Hasselt
Beringen
Genk
Heerlen
Maastricht
Vaals
Aachen
Geleen
Verviers
Liège
Seraing
Andenne
Werbomont
Malmédy
Marche-en-Famenne
Neufchâteau
Bastogne
Welswampach
Clervaux
Hosingen
Borscheid
Diekirch
Ettelbruck
Grevenmacher
Arlon
Virton
Aubange
Pétange
Esch-sur-Alzette
Dudelange

N E S W

0 miles   40
0 kilometers   40

51°   50°   3°   4°   5°   6°

The Low Countries

NETHERLANDS LAND AREA	16,033 sq miles (41,526 sq km)
OFFICIAL LANGUAGE	Dutch
MAIN RELIGION	Christian
LIFE EXPECTANCY	79 years
LITERACY	99%

BELGIUM LAND AREA	11,780 sq miles (30,510 sq km)
OFFICIAL LANGUAGE	Dutch/French/German
MAIN RELIGION	Christian
LIFE EXPECTANCY	78 years
LITERACY	98%

Luxembourgish is the national language of Luxembourg.

WHERE PEOPLE LIVE

Urban — Rural

BELGIUM
97% — 3%

NETHERLANDS
89% — 11%

USING THE LAND

Forest and woodland
Arable land
Grazing

Cereals
Potatoes
Vegetables
Sugar beet
Flowers
Beef cattle
Dairy cattle
Pigs
Gas production
Timber
Industrial center

Groningen

AMSTERDAM

Enschede

The Hague

Utrecht

Rotterdam

Eindhoven

Antwerp

Ghent

BRUSSELS

Liège

LUXEMBOURG

Fishing
In the Netherlands, fishing for herring, mackerel and flatfishes is mostly carried out in the North Sea and in some inland fisheries. In Belgium, the fishing industry is suffering because of fishing quotas imposed by the EU. Traditional coastal fishing now plays only a small part in Belgium's economy.

Farming
Cattle are raised on many farms throughout the Netherlands. Dairy cows, especially the black-and-white Holstein and Friesian, are the most popular varieties. The country's fertile polders are perfect for dairy farming.

Sugar beet
Although most farms in the Netherlands are small, their yields are among the world's highest. Leading crops include potatoes and sugar beet (*below*). Many farmers grow their crops in glasshouses during the winter.

NATURAL FEATURES

Ardennes BELGIUM–LUXEMBOURG
This chain of wooded hills covers 3,860 square miles (10,00 sq km) in northern Luxembourg, southern Belgium and northeast France. Under many of the hills are extensive cave systems, which are just one of the tourist attractions. The Ardennes is Belgium's most heavily forested region and also its least populated.

Beemster Polder
THE NETHERLANDS
Reclaimed in the 17th century from an area that used to be an inland sea, this oldest polder (reclaimed land) in the Netherlands is still divided into the rectangular plots of land that were drawn up in 1612.

Soignes Forest

Waddenzee
THE NETHERLANDS
This is the part of the North Sea between the Dutch mainland and the West Frisian Islands. Texel, the largest of these islands, is home to more than 300 species of birds, including the Eurasian spoonbill, and many migratory birds. It is one of the most important breeding grounds in Europe.

Eurasian spoonbill

Soignes Forest BELGIUM
Covering an area of about 10,000 acres (4,000 ha), this forest contains five nature reserves. Originally part of the ancient Charbonnière forest of Gaul, in which aurochs and elk roamed, it is known for its lofty beech trees.

Cheese markets
Many cheese-producing towns, such as Edam, Gouda and Alkmaar, retain their traditional cheese markets. Large, round balls of cheese are carried from the public weighing house to the cheese market, or *kaasmarkt*, on wooden sledges. The porters dress in white shirts and trousers, and wear leather slings to help them carry the heavy sledge. Gouda and Edam cheeses are world famous.

Edam cheese

LARGEST CITIES

Brussels 1,044,000

Amsterdam 747,000

Rotterdam 597,000

The Hague 485,000

Antwerp 466,000

Great painters

The 16th and 17th centuries were golden years for painting in Belgium and the Netherlands. The Flemish master Peter Paul Rubens painted for royal families, and is famous for his portraits, such as the *Portrait of a Boy* (above). Rembrandt, one of the most gifted Dutch painters, also specialized in portraits, using light and shade for dramatic effect.

TRADITIONS AND CULTURE

Belgian chocolate

Belgium is the world's third-largest producer of chocolates, which are exported all over the world. Some fine chocolate makers still fill and decorate their chocolates by hand.

Wooden shoes

Some Dutch people wear traditional wooden shoes that are shaped like ordinary shoes to help keep their feet warm and dry in the damp. Clogs, the pointy-toed, wooden shoes that are sold as tourist souvenirs, are not worn.

St Nicholas

Each year the people of the Netherlands celebrate the festival of Sinterklaas, or St Nicholas, the patron saint of sailors. On 6 December, the children exchange presents. Over the years, "Sinterklaas" became "Santa Claus."

Elfstedentocht

Also called the "Eleven Cities' Journey," this skating competition takes place on frozen canals that pass through 11 towns in Friesland, covering a distance of 125 miles (200 km).

Moules-frite—mussels with fries—is the national dish of Belgium.

PEOPLE

Desiderius Erasmus 1466–1536

Born in Rotterdam, Erasmus was a thinker and writer of the Renaissance period. He spent his life studying and writing about Christianity.

Abel Tasman c 1603–59

This navigator was chosen by the governor-general of the Dutch East Indies to explore the south Pacific. In 1642 he discovered what is now Tasmania, Australia, naming it Van Diemen's Land for his patron.

Vincent van Gogh 1853–90

Van Gogh's early paintings were mostly of farms and peasants. His later works were of orchards and sunflowers (*left*).

He had a unique brush style and loved to use bright, vivid colors. He is the greatest Dutch painter since Rembrandt.
Sunflowers

Mata Hari 1876–1917

Born in Friesland, Mata Hari's real name was Margarethe Geertruide Zelle. Well known as a dancer, she was accused of being a spy for Germany during World War I and was executed by the French.

Hergé 1907–83

Born in Brussels, Georges Rémi (known as Hergé) was a cartoonist. He created the children's cartoon series *The Adventures of Tintin* (*left*), which tells of the journeys of a boy reporter called Tintin and his white terrier, Snowy.

Anne Frank 1929–45

In 1942, during World War II, Anne Frank and her family hid for two years in an Amsterdam warehouse to avoid capture. Anne kept a diary of her life until taken to Auschwitz.
Anne Frank

PLACES

Amsterdam THE NETHERLANDS

Amsterdam is one of the Netherlands' two capitals (the other is The Hague). It began as a fishing village, and is now a busy port and commercial center.

Amsterdam

City of Luxembourg LUXEMBOURG

The capital of Luxembourg, which is one of Europe's oldest and smallest countries, this city is one of Europe's most important financial centers.

Brussels BELGIUM

Belgium's capital Brussels (*below*) is home to the headquarters of the European Union (EU) and the North Atlantic Treaty Organization (NATO).

Bruges BELGIUM

In the Middle Ages, Bruges was one of the largest and most influential of all European cities. An extensive network of canals runs through the city, which has beautiful gabled buildings and cobblestone streets.

The Hague THE NETHERLANDS

This city is the seat of government of the Netherlands. It is home to the Dutch parliament building and is the official residence of the Dutch royal family.

European Union

The European Union (EU) is an organization of democratic European countries that promotes cooperation among its members. Originally, this cooperation was mostly in the areas of politics, trade and economics, but now it involves such issues as human rights, international security and environmental protection.

HISTORY AT A GLANCE

c 50 BC
Julius Caesar invades the areas now known as the Low Countries. He conquers the land south of the Rhine, but the Frisians north of the Rhine are unconquered.

AD 406–511
Germanic tribes, called the Franks, end Roman rule in the Low Countries. Under Clovis I (king from c 481 to 511) the Franks rule most of Gaul.

AD 713–814
Charles Martel, a Frankish prince, conquers the Frisians and controls the Frankish empire, which reaches its peak between AD 768 and 814 under Charles's grandson, Charlemagne.

AD 925–1350
The Netherlands is ruled by the king of Germany, except for Flanders, which is ruled by France.

1350–1420
The dukes of French Burgundy, such as John the Fearless, become powerful, and the area is called the "Burgundian Netherlands."

1504
The Low Countries again become part of the Holy Roman Empire.
John the Fearless

1579
Seven provinces break away from Spanish rule and form the Union of Utrecht. This union is called the United Provinces of the Netherlands.

1602
The Dutch East India Company is formed and establishes profitable trade routes throughout Europe and East Asia.

1795–1813
The French, led by Napoleon Bonaparte, invade the Netherlands and control the United Provinces.

1814
The Congress of Vienna approves the United Kingdom of the Netherlands, including Belgium and Luxembourg. William I of Orange is king.

Congress of Vienna

1830
Belgians gain their independence after revolting against King William's control. Luxembourg becomes independent nine years later.

1847–48
Belgium and the Netherlands adopt important constitutional reforms.

1940–44
The Germans invade and occupy the Netherlands and Belgium until the end of World War II.

1957
Belgium, France, Italy, Luxembourg, West Germany and the Netherlands form the European Economic Community (EEC) to help free up trade among its members.

1967
The North Atlantic Treaty Organization (NATO) moves its headquarters from France to Belgium.

1992
The members of the European Community sign the Maastricht Treaty, which later establishes the European Union.

2002
Members of the European Union adopt euro notes and coins as their common currency.
Euro

Western Central Europe

Switzerland is one of the world's most rugged countries. Mountains make up more than 70 percent of its area.

Barge on Rhine River

GERMANY
POPULATION 82,422,000 ✳ CAPITAL BERLIN

AUSTRIA
POPULATION 8,193,000 ✳ CAPITAL VIENNA

SWITZERLAND
POPULATION 7,524,000 ✳ CAPITAL BERN

LIECHTENSTEIN
POPULATION 34,000 ✳ CAPITAL VADUZ

Brandenburg Gate
This monumental gateway in Berlin was built between 1788 and 1791. On its top is a statue of a chariot drawn by four horses, representing victory. The gate was damaged in World War II but has since been restored.

Farming
Wheat, barley, corn and sugar beets are grown in the region's richer soils. In the poorer soils of north Germany, rye, oats and potatoes are the main crops.

Car manufacture
The Ruhr valley in Germany is the world's largest car producer after the USA and Japan. German cars are noted for their style and reliability.

Hohensalzburg Castle
This massive fortress dominates the city of Salzburg in Austria. It was built by Archbishop Gebhard in the 11th century to protect the city from attacks by the neighboring Bavarians.

Tugboat
In the North Sea, tugboats bring ships and tankers safely through narrow or shallow waterways, and maneuver them into tight docking bays.

Bavarian folk costume

Map labels

POLAND

GERMANY

DENMARK

NETHERLANDS

Baltic Sea

North Sea

Pommersche Bay

Kap Arkona

Kieler Bay

Fehmarn Belt

Fehmarn

Mecklenburger Bay

Lübecker Bucht

Helgoländer Bay

North Frisian Islands

East Frisian Islands

BERLIN
Potsdam
Frankfurt an der Oder
Cottbus
Hoyerswerda
Bautzen
Görlitz
Dresden
Chemnitz
Zwickau
Gera
Jena
Weimar
Erfurt
Gotha
Eisenach
Göttingen
Nordhausen
Halle
Leipzig
Lutherstadt Wittenberg
Dessau
Magdeburg
Brandenburg
Stendal
Wittenberge
Schwedt
Eberswalde
Finow
Oderhaff
Neubrandenburg
Greifswald
Stralsund
Rostock
Wismar
Schwerin
Schweriner See
Müritz
Plauer See
Kummerower See
Peene
Oder
Elbe
Saale
Werra
Fulda
Weser
Leine
Weser
Ems

Flensburg
Heide
Neumünster
Kiel
Lübeck
Hamburg
Elmshorn
Bremervörde
Lüneburg
Uelzen
Celle
Braunschweig
Wolfsburg
Salzgitter
Goslar
Hannover
Hildesheim
Hameln
Detmold
Paderborn
Lippstadt
Gütersloh
Bielefeld
Minden
Osnabrück
Bremen
Delmenhorst
Oldenburg
Bremerhaven
Cuxhaven
Wilhelmshaven
Nordhorn
Rheine
Münster
Hamm
Herne
Bochum
Dortmund
Hagen
Wuppertal
Remscheid
Solingen
Essen
Bottrop
Moers
Duisburg
Krefeld
Düsseldorf
Neuss
Leverkusen
Bergisch Gladbach
Mönchengladbach
Cologne
Bergheim
Düren
Aachen
Siegen
Marburg
Kassel

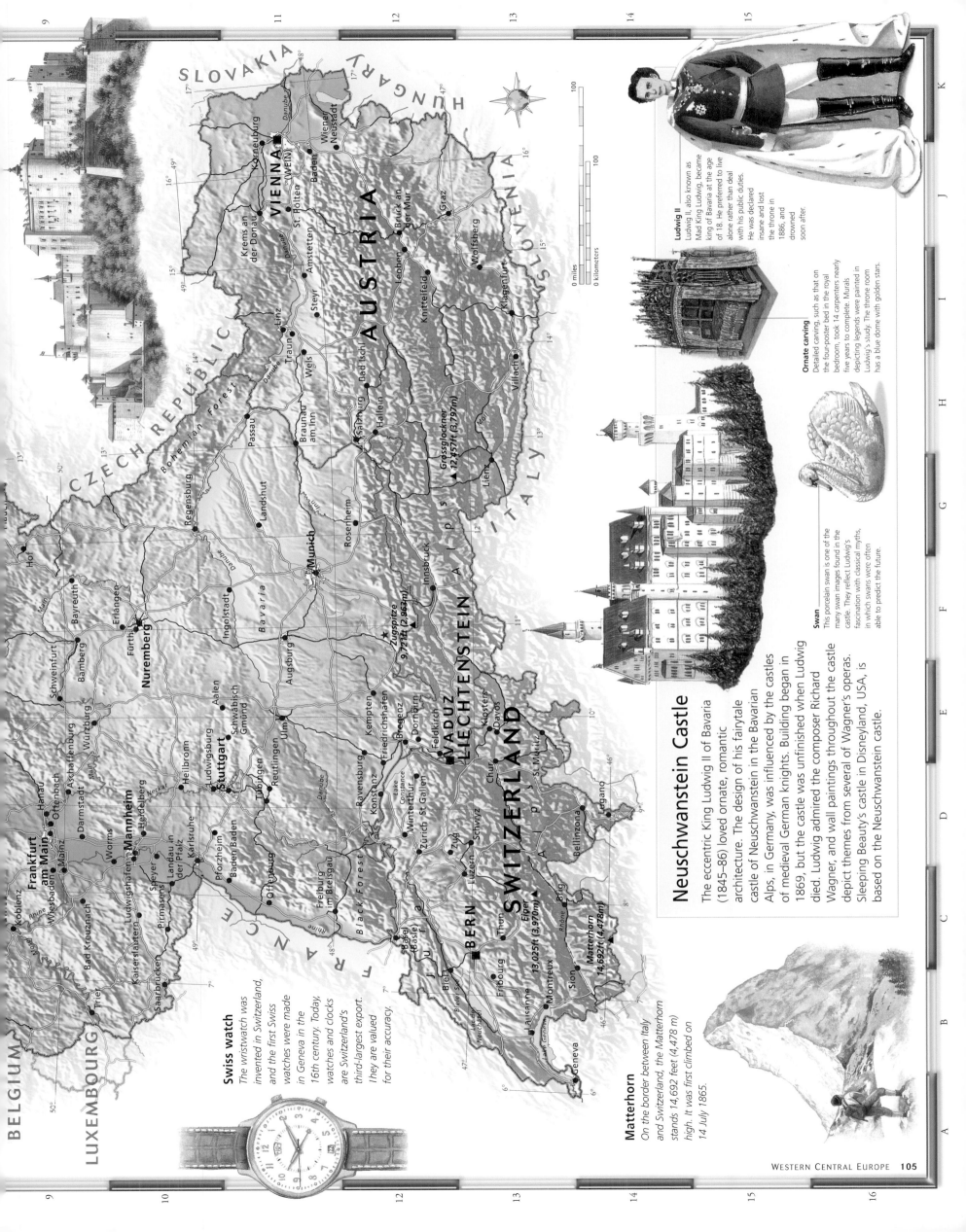

SLOVAKIA

HUNGARY

CZECH REPUBLIC

AUSTRIA

SLOVENIA

ITALY

SWITZERLAND

LIECHTENSTEIN

FRANCE

BELGIUM

LUXEMBOURG

VIENNA (WIEN)

BERN

VADUZ

Korneuburg • Krems an der Donau • St. Pölten • Amstetten • Baden • Wiener Neustadt • Bruck an der Mur • Graz • Leoben • Knittelfeld • Wolfsberg • Klagenfurt • Villach • Lienz

Linz • Steyr • Wels • Traun • Bad Ischl • Salzburg • Hallein

Passau • Braunau am Inn • Regensburg • Landshut • Rosenheim

Munich

Hof • Bayreuth • Bamberg • Schweinfurt • Erlangen • Fürth • **Nuremberg** • Ingolstadt • Augsburg

Aschaffenburg • Würzburg • Darmstadt • **Mannheim** • Heidelberg • Heilbronn • Ludwigsburg • **Stuttgart** • Aalen • Schwäbisch Gmünd • Reutlingen • Tübingen • Ulm • Kempten

Frankfurt am Main • Hanau • Offenbach • Mainz • Wiesbaden • Worms • Speyer • Ludwigshafen • Landau in der Pfalz • Karlsruhe • Pforzheim • Baden Baden • Offenburg • Freiburg im Breisgau

Koblenz • Trier • Bad Kreuznach • Kaiserslautern • Pirmasens • Saarbrücken

Ravensburg • Friedrichshafen • Bregenz • Dornbirn • Feldkirch • Chur • Klosters • Davos • St. Moritz

Konstanz • Winterthur • St. Gallen • Zürich • Zug • Schwyz • Luzern • Brig • Lugano • Bellinzona

Basle/Bâle • Biel • Neuchâtel • Fribourg • Thun • Lausanne • Montreux • Sion • Geneva

Lake Constance • Lake Geneva • Lac de Neuchâtel • Bieler See

Bohemian Forest • Black Forest • Bavaria • Danube • Rhine • Main • Inn • Alps • Jura

Zugspitze 9,721ft (2,963m) ▲

Grossglockner 12,457ft (3,797m) ▲

Eiger 13,025ft (3,970m) ▲

Matterhorn 14,692ft (4,478m) ▲

0 miles   100
0 kilometers 100

Swiss watch

The wristwatch was invented in Switzerland, and the first Swiss watches were made in Geneva in the 16th century. Today, watches and clocks are Switzerland's third-largest export. They are valued for their accuracy.

Matterhorn

On the border between Italy and Switzerland, the Matterhorn stands 14,692 feet (4,478 m) high. It was first climbed on 14 July 1865.

Neuschwanstein Castle

The eccentric King Ludwig II of Bavaria (1845–86) loved ornate, romantic architecture. The design of his fairytale castle of Neuschwanstein in the Bavarian Alps, in Germany, was influenced by the castles of medieval German knights. Building began in 1869, but the castle was unfinished when Ludwig died. Ludwig admired the composer Richard Wagner, and wall paintings throughout the castle depict themes from several of Wagner's operas. Sleeping Beauty's castle in Disneyland, USA, is based on the Neuschwanstein castle.

Swan
This porcelain swan is one of the many swan images found in the castle. They reflect Ludwig's fascination with classical myths, in which swans were often able to predict the future.

Ornate carving
Detailed carving, such as that on the four-poster bed in the royal bedroom, took 14 carpenters nearly five years to complete. Murals depicting legends were painted in Ludwig's study. The throne room has a blue dome with golden stars.

Ludwig II
Ludwig II, also known as Mad King Ludwig, became king of Bavaria at the age of 18. He preferred to live alone rather than deal with his public duties. He was declared insane and lost the throne in 1886, and drowned soon after.

Tim Burners-Lee developed the world wide web in 1989 while working near Geneva.

Western Central Europe

GERMANY LAND AREA	134,836 sq miles (349,223 sq km)
OFFICIAL LANGUAGE	German
MAIN RELIGION	Christian
LIFE EXPECTANCY	78 years
LITERACY	99%

AUSTRIA LAND AREA	31,945 sq miles (82,738 sq km)
OFFICIAL LANGUAGE	German
MAIN RELIGION	Christian
LIFE EXPECTANCY	78 years
LITERACY	98%

SWITZERLAND LAND AREA	15,355 sq miles (39,770 sq km)
OFFICIAL LANGUAGE	German/French/Italian
MAIN RELIGION	Christian
LIFE EXPECTANCY	80 years
LITERACY	99%

WHERE PEOPLE LIVE

| | Urban | Rural | |

GERMANY
87% | 13%

SWITZERLAND
68% | 32%

AUSTRIA
65% | 35%

Neanderthals

Named for the Neander Valley near Düsseldorf in Germany, where their remains were discovered in 1856, the Neanderthals lived in Europe between 60,000 and 35,000 years ago. They had a thick brow line and sloping forehead, and were shorter and stockier than other early humans. Their disappearance is a mystery—perhaps it was because they did not develop technology.

USING THE LAND

Cereals
Potatoes
Wine
Sugar beet
Beef cattle
Dairy cattle
Sheep
Pigs

Industrial center
Mining
Timber
Winter sports

NATURAL FEATURES

Eisriesenwalt caves AUSTRIA
Discovered in 1879, these huge ice caves in Salzburg have more than 25 miles (40 km) of explored passageways and 39,000 cubic yards (30,000 m³) of ice.

Lake Geneva SWITZERLAND–FRANCE
Lake Geneva is one of the largest and most beautiful lakes in Europe. Sixty percent of its waters belong to Switzerland, the remainder to France. Château de Chillon (*below*) is a fortress built on the shores in the 11th century.

The Alps
Europe's most impressive mountain range extends along Germany's southern border with Austria, into the state of Bavaria. Although the peaks are snow-covered during winter, masses of edelweiss (*left*) blanket the alpine meadows in spring.

The Black Forest GERMANY
Named for its dense growth of spruce and fir trees that let little light into the area, this dramatic forest in southwest Germany has been the backdrop for many magical tales. Pollution, such as acid rain, has recently threatened the forest.

LARGEST CITIES

Berlin 3,371,000

Hamburg 1,748,000

Vienna 1,573,000

Munich 1,282,000

Cologne 959,000

Kiel
Hamburg
BERLIN
Hannover
Essen
Leipzig
Dresden
Cologne
Frankfurt am Main
Nuremberg
Stuttgart
Linz
VIENNA
Munich
Salzburg
Basel
Zurich
VADUZ
Innsbruck
Graz
BERN
Klagenfurt
Geneva
Lugano

Forest and woodland
Arable land
Grazing
Arid or marginal

Chemicals
Germany is one of the world's leaders in chemicals production for both the local and export markets. Many corporations are developing measures to ensure that the environment is protected while chemicals are being manufactured.

Winter sports
The mountainous landscape of much of this region, as well as the extremely cold winters, make snow- and ice-related sports very popular. Many Germans, Swiss and Austrians love skiing, especially the cross-country style called *langlaufing*. In recent years, snowboarding (*right*) has also become popular.

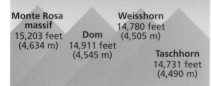

HIGHEST MOUNTAINS

Monte Rosa massif
15,203 feet (4,634 m)

Dom
14,911 feet (4,545 m)

Weisshorn
14,780 feet (4,505 m)

Taschhorn
14,731 feet (4,490 m)

Classical music

Between 1750 and 1820, Vienna, Austria's capital, was the center of classical music. Two of the most gifted composers from this time were Ludwig van Beethoven (1770–1827), who at the age of 30 began to go deaf, and Wolfgang Amadeus Mozart (1756–91), who died at age 35 at the height of his musical powers. Both relied on the support of wealthy patrons, who provided the funds that enabled them to write music.

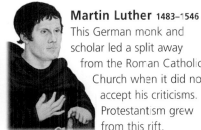

Ludwig van Beethoven

PEOPLE

Martin Luther 1483–1546
This German monk and scholar led a split away from the Roman Catholic Church when it did not accept his criticisms. Protestantism grew from this rift.

Gregor Mendel 1822–84
Known as the father of modern genetics, this Austrian monk, and later scientist, discovered why some plants and animals share the same characteristics.

Jean-Henri Dunant 1828–1910
In 1862, this Swiss journalist gathered together 36 people from 14 nations to form the International Red Cross. The Red Cross flag—a red cross on a white background—is the reverse of the Swiss flag.

Albert Einstein 1879–1955
Born in Germany, Einstein, a physicist, became a Swiss citizen in 1901. He published four research papers in 1905, the most influential being on his theory of relativity.

Albert Einstein

Maria von Trapp 1905–87
With her seven stepchildren and husband, this Austrian singer formed the Trapp Family Singers, who sang to audiences the world over. The film *The Sound of Music* is based on Maria's life.

Julie Andrews as Maria in *The Sound of Music*

TRADITIONS AND CULTURE

Oktoberfest
For 16 days during this beer festival in October, beer halls are filled with people drinking steins (*right*) of beer and enjoying oom-pah band music. The festival attracts more than 7 million visitors to Munich.

Fairy tales
Grimms' fairy tales were written by the brothers Grimm—two Germans who collected folktales about kings, magic and talking animals. The tales were often set in the forests and mountains of Germany.

Saint Bernard dog
This shaggy, densely coated dog breed was first reared in the 17th century by monks in the Saint Bernard Monastery, high in the Swiss Alps. Because of the dogs' ability to withstand very cold weather and their excellent sense of direction, they were able to help the guides who led people across the often dangerous Saint Bernard Pass.

Lipizzaner horses
This classic horse breed dates from 1580, and is a mix of Spanish, Arabian and Berber. It features in the dressage performances at the Spanish Riding School in Vienna.

Cuckoo clocks
Made in Germany since the 18th century, these decorative clocks (*right*) feature a mechanized cuckoo bird, which appears and sings as the clock strikes. The clock face can also be carved or painted.

Swiss cheese
Switzerland has a thriving dairy industry, and cheese-making is a family tradition that takes great skill. Emmentaler and Gruyère are the most popular varieties. A favorite Swiss dish is fondue, in which cheese is melted in a pot over a gentle flame, and pieces of bread are dipped into the pot.

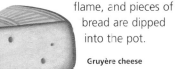

Gruyère cheese

Liechtenstein is the world's largest exporter of false teeth.

PLACES

Berlin GERMANY
This capital city, divided into east and west after World War II but becoming one city again in 1989, began as a trading center in the 13th century. Its most famous landmark is the Brandenberg Gate.

Zurich SWITZERLAND
Situated either side of the Limmat River on Lake Zurich is Switzerland's financial capital, a bustling business and cultural center, which earns one-fifth of the national income and has many visitors each year.

Vaduz LIECHTENSTEIN
This small capital city, although wealthy, has an atmosphere more like a village than a thriving center. Liechtenstein Castle, home of the prince, overlooks the city.

Cologne Cathedral

Cologne Cathedral GERMANY
One of the world's largest Gothic structures, this cathedral is the most visited monument in Germany. Building started in 1248, but the cathedral was not completed until 1880. Its two large towers rise to 515 feet (157 m).

Vienna AUSTRIA
Vienna, on the Danube River, was once the capital of the Holy Roman Empire. It is now known for its architecture, much of which dates from the Habsburg period, and its music. Vienna is the birthplace of the noted composers Franz Schubert, Johann Strauss and Arnold Schoenberg.

Vienna

AD 962
King Otto of Saxony rules the Holy Roman Empire as the first Holy Roman Emperor.

1200s
Three German cantons (districts) combine to form the Swiss Federation. More join over time. Zurich joins in 1351.

1278
Robert de Habsburg begins the Habsburg dynasty after taking control of Austria. By the 1500s this dynasty dominates most of Europe.

1455
Johann Gutenberg produces the Gutenberg Bible, the first European book printed with movable type.

Gutenberg Bible

1517
Martin Luther speaks out against the Roman Catholic Church. The Reformation follows. Luther establishes the Protestant Church.

1529
Ottoman Turks besiege Vienna but fail to take over the city.

1618–48
Protestants start the Thirty Years War as a protest against the Habsburg Holy Roman emperors. The Treaty of Westphalia ends the war.

1713
Liechtenstein becomes a principality under the Holy Roman Empire and gains independent sovereignty 150 years later.

1781
Joseph II of Austria abolishes serfdom in the Austrian empire.

1871
Prussian leader Otto von Bismarck forms the new German empire. The Victory column is built two years later in Berlin to commemorate unification and past victories.

Victory column

1914–18
Germany is defeated in World War I by the Allies and becomes a republic.

1933
Adolf Hitler leads the Nazi party into power. The following year Hitler gains total control and imposes his rule on the German people.

1938
Under Hitler's direction, tanks move into Vienna and occupy the city. Austria unites with Germany.

Adolf Hitler

1939–45
World War II occurs between Germany and the Allied forces. Millions of Jews are killed by Nazis during the Holocaust. Many German cities are bombed by the Allies. Germany is defeated and divided into East and West.

1961–89
The Berlin Wall separates the two halves of Berlin into East and West, and isolates West Berlin. The wall comes down in 1989, following the collapse of communism. Germany reunites.

Italy

Football players

ITALY
POPULATION 58,134,000 ✳ CAPITAL ROME

MALTA
POPULATION 400,000 ✳ CAPITAL VALLETTA

SAN MARINO
POPULATION 29,000 ✳ CAPITAL SAN MARINO

VATICAN CITY
POPULATION 932 ✳ CAPITAL VATICAN CITY

The Colosseum of Rome

In AD 72 the Roman emperor Vespasian began building a massive amphitheater (theater in the round). It took eight years to complete. The arena was used for the cruel and bloody gladiatorial games, the Romans' favorite popular entertainment. More than 5,000 animals and gladiators died in the opening 123 days of celebration.

Awning
An enormous canvas was attached to the top in the summer.

Size and capacity
The Colosseum is four stories high with 80 entrances. It could seat 50,000 spectators.

Under the floor
The gladiators and animals were kept in chambers underneath the arena's wooden floor until their performance began.

Arches
There are 80 arches on every floor, each separated by columns.

The Colosseum today
After 400 years the arena fell into disuse. Today, thousands of tourists visit the ruins every year.

Program of events

The arena of the Colosseum was sometimes flooded for mock sea battles. Wild animal hunts also took place. A setting of hills, trees and small lakes was created to make the event more realistic. The fights of the gladiators were the main attraction.

Villa Capra
Andrea Palladio designed the Villa Capra in Vicenza in 1566. It was based on the architecture of ancient Greece and Rome. Squares, circles and rectangles were combined to create a formal building that became the model for many stately homes throughout Europe.

Carnevale celebrations
Carnevale is held each year in February. This tradition dates from the 14th century. People wear bright costumes and enjoy parades and masked balls. Venice is famous for its carnevale masks. Many depict characters from Italian folktales.

Vatican City, where the Pope lives, is the smallest country in the world. It is so small that it takes less than an hour to walk around the whole country.

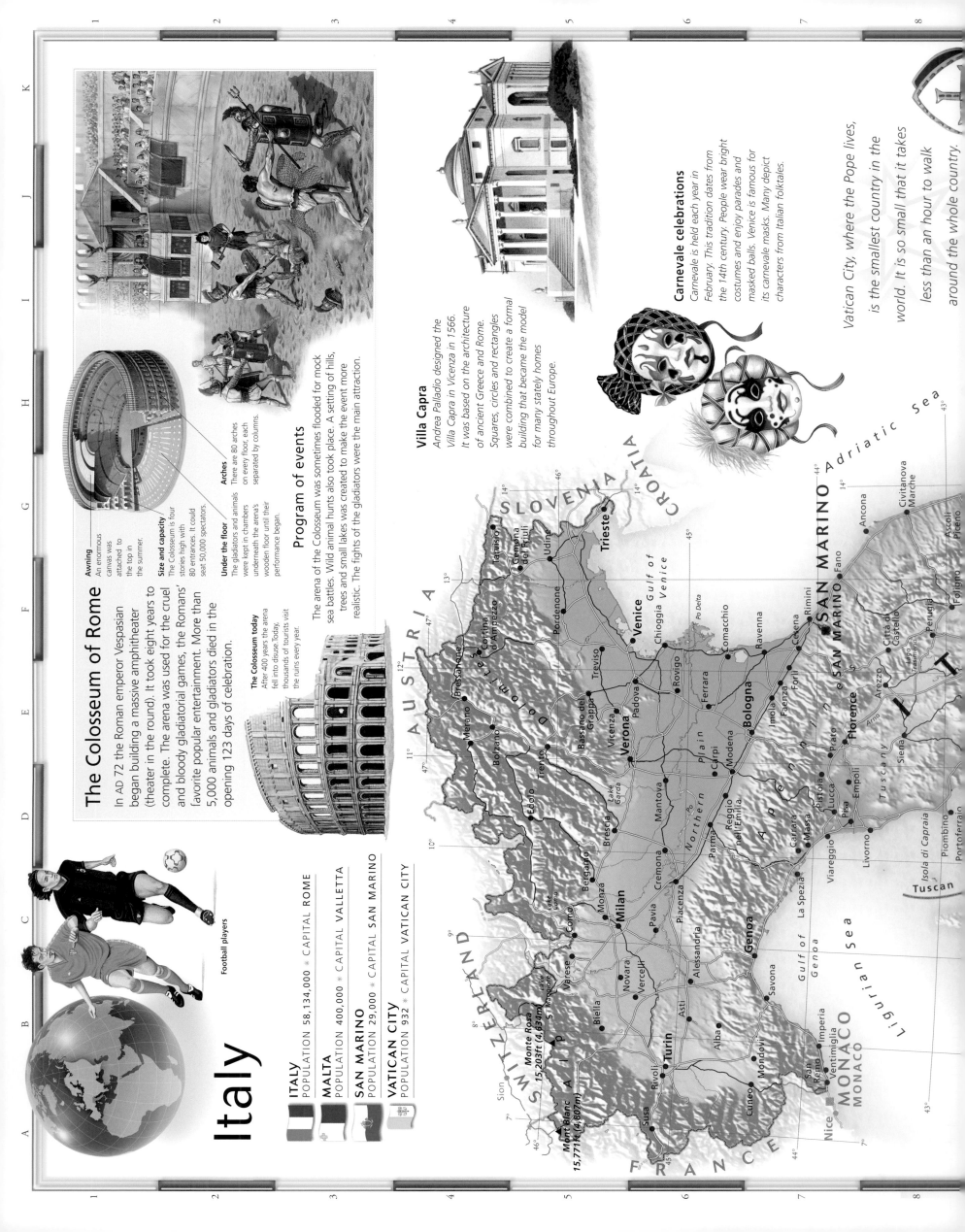

SWITZERLAND

AUSTRIA

SLOVENIA

CROATIA

FRANCE

MONACO

Mont Blanc 15,771ft (4,802m)
Monte Rosa 15,203ft (4,634m)

Nice
Ventimiglia
San Remo
Imperia
Cuneo
Susa
Rivoli
Turin
Mondovi
Alba
Asti
Savona
Alessandria
Biella
Vercelli
Novara
Varese
Como
Lake Como
Lake Maggiore
Lake Garda
Bergamo
Monza
Milan
Pavia
Piacenza
Cremona
Mantova
Brescia
Edolo
Bolzano
Merano
Brixen
Bressanone
Trento
Vicenza
Verona
Padova
Rovigo
Treviso
Cortina d'Ampezzo
Tarvisio
Gemona del Friuli
Udine
Pordenone
Trieste
Venice
Chioggia
Po Delta
Comacchio
Ravenna
Ferrara
Bologna
Modena
Carpi
Reggio nell'Emilia
Parma
Imola
Faenza
Forlì
Cesena
Rimini
Fano
SAN MARINO
Ancona
Civitanova Marche
Ascoli Piceno
Foligno
Perugia
Città di Castello
Arezzo
Florence
Prato
Pistoia
Lucca
Pisa
Empoli
Siena
Lago Trasimeno
Livorno
Viareggio
Massa
Carrara
La Spezia
Genoa
Piombino
Portoferraio
Isola di Capraia
Tuscan

Gulf of Genoa
Ligurian Sea
Gulf of Venice
Adriatic Sea
Tuscany
Northern Plain
Dolomites
Apennines
Arno
Po

Sion

ITALY

Pope's ceremonial headdress

Red mullet

Octopus

Pompei
In AD 79, Mount Vesuvius, near Naples, erupted. The people of the city of Pompei looked up to see a tower of thick black smoke. Ash 20 feet (6 m) deep quickly covered the city. More than 1,600 years later, the city was unearthed and its secrets were revealed.

Scooter transport
In 1946, the first commercially successful motor scooter was made in Italy. Called the Vespa (Latin for wasp), it is still popular. Scooters are easy to drive in crowded cobbled streets.

Michelangelo's David
In 1501, the artist Michelangelo was commissioned to create a monument to represent the city of Florence. Three years later, the famous statue was finished. Carved from a single piece of marble, it shows the biblical hero David just before he defeats the giant Goliath.

Cruise ship

Sardinian woman

Sardines

ITALY 109

Italy

LAND AREA	113,522 sq miles (294,020 sq km)
OFFICIAL LANGUAGE	Italian
MAIN RELIGION	Christian
LIFE EXPECTANCY	79 years
LITERACY	98%

USING THE LAND

NATURAL FEATURES

Blue Grotto
On a clear day, the waters of this huge underground cave on the shore of the island of Capri reflect a beautiful deep blue. In Roman times, the grotto was a water monument for Emperor Tiberius, but it lay unused until the 1800s because local fishermen believed that it was haunted by evil spirits.

Sicily and Sardinia
These two Italian islands are off Italy's west coast. Sicily lies at the southern tip and Sardinia sits between Naples and Rome. Sicily has a mix of fine beaches and local historical treasures while Sardinia's windswept coastline is popular for fishing and water sports.

Dolomites
These majestic mountains, made of dolomite limestone, lie near the Austrian border on the edge of the Alps, in the northwest of Italy. Eighteen of the peaks rise to more than 10,000 feet (3,050 m).

Appennines
This steep mountain range extends for 860 miles (1,376 km) like a backbone down the center of Italy, between the east and west coasts. Most of Italy's rivers have their source in this range.

WHERE PEOPLE LIVE

Urban		Rural
67%		33%

LARGEST CITIES

Rome 2,548,000

Milan 1,324,000

Naples 978,000

Torino 872,000

Palermo 663,000

Mount Etna
Perched above the Sicilian town of Catania, Mount Etna is one of the world's most active volcanoes. Eruptions have occurred for more than 2.5 million years. Lava flows destroy villages and farmland every few years, and smaller eruptions happen even more often. Etna's name comes from the Greek for "I burn."

PEOPLE

Marco Polo 1254–1324
Born in Venice, Marco Polo set sail for China in 1271. He completed his journey by camel along the Silk Road and spent time in the emperor Kublai Khan's court. He did not return to Italy for 24 years.

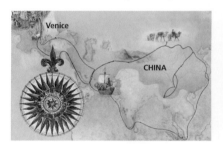

Leonardo da Vinci 1452–1519
A brilliant inventor, engineer, architect, scientist and artist, da Vinci was a leading figure of the Renaissance. He designed flying machines, such as the one below, based on his belief that humans could fly. His paintings, such as *Mona Lisa* and *The Last Supper*, are masterpieces.

Leonardo's flying machine

Galileo Galilei 1564–1642
Mathematician, astronomer, scientist: this genius made sense of the world by inventing the telescope, through which he viewed the planets.

Maria Montessori 1870–1952
Maria Montessori, Italy's first female medical student and later, a teacher, paved the way for a new way of teaching—the Montessori method.

Benito Mussolini 1883–1945
Prime minister from 1922 to 1943 and founder of fascism, this dictator carried out many social reforms and public works, but abolished democracy and banned trade unions and the free press.

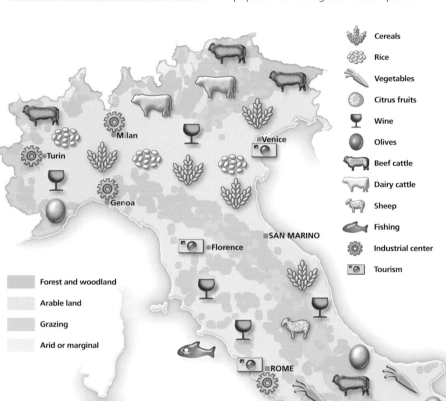

Cereals
Rice
Vegetables
Citrus fruits
Wine
Olives
Beef cattle
Dairy cattle
Sheep
Fishing
Industrial center
Tourism

Forest and woodland
Arable land
Grazing
Arid or marginal

Milan
Turin
Venice
Genoa
SAN MARINO
Florence
ROME
Bari
Naples
Cagliari
Palermo
VALLETTA

Fruit and vegetables
Olive oil, garlic and tomatoes are a tasty basis for many of Italy's dishes. The country produces olives and vegetables of a very high quality. This is due to its Mediterranean climate of hot, dry summers and cool winters.

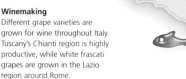

Winemaking
Different grape varieties are grown for wine throughout Italy. Tuscany's Chianti region is highly productive, while white frascati grapes are grown in the Lazio region around Rome.

Fishing
The waters of the Mediterranean Sea are home to sardines, tuna and anchovies. Fishing is an important industry for Italy.

PLACES

St Peter's Basilica VATICAN CITY

Each year, tourists flock to St Peter's Basilica (*above*). Built between 1506 and 1615, it is the church of the popes and a pilgrimage site for Roman Catholics. In front of it is a vast colonnaded square in which crowds gather to hear the pope speak.

Rome ITALY

Set on seven hills around the Tiber River, Rome is a thriving blend of ancient traditions and modern lifestyle. Italy's capital, it attracts millions of visitors who walk the city in search of its architectural treasures and appreciate its lively, buzzing atmosphere. Its attractions include ancient sites such as the Pantheon and the ruins of the Forum.

Milan ITALY

This northern city is a center of fashion, showcased each year at the Milan Fashion Show. Italian designers such as Miuccia Prada and Giorgio Armani are known all over the world.

Valletta MALTA

This seaport, Malta's capital, has been ruled by many different powers over the centuries. Once an important naval base, it was heavily bombed in World War II.

The Leaning Tower of Pisa

The most unusual feature of this bell tower in Pisa is its lean. Building stopped shortly after it began in 1173 as the subsiding ground below the tower caused it to tilt. Almost 200 years later, it was finally completed to a height of 180 feet (55 m), with 294 steps leading to the top. The bells in the tower are no longer rung, and concrete now supports the foundations under the ground.

Naples ITALY

Italy's most densely populated city, the seaport of Naples sits on the west coast's Bay of Naples, close to possible earthquake and volcano activity.

Florence ITALY

Florence is the cultural heart of Italy, showcasing such architectural marvels as the imposing Duomo (*below*). A center of the Renaissance, the city is home to the Uffizi gallery, which displays Italy's rich heritage of art. Notable Florentines include Michelangelo, Leonardo da Vinci, Galileo, Machiavelli, Dante and the city's most famous rulers, the Medici family.

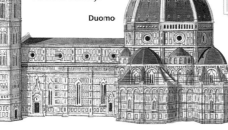

Duomo

Venice

This city consists of 118 small islands, linked by waterways and bridges, including the famous Rialto Bridge (*above*). In the 14th century, Venice was Europe's greatest seaport, and it is still a major Italian port today. Cars are banned from most of the city; water transport is provided by gondolas, vaporettos and power boats. Floods frequently bring the city to a halt. Industries include boatbuilding, textiles, furniture and glassworking. Tourism is an important source of income.

San Marino is the smallest republic in Europe and the oldest republic in the world.

TRADITIONS AND CULTURE

Pinocchio

This world-famous story of the wooden boy puppet who comes to life was written by Carlo Collodi and first published in 1890. Pinocchio learns about life through his adventures. His nose grows whenever he tells a lie.

Pinocchio

The Renaissance

In the 14th century there was a rebirth in art and classical knowledge, first in northern Italy and then throughout Europe. Ancient Greek thought was rediscovered and people began to view the world differently. There were great advances in art, science, literature and architecture. Michelangelo, one of the greatest Renaissance painters, brought a realism to art not seen before. His masterpiece, a series of frescoes painted on the ceiling of the Vatican's Sistine Chapel (*below*), took five years to complete.

Football (soccer)

Football is Italy's national sport. Most cities have their own first-grade teams, and some import highly paid players from other countries to play for them. Matches attract huge crowds.

Italian tastes

Italian people love their food. Their favorites are pizza (*right*) and pasta, which are both made from a dough of wheat grain mixed with water. There are hundreds of pasta varieties, from long spaghetti to small ravioli, served with many different sauces. Another favorite is Italian ice cream, or gelato.

Pizza

Italian design

Italian firms such as Alessi and Cappellini are known for their stylish and innovative designs, particularly in the areas of homewares, furniture and cars. Italy encourages good design through its design schools and exhibitions.

Alessi bottle opener

Opera

This combination of singing and drama originated in Italy in the 16th century. Italian operas include Verdi's *Rigoletto* and Puccini's *Tosca*. Famous modern opera singers include Luciano Pavarotti.

HISTORY AT A GLANCE
ANCIENT ROME

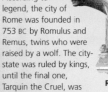

BEGINNINGS

According to legend, the city of Rome was founded in 753 BC by Romulus and Remus, twins who were raised by a wolf. The city-state was ruled by kings, until the final one, Tarquin the Cruel, was defeated in 509 BC by the Etruscans.

Romulus and Remus

THE REPUBLIC 509–27 BC

Two elected consuls ruled instead of the former kings. The consuls were advised by a council called the Senate, composed of wealthy citizens. During the 6th century BC, Rome became more powerful and by 275 BC controlled all of Italy. In the Punic Wars (264–146 BC), Rome fought Carthage for control of the Mediterranean and won. Further battles against Greece, Syria, Egypt and Macedonia were also successful.

JULIUS CAESAR

In 49 BC, as a popular general during the Roman Republic period, Julius Caesar led his army to victory over England and Germany. He made himself dictator of Rome and was murdered on 15 March 44 BC, known as the "ides of March."

THE EMPIRE 27 BC – AD 476

Rome's first emperor, Augustus, was Julius Caesar's nephew. He was crowned in 27 BC. The Roman empire continued to grow until it reached its largest point under Trajan (ruled AD 98–117). Rome ruled most of western Europe, including Britain, northern Africa and the Mediterranean Basin. However, the empire grew weaker and eventually split into two, with its eastern capital in Constantinople in 395. The fall of Rome was completed in 476 when Germanic tribes overran the city. The eastern empire continued until 1453, when the Ottomans captured Constantinople.

Roman soldiers

THE ARMY

The backbone of Rome's empire was its army—the most advanced and well-organized army of the ancient world. It was divided into 60 units, or legions, of foot soldiers, called legionaries. Each legion contained about 5,000 men. The army conquered many lands, expanding Rome's territory. Military life was harsh, but retired soldiers were given money or land to farm.

ROMAN ACHIEVEMENTS

The Romans invented concrete, which made it possible to build large, strong structures such as domed roofs and arched bridges. Roman roads were paved, and were known for their durability and straightness. Aqueducts supplied cities with water for public lavatories, fountains and bathhouses. The water flowed gently from a higher level to a lower one. Tiers of arches supported the pipes across steep valleys. Rome had an extensive and efficient sewerage system that was not bettered until the late 19th century.

Roman aqueduct

Southeastern Europe

Diocletian's palace
This massive palace on the Adriatic coast in Split, Croatia, was built for the Roman emperor Diocletian in the late 3rd century AD. The palace is set out like a Roman fort, and now forms the city center.

Folk dancing
Ranging from simple, quick steps and gentle turns to lively jumping, traditional folk dances are enjoyed throughout Romania. Music and loud shouts accompany the dancers.

Rural life
Farming methods are changing as more country people move to the cities to find work. However, in some areas, the traditional way of life continues.

Greek evzones guards

The dalmatian is a breed of dog named for the Adriatic coastal region of Dalmatia, its first known home. These dogs once ran beside horsedrawn carriages to frighten highwaymen.

ROMANIA POPULATION 22,304,000 * CAPITAL BUCHAREST

GREECE POPULATION 10,688,000 * CAPITAL ATHENS

SERBIA POPULATION 9,396,000 * CAPITAL BELGRADE

BULGARIA POPULATION 7,385,000 * CAPITAL SOFIA

BOSNIA–HERZEGOVINA POPULATION 4,499,000 * CAPITAL SARAJEVO

CROATIA POPULATION 4,495,000 * CAPITAL ZAGREB

ALBANIA POPULATION 3,582,000 * CAPITAL TIRANA

MACEDONIA POPULATION 2,051,000 * CAPITAL SKOPJE

SLOVENIA POPULATION 2,010,000 * CAPITAL LJUBLJANA

MONTENEGRO POPULATION 631,000 * CAPITAL PODGORICA

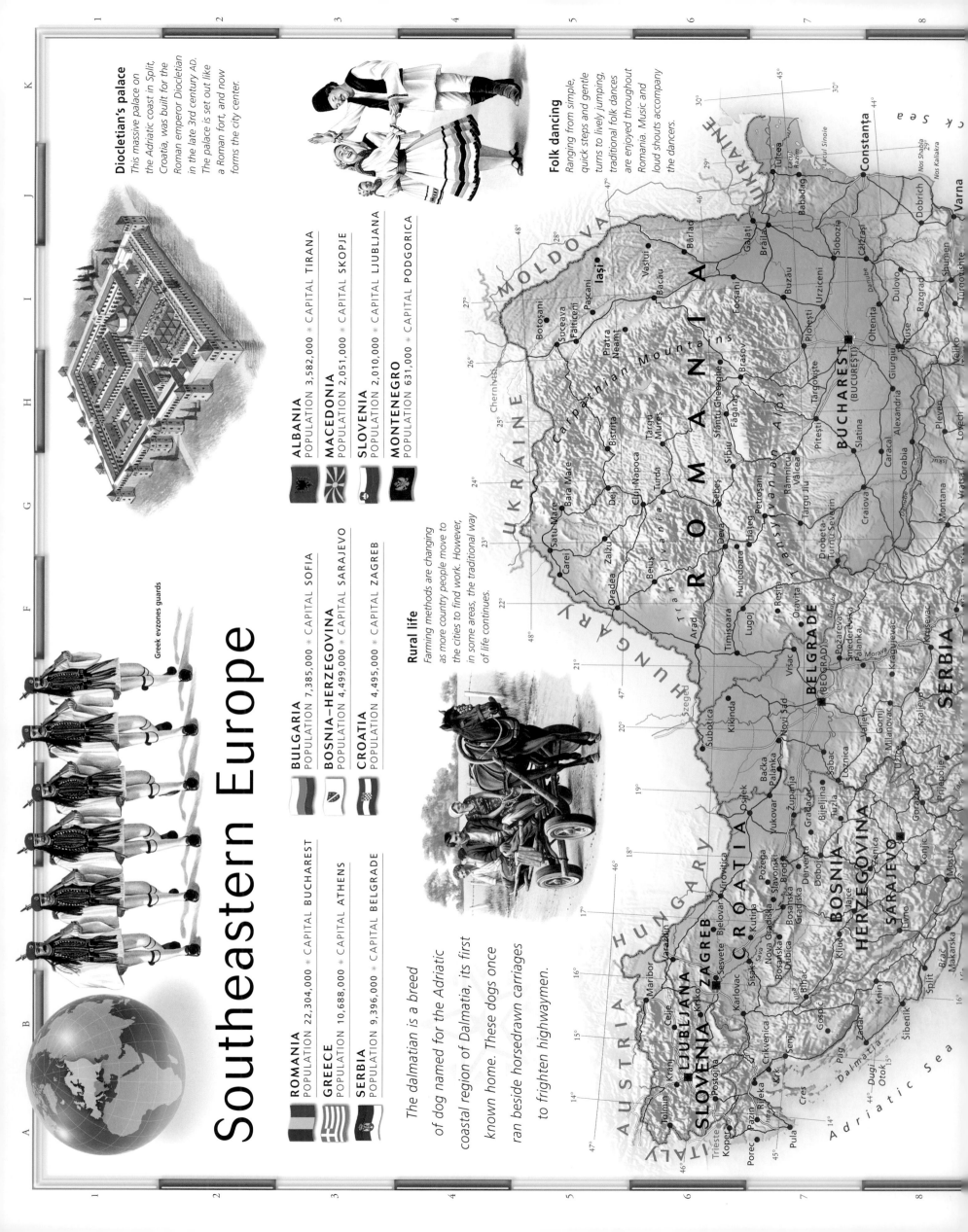

Map labels

UKRAINE

MOLDOVA

ROMANIA

HUNGARY

AUSTRIA

ITALY

SLOVENIA

CROATIA

BOSNIA–HERZEGOVINA

SERBIA

Carpathian Mountains

Transylvanian Alps

Transylvania

Dalmatia

Adriatic Sea

ck Sea

Chernivtsi, Botoşani, Suceava, Fălticeni, Iaşi, Vaslui, Paşcani, Piatra Neamţ, Bistriţa, Bacău, Bârlad, Galaţi, Brăila, Buzău, Focşani, Urziceni, Ploeşti, BUCHAREST (BUCUREŞTI), Oltenita, Giurgiu, Constanţa, Tulcea, Lacul Razim, Lacul Sinoie, Babadag, Slobozia, Călăraşi, Dulovo, Razgrad, Dobrich, Shumen, Tărgovishte, Varna, Targovişte, Nos Shabla, Nos Kaliakra

Satu Mare, Carei, Zalău, Oradea, Beiuş, Cluj-Napoca, Dej, Baia Mare, Turda, Sebeş, Deva, Hunedoara, Haţeg, Petroşani, Târgu Mureş, Sibiu, Făgăraş, Sfântu Gheorghe, Braşov, Piteşti, Râmnicu Vâlcea, Târgu Jiu, Craiova, Slatina, Caracal, Corabia, Alexandria, Pleven, Lovech, Ruse, Montana, Iskür

Arad, Timişoara, Lugoj, Reşiţa, Oraviţa, Drobeta-Turnu-Severin, Orşova, Danube, Morava, Negotin, Vidin

Szeged, Kikinda, Subotica, Bačka Palanka, Novi Sad, BELGRADE (BEOGRAD), Pančevo, Smederevo, Požarevac, Kragujevac, Jagodina, Kruševac

Maribor, Celje, Kranj, LJUBLJANA, Postojna, Koper, Trieste, Porec, Pazin, Pula, Rovinj, Rijeka, Crikvenica, Senj, Krk, Cres, Pag, Zadar, Dugi Otok, Šibenik, Split, Brač, Makarska, Knin, Gospić, Karlovac, Sisak, Sesvete, ZAGREB, Varaždin, Čakovec, Bjelovar, Kutina, Nova Gradiška, Bosanska Gradiška, Bosanska Dubica, Bihać, Banja Luka, Slavonski Brod, Požega, Osijek, Vukovar, Županja, Bijeljina, Tuzla, Loznica, Šabac, Valjevo, Gornji Milanovac, Zvornik, Derventa, Doboj, Zenica, SARAJEVO, Jajce, Livno, Mostar, Konjic, Goražde, Priboj, Prijepolje, Pljevlja

Ulcinj, Tirana

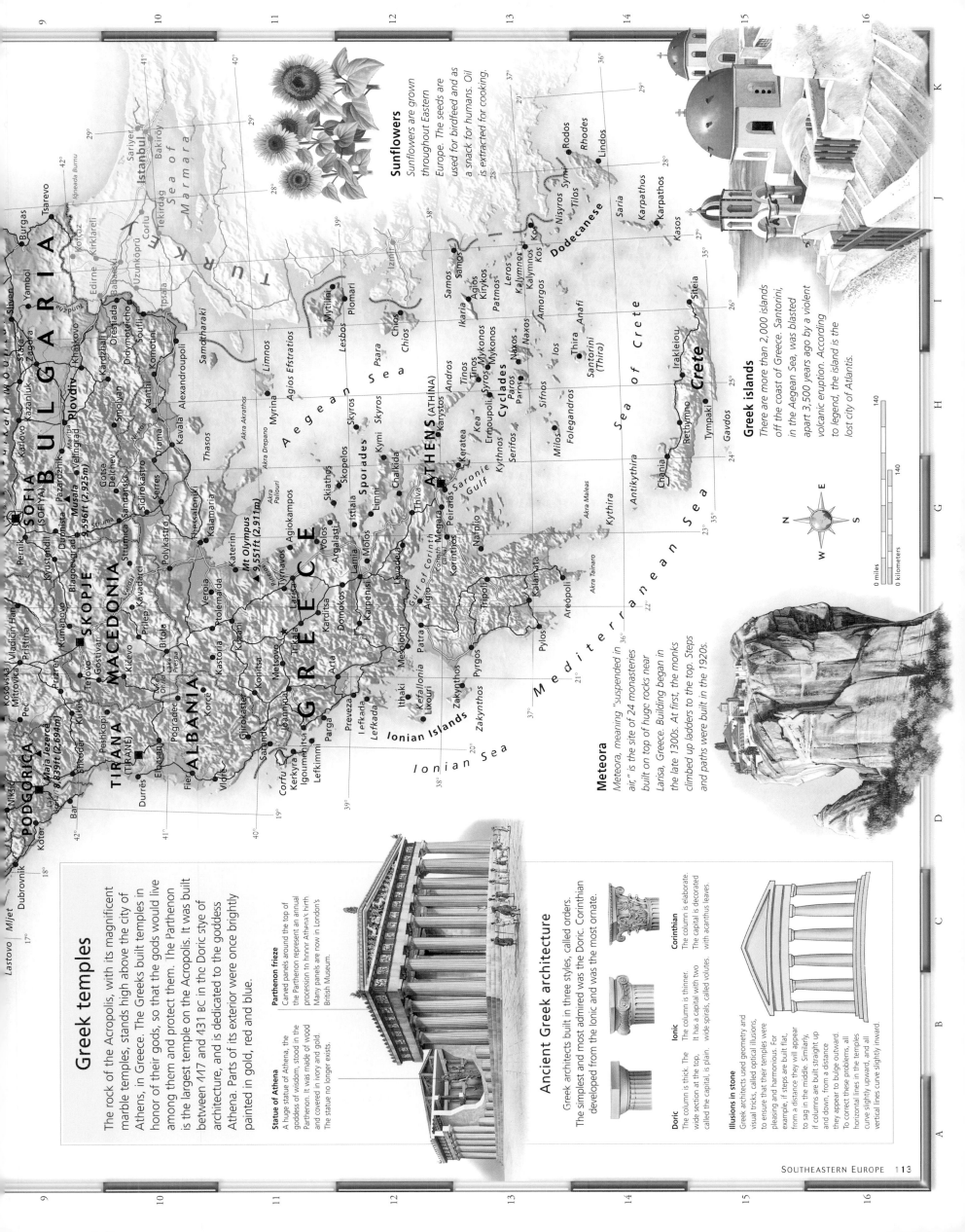

Greek temples

The rock of the Acropolis, with its magnificent marble temples, stands high above the city of Athens, in Greece. The Greeks built temples in honor of their gods, so that the gods would live among them and protect them. The Parthenon is the largest temple on the Acropolis. It was built between 447 and 431 BC in the Doric stye of architecture, and is dedicated to the goddess Athena. Parts of its exterior were once brightly painted in gold, red and blue.

Statue of Athena
A huge statue of Athena, the goddess of wisdom, stood in the Parthenon. It was made of wood and covered in ivory and gold. The statue no longer exists.

Parthenon frieze
Carved panels around the top of the Parthenon represent an annual procession to honor Athena's birth. Many panels are now in London's British Museum.

Ancient Greek architecture

Greek architects built in three styles, called orders. The simplest and most admired was the Doric. The Corinthian developed from the Ionic and was the most ornate.

Doric
The column is thick. The wide section at the top, called the capital, is plain.

Ionic
The column is thinner. It has a capital with two wide spirals, called volutes.

Corinthian
The column is elaborate. The capital is decorated with acanthus leaves.

Illusions in stone
Greek architects used geometry and visual tricks, called optical illusions, to ensure that their temples were pleasing and harmonious. For example, if steps are built flat, from a distance they will appear to sag in the middle. Similarly, if columns are built straight up and down, from a distance they appear to bulge outward. To correct these problems, all horizontal lines in the temples curve slightly upward, and all vertical lines curve slightly inward.

Sunflowers

Sunflowers are grown throughout Eastern Europe. The seeds are used for birdfeed and as a snack for humans. Oil is extracted for cooking.

Meteora

Meteora, meaning "suspended in air," is the site of 24 monasteries built on top of huge rocks near Larisa, Greece. Building began in the late 1300s. At first, the monks climbed up ladders to the top. Steps and paths were built in the 1920s.

Greek islands

There are more than 2,000 islands off the coast of Greece. Santorini, in the Aegean Sea, was blasted apart 3,500 years ago by a violent volcanic eruption. According to legend, the island is the lost city of Atlantis.

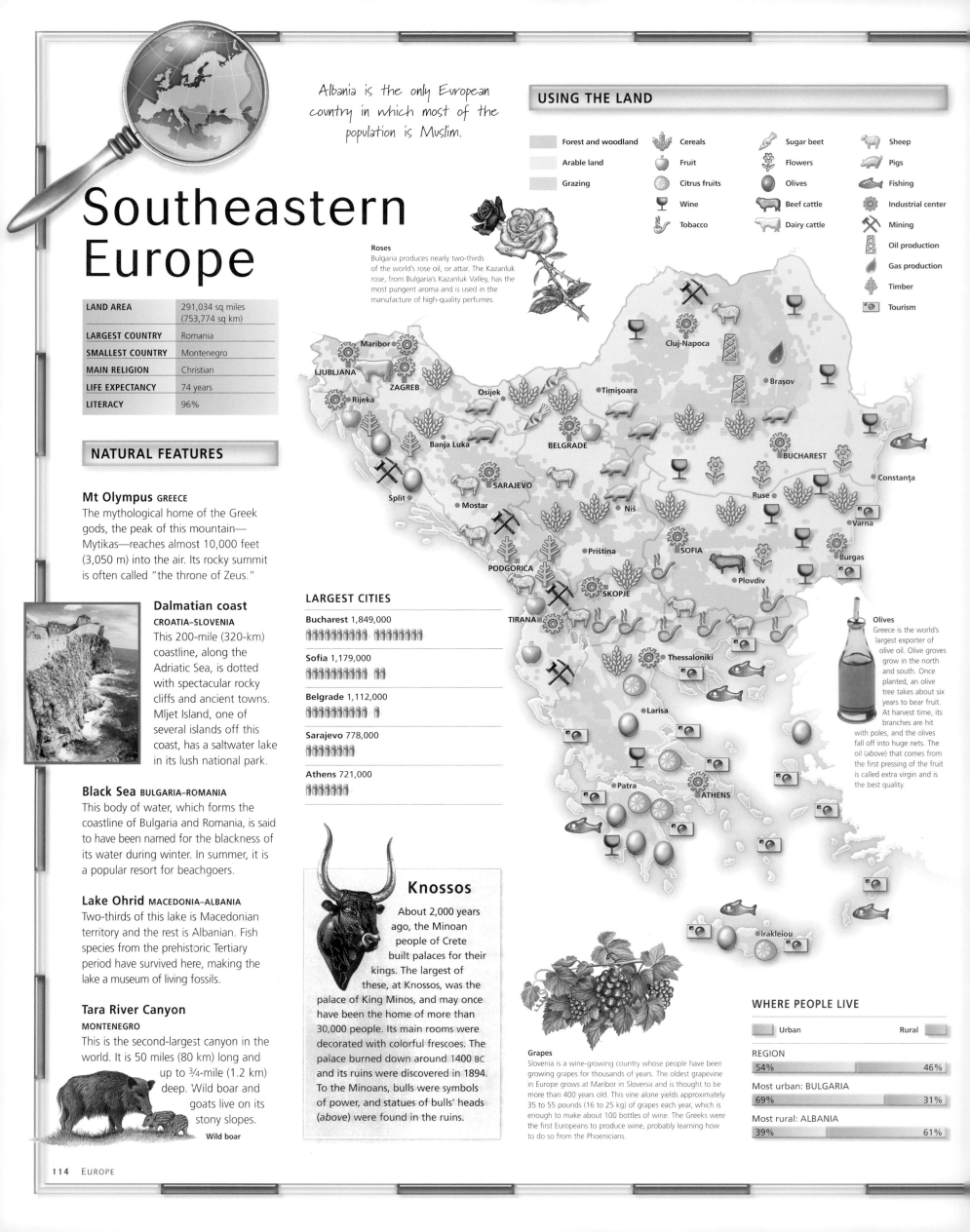

Albania is the only European country in which most of the population is Muslim.

Southeastern Europe

LAND AREA	291,034 sq miles (753,774 sq km)
LARGEST COUNTRY	Romania
SMALLEST COUNTRY	Montenegro
MAIN RELIGION	Christian
LIFE EXPECTANCY	74 years
LITERACY	96%

NATURAL FEATURES

Mt Olympus GREECE
The mythological home of the Greek gods, the peak of this mountain—Mytikas—reaches almost 10,000 feet (3,050 m) into the air. Its rocky summit is often called "the throne of Zeus."

Dalmatian coast
CROATIA–SLOVENIA
This 200-mile (320-km) coastline, along the Adriatic Sea, is dotted with spectacular rocky cliffs and ancient towns. Mljet Island, one of several islands off this coast, has a saltwater lake in its lush national park.

Black Sea BULGARIA–ROMANIA
This body of water, which forms the coastline of Bulgaria and Romania, is said to have been named for the blackness of its water during winter. In summer, it is a popular resort for beachgoers.

Lake Ohrid MACEDONIA–ALBANIA
Two-thirds of this lake is Macedonian territory and the rest is Albanian. Fish species from the prehistoric Tertiary period have survived here, making the lake a museum of living fossils.

Tara River Canyon
MONTENEGRO
This is the second-largest canyon in the world. It is 50 miles (80 km) long and up to ¾-mile (1.2 km) deep. Wild boar and goats live on its stony slopes.

Wild boar

USING THE LAND

Forest and woodland	
Arable land	
Grazing	

- Cereals
- Fruit
- Citrus fruits
- Wine
- Tobacco
- Sugar beet
- Flowers
- Olives
- Beef cattle
- Dairy cattle
- Sheep
- Pigs
- Fishing
- Industrial center
- Mining
- Oil production
- Gas production
- Timber
- Tourism

Roses
Bulgaria produces nearly two-thirds of the world's rose oil, or attar. The Kazanluk rose, from Bulgaria's Kazanluk Valley, has the most pungent aroma and is used in the manufacture of high-quality perfumes.

LARGEST CITIES

Bucharest 1,849,000

Sofia 1,179,000

Belgrade 1,112,000

Sarajevo 778,000

Athens 721,000

Knossos
About 2,000 years ago, the Minoan people of Crete built palaces for their kings. The largest of these, at Knossos, was the palace of King Minos, and may once have been the home of more than 30,000 people. Its main rooms were decorated with colorful frescoes. The palace burned down around 1400 BC and its ruins were discovered in 1894. To the Minoans, bulls were symbols of power, and statues of bulls' heads (above) were found in the ruins.

Grapes
Slovenia is a wine-growing country whose people have been growing grapes for thousands of years. The oldest grapevine in Europe grows at Maribor in Slovenia and is thought to be more than 400 years old. This vine alone yields approximately 35 to 55 pounds (16 to 25 kg) of grapes each year, which is enough to make about 100 bottles of wine. The Greeks were the first Europeans to produce wine, probably learning how to do so from the Phoenicians.

Olives
Greece is the world's largest exporter of olive oil. Olive groves grow in the north and south. Once planted, an olive tree takes about six years to bear fruit. At harvest time, its branches are hit with poles, and the olives fall off into huge nets. The oil (above) that comes from the first pressing of the fruit is called extra virgin and is the best quality.

WHERE PEOPLE LIVE

	Urban	Rural
REGION	54%	46%
Most urban: BULGARIA	69%	31%
Most rural: ALBANIA	39%	61%

TRADITIONS AND CULTURE

Iliad and *Odyssey*

These two epic poems, written by the Greek poet Homer, tell the story of the Trojan War—a battle between Greece and Troy, in Asia Minor. The two poems are the earliest surviving examples of Greek literature.

Greek vase

Roma people

In the villages of Romania, these Gypsies perform their traditional folk music and dancing. Although little of their history is written down, their past is remembered through story-telling, usually in the Gypsy language called Romany.

Wagons at a Roma camp

Festivals

Many festivals are held throughout the year in southeastern Europe. In Bulgaria, at the *Martenitsa*, tiny red and white trims are tied to clothes to celebrate winter's end and the start of summer. For Greek Easter, red eggs are exchanged as gifts.

Macedonian folk music

The folk music of Macedonia has Turkish and Bulgarian influences. It is always linked to dancing. In the villages, the men play traditional instruments such as the *gaida*, or bagpipe, to accompany the folk dances.

Olympic Games

The Olympic Games have taken place since ancient Greek times, when they were held over five days every four years at Olympia, to honor the god Zeus. The best all-round athlete had to succeed in five events—discus and javelin throwing, running, jumping and wrestling. Chariot racing was the most popular event for the spectators.

Discus thrower

PLACES

Dubrovnik CROATIA

This capital city, on the Dalmatian coast, was founded by Roman refugees in the 7th century. In the 1991–92 civil war, much of the city was destroyed by shell fire, but many of its historic buildings have now been restored.

Mostar BOSNIA–HERZOGOVINA

This medieval town is set in the Neretva River's valley. Its name means "bridge," for the 16th-century bridge that was destroyed in the shelling raids of the 1990s. Mostar is now divided into Muslim and Croat areas.

Bucharest ROMANIA

The tree-lined boulevards of this capital city have taken their inspiration from Paris. Monasteries and churches are clustered into the back streets of the city, and on a small island in Snagov Lake, to the city's north, is the supposed tomb of Dracula.

Predjama Castle

Predjama Castle SLOVENIA

Perched on a steep cliff, this stately castle sits at the entrance to a huge cave. Castle treasure, dating back to the 16th century when the legendary knight Erasmus of Predjama lived, has been found during recent restoration of the site.

Rhodes GREECE

The city of Rhodes, founded in 408 BC, is capital of the island of the same name. The city was home to the Colossus of Rhodes, a massive statue and one of the Seven Wonders of the World. The Old Town in the city is the oldest inhabited medieval town in Europe.

Shipka Memorial Church BULGARIA

The five golden domes of this huge church, built in 1902 after the Russo-Turkish war, tower over Shipka village. The church is dedicated to Russian leader Alexander Nevsky. Its crypt is the resting place for soldiers lost in battle.

Shipka Memorial Church

PEOPLE

Archimedes c 290–212 BC

This Greek inventor is famous for his discovery that the force weighing down on a submerged object is equal to the weight of the fluid the object displaces. He was also skilled in astronomy, mathematics and mechanics.

Constantin Brancusi 1876–1957

This Romanian sculptor is known for the dramatic, yet simple, lines and shapes in his work, made from bronze or wood. He designed a memorial (*left*) in Tirgu Jui Memorial Park in Romania, which gives the effect of an endless column.

Josip Tito 1892–1980

Born in Croatia, this revolutionary statesman led the former country of Yugoslavia (now Slovenia) from 1943 to 1980 under communist rule. He disagreed with many of Stalin's severe communist ideas.

Dracula

The legend of Dracula was inspired by the 15th-century Romanian prince Vlad Tepesset, also known as Vlad the Impaler. This brutal ruler led his people in raids against the Turks and punished his captured enemies harshly. He died in battle in 1476.

Dracula's castle

Mother Teresa 1910–97

Born in Macedonia, this nun dedicated her life to helping the sick and poor in Calcutta, India. She first went to India in 1928 and, in 1950, set up the Missionaries of Charity, which now has more than 450 centers around the world.

Mother Teresa

HISTORY AT A GLANCE

ANCIENT GREECE

GREEK MYTHOLOGY

The ancient stories about Greek gods and goddesses, and their adventures with magic and monsters, are among the best known in the world. Zeus was the king of gods and Hercules, the son of Zeus, was the most popular hero. In one of his feats, Hercules strangled the Nemean lion, then wore its skin as a cloak. Many of the gods were depicted in artworks (*above*).

GREEK THINKERS

Some of the greatest philosophers, or thinkers, of all time were from ancient Greece. They tried to work out how people should live and how the world worked. Socrates' ideas were about goodness, known as ethics. Plato, one of Socrates' students, developed a theory of ideals. Aristotle was taught by Plato. Pythagoras' theories have formed the basis for many of today's scientific understandings.

ATHENS

Spreading out from the Acropolis, a rocky hill that created natural protection from enemies, Athens had become the most powerful city-state by 500 BC. Athens is known as the birthplace of democracy, as its free male citizens were able to vote for the city's leaders.

SPARTA

The city-state of Sparta was established in the 10th century BC. Spartan warriors were known to be tough and strong in battle, and they fought to increase their territory. All Spartan men were soldiers, while girls were trained for outdoor life.

Temple of Apollo at Delphi

DELPHI

The ancient Greeks often received advice from oracles, or representatives of the gods. Apollo offered advice from his temple at Delphi by speaking through the most honored oracle, the Pythia. A road led up to Apollo's temple, lined with buildings that were filled with gifts for him.

PERSIAN WARS

The Persians, from the area in western Asia now known as Iran, tried to take over many of the Greek city-states to gain more power. They captured the state of Ionia but were fought off by soldiers of the Greek army, called hoplites, in the Battle of Marathon. The account of the Persian War, where the historian Herodotus interviewed survivors, was the first accurate written record of history.

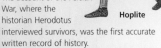

Hoplite

ALEXANDER THE GREAT 356–323 BC

After King Philip II of Macedonia died in 337 BC, his son Alexander reigned. This young leader decided to conquer the Persian territories and beyond, creating the largest empire the world had ever seen. He was clever and courageous and his cavalry of 5,000 horsemen had great respect for him. He died at 32, which fragmented his empire and brought his era to an end.

Tobogganing

A toboggan is a long, flat-bottomed sled made of thin boards curved up at the front. The curved runners of the sled move easily over snow and ice. Tobogganing is a popular sport during the cold winters of Eastern Europe.

Eastern Europe

UKRAINE
POPULATION 46,711,000 * CAPITAL KIEV

POLAND
POPULATION 38,537,000 * CAPITAL WARSAW

BELARUS
POPULATION 10,293,000 * CAPITAL MINSK

CZECH REPUBLIC
POPULATION 10,235,000 * CAPITAL PRAGUE

HUNGARY
POPULATION 9,981,000 * CAPITAL BUDAPEST

SLOVAKIA
POPULATION 5,439,000 * CAPITAL BRATISLAVA

MOLDOVA
POPULATION 4,467,000 * CAPITAL CHISINAU

LITHUANIA
POPULATION 3,586,000 * CAPITAL VILNIUS

LATVIA
POPULATION 2,275,000 * CAPITAL RIGA

ESTONIA
POPULATION 1,324,000 * CAPITAL TALLINN

Gdańsk shipyards

Gdańsk, a port on the Baltic Sea, was once Poland's most prosperous city. In the 1980s, the shipyards were the base of the trade union group called Solidarity, which successfully opposed the communist government.

Astronomical clock

Prague's astronomical clock, on a wall of the city's town hall, was built in 1410. It includes an astrolabe (an early scientific instrument for measuring time), signs of the zodiac, sculptures and moving figures of the 12 apostles.

Budapest parliament

One of the largest parliament buildings in the world overlooks the Danube River in Budapest. It was built between 1884 and 1902, and has 691 rooms and more than 12 miles (19 km) of corridors.

The Estonian islands in the Gulf of Finland are a resting place for hundreds of species of birds migrating from the north to the Baltic Sea.

Wildcat

Tallinn

Tallinn, on the Gulf of Finland, is the capital of Estonia. The city started as a Danish fort in 1219. It became a thriving trade center in the mid-1300s, and merchants from around Europe sold their goods in its busy marketplace. Tallinn's medieval buildings, such as St Olaf's church and the town hall, are among the best preserved in Europe. The city is now a commercial fishing port.

Built to protect

Wealthy cities like Tallinn were often threatened by invaders. Dating from the 16th century, the imposing wall surrounding Tallinn's Old Town protected its citizens from enemies.

St Olaf's church
St Olaf's spire is a Tallinn landmark. The church, built in the 12th century, was the tallest in medieval Europe.

Watchtowers
There are 26 watchtowers. Soldiers armed with crossbows stood guard in them.

The town wall
Tallinn's massive wall was the strongest in Northern Europe.

Latvian folk dancers
Latvia proudly maintains its traditional folk songs and dances. One kind of folk song, called daina, tells stories that date back many hundreds of years.

Harvesting wheat
Wheat is grown throughout Eastern Europe. In some countries, such as Ukraine and Belarus, where there are many small farms, much of the work is done by hand.

Cossack dancer
The Cossacks are a group of people who live north of the Black Sea. They are known for their lively folk dances, which include athletic jumps, kicks and balancing acts.

Eastern Europe

LAND AREA	594,413 sq miles (1,539,522 sq km)
LARGEST COUNTRY	Ukraine
SMALLEST COUNTRY	Moldova
MAIN RELIGION	Christian
LIFE EXPECTANCY	71 years
LITERACY	88%

Sweet peppers
Peppers (left) are the main crop in some regions of Hungary, especially in the fertile district between Szeged and Kalocsa near the Danube River. Hungarians grow red peppers to make a seasoning called paprika, which is used in the dish Hungarian goulash.

WHERE PEOPLE LIVE

Urban	Rural

REGION

65%	35%

Most urban: CZECH REPUBLIC

75%	25%

Most rural: MOLDOVA

46%	54%

Chernobyl

In April 1986, an explosion and fire in the Chernobyl nuclear power plant, Ukraine, released huge amounts of radiation into the air. This poisoned food and water supplies, and caused health problems in Ukraine and surrounding areas. The pink in the image above shows how far the radioactivity had spread around the Northern Hemisphere by the tenth day after the explosion.

USING THE LAND

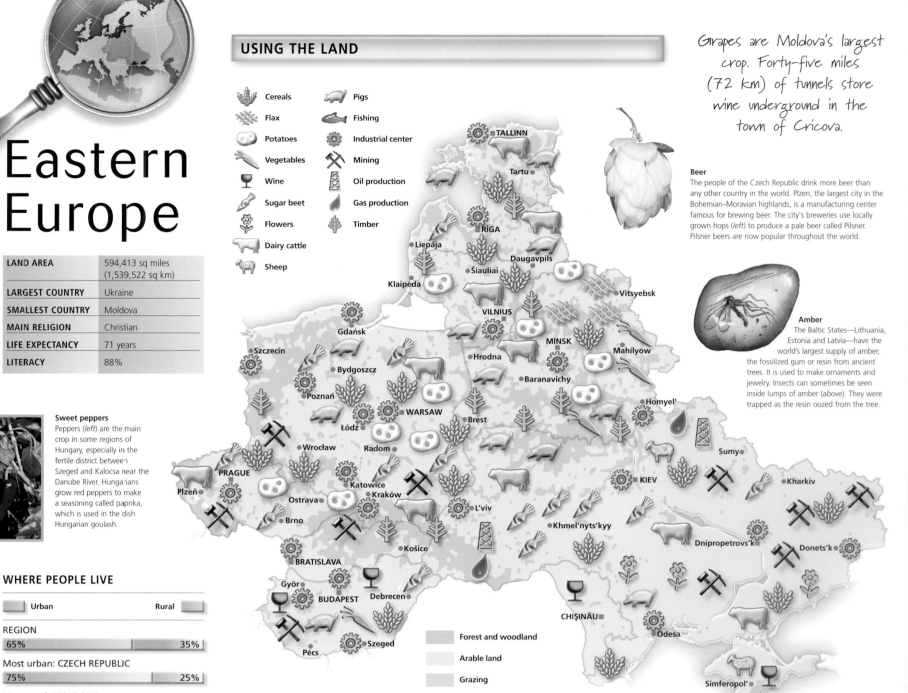

- Cereals
- Flax
- Potatoes
- Vegetables
- Wine
- Sugar beet
- Flowers
- Dairy cattle
- Sheep
- Pigs
- Fishing
- Industrial center
- Mining
- Oil production
- Gas production
- Timber

Forest and woodland
Arable land
Grazing

Map cities: TALLINN, Tartu, RIGA, Liepāja, Daugavpils, Šiauliai, Klaipėda, Vitsyebsk, VILNIUS, Gdańsk, MINSK, Mahilyow, Szczecin, Hrodna, Bydgoszcz, Baranavichy, Poznań, WARSAW, Brest, Homyel', Łódź, Radom, Wrocław, Sumy, Plzeň, PRAGUE, Katowice, KIEV, Kharkiv, Ostrava, Kraków, Brno, L'viv, Khmel'nyts'kyy, Dnipropetrovs'k, Donets'k, Košice, BRATISLAVA, Győr, BUDAPEST, Debrecen, CHIŞINĂU, Odesa, Pécs, Szeged, Simferopol'

Grapes are Moldova's largest crop. Forty-five miles (72 km) of tunnels store wine underground in the town of Cricova.

Beer
The people of the Czech Republic drink more beer than any other country in the world. Plzen, the largest city in the Bohemian–Moravian highlands, is a manufacturing center famous for brewing beer. The city's breweries use locally grown hops (left) to produce a pale beer called Pilsner. Pilsner beers are now popular throughout the world.

Amber
The Baltic States—Lithuania, Estonia and Latvia—have the world's largest supply of amber, the fossilized gum or resin from ancient trees. It is used to make ornaments and jewelry. Insects can sometimes be seen inside lumps of amber (above). They were trapped as the resin oozed from the tree.

NATURAL FEATURES

Courland Lagoon LITHUANIA
Courland Lagoon, or Kursky Zaliv, is 56 miles (90 km) long and 28 miles (45 km) wide. It is separated from the Baltic Sea by the Courland Spit, a strip of sand dunes that is classified as a UNESCO World Heritage Site.

Bialowieza Forest POLAND–BELARUS
This nature reserve along the borders of Poland and Belarus is administered by both nations. The forest is home to many animals, such as lynx, boar, tarpan horses and a large herd of rare European bison called wisent (below).

Tatra mountains POLAND–SLOVAKIA
The Tatras, the highest of the central Carpathian Mountains, mark part of the border between Poland and Slovakia. Forests of spruce and firs thrive in the alpine climate. The chamois (left) lives in the high mountains, and is hunted for its skin, which is made into soft leather.

Chamois

Danube River
The second-longest river in Europe, the Danube flows through nine countries from southern Germany through eastern Europe to the Black Sea. It is a transport route for agricultural and industrial freight. Chemical pollution in the Danube has affected its wildlife and the water supply of farmlands on its banks.

LONGEST RIVERS

Danube 1,770 miles (2,850 km)

Dnieper 1,420 miles (2,285 km)

Vistula 651 miles (1,047 km)

Western Dvina 632 miles (1,020 km)

LARGEST CITIES

Kiev 2,470,000

Minsk 1,753,000

Budapest 1,692,000

Warsaw 1,619,000

Kharkiv 1,412,000

PLACES

Warsaw POLAND
Located on the Vistula River in the center of Poland, Warsaw is Poland's capital and its largest city. The Old Town, built in the 13th century, is a mix of architectural styles and cobbled streets. Much of the city had to be rebuilt after World War II.

Bratislava SLOVAKIA
Bratislava, Slovakia's capital, is dominated by its huge castle that stands 300 feet (90 m) above the Danube. This was once the home of the Austrian royal family. Modern Bratislava is a center for learning, a transport hub and river port.

St Stephen's crown
When Stephen was crowned king of Hungary in AD 1000, he received a jeweled crown from Pope Sylvester II. That crown forms part of what is now called the Hungarian Holy Crown, held as a national treasure and relic. Stephen was made the patron saint of Hungary, and his crown is a symbol of Hungarian nationhood.

St Sophia's Cathedral UKRAINE
Completed in 1037, this is the oldest church in Kiev, the capital of Ukraine. It had fallen into ruin by the 13th century and was rebuilt between 1685 and 1707.

Budapest HUNGARY
The capital of Hungary, this city is divided by the Danube, with Buda on the east and Pest on the west. Buda is the city's historical heart and Pest is its economic, commercial and political center.

Vilnius LITHUANIA
The capital of Lithuania, the first Soviet Republic to gain independence in 1990, this city stands a few miles from the geographical center of Europe.

Prague CZECH REPUBLIC
One of the oldest cities in Europe, Prague is situated on the Vltava River. It is the capital city, business hub and cultural center of the Czech Republic, and is known for its historic buildings.

Prague

Copernicus
Nicolaus Copernicus was born in Poland in 1473. An astronomer, physician and economist, he proposed the idea that Earth and other planets in the solar system revolved around the Sun. Until then, people believed that Earth was the center of the universe and everything revolved around it. He died in 1543, just after his theory was published.

Copernican solar system

PEOPLE

Attila the Hun c AD 406–53
In 434, Attila became king of the Huns. He united them and ruled their kingdom in present-day Hungary. He conquered lands from the Baltic to the Caspian Sea but failed to keep them under his control.

Frédéric Chopin 1810–49
Polish-born Frédéric Chopin gave his first public piano concert at the age of eight, and by 15 was composing music. He composed more than 200 pieces of music for the solo piano.

Rain by Marc Chagall

Marc Chagall 1887–1985
Born in present-day Belarus, Chagall moved to Paris in 1910. He is known for his unusual, dreamlike paintings, in which his figures sometimes float upside down. He was also a printmaker and stage designer.

Pope John Paul II born 1920
In 1978, Polish-born Karol Wojtyla became the first non-Italian pope since 1522 and took the name Pope John Paul II. He has visited more countries than any other pope in history.

Martina Navratilova born 1956
Born in Prague, Navratilova became a US citizen in 1981. She is one of the world's top women's tennis players, and has won a record 167 singles championships.

1918–20
Poland fights Russia, winning the Battle of Warsaw and gaining independence in 1920. Hungary, Estonia, Belarus, Latvia, Ukraine, Lithuania and Czechoslovakia also gain their independence in this period.

1938–39
Nazi Germany annexes first Sudetenland, the German-speaking part of Czechoslovakia, then the rest of Czechoslovakia. It then invades Poland, which leads the UK to declare war on Germany.

Polish cavalry (1939)

1939–45
The Soviet Union and Germany either invade or annex Estonia, Belarus, Latvia, Lithuania, Ukraine, Moldova (then part of Bessarabia) and Czechoslovakia. World War II breaks out.

1945–46
The victory of the Allies leads to the Soviet Union annexing western Ukraine, Estonia, part of Poland, western Belarus and part of Bessarabia (now Moldova). Poland regains some territory from Germany and Warsaw begins to rebuild.

1956
Hungary revolts against the Soviet Union. The revolt is put down by Soviet troops, who execute many of the revolution's leaders. The Soviets form a new government with János Kádár as prime minister.

Demonstration in Prague

1989
Protests, now known as the "velvet revolution," are held in Czechoslovakia to end communist rule. After nearly a decade of struggle, the Polish Solidarity campaign for independence is successful, and the first free elections are held. The border with Austria reopens.

1991
Moldova, Estonia, Lithuania, Latvia, Ukraine and Belarus gain their independence. Soviet forces withdraw from Czechoslovakia, and the country prepares to divide politically.

1993
Czechoslovakia forms two independent countries—the Czech Republic and Slovakia. Michal Kovac is elected president of Slovakia, and Vaclav Havel becomes president of the Czech Republic.

1999
Vaira Vike-Freiberga is elected president of Latvia, and becomes Eastern Europe's first female president. Hungary, the Czech Republic and Poland join as members of NATO.

Vaira Vike-Freiberga

2002
The European Union invites Hungary, Poland, Latvia, Lithuania, Estonia, Slovakia and the Czech Republic to join in 2004. Lithuania agrees to close Ignalina nuclear power station.

TRADITIONS AND CULTURE

Midsummer's Eve LATVIA
This important festival in Latvia, also called St John's Eve, celebrates the middle of summer on 23–24 June. People light bonfires, sing and dance. They feast on special foods, such as caraway cheese and barley beer.

Puppetry CZECH REPUBLIC
A Czech tradition since medieval times, puppetry entertained and educated children. Czech puppeteers also used puppets to comment on the social and political concerns of the people. Puppetry remains very popular today.

Bohemian crystal CZECH REPUBLIC
Since the 15th century, the region of Bohemia in the western Czech Republic has manufactured Bohemian crystal. This is some of the world's finest and most expensive glassware.

Painted eggs UKRAINE
Exchanging hand-painted, decorated eggs as gifts has been an Easter tradition in Ukraine for centuries. Painting the eggs coincides with the arrival of spring. They are a symbol of rebirth, or the creation of new life.

Cowboys HUNGARY
Hungarian cowboys, or *csikósok*, manage herds of horses and cattle on the plains and grasslands of Hungary. They are admired for their skills on horseback.

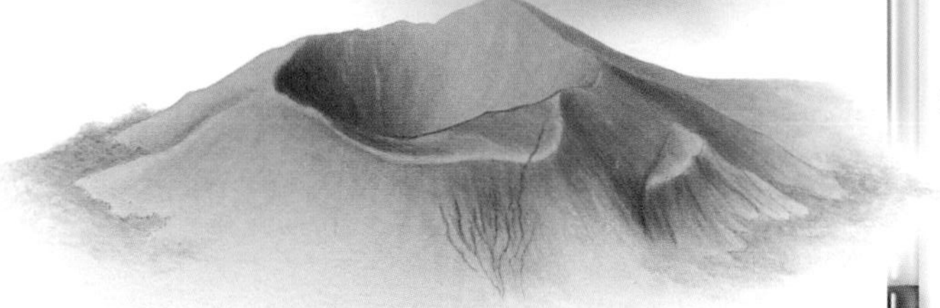

Northern Europe

Iceland is known as the land of ice and fire. In just over 1,000 years, it has had more than 30 volcanic eruptions. One-third of all the lava that has erupted on land since 1500 has come from Iceland.

SWEDEN POPULATION 9,017,000 ∗ CAPITAL STOCKHOLM

DENMARK POPULATION 5,451,000 ∗ CAPITAL COPENHAGEN

FINLAND POPULATION 5,231,000 ∗ CAPITAL HELSINKI

NORWAY POPULATION 4,611,000 ∗ CAPITAL OSLO

ICELAND POPULATION 299,000 ∗ CAPITAL REYKJAVÍK

Reindeer

Reindeer, or caribou, travel great distances in search of food. They use their long antlers to scrape away snow to expose the grasses on which they feed. Reindeer have four toes on each foot, which they spread out to keep their balance on soft snow.

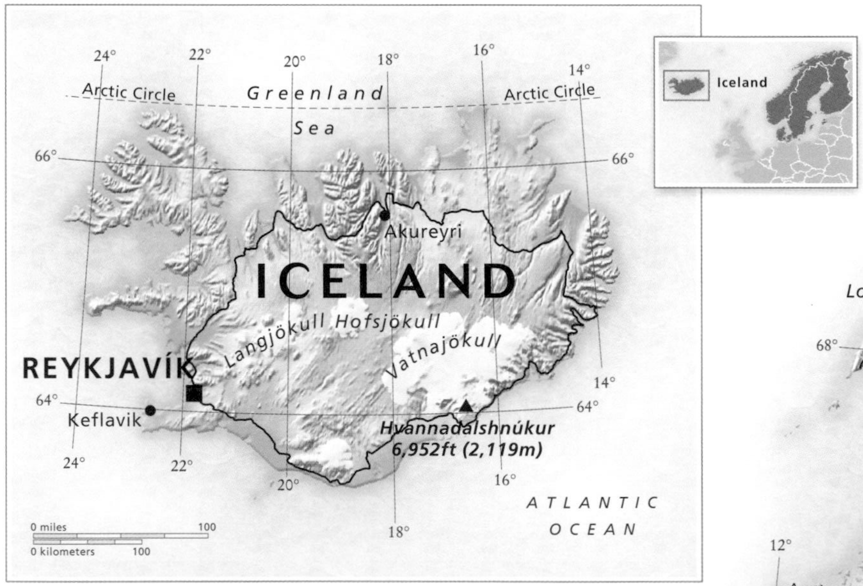

Puffin

Skiing

People have used skis as a form of winter transport for thousands of years. Today, they mostly use them for sport. Ski sports include ski-jumping, slalom and downhill racing.

Breaking the ice

An icebreaker has a special steel hull to help it rise up on thick polar ice and then crush down through it. Powerful engines propel the ship up and forward.

Iceland (inset map)

ATLANTIC OCEAN

Arctic Circle

Greenland Sea

ICELAND

Akureyri

Langjökull Hofsjökull Vatnajökull

Hvannadalshnúkur 6,952ft (2,119m)

REYKJAVÍK

Keflavík

0 miles 100
0 kilometers 100

Main map labels

Barents Sea

RUSSIA

FINLAND

ARCTIC OCEAN

Arctic Circle

Varanger Fjord
Kirkenes
Tana Bru
Lakse Fjord
Lakselv
Porsangen
North Cape
Magerøya
Alta
Karasjok
Karigasniemi
Kaamanen
Ivalo
Inari
Kemijärvi
Rovaniemi
Kemi
Kuusamo
Suomussalmi
Kajaani
Kuhmo
Oulujoki
Oulu
Raahe
Hailuoto
Luleå
Tornio
Kittilä
Sodankylä
Muonio
Kolari
Karesuando
Konkämäeno
Jukkasjärvi
Kiruna
Kebnekaise 6,926ft (2,111m)
Gällivare
Jokkmokk
Boden
Piteå
Skellefteå
Luleälven
Arvidsjaur
Lycksele
Vilhelmina
Storuman
Dorotea
Sørøya
Arnøya
Ringvassøy
Kvaløya
Senja
Tromsø
Harstad
Narvik
Vesterålen
Lofoten
Vestfjord
Fauske
Bodø
Mo i Rana
Mosjøen
Vega
Sømna
Namsos
Vikna
Namdalen
Trøndelag

Greenland Sea

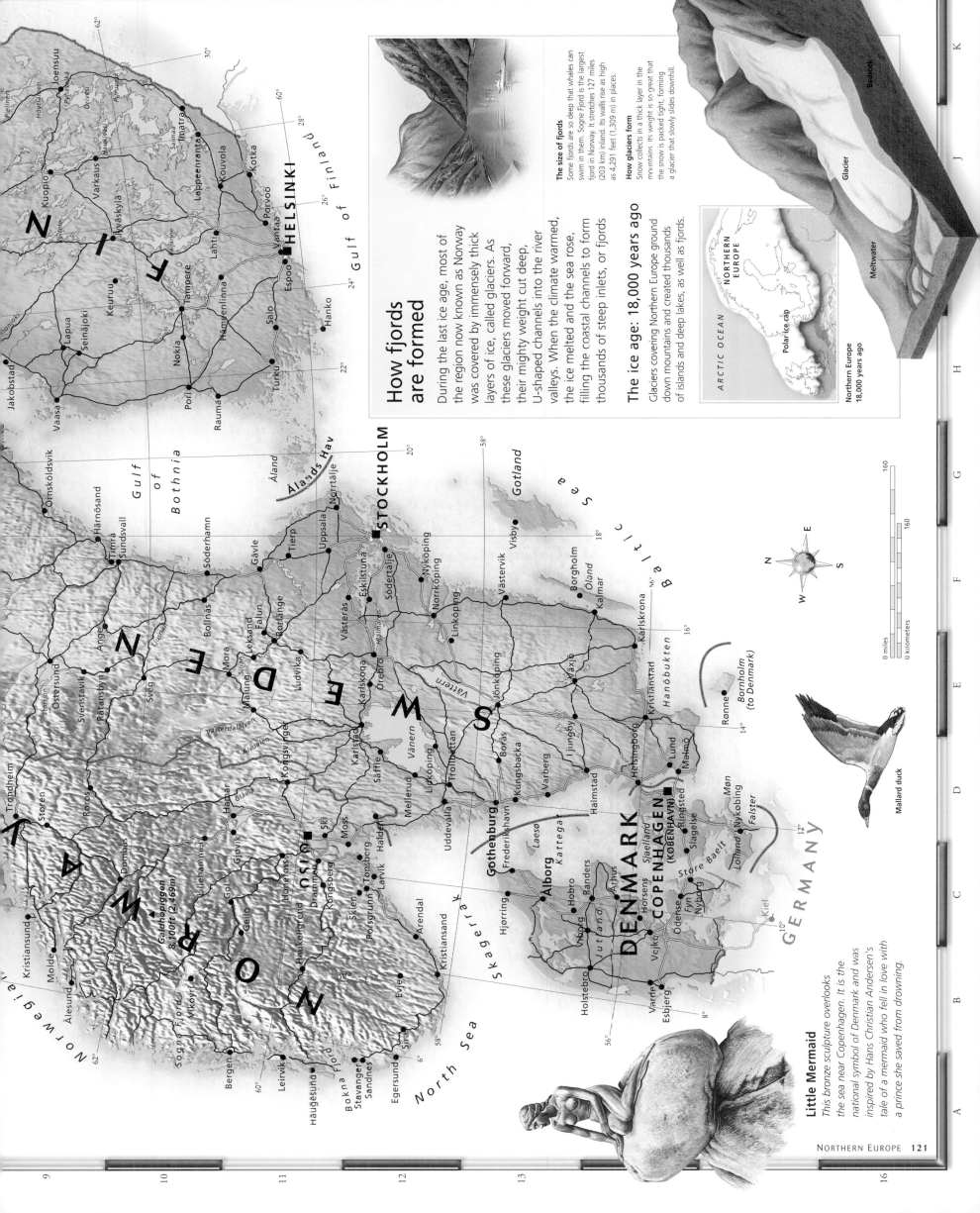

How fjords are formed

During the last ice age, most of the region now known as Norway was covered by immensely thick layers of ice, called glaciers. As these glaciers moved forward, their mighty weight cut deep, U-shaped channels into the river valleys. When the climate warmed, the ice melted and the sea rose, filling the coastal channels to form thousands of steep inlets, or fjords.

The ice age: 18,000 years ago

Glaciers covering Northern Europe ground down mountains and created thousands of islands and deep lakes, as well as fjords.

The size of fjords
Some fjords are so deep that whales can swim in them. Sogne Fjord is the largest fjord in Norway. It stretches 127 miles (203 km) inland. Its walls rise as high as 4,291 feet (1,309 m) in places.

How glaciers form
Snow collects in a thick layer in the mountains. Its weight is so great that the snow is packed tight, forming a glacier that slowly slides downhill.

Bedrock

Glacier

Meltwater

ARCTIC OCEAN

NORTHERN EUROPE

Polar ice cap

Northern Europe
18,000 years ago

Little Mermaid

This bronze sculpture overlooks the sea near Copenhagen. It is the national symbol of Denmark and was inspired by Hans Christian Andersen's tale of a mermaid who fell in love with a prince she saved from drowning.

Mallard duck

N E S W

0 miles   160
0 kilometers   160

FINLAND

Joensuu
Pyhäselkä
Pielinen
Höytiäinen
Orivesi
Kuopio
Varkaus
Pyhäjärvi
Savonlinna
Iisalmi
Saimaa
Jyväskylä
Imatra
Lappeenranta
Kouvola
Kotka
Keuruu
Äänekoski
Lahti
HELSINKI
Tampere
Hämeenlinna
Porvoo
Vantaa
Espoo
Nokia
Salo
Hanko
Turku
Rauma
Pori
Seinäjoki
Lapua
Vaasa
Jakobstad

Gulf of Finland

SWEDEN

Örnsköldsvik
Härnösand
Timrå
Sundsvall
Ångermanälven
Östersund
Storsjön
Svenstavik
Rätansbyn
Sveg
Ljusnan
Bollnäs
Ånge
Mora
Malung
Siljan
Leksand
Falun
Borlänge
Ludvika
Kongsvinger
Gävle
Tierp
Uppsala
Norrtälje
Åland
Ålands Hav
STOCKHOLM
Eskilstuna
Södertälje
Västerås
Hjälmaren
Örebro
Karlskoga
Karlstad
Säffle
Mellerud
Lidköping
Trollhättan
Vänern
Nyköping
Norrköping
Linköping
Vättern
Jönköping
Västervik
Visby
Gotland
Borås
Kungsbacka
Varberg
Ljungby
Växjö
Halmstad
Helsingborg
Lund
Malmö
Kristianstad
Hanöbukten
Karlskrona
Borgholm
Öland
Kalmar
Bornholm
(to Denmark)
Ronne

Gulf of Bothnia

Baltic Sea

NORWAY

Trondheim
Støren
Røros
Storen
Molde
Ålesund
Kristiansund
Dombås
Vinstra
Gol
Hamar
Lillehammer
Gjøvik
Galdhøpiggen
8,100ft (2,469m)
Bergen
Leirvik
Haugesund
Stavanger
Sandnes
Sira
Bokna Fjord
Sogna Fjord
Vikøyri
Haukeligrend
Hønefoss
Drammen
OSLO
Kongsberg
Ski
Moss
Halden
Larvik
Tønsberg
Skien
Porsgrunn
Notodden
Kongsberg
Arendal
Kristiansand
Evje

North Sea

Skagerrak

Norwegian Sea

DENMARK

Hjørring
Hobro
Randers
Ålborg
Viborg
Holstebro
Vejle
Horsens
Århus
Vardø
Esbjerg
Odense
Fyn
Nyborg
Slagelse
Ringsted
Sjælland
COPENHAGEN
(KØBENHAVN)
Nykøbing
Møn
Falster
Lolland
Store Baelt
Kattegat
Læsø
Frederikshavn
Jutland
Kiel

GERMANY

Northern Europe

- Forest and woodland
- Arable land
- Grazing
- Arid or marginal

REYKJAVÍK

SWEDEN LAND AREA	173,732 sq miles (449,964 sq km)
OFFICIAL LANGUAGE	Swedish
MAIN RELIGION	Christian
LIFE EXPECTANCY	80 years
LITERACY	99%

DENMARK LAND AREA	16,639 sq miles (43,094 sq km)
OFFICIAL LANGUAGE	Danish
MAIN RELIGION	Christian
LIFE EXPECTANCY	77 years
LITERACY	99%

FINLAND LAND AREA	130,128 sq miles (337,030 sq km)
OFFICIAL LANGUAGE	Finnish
MAIN RELIGION	Christian
LIFE EXPECTANCY	78 years
LITERACY	99%

NORWAY LAND AREA	125,182 sq miles (324,220 sq km)
OFFICIAL LANGUAGE	Norwegian
MAIN RELIGION	Christian
LIFE EXPECTANCY	79 years
LITERACY	99%

Reykjavik in Iceland is the world's northernmost capital. At midnight, you can see the Sun go down.

Fishing
The waters of Northern Europe are full of both freshwater and saltwater fishes. Salmon, trout and perch are found in the inland rivers and lakes, while mackerel, cod and herring live in coastal waters. Norway is one of the world's leading fishing countries, and has fish farms for salmon and trout in the fjord areas.

Oulu

Trondheim

Umea

Bergen

OSLO

STOCKHOLM

Gothenburg

Turku · HELSINKI

Århus

COPENHAGEN

Timber
Much of Northern Europe is forested with coniferous, or cone-bearing, trees, including spruce and pine. Deciduous trees, such as birch, are grown in the southern regions. The timber from these forests is produced largely for export.

NATURAL FEATURES

Lake Vänern SWEDEN
This inland lake, the largest in Sweden and dating back to 6500 BC, is situated near the Göta Canal, an inland waterway connecting Stockholm and Gothenberg.

Aurora borealis
Auroras are streaks or curtains of colored light, caused when electrically charged particles from the Sun collide with Earth's atmosphere. The aurora borealis, or northern lights, is especially bright near the Arctic Circle. It can be seen many times a year in Northern Europe.

Arctic fox

Lappland
Pine and spruce trees cover most of this region, which takes in parts of Sweden, Norway, Russia and Finland. Lappland falls within the Arctic Circle and is home to animals such as the Arctic fox, whose coat changes color with the seasons.

Åland Islands FINLAND
Thousands of islands lie in Finland's Coastal Islands region—one of its four geographic areas. Although most of them are uninhabited, about 80 of the 6,500 islands in the Åland group, off the southwest coast, are home to Swedish-speaking Finns. In this group, the island of Åland is the largest.

- Cereals
- Sugar beet
- Beef cattle
- Sheep
- Pigs
- Reindeer
- Fishing
- Industrial center
- Mining
- Oil production
- Gas production
- Timber

WHERE PEOPLE LIVE

Urban		Rural

DENMARK
85% | 15%

SWEDEN
83% | 17%

NORWAY
75% | 25%

FINLAND
67% | 33%

LARGEST CITIES

Stockholm 1,269,000

Copenhagen 1,094,000

Oslo 880,000

Helsinki 559,000

Gothenburg 522,000

Tollund Man

In 1950, two brothers from the small village of Tollund on Denmark's Jutland Peninsula, while digging up peat, discovered a well-preserved body from about 2,000 years ago. The peat covering Tollund Man was removed, revealing that he wore a pointed hat, tied under his chin.

Sami people

These traditional people live mainly in Lappland, which stretches across northern Norway, Sweden and Finland into the western part of Russia. They are the only people in Northern Europe allowed to herd reindeer, and many are now involved in fishing and handicrafts.

PEOPLE

Saint Bridget c 1303–73

The patron saint of Sweden, Saint Bridget is the most celebrated saint of Northern Europe. She founded the Brigittine order of nuns and monks, and helped sick and poor people.

Hans Christian Andersen 1805–75

The stories of this Danish fairy-tale writer often had characters who went through hard times in their search for happiness. One of Andersen's most famous tales is *The Ugly Duckling*.

Edvard Munch
1863–1944

This Norwegian artist created paintings, such as *The Scream* (*right*), which usually showed extremes of emotion. He moved to Paris in 1889 and learned from great French artists such as Paul Gauguin.

Roald Amundsen 1872–1928

In 1911, this Norwegian explorer, in an expedition with four others, was the first person to reach the South Pole. He was also the first to fly over the North Pole.

ABBA

ABBA 1973–83

In 1974, this Swedish pop music band won the Eurovision Song Contest. For the next six years, they topped music charts the world over with one hit after another.

TRADITIONS AND CULTURE

Nobel Prize

Annual prizes in literature, science and peace are awarded by the Nobel Foundation, which was established in 1900 using funds from Alfred Nobel, the Swedish inventor of dynamite.

Saunas

Many Swedish and Finnish people have saunas about once a week. They lie or sit on wooden slats in a hot, enclosed room, then plunge into cold water.

Runes

These are the characters, made up of sticks, in the Viking alphabet. Stones were carved with runic letters and stories in memory of events.

Trolls

These odd creatures are part of Norway's rich folklore. In early tales, trolls were very large creatures who turned to stone if they went out in the sun. The nokken is a water spirit troll and the hulder troll is female.

The *Kalevala*

Elias Lönnrot compiled this Finnish national epic from ancient spoken poetry he collected in Finland and Karelia. It was published in 1835.

Legoland, built with more than 45 million Lego bricks, is Denmark's most visited attraction.

PLACES

Reykjavík ICELAND

This lively capital city, founded in AD 874, was a small fishing village until the 20th century. It was a naval base in World War II. Today it is a fishing port and home to half of Iceland's industries.

Copenhagen DENMARK

Mostly situated on the east coast of Zealand, this thriving city is Denmark's center for industry, education and culture.

Helsinki FINLAND

Much of this city was rebuilt after fire destroyed it in the 19th century. The Helsinki Cathedral, a grand, domed building, was one of the main projects.

Bergen waterfront

Bergen NORWAY

As Norway's second-largest city and one of the country's chief ports, Bergen is a center for manufacture and trade. The waterfront is lined with wharves from the 13th century.

Stockholm SWEDEN

This picturesque city, Sweden's capital, is a blend of old and new. Its Old Town reflects the Middle Ages, sitting alongside modern life in the rest of the city.

Kronborg Castle DENMARK

This noble castle in Elsinore provided the setting for Hamlet's home in Shakespeare's play. It's one of Northern Europe's most renowned buildings.

Stavkirks

These wooden places of worship, known as stave churches, were built in Norway about 1,000 years ago after the Vikings converted to Christianity. They have high-pitched roofs and are decorated with a mix of Viking and Christian symbols. Dragons (a Viking symbol) often appear at the ends of the gables and crosses (a Christian symbol) are placed at the doors and windows.

Stavkirk in Vikøyri, built in 1130

HISTORY AT A GLANCE
THE VIKINGS

Viking pendants, worn in battle

NORSE MYTHS

Many myths and legends evolved during Viking times. The Vikings believed in gods and goddesses who lived in a place called Asgard. Each god had its own characteristics—Thor was the god of thunder and was very strong; Odin was the god of wisdom and war, and had magic powers; and Frey, a fertility god, had a boat in which all the gods could travel.

VIKING RAIDS

Between the 8th and 11th centuries, fierce Vikings from Norway, Sweden and Denmark, in search of more territory, metals and slaves, raided the far-flung lands of Europe and even North America. They were clever traders and craftsmen who told wonderful stories.

LONGSHIPS

The Vikings were skilled navigators who traveled in longships. The wooden hull was built from 16 overlapping planks. A carved figure, often a dragon, sat at the prow, or front, of the ship.

Viking longship

WEAPONS

A Viking warrior valued his weapons greatly. With his ax, shield and spear at his side, he was armed for any battle. Shields were usually wooden with an iron center to protect the warrior's hand, and the ax, made from iron, had engraved silver patterns on it.

HOUSES

Timber, straw or stone was used to make long, narrow houses, called longhouses. Early in the Viking age, houses did not have windows and were dark but, later, animal bladders were stretched across openings in the wall to let in some light. A hearth was always in the center.

BURIALS

Viking graves were often marked out in the shape of boats. Before Christianity, possessions were buried with the body for use in the next life. According to legend, dead warriors were taken by women to Valhalla—the Viking heaven.

Leif Eriksson sighting America

EXPLORERS

The Vikings were great adventurers, keen to explore lands near and far. In AD 982, Erik the Red discovered Greenland after he left Iceland in search of a new land. Leif Eriksson, one of Eric's sons, is thought to have been the first Viking to land in North America. Harald Haardraade, a member of the Byzantine fighting Vikings called the Varangian Guard, was the last Viking to land in England. The last of the warrior Viking kings, he was killed in battle in 1066.

OCEAN

Severnaya Zemlya

Laptev Sea

New Siberia Islands

East Siberian Sea

Bering Strait

Gulf of Anadyr

Central Siberian Plateau

Siberia

Lena

Kirenga

Varkhoyanskiy Khrebet

Khrebet Cherskogo

Kamchatka Peninsula

Stanovoy Khrebet

Sea of Okhotsk

Lake Baikal

Heilong Jiang (Amur)

Sakhalin

Kuril Islands

Argun

Manchurian Plain

Sikhote-Alin

Mongolian Plateau

Sea of Japan

Hokkaidō

Gobi Desert

Yellow

Bo Hai

Korea Bay

Korean Peninsula

Honshū

Yellow Sea

Great Plain of China

Yangtze

Korea Strait

Shikoku

Sichuan Basin

Yangtze

East China Sea

Kyūshū

Ryukyu Islands

Taiwan Strait

Taiwan

Hainan

Luzon

Philippine Sea

PACIFIC OCEAN

Khorat Plateau

Mekong

Mindoro

Philippines

Samar

Indochina Peninsula

Palawan

Panay

Negros

Cebu

South China Sea

Sulu Sea

Mindanao

Gulf of Thailand

Malay Peninsula

Celebes Sea

Strait of Malacca

Greater Sunda Islands

Sumatra

Borneo

Moluccas

New Guinea

Malay Archipelago

Sulawesi

Banda Sea

Java Sea

Flores Sea

Arafura Sea

Java

Lesser Sunda Islands

Timor

Timor Sea

Asia

Russia

Sputnik

🏳 **RUSSIA**
POPULATION 142,894,000 ✳ CAPITAL **MOSCOW**

Nenets' camp
The Nenets live in the far northwest region of Russia. They are hunters and reindeer herders. Each season, when the reindeer migrate, the Nenets set up tents and cover them with animal skins for warmth.

St Basil's Cathedral
This ornate cathedral in Moscow was built by Czar Ivan the Terrible. Work began in 1554. When first built, the cathedral was painted white. The eight colorful domes are shaped rather like onions to shed heavy snow and rain.

Wolf

Russia is the largest country in the world. It covers two-thirds of Asia and one-third of Europe, and has 11 time zones. Russia was once part of a much larger country called the Soviet Union.

Sturgeon
Up to 90 percent of the world's sturgeon comes from the Caspian Sea. The giant sturgeon grows to 19 feet (6 m) long and can live for 150 years. Sturgeon roe, or eggs, is called caviar. It is an expensive delicacy.

Siberian timber house
The homes of wealthy Siberians in the early 1800s were built of timber. Some of the finest are in Irkutsk, near Lake Baikal. They have shuttered windows and ornate decoration.

Map labels

Franz Josef Land
Barents Sea
Novaya Zemlya
Kara Sea
Ostrov Kolguyev
Ostrov Belyy
Ostrov Vaygach
Yamal Peninsula
Gydanskiy Peninsula
Arctic Erde
North Cape
FINLAND
White Sea
Pechorskoye More
Baydaratskaya Guba
Obsakaya Guba
ESTONIA
LATVIA
Murmansk
Kandalaksha
Kola Peninsula
Severodvinsk
Arkhangel'sk
Vorkuta
Noril'sk
Gulf of Finland
St Petersburg
Lake Ladoga
Lake Onega
Petrozavodsk
Pskov
Velikiye Novgorod
Velikiye Luki
Smolensk
Tver'
Cherepovets
Vologda
Rybinsk
Yaroslavl'
Ukhta
Syktyvkar
BELARUS
UKRAINE
Bryansk
Kaluga
Kolomna
Vladimir
MOSCOW (MOSKVA)
Orel
Tula
Novomoskovsk
Kursk
Ryazan'
Nizhniy Novgorod
Kirov
Belgorod
Lipetsk
Arzamas
Yoshkar-Ola
Solikamsk
Staryy Oskol
Voronezh
Michurinsk
Tambov
Cheboksary
Glazov
Kazan'
Berezniki
Penza
Saransk
Izhevsk
Perm'
Serov
West Siberian Plain
Surgut
Nizhnevartovsk
Donets'k
Kuznetsk
Ul'yanovsk
Sarapul
Nizhniy Tagil
Sea of Azov
Kerch
Saratov
Naberezhnyye Chelny
Neftekamsk
Pervoural'sk
Yekaterinburg
Rostov-na-Donu
Shakhty
Engel's
Syzran' Chelny
Oktyabr'skiy
Kamensk-Ural'skiy
Novorossiysk
Balakovo
Tol'yatti
Samara
Ufa
Tobol'sk
Krasnodar
Volgograd
Sterlitamak
Zlatoust
Tyumen'
Maykop
Armavir
Elista
Ural'sk
Orenburg
Miass
Chelyabinsk
Sochi
Nevinnomyssk
Stavropol
Magnitogorsk
Kurgan
Cherkessk
Elbrus 18,510ft (5,642m)
Pyatigorsk
Nal'chik
Caspian Depression
Orsk
Petropavlovsk
Omsk
Black Sea
GEORGIA
Groznyy
Astrakhan'
Atyrau
KAZAKHSTAN
Tomsk
Achinsk
T'BILISI
Caspian Sea
Makhachkala
Novosibirsk
Kemerovo
Krasnoyarsk
AZERBAIJAN
Caucasus
Barnaul
Kiselevsk
Novokuznetsk
Abakan
BAKU (BAKI)
Semipalatinsk
Rubtsovsk
Biysk
Zapadnyy
Gora Belukha 14,783ft (4,506m)
Kyzyl
Yenisey
Irtysh
Ob
Volga
Ural Mountains
R U S ...

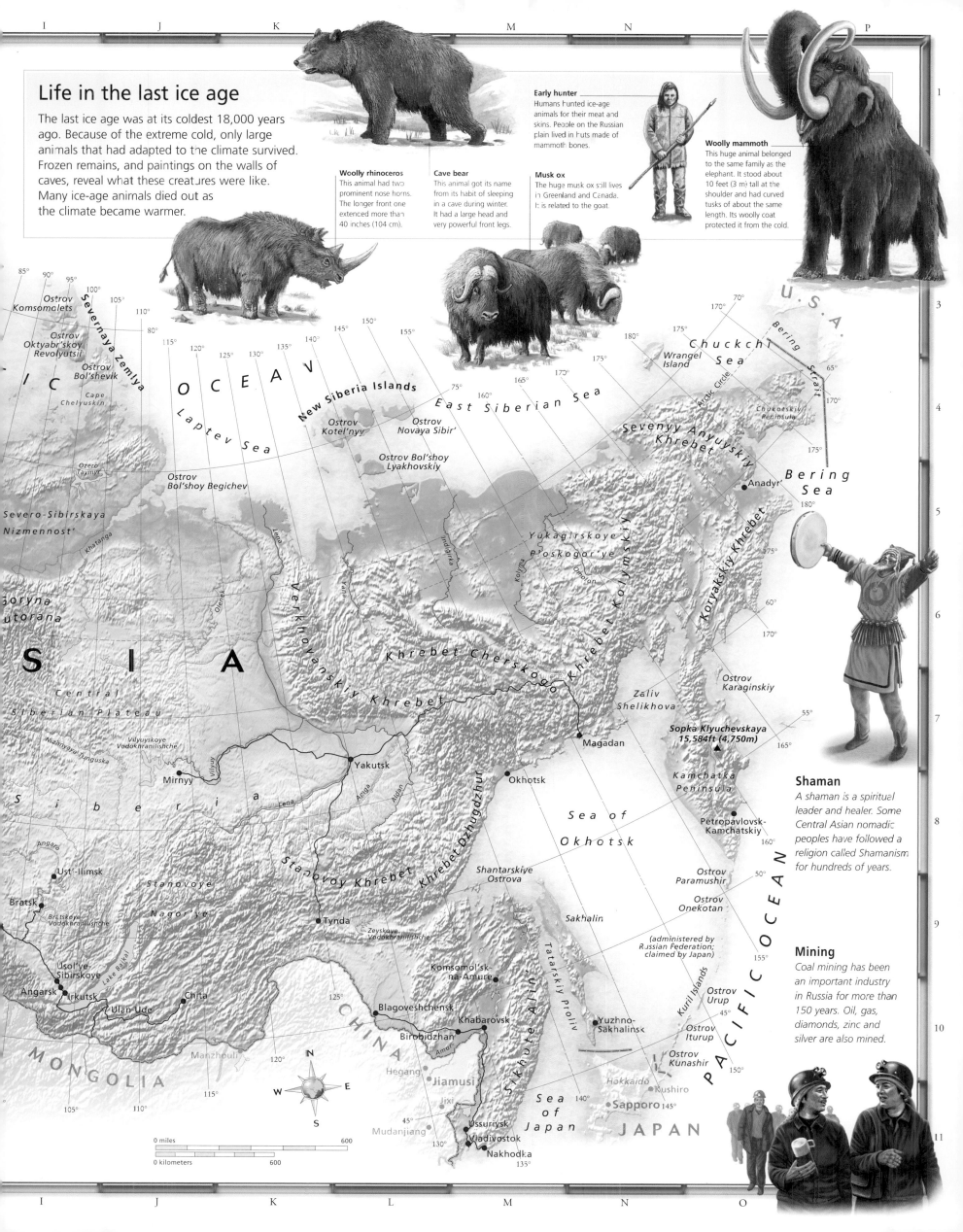

Life in the last ice age

The last ice age was at its coldest 18,000 years ago. Because of the extreme cold, only large animals that had adapted to the climate survived. Frozen remains, and paintings on the walls of caves, reveal what these creatures were like. Many ice-age animals died out as the climate became warmer.

Woolly rhinoceros
This animal had two prominent nose horns. The longer front one extended more than 40 inches (104 cm).

Cave bear
This animal got its name from its habit of sleeping in a cave during winter. It had a large head and very powerful front legs.

Musk ox
The huge musk ox still lives in Greenland and Canada. It is related to the goat.

Early hunter
Humans hunted ice-age animals for their meat and skins. People on the Russian plain lived in huts made of mammoth bones.

Woolly mammoth
This huge animal belonged to the same family as the elephant. It stood about 10 feet (3 m) tall at the shoulder and had curved tusks of about the same length. Its woolly coat protected it from the cold.

Shaman
A shaman is a spiritual leader and healer. Some Central Asian nomadic peoples have followed a religion called Shamanism for hundreds of years.

Mining
Coal mining has been an important industry in Russia for more than 150 years. Oil, gas, diamonds, zinc and silver are also mined.

U.S.A.

ARCTIC OCEAN

Ostrov Komsomolets
Severnaya Zemlya
Ostrov Oktyabr'skoy Revolyutsii
Ostrov Bol'shevik
Cape Chelyuskin
Ozero Taymyr

Laptev Sea
New Siberia Islands
Ostrov Kotel'nyy
Ostrov Novaya Sibir'
Ostrov Bol'shoy Lyakhovskiy
Ostrov Bol'shoy Begichev

East Siberian Sea
Chuckchi Sea
Wrangel Island
Arctic Circle
Bering Strait
Chukotskiy Peninsula
Sevenyy Anyuyskiy Khrebet
Anadyr'
Bering Sea

Severo-Sibirskaya Nizmennost'
Khatanga

Yukagirskoye Ploskogor'ye
Kolyma
Omolon
Khrebet Kolymskiy
Koryakskiy Khrebet
Ostrov Karaginskiy

Goryna utorana

S I B E R I A (SIA)

Central Siberian Plateau
Nizhnyaya Tunguska
Vilyuyskoye Vodokhranilishche

Verkhoyanskiy Khrebet
Lena
Yana
Indigirka
Olenek

Khrebet Cherskogo

Zaliv Shelikhova

Sopka Klyuchevskaya 15,584ft (4,750m)

Kamchatka Peninsula

Mirnyy
Vilyuy
Yakutsk
Lena
Aldan
Anga

Magadan
Okhotsk

Petropavlovsk-Kamchatskiy

Siberia

Angara

Stanovoye Nagor'ye
Ust'-Ilimsk
Bratsk
Bratskoye Vodokhranilishche

Stanovoy Khrebet
Khrebet Dzhugdzhur

Sea of Okhotsk

Shantarskiye Ostrova

Ostrov Paramushir
Ostrov Onekotan

Tynda
Zeyskoye Vodokhranilishche

Sakhalin

Usol'ye-Sibirskoye
Angarsk
Irkutsk
Ulan Ude
Lake Baikal
Chita

Komsomol'sk-na-Amure
Khabarovsk
Birobidzhan
Amur

Tatarskiy proliv

Yuzhno-Sakhalinsk

Kuril Islands
Ostrov Urup
Ostrov Iturup
Ostrov Kunashir

(administered by Russian Federation; claimed by Japan)

MONGOLIA
Manzhouli
Hegang
Jiamusi
Jixi
Mudanjiang

CHINA

Blagoveshchensk

Sikhote Alin'

Ussuriysk
Vladivostok
Nakhodka

Sea of Japan

Hokkaido
Kushiro
Sapporo

JAPAN

PACIFIC OCEAN

N
W   E
S

0 miles   600
0 kilometers   600

Russia

LAND AREA	6,562,115 sq miles (16,995,800 sq km)
OFFICIAL LANGUAGE	Russian
MAIN RELIGION	Christian
LIFE EXPECTANCY	73 years
LITERACY	99%

NATURAL FEATURES

Russian steppe
The Russian steppe is a vast, low-lying plain in southern Russia. Much of the plain lies less than 650 feet (200 m) above sea level. The natural vegetation includes grasses, mosses, lichen and trees.

Ural Mountains
These mountains divide European Russia from Siberia, and form the traditional border between Europe and Asia. The Urals extend from the Arctic Circle south for 1,550 miles (2,500 km) to the arid region near the Kazakhstan border.

Russian taiga
An area of coniferous forest, lakes, bogs and rivers in northern Russia, the taiga is home to many small mammals as well as moose, wolves and the rare Siberian tiger.

Siberian tiger

Lake Baikal
Formed more than 25 million years ago, Lake Baikal, in Siberia, is the oldest and deepest lake in the world. More than 1 mile (1,620 m) deep, it holds one-fifth of Earth's freshwater supplies. Home to more than 1,200 native plant and animal species, it is threatened by industrial wastewater pollution.

Tunguska meteorite
On 30 June 1908, a huge area of the forest in Tunguska, in a remote part of Siberia, was destroyed by an enormous fireball. Many scientists believe it was the largest meteorite to fall to Earth in the last 2,000 years. No fragments of it were left behind.

USING THE LAND

Natural resources
Russia has enormous deposits of iron, coal, oil and natural gas (*left*). However, two-thirds of the country's oil and natural gas deposits are in Siberia, which is a long way from the major population centers. Siberia's harsh climate makes it difficult to extract them.

- Forest and woodland
- Arable land
- Grazing
- Arid or marginal

Lake Baikal

- Cereals
- Potatoes
- Beef cattle
- Reindeer
- Fishing
- Industrial center
- Mining
- Oil production
- Gas production
- Timber

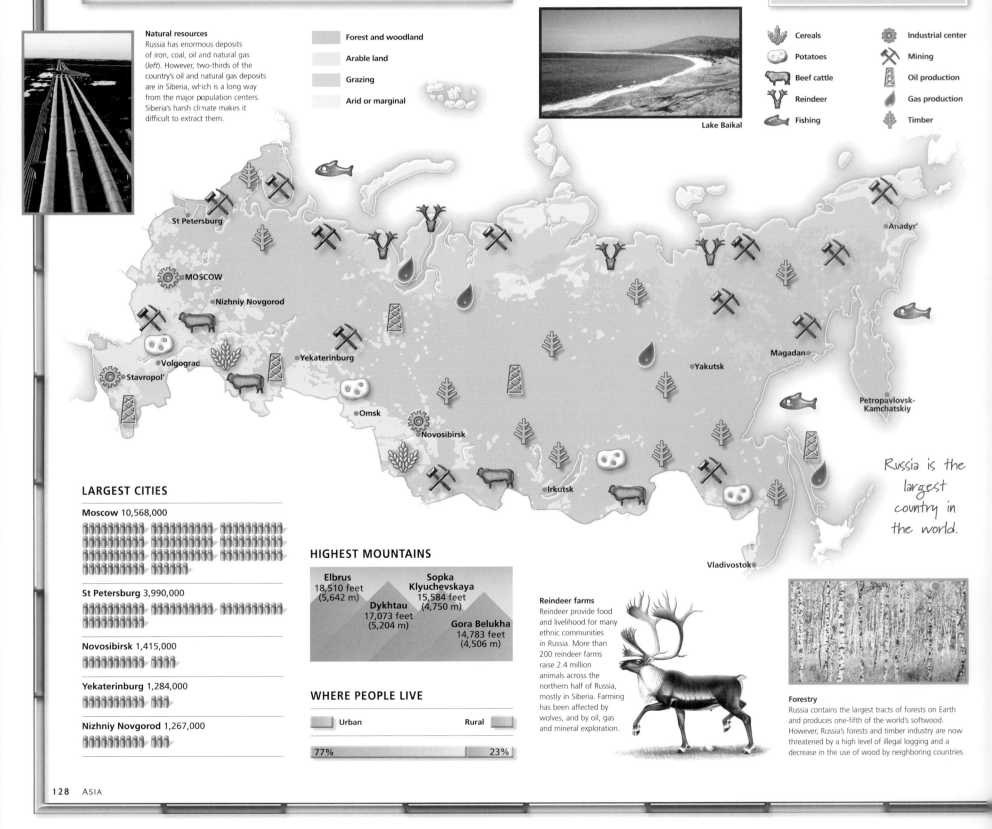

St Petersburg · *Anadyr'*
MOSCOW · *Nizhniy Novgorod* · *Magadan*
Volgograd · *Yekaterinburg* · *Yakutsk* · *Petropavlovsk-Kamchatskiy*
Stavropol' · *Omsk* · *Novosibirsk* · *Irkutsk* · *Vladivostok*

Russia is the largest country in the world.

LARGEST CITIES

Moscow 10,568,000

St Petersburg 3,990,000

Novosibirsk 1,415,000

Yekaterinburg 1,284,000

Nizhniy Novgorod 1,267,000

HIGHEST MOUNTAINS

Elbrus 18,510 feet (5,642 m)

Sopka Klyuchevskaya 15,584 feet (4,750 m)

Dykhtau 17,073 feet (5,204 m)

Gora Belukha 14,783 feet (4,506 m)

WHERE PEOPLE LIVE

Urban	Rural
77%	23%

Reindeer farms
Reindeer provide food and livelihood for many ethnic communities in Russia. More than 200 reindeer farms raise 2.4 million animals across the northern half of Russia, mostly in Siberia. Farming has been affected by wolves, and by oil, gas and mineral exploration.

Forestry
Russia contains the largest tracts of forests on Earth and produces one-fifth of the world's softwood. However, Russia's forests and timber industry are now threatened by a high level of illegal logging and a decrease in the use of wood by neighboring countries.

PEOPLE

Ivan the Terrible 1530–84
Ivan IV became the first czar (emperor) of Russia in 1547. Balanced against his political reform and territorial expansion was the fact that he instituted a reign of terror among the Russian nobility, killing thousands of people.

Catherine the Great 1729–96
Catherine II became czarina (empress) of Russia in 1796 as a result of a coup in which her husband (Peter the Great) was murdered. She successfully waged war against Turkey and Poland, increasing Russia's territory. During her reign, Russia enjoyed a period of stability.

Leo Tolstoy 1828–1910
One of the world's literary masters, Leo Tolstoy had a strong belief in the virtues of the simple peasant life—a belief that was reflected in his work. His most famous novel is *War and Peace*, an epic tale about Russia's struggle against France in the Napoleonic Wars.

Peter Tchaikovsky 1840–93
The compositions of the classical composer Peter Tchaikovsky are still played in concerts all over the world. His works include the ballets *Swan Lake* and *The Nutcracker*.

Grigory Rasputin 1871–1916
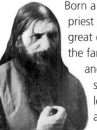
Born a Siberian peasant, this priest and mystic exerted a great deal of influence over the family of Czar Nicholas II and the court. Scandals surrounding Rasputin led to his murder by a group of nobles.

Trans-Siberian railroad
Stretching almost one-fourth of the way around the globe, the Trans-Siberian railroad is the longest rail system in the world. The journey from Moscow to Vladivostok makes 92 stops, takes eight days and covers 5,778 miles (9,244 km). The railroad was built between 1891 and 1904, in the reign of Alexander III.

TRADITIONS AND CULTURE

Icon painting

Icons are small religious images. Russia developed its own style of icon painting in the 15th century, using local saints and backgrounds. The icons illustrate legends, parables or rites of the Russian Orthodox Church. Painted icons are noted for their bright colors, including gold, and emphasis on strong outlines.

Matryoshka dolls
Also called "nesting dolls," these brightly painted, hollow wooden dolls are shaped so that they fit inside one another. They are an example of traditional Russian folk art. Sometimes matryoshka dolls represent a whole family, with some sets including more than 12 dolls.

Fabergé eggs
Created by Russian goldsmith and jeweler Peter Faberge, these Easter eggs are his finest work. Fabergé made the first egg in 1884 as an Easter present for Czar Alexander III to give to his wife—thus beginning a tradition in the royal family. Each ornate jeweled egg contained an elaborate surprise gift for the czarina.

Russian ballet
Russia's ballet schools have produced many of the world's greatest ballet dancers, such as Rudolph Nureyev and Anna Pavlova. The Bolshoi Ballet, meaning "great ballet" in Russian, in Moscow is one of the world's leading ballet companies.

Troika rides
Far from being a thing of the past, horse-drawn sleighs in winter (and carriages in summer) are becoming more popular in Russia, not just as a novelty ride, but as transport for well-to-do business people and politicians.

Lenin

Born Vladimir Ilyich Ulyanov in 1870, Lenin founded the Communist Party, led the Russian Revolution and created the Soviet state, the world's first communist regime. His aim was to create a classless society ruled by workers, soldiers and peasants. He died in 1924 and people visit his tomb in the Kremlin, where his body is preserved.

PLACES

The Kremlin MOSCOW
This is a large walled area in the center of Moscow (*below*). Built in 1156 and much enlarged since, the Kremlin is the seat of the Russian government and the center of the Russian Orthodox Church. It also has magnificent palaces and churches that are open to the public.

The Kremlin

Velikiy Novgorod
This northwestern city is one of the oldest in Russia. It was a thriving cultural and trading center in medieval times. With its many fine historic buildings, it is a popular tourist destination.

Vladivostok
This major port and naval base is located on a peninsula in the Sea of Japan. Its name means "rule the East." Founded in 1860 as a military outpost, it was closed to foreigners during the Cold War.

St Petersburg
This city, built in 1703 by Peter the Great, is the second-largest city in Russia. For 200 years up to 1918, it was Russia's capital city. St Petersburg is a major industrial and commercial center and its port, although frozen for part of the year, is one of the largest in the world. Constructed in the 18th century for Catherine the Great as her winter palace, the Hermitage Museum (*below*) is the largest museum and art gallery in Russia.

Hermitage Museum, St Petersburg

HISTORY AT A GLANCE
RUSSIA SINCE 1917

Russian Revolution poster

RUSSIAN REVOLUTION
Czar Nicholas II was a poor leader in World War I, and his government collapsed in 1917. The Bolsheviks seized power in October of that year and brought Russia under communist control, with Lenin as leader. After a series of wars, the communists formed the Union of Soviet Socialist Republics (USSR), or Soviet Union, in 1922.

JOSEPH STALIN
By 1928, Stalin had assumed sole power over the USSR and remained as dictator until his death in 1953. He centralized industries and set up state farms. His rule was noted for its harshness.

WORLD WAR II
In 1941, Germany invaded the USSR and encircled the city of Leningrad. After much suffering, the Soviets broke the siege in 1944. At the end of the war, the USSR occupied much of eastern Europe.

The Battle of Leningrad memorial

COLD WAR
The so-called cold war between the USSR and the USA climaxed in October 1962, with the Cuban missile crisis—the USA's discovery of Soviet missiles in Cuba. Nuclear war was averted.

YURI GAGARIN
On 12 April 1961, this Soviet cosmonaut became the first man in space. Flying at a maximum altitude of 187 miles (299 km) in the Vostok I spacecraft, Gagarin orbited Earth once before landing. He never flew into space again.

Yuri Gagarin

POLITICAL REFORM
Mikhail Gorbachev, president of the USSR (1990–91), was a reformer within the Communist Party who worked to decentralize power in the USSR and improve ties with the USA.

BREAKUP OF THE USSR
Gorbachev's quest for openness (*glasnost*) and restructuring (*perestroika*) led to the breakup of the USSR and ended its control of eastern Europe. The USSR ceased to exist on 31 December 1991.

RUSSIAN FEDERATION
Russia faced many problems as it tried to become more democratic and develop a freer economy. In 1994, Russia invaded Chechnia to reassert its control over its former territory. In 2000, Vladimir Putin became president.

Western Asia

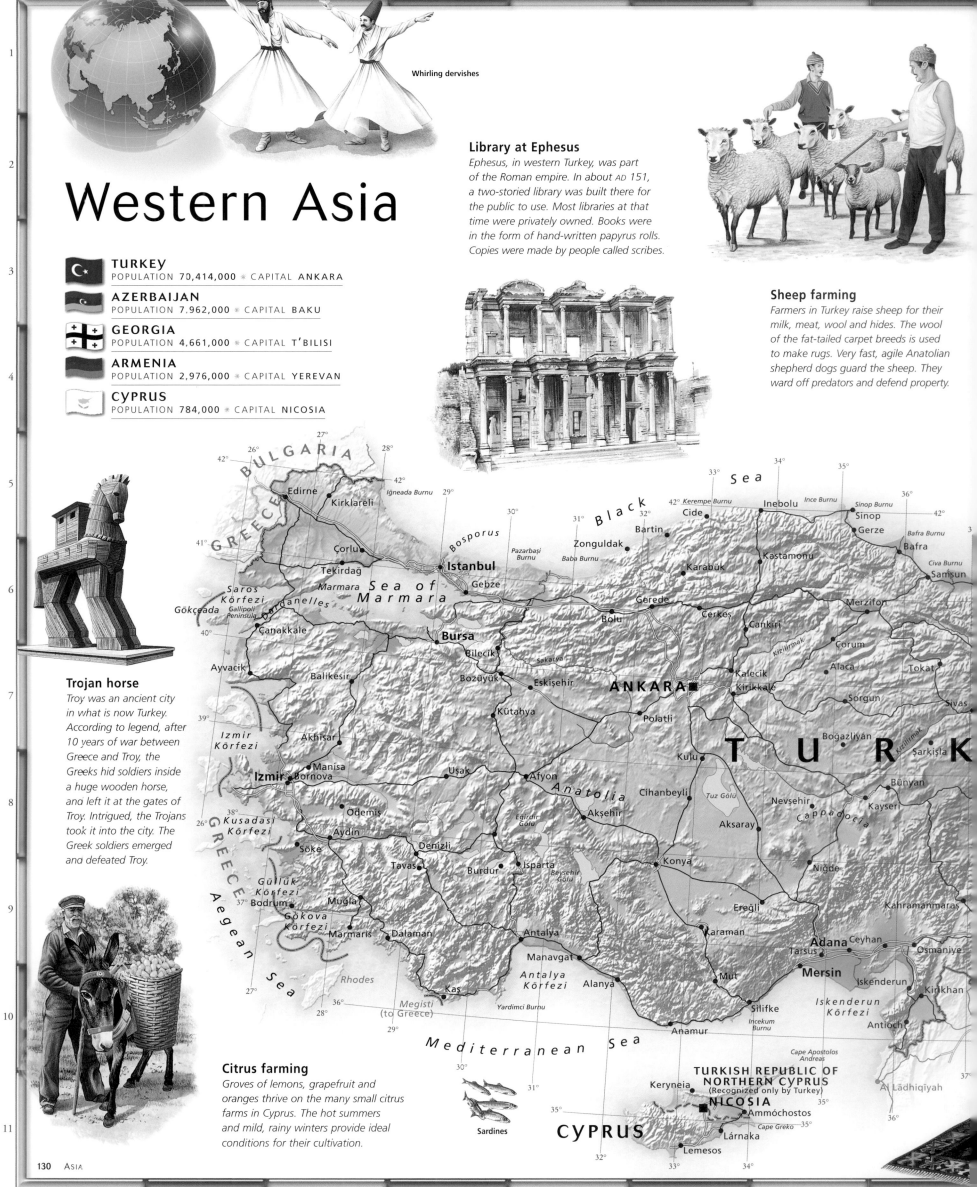

Whirling dervishes

TURKEY
POPULATION 70,414,000 ∗ CAPITAL ANKARA

AZERBAIJAN
POPULATION 7,962,000 ∗ CAPITAL BAKU

GEORGIA
POPULATION 4,661,000 ∗ CAPITAL T'BILISI

ARMENIA
POPULATION 2,976,000 ∗ CAPITAL YEREVAN

CYPRUS
POPULATION 784,000 ∗ CAPITAL NICOSIA

Library at Ephesus
Ephesus, in western Turkey, was part of the Roman empire. In about AD 151, a two-storied library was built there for the public to use. Most libraries at that time were privately owned. Books were in the form of hand-written papyrus rolls. Copies were made by people called scribes.

Sheep farming
Farmers in Turkey raise sheep for their milk, meat, wool and hides. The wool of the fat-tailed carpet breeds is used to make rugs. Very fast, agile Anatolian shepherd dogs guard the sheep. They ward off predators and defend property.

Trojan horse
Troy was an ancient city in what is now Turkey. According to legend, after 10 years of war between Greece and Troy, the Greeks hid soldiers inside a huge wooden horse, and left it at the gates of Troy. Intrigued, the Trojans took it into the city. The Greek soldiers emerged and defeated Troy.

Citrus farming
Groves of lemons, grapefruit and oranges thrive on the many small citrus farms in Cyprus. The hot summers and mild, rainy winters provide ideal conditions for their cultivation.

Sardines

BULGARIA
GREECE

Edirne
Kırklareli
Igneada Burnu
Çorlu
Tekirdağ
Bosporus
Istanbul
Gebze
Saros Körfezi
Marmara
Sea of Marmara
Gökçeada
Gallipoli Peninsula
Dardanelles
Çanakkale
Ayvacık
Balıkesir
Bilecik
Bozüyük
Eskişehir
Kütahya
Akhisar
İzmir Körfezi
İzmir
Manisa
Bornova
Uşak
Afyon
Anatolia
Ödemiş
Akşehir
Kuşadası Körfezi
Aydın
Söke
Denizli
Tavas
Egirdir Gölü
Isparta
Burdur
Güllük Körfezi
Bodrum
Muğla
Gökova Körfezi
Marmaris
Dalaman
Antalya
Aegean Sea
Rhodes
Kaş
Megisti (to Greece)
Yardimci Burnu
Antalya Körfezi
Alanya
Manavgat
Mut
Mediterranean Sea
Anamur
Incekum Burnu

Black Sea
Kerempe Burnu
Cide
Bartin
Zonguldak
Ince Burnu
Inebolu
Sinop Burnu
Sinop
Gerze
Bafra Burnu
Bafra
Civa Burnu
Samsun
Karabük
Kastamonu
Gerede
Bolu
Çerkeş
Çankırı
Merzifon
Corum
Alaca
Tokat
ANKARA
Kalecik
Kırıkkale
Sorgun
Sivas
Polatli
Boğazliyan
Şarkışla
TURKEY
Kulu
Kızılırmak
Cihanbeyli
Tuz Gölü
Nevşehir
Bünyan
Kayseri
Aksaray
Cappadocia
Konya
Niğde
Beyşehir Gölü
Ereğli
Kahramanmaraş
Karaman
Adana
Ceyhan
Tarsus
Osmaniye
Mersin
İskenderun
İskenderun Körfezi
Kırıkhan
Antioch
Silifke
Al Ladhiqiyah

Keryneia
TURKISH REPUBLIC OF NORTHERN CYPRUS
(Recognized only by Turkey)
NICOSIA
Ammóchostos
Cape Apostolos Andreas
Cape Greko
CYPRUS
Lárnaka
Lemesos

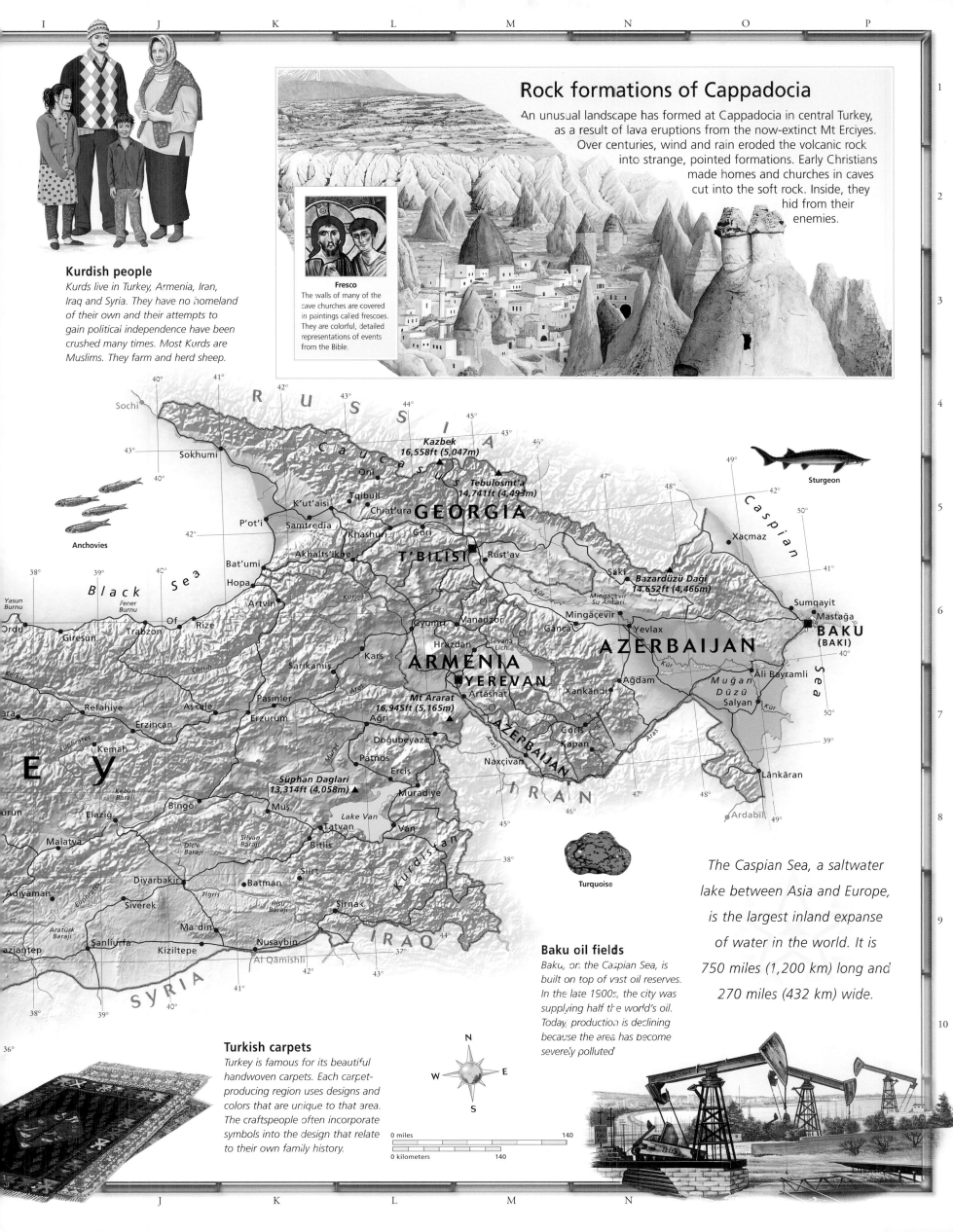

Rock formations of Cappadocia

An unusual landscape has formed at Cappadocia in central Turkey, as a result of lava eruptions from the now-extinct Mt Erciyes. Over centuries, wind and rain eroded the volcanic rock into strange, pointed formations. Early Christians made homes and churches in caves cut into the soft rock. Inside, they hid from their enemies.

Fresco
The walls of many of the cave churches are covered in paintings called frescoes. They are colorful, detailed representations of events from the Bible.

Kurdish people

Kurds live in Turkey, Armenia, Iran, Iraq and Syria. They have no homeland of their own and their attempts to gain political independence have been crushed many times. Most Kurds are Muslims. They farm and herd sheep.

Sturgeon

Anchovies

Turquoise

The Caspian Sea, a saltwater lake between Asia and Europe, is the largest inland expanse of water in the world. It is 750 miles (1,200 km) long and 270 miles (432 km) wide.

Baku oil fields

Baku, on the Caspian Sea, is built on top of vast oil reserves. In the late 1900s, the city was supplying half the world's oil. Today, production is declining because the area has become severely polluted

Turkish carpets

Turkey is famous for its beautiful handwoven carpets. Each carpet-producing region uses designs and colors that are unique to that area. The craftspeople often incorporate symbols into the design that relate to their own family history.

N
W E
S

0 miles 140
0 kilometers 140

Map labels:
Sochi, Sokhumi, Oni, Kazbek 16,558ft (5,047m), Tebulosmt'a 14,741ft (4,493m), K'ut'aisi, Chiat'ura, GEORGIA, Tqibuli, Samtredia, Khashuri, Gori, Rust'avi, P'ot'i, Akhalts'ikhe, T'BILISI, Xaçmaz, Bat'umi, Hopa, Bazardüzü Daği 14,652ft (4,466m), Sumqayit, Mastağa, BAKU (BAKI), Black Sea, Artvin, Mingäçevir Su Anbari, Mingäçevir, Yasun Burnu, Fener Burnu, Ordu, Of, Rize, Gyumri, Vanadzor, Ganca, Yevlax, AZERBAIJAN, Giresun, Trabzon, Hrazdan, Sevana Lich, Ali Bayramli, Kars, ARMENIA, Sarikamiş, YEREVAN, Xankändi, Muğan Düzü, Salyan, Refahiye, Aşkale, Pasinler, Artashat, Mt Ararat 16,945ft (5,165m), Ağdam, Goris, Erzincan, Erzurum, Kapan, Kemah, Ağri, AZERBAIJAN, Keban Baraji, Doğubeyazit, Naxçivan, Lānkäran, Patnos, IRAN, Süphan Daglari 13,314ft (4,058m), Erciş, Bingöl, Muradiye, Elaziğ, Muş, Lake Van, Tatvan, Van, Malatya, Dicle Baraji, Silvan Baraji, Bitlis, Ilisu Baraji, Siirt, Kurdistan, Diyarbakir, Batman, Şirnak, Siverek, Tigris, Ma'din, Nusaybin, Aratük Baraji, Şanliurfa, Kiziltepe, Al Qāmishli, IRAQ, aziantep, SYRIA

RUSSIA
Caucasus
Kür
Aras
Çoruh
Murat
Euphrates

Coordinate labels:
40°, 41°, 42°, 43°, 44°, 45°, 46°, 47°, 48°, 49°, 50°
36°, 37°, 38°, 39°, 40°, 41°, 42°

Bactrian camel train
The two-humped bactrian camel can travel for four days without water. These camels have been used since ancient times to transport goods across the deserts of Central Asia.

Central Asia

PAKISTAN
POPULATION 165,804,000 ✴ CAPITAL ISLAMABAD

AFGHANISTAN
POPULATION 31,057,000 ✴ CAPITAL KABUL

UZBEKISTAN
POPULATION 27,307,000 ✴ CAPITAL TASHKENT

KAZAKHSTAN
POPULATION 15,233,000 ✴ CAPITAL ASTANA

TAJIKISTAN
POPULATION 7,321,000 ✴ CAPITAL DUSHANBE

KYRGYZSTAN
POPULATION 5,214,000 ✴ CAPITAL BISHKEK

TURKMENISTAN
POPULATION 5,043,000 ✴ CAPITAL ASHGABAT

The Aral Sea is an environmental disaster area. Harmful irrigation practices have turned two-thirds of the sea into desert over 30 years. The fishing industry is now in ruins.

Stranded fishing boats, Aral Sea

Uzbek clothing
The traditional layered clothing of the women of Uzbekistan is made from a multicolored silk fabric known as "the king of satins." Jewelry included a tiara with delicate pendants that followed the curve of the eyebrows.

The Silk Road

The Silk Road is one of the most important trade routes in history. It was not a single road, but a network of shorter routes that linked scattered oasis settlements and market towns. From about 130 BC, goods from China were taken across the vast continent of Asia to the shores of the Mediterranean. Traders battled along the edges of deserts and braved dangerous mountain passes. Sometimes, camel trains were attacked by bandits. As well as goods, ideas, skills and religion also moved along the routes. Buddhism reached China from India in this way. The Silk Road declined in importance when a sea route from Europe to Asia was discovered in the late 15th century.

— Silk Road ■ Central Asia

Trading along the Silk Road

Few merchants ever traveled the full length of the route. Most covered just part of the journey, trading their wares for products from other countries, then returning home. Goods moved slowly and changed hands many times. Camel trains heading toward China carried gold, ivory, gems and glass.

Goods from Asia
Traders from Asia carried silk, furs, ceramics, jade and finely worked objects of bronze. Even in Roman times small quantities of Chinese goods were reaching Europe.

Registan Square
This square in the ancient city of Samarkand, in Uzbekistan, was once a marketplace for traders traveling the Silk Road. Majestic Islamic buildings dating from the 14th century line the square.

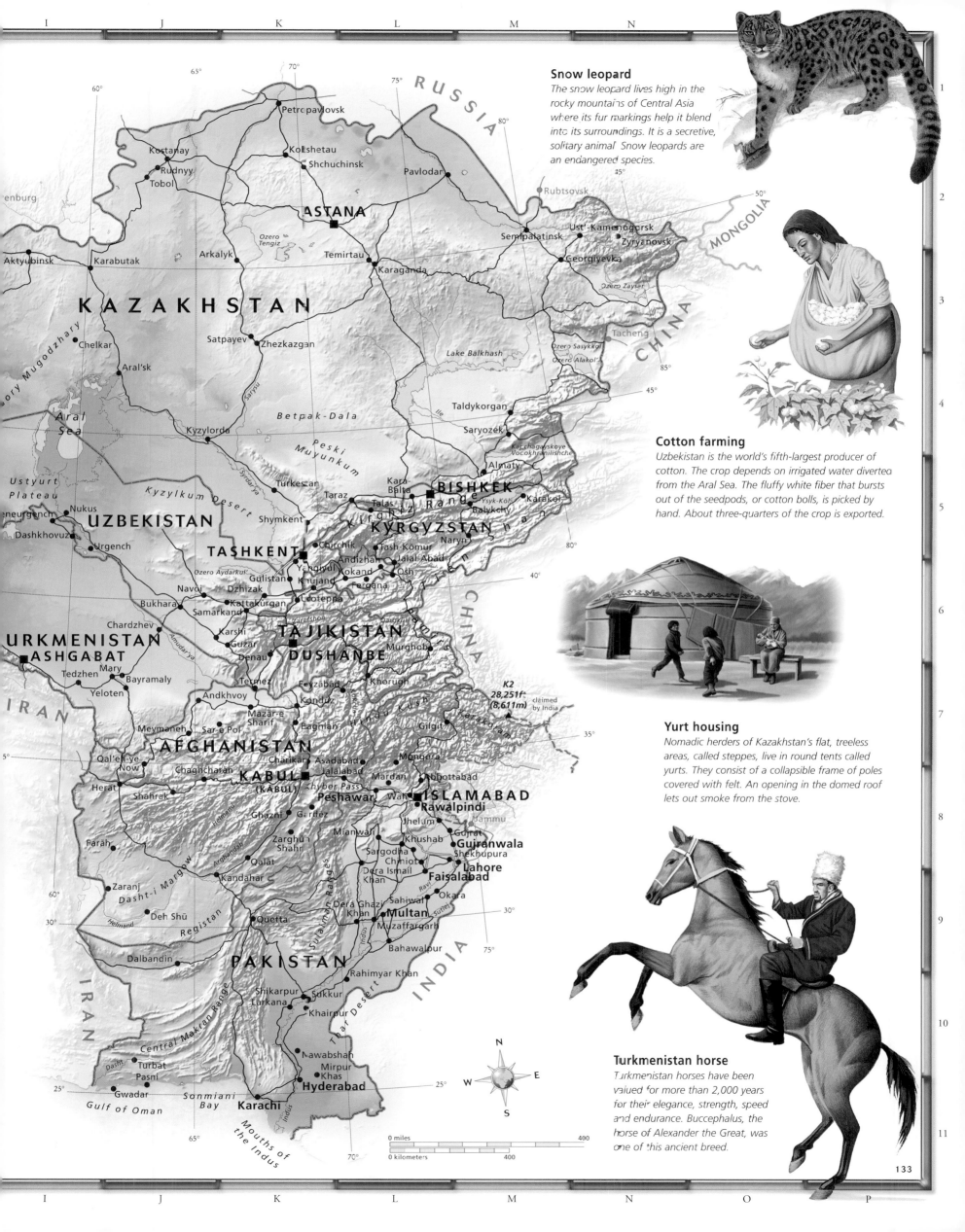

Snow leopard

The snow leopard lives high in the rocky mountains of Central Asia where its fur markings help it blend into its surroundings. It is a secretive, solitary animal. Snow leopards are an endangered species.

Cotton farming

Uzbekistan is the world's fifth-largest producer of cotton. The crop depends on irrigated water diverted from the Aral Sea. The fluffy white fiber that bursts out of the seedpods, or cotton bolls, is picked by hand. About three-quarters of the crop is exported.

Yurt housing

Nomadic herders of Kazakhstan's flat, treeless areas, called steppes, live in round tents called yurts. They consist of a collapsible frame of poles covered with felt. An opening in the domed roof lets out smoke from the stove.

Turkmenistan horse

Turkmenistan horses have been valued for more than 2,000 years for their elegance, strength, speed and endurance. Buccephalus, the horse of Alexander the Great, was one of this ancient breed.

133

The city of Kandahar in Afghanistan was founded by Alexander the Great in the 4th century BC.

Western and Central Asia

LAND AREA	2,435,424 sq miles (6,307,720 sq km)
LARGEST COUNTRY	Kazakhstan
SMALLEST COUNTRY	Cyprus
MAIN RELIGION	Muslim
LIFE EXPECTANCY	64 years
LITERACY	88%

Opium poppies
Opium poppies, used to make drugs such as morphine and codine, are grown widely in Afghanistan. Sap from the seedpods is often traded illegally, and is used to produce the banned drug, heroin.

- Forest and woodland
- Arable land
- Grazing
- Arid or marginal

USING THE LAND

- Cereals
- Rice
- Wheat
- Fruit and vegetables
- Fruit
- Citrus fruits
- Wine
- Cotton
- Tobacco
- Sugar beet
- Dates
- Beef cattle
- Sheep
- Fishing
- Industrial center
- Mining
- Oil production
- Gas production

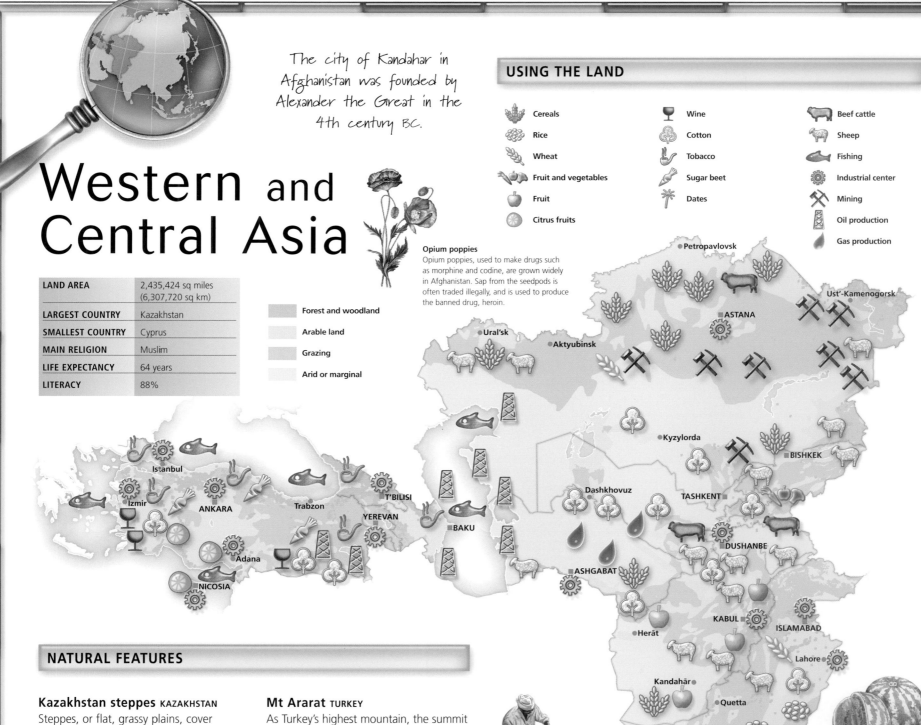

NATURAL FEATURES

Kazakhstan steppes KAZAKHSTAN
Steppes, or flat, grassy plains, cover most of Kazakhstan's north—about half of this country's total area. Farmers raise sheep and cattle in some parts.

Pammukale TURKEY
These chalk-coated cliffs look like a frozen waterfall. Calcium-rich spring waters flow over the cliffs to form pools, overhangs, stalactites and other formations.

Tien Shan
These largely unexplored, snow-capped mountains run for 1,500 miles (2,410 km) between Kazakhstan, Kyrgyzstan and China, along the steppe's southern edge.

North Anatolian Fault TURKEY
This fault, or deep crack in Earth's surface, runs from the Sea of Marmara to Lake Van. Shifting land either side of the fault can cause earthquakes, most recently in 1999, when more than 18,000 people died.

Mt Ararat TURKEY
As Turkey's highest mountain, the summit of this imposing landmark is 16,945 feet (5,165 m) above sea level. A glacier stretches down its northern face. The mountain is thought to be the resting place of Noah's Ark, referred to in the Old Testament of the Bible.

Khyber Pass
The Khyber Pass links Pakistan and Afghanistan through the Hindu Kush mountains. It is 33 miles (53 km) long. Invading armies have used it as a passage for centuries. The pass was well defended, and ancient fortresses and watchtowers still stand. It is walled by steep cliffs, and narrows to less than 10 feet (3 m) in parts.

Wheat
Wheat, which is grown extensively throughout this region, is used to make flat bread. The bread is sometimes cooked in a clay oven under the ground (*above*). Regional varieties include *nan*, *pide* and *chapatti*. *Jelabi* is an Afghan sweet bread that is deep-fried and coated in sugar syrup. Rice and other cereals are also grown in Western and Central Asia.

"Stan" at the end of a country's name means country.

Watermelons
In spring, snow from the Tien Shan mountains melts, providing water for irrigation. The fertile valleys of Kazakhstan are excellent for growing fruit crops, such as watermelons and citrus fruits.

WHERE PEOPLE LIVE

Urban	Rural

REGION
| 48% | 52% |

Most urban: TURKEY
| 74% | 26% |

Most rural: AFGHANISTAN
| 20% | 80% |

LARGEST CITIES

Karachi 12,316,000

Istanbul 10,291,000

Lahore 6,660,000

Hagia Sophia

Hagia Sophia, in Istanbul, Turkey, is one of the most spectacular examples of domed architecture in the world. It was built as a Christian church in the 6th century, in the Byzantine period. From 1453 until the 1930s, Hagia Sophia was used as a mosque. Many of its features—from the intricate mosaics and fountain, to the minarets (tall towers) built on each corner—are from this period. Today, it is used as a museum.

PEOPLE

Ismail al-Bukhari AD 810–870
This Arabic scholar wrote a book of sayings of the prophet Muhammad. Muslims believe it is second in value only to their holy book, the Koran.

Öz Beg ruled 1312–41
As khan, or ruler, of the Golden Horde—an area under Mongol rule—Öz Beg adopted Islam as his religion. The Uzbek people derive their name from his.

Timur the Great 1336–1405

Some say this Mongol ruler, known as Tamerlane in Europe, was one of history's most bloodthirsty tyrants, while others believe he was wise and just. Today, pilgrims and tourists flock to his tomb in Samarkand.

Roxelana died 1558
Chosen from the sultan's harem as his favorite, Roxelana became the wife of the Ottoman ruler Süleyman, and advised him on political and social matters.

Mustafa Kemal Atatürk 1881–1938
This military hero became Turkey's first president and prime minister in 1923, after he led a nationalist movement to abolish Ottoman rule.

Mustafa Kemal Atatürk

Imran Khan born 1952
This world-class Pakistani cricketer first captained his country's cricket team in 1982. He is now a politician.

PLACES

Kabul AFGHANISTAN
Afghanistan's capital, Kabul, has been under constant attack over the centuries. Following Soviet occupation in the 1980s, civil war broke out, with warlords fighting for control of the city. From 1996 to 2002, Kabul was controlled by the repressive Taliban.

Istanbul TURKEY
Called Constantinople until its capture by the Ottomans in the 15th century, Istanbul is Turkey's grandest city. Much of its architecture is from Byzantine times.

Samarkand UZBEKISTAN
Samarkand, Uzbekistan's second-largest city, is also one of the world's oldest. Its culture is a blend of Iranian, Indian and Mongolian traditions.

Badshahi Mosque PAKISTAN
This 5,000-seat mosque (below) at Lahore is the largest in the Indian subcontinent. Its enclosed central space and beautiful pool are typical of Islamic architecture.

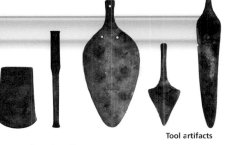
Tool artifacts

Mohenjo-daro PAKISTAN
The ruins of this ancient city lie on the banks of the Indus River. The well-planned city was built around 3000 BC, with buildings made from unbaked mud bricks. It was the largest city of the ancient Indus civilization.

Topkapi harem

In the 15th century, part of Turkey's Topkapi Palace (above) was home to a group of women chosen to look after the padishah, or ruler. Women in the Topkapi harem lived in the palace for life, and were forbidden to leave. At times, there were several thousand women in the harem.

TRADITIONS AND CULTURE

Shari'a law
Often called Islamic law, this legal system has been inspired by religious traditions and writings, notably the Koran. Many of the laws relate to worship, politics, criminal acts and family life.

Buzkashi
In this regional sport, players compete on horseback to bring an animal carcass into a scoring circle. *Buzkashi* means "goat grabbing."

An imam, or Muslim leader

Hamam
These are traditional baths Turkish men and women still visit regularly. Bathers go through three stages—they lie on hot marble, making them sweat, then have a body massage, followed by a drink.

In Greek mythology, the goddess Aphrodite was born in the waves of Cyprus.

Islamic art
Islamic art is brightly colored, with strong patterns and shapes. Calligraphy, or decorative handwriting, and geometric patterns (above) are typical features of this style. Islamic designs decorate ceramics, glass, textiles, metalwork and woodwork.

Grand Bazaar
This shopping market in Istanbul's center, which started as just a few stalls in the 15th century, now contains 4,000 shops stretching through 60 streets. Everything from leather and carpets to sweets and spices (below) is for sale.

Constantinople

AD 330
The emperor Constantine I renames Byzantium as Constantinople and makes it the capital of the Eastern Roman and Byzantine empires. The city becomes the new financial and political center and remains powerful for the next 1,000 years, but slowly declines by the 12th century.

1401
The Safavid dynasty in Persia is founded by Shah Ismail I. In the years to come, wars are fought between the Safavids and Ottoman Turks.

1453
The Ottoman Turks, headed by Sultan Mehmet, capture Constantinople. During Mehmet's reign, the Grand Bazaar is redeveloped, which improves the city's economy. The architectural masterpiece, the Topkapi Palace, is built.

1457
The Ottomans rename the city of Constantinople as Istanbul, and declare it the capital of their growing empire. Five years later, the Ottoman Turks take over Bosnia.

1520
Süleyman I, known as Süleyman the Magnificent because of his successes in expanding the empire, is crowned ruler over the Ottoman empire. Art and architecture expand during his reign.

Süleyman the Magnificent

1522
The Turks capture the Greek Island of Rhodes in the Aegean Sea and by 1524 it becomes part of the Ottoman empire.

1526
The Turks invade Hungary in the Battle of Mohacs. The battle lasts only two hours and the Turks gain victory, claiming Hungary for the Ottomans.

1529
The Turks fail to capture the city of Vienna, capital of Austria. The Ottoman empire shows signs of losing power.

1571
The Turks are defeated at the Battle of Lepanto, a huge sea battle fought off the coast of Greece between a Turkish and a Christian fleet.

1590
The Turks and Persians make peace after years of fighting with each other. Shortly after this, the Ottoman empire starts to decline.

1909
The last of the 36 Ottoman sultans, Muhammed Vahiduddin starts his reign. His rule ends in 1922 after Mustafa Kemal Atatürk abolishes the Muslim rank of sultan and founds the Republic of Turkey in 1924.

Muhammed Vahiduddin

Desert oasis

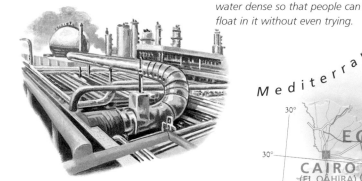

The Middle East

IRAN
POPULATION 68,688,000 * CAPITAL TEHRAN

SAUDI ARABIA
POPULATION 27,020,000 * CAPITAL RIYADH

IRAQ
POPULATION 26,783,000 * CAPITAL BAGHDAD

YEMEN
POPULATION 21,456,000 * CAPITAL ŞAN'Ā'

SYRIA
POPULATION 18,881,000 * CAPITAL DAMASCUS

ISRAEL
POPULATION 6,352,000 * CAPITAL JERUSALEM

JORDAN
POPULATION 5,907,000 * CAPITAL AMMĀN

LEBANON
POPULATION 3,874,000 * CAPITAL BEIRUT

OMAN
POPULATION 3,102,000 * CAPITAL MUSCAT

UNITED ARAB EMIRATES
POPULATION 2,603,000 * CAPITAL ABU DHABI

KUWAIT
POPULATION 2,418,000 * CAPITAL KUWAIT

QATAR
POPULATION 885,000 * CAPITAL DOHA

BAHRAIN
POPULATION 699,000 * CAPITAL AL MANĀMAH

Dead Sea
This landlocked sea, between Israel and Jordan, contains large amounts of salt. This makes the water dense so that people can float in it without even trying.

The world's largest known reserves of oil are in the Middle East. Saudi Arabia, Iraq, Iran, the United Arab Emirates and Kuwait are among the world's leading oil producers.

Jerusalem's holy sites

Jerusalem is one of the holiest cities in the world. Within its boundaries are sites central to the beliefs of the Jewish, Christian and Islamic faiths. Jews consider Jerusalem a holy city because it was the religious center and capital of the ancient Israelite nation. For Christians, it is the place where Jesus Christ taught and was crucified. Muslims believe that Muhammad, the founder of Islam, rose to heaven from Jerusalem. Over the centuries, followers of these faiths have often disagreed about who controls Jerusalem, and conflicts have occurred as a result.

Jewish rabbi

Western Wall
This wall is all that remains of the Jewish Temple destroyed by the Romans in AD 70. It is the Jews' holiest site. They pray here and leave prayers on pieces of paper between the stones.

Temple Mount
Muslims believe Muhammad was lifted to heaven from the rock that lies directly beneath the golden dome. It is one of the most sacred Islamic sites. Jews believe the rock is the place where Abraham prepared to sacrifice his son, Isaac.

Church of the Holy Sepulchre
This church is built over the site where many Christians believe Jesus Christ was crucified. It is said to contain the sepulchre (tomb) where he was buried. The building dates from 1149, the time of Crusades.

Muslim praying

Christian nun

Hunting with falcons
This is a traditional sport in Saudi Arabia. Young, preferably female, wild falcons are trained to kill prey and return it to their handler. A leather glove protects the handler's arm from sharp talons.

Map labels
Manbij, Antioch, Aleppo, Al Lādhiqīyah, Idlib, Ar Raqqa, Hamah, Tartūs, Tripoli, Ḩimş, Palmyra, SYRIA, LEBANON, Ba'albek, BEIRUT (BAYRŪT), DAMASCUS (DIMASHQ), Soûr, Saida, As Suwaydā', Haifa, Nazareth, ISRAEL, Muqa, Tel Aviv-Jaffa, Nablus, Az Zarqā', Turay, JERUSALEM, AMMĀN, Gaza, Kāf, EGYPT, JORDAN, Ma'an, Suez Canal, Suez, Negev, Wadi Rum, CAIRO (EL QAHIRA), Sinai, Elat, Al 'Aqabah, At Tubayq, Jabal al Lawz 8,461ft (2,579m), Tabūk, Rās Karkūmā, Hurghada, Rās Abū Madd, Rās Baridi, Yanbu' al Baḥr, Nile, Mediterranean Sea, Gulf of Aqaba, Gulf of Suez, Tropic of Cancer, Medin, Rābigh, Jeddah, Me, Nubian Desert, SUDAN, Port Sudan, Suakin, ERITREA, Massawa, ASMARA, Red

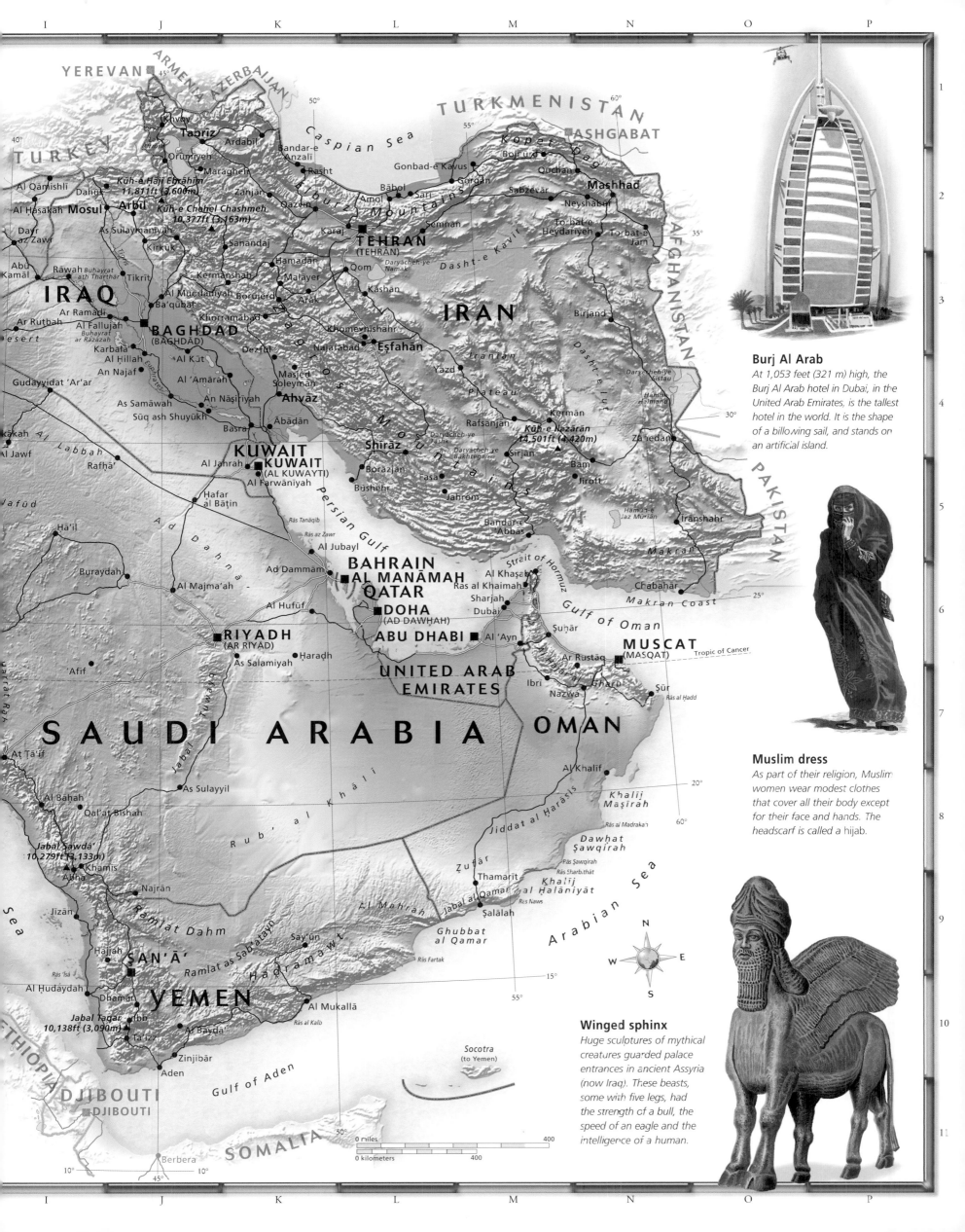

Burj Al Arab

At 1,053 feet (321 m) high, the Burj Al Arab hotel in Dubai, in the United Arab Emirates, is the tallest hotel in the world. It is the shape of a billowing sail, and stands on an artificial island.

Muslim dress

As part of their religion, Muslim women wear modest clothes that cover all their body except for their face and hands. The headscarf is called a hijab.

Winged sphinx

Huge sculptures of mythical creatures guarded palace entrances in ancient Assyria (now Iraq). These beasts, some with five legs, had the strength of a bull, the speed of an eagle and the intelligence of a human.

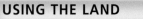

The Middle East

LAND AREA	1,971,313 sq miles (5,105,677 sq km)
LARGEST COUNTRY	Iran
SMALLEST COUNTRY	Bahrain
MAIN RELIGION	Muslim
LIFE EXPECTANCY	73 years
LITERACY	78%

NATURAL FEATURES

Elburz and Zagros mountains IRAN

There are two mountain ranges in Iran, the Zagros and the Elburz. Mt Damavand, at more than 18,638 feet (5,681 m) above sea level, is Iran's highest peak. It is an almost extinct volcano, which still spouts occasional plumes of gas.

Mt Damavand

Mesopotamia IRAQ

Mesopotamia (from a Greek word that means "between the rivers") was the site of the world's earliest civilizations, from about 10,000 BC. It lay between the Tigris and Euphrates rivers. The northern region had a mild climate and fertile land, while the southern had lush, marshy areas.

Arz el Rab LEBANON

Arz el Rab, or Cedars of the Lord, is the oldest cedar grove in Lebanon. The mountains were once covered with cedar trees, since cut down over the centuries.

Wadi Rum JORDAN

This wadi, or river valley, is unusual for its deep, pinkish sands covered in small shrubs, and its occasional enormous rock formations, called *jebels,* that rise up into the sky, making the wadi look rather like the surface of the Moon.

USING THE LAND

- Forest and woodland
- Arable land
- Grazing
- Arid or marginal

- 🌾 Rice
- 🌾 Wheat
- 🍎 Fruit
- 🍊 Citrus fruits
- 🌿 Cotton
- ☕ Coffee
- ✳ Dates
- 🐑 Sheep
- 🐐 Goats
- 🐟 Fishing
- ⚙ Industrial center
- Oil production
- Gas production

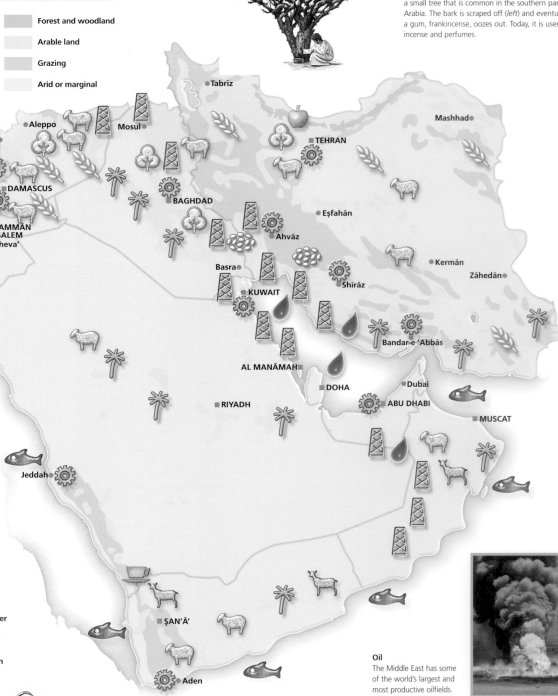

Grain

Wheat, millet and barley are the main grain crops of the Middle East. The greatest problem is the lack of water but the area suitable for growing these crops has been extended by irrigation. Small crops are even planted in moist wadis (river valleys) in the desert.

WHERE PEOPLE LIVE

Urban	Rural

REGION
76% | 24%

Most urban: KUWAIT
97% | 3%

Most rural: YEMEN
24% | 76%

Frankincense

Thousands of years ago, frankincense was used for religious ceremonies and embalming. It comes from a small tree that is common in the southern part of Arabia. The bark is scraped off (*left*) and eventually a gum, frankincense, oozes out. Today, it is used in incense and perfumes.

Oil

The Middle East has some of the world's largest and most productive oilfields. The most important are in Saudi Arabia, Iran, Iraq and Kuwait. Kuwait is the second-largest oil producer (Saudi Arabia is the largest) in the Middle East. During the 1991 Gulf War, the Iraqis set fire to many of the oil wells and oil refineries in Kuwait (*above*).

The Crusades

In the 11th century, Palestine was under the control of the Muslims. In 1095, Pope Urban II joined with the Byzantine emperor to recapture the Holy Land (Palestine) from the Muslims for the Christians. For almost 200 years, until 1294, the armies of eight separate crusades raided Palestine. In periods of peace, the crusaders were accepted and entertained by the Muslims (*above*).

LARGEST CITIES

Tehran 7,186,000

Baghdad 5,832,000

Riyadh 4,453,000

Jeddah 3,003,000

Mashhad 2,463,000

Map labels: Tabrīz, Mashhad, Aleppo, Mosul, Al Lādhiqīyah, TEHRAN, BEIRUT, DAMASCUS, BAGHDAD, Eşfahān, Haifa, Tel Aviv-Jaffa, AMMAN, JERUSALEM, Be'ér Sheva', Ahvāz, Kermān, Basra, Zāhedān, KUWAIT, Shīrāz, AL MANĀMAH, Bandar-e 'Abbās, RIYADH, DOHA, Dubai, ABU DHABI, MUSCAT, Jeddah, ŞAN'Ā', Aden

TRADITIONS AND CULTURE

Damascus souks
Souks, or market stalls, are a common sight in the old section of Damascus, Syria. Famous for their crafts, the souks sell fine damask tapestries, glassware and carvings inlaid with mother-of-pearl.

Kibbutzim
These are groups of farms in Israel in which the owners share the work, the decision-making, the food and the earnings in return for the work they do for the community.

Camel racing
Camel races are popular in Saudi Arabia. Every year, more than 2,000 camels and riders compete in the grueling King's Cup Camel Race in Riyadh.

Camel racing

Over 95 percent of Saudi Arabia is desert. The Rub' al Khāli desert is known as the Empty Quarter.

Five pillars of Islam
Mecca, in Saudi Arabia, is the holiest city of Islam. One of the five duties (or pillars) of faith for Muslims is that they make a pilgrimage to Mecca (a hajj, *above*) at least once in their lifetime.

Birthplace of religions
The Middle East is the birthplace of three of the world's major religions: Christianity, Judaism and Islam. Judaism, which began in the area around 2000 BC, is the world's oldest major religion. Christianity, based on the teachings of Jesus Christ around 2,000 years ago, also reveres some of Judaism's scriptures as holy. Islam arose in the 7th century from the teachings of the prophet Muhammad.

PLACES

Jericho ISRAEL
The ancient walled city of Jericho was first settled around 8350 BC. Now situated in the West Bank area, Jericho was handed over to Palestinian control in 1994 after years of unrest.

Petra JORDAN
Once a wealthy trading center, the city of Petra (*left*) was carved from red sandstone cliffs more than 2,000 years ago. It seems to have been abandoned at some time in the 6th century.

Baghdad IRAQ
The capital of Iraq and its largest city, Baghdad is situated near the Tigris River. The site has been settled since ancient times, and Baghdad was once one of the world's richest cities. Much of the city has been destroyed by recent wars.

Mecca SAUDI ARABIA
Every year, millions of Muslims make the pilgrimage to Mecca, the birthplace of Muhammad, to pray. Muslims think of Mecca as their homeland and even when they are elsewhere in the world, they face in the direction of Mecca to pray.

Esfahan IRAN
One of the largest cities in Iran, Esfahan is famous for its mosques, such as the 17th-century Royal Mosque, now called Masjid-e Iman, its medieval Islamic architecture and its public gardens.

Royal Mosque

PEOPLE

Solomon c 1000 BC
Solomon, son of King David, was the third king of ancient Israel. He was known as a wise and clever king who established peace and unity in Israel.

King Solomon

Harun Al-Rashid AD 766–809
A ruler of the Abbasid dynasty, Harun Al-Rashid supported the arts, literature, mathematics and medicine. The capital, Baghdad, flourished under his rule.

Saladin 1138–93
Saladin, a Muslim sultan, captured Jerusalem from the Christians in 1187. The English king Richard the Lionheart fought against him in the Third Crusade, which ended in a truce in 1192.

Ibn Saud 1880–1953
From 1902, when he first attacked Riyadh, Ibn Saud's aim was to unify Arabia. He achieved this in 1932, when he brought tribal conflicts under control and became the king of Arabia

Ayatollah Khomeini 1900–89
In 1979, this Muslim leader took control of Iran from the king and changed its government to an Islamic republic. Khomeini was its first leader.

Flying carpet

Arabian Nights
Also called *The Thousand and One Nights*, this collection of almost 200 folktales first appeared around the year AD 800. The stories tell of the heroic and romantic adventures of well-known characters, such as Sinbad the Sailor, Aladdin and Ali Baba. These tales have been collected from several countries, including Arabia, India, Egypt and Persia.

HISTORY AT A GLANCE
ANCIENT MESOPOTAMIA

c 5000 BC
Tribes, probably from Arabia, begin to settle into village life along the banks of the Tigris and Euphrates rivers—the area called Mesopotamia.

c 3000 BC
The Sumerians, an advanced culture whose inventions include writing, a calendar, systems of measurement and the wheel, live in this area.

c 2340 BC
Sargon of Agade, a military ruler from central Mesopotamia, conquers Syria and the Sumer, forming the kingdom of Akkad, the first nation-state in world history.

c 1760 BC
King Hammurabi, of the Amorite dynasty, establishes Babylon as an important trading center and the capital of Mesopotamia. He introduces laws, called the Code of Hammurabi, which are carved into a black stone called a stela (*right*).

Hammurabi

c 1600 BC
The Hittites, a people from an area that is now part of Turkey, sweep down into Babylon, conquer and plunder the city, and bring the dynasty of Hammurabi to an end.

c 1240 BC
The Assyrians, a people from the northern part of what is now Iraq, decide to expand into Babylon. After a series of battles, Hittite power collapses and the Assyrians control Babylon.

c 1200 BC
One of the oldest epics in world literature, *The Epic of Gilgamesh*, is written, telling the tale of Gilgamesh, a powerful king in ancient Sumeria.

c 1155 BC
The Assyrians create a unified empire by installing Assyrian rulers in each capital they conquer.

706–681 BC
Sennacherib succeeds his father, Sargon II, as king of Assyria. He makes Nineveh the capital city, and sets up a library of thousands of clay tablets of technical and scientific writings. In 689, he destroys the city of Babylon.

612 BC
The Medes, a people from Iran, join forces with the Babylonians to destroy the Assyrian empire.

Ishtar Gate

605–562 BC
King Nebuchadnezzar II captures Jerusalem and controls the southern area of Mesopotamia. He rebuilds Babylon and fortifies it with walls. One of its eight gates is the Ishtar Gate (*above*), named after Ishtar, goddess of love and war.

539 BC
The Persian king, Cyrus the Great, and his soldiers (*right*), incorporate Babylon into the rapidly growing Persian empire. Persia rules much of the Middle East until it is conquered by Alexander the Great.

331 BC
Macedonian general Alexander the Great conquers Babylon, ruling until his death in 323.

Persian soldier

Southern Asia

INDIA POPULATION 1,095,392,000 ✷ CAPITAL NEW DELHI

BANGLADESH POPULATION 147,365,000 ✷ CAPITAL DHAKA

NEPAL POPULATION 28,287,000 ✷ CAPITAL KATHMANDU

SRI LANKA POPULATION 20,222,000 ✷ CAPITAL COLOMBO

BHUTAN POPULATION 2,280,000 ✷ CAPITAL THIMPHU

MALDIVES POPULATION 359,000 ✷ CAPITAL MALE

The Himalayas

The Himalayas extend more than 1,600 miles (2,600 km) from northern Pakistan, through Kashmir and northern India, across Tibet and Nepal and into Bhutan. Although the mountains are known as the Himalayas, they are three separate ranges. The Great Himalaya range includes Mount Everest. Nearly a third of the world's mammal species live in the Himalayas. They include the snow leopard and the red panda. Rhododendrons bloom on the lower slopes and there are more than 250 species of orchids.

On the move
The continents are carried along by Earth's tectonic plates. The plates are moving up to 8 inches (20 cm) per year in some places.

10 million years ago
38 million years ago
55 million years ago
71 million years ago

EURASIAN PLATE
INDIA today
Equator
INDIAN OCEAN
"INDIA" landmass
Sri Lanka

How the Himalayas were formed

The Himalayas were formed by the collision of two tectonic plates. The Indian Plate and the Eurasian Plate started on their collision course about 60 million years ago.

Continents in collision
One continent pushes over the top of the other and the rocks start to crumple and fold.

Rising mountains
Peaks are thrust upward as pressure continues. Fossils from the seabed move to the top of the mountains.

Growing sideways
Some land is pushed outward, so the mountain range then extends sideways.

Indian elephants

The Indian, or Asian, elephant is smaller than the African elephant. It is a strong, calm animal that can carry people, logs and food.

Taj Mahal

The Taj Mahal near Agra, in northern India, was built in the mid-1600s by Mughal emperor Shah Jahan as a monument to his favorite wife. It is made of white marble and decorated with jewels and carvings.

The largest, most famous sapphire in the world was discovered in Sri Lanka more than 300 years ago. Surprisingly, it is called the Star of India.

Indian dancer

Dancing takes place at festivals throughout India. Some dances tell stories or are associated with a particular religion This dancer in Jaipur, in Rajasthan, is celebrating Holi, the festival that welcomes spring and honors elephants.

CHINA
CHINA
NEPAL
BHUTAN
THIMPHU
KATHMANDU
Kula Kangri 24,783ft (7,554m)
Mt Everest 29,035ft (8,850m)
Annapurna 26,545ft (8,091m)
Dhangadhi
Dhaulagiri
Mizoram Hills
Digboi
Tinsukia
Silchar
Bongaigaon
Dhubri
Gorakhpur
Faizabad
Lucknow
Bahraich
Sitapur
Shahjahanpur
Pilibhit
Bareilly
Budaun
Moradabad
Rampur
Haldwani
Dehra Dun
Haridwar
Roorkee
Muzaffarnagar
Meerut
Aligarh
Hathras
Mathura
Agra
Firozabad
Bhind
NEW DELHI
Delhi
Faridabad
Rohtak
Ghaziabad
Panipat
Karnal
Ambala
Chandigarh
Patiala
Ludhiana
Jalandhar
Hoshiarpur
Pathankot
Amritsar
Jammu
Srinagar
Kashmir
Ladakh
Karakoram Range
K2 28,251ft (8,611m)
(Administered by China, claimed by India)
(Administered by China, claimed by India)
(Administered by China, claimed by India)
(Administered by China, claimed by India)
Himalaya Range
Himalayan Range
Jaipur
Sikar
Rajasthan
Bikaner
Thar Desert
Bhiwani
Hisar
Sirsa
Ganganagar
Abohar
Moga
Bathinda
Hindu Kush
ISLAMABAD
Lahore
Gujranwala
Jhelum
PAKISTAN

96° 94° 92° 90° 88° 86° 84° 82° 80° 78° 76° 74° 72° 70°
28° 30° 32° 34° 36°

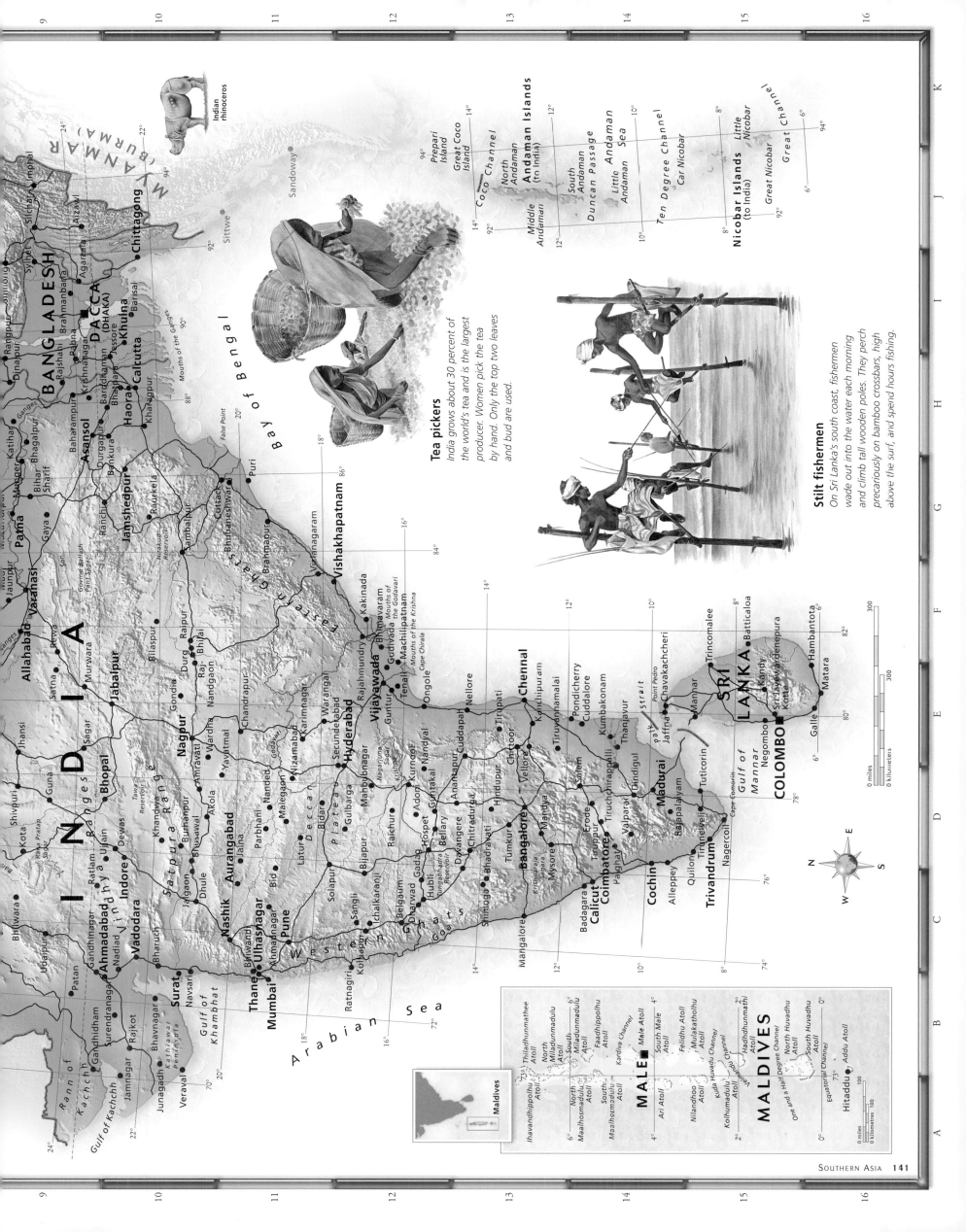

Indian rhinoceros

Tea pickers
India grows about 30 percent of the world's tea and is the largest producer. Women pick the tea by hand. Only the top two leaves and bud are used.

Stilt fishermen
On Sri Lanka's south coast, fishermen wade out into the water each morning and climb tall wooden poles. They perch precariously on bamboo crossbars, high above the surf, and spend hours fishing.

Southern Asia

The Maldives has over 1,200 islands, but only about 80 are open to foreigners.

Bhutan is the only country with a national park formed to protect the yeti.

One-fifth of the world's people live in Southern Asia.

INDIA	
TOTAL AREA	1,147,955 sq miles (2,973,190 sq km)
OFFICIAL LANGUAGE	English, Hindu and others
MAIN RELIGION	Hinduism
LIFE EXPECTANCY	63 years
LITERACY	59%

BANGLADESH	
TOTAL AREA	51,703 sq miles (133,910 sq km)
OFFICIAL LANGUAGE	Bangla (Bengali)
MAIN RELIGION	Muslim
LIFE EXPECTANCY	61 years
LITERACY	43%

NEPAL	
TOTAL AREA	52,819 sq miles (136,800 sq km)
OFFICIAL LANGUAGE	Nepali
MAIN RELIGION	Hinduism
LIFE EXPECTANCY	59 years
LITERACY	41%

SRI LANKA	
TOTAL AREA	24,996 sq miles (64,740 sq km)
OFFICIAL LANGUAGE	Sinhala
MAIN RELIGION	Buddhism
LIFE EXPECTANCY	72 years
LITERACY	92%

BHUTAN	
TOTAL AREA	18,147 sq miles (47,000 sq km)
OFFICIAL LANGUAGE	Dzongkha
MAIN RELIGION	Buddhism
LIFE EXPECTANCY	53 years
LITERACY	42%

WHERE PEOPLE LIVE

Urban | Rural

INDIA	
28%	72%
BANGLADESH	
24%	76%
SRI LANKA	
23%	77%
NEPAL	
12%	88%
BHUTAN	
7%	93%

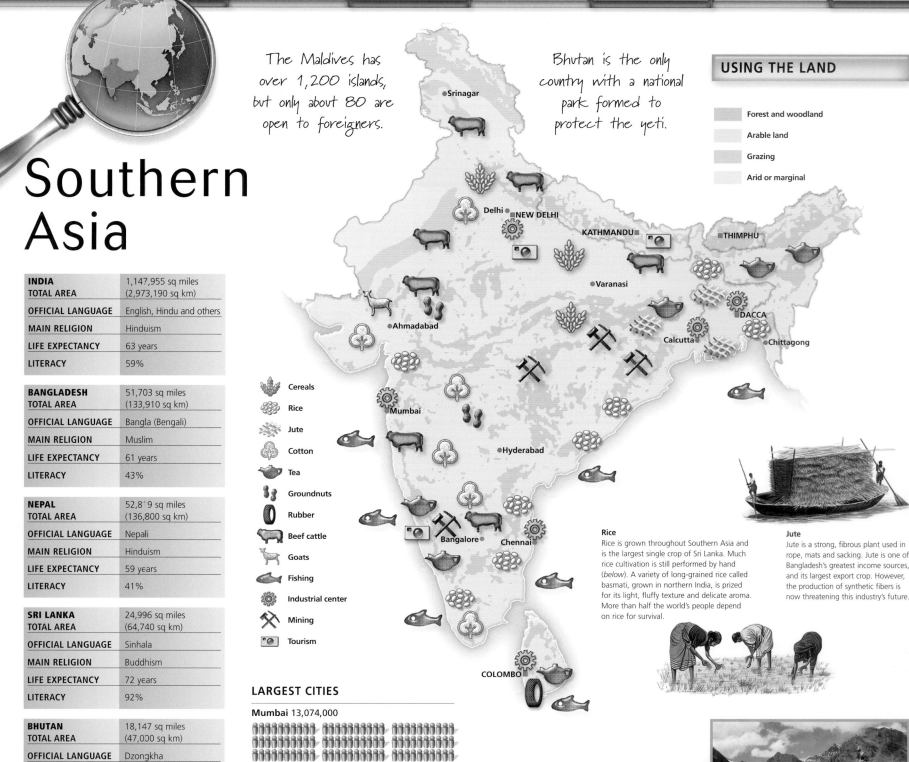

Map legend

- Cereals
- Rice
- Jute
- Cotton
- Tea
- Groundnuts
- Rubber
- Beef cattle
- Goats
- Fishing
- Industrial center
- Mining
- Tourism

Map labels: Srinagar, Delhi, NEW DELHI, KATHMANDU, THIMPHU, Varanasi, Ahmadabad, DACCA, Calcutta, Chittagong, Mumbai, Hyderabad, Bangalore, Chennai, COLOMBO

USING THE LAND

- Forest and woodland
- Arable land
- Grazing
- Arid or marginal

LARGEST CITIES

Mumbai 13,074,000

Delhi 11,505,000

Dacca 6,969,000

Bangalore 5,282,000

HIGHEST MOUNTAINS

Kangchenjunga
28,169 feet
(8,586 m)

Mt Everest
29,035 feet
(8,850 m)

Lhotse
27,940 feet
(8,516 m)

Makalu
27,765 feet
(8,462 m)

Rice
Rice is grown throughout Southern Asia and is the largest single crop of Sri Lanka. Much rice cultivation is still performed by hand (*below*). A variety of long-grained rice called basmati, grown in northern India, is prized for its light, fluffy texture and delicate aroma. More than half the world's people depend on rice for survival.

Jute
Jute is a strong, fibrous plant used in rope, mats and sacking. Jute is one of Bangladesh's greatest income sources, and its largest export crop. However, the production of synthetic fibers is now threatening this industry's future.

NATURAL FEATURES

Thar Desert INDIA
Also known as the Great Indian Desert, the Thar covers 74,000 square miles (192,000 sq km) in northwest India. High winds erode the desert's sand dunes into constantly changing forms.

The Sundarbans INDIA–BANGLADESH
One of the largest mangrove swamps on Earth, the Sundarbans span the border between India and Bangladesh on the Bay of Bengal. They are home to rare species of animals, such as the Bengal tiger (*below*) and the Indian python.

Bengal tiger

Ladakh KASHMIR
The remote region of Ladakh, often called the Land of High Passes, lies across the disputed Kashmir Valley in the rainshadow of the Indian Himalayas. High plains and deep valleys dominate the landscape. It is one of the highest and driest regions in the world.

Ladakh

Mt Everest NEPAL
Located in the Himalayas on the border between Nepal and Tibet, Mt Everest is the highest point on Earth. The ultimate challenge for any mountain climber is to reach its summit, a steep and rugged area 29,035 feet (8,850 m) above sea level.

Shiva

Hindu gods

Hindus believe that their gods, even though they appear in separate forms, are part of one supreme god, Brahman. The three most important gods reflect the circle of life. First is Brahma, the creator of the world; then Vishnu, the preserver of the existing world; and finally, Shiva, the destroyer of the world.

PEOPLE

The Buddha c 566–486 BC
Siddhartha Gautama, founder of the Buddhist religion and known as the Buddha, began life as a Hindu. Dissatisfied with many Hindu teachings, he searched for spiritual answers and received "enlightenment," after which he taught about the true nature of the world.

Akbar 1542–1605
The grandson of the Mughal founder Babur, Akbar (right) was the greatest of India's Mughal emperors. He tolerated all religions and supported the arts.

Mahatma Gandhi 1869–1948
Called the Mahatma, or great soul, Gandhi helped to gain India's independence from Britain in 1947. Later, as head of the Indian National Congress, he led peaceful protests in an effort to unify the country. He was shot dead by a Hindu rebel.

Tenzing Norgay 1914–86
After six failed attempts, Tenzing Norgay, a Sherpa from Nepal, joined Edmund Hillary to become the first to conquer Mt Everest and return, in May 1953.

Indira Gandhi 1917–84
The first female prime minister of India, Indira Gandhi led her country twice, from 1966 to 1967, and from 1980 until she was assassinated by her guards in 1984. She supported social changes that improved the lives of many Indians.

PLACES

Mumbai INDIA
Located on an island connected by bridges to the mainland, Mumbai, India's largest city, provides much of the country's wealth through its port trade and film industry. In contrast, many of its citizens are poor and homeless.

Meenakshi Temple INDIA
Towering above the heart of Madurai is this temple complex (below), built by the Nayaks in the 16th century. Towers carved with mythical figures enclose the main shrine, which honors the god Shiva and his wife Meenakshi.

Colombo SRI LANKA
The administrative capital of Sri Lanka, Colombo was founded in the mid-1300s at the mouth of the Kelani River. Many of Colombo's buildings date from its 450 years of European colonization.

TRADITIONS AND CULTURE

Tsechus BHUTAN
These annual festivals are held to celebrate Buddhism's arrival in Bhutan. Dancers wearing silk costumes and animal masks (right) act out traditional legends in the streets.

Sacred cows
For Hindus, many of whom live in southern Asia, cows are sacred beasts. No Hindu eats beef, and cows are free to roam.

Varanasi ghats INDIA
In Varanasi, India's most holy city, the ghats, or steps, of the Ganges River attract millions of pilgrims who bathe in the river's sacred waters. First light is the most blessed time to bathe.

Bollywood INDIA
Mumbai has the largest film industry in the world, producing about 800 films a year. Watching Bollywood films is one of the most popular pastimes for Southern Asians.

Golden Temple

Golden Temple INDIA
This holiest of Sikh shrines (above) stands in the middle of a pool of water at Amritsar. It was built by Guru Arjun, one of the 10 Sikh gurus, and houses his original writings on the Sikh faith.

Thimpu BHUTAN
Located in the heart of the Himalayas, this small Buddhist city is the capital of the kingdom of Bhutan. Buildings constructed in the traditional Bhutanese style dominate the skyline.

Kathmandu NEPAL
The capital of Nepal, Kathmandu has a rich architectural heritage from several religions. This Buddhist temple, the Bodhnath Stupa (left), looks like a mandala from above, and is the largest of its kind.

Kandy perahera SRI LANKA
Decorated elephants and hundreds of dancers take part in the 10-day perahera Buddhist festival, at Kandy. The sacred tooth, a relic of the Buddha, is displayed.

Sikhism INDIA
This religion, founded by Guru Nanak in the 15th century, combines Hindu and Islamic beliefs. Nine gurus succeeded Nanak and each added his mark to the Sikh faith, now followed by millions.

Indian cobra
Found in the rain forests, rice paddies and cultivated fields of India, the Indian cobra is highly venomous. When threatened, the snake rises up and spreads its neck vertebrae (above). To attack, the cobra "spits" by pressing on its venom glands, forcing venom out through its fangs. It can spit venom over 6½ feet (2 m).

HISTORY AT A GLANCE
INDIA SINCE 1525

THE MUGHALS 1526–1857
Babur (above), a Muslim leader from Afghanistan, founded the Mughal dynasty. Babur's grandson Akbar, a ruler at 15, brought more power and strength to the empire and formed his own religion. Shah Jahan, the grandson of Akbar, developed art and architecture, and created the Taj Mahal. The dynasty slowly declined after his rule, and was ended by Britain in 1857.

RIVAL STATES
As the Mughal empire became less powerful, other countries tried to take control of India. Portuguese seaman Vasco de Gama was the first European to land there, in Calicut in 1498, and Dutch, French and British ships arrived soon after. The Portuguese set up a factory in Goa and took control of Indian trade during the 16th century. Britain then gained trading control through the East India Company, set up in 1600.

SPICE TRADE
In the 17th century, trading companies were set up by other Europeans keen to trade with India for silk and spices. The British East India Company took spices, and later silks, back to England. France also competed for trade.

Indian spice market

THE BRITISH RAJ
In 1756, the prince of Bengal tried to regain power from the English. A year later, Britain, led by Robert Clive, won the Battle of Plassey, and took over the rule of Bengal and India. In 1858, Indian rule passed to the British crown. Many British people went to India and lived as they would in their homeland. In 1947, Britain agreed to release India from its control and it became independent.

Indians served the British during the Raj

SINCE INDEPENDENCE
Once India gained independence, Pakistan, a Muslim nation, wanted to split away. Riots broke out, and millions were killed as they tried to flee the unrest in the "partition" of India. Kashmir joined India, which has caused warring with Pakistan ever since. In 1971, with the support of India's army, East Pakistan gained independence from Pakistan and formed Bangladesh. In 1950, India became a democratic republic and is now governed by a coalition, or joint, government, headed by its own prime minister.

Southeast Asia

Shadow puppet
Indonesian puppet masters play out traditional stories using puppets made from buffalo or goat skin. The moving puppets cast large shadows onto a screen. The puppet master operates the arms with rods, and speaks all the voices.

Inlay Lake
The fishing people who live by the shallow waters of Inlay Lake, in Myanmar, have a unique rowing style. They use a single oar, powered by one leg.

INDONESIA
POPULATION 245,453,000 * CAPITAL JAKARTA

PHILIPPINES
POPULATION 89,469,000 * CAPITAL MANILA

VIETNAM
POPULATION 84,403,000 * CAPITAL HANOI

THAILAND
POPULATION 64,632,000 * CAPITAL BANGKOK

MYANMAR (BURMA)
POPULATION 47,383,000 * CAPITAL RANGOON

MALAYSIA
POPULATION 24,386,000 * CAPITAL KUALA LUMPUR

CAMBODIA
POPULATION 13,881,000 * CAPITAL PHNOM PENH

LAOS
POPULATION 6,368,000 * CAPITAL VIENTIANE

SINGAPORE
POPULATION 4,492,000 * CAPITAL SINGAPORE

EAST TIMOR
POPULATION 1,063,000 * CAPITAL DILI

BRUNEI
POPULATION 379,000 * CAPITAL BANDAR SERI BEGAWAN

Buddhist monk

Becak taxi
These cycle taxis are common in the small towns and rural areas of Indonesia. They take people to school and to market, and also carry goods. They were once popular in large cities, but were banned because they caused traffic jams.

Thai dancers
Elaborately costumed dancers perform plays depicting Thai myths and religious stories. The dancers' faces are either masked or expressionless. Emotions are communicated through hand and body movements. These performances were originally seen only in the royal courts.

The merlion is the symbol of Singapore, the busiest port in Southeast Asia. It is half-fish, to pay tribute to Singapore's beginnings as a fishing village.

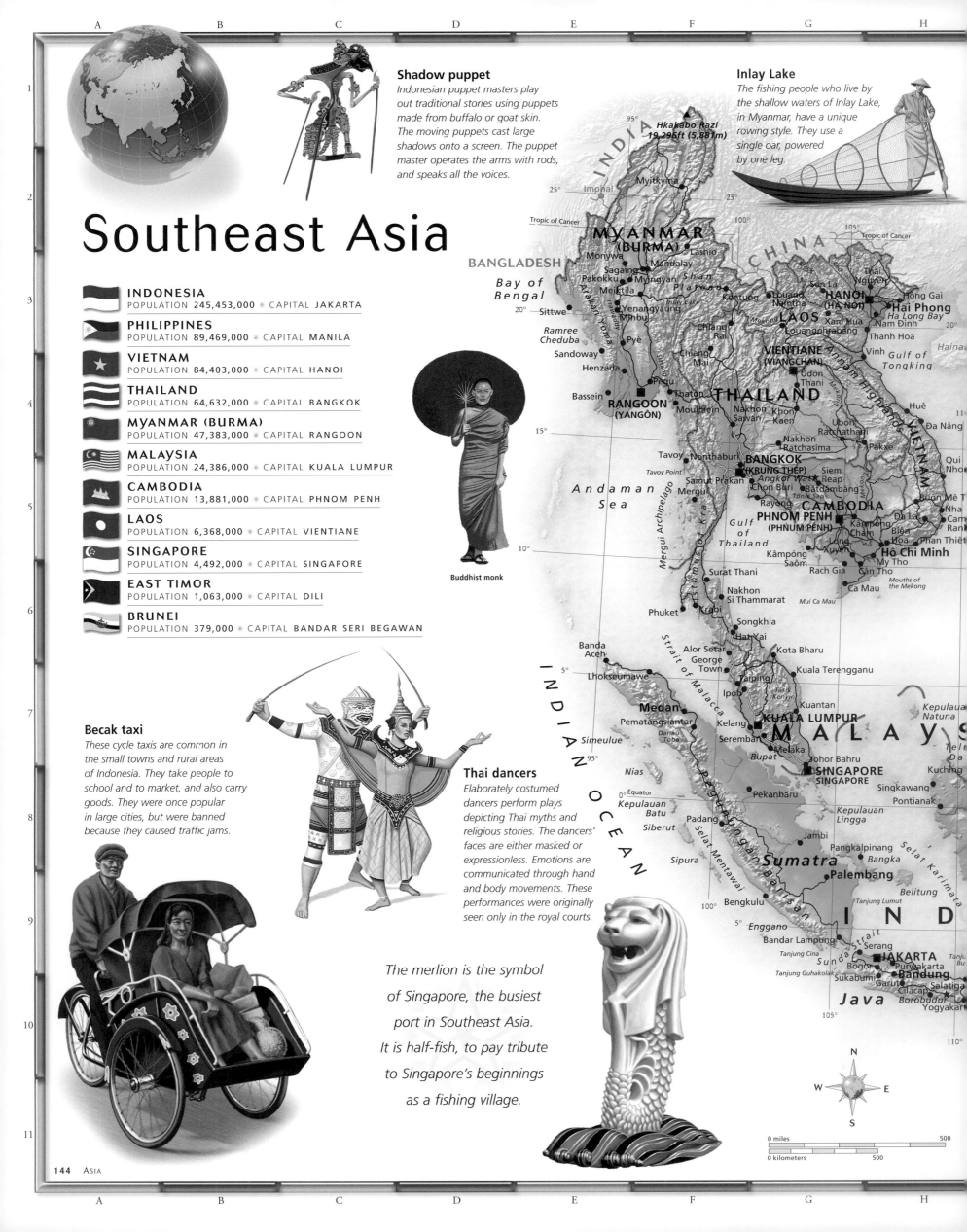

Map labels: INDIA, Hkakabo Razi 19,295ft (5,881m), Imphal, Myitkyina, CHINA, Tropic of Cancer, MYANMAR (BURMA), BANGLADESH, Monywa, Lashio, Sagaing, Mandalay, Son La, Thai Nguyen, Bay of Bengal, Pakokku, Myingyan, Shan Plateau, Kentung, Louang Namtha, HANOI (HA NOI), Hong Gai, Meiktila, Yenangyaung, Minbu, Sittwe, Chiang Rai, LAOS, Louangphrabang, Ha Long Bay, Nam Dinh, Ramree Cheduba, Pye, Chiang Mai, VIENTIANE (VIANGCHAN), Thanh Hoa, Sandoway, Henzada, Udon Thani, Vinh, Gulf of Tongking, Hainan, Bassein, Pegu, Thaton, THAILAND, Huê, Da Nang, RANGOON (YANGÔN), Moulmein, Nakhon Sawan, Khon Kaen, Ubon Ratchathani, Pakxe, VIETNAM, Tavoy, Nonthaburi, Nakhon Ratchasima, Qui Nhon, Tavoy Point, BANGKOK (KRUNG THÉP), Siem Reap, Andaman Sea, Samut Prakan, Angkor Wat, Batdambang, Buôn Mê Thuôt, Mergui, Chon Buri, Tônlé Sap, Nha Trang, Mergui Archipelago, Rayong, CAMBODIA, Da Lat, Cam Ranh, Gulf of Thailand, PHNOM PENH (PHNUM PÉNH), Kâmpong Cham, Biên Hoa, Phan Thiêt, Kâmpóng Saôm, Long Xuyen, Hô Chi Minh, Surat Thani, Rach Gia, Cân Tho, My Tho, Mouths of the Mekong, Nakhon Si Thammarat, Ca Mau, Mui Ca Mau, Phuket, Krabi, Songkhla, Banda Aceh, Hat Yai, Kota Bharu, Lhokseumawe, Alor Setar, George Town, Kuala Terengganu, Ipoh, Taiping, Kepulauan Natuna, Kuantan, MALAYSIA, Medan, Pematangsiantar, Kelang, KUALA LUMPUR, Simeulue, Danau Toba, Seremban, Melaka, Kuching, Rupat, Johor Bahru, SINGAPORE, Nias, SINGAPORE, Singkawang, Pekanbaru, Pontianak, Equator, Kepulauan Batu, Kepulauan Lingga, Siberut, Padang, Jambi, Sipura, Pangkalpinang, Bangka, Selat Karimata, Sumatra, Palembang, Belitung, Bengkulu, Tanjung Lumut, INDONESIA, Enggano, Bandar Lampung, Serang, JAKARTA, Purwakarta, Tanjung Cina, Sunda Strait, Bogor, Bandung, Tanjung Guhakolak, Sukabumi, Garut, Cilacap, Salatiga, Java, Borobudur, Yogyakarta

0 miles 500
0 kilometers 500

N W E S

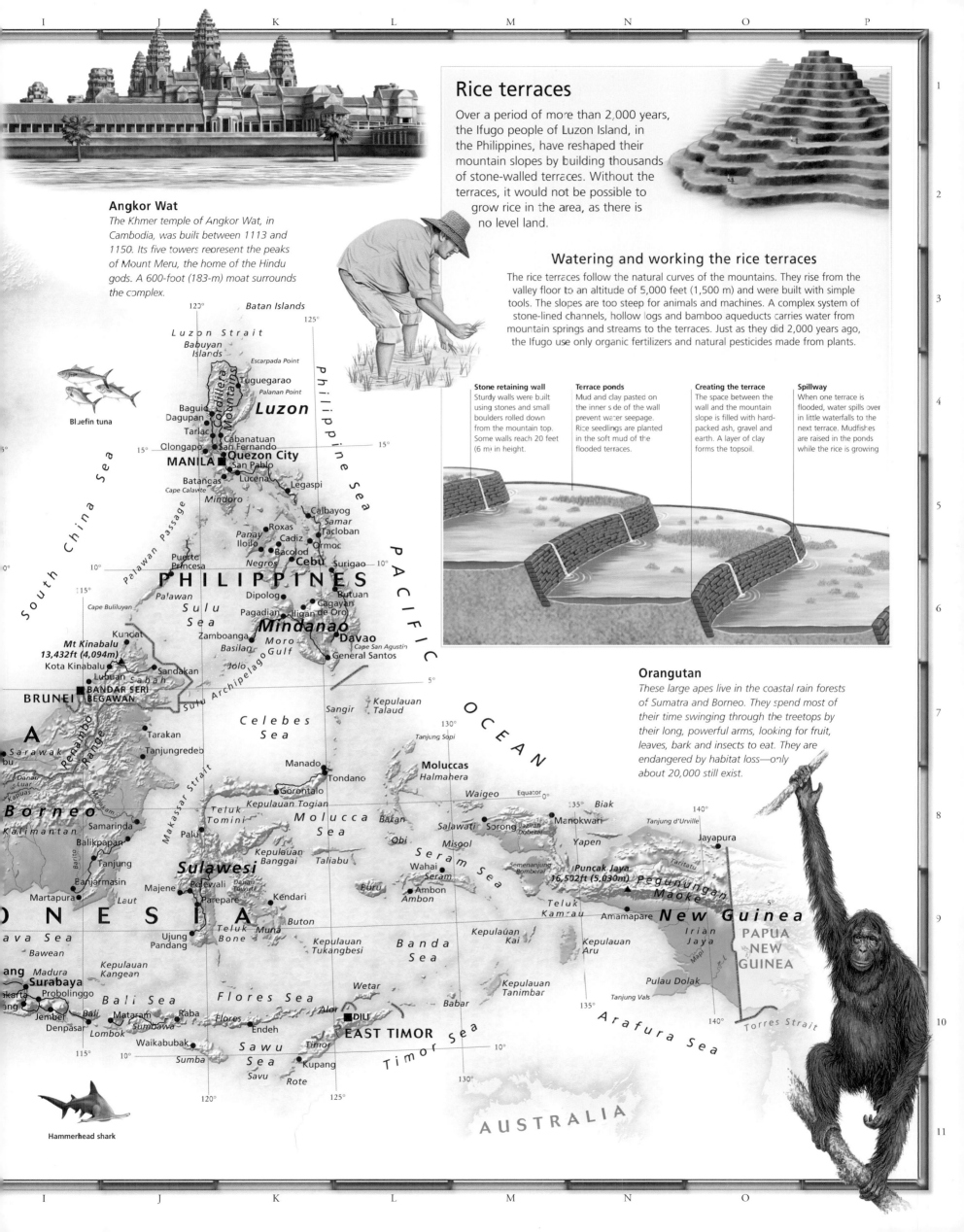

Angkor Wat

The Khmer temple of Angkor Wat, in Cambodia, was built between 1113 and 1150. Its five towers represent the peaks of Mount Meru, the home of the Hindu gods. A 600-foot (183-m) moat surrounds the complex.

Rice terraces

Over a period of more than 2,000 years, the Ifugo people of Luzon Island, in the Philippines, have reshaped their mountain slopes by building thousands of stone-walled terraces. Without the terraces, it would not be possible to grow rice in the area, as there is no level land.

Watering and working the rice terraces

The rice terraces follow the natural curves of the mountains. They rise from the valley floor to an altitude of 5,000 feet (1,500 m) and were built with simple tools. The slopes are too steep for animals and machines. A complex system of stone-lined channels, hollow logs and bamboo aqueducts carries water from mountain springs and streams to the terraces. Just as they did 2,000 years ago, the Ifugo use only organic fertilizers and natural pesticides made from plants.

Stone retaining wall
Sturdy walls were built using stones and small boulders rolled down from the mountain top. Some walls reach 20 feet (6 m) in height.

Terrace ponds
Mud and clay pasted on the inner side of the wall prevent water seepage. Rice seedlings are planted in the soft mud of the flooded terraces.

Creating the terrace
The space between the wall and the mountain slope is filled with hard-packed ash, gravel and earth. A layer of clay forms the topsoil.

Spillway
When one terrace is flooded, water spills over in little waterfalls to the next terrace. Mudfishes are raised in the ponds while the rice is growing

Orangutan

These large apes live in the coastal rain forests of Sumatra and Borneo. They spend most of their time swinging through the treetops by their long, powerful arms, looking for fruit, leaves, bark and insects to eat. They are endangered by habitat loss—only about 20,000 still exist.

Bluefin tuna

Hammerhead shark

Batan Islands

Luzon Strait
Babuyan Islands
Escarpada Point

Tuguegarao
Cordillera Mountains
Palanan Point
Baguio
Dagupan
Tarlac
Cabanatuan
Olongapo
San Fernando
Quezon City
MANILA
San Pablo
Batangas
Lucena
Cape Calavite
Legaspi
Mindoro

Luzon

Philippine Sea

PACIFIC OCEAN

Calbayog
Samar
Roxas
Tacloban
Panay
Cadiz
Iloilo
Bacolod
Ormoc
Cebu
Negros
Surigao
Butuan

PHILIPPINES

Dipolog
Cagayan
Pagadian
Iligan de Oro
Mindanao
Davao
Cape San Agustín

Palawan
Sulu Sea
Zamboanga
Moro Gulf
Basilan
General Santos
Jolo

Cape Buliluyan

South China Sea

Palawan Passage

Puerto Princesa

Mt Kinabalu
13,432ft (4,094m)
Kuncat
Kota Kinabalu
Sabah
Lubuan
Sandakan
Sulu Archipelago

BRUNEI
BANDAR SERI BEGAWAN

Penambo Range
Sarawak
bu
Danau Luar
Kapuas

Borneo
Kalimantan
Samarinda
Balikpapan
Barito
Tanjung
Banjarmasin
Martapura
Laut

ONESIA
Tarakan
Tanjungredeb
Makassar Strait
Mahakam
Palu
Teluk Tomini
Gorontalo
Kepulauan Togian
Celebes Sea
Manado
Tondano

Sangir
Kepulauan Talaud

Tanjung Sopi

Moluccas
Halmahera

Waigeo
Equator 0°
Biak
Molucca Sea
Batan
Salawati
Sorong
Manokwari
Jazirah Doberai
Yapen
Jayapura
Obi

Misool
Seram Sea
Wahai
Semenanjung Bomberai
Puncak Jaya
16,502ft (5,030m)
Seram
Buru
Ambon
Ambon
Teluk Kamrau
Amamapare
Pegunungan Maoke

New Guinea

Irian Jaya
PAPUA NEW GUINEA

Majene
Polewali
Danau Towuti
Sulawesi
Parepare
Kendari
Euru
Teluk Bone
Banda Sea
Kepulauan Kai
Kepulauan Aru
Mapi
Pulau Dolak

Ujung Pandang
Muna
Buton
Kepulauan Tukangbesi

ESIA
ava Sea
Bawean
Kepulauan Kangean
Madura
ang
Surabaya
Probolinggo
akarta
ang
Jember
Bali
Mataram
Sumbawa
Raba
Flores Sea
Kepulauan Tanimbar
Denpasar
Lombok
Waikabubak
Waingapu
Sumba
Sawu Sea
Savu
Rote
Bali Sea

Alor
Wetar
Babar
DILI
Endeh
Flores
Timor
EAST TIMOR
Kupang

Tanjung Vals

Tanjung d'Urville

Arafura Sea

Timor Sea

Torres Strait

AUSTRALIA

Southeast Asia

LAND AREA	1,689,703 sq miles (4,376,310 sq km)
LARGEST COUNTRY	Indonesia
SMALLEST COUNTRY	Singapore
MAIN RELIGION	Muslim
LIFE EXPECTANCY	70 years
LITERACY	76%

The small country of Brunei became rich when oil was discovered in 1929. The Sultan of Brunei owns the largest fleet of Rolls Royce cars in the world.

WHERE PEOPLE LIVE

Urban   Rural

REGION
43%   57%

Most urban: SINGAPORE
100%

Most rural: CAMBODIA
16%   84%

USING THE LAND

Forest and woodland

Arable land

Grazing

Arid or marginal

Krakatoa

In 1883, Krakatoa, a volcano on a small Indonesian island, erupted. The noise from the explosion was heard as far away as Australia and Japan. Several tsunamis (giant tidal waves) killed thousands of people—the largest killed 36,000. A steamship called the *Berouw* (*above*) was swept inland 1½ miles (2.4 km) by the force of one of the waves.

NATURAL FEATURES

Irian Jaya

Occupying the western half of New Guinea, Irian Jaya is an area of high mountains and dense rain forests. It is home to many animals, including the tree kangaroo, and the Arfak butterflies, which are found only in this region.   Tree kangaroo

Spice Islands

Lying between Sulawesi and New Guinea, the Spice Islands (Moluccas Islands) were the only source of spices, such as cloves, nutmeg and pepper, from the early 1500s to the late 1800s.

Lake Tonle Sap CAMBODIA

During the wet season, Lake Tonle Sap, the largest inland lake in Southeast Asia, floods. When the water subsides, the farmland is covered with rich, fertile soil.

Ha Long Bay VIETNAM

Ha Long Bay, or the Bay of the Descending Dragon, includes more than 1,600 rocky islands whose limestone cliffs are full of alcoves, caves and tunnels.

Timber
Timber is a prized resource in Southeast Asia, but its logging (*left*) has led to serious environmental problems in countries such as Thailand, Myanmar and Malaysia. Careless and often illegal logging has destroyed forests. Many species of animals have therefore lost their habitats and some may become extinct.

Rice

Tobacco

Coconuts

Palm oil

Rubber

Beef cattle

Fishing

Shellfish

Industrial center

Mining

Oil production

Gas production

Timber

Tourism

Mandalay
Louangphrabang
HANOI
Chiang Mai
VIENTIANE
RANGOON
Đa Nẵng
Tavoy
BANGKOK
Bătdâmbăng
PHNOM PENH
Hồ Chí Minh
MANILA
Phuket
Hat Yai
Cebu
Davao
Phuket
BANDAR SERI BEGAWAN
KUALA LUMPUR
SINGAPORE
Padang
Palembang
Banjarmasin
Ujung Pandang
Ambon
Jayapura
JAKARTA
Surabaya
Denpasar
DILI

Fruits
An amazing variety of fruits are grown in the plantations of Southeast Asia. Tropical fruits, such as pineapples (*left*), bananas, melons and mangoes, are sold at local markets. Some countries, including Vietnam and Malaysia, export fruits to other countries, often in canned form.

LARGEST CITIES

Manila 10,666,000

Jakarta 8,569,000

Bangkok 4,819,000

Rangoon 4,669,000

PLACES

Jakarta INDONESIA
Jakarta, situated on the island of Java, was settled in the 5th century. It is the capital of Indonesia, its largest city and its industrial and commercial center.

Rangoon MYANMAR
Rangoon is the political center of Myanmar. Located on the Ayeyarwady delta, it is also a major trading port and industrial city.

Ho Chi Minh VIETNAM
Formerly called Saigon, this is the largest city in Vietnam. The busy streets are filled with people, market stalls and traffic. Its architecture is a mix of French colonial and Asian.

Getting around Ho Chi Minh

Grand Palace BANGKOK
Built in 1782, this palace on the east bank of the Choa Phraya River was the home of the Thai royal family until the late 1800s. It is now used for ceremonial purposes.

Borobodur INDONESIA
This is the largest Buddhist monument in the world. It was built on the island of Java in the 700s and 800s, and is shaped like a pyramid, with a square base and five tiers topped with three circular terraces.

Komodo dragon

The Komodo dragon is the biggest lizard in the world. It is an excellent swimmer and moves freely between several Indonesian islands. It can grow up to 10 feet (3 m) and weigh up to 200 pounds (90 kg). It has strong, thick legs with sharp claws, fanglike teeth and a lashing tail. Despite its size, it moves fast and can kill deer, goats and wild boar.

The Petronas Towers, 1,483 feet (452 m) high, in Kuala Lumpur, Malaysia, are the tallest buildings in the world.

TRADITIONS AND CULTURE

White elephants
In ancient times, the kings of Siam (now Thailand) and Burma (Myanmar) valued and protected these animals because they believed that they would bring them peace, power and riches.

Balinese festivals
Many Balinese festivals are based on religious traditions and feature elaborate costumes (*below*). Galungan, or Balinese New Year, begins on the first day of the Hindu calendar year and lasts for 10 days. Villages honor dead ancestors and celebrate good defeating evil.

Stilt villages
In many countries in Southeast Asia, houses are built up on stilts. In some regions, this is because the houses are built over water, but in others, it is to provide shelter and living quarters underneath for the farm animals, such as pigs, chicken and water buffalo.

Stilt village

Ceremonial silks
For centuries, Thai people have been weaving silk that is famous worldwide. The colors and patterns have symbolic meanings and the silks are worn in ceremonies. Thai silk is printed by a process called silk-screen printing.

Islamic traders
Arab merchants brought Islam to Southeast Asia in the 7th century. By the 13th century, sailing in ships called dhows (*above*), these Muslim sailors had set up a spice-trading network across Asia. Muhammad, the prophet and founder of Islam, had himself been a merchant, so Islamic merchants were well respected as honest traders.

PEOPLE

King Mongkut 1804–68
Also known as Rama IV, Thailand's King Mongkut was a Buddhist monk for 27 years before becoming king. In 1862, he hired a British governess to teach his children English. The musical *The King and I* was based on her journals.

Tunku Abdul Rahman 1903–90
Rahman, the prime minister of Malaya from 1957 to 1963, led the movement to set up the independent country of Malaysia. He then became Malaysia's prime minister from 1963 to 1970.

King Norodom Sihanouk born 1922
Born in Cambodia, Sihanouk became king in 1941 when he was 18. In 1955, he gave up his throne to form a political party and become prime minister. After many years of political unrest, Sihanouk became king again in 1993.

Aung San Suu Kyi born 1945
Aung San helped found the National League for Democracy and was awarded the Nobel Peace Prize in 1991 for her work toward democracy for Myanmar.

Aung San Suu Kyi

Xanana Gusmão born 1946
Gusmão, a former guerilla leader who fought against Indonesian rule, and was imprisoned for it, was elected president of East Timor in 2002.

HISTORY AT A GLANCE

C 1,600,000 BC
Humanlike people live in Java. They are about 5 feet (150 cm) tall, with large eyebrow ridges, a heavy jaw, a small chin and a thick skull.

C 2100 BC
Humans live in Ban Chiang, a settlement in the Udon Thani province in Thailand. They cultivate rice and raise animals for food. They also make and use metal tools.

Pagan palace

AD 1044
King Anawratha comes to the throne of Burma and rules from its capital, Pagan. Over the next 13 years he defeats the Mon, who are an Austro-Asian people, and unifies Burma.

1350
King Ramathibodi I founds the new kingdom of Ayutthaya in Thailand. He sets up his capital on an island near the Chao Phraya River just north of present-day Bangkok. He unifies the people and establishes a legal system. The kingdom lasts until 1767.

Ayutthayan Buddha

1595–98
The first Dutch trading missions arrive in Indonesia and, several years later, the powerful Dutch East India Company is founded.

1782
King Rama I becomes king of Thailand. He is the first of the Chakri dynasty, which rules Thailand today. He moves the court to Bangkok, turning it from a small village to a royal city.

1959
The island of Singapore, previously a colony of Britain, gains self-government for its internal affairs. Britain remains responsible for its defense and foreign affairs.

Vietnam War

1965–73
The USA joins the South Vietnamese in their efforts to prevent the North Vietnamese and South Vietnamese rebels from taking over Vietnam. The USA is involved for eight years, the longest war in which it has taken part.

1967
Suharto takes over from Sukarno as president of Indonesia. He makes peace with Malaysia and helps form the Association of Southeast Asian States (ASEAN), which promotes trade and cooperation with western countries.

1975–79
Cambodia is ravaged by the dictator Pol Pot, the leader of the Khmer Rouge soldiers. Temples and mosques are destroyed, and thousands of Cambodians are tortured, executed and buried.

2002
East Timor, which has been ruled by force by Indonesia since 1975, becomes independent, elects Xanana Gusmão as president and joins the United Nations.

Eastern Asia

Farmer with buffalo plow

Tibet, in southwest China, is known as "the roof of the world." The Himalayas, on the border between Tibet and Nepal, are Earth's highest mountains.

Traditional costume, Mongolia

CHINA
POPULATION 1,313,974,000 ⁕ CAPITAL BEIJING

SOUTH KOREA
POPULATION 48,847,000 ⁕ CAPITAL SEOUL

NORTH KOREA
POPULATION 23,113,000 ⁕ CAPITAL PYONGYANG

TAIWAN
POPULATION 23,036,000 ⁕ CAPITAL TAIPEI

MONGOLIA
POPULATION 2,832,000 ⁕ CAPITAL ULAANBAATAR

The Great Wall of China

For thousands of years, the people of China built walls along their northern frontier. They all had one purpose: to keep Mongolian tribes from invading China's farmlands. The first wall—known as the Long Wall—was built between 217 and 208 BC by Emperor Qin Shi Huangdi, and stretched for 1,800 miles (2,900 km), with 25,000 watchtowers along its length.

Today's wall, snaking like a dragon through northern China's mountains and plains, is the fourth one. Emperor Zhu Yuanzhang ordered work to begin in 1368, and building continued for almost 300 years until 1644. The wall was made of earth rammed between stone and brick, with watchtowers, gateways and forts along the way.

Length
The Great Wall of China is the longest structure ever built. The main wall and its branches are about 4,000 miles (6,400 km) long.

CHINA

China's first emperor, Qin Shi Huangdi

Building the wall
Millions of prisoners, soldiers and peasants were forced to work on the wall. So many of them died that the wall has been called "the world's longest graveyard."

Defending the wall
Archers on each tower could cover half the distance between them. This meant that enemy soldiers storming the wall were never out of arrow range.

Chinese lion dance
The lion dance is about 2,000 years old, and is part of Chinese New Year and other festivals. Two dancers are inside the lion costume. One handles the head; the other plays the body and the tail. Three musicians accompany the lion.

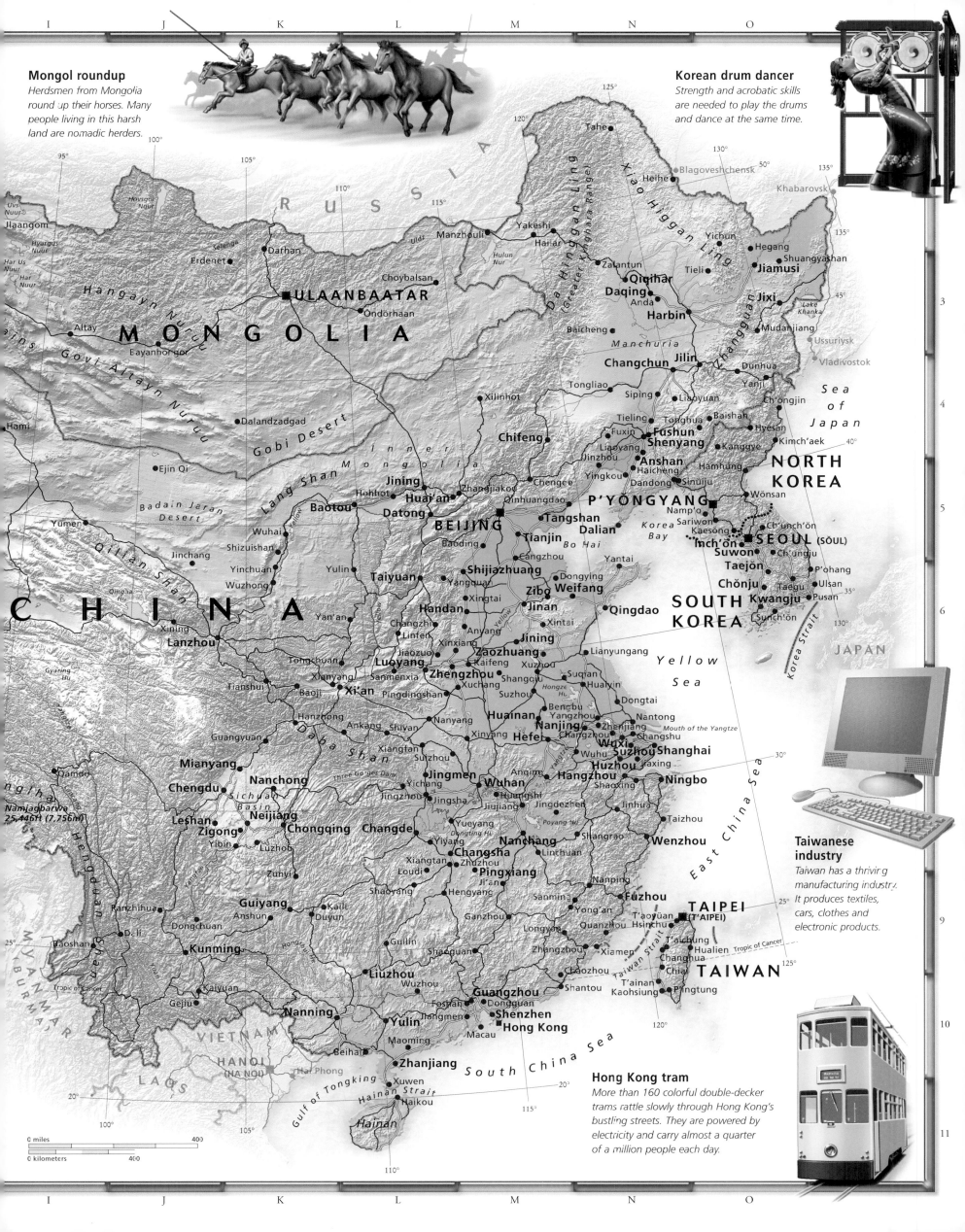

Mongol roundup
Herdsmen from Mongolia round up their horses. Many people living in this harsh land are nomadic herders.

Korean drum dancer
Strength and acrobatic skills are needed to play the drums and dance at the same time.

Taiwanese industry
Taiwan has a thriving manufacturing industry. It produces textiles, cars, clothes and electronic products.

Hong Kong tram
More than 160 colorful double-decker trams rattle slowly through Hong Kong's bustling streets. They are powered by electricity and carry almost a quarter of a million people each day.

Eastern Asia

Tea plantations
During the 17th century, European traders came to China's coast to buy tea and other goods. Today, Chinese tea remains popular. Plantations in more than 20 provinces grow crops for local use and for export.

USING THE LAND

- Cereals
- Rice
- Tea
- Sugarcane
- Soybeans
- Beef cattle
- Sheep
- Pigs
- Fishing
- Industrial center
- Mining
- Oil production
- Timber

- Forest and woodland
- Arable land
- Grazing
- Arid or marginal

CHINA LAND AREA	3,705,195 sq miles (9,596,410 sq km)
OFFICIAL LANGUAGE	Chinese/Mandarin
MAIN RELIGION	Buddhist/Taoist
LIFE EXPECTANCY	72 years
LITERACY	86%

SOUTH KOREA LAND AREA	37,911 sq miles (98,190 sq km)
OFFICIAL LANGUAGE	Korean
MAIN RELIGION	Christian
LIFE EXPECTANCY	75 years
LITERACY	98%

NORTH KOREA LAND AREA	46,491 sq miles (120,410 sq km)
OFFICIAL LANGUAGE	Korean
MAIN RELIGION	Buddhist
LIFE EXPECTANCY	70 years
LITERACY	99%

TAIWAN LAND AREA	12,456 sq miles (32,260 sq km)
OFFICIAL LANGUAGE	Mandarin
MAIN RELIGION	Buddhist/Taoist
LIFE EXPECTANCY	76 years
LITERACY	86%

MONGOLIA LAND AREA	600,543 sq miles (1,555,400 sq km)
OFFICIAL LANGUAGE	Khalkha Mongol
MAIN RELIGION	Buddhist
LIFE EXPECTANCY	63 years
LITERACY	99%

Map labels: ULAANBAATAR, Ürümqi, Kashi, Harbin, Changchun, BEIJING, Tianjin, P'YONGYANG, SEOUL, Lanzhou, Zhengzhou, Shanghai, Lhasa, Wuhan, Chongqing, TAIPEI, Hong Kong, Haikou

LARGEST CITIES

Shanghai 15,435,000

Seoul 10,451,000

Beijing 7,725,000

NATURAL FEATURES

Plateau of Tibet CHINA
This high, flat and dry region in southwest China, north of the Himalayas, is the largest plateau in the world. It is home to Tibetan farmers, who keep yaks (right) for meat and dairy products.

Yellow River CHINA
The name of this river comes from the yellow silt that gathers on its bed as it flows downstream. Because its floods cause so much damage, the Yellow River is also called "China's Sorrow."

Gobi Desert MONGOLIA–CHINA
Vast areas of the Gobi Desert are covered in rugged, bare rock, with little vegetation. The desert stretches across 500,000 square miles (1,300,000 sq km).

Guilin CHINA
Tourists flock to this scenic area in Guangxi province to see its unusual limestone mountain peaks, known as karst formations. These landscapes have inspired artists and poets for centuries.

Guilin mountains

WHERE PEOPLE LIVE

	Urban	Rural
SOUTH KOREA	81%	19%
TAIWAN	69%	31%
NORTH KOREA	60%	40%
MONGOLIA	58%	42%
CHINA	32%	68%

LONGEST RIVERS

Yangtze (Chang Jiang) 3,964 miles (6,380 km)

Yellow (Huang He) 3,395 miles (5,464 km)

Lancang Jiang (Mekong) 2,749 miles (4,425 km)

Heilong Jiang (Amur) 1,786 miles (2,874 km)

Rice paddies
Rice, China's main crop, is grown in flooded fields called paddies. The seeds are sown elsewhere, and once the rice shoots appear, women plant them out into the paddies. When the rice stalks are ripe, they are harvested. The grains are shaken from the stalks and left to dry in the sun. Water buffalo are sometimes used to plow the rice fields.

Three Gorges Dam

A massive dam is being built across the Yangtze River at Sandouping. Work began in 1993, and when complete, water from the dam will generate hydroelectricity to power China's industries. The water will flood an area the size of Singapore, washing away the homes of more than a million people, and destroying historic sites and magnificent scenery.

TRADITIONS AND CULTURE

Tai chi

Each morning, people all over China start their day outdoors with a series of gentle movements that they believe will help develop their mind, body and spirit. Tai chi started in the 3rd century AD.

Moon Festival

At this mid-autumn festival during the eighth full moon of the Chinese lunar year, people let off loud fireworks when the moon appears, and eat moon cakes (*left*).

Woodblock printing

People in Eastern Asia invented the first form of printing in the 8th century. They carved characters from printed blocks, covered them with ink, and pressed the inked block onto paper.

There are 300 million bicycles in China, and people need a licence to ride one.

Dragon boat racing

As part of the Dragon Boat Festival, celebrated in Taiwan as well as China, long, decorated boats race on waterways to commemorate the death of the poet Chu Yuan, who drowned in 299 BC. Rice dumplings are served on the day.

Dragon boat

Chinese art

For centuries, Chinese painters have created landscapes using ink and brush on silk or paper. Plants and animals, combined with calligraphy, are popular subjects for scrolls, fans or folded albums.

PEOPLE

Confucius 551–479 BC

The values of this great thinker and teacher still form part of the Chinese way of life. Although he lived 2,500 years ago, his ideas on the family, school and nation are respected throughout China.

Zhang Heng AD 78–139

This Chinese mathematician and astronomer invented a seismoscope (*right*), for recording earthquakes. A ball fell out of a dragon's mouth into a frog's mouth when an earthquake occurred, making a loud noise, which woke the emperor.

Genghis Khan 1162–1227

One of the great Mongol leaders, Genghis Khan brought together the tribes of central Asia in 1209, and was crowned lord of all. His grandson was Kublai Khan.

Mao Zedong 1893–1976

The son of a peasant, Mao Zedong was a revolutionary leader. As head of the People's Republic of China, formed in 1949, Chairman Mao led China for almost 30 years under communist rule.

Dalai Lama born 1935

This spiritual leader of Tibet, now the 14th, has lived in exile in India since 1959. His title means "Ocean of Wisdom." In 1989, he received the Nobel Peace Prize.

Giant pandas

The number of giant pandas in China has dropped to 700 because the fountain bamboo forests that provide their food are being cleared for housing. These bears live in Sichuan province in central China.

Terra-cotta warriors

In 1974, workers in Shaanxi province, China, discovered a pit of life-size pottery statues. Emperor Qin Shi Huangdi had ordered the terra-cotta warriors to be made so that they could protect him after his death. In one pit, 7,000 soldiers and 600 horses, originally painted in bright colors, were found. Although they were made from molds, no two faces are the same.

Koumiss, the national drink of Mongolia, is made from fermented mare's milk.

PLACES

Shanghai CHINA

Shanghai, on the Huangpu River, was first settled in AD 1000. This thriving port is China's chief industrial and commercial city, and has long been a center for foreign investment and trade.

The Forbidden City CHINA

The emperor once lived behind the walls of this elaborate complex, whose intricate features date from the Ming dynasty. Today, tourists are able to enter the area and walk around its grounds.

The Forbidden City

Seoul SOUTH KOREA

South Korea's capital, Seoul, is a modern city on the Han River. Many businesses have their headquarters in the center and the streets bustle with a quarter of the nation's population.

Potala Palace TIBET

This traditional home of the Dalai Lama, or priest-king, of Tibet sits on a rocky hill above the city of Lhasa. The 1,000-room palace was built in the 17th century.

Potala Palace

HISTORY AT A GLANCE
THE CHINESE DYNASTIES

XIA c 2205–c 1700 BC
People are living in communities and use tools by the time this first dynasty develops, but few records exist. Yu, a Xia emperor, builds the first of China's canals.

SHANG 1600–1050 BC
The Shang dynasty overthrows the Xia. People use bronze for the first time, for tools and pottery. The Shang develop a 12-month, 360-day calendar.

Bronze Shang pot

ZHOU 1050–221 BC
Local armies fight for land, with much bloodshed. Confucianism develops. Iron is used and ox-drawn plows, crossbows and irrigation are invented.

QIN 221–207 BC
The ruler of the Qin state overthrows the Zhou ruler. Local states are destroyed and unified into one nation. The word China comes from "Qin."

HAN 206 BC – AD 220
The country is run by a new national civil service, based on the teachings of Confucius. Factories produce silk, cloth, paper and farm tools.

JIN AD 265–420
Two Jin dynasties emerge—northern and southern—under the rule of the Emperor Sima Yan. China cannot maintain its unity.

SUI AD 581–618
China is reunified after three centuries of disunity. The Great Wall is rebuilt and planning for the Grand Canal begins. Defeat by the Turks causes this short dynasty to collapse.

Fashions from the Tang dynasty

TANG AD 618–907
A lively emperor brings a new age of prosperity and opportunity in art and culture. Paper money is introduced and Buddhism becomes popular.

LIAO AD 907–1125
China disintegrates during these years, following attacks from the north. Many areas fall into foreign hands. The south divides into small states.

SONG AD 960–1279
The country is once again united. Cities grow. This is a golden age for architecture, craft, science, painting and learning.

YUAN 1206–1368
Kublai Khan sets up the Mongol emperors in Beijing to rule the Silk Road. The Chinese resent their Mongol invaders.

MING 1368–1644
The ideals of the Tang and Song dynasties return under Zhou Yuanzhang. This is a time of stability and order.

The last emperor

QING 1644–1911
The Manchus seize China. The empire gradually weakens and the Manchus are overthrown. Still a child, Pu Yi is the last emperor of China.

MODERN CHINA 1949
After civil war, China becomes a communist regime and is renamed the People's Republic of China. Industry and agriculture are modernized.

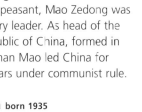

Japan

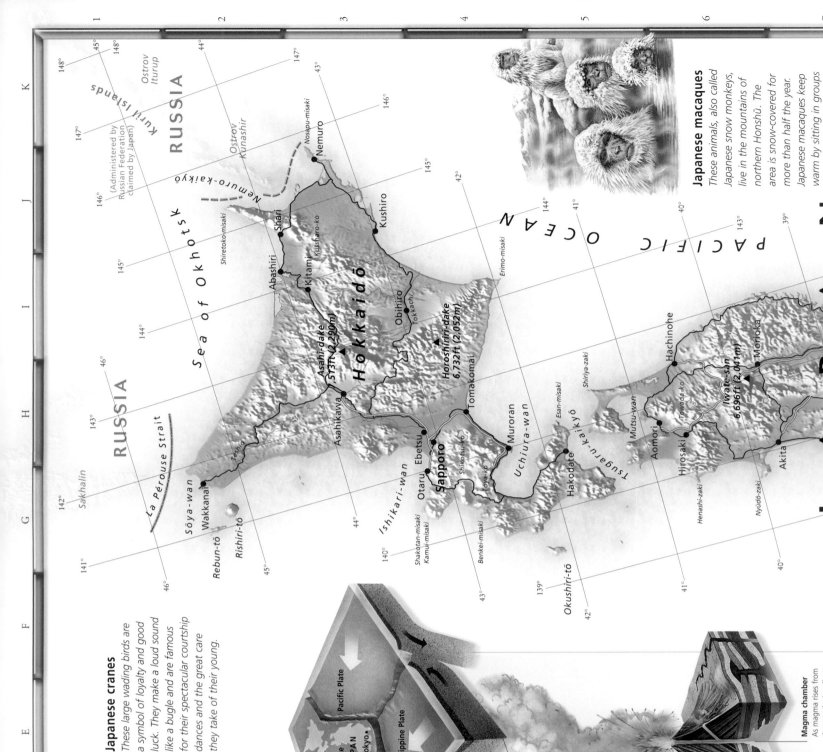

🗾 **JAPAN**
POPULATION 127,464,000 ✴ CAPITAL TOKYO

Earthquakes and volcanoes

Earth's crust is broken into pieces, called tectonic plates, that constantly move around. When a thick plate rides up over a thinner plate, the thinner one is forced down into the layer between Earth's crust and its core, a process called subduction. On the surface, volcanoes and earthquakes occur. There are three tectonic plates beneath Japan, and regular, sometimes devastating, earthquakes and volcanic eruptions take place on land.

The Ring of Fire

Japan sits on the Ring of Fire (in red). This chain includes more than half Earth's volcanoes and is the source of more than half its earthquakes.

Equator

PACIFIC OCEAN

JAPAN

PACIFIC OCEAN

— Ring of Fire

Double trouble

Japan lies on both the Pacific and the Philippine plates. The Pacific Plate moves 4 inches (10 cm) each year. The Philippine Plate moves at half that speed. These two plates cause many of Japan's earthquakes and volcanoes.

Pacific Plate

Eurasian Plate

JAPAN
Tokyo
Kobe

Philippine Plate

How volcanoes form

Forces deep within Earth cause magma to burst through the crust and spit ash and fire.

Mid-ocean ridge
When plates under the ocean are pushed apart, magma rises through the gap. It cools and hardens to form a series of ridges on the ocean floor.

Island arc volcano
When two plates with ocean crust collide, island arc volcanoes form.

Hot-spot volcano
Sometimes, magma from a spot deep in the mantle forces its way through a weak spot in the middle of a plate to form a series of hot-spot volcanoes.

Continental volcano
When thin ocean crust meets thicker continental crust, the thin crust slides under the thicker one. This process forms a line of volcanoes.

Magma chamber
As magma rises from the mantle, it collects in the crust in large pockets called magma chambers.

Trench

Magma upwelling

Direction of plate movement

Ocean crust

Magma upwelling

Japanese cranes
These large wading birds are a symbol of loyalty and good luck. They make a loud sound like a bugle and are famous for their spectacular courtship dances and the great care they take of their young.

Japanese macaques
These animals, also called Japanese snow monkeys, live in the mountains of northern Honshū. The area is snow-covered for more than half the year. Japanese macaques keep warm by sitting in groups in hot volcanic springs.

Fishing

Kuril Islands

Ostrov Iturup

Ostrov Kunashir

(Administered by Russian Federation claimed by Japan)

RUSSIA

RUSSIA

Sea of Okhotsk

Nemuro-kaikyo

Nosapu-misaki
Nemuro

Shiretoko-misaki

Shari
Abashiri
Kitami
Kushiro-ko
Kushiro

Kamikawa

Hokkaidō

Asahi-dake
5,131ft (2,290m)

Horoshiri-dake
6,732ft (2,052m)

Obihiro

Tokachi

Asahikawa

Tomakomai

Muroran
Uchiura-wan

Esan-misaki

Sapporo
Otaru Ebetsu
Shikotsuko

Toya-ko
Toya-ko

Hakodate

Erimo-misaki

Tsugaru-kaikyō

Tsugaru-kaikyō

Okushiri-tō

Shiriya-zaki

Ō-dōmari
Aomori

Mutsu-wan

Henashi-zaki

Nyūdō-zaki

Hirosaki

Hachinohe

Towada-ko

Iwate-san
6,696ft (2,041m)

Morioka

Kinka-san

Akita

Sakata

Ishinomaki

Yamagata

Sendai
Sendai-wan

Tsuruoka

JAPAN

Niigata

Fukushima

Sadoga-shima

PACIFIC OCEAN

La Pérouse Strait

Sōya-wan
Wakkanai

Sakhalin

Rebun-tō

Rishiri-tō

Ishikari-wan

Shakotan-misaki
Kamui-misaki

Benkei-misaki

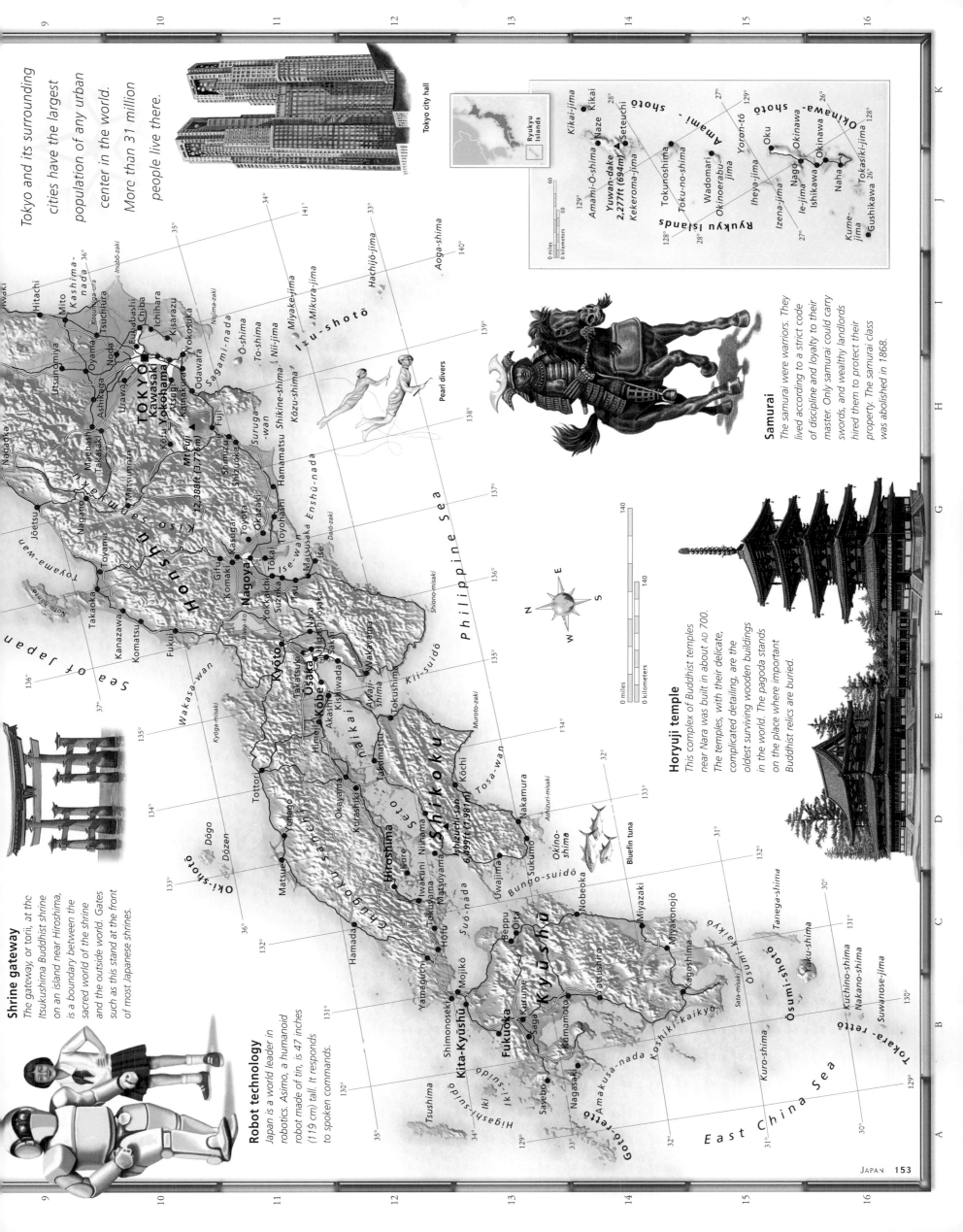

Tokyo and its surrounding cities have the largest population of any urban center in the world. More than 31 million people live there.

Tokyo city hall

Shrine gateway

The gateway, or torii, at the Itsukushima Buddhist shrine on an island near Hiroshima, is a boundary between the sacred world of the shrine and the outside world. Gates such as this stand at the front of most Japanese shrines.

Robot technology

Japan is a world leader in robotics. Asimo, a humanoid robot made of tin, is 47 inches (119 cm) tall. It responds to spoken commands.

Samurai

The samurai were warriors. They lived according to a strict code of discipline and loyalty to their master. Only samurai could carry swords, and wealthy landlords hired them to protect their property. The samurai class was abolished in 1868.

Horyuji temple

This complex of Buddhist temples near Nara was built in about AD 700. The temples, with their delicate, complicated detailing, are the oldest surviving wooden buildings in the world. The pagoda stands on the place where important Buddhist relics are buried.

Pearl divers

Bluefin tuna

JAPAN 153

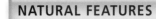

Japan

LAND AREA	144,689 sq miles (374,744 sq km)
OFFICIAL LANGUAGE	Japanese
MAIN RELIGION	Shinto/Buddhism
LIFE EXPECTANCY	81 years
LITERACY	99%

Japan has an average of 546 residents per square mile (337 per sq km)—one of the world's highest population densities.

WHERE PEOPLE LIVE

Urban		Rural
79%		21%

Rice plantations
About half the country's farmland is planted with rice, Japan's main food. Japan has abundant rainfall and many rivers that can be used for irrigation, allowing rice to be cultivated in paddies—fields that have been submerged under 2–4 inches (5–10 cm) of water. Farmers harvest their crops quickly with efficient machinery.

USING THE LAND

- Forest and woodland
- Arable land

- Rice
- Fruit
- Tobacco
- Beef cattle
- Fishing
- Industrial center
- Winter sports

Fruit and vegetables
Although four-fifths of the country is mountainous, and the soils are poor, Japan grows a wide variety of crops, including tomatoes, strawberries, cherries and carrots. Because of the limited amount of suitable farming land, Japanese farms are very small—seldom more than 2 acres (1 ha)—and every usable piece of land is planted.

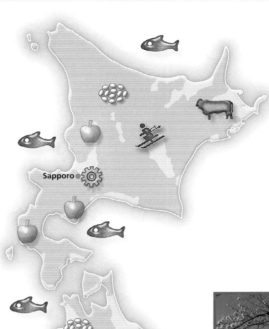

Sapporo

Sendai

TOKYO
Yokohama

Nagoya

Kyōto

Ōsaka

Hiroshima

Fukuoka

Nakamura

Kagoshima

Fishing
Since earliest times, the Japanese have relied on the sea and waterways for food. Deep-sea fishes, such as mackerel and tuna, are plentiful. However, to keep up with the demand for freshwater species, such as trout and eel, fish farms have been developed. Seaweed is also part of many Japanese dishes—fishermen gather kelp along Hokkaido's coast, and laver seaweed, or *nori*, is grown in Kyushu.

LARGEST CITIES

Tokyo 8,404,000

Yokohama 3,632,000

Osaka 2,589,000

Nagoya 2,198,000

Sapporo 1,981,000

NATURAL FEATURES

Earthquake damage

Earthquakes
Japan experiences about 1,000 mostly minor Earth tremors each year. In 1923, an earthquake in the Tokyo–Yokohama area killed 140,000 people. The 1995 Kobe quake lasted only 20 seconds, but caused US$200 billion worth of damage and killed more than 5,000 people.

Mt Fuji
This volcano, which last erupted in 1707, is the highest peak in Japan, at 12,388 feet (3,776 m). Its name means "everlasting life." Regarded as sacred, it is a place of pilgrimage and the subject of many paintings and poems.

Mt Fuji

Ryukyu islands
This archipelago of 55 islands—some flat and built from coral, others mountainous and volcanic—extends 400 miles (640 km). Agriculture is the main occupation. The main crops are rice, sweet potatoes, sugar and pineapples. The islanders have their own language.

Shirakami mountains
This uninhabited, mountainous area in northern Honshū contains Japan's last beech forest. Many plants and animals are found here, including the Asiatic bear.

Asiatic bear

Bullet train
The first section of the *Shinkansen*—a high-speed electric rail line between Tokyo and Fukuoka—opened in 1964. About 250 "bullet trains" operate along the line daily. On some sections they can reach speeds of 160 miles (260 km) per hour. The fastest trains can complete the 664-mile (1,062-km) trip in less than seven hours.

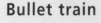

Great Buddha

Erected in 1252, this 37-foot (11-m) tall bronze statue is in the grounds of Kotokuin Temple in Kamakura. The wooden building that once housed it was destroyed by a tsunami in 1495. Today, more than 96 million people follow Buddhism, which came to Japan from China in the 6th century. This Buddha faces the ocean, thought to be an ideal place to meditate.

PEOPLE

Murasaki Shikibu AD 978–1014
This Japanese noblewoman created *The Tale of Genji*—one of the world's first novels. The story was painted on a scroll, with intricately detailed illustrations. She also kept a diary of her life at court.

Toyotomi Hideyoshi 1536–98
The son of a peasant, Hideyoshi rose to be a samurai, then a feudal lord. He conquered Japan and unified the country after more than a century of warfare.

The Great Wave Off Kanagawa

Katsushika Hokusai 1760–1849
This artist produced thousands of artworks by printing from carved wood blocks. His series "Thirty-six Views of Mount Fuji," which includes *The Great Wave Off Kanagawa*, is famous.

Emperor Hirohito 1901–89
Japan's longest-reigning monarch, Hirohito oversaw dramatic changes in Japan, through an era of military expansion that ended with defeat in World War II, to the country's emergence as an economic superpower.

TRADITIONS AND CULTURE

Cherry blossoms
The brief season of Japan's national flower, the cherry blossom, is eagerly awaited each spring. Many poems have been written about these flowers. During World War II, they symbolized the soldiers who died in the war. In peacetime, they represent the start of the school year.

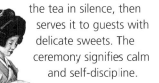

Shinto
Shinto is an ancient Japanese religion, based on the worship of spirits. There are more than 80,000 Shinto shrines in Japan. Before entering a shrine to pay their respects to the spirits, people wet their fingertips and rinse out their mouth.

Tea ceremony
This ancient ceremony takes great skill and concentration. The host prepares the tea in silence, then serves it to guests with delicate sweets. The ceremony signifies calm and self-discipline.

Hari-kiri, or seppuku, is a traditional form of ritual suicide.

Theater
Japan has three main types of traditional theater. Noh plays are short, with more symbolism than action. Lively Kabuki plays combine music, dance and mime with elaborate staging and costuming. Bunraku is a sophisticated form of puppet theater.

Noh mask

Rock gardens
The 2,000-year-old Japanese art of rock gardening follows strict rules to create serene spaces through harmony of the various elements. The patterns have spiritual and symbolic significance.

Sumo wrestling
Sumo wrestling, the national sport, is a popular spectacle in Japan. Following centuries-old rules and rituals, the two opponents, who eat special food to bulk up their size, use their strength and weight to try to knock each other out of a ring.

PLACES

Tokyo
Tokyo, Japan's largest city, was founded in 1457 as the fortified town of Edo. In 1868, it became the capital and was renamed Tokyo. This bustling, crowded city is where much of the nation's political, economic and social activity takes place, and is home to one-fourth of the nation's people.

Kyoto
Founded in AD 794, Kyoto was the capital and home of the emperor's family for more than 1,000 years. A center of Buddhism and traditional culture, it is known for its historic temples and gardens, schools of tea ceremony and flower arranging, museums, geisha houses, artisans, theaters and festivals.

Golden Pavilion, Kyoto

Hiroshima
On 6 August 1945, the USA dropped an atomic bomb on Hiroshima. Some 70,000 people died instantly or soon after the blast; a similar number died later of radiation sickness. The Atomic Bomb Dome (*above*) was one of the few buildings not completely destroyed. The city has been rebuilt, and is now a center of the peace movement.

Atomic Bomb Dome

Osaka
Japan's second city, Osaka has long been a cultural center, and has several universities. Its castle was built in the 16th century by the warlord Toyotomi Hideyoshi. Today, the city is a financial center with a busy port. Its industries include machinery, chemicals, metal production, textiles, paper and printing.

HISTORY AT A GLANCE

Jomon pottery

13,000 BC
Hunters and gatherers form the Jomon period. The first pottery is created.

300 BC
Settlers from Southeast Asia and Korea arrive, bringing their knowledge of rice-farming.

AD 500
The Yamato period starts. *Daimyo* (rulers) take control of large areas.

AD 710
The Nara period starts. Later this century, Japanese culture evolves, with a new writing system. Buddhism becomes the state religion.

AD 794
Kyoto is built as the new capital city. It remains Japan's principal city for more than 1,000 years.

1185
After defeating the Taira family, Minamoto Yoritomo establishes a rival government and becomes the first shogun.

1274
The Mongols invade Japan. A "divine wind" (kamikaze) sinks their ships and they retreat. A second Mongol invasion also fails.

1542
The first Europeans arrive in search of spices and silk to trade. Missionaries spread the Christian faith. Firearms are introduced.

Imperial Palace

1590
After a series of wars, Toyotomi Hideyoshi unifies Japan and takes control. Guns are banned and the samurai gain status.

1600
The Tokugama period starts. Edo (Tokyo) becomes the new capital. All foreigners are expelled from 1637—only the Dutch and Chinese are allowed to trade from Nagasaki. Christianity is banned in 1614.

1868
Emperor Meiji is made head of state and moves to Tokyo. A period of rapid modernization begins. Japan's national pride grows.

Zero plane

1941
Japan launches a surprise attack on Pearl Harbor and fights the USA and Allies in World War II.

1945
Japan surrenders after the USA drops atomic bombs over Hiroshima and Nagasaki.

1997
After a period of rapid growth, the Japanese economy enters a severe recession.

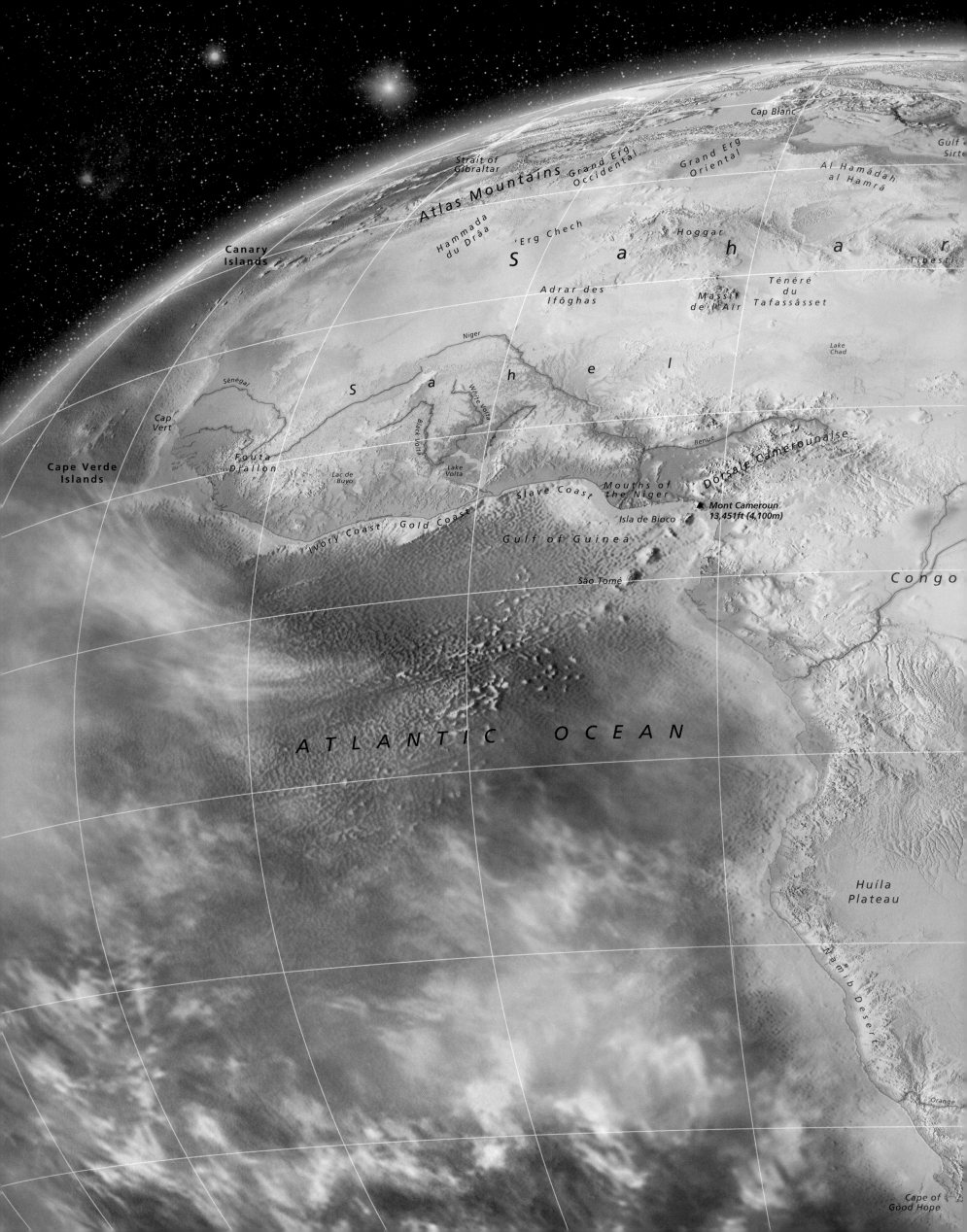

Cap Blanc

Gulf of Sirte

Strait of Gibraltar

Atlas Mountains

Grand Erg Occidental

Grand Erg Oriental

Al Hamádah al Hamrá

Canary Islands

Hammada du Drâa

'Erg Chech

Hoggar

S a h a r a

Tibesti

Adrar des Ifôghas

Massif de l'Aïr

Ténéré du Tafassâsset

Niger

Lake Chad

Sénégal

S a h e l

Cape Verde Islands

Cap Vert

White Volta

Fouta Djallon

Black Volta

Benue

Dorsale Camerounaise

Lac de Buyo

Lake Volta

Slave Coast

Mouths of the Niger

Mont Cameroun 13,451ft (4,100m)

Ivory Coast

Gold Coast

Isla de Bioco

Gulf of Guinea

Congo

São Tomé

ATLANTIC OCEAN

Huíla Plateau

Namib Desert

Orange

Cape of Good Hope

Mediterranean Sea

Libyan
Desert

Qattára
Depression

Nile
Delta

Sinai

Nile

Eastern Desert

Western Desert

a

Massif
Ennedi

Marra
Plateau

Nubian
Desert

Red Sea

Blue Nile

White Nile

Lake
Tana

Ethiopian

Highlands

Ahmar
Mountains

Gulf of Aden

Rās Xaafuun

Mendebo
Mountains

Horn of
Africa

Ubangi

Congo

Lake
Turkana

Great Rift Valley

Shebeli

Basin

Lake
Albert

Lake
Victoria

Serengeti
Plain

Mt Kenya
17,057ft (5,199m)

Plateau
du Kasai

Lake
Tanganyika

Great Rift Valley

East African
Plateau

Kilimanjaro
19,331ft (5,892m)

Pemba Island

Africa

Zanzibar Island

Lake
Malawi

INDIAN   OCEAN

Zambezi

Lake
Kariba

Comoros
Islands

Okavango
Delta

Zambezi

Mozambique Channel

K a l a h a r i

B a s i n

Limpopo

Madagascar

K a l a h a r i

D e s e r t

Drakensberg

Great Karoo

Little Karoo

ape
gulhas

Cape
Agulhas

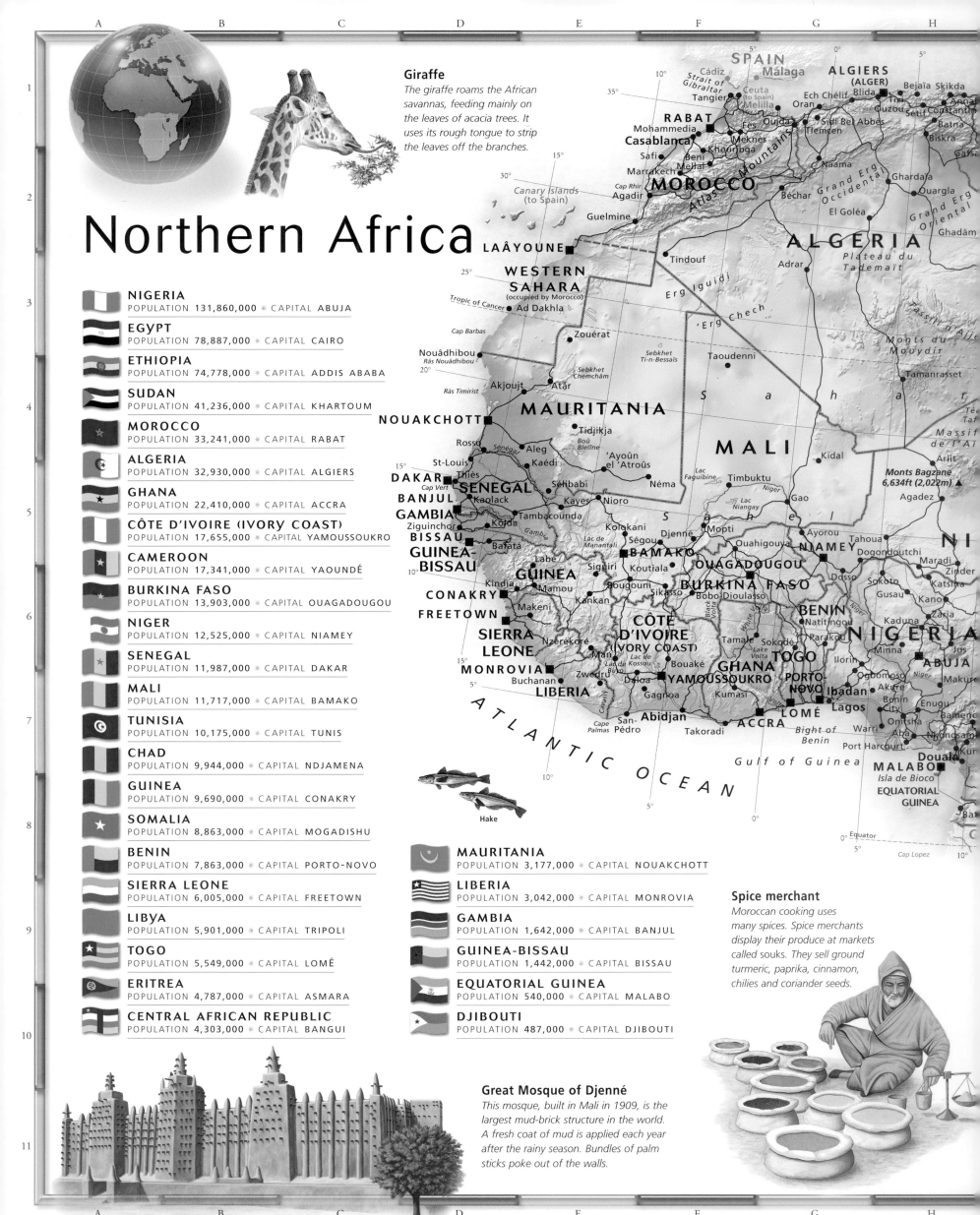

Northern Africa

Giraffe
The giraffe roams the African savannas, feeding mainly on the leaves of acacia trees. It uses its rough tongue to strip the leaves off the branches.

NIGERIA
POPULATION 131,860,000 * CAPITAL ABUJA

EGYPT
POPULATION 78,887,000 * CAPITAL CAIRO

ETHIOPIA
POPULATION 74,778,000 * CAPITAL ADDIS ABABA

SUDAN
POPULATION 41,236,000 * CAPITAL KHARTOUM

MOROCCO
POPULATION 33,241,000 * CAPITAL RABAT

ALGERIA
POPULATION 32,930,000 * CAPITAL ALGIERS

GHANA
POPULATION 22,410,000 * CAPITAL ACCRA

CÔTE D'IVOIRE (IVORY COAST)
POPULATION 17,655,000 * CAPITAL YAMOUSSOUKRO

CAMEROON
POPULATION 17,341,000 * CAPITAL YAOUNDÉ

BURKINA FASO
POPULATION 13,903,000 * CAPITAL OUAGADOUGOU

NIGER
POPULATION 12,525,000 * CAPITAL NIAMEY

SENEGAL
POPULATION 11,987,000 * CAPITAL DAKAR

MALI
POPULATION 11,717,000 * CAPITAL BAMAKO

TUNISIA
POPULATION 10,175,000 * CAPITAL TUNIS

CHAD
POPULATION 9,944,000 * CAPITAL NDJAMENA

GUINEA
POPULATION 9,690,000 * CAPITAL CONAKRY

SOMALIA
POPULATION 8,863,000 * CAPITAL MOGADISHU

BENIN
POPULATION 7,863,000 * CAPITAL PORTO-NOVO

SIERRA LEONE
POPULATION 6,005,000 * CAPITAL FREETOWN

LIBYA
POPULATION 5,901,000 * CAPITAL TRIPOLI

TOGO
POPULATION 5,549,000 * CAPITAL LOMÉ

ERITREA
POPULATION 4,787,000 * CAPITAL ASMARA

CENTRAL AFRICAN REPUBLIC
POPULATION 4,303,000 * CAPITAL BANGUI

MAURITANIA
POPULATION 3,177,000 * CAPITAL NOUAKCHOTT

LIBERIA
POPULATION 3,042,000 * CAPITAL MONROVIA

GAMBIA
POPULATION 1,642,000 * CAPITAL BANJUL

GUINEA-BISSAU
POPULATION 1,442,000 * CAPITAL BISSAU

EQUATORIAL GUINEA
POPULATION 540,000 * CAPITAL MALABO

DJIBOUTI
POPULATION 487,000 * CAPITAL DJIBOUTI

Hake

Spice merchant
Moroccan cooking uses many spices. Spice merchants display their produce at markets called souks. They sell ground turmeric, paprika, cinnamon, chilies and coriander seeds.

Great Mosque of Djenné
This mosque, built in Mali in 1909, is the largest mud-brick structure in the world. A fresh coat of mud is applied each year after the rainy season. Bundles of palm sticks poke out of the walls.

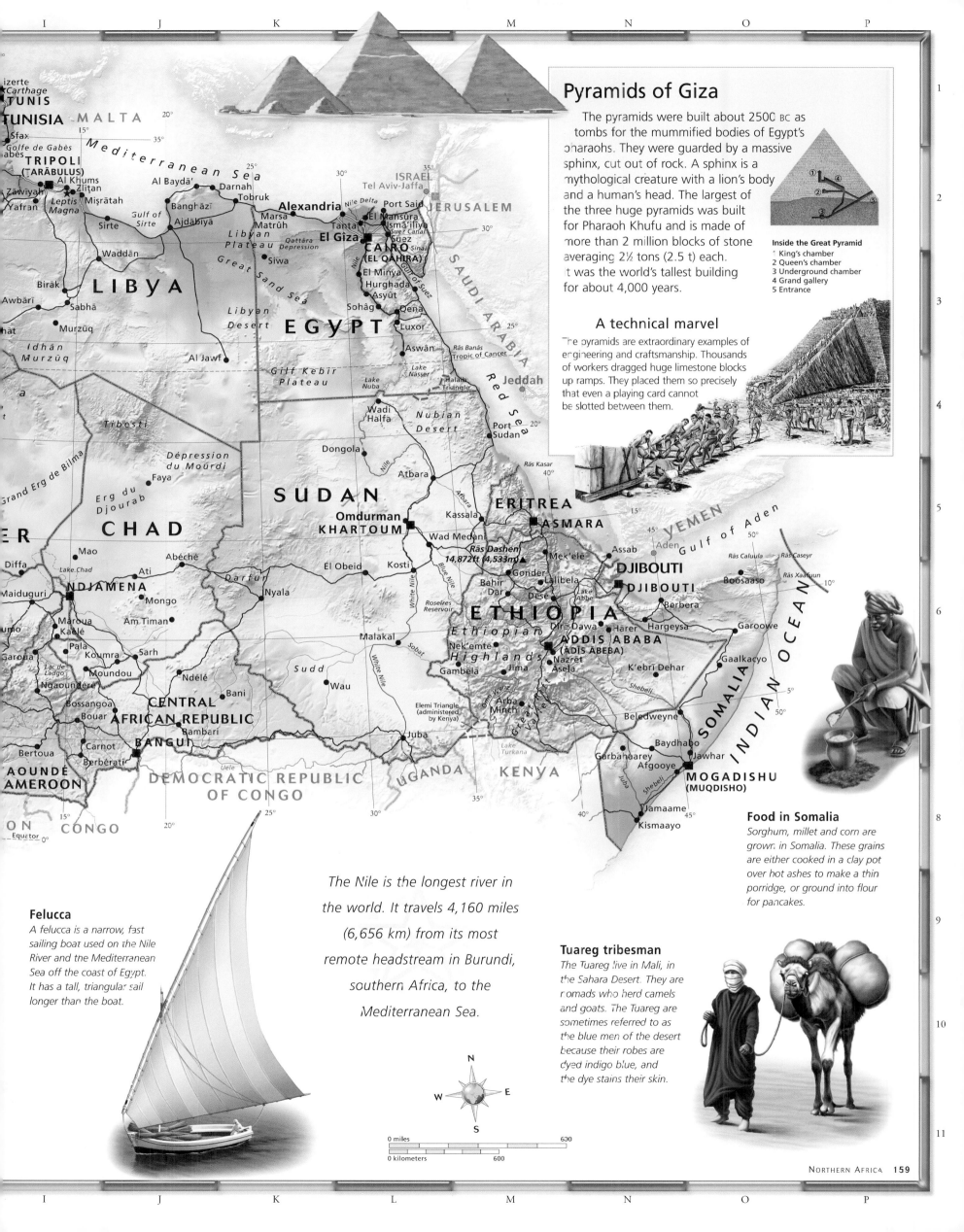

Pyramids of Giza

The pyramids were built about 2500 BC as tombs for the mummified bodies of Egypt's pharaohs. They were guarded by a massive sphinx, cut out of rock. A sphinx is a mythological creature with a lion's body and a human's head. The largest of the three huge pyramids was built for Pharaoh Khufu and is made of more than 2 million blocks of stone averaging 2½ tons (2.5 t) each. It was the world's tallest building for about 4,000 years.

Inside the Great Pyramid
1 King's chamber
2 Queen's chamber
3 Underground chamber
4 Grand gallery
5 Entrance

A technical marvel

The pyramids are extraordinary examples of engineering and craftsmanship. Thousands of workers dragged huge limestone blocks up ramps. They placed them so precisely that even a playing card cannot be slotted between them.

The Nile is the longest river in the world. It travels 4,160 miles (6,656 km) from its most remote headstream in Burundi, southern Africa, to the Mediterranean Sea.

Felucca

A felucca is a narrow, fast sailing boat used on the Nile River and the Mediterranean Sea off the coast of Egypt. It has a tall, triangular sail longer than the boat.

Food in Somalia

Sorghum, millet and corn are grown in Somalia. These grains are either cooked in a clay pot over hot ashes to make a thin porridge, or ground into flour for pancakes.

Tuareg tribesman

The Tuareg live in Mali, in the Sahara Desert. They are nomads who herd camels and goats. The Tuareg are sometimes referred to as the blue men of the desert because their robes are dyed indigo blue, and the dye stains their skin.

0 miles 600
0 kilometers 600

Northern Africa

LAND AREA	6,482,026 sq miles (16,788,371 sq km)
LARGEST COUNTRY	Algeria
SMALLEST COUNTRY	Djibouti
MAIN RELIGION	Muslim
LIFE EXPECTANCY	52 years
LITERACY	53%

USING THE LAND

- Wheat
- Citrus fruits
- Wine
- Cotton
- Coffee
- Cocoa
- Sugarcane
- Groundnuts
- Dates
- Olives
- Beef cattle
- Sheep
- Goats
- Fishing
- Industrial center
- Mining
- Oil production
- Gas production
- Tourism
- Forest and woodland
- Arable land
- Grazing
- Arid or marginal

Suez Canal
In 1869, the Suez Canal was opened, joining the Red Sea, which lies to the east of Egypt, with the Mediterranean Sea, which lies to the north. This shortened the distance for ships moving between Europe and Asia. The canal took 11 years to build and is one of the busiest waterways in the world.

LARGEST CITIES

Lagos 9,230,000

Cairo 7,933,000

Abidjan 3,918,000

Alexandria 3,917,000

Grinding millet
Africa is becoming one of the world's leading producers of millet. Much is used within the continent—each African eats an average of 44 pounds (20 kg) of millet grain each year. Millet stalks are valuable as livestock feed, building material and fuel.

Cacao beans
Cacao beans are the seeds inside the pods of the cacao tree. All chocolate products, including cocoa, are made from cacao beans. Most of the world's cacao beans come from forests on the west coast of Africa, especially Ghana, Nigeria and Côte d'Ivoire.

Liberia and Ethiopia are the only countries in Africa that have never been colonized.

Map labels: ALGIERS, TUNIS, RABAT, Casablanca, TRIPOLI, Banghāzī, LAÂYOUNE, Alexandria, CAIRO, Aswân, NOUAKCHOTT, Port Sudan, DAKAR, BANJUL, KHARTOUM, ASMARA, BISSAU, BAMAKO, NIAMEY, NDJAMENA, DJIBOUTI, OUAGADOUGOU, ADDIS ABABA, CONAKRY, FREETOWN, ABUJA, YAMOUSSOUKRO, PORTO-NOVO, MONROVIA, ACCRA, LOMÉ, Lagos, Abidjan, BANGUI, MALABO, YAOUNDÉ, MOGADISHU

Gelada

NATURAL FEATURES

Sinai Desert EGYPT
The Sinai Desert is in northeastern Egypt, east of the Suez Canal and the Gulf of Suez. It is a barren area, but it does have a number of oases, such as Wadi Ferain in the southwest, which has been used by the Bedouin for thousands of years.

Atlas Mountains MOROCCO–TUNISIA
These mountains are made up of three ranges that run from the northeast to the southwest and extend for 1,200 miles (2,000 km). The land between the mountains and the coast is fertile.

Ethiopian highlands ETHIOPIA
Covering two-thirds of the country and divided by the Great Rift Valley, the highlands have the country's richest farmland. A wide variety of animals live in the highlands—the gelada baboon is found only in this region.

Jungle CÔTE D'IVOIRE
Côte d'Ivoire is on the west coast of Africa along the Gulf of Guinea. Almost one-third of the country is a densely forested tropical jungle. The region's elephants are threatened because their habitat is being destroyed and animals are being killed to supply the ivory market.

Sahara Desert
The Sahara is the largest desert in the world. It stretches across more than half of northern Africa, from the Atlantic Ocean to the Red Sea. Its rocky plains are barren and not suitable for farming. Most of the Saharan people are nomads who move their herds of camels, sheep and goats around to take advantage of available water and pasture land.

Cassava
Cassava, the starchy root of a small shrub, grows well in the hot climates of western Africa. The bark of the root is peeled off, the juice squeezed out and the remaining pulp is baked to make flat cakes. Cassava can also be dried and deep-fried, or fermented and made into an alcoholic drink. Cassava is also known as manioc or yuca.

WHERE PEOPLE LIVE

Urban		Rural

REGION
42% — 58%

Most urban: LIBYA
87% — 13%

Most rural: ETHIOPIA
17% — 83%

Aswan High Dam

Before the Aswan High Dam was completed in 1970, Egyptian farmers depended on the River Nile to water their crops. The dam now provides Egypt with regular water supplies, but its construction was difficult. In the 1960s, Abu Simbel (*below*), the temple of Ramses II, had to be moved to save it from the rising waters.

TRADITIONS AND CULTURE

Musical storytelling ALGERIA
The Berbers of Algeria (*below*) use music and song to tell stories and record their history. They play their many instruments, including various kinds of drums, at traditional festivals and weddings.

Dinka people SUDAN
These are a group of closely related cattle-herding peoples living in central Africa. The women plant and raise most of the crops and the men are responsible for the goats, sheep and cattle.

Tribal religions
Followers of tribal religions worship spirits that they believe are in all living things. These spirits communicate through shamans (priests), who honor them in rituals.

Minarets
A minaret is a tall tower attached to a mosque. A *muezzin*, or crier, calls the followers of Islam to prayer five times each day from the balcony of the minaret.

Ethiopia uses the Julian calendar, and its dates are therefore seven years behind those used in most countries.

PLACES

Cairo EGYPT
Cairo, the capital of Egypt, is one of the oldest cities in Africa and among the world's most crowded. Its noisy and colorful streets have a mix of mosques, monuments, museums and bazaars.

Timbuktu MALI
Timbuktu began as a nomad camp in 1100, and later became a trading post for merchants crossing the Sahara. Today, the city is a center of Islamic learning.

Carthage TUNISIA
Carthage, founded in the 8th century BC, was one of the greatest cities and busiest seaports of ancient times. It was destroyed by the Romans in 146 BC.

Lalibela churches ETHIOPIA
These 11 churches, carved out of rock in the 13th century, were named for King Lalibela of the Zagwe dynasty. They are joined by a maze of tunnels and passages.

Nomadic Wodaabe people have male beauty contests.

Leptis Magna LIBYA
Originally a Phoenician port, Leptis Magna became part of the Roman empire in 111 BC. Its ruined buildings show that it was once a large and bustling city.

Leptis Magna

Marrakech MOROCCO
Marrakech, on the plains below the Atlas Mountains, was founded in 1062 by the Almoravid dynasty as the capital of its empire. It became one of Islam's great cities and today is a popular tourist resort, famous for its bazaars.

Liberia
Liberia, a small country on the west coast, is Africa's oldest republic. It was founded in 1822 by freed slaves from the USA, but today most of its people are native Africans. The name Liberia means "free land." Less than 4 percent of the land can be farmed, but there are rich reserves of iron ore.

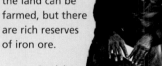
Freed slave

PEOPLE

Queen of Sheba c 1000 BC
The Queen of Sheba features in the traditional stories of Muslims and Christians, but her homeland is not known. Ethiopians claim that their first emperor, Menelik I, was the son of the Queen of Sheba and King Solomon of Israel.

Hannibal c 287–c 183 BC
The Carthaginian general Hannibal led his army across the Alps by elephant in 218 BC to fight his enemies, the Romans. Many years later, he poisoned himself rather than surrender to Rome.

Ibn Batuta c AD 303–c 377
Born in Tangier, Morocco, Arab traveler and author Ibn Batuta visited western Africa, western Europe and Asia. He journeyed for 29 years recording his travels in his book *Rihla* (Journey).

Haile Selassie 1892–1975
Haile Selassie became emperor of Ethiopia in 1930 and set about modernizing his country. After a military rebellion, he was removed from power in 1974.

Kofi Annan born 1938
Kofi Annan was born in Kumasi, Ghana, and studied in the USA and Switzerland. He joined the United Nations in 1962 and was head of its peacekeeping department from 1993 to 1995. In 1997, he became the seventh Secretary General of the United Nations.

Kofi Annan

The Sphinx

RIVER NILE
Life in ancient Egypt revolved around the River Nile. Every year the river flooded its banks, watering the land and leaving behind rich, fertile soil in which the people grew crops.

PHARAOHS
Ancient Egyptians believed that their rulers, the pharaohs, were god-kings. They believed the pharaohs could control the weather, their crops and even Egypt's success in war and trade.

GODS AND GODDESSES
Ancient Egyptians worshiped hundreds of gods and goddesses. Some, such as the sun-god Re, were honored as great gods throughout the country, but others were recognized only in particular regions. Many gods appeared in animal form.

Gods and goddesses

HIEROGLYPHICS
The ancient Egyptians used hieroglyphics, a form of writing in which picture symbols represented objects, people, and even ideas and sounds.

PAPYRUS
Papyrus is a water plant. Egyptians sliced the stems to make paper. When one layer was placed on another, the plant's juices glued them together.

MUMMIES
A mummy is a dead body that has been dried out to stop it from decaying. The bodies were preserved by a special embalming process and stored inside a decorated coffin or case.

Mummy case

SPHINXES
The Egyptians built sphinxes to guard their temples or tombs. They usually had a human head (as a sign of intelligence) and a lion's body (as a sign of strength).

NEFERTITI
Nefertiti, an Egyptian queen of the 14th century BC, was the wife of the pharaoh Akhenaton. With her husband, she established a new religion based on Sun worship.

TUTANKHAMEN
Tutankhamen (*right*) was pharaoh of Egypt from about 1347 to 1339 BC. In 1922, his tomb containing thousands of golden treasures was discovered near Luxor.

CLEOPATRA
Cleopatra became queen of Egypt in 51 BC. She was the last pharaoh to rule Egypt. She was clever and ambitious, and was supported in battle by two Roman generals, Mark Antony and Julius Caesar.

Southern Africa

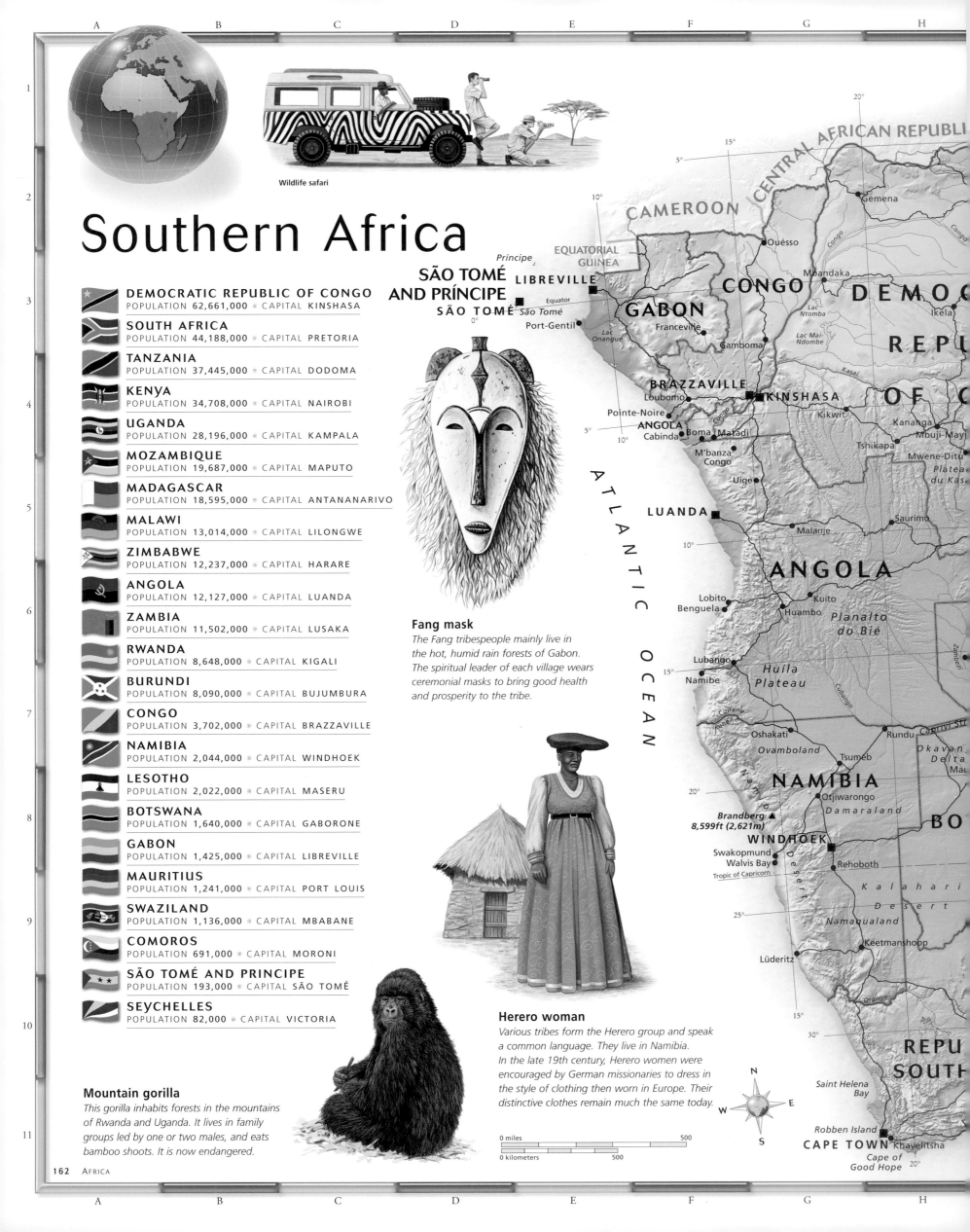

Wildlife safari

DEMOCRATIC REPUBLIC OF CONGO
POPULATION 62,661,000 * CAPITAL KINSHASA

SOUTH AFRICA
POPULATION 44,188,000 * CAPITAL PRETORIA

TANZANIA
POPULATION 37,445,000 * CAPITAL DODOMA

KENYA
POPULATION 34,708,000 * CAPITAL NAIROBI

UGANDA
POPULATION 28,196,000 * CAPITAL KAMPALA

MOZAMBIQUE
POPULATION 19,687,000 * CAPITAL MAPUTO

MADAGASCAR
POPULATION 18,595,000 * CAPITAL ANTANANARIVO

MALAWI
POPULATION 13,014,000 * CAPITAL LILONGWE

ZIMBABWE
POPULATION 12,237,000 * CAPITAL HARARE

ANGOLA
POPULATION 12,127,000 * CAPITAL LUANDA

ZAMBIA
POPULATION 11,502,000 * CAPITAL LUSAKA

RWANDA
POPULATION 8,648,000 * CAPITAL KIGALI

BURUNDI
POPULATION 8,090,000 * CAPITAL BUJUMBURA

CONGO
POPULATION 3,702,000 * CAPITAL BRAZZAVILLE

NAMIBIA
POPULATION 2,044,000 * CAPITAL WINDHOEK

LESOTHO
POPULATION 2,022,000 * CAPITAL MASERU

BOTSWANA
POPULATION 1,640,000 * CAPITAL GABORONE

GABON
POPULATION 1,425,000 * CAPITAL LIBREVILLE

MAURITIUS
POPULATION 1,241,000 * CAPITAL PORT LOUIS

SWAZILAND
POPULATION 1,136,000 * CAPITAL MBABANE

COMOROS
POPULATION 691,000 * CAPITAL MORONI

SÃO TOMÉ AND PRINCIPE
POPULATION 193,000 * CAPITAL SÃO TOMÉ

SEYCHELLES
POPULATION 82,000 * CAPITAL VICTORIA

Fang mask
The Fang tribespeople mainly live in the hot, humid rain forests of Gabon. The spiritual leader of each village wears ceremonial masks to bring good health and prosperity to the tribe.

Herero woman
Various tribes form the Herero group and speak a common language. They live in Namibia. In the late 19th century, Herero women were encouraged by German missionaries to dress in the style of clothing then worn in Europe. Their distinctive clothes remain much the same today.

Mountain gorilla
This gorilla inhabits forests in the mountains of Rwanda and Uganda. It lives in family groups led by one or two males, and eats bamboo shoots. It is now endangered.

0 miles 500
0 kilometers 500

CENTRAL AFRICAN REPUBLIC

CAMEROON

Gemena

SÃO TOMÉ AND PRÍNCIPE

Príncipe

EQUATORIAL GUINEA

LIBREVILLE

SÃO TOMÉ

São Tomé

Port-Gentil

GABON

Franceville

CONGO

Ouésso

Mbandaka

Ikela

Lac Ntomba

Lac Mai-Ndombe

DEMO

REPU

OF C

BRAZZAVILLE

Loubomo

Pointe-Noire

ANGOLA

Cabinda

Boma Matadi

M'banza Congo

Uíge

KINSHASA

Kikwit

Kasai

Kananga

Mbuji-Mayi

Tshikapa

Mwene-Ditu

Plateau du Kas

LUANDA

Malanje

Saurimo

ATLANTIC OCEAN

ANGOLA

Lobito

Benguela

Kuito

Huambo

Planalto do Bié

Lubango

Namibe

Huíla Plateau

Cubango

Zambezi

Cunene

Cubango

Oshakati

Ovamboland

Rundu

Caprivi Str

Okavango Delta

NAMIBIA

Tsumeb

Otjiwarongo

Damaraland

BO

Brandberg ▲
8,599ft (2,621m)

WINDHOEK

Swakopmund
Walvis Bay

Tropic of Capricorn

Rehoboth

Kalahari

Desert

Namib Desert

Namaqualand

Lüderitz

Keetmanshoop

Orange

REPU

SOUTH

Saint Helena Bay

Robben Island

CAPE TOWN

Khayelitsha

Cape of Good Hope

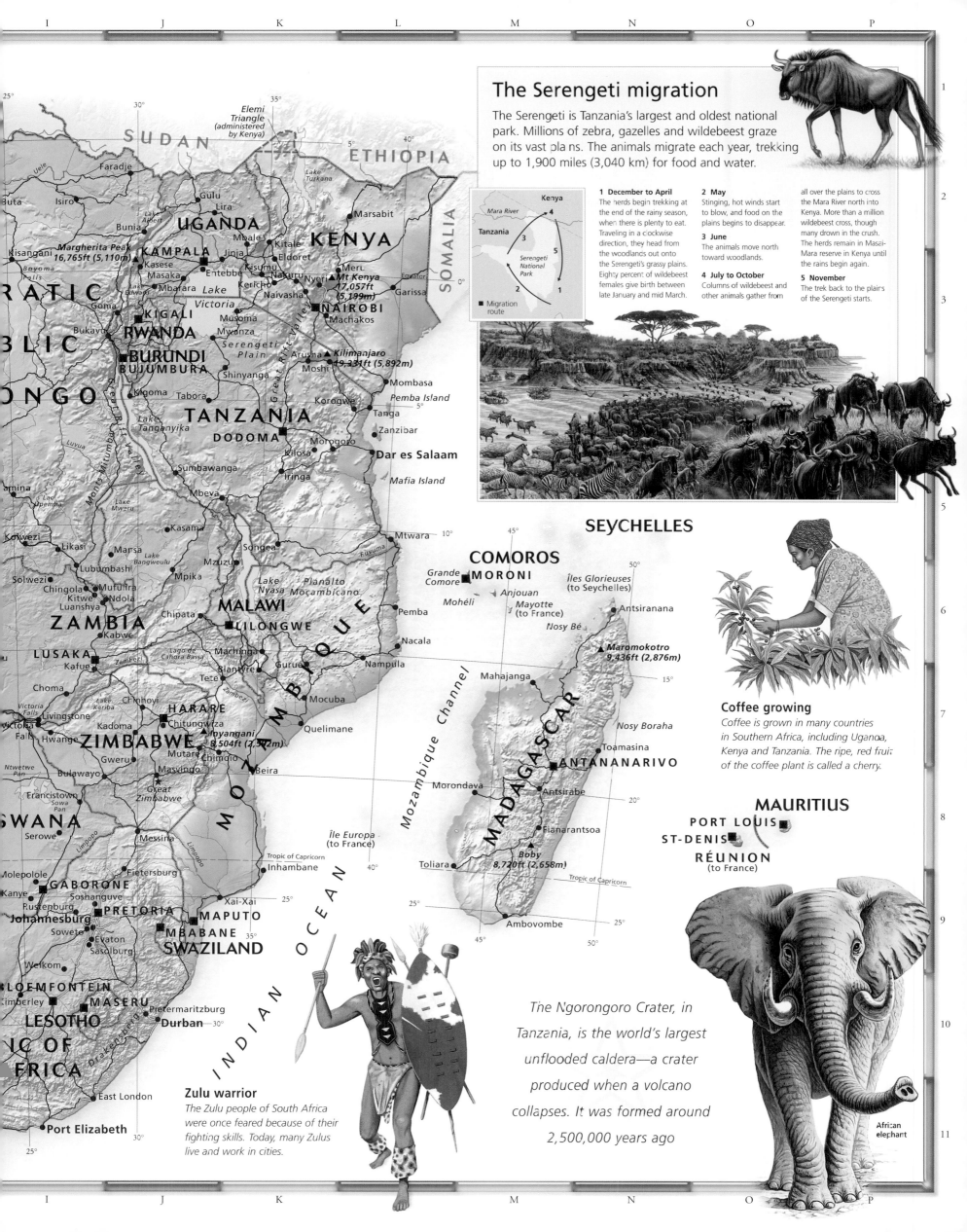

The Serengeti migration

The Serengeti is Tanzania's largest and oldest national park. Millions of zebra, gazelles and wildebeest graze on its vast plains. The animals migrate each year, trekking up to 1,900 miles (3,040 km) for food and water.

Kenya

Mara River

Tanzania

Serengeti National Park

■ Migration route

1 December to April
The herds begin trekking at the end of the rainy season, when there is plenty to eat. Traveling in a clockwise direction, they head from the woodlands out onto the Serengeti's grassy plains. Eighty percent of wildebeest females give birth between late January and mid March.

2 May
Stinging, hot winds start to blow, and food on the plains begins to disappear.

3 June
The animals move north toward woodlands.

4 July to October
Columns of wildebeest and other animals gather from all over the plains to cross the Mara River north into Kenya. More than a million wildebeest cross, though many drown in the crush. The herds remain in Masai-Mara reserve in Kenya until the rains begin again.

5 November
The trek back to the plains of the Serengeti starts.

Coffee growing

Coffee is grown in many countries in Southern Africa, including Uganda, Kenya and Tanzania. The ripe, red fruit of the coffee plant is called a cherry.

Zulu warrior

The Zulu people of South Africa were once feared because of their fighting skills. Today, many Zulus live and work in cities.

The Ngorongoro Crater, in Tanzania, is the world's largest unflooded caldera—a crater produced when a volcano collapses. It was formed around 2,500,000 years ago

African elephant

Map labels

SUDAN
ETHIOPIA
UGANDA
KENYA
SOMALIA
RWANDA
BURUNDI
TANZANIA
ZAMBIA
MALAWI
MOZAMBIQUE
ZIMBABWE
BOTSWANA
SWAZILAND
LESOTHO
SOUTH AFRICA
MADAGASCAR
COMOROS
SEYCHELLES
MAURITIUS

Elemi Triangle (administered by Kenya)

Margherita Peak 16,765ft (5,110m) ▲
Mt Kenya 17,057ft (5,199m) ▲
Kilimanjaro 19,331ft (5,892m) ▲
Inyangani 8,504ft (2,592m) ▲
Maromokotro 9,436ft (2,876m) ▲
Boby 8,720ft (2,658m) ▲

KAMPALA
KIGALI
BUJUMBURA
DODOMA
Dar es Salaam
LUSAKA
LILONGWE
HARARE
MAPUTO
MBABANE
PRETORIA
GABORONE
Johannesburg
MASERU
BLOEMFONTEIN
MORONI
ANTANANARIVO
PORT LOUIS
ST-DENIS
RÉUNION (to France)

Faradje, Isiro, Gulu, Lira, Marsabit, Bunia, Mbale, Kitale, Eldoret, Kasese, Jinja, Kisumu, Kericho, Nakuru, Nyeri, Masaka, Entebbe, Naivasha, Machakos, Garissa, Mbarara, NAIROBI, Goma, Bukavu, Musoma, Mwanza, Meru, Arusha, Moshi, Kigoma, Tabora, Shinyanga, Mombasa, Korogwe, Tanga, Zanzibar, Morogoro, Kilosa, Iringa, Sumbawanga, Mbeya, Kasama, Mtwara, Songea, Mzuzu, Mpika, Chipata, Pemba, Nacala, Machinga, Blantyre, Gurue, Nampula, Tete, Mocuba, Quelimane, Mahajanga, Toamasina, Antsirabe, Fianarantsoa, Morondava, Toliara, Ambovombe, Antsiranana, Grande Comore, Anjouan, Mohéli, Mayotte (to France), Nosy Bé, Nosy Boraha

Lake Turkana, Lake Albert, Lake Edward, Lake Victoria, Lake Tanganyika, Lake Nyasa, Lake Mweru, Lake Bangweulu, Lake Kariba, Lake Malombe, Great Rift Valley, Serengeti Plain, Planalto Moçambicano, Mozambique Channel, INDIAN OCEAN, Îles Glorieuses (to Seychelles), Île Europa (to France), Pemba Island, Mafia Island, Zanzibar

Equator
Tropic of Capricorn

Southern Africa

Forest and woodland
Arable land
Grazing
Arid or marginal

Kenya has the world's youngest population. The average age is 18 years.

Rubber
The people of the Democratic Republic of Congo cut into the bark of the rubber tree to drain off the fluid that is made into rubber. This is called tapping. Some species of rubber trees grow only in the Democratic Republic of Congo. Rubber is one of the country's main exports. However, the use of synthetic rubber has led to a decline in demand.

LAND AREA	4,281,904 sq miles (11,090,080 sq km)
LARGEST COUNTRY	Democratic Republic of Congo
SMALLEST COUNTRY	Seychelles
MAIN RELIGION	Christian
LIFE EXPECTANCY	45 years
LITERACY	66%

NATURAL FEATURES

Congo River
The Congo, the eighth-longest river in the world, flows through western central Africa. People along its banks rely on the river for transport and trade.

Mt Kilimanjaro TANZANIA
Kilimanjaro is Africa's highest mountain. Although it is near the Equator in Tanzania, its summit is always covered in snow. It was once an active volcano.

Mt Kilimanjaro

Kalahari Desert
Most of the large Kalahari Desert is in Botswana, but it also extends to Namibia and South Africa. Although little rain falls, trees and grasses grow in the desert.

Victoria Falls
Victoria Falls forms part of the border between Zambia and Zimbabwe. The falls are fed by the Zambezi River. Their local name, *mosi-oa-tunya*, means "smoke that thunders" because the water can be heard 10 miles (16 km) away.

Ngorongoro Crater TANZANIA
The Ngorongoro Crater, at the eastern edge of the Serengeti Plain, is home to more than 30,000 animals. The crater has a constant supply of spring water.

Map legend:
- Corn (maize)
- Citrus fruits
- Wine
- Cotton
- Coffee
- Tea
- Cocoa
- Tobacco
- Beef cattle
- Sheep
- Fishing
- Industrial center
- Mining
- Oil production
- Timber

Map labels: SÃO TOMÉ, LIBREVILLE, BRAZZAVILLE, KINSHASA, LUANDA, Namibe, WINDHOEK, Cape Town, Port Elizabeth, GABORONE, PRETORIA, Johannesburg, Bloemfontein, MASERU, Durban, MBABANE, MAPUTO, HARARE, Beira, LUSAKA, LILONGWE, Lubumbashi, DODOMA, Zanzibar, Dar es Salaam, BUJUMBURA, KIGALI, KAMPALA, NAIROBI, MORONI, MORONI, ANTANANARIVO

Vanilla beans
Vanilla beans are harvested from the vanilla plant, which is a tropical orchid that takes about three years to flower. The world's leading producer of vanilla beans is the island of Madagascar.

Diamond mining
South Africa's diamond mining industry began in 1867 with the discovery of a single diamond on the banks of the Orange River. Today, South Africa produces 9 percent of the world's diamonds, and exports 90 percent of what it mines. It is the world's fifth-largest rough diamond producer.

Great Rift Valley

The Great Rift Valley cuts across the entire length of Kenya, and extends north into Ethiopia and south into Tanzania. Millions of years ago, the land slowly moved apart, creating the valley. The area is rich in fossils, and is famous for the discovery of the bones of an early human, nicknamed Lucy, who lived 3 million years ago.

Reconstruction of Lucy

Boyoma Falls in the Democratic Republic of Congo has the world's greatest waterfall flow.

WHERE PEOPLE LIVE

Urban	Rural

REGION
36% — 64%

Most urban: GABON
80% — 20%

Most rural: RWANDA
6% — 94%

LARGEST CITIES

Kinshasa 8,419,000

Cape Town 3,660,000

Dar es Salaam 2,916,000

Durban 3,369,000

PLACES

Cape Town SOUTH AFRICA
Cape Town is South Africa's oldest city and legislative capital. It was the first white settlement in South Africa, founded in 1652. Set between the coast and Table Mountain, Cape Town is a shipping and commercial center.

Stone Town TANZANIA
In historical Stone Town, on Zanzibar Island, African and Arabic cultures are brought together in a mix of cathedrals, mosques, temples and houses built in the 19th century on the island.

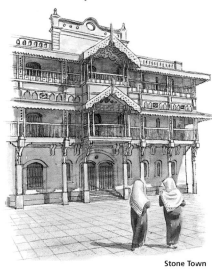

Stone Town

Nairobi KENYA
The capital of Kenya, Nairobi is a center of trade, industry, business and tourism, and one of the largest cities in Africa. It is home to several museums of African history, art and natural history.

Source of the Nile
For hundreds of years, explorers were puzzled about the starting point of the world's longest river, the Nile. In 1862, John Hanning Speke discovered that its primary source is Lake Victoria, whose waters rise from the Ruvironza River in the mountains of Burundi. The River Nile flows northward through a total of eight African countries from central Africa to the Mediterranean Sea.

Robben Island SOUTH AFRICA
Used for more than 400 years as a prison, Robben Island is best known for two ex-prisoners: anti-apartheid activists Nelson Mandela and Walter Sisulu.

Great Zimbabwe ZIMBABWE
This city, built by the Shona people in the 1100s, was once the center of a great empire. Its structures were made from stones put together without mortar.

PEOPLE

Shaka c 1787–1828
The son of a Zulu chieftain, Shaka was a fierce warrior. When his father died, Shaka took over the Zulu clan. Under his leadership, the Zulus established one of Africa's most powerful empires.

Louis Leakey 1893–1976
Archaeologist Louis Leakey and his wife Mary discovered fossils believed to be early human beings that lived in Africa about 2 million years ago. They found these fossils (called hominids) in Olduvai Gorge in Tanzania.

Nelson Mandela born 1918
After working as a lawyer, Mandela joined the African National Congress in 1944. He organized protests against the government and was sentenced to life in prison in 1964. Mandela was released in 1990, and in 1994 he became South Africa's first black president.

Christiaan Barnard 1922–2001
Born in South Africa, Christiaan Barnard was a heart surgeon in Cape Town. He pioneered open-heart surgery, and in 1967 became the first surgeon to transplant a human heart from one person to another.

Animals of Madagascar
The forests of Madagascar, an island off the east coast of Africa, are home to an amazing variety of animals. Many species of birds, reptiles, insects and mammals exist only on this island. The best known are the lemurs, which have survived there for 58 million years. There are more than 20 species, ranging in size from the 11-inch (29-cm) mouse lemur to the 3-foot (90-cm) indri. Many are now endangered.

Ring-tailed lemur

Elephants can walk under water by sticking their trunks up in the air above the water like a snorkel.

1488
Portuguese explorer Bartholomew Diaz rounds the Cape of Good Hope and calls it the "Cape of Storms" because of the terrible weather.

1652
The Dutch East India Company establishes a settlement at the Cape to supply its ships sailing between the East Indies and the Netherlands.

Dutch East India crest

1779
First war between the Xhosa tribe, who had been tending cattle and raising crops at the Cape since the 1500s, and the British and Dutch settlers.

1795
Britain annexes the Cape for the first time and many of the Afrikaner (Dutch-supporting) settlers go north to gain freedom from British rule.

1852
Afrikaners in the Transvaal gain independence from Britain. Shortly afterward, the Afrikaners establish the Orange Free State, one of the four provinces of the Union of South Africa.

1879
After many fierce battles, the Zulu kingdom finally loses its independence and is defeated by the British armies.

1880
The first Boer War between the British and the Afrikaners begins. The Afrikaners are victorious.

The second Boer War

1899–1902
The second Boer War, also called the South African War, takes place between the British and the Afrikaners. Although the Afrikaners fight fiercely, the British defeat them, and the Transvaal and the Orange Free State become British colonies.

1950
A policy of segregation, called apartheid, is implemented. People are officially classified into four distinct racial groups: black, white, colored and Asian.

Apartheid sign

1961
South Africa leaves the Commonwealth of Nations and becomes a republic. The African National Congress (ANC) begins to use weapons in its protests against the government.

1990
Nelson Mandela is released from prison; negotiations begin on voting rights for blacks.

1994
The ANC wins the first election after apartheid is abolished and Nelson Mandela becomes president. After an absence of 20 years, South Africa rejoins the United Nations.

1999
The ANC wins the general elections and Thabo Mbeki takes over as president.

TRADITIONS AND CULTURE

Chokwe masks
Masks once played an important role in the rituals of the Chokwe people of the Democratic Republic of Congo. Today, they are used mostly for entertainment.

Masai people
The Masai are a nomadic people who live in the grasslands of southern Kenya and northern Tanzania. Their daily life centers around the herding of cattle. Families and their herds live together in a compound known as a *kraal*.

San people of the Kalahari
The San live in the Kalahari region of Botswana and Namibia. In the past, the San survived by hunting animals with bows and snares, and gathering desert berries and insects. Today, few of them follow this traditional way of life.

San hunters

Zionist church
About 6 million people in southern Africa are followers of this faith, which combines the teachings of Christianity with traditional African beliefs and forms of worship such as dancing.

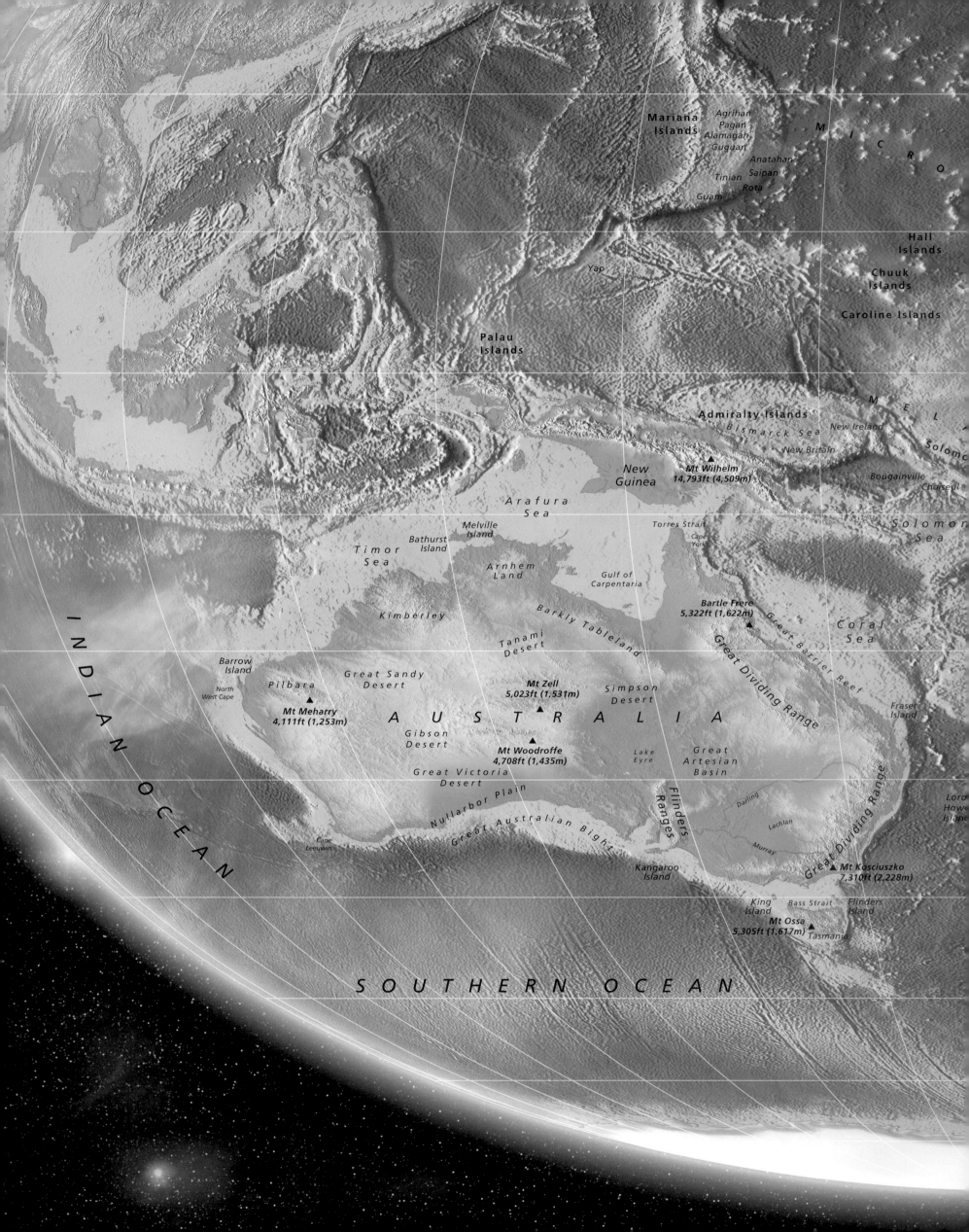

Australia and Papua New Guinea

Bird-of-paradise
Birds-of-paradise live in the forests of Papua New Guinea. To attract a mate, male birds gather in the treetops and call loudly, dance and display their long, brightly colored tail feathers. Female birds are drab and have short feathers.

AUSTRALIA
POPULATION 20,264,000 * CAPITAL CANBERRA

PAPUA NEW GUINEA
POPULATION 5,671,000 * CAPITAL PORT MORESBY

Iron ore mining
Australia is one of the world's largest producers of iron ore. Most comes from the Hamersley Range, in Western Australia. The massive trucks that cart iron ore are too big for public roads and never leave the mine.

Aboriginal dancers
Aboriginal Australians use dancing to express their beliefs and represent their lives. Some of the dances tell the stories of the Dreamtime—the time of the creation of all things. These dances and stories have been handed down by tribal elders over thousands of years.

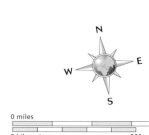

Uluru rises 2,844 feet (867 m) above sea level and measures nearly 6 miles (9.5 km) around its base. It is the largest monolith (single piece of rock) in the world.

Red kangaroo

Dugongs

Arafura Sea

Timor Sea

Melville Island
Bathurst Island
Cobourg Peninsula
Goulbur Islands
Van Diemen Gulf
DARWIN
Palmerston
Kakadu ★ National Park
Cape Ford
Joseph Bonaparte Gulf
Pine Creek
Arnhem Land
Katherine
Daly

Bonaparte Archipelago
Wyndham
Kununurra
Lake Argyle
Daly Waters

Cape Leveque
King Sound
Kimberley Plateau
King Leopold Ranges
Fitzroy
Bungle Bungles
Top Springs
Victoria

Broome
Fitzroy Crossing
Halls Creek
Tanami Desert
Tennant Creek

INDIAN OCEAN
Eighty Mile Beach
Great Sandy Desert
Lake Gregory
Lake White
Lake Mackay
NORTHERN TERRITORY

Dampier
Port Hedland
Percival Lakes
A U S T R
MacDonnell Ranges
Alice Springs

Barrow Island
Onslow
Newman
Lake Disappointment
Lake Neale
Lake Amadeus
Uluru (Ayers Rock)
2,844ft (867m)

North West Cape
Exmouth
Hamersley Range
Gibson Desert

Tropic of Capricorn
Lake MacLeod
W E S T E R N   A U S T R A L I A
Great Victoria
Desert

Gascoyne
Carnarvon
Lake Carnegie

Dirk Hartog Island
Shark Bay
Denham
Murchison
Lake Wells
Coober Pedy

Meekatharra
Lake Noondie
Lake Carey
Lake Minigwal

Lake Austin
SOUTH AUSTRALIA

Mount Magnet
Lake Ballard
Tarcoola

Geraldton
Lake Barlee
Nullarbor Plain

Dongara
Lake Moore
Kalgoorlie

Moora
Coolgardie
Lake Lefroy
Eucla
Cedur

PERTH
Northam
Norseman
Lake Cowan
Balladonia
Great Australian Bight
Penong

Fremantle
Mandurah
Brookton
Wagin
Ravensthorpe
Esperance
Elliston

Bunbury
Busselton
Augusta
Albany

SOUTHERN OCEAN

Uluru

N
W E
S

0 miles   500
0 kilometers   500

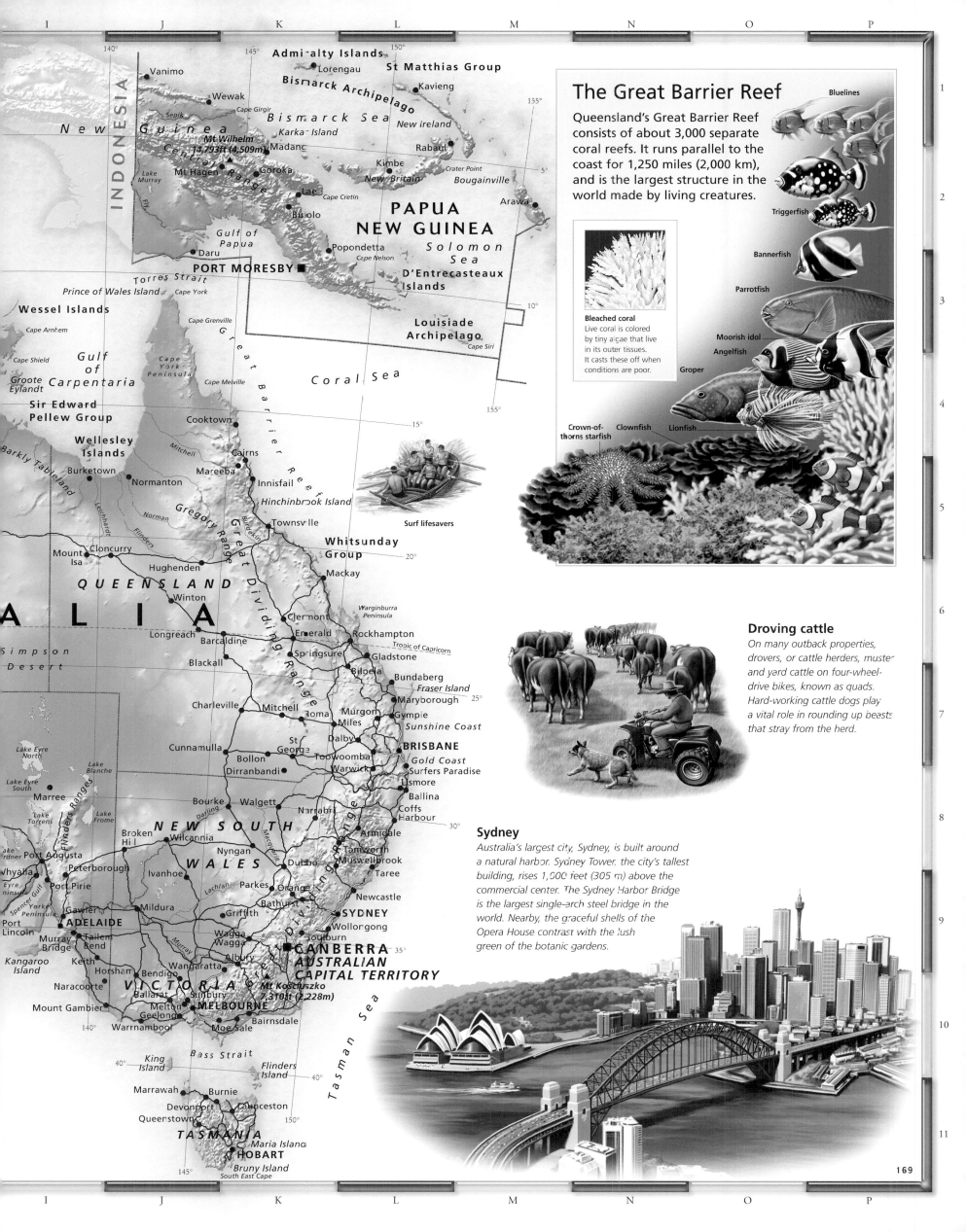

Grid labels top: I J K L M N O P
Grid labels right: 1 2 3 4 5 6 7 8 9 10 11

Map labels:

140° 145° 150° 155°

Vanimo
Admiralty Islands
Lorengau
St Matthias Group
Wewak
Bismarck Archipelago
Kavieng
Cape Girgir
Bismarck Sea
New Ireland
Sepik
New Guinea
Karkar Island
Central Range
Mt Wilhelm
14,793ft (4,509m)
Madang
Rabaul
Lake Murray
Mt Hagen
Goroka
Kimbe
New Britain
Crater Point
Bougainville
Lae
Cape Cretin
Fly
Buolo
PAPUA NEW GUINEA
Arawa
Daru
Gulf of Papua
Popondetta
Cape Nelson
Solomon Sea
PORT MORESBY
Torres Strait
D'Entrecasteaux Islands
Prince of Wales Island
Cape York
Wessel Islands
Cape Grenville
Louisiade Archipelago
Cape Arnhem
Great Barrier Reef
Cape Siri
Cape Shield
Gulf of Carpentaria
Cape York Peninsula
Coral Sea
Groote Eylandt
Cape Melville
Sir Edward Pellew Group
Wellesley Islands
Cooktown
Barkly Tableland
Burketown
Cairns
Leichhardt
Mareeba
Innisfail
Mitchell
Gregory Range
Hinchinbrook Island
Normanton
Norman
Townsville
Flinders
Whitsunday Group
Mount Isa
Cloncurry
Hughenden
Mackay
QUEENSLAND
Winton
Warginburra Peninsula
Longreach
Clermont
Simpson Desert
Barcaldine
Emerald
Rockhampton
Tropic of Capricorn
Blackall
Springsure
Gladstone
Biloela
Bundaberg
Charleville
Mitchell
Roma
Murgon
Fraser Island
Maryborough
Lake Eyre North
Cunnamulla
Miles
Gympie
Sunshine Coast
St George
Dalby
BRISBANE
Lake Eyre South
Bollon
Toowoomba
Gold Coast
Marree
Dirranbandi
Warwick
Surfers Paradise
Lake Blanche
Bourke
Walgett
Lismore
Lake Torrens
Narrabri
Ballina
Lake Frome
Coffs Harbour
NEW SOUTH
Broken Hill
Wilcannia
Armidale
Port Augusta
Nyngan
Tamworth
WALES
Dubbo
Muswellbrook
Whyalla
Ivanhoe
Taree
Peterborough
Parkes
Eyre Peninsula
Orange
Newcastle
Port Pirie
Bathurst
Port Lincoln
Mildura
Griffith
SYDNEY
Yorke Peninsula
Wagga Wagga
Wollongong
Gawler
ADELAIDE
Albury
CANBERRA
Southbound
Murray Bridge
Wangaratta
AUSTRALIAN
Kangaroo Island
Tailem Bend
Bendigo
CAPITAL TERRITORY
Keith
Horsham
VICTORIA
Mt Kosciuszko
7,310ft (2,228m)
Naracoorte
Ballarat
Sunbury
Tasman Sea
Melton
MELBOURNE
Mount Gambier
Geelong
Bairnsdale
Warrnambool
Moe Sale
King Island
Bass Strait
Flinders Island
Marrawah
Burnie
Devonport
Launceston
Queenstown
TASMANIA
Maria Island
HOBART
Bruny Island
South East Cape

INDONESIA
ALIA

The Great Barrier Reef

Queensland's Great Barrier Reef consists of about 3,000 separate coral reefs. It runs parallel to the coast for 1,250 miles (2,000 km), and is the largest structure in the world made by living creatures.

Bluelines

Triggerfish

Bannerfish

Parrotfish

Moorish idol

Angelfish

Groper

Bleached coral
Live coral is colored by tiny algae that live in its outer tissues. It casts these off when conditions are poor.

Crown-of-thorns starfish
Clownfish
Lionfish

Surf lifesavers

Droving cattle

On many outback properties, drovers, or cattle herders, muster and yard cattle on four-wheel-drive bikes, known as quads. Hard-working cattle dogs play a vital role in rounding up beasts that stray from the herd.

Sydney

Australia's largest city, Sydney, is built around a natural harbor. Sydney Tower, the city's tallest building, rises 1,000 feet (305 m) above the commercial center. The Sydney Harbor Bridge is the largest single-arch steel bridge in the world. Nearby, the graceful shells of the Opera House contrast with the lush green of the botanic gardens.

On the Aboriginal flag, the color black represents the people, red is the land, and yellow represents the Sun.

Australia and Papua New Guinea

USING THE LAND

- 🌾 Cereals
- 🍷 Wine
- ☕ Coffee
- 🌾 Sugarcane
- 🥥 Coconuts
- 🌴 Palm oil
- Rubber
- 🐄 Beef cattle
- 🐑 Sheep
- Fishing
- ⚙ Industrial center
- ⛏ Mining
- 🛢 Oil production
- Gas production
- 🌲 Timber
- 📷 Tourism

AUSTRALIA LAND AREA	2,941,299 sq miles (7,617,930 sq km)
OFFICIAL LANGUAGE	English
MAIN RELIGION	Christian
LIFE EXPECTANCY	80 years
LITERACY	99%

PAPUA NEW GUINEA LAND AREA	174,850 sq miles (452,860 sq km)
OFFICIAL LANGUAGE	English
MAIN RELIGION	Christian
LIFE EXPECTANCY	64 years
LITERACY	66%

Legend:
- Forest and woodland
- Arable land
- Grazing
- Arid or marginal

New Guinea, the second largest island in the world, has over 750 languages—more than any other country.

Map labels: Rabaul, PORT MORESBY, Darwin, Cairns, Alice Springs, Brisbane, Perth, Adelaide, Sydney, CANBERRA, Melbourne, Hobart

LARGEST CITIES

Sydney 4,491,000

Melbourne 3,829,000

Brisbane 1,939,000

Perth 1,497,000

Adelaide 1,080,000

Sugarcane
Queensland produces most of Australia's sugarcane, grown on more than 6,000 farms for export as well as local use. Raw sugar comes from the juice inside the cane, which is extracted after the long stalks (above) are harvested and stripped of leaves. Ethanol, a renewable fuel, is produced from sugarcane waste.

Gold
This precious metal, discovered in Victoria and New South Wales in 1851, brought gold seekers from all over the world in search of their fortune. Today, Australia is the world's third-largest gold-mining country, with more than 300 tons (300 t) mined annually.

NATURAL FEATURES

Lake Eyre AUSTRALIA
This usually dry salt lake in the Simpson Desert fills with water only a few times each century, after heavy rains. Millions of birds gather around the lake to breed.

Tasmanian forests AUSTRALIA
The dense forests of the Tasmanian wilderness contain some of the world's oldest living plants. The Tasmanian tiger roamed the forests until last century.

Highlands PAPUA NEW GUINEA

The Southern Highlands have spectacular natural scenery. The Baiyer Wildlife Sanctuary is in the Western Highlands and Mt Wilhelm lies in the Eastern Highlands.

Bungle Bungles AUSTRALIA
These massive rock domes in Western Australia formed 350 million years ago. Their distinctive orange and black bands are best seen from the air. Pools and gorges lie among the domes.

Kakadu National Park AUSTRALIA
Lagoons and billabongs, or waterholes, are a common sight in the Kakadu National Park in Australia's Northern Territory. Much of the land in the park, which supports many animals and birds, floods every year for several months.

Waterlilies at Kakadu

WHERE PEOPLE LIVE

	Urban		Rural
AUSTRALIA	85%		15%
PAPUA NEW GUINEA	17%		83%

LONGEST RIVERS

Murray 1,566 miles (2,520 km)

Murrumbidgee 979 miles (1,575 km)

Darling 864 miles (1,390 km)

Lachlan 851 miles (1,370 km)

Koala and baby

Australian wildlife
Australia is home to two unusual groups of animals. Marsupials are mammals that carry their newborn in a pouch. Koalas, kangaroos and wombats are the most common marsupials. Kangaroos have strong hind legs and can bound along at great speed. Monotremes—platypus and echidnas—are unique animals that lay eggs. When the eggs hatch, they feed their young with milk.

PLACES

Parliament House AUSTRALIA
This modern concrete building, with its imposing flagpole, was opened in 1988 in Canberra, Australia's capital city. It is the seat of national government.

Parliament House

Melbourne AUSTRALIA
This cosmopolitan city, established in 1835, holds several world-renowned sporting events each year, including the Melbourne Cup horse race and the Australian Open tennis grand slam.

Adelaide AUSTRALIA
Named for Queen Adelaide in 1836, this small Australian city hosts the nation's most popular arts festival every two years. The city is surrounded by hills.

Darwin AUSTRALIA
This tropical city in the Northern Territory is Australia's closest point to Southeast Asia. In 1974, Cyclone Tracy devastated the city and it had to be rebuilt.

Sydney Opera House
Jutting into Sydney's harbor, this unique structure, with its curved sail-like roofs, has become one of Australia's most famous landmarks. In 1958, the designs of Danish architect Jørn Utzon were chosen from more than 200 competition entries, and work on the Opera House began. It took 15 years to complete. Musicians and actors from all over the world perform in its theaters and concert halls.

Port Moresby PAPUA NEW GUINEA
Local business people and foreigners populate this city, the largest in Papua New Guinea. The parliament building is in the style of a traditional spirit house.

Coober Pedy AUSTRALIA
Most buildings in this opal-mining town are underground, often in unused mines. Temperatures are so hot for much of the year that people prefer to live, and sometimes work, underground.

Underground house, Coober Pedy

PEOPLE

Captain Arthur Philip 1738–1814
As captain of the British fleet that landed on Australian soil in 1788, and first governor, Arthur Philip chose Sydney Cove as the site of a convict settlement.

Caroline Chisholm 1808–77
Called "the immigrants' friend," Caroline Chisholm set up quarters for 11,000 homeless convict women who came to Australia. She found work for many of these women on farms.

Ned Kelly 1854–80
This Victorian bushranger from an Irish convict family stole money from banks and animals from farms. He was found guilty of his crimes in 1880, and was hanged in Melbourne jail. He wore a metal face shield and suit of armor (right) to disguise himself, as well as for protection.

Ned Kelly

Sir Donald Bradman 1908–2001
Regarded as one of the best cricketers in the world, "the Don" (right) scored a batting average of 99.94. He played for Australia in 52 test matches over 20 years.

Edward Mabo 1936–92
This Aboriginal rights activist, in the Mabo decision of 1993, convinced the High Court of Australia to rule that ownership of land by Australian Aborigines before European settlement should be legally recognized.

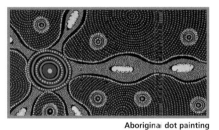

Sir Michael Somare born 1936
This politician was the leader of Papua New Guinea's fight for independence. He became the country's first prime minister after independence in 1975. Over 10 years, the "big chief," as he was called, was twice voted into office, then out again.

TRADITIONS AND CULTURE

Sing-sings PAPUA NEW GUINEA
Dance, music and drama are combined at cultural festivals, called sing-sings. People wear elaborate costumes, and display carved masks outside spirit houses to protect the community. One tribe, the mudmen of Asaro (right), wear huge clay masks to imitate dead people in their dances.

Aboriginal art AUSTRALIA
The earliest Aboriginal paintings have been found in caves, drawn with yellow ocher and charcoal. Artists from different areas use a variety of styles, including dots (below), to create pictures that tell stories of their lives.

Aboriginal dot painting

Beaches
Most Australians live near the coast, so the beach is a popular destination for many families, especially at Christmas time. Ocean waves can be dangerous so surf lifesavers patrol the beach to keep swimmers safe.

Surf lifesavers

Four of the world's five deadliest snakes are found in Australia. The inland taipan is 50 times more venomous than the Indian cobra.

The Royal Flying Doctor Service

The outback
Australia is a vast country. People who live in the remote and sparsely populated outback areas rely on distance services to link them with the rest of the country. Doctors and nurses of the Royal Flying Doctor Service visit their outback patients by air. Many outback children are educated by lessons from the correspondence school or by two-way radio via the School of the Air.

HISTORY AT A GLANCE

c 50,000 BC
Aborigines arrive in Australia from New Guinea by crossing a land bridge. They occupy Fraser Cave, on the southern tip of Tasmania, about 30,000 years later.

Aboriginal tools

c 8000–6000 BC
New Guinea separates from Australia. Tribes develop in New Guinea's high mountain valleys.

AD 1688
William Dampier lands on the northwest coast of Australia in his ship *Cygnet*—the first European to land on Australian soil. Almost 100 years later, Captain James Cook lands at Botany Bay on the east coast and claims it for Britain.

1788
The First Fleet, of 11 ships carrying 1,500 convicts and soldiers, arrives in Sydney Cove.

1851
Gold is discovered in Victoria and New South Wales, and the gold rush begins.

Convicts

1868
The last convicts are sent from Britain. They arrive in Western Australia. Free settlers migrate to Australia and the population grows.

1884
Britain annexes the southeast of New Guinea and Germany controls the northeast. Australia takes over the British area 20 years later.

1901
The six British colonies of Australia join to form a single federation of states, to be governed as one nation—the Commonwealth of Australia.

1914–18
Australia fights for Britain in World War I, along with New Zealand soldiers. They become known as ANZACs.

1921
German New Guinea comes under the control of Australia.

1939–45
Britain declares war on Germany, and Australia supports Britain in World War II. Japan occupies New Guinea from 1942 to 1945.

1975
Papua New Guinea gains its independence from Australia. Michael Somare is its first prime minister.

2000
Sydney hosts the Olympic Games. Sprinter Cathy Freeman wins a gold medal for Australia.

Cathy Freeman

New Zealand and the Pacific Islands

Brown kiwi
The kiwi cannot fly. Instead, it has strong legs for running, kicking and burrowing. Nostrils at the end of its long beak help it to sniff out insects to eat.

Parliament House
New Zealand's Parliament House is in Wellington. The circular building behind, known as the Beehive, contains the offices of government ministers.

NEW ZEALAND
POPULATION 4,076,000 ✳ CAPITAL WELLINGTON

FIJI
POPULATION 906,000 ✳ CAPITAL SUVA

SOLOMON ISLANDS
POPULATION 552,000 ✳ CAPITAL HONIARA

VANUATU
POPULATION 209,000 ✳ CAPITAL PORT VILA

SAMOA
POPULATION 177,000 ✳ CAPITAL APIA

TONGA
POPULATION 115,000 ✳ CAPITAL NUKU'ALOFA

FEDERATED STATES OF MICRONESIA
POPULATION 108,000 ✳ CAPITAL PALIKIR

KIRIBATI
POPULATION 105,000 ✳ CAPITAL TARAWA

MARSHALL ISLANDS
POPULATION 60,000 ✳ CAPITAL MAJURO

PALAU
POPULATION 21,000 ✳ CAPITAL KOROR

NAURU
POPULATION 13,000 ✳ CAPITAL YAREN

TUVALU
POPULATION 12,000 ✳ CAPITAL FUNAFUTI

Farming
Lush pastures grow in New Zealand's rich volcanic soil. They support large numbers of sheep, deer and cattle. Meat, wool and dairy products are the main exports.

Tiki
The tiki is a Maori fertility symbol. Tiki are carved from nephrite, a hard stone similar to jade that can be found on New Zealand's South Island.

Traditional house, Solomon Islands

Conch shell blower

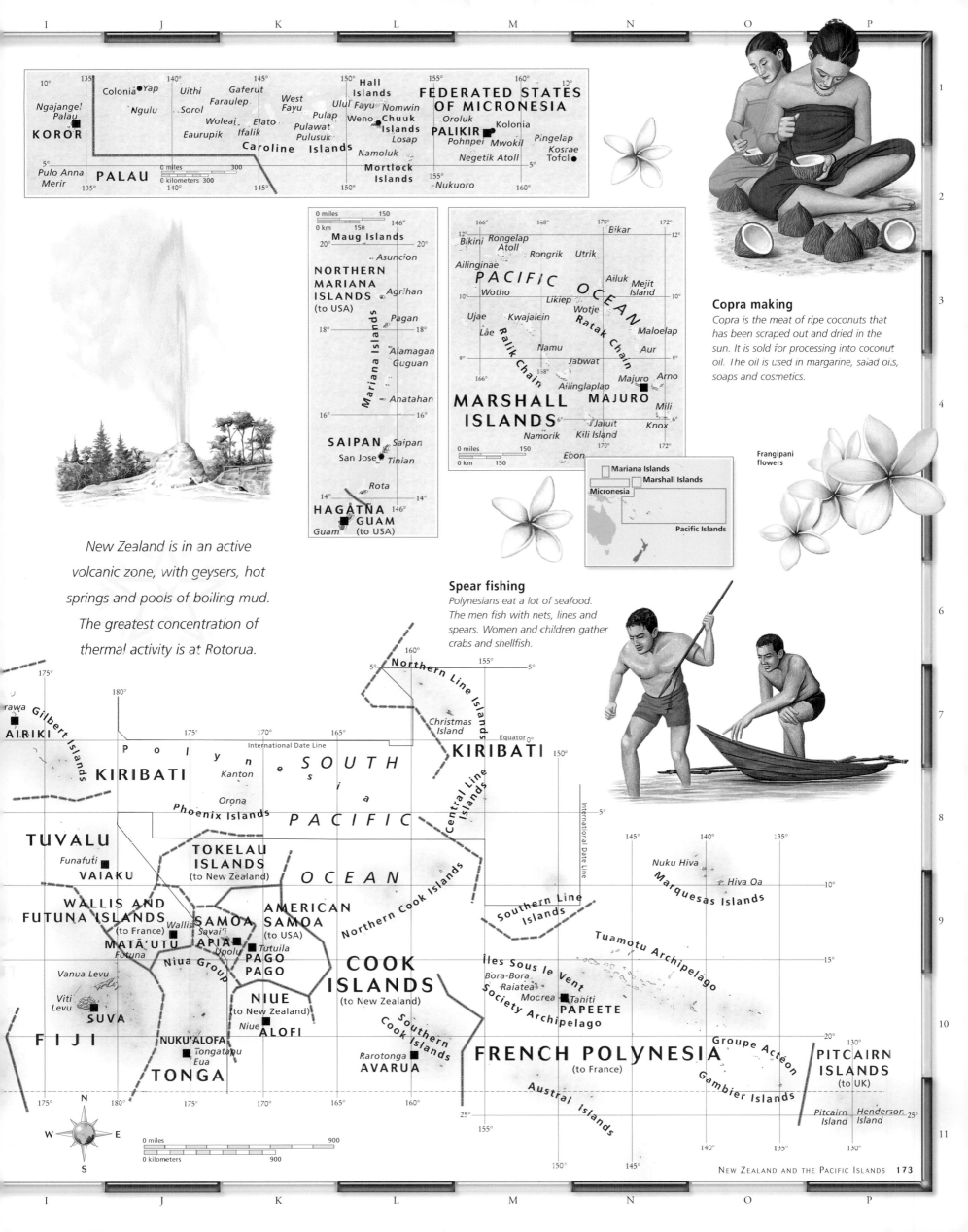

Map labels and text

FEDERATED STATES OF MICRONESIA

Colonia • Yap
Ngajangel
Palau
KOROR

Uithi
Ngulu
Sorol
Woleai
Eauripik
Ifalik

Gaferut
Faraulep
Elato
Pulawat
Pulusuk

West
Fayu
Ulul Fayu
Pulap
Weno

Hall
Islands
Nomwin
Chuuk
Islands
Losap
Namoluk

Oroluk
Kolonia
Pohnpei
Mwokil
Pingelap
Kosrae
Negetik Atoll
Tofol

PALIKIR

Caroline Islands
Mortlock
Islands
Nukuoro

Pulo Anna
Merir
PALAU

0 miles 300
0 kilometers 300

Maug Islands

NORTHERN
MARIANA
ISLANDS
(to USA)

Asuncion
Agrihan
Pagan
Alamagan
Guguan
Anatahan

Mariana Islands

SAIPAN
San Jose Tinian
Saipan
Rota

HAGÅTÑA
GUAM
Guam (to USA)

0 miles 150
0 km 150

PACIFIC OCEAN

Bikini
Rongelap
Atoll
Ailinginae
Wotho
Ujae
Lae
Kwajalein
Namu
Ailinglaplap
Namorik
Kili Island
Ebon

Rongrik
Likiep
Wotje
Jabwat
Jaluit

Utrik
Ailuk
Mejit
Island
Maloelap
Aur
Majuro
Mili
Knox

Bikar
Ratak Chain
Ralik Chain

MARSHALL
ISLANDS
MAJURO
Arno

0 miles 150
0 km 150

Copra making

Copra is the meat of ripe coconuts that has been scraped out and dried in the sun. It is sold for processing into coconut oil. The oil is used in margarine, salad oils, soaps and cosmetics.

Spear fishing

Polynesians eat a lot of seafood. The men fish with nets, lines and spears. Women and children gather crabs and shellfish.

Frangipani flowers

Mariana Islands
Marshall Islands
Micronesia
Pacific Islands

New Zealand is in an active volcanic zone, with geysers, hot springs and pools of boiling mud. The greatest concentration of thermal activity is at Rotorua.

Lower map:

Tarawa
Gilbert Islands
AIRIKI
KIRIBATI

Polynesia

SOUTH PACIFIC OCEAN

Kanton
Orona
Phoenix Islands

Northern Line Islands
Christmas Island
KIRIBATI
Equator 0°

International Date Line

TUVALU
Funafuti
VAIAKU

TOKELAU
ISLANDS
(to New Zealand)

WALLIS AND
FUTUNA ISLANDS
(to France)
Wallis
MATÃ'UTU
Futuna

SAMOA
Savai'i
APIA
Upolu

AMERICAN
SAMOA
(to USA)
Tutuila
PAGO
PAGO

Niua Group

Vanua Levu
Viti
Levu
SUVA
FIJI

NUKU'ALOFA
Tongatapu
Eua
TONGA

NIUE
(to New Zealand)
Niue
ALOFI

COOK
ISLANDS
(to New Zealand)

Northern Cook Islands

Southern
Cook Islands
Rarotonga
AVARUA

Central Line Islands
International Date Line

Southern Line Islands

Îles Sous le Vent
Bora-Bora
Raiatea
Moorea Tahiti
PAPEETE
Society Archipelago

Nuku Hiva
Hiva Oa
Marquesas Islands

Tuamotu Archipelago

FRENCH POLYNESIA
(to France)

Groupe Actéon
Gambier Islands

Austral Islands

PITCAIRN
ISLANDS
(to UK)

Pitcairn
Island
Henderson
Island

N
W E
S

0 miles 900
0 kilometers 900

In 1893, New Zealand became the first country to grant women the right to vote.

New Zealand and the Pacific Islands

LAND AREA	128,126 sq miles (331,846 sq km)
LARGEST COUNTRY	New Zealand
SMALLEST COUNTRY	Nauru
MAIN RELIGION	Christian
LIFE EXPECTANCY	68 years
LITERACY	89%

The word "maori" means local, or original, people. White settlers were called "paheka."

NATURAL FEATURES

Yasawa Islands FIJI
This chain of coral islands, protected by reefs, lies off the northwest coast of Fiji's main island, Viti Levu. Beaches of white sand fringe the islands (below).

Tahitian mountains FRENCH POLYNESIA
The volcanic mountains of Tahiti run along the island's north and south coasts. The dense tropical rain forests that cover the mountains have provided inspiration for artists such as Paul Gauguin.

Milford Sound

Milford Sound NEW ZEALAND
These deep, fjordlike waterways (above), in South Island, are the final destination for trampers on the Milford Track, a famous walking trail through spectacular mountains and river valleys.

Tongariro National Park NEW ZEALAND
In the center of New Zealand's North Island lies a Maori sacred area, situated on several active volcanoes, notably Mt Ruapehu (left), which erupted in 1995.

Kiwifruit
First called a Chinese gooseberry after its place of origin, but now named after New Zealand's national bird, this delicious fruit is mainly grown near the Bay of Plenty in the north. The fruit, which grows on a vine, needs sunny conditions and rich soil to grow. New Zealand is the world's leading producer of kiwifruit.

Wood and paper products
New Zealand is one of the largest paper and wood producers in the Pacific region. Kauri trees (above), which take more than 1,000 years to mature, were plentiful in New Zealand before European settlement, but are now protected because of years of logging. Many smaller islands in the Pacific region grow coconut trees for wood, copra (dried coconut meat) and palm oil production.

Wellington is the southernmost national capital in the world.

Dairy food
New Zealand is the world's largest exporter of butter and cheese. Most dairy foods are exported, as more goods are produced than the small population needs. New Zealand's rich soils and grasslands provide fodder for the country's herds of cattle.

USING THE LAND

- Forest and woodland
- Arable land
- Grazing
- Arid or marginal

Auckland
Manukau
Hamilton
Napier
WELLINGTON
Christchurch
Queenstown
Dunedin
Invercargill

- Cereals
- Fruit
- Wine
- Beef cattle
- Dairy cattle
- Sheep
- Pigs
- Fishing
- Industrial center
- Timber
- Tourism

Tourism
Millions of tourists are attracted to the South Pacific islands each year, because of their beautiful beaches, coral reefs teeming with fishes and relaxed lifestyle. Most countries in the region rely on the income tourism brings. However, the high number of tourists can cause environmental problems, both on land and in the sea. Clean, fresh water is often in short supply, and an increased demand from visitors can reduce the amount available for local islanders.

LARGEST CITIES

Auckland 442,000

Manukau 411,000

Christchurch 375,000

Wellington 186,000

Hamilton 158,000

WHERE PEOPLE LIVE

Urban		Rural

REGION
49% | 51%

Most urban: NAURU
100%

Most rural: SOLOMON ISLANDS
19% | 81%

Flightless birds

Several birds of New Zealand cannot fly. Before European settlement, the Maoris hunted the giant moa (*above*) to extinction. The kiwi, New Zealand's national bird, is like a hen but has stumps instead of wings. Flightless species of parrots include the kea, kaka and kakapo.

PEOPLE

Fletcher Christian 1764–93
Christian led the crew of the *Bounty* in a mutiny against Captain Bligh in 1789, and sailed for Pitcairn Island in the Pacific. His descendants still live there.

Te Rauparaha c 1768–1849
This fearless warrior and Maori chief signed the Treaty of Waitangi in 1840. New Zealand's rugby teams perform his haka (war song) before their matches.

Ernest Rutherford 1871–1937
Many call this New Zealand-born scientist the father of nuclear physics. He received world recognition for his discoveries relating to nuclear atoms.

Queen Salote Tupou III 1900–65
Queen Salote ruled the Kingdom of Tonga from 1918 until her death in 1965. She improved health and education, and helped to develop national pride.

Sir Edmund Hillary born 1919
This mountain climber from Auckland, New Zealand, made several attempts to climb the world's highest peak, Mt Everest. With the Sherpa Tenzing Norgay, he was first to reach the summit in May 1953.

Jonah Lomu born 1975
Jonah Lomu was a player in New Zealand's rugby team from 1994 to 2002. He played 63 international test matches in his 73 games.

TRADITIONS AND CULTURE

Family life SAMOA
In Samoa, the *aiga* (extended family) is all important. Each village is comprised of several *aiga*. The larger the extended family, the more important it is and the more influence it has in village affairs.

Maori culture NEW ZEALAND
As part of their traditional ceremonies, Maori men chant loudly in a haka, while women in traditional dress (*below*) perform a dance with twirling balls, called *poi*. The striking patterns painted on their faces are symbolic of the tattoos their ancestors wore.

PLACES

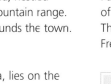

Sky Tower AUCKLAND
This striking structure in Auckland, New Zealand, is the tallest building in the Southern Hemisphere. It towers more than 1,075 feet (328 m) above the ground.

Queenstown NEW ZEALAND
Queenstown is a popular ski resort on Lake Wakatipu, South Island, nestled below the Remarkables mountain range. Breathtaking scenery surrounds the town.

Port Vila VANUATU
Vanuatu's capital, Port Vila, lies on the southwest coast of the island of Efate. The city's daily markets and bustling harbor attract many visitors.

Jean-Marie Tjibaou Cultural Center NOUMEA
This structure (*below*) was built on Tina Peninsula, Noumea, in 2000. It was designed by architect Renzo Piano and the unusual shapes reflect the traditional buildings of the local Kanak people.

War clubs MELANESIA
During the 18th and 19th centuries, warriors carried clubs to fight the enemy. A throwing club was strapped to the waist and thrown in battle. A bladed club was used to cut down the enemy. A chief's club, however, was ornamental.

Village chieftains SOUTH PACIFIC
As the village leader and part of a council of chiefs, the chieftain is responsible for the problems that arise in his community and has authority over the people.

Tramping NEW ZEALAND
Keen walkers from all over the world head for the many tracks in New Zealand to go tramping through the country's spectacular natural landscape. The summer months from November to April are the best times to tramp.

Royal Palace TONGA
This stately waterfront palace (*above*), built in 1867 in the capital Nuku'alofa, on the island of Tongatapu, is home to the royal family of Tonga.

Papeete FRENCH POLYNESIA
Papeete is the chief port of the island of Tahiti, and capital of French Polynesia. The lifestyle of this city is a lively mix of French, Polynesian and Chinese cultures.

Cook's voyages
Captain James Cook set sail from England three times between 1768 and 1779 on scientific expeditions to the South Pacific. On his first trip, he charted the coastlines of Tahiti, New Zealand and eastern Australia, claiming them as part of Britain. On his later trips he visited Tonga and many more Pacific islands. He was the first captain to give his crew fresh fruit to prevent the disease, scurvy.

Cook's ship *Endeavour*

HISTORY AT A GLANCE

40,000 BC
Early peoples begin to inhabit the island chains of the Pacific Ocean region.

4000 BC
Sea vessels are developed, which makes travel between island chains possible. Expert navigators follow the paths of birds to find new islands.

Double-hulled canoe used for exploration

AD 1000
Most Pacific islands are inhabited, and the first Maori settle in New Zealand.

1513
Spanish conquistador Vasco Nuñez de Balboa is the first European to sight the Pacific Ocean, on his voyage from Panama.

1560s
Alvaro de Mendana discovers the Marquesas Islands. He lands on the Solomon Islands, naming them for the biblical King Solomon.

1606
Pedro Fernandez de Quiros, from Portugal, discovers the Cook Islands and the New Hebrides

1642
Dutch explorer Abel Tasman is the first European to sight New Zealand. He visits the mainland. More than 100 years later, James Cook maps the New Zealand coastline.

1818
The musket wars start in New Zealand, between British settlers and the Maori.

1840
The Treaty of Waitangi is signed between the Maori and British. The treaty protected Maori rights if they sold their land to the British. New Zealand becomes a British colony.

Treaty House, Waitangi

1843–72
The Maori wars, also known as the land wars, flare up in New Zealand over issues arising from the Treaty of Waitangi

1893
Social reforms are introduced in New Zealand, including the suffrage (right to vote) for women.

1941–45
Parts of World War II are fought in the Pacific region. At the end of the war, the USA begins to test its nuclear weapons on Bikini atoll.

1962
Western Samoa (now Samoa) becomes the first independent Pacific nation. Eight years later, Fiji and Tonga gain independence from Britain.

1985
The Treaty of Rarotonga declares the South Pacific a nuclear-free zone. New Zealand bans all nuclear trade.

1995
The Waikato-Raupatu Claims Settlement Act for Maori land claims is passed.

Nuclear testing

United States of America:

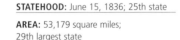

ALABAMA

Half of all the peanuts grown in the USA are grown within 100 miles (161 km) of Dothan, Alabama, the Peanut Capital of the World.

ALABAMA (AL)
CAPITAL: MONTGOMERY

Alabama, the heart of the Deep South, has borders with four other states. Millions of years ago, the waters of the Gulf of Mexico covered the southern part of the state. When the waters receded they left a black belt of fertile soil between the forests of the north and south of Alabama.

STATEHOOD: December 14, 1819; 22nd state

AREA: 52,419 square miles; 30th largest state

STATE FLOWER: Camellia

STATE TREE: Southern pine

STATE BIRD: Yellowhammer

ALASKA

In summer, the sun shines in Alaska 20 to 24 hours a day. Fruit and vegetables can grow to three or four times their normal weight and 90-pound (41-kg) cabbages are common.

ALASKA (AK)
CAPITAL: JUNEAU

Alaska is geographically nearer to Russia—51 miles (82 km) at the nearest point—than it is to the other 49 states. Almost one-third of the state is in the Arctic Circle and there are more glaciers and ice fields in Alaska than in the rest of the inhabited world. At the southern end of the state is the volcanic Aleutian Island arc in the Pacific Ocean.

STATEHOOD: January 3, 1959; 49th state

AREA: 663,267 square miles; the largest state

STATE FLOWER: Forget-me-not

STATE TREE: Sitka spruce

STATE BIRD: Willow ptarmigan

ARIZONA

Arizona has both the sunniest city in the USA, Yuma, and the city with the hottest apparent temperature, Phoenix.

ARIZONA (AZ)
CAPITAL: PHOENIX

Arizona is a land of rugged canyons, mountains, desert scrub, and the Sonoran Desert. It is also one of the fastest-growing states with three-quarters of the state's population living in just two cities—Phoenix and Tucson. Outside these cities, farming of cotton and sorghum, copper mining, and tourism are the major industries.

STATEHOOD: February 14, 1912; 48th state

AREA: 113,998 square miles; 6th largest state

STATE FLOWER: Saguaro blossom

STATE TREE: Paloverde

STATE BIRD: Cactus wren

ARKANSAS

Bauxite, a town in Arkansas, produces 95 percent of all the aluminum ore in the USA. The ore is often called bauxite, which gave the town its name.

ARKANSAS (AR)
CAPITAL: LITTLE ROCK

From the lowlands around the Mississippi River, Arkansas stretches west through prairies and dense forests to the high lands of the Ouachita and Ozark Mountains. The smallest state west of the Mississippi, Arkansas is the leading producer of rice and chickens. Food processing is now a major industry along with mining (mainly bauxite and coal).

STATEHOOD: June 15, 1836; 25th state

AREA: 53,179 square miles; 29th largest state

STATE FLOWER: Apple blossom

STATE TREE: Pine

STATE BIRD: Mockingbird

CALIFORNIA

The highest and lowest points in continental USA are both in California. Mt Whitney, 14,494 feet (4,420 m) above sea level, is the highest and, only 75 miles (120 km) away in Death Valley, is the lowest point, 282 feet (86 m) below sea level.

CALIFORNIA (CA)
CAPITAL: SACRAMENTO

Between the Coastal Ranges and the Sierra Nevada lies California's fertile central valley. Forty percent of the USA's canned or frozen fruit and vegetables, and most of the country's wine, come from here. In the major cities—on the Pacific coast where there are breaks in the Coastal Ranges—high-tech industries and the movie industry predominate.

STATEHOOD: September 9, 1850; 31st state

AREA: 163,696 square miles; 3rd largest state

STATE FLOWER: Golden poppy

STATE TREE: California redwood

STATE BIRD: California valley quail

COLORADO

In 1894, at Smuggler Mine in Aspen, Colorado, miners found the world's largest silver nugget. It weighed 1,840 pounds (835 kg).

COLORADO (CO)
CAPITAL: DENVER

More than half of all the mountains over 14,000 feet (4,270 m) in the USA are in Colorado's mineral-rich Rocky Mountains. To the west of these are the high plains of the Colorado Plateau, with their cattle and sheep ranches. But it is on the edge of the Great Plains, in eastern Colorado, that 80 percent of the population lives.

STATEHOOD: August 1, 1876; 38th state

AREA: 104,094 square miles; 8th largest state

STATE FLOWER: Rocky Mountain columbine

STATE TREE: Blue spruce

STATE BIRD: Lark bunting

50 States Fact File

CONNECTICUT

The Connecticut Courant newspaper, first published in 1764 and still published today (as the Hartford Courant) is the USA's longest continuously published newspaper.

CONNECTICUT (CT)
CAPITAL: HARTFORD

Most of Connecticut's bigger cities are along the 250 miles (403 km) of Atlantic coastline or in the Connecticut River valley. Small farms dotted around the countryside grow vegetables, flowers, and special tobacco leaves for covering cigars. But it is trade and commerce that have made the people of Connecticut the wealthiest in the USA.

STATEHOOD: January 9, 1788; 5th state

AREA: 5,543 square miles; 3rd smallest state

STATE FLOWER: Mountain laurel

STATE TREE: White oak

STATE BIRD: American robin

DELAWARE

Pea Patch Island was a mudbank when a ship carrying peas ran aground on it. The peas grew on the mudbank to form a new island, which is now home to thousands of heron.

DELAWARE (DE)
CAPITAL: DOVER

Most of Delaware lies south of the Chesapeake and Delaware Canal. Commercial fishing on the Atlantic Coast, and poultry, fruit, and vegetable farming inland are the main activities. The much smaller industrial north of the state is where two-thirds of the population lives. The main industries are chemicals and products made from chemicals.

STATEHOOD: December 7, 1787; 1st state

AREA: 2,489 square miles; 2nd smallest state

STATE FLOWER: Peach blossom

STATE TREE: American holly

STATE BIRD: Blue hen chicken

FLORIDA

St Augustine in Florida was settled by the Spanish in 1565. It is the oldest European settlement in the USA.

FLORIDA (FL)
CAPITAL: TALLAHASSEE

Florida is the most recent geological region of continental USA, emerging from the ocean 45,000 years ago. With more coastline than any other state except Alaska, but with more sunshine and beaches, Florida attracts 25 million tourists each year. Sunshine is also why three-quarters of the country's oranges and grapefruit come from Florida.

STATEHOOD: March 3, 1845; 27th state

AREA: 65,755 square miles; 22nd largest state

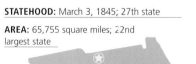

STATE FLOWER: Orange blossom

STATE TREE: Cabbage palm (Sabal palmetto)

STATE BIRD: Mockingbird

GEORGIA

The Okefenokee swamp in Georgia is the largest freshwater swamp in the USA. Once part of the Atlantic Ocean, it is now 100 feet (30 m) above sea level.

GEORGIA (GA)
CAPITAL: ATLANTA

Georgia's rivers flow in three directions— east to the Atlantic, south to the Gulf of Mexico, or west to the Mississippi. In the forested Appalachian Mountains of the north, timber, quarrying, and carpet making are the main industries. In the southern and coastal plains, wealth comes from farming peanuts, pecans, and peaches.

STATEHOOD: January 2, 1788; 4th state

AREA: 59,425 square miles; 24th largest state

STATE FLOWER: Cherokee rose

STATE TREE: Live oak

STATE BIRD: Brown thrasher

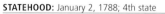

HAWAII

The wettest place in the USA (and possibly the wettest place in the world) is Mt Waialeale on the island of Kauai, Hawaii. Average rainfall is 460 inches (11,684 mm).

HAWAII (HI)
CAPITAL: HONOLULU

Hawaii is the only state that is not in the continent of North America. Of Hawaii's 132 volcanic islands stretching across the Pacific Ocean, only eight are populated. Three-quarters of the population live on Oahu, while Hawaii—the largest island— has most of the pineapple, coffee, and sugar plantations. Tourism is Hawaii's major industry.

STATEHOOD: August 21, 1959; 50th state

AREA: 10,931 square miles; 8th smallest state

STATE FLOWER: Hibiscus

STATE TREE: Kukui or candlenut

STATE BIRD: Nene or Hawaiian goose

IDAHO

Around 27 billion potatoes grow in Idaho each year—that is 90 potatoes for every person in the USA.

IDAHO (ID)
CAPITAL: BOISE

Most of Idaho is a pristine wilderness of mountains, forests, lakes, and streams where minerals, timber, and tourism are the main industries. The southern part of the state is flatter and three-quarters of the population live within 30 miles (48 km) of the Snake River. Potatoes, beets, and farmed trout are the main produce in the fertile south

STATEHOOD: July 3, 1890; 43rd state

AREA: 83,570 square miles; 14th largest state

STATE FLOWER: Syringa

STATE TREE: Western white pine

STATE BIRD: Mountain bluebird

ILLINOIS

Illinois had the world's very first skyscraper—the ten-story Home Insurance Building in Chicago (1885). Now it has the tallest skyscraper in the USA—Sears Tower in Chicago.

ILLINOIS (IL)
CAPITAL: SPRINGFIELD

Illinois is a flat inland state surrounded by water—Lake Michigan to the northeast, the Wabash and Ohio rivers to the southeast, and the Mississippi River to the west. Chicago, the biggest city, is a water, land, and air transportation hub. Outside the main cities, less than 20 percent of the Illinois population farms 80 percent of the state's land.

STATEHOOD: December 3, 1818; 21st state

AREA: 57,914 square miles; 25th largest state

STATE FLOWER: Native violet

STATE TREE: White oak

STATE BIRD: Cardinal

INDIANA

Indiana has a "lost" river that flows underground through limestone for 21 miles (34 km). Only after torrential rain does the river flow along its usually dry river bed on the surface.

INDIANA (IN)
CAPITAL: INDIANAPOLIS

Industry in Indiana—mainly steelmaking—is concentrated around Gary in the north. The rest of the state's north is taken up by 85,000 farms, with corn the number one crop. In the center is Indianapolis, which has more major highways leading from it than any other city. In the south, Indiana's only remaining forest is rich in coal and limestone deposits.

STATEHOOD: December 11, 1816; 19th state

AREA: 36,418 square miles; 38th largest state

STATE FLOWER: Peony

STATE TREE: Tulip tree

STATE BIRD: Cardinal

IOWA

Farms take up almost 95 percent of the land in Iowa. These Iowa farms raise more hogs than anywhere else in the world and a billion bushels of corn each year.

IOWA (IA)
CAPITAL: DES MOINES

Iowa is a state of rolling plains rather than flatlands. Black loam, deposited by melting glaciers, is fertile farming soil. Iowa's many rivers provide irrigation and transport for the corn, alfalfa, and soybean crops. Many Iowans who are not farmers work in farm-related industries such as food processing, meat packing, and farm machinery.

STATEHOOD: December 28, 1846; 29th state

AREA: 56,272 square miles; 26th largest state

STATE FLOWER: Wild rose

STATE TREE: Oak

STATE BIRD: Eastern goldfinch

KANSAS

In 1970, the heaviest hailstone ever recorded fell in Coffeyville, Kansas. The hailstone weighed 1.7 pounds (772 g).

KANSAS (KS)
CAPITAL: TOPEKA

The center of continental USA is just outside Lebanon in Kansas. The "cowboy state" is now a major wheat-growing state. Russian Mennonite immigrants introduced a hardy strain of wheat that would grow in the dry, hard soil of Kansas. Grain milling, beef cattle, and aircraft construction, in Wichita, are the other major industries.

STATEHOOD: January 29, 1861; 34th state

AREA: 82,277 square miles; 15th largest state

STATE FLOWER: Sunflower

STATE TREE: Cottonwood

STATE BIRD: Western meadowlark

KENTUCKY

The Mammoth Cave system in Kansas is the world's largest cave system. There are more than 360 miles (580 km) of winding tunnels . . . and 130 different species of animals.

KENTUCKY (KY)
CAPITAL: FRANKFORT

The bluegrass region of northern Kentucky is ideal for horse breeding. Underground limestone feeds the lush, calcium-rich grass, and grass seed is a major product of the state. One of the top producers of coal and tobacco, Kentucky's more recent industries include leather tanning and farm equipment.

STATEHOOD: June 1, 1792; 15th state

AREA: 40,409 square miles; 37th largest state

STATE FLOWER: Goldenrod

STATE TREE: Kentucky coffee tree

STATE BIRD: Cardinal

LOUISIANA

P.B.S. Pinchback became the USA's first African-American governor in 1872 when he served as Governor of Louisiana for 35 days.

LOUISIANA (LA)
CAPITAL: BATON ROUGE

Louisiana is the lowest-lying state, especially in the Mississippi River delta where levees (small dams) are used to prevent flooding. In the past, sugar, salt, cotton, rice, and commercial fishing were the main products but now much of Louisiana's wealth comes from oil and natural gas, found throughout the state and offshore in the Gulf of Mexico.

STATEHOOD: April 30, 1812; 18th state

AREA: 51,840 square miles; 31st largest state

STATE FLOWER: Magnolia

STATE TREE: Bald cypress

STATE BIRD: Eastern brown pelican

MAINE

MAINE (ME)
CAPITAL: AUGUSTA

Maine is the easternmost state—Mount Katahdin, the highest point, is the first place in the USA that the rising sun strikes. With 3,500 miles (5,635 km) of coastline, tourism and commercial fishing, mainly for lobsters, are major industries. Ninety percent of the state is forest wilderness and the principal manufacturing industries are wood pulp and paper.

STATEHOOD: March 15, 1820; 23rd state

AREA: 35,385 square miles; 12th smallest state

STATE FLOWER: White pine cone and tassel

STATE TREE: Eastern white pine

STATE BIRD: Chickadee

MARYLAND

MARYLAND (MD)
CAPITAL: ANNAPOLIS

Chesapeake Bay, famous for its blue crabs and oysters, divides Maryland in two. The major cities and the suburbs of Washington D.C. are on the Western Shore. Tobacco is grown in the southern part of the Western Shore. Poultry farms and market gardens are common on the less-populated Eastern Shore.

STATEHOOD: April 28, 1788; 7th state

AREA: 12,407 square miles; 9th smallest state

STATE FLOWER: Black-eyed Susan

STATE TREE: White oak

STATE BIRD: Baltimore oriole

MASSACHUSETTS

MASSACHUSETTS (MA)
CAPITAL: BOSTON

Only 47 miles (76 km) from north to south at its western border, Massachusetts has a bigger population than any of the other New England states, with Greater Boston the most densely populated area. Fishing and tourism predominate on the east coast while cranberries are farmed in the shallow marshes of Cape Cod.

STATEHOOD: February 6, 1788; 6th state

AREA: 10,555 square miles; 7th smallest state

STATE FLOWER: Mayflower

STATE TREE: American elm

STATE BIRD: Chickadee

MICHIGAN

MICHIGAN (MI)
CAPITAL: LANSING

Water makes up more than 40 percent of the total area of Michigan. It has the longest freshwater shoreline in the world—longer than the Atlantic coastline from Maine to Florida. The state is split into two peninsulas connected by the Mackinac Bridge. The state's largest city, Detroit, is the country's major producer of automobiles and trucks.

STATEHOOD: January 26, 1837; 26th state

AREA: 96,716 square miles; 11th largest state

STATE FLOWER: Apple blossom

STATE TREE: White pine

STATE BIRD: Robin

MINNESOTA

In 1931, a construction crew, working near Pelican Lake in Minnesota, found the oldest fossilized human remains ever found in the USA. But "Minnesota Man" turned out to be a woman.

MINNESOTA (MN)
CAPITAL: ST PAUL

Minnesota, on Lake Superior, is also the source of the Mississippi River. The state's two largest cities—Minneapolis and St. Paul—stand on either side of the Mississippi. These waterways make Minnesota a major transportation and distribution center. Minnesota is the second northernmost state in the USA, after Alaska, and winters can be freezing cold.

STATEHOOD: May 11, 1858; 32nd state

AREA: 86,939 square miles; 12th largest state

STATE FLOWER: Pink and white lady's slipper

STATE TREE: Red (Norway) pine

STATE BIRD: Common loon

MISSISSIPPI

The world's first lung transplant and first heart transplant (using a chimpanzee's heart) were performed at the University of Mississippi Medical Center in the early 1960s.

MISSISSIPPI (MS)
CAPITAL: JACKSON

Mississippi in the Deep South is a rural state—more than half the population lives in small towns or in the countryside. The regular flooding of the Mississippi has created ideal soil for the farming of cotton, soybeans, rice, and wheat. Catfish are caught in the rivers and, offshore in the Gulf of Mexico, the state has many oil and natural gas wells.

STATEHOOD: December 10, 1817; 20th state

AREA: 48,430 square miles; 32nd largest state

STATE FLOWER: Magnolia flower

STATE TREE: Magnolia tree

STATE BIRD: Mockingbird

MISSOURI

Three of the strongest earthquakes ever recorded in the USA occurred near New Madrid, Missouri in 1811 and 1812. The earthquakes caused the Mississippi River to flow backward—temporarily—before the River again flowed forward but on a different course.

MISSOURI (MO)
CAPITAL: JEFFERSON CITY

Missouri's wealth comes from manufacturing and it is the USA's third largest state in terms of manufactured goods, which include aircraft, spacecraft, chemicals, and beer. Wealth also comes from farming—corn in the north, cotton and rice in the southeast—timber from the forests of the Ozark Plateau, and lead mining.

STATEHOOD: August 10, 1821; 24th state

AREA: 69,704 square miles; 21st largest state

STATE FLOWER: Hawthorn

STATE TREE: Flowering dogwood

STATE BIRD: Eastern Bluebird

MONTANA

Millions of grasshoppers remain frozen in the Grasshopper Glacier in Montana. The large migrating swarm was caught in a severe storm, deposited in the glacier, and then buried by snow and ice.

 MONTANA (MT)
CAPITAL: HELENA

Although the name Montana comes from the Spanish for mountains, only two-fifths of the state is mountainous. In Montana's Rocky Mountains are peaks so steep and rugged they have never been climbed. Most of Montana is relatively flat land where vast herds of cattle and sheep roam. Although large in size, Montana only has five people per square mile.

STATEHOOD: November 8, 1889; 41st state

AREA: 147,042 square miles; 4th largest state

STATE FLOWER: Bitterroot

STATE TREE: Ponderosa pine

STATE BIRD: Western meadowlark

NEBRASKA

Nebraska is the only state with a one-house legislature instead of the two-house system of the US government and the other 49 states. All 49 members are "senators."

NEBRASKA (NE)
CAPITAL: LINCOLN

One of the great agricultural states, 95 percent of Nebraska's land is devoted to farming. Nebraska's 50,000 farms produce corn and wheat but also raise 6 million cattle, 4 million hogs, and 2 million turkeys. Most industry is farm-related (grain processing and meat packing) but income from farming is greater than industry, timber, and mining together.

STATEHOOD: March 1, 1867; 37th state

AREA: 77,354 square miles; 16th largest state

STATE FLOWER: Goldenrod

STATE TREE: Cottonwood

STATE BIRD: Western meadowlark

NEVADA

Nevada is the driest state in the USA with less than 8 inches (203 mm) of rain each year on average.

 NEVADA (NV)
CAPITAL: CARSON CITY

Gold and silver brought prospectors to this otherwise hostile landscape of wild rugged mountains and desert; gold and silver are still important industries. Much of the barren land in Nevada is used by the federal government for weapons testing. The biggest industries in Nevada are gambling and entertainment in Las Vegas and Reno.

STATEHOOD: October 31, 1864; 36th state

AREA: 110,561 square miles; 7th largest state

STATE FLOWER: Sagebrush

STATE TREE: Single-leaf piñon

STATE BIRD: Mountain bluebird

NEW HAMPSHIRE

The fastest surface winds ever recorded blew across the top of Mt Washington in April 1934. The climate research station on top of Mt. Washington recorded winds of 231 miles an hour (372 km/h).

 NEW HAMPSHIRE (NH)
CAPITAL: CONCORD

The granite-rich White Mountains in the north are the center of tourism and timber production. Most of the population is concentrated in the south of the state with its machinery, plastics, metal, and electrical goods factories. Every four years, New Hampshire is the first state to hold the presidential primary elections.

STATEHOOD: June 21, 1788; 9th state

AREA: 9,350 square miles; 5th smallest state

STATE FLOWER: Purple lilac

STATE TREE: White birch

STATE BIRD: Purple finch

NEW JERSEY

New Jersey is the fourth smallest state but has the highest population density—1,134 people per square mile.

 NEW JERSEY (NJ)
CAPITAL: TRENTON

This very metropolitan state between two of the USA's biggest cities—New York and Philadelphia—is also known as the Garden State because of the large number of market gardens. Most of the population lives in the north where finance, services, retail, and manufacturing provide employment. Tourism and fishing are the main industries along the Atlantic coastline.

STATEHOOD: December 18, 1787; 3rd state

AREA: 8,721 square miles; 4th smallest state

STATE FLOWER: Purple violet

STATE TREE: Red oak

STATE BIRD: Eastern goldfinch

NEW MEXICO

Mew Mexico's state bird, the roadrunner, can fly for a few seconds if it gets a good run downhill for takeoff. But the roadrunner prefers to run at speeds of up to 17 miles an hour (27 km/h).

 NEW MEXICO (NM)
CAPITAL: SANTA FE

New Mexico was controlled by Spain for hundreds of years before 1848, when the USA took over. Many of the people are still of Spanish, Mexican, or Native American descent. New Mexico has a varied landscape of mountains in the north, plains in the east, and deserts in the south. Mining, and oil and natural gas, are the major industries.

STATEHOOD: January 6, 1912; 47th state

AREA: 121,589 square miles; 5th largest state

STATE FLOWER: Yucca

STATE TREE: Piñon

STATE BIRD: Roadrunner

NEW YORK

Between 1892 and 1954, 12 million immigrants passed through Ellis Island in New York Harbor. Today, 40 percent of US citizens have an ancestor who passed through Ellis Island.

 NEW YORK (NY)
CAPITAL: ALBANY

New York borders the Atlantic Ocean and Lake Ontario, which is connected to New York City Harbor by rivers and canals. Away from the skyscrapers of the USA's largest city, "upstate" New York has millions of acres of dairy farms, mountain ranges, and Adirondack Park, the largest state park in the lower 48 states.

STATEHOOD: July 26, 1788; 11th state

AREA: 54,556 square miles; 27th largest state

STATE FLOWER: Rose

STATE TREE: Sugar maple

STATE BIRD: Bluebird

OHIO

Ohio had the first ambulance service, the first police cars, first traffic light, and first electric lighting in the USA.

 **OHIO (OH)**
CAPITAL: COLUMBUS

The manufacturing cities are located near Lake Erie in the north or the Ohio River in the south. Cleveland steel, Cincinnati soap, Akron rubber, and Toledo glass are transported by barge or ship out of Ohio, which has the second highest number of manufacturing jobs in the USA. More than half of Ohio is farmland; soybeans, winter wheat, and corn are the major crops.

STATEHOOD: March 1, 1803; 17th state

AREA: 44,825 square miles; 34th largest state

STATE FLOWER: Scarlet carnation

STATE TREE: Buckeye

STATE BIRD: Cardinal

NORTH CAROLINA

The Cape Hatteras Lighthouse, built in 1870, is America's tallest brick lighthouse at 208 feet (63 m). It warns ships of the treacherous Diamond Shoals.

 NORTH CAROLINA (NC)
CAPITAL: RALEIGH

Between the Appalachian Mountains and the Atlantic Ocean lies the Piedmont Plateau where most of North Carolina's population lives and where furniture and textile factories are located. In Research Triangle Park, founded by the universities in Durham, Raleigh, and Chapel Hill, supercomputing and biotechnology are the focus. But it is tobacco that is still the state's major industry.

STATEHOOD: November 21, 1789; 12th state

AREA: 53,819 square miles; 28th largest state

STATE FLOWER: Dogwood

STATE TREE: Pine

STATE BIRD: Cardinal

OKLAHOMA

Oil wells were dug all over the state of Oklahoma, including one in the grounds of the State Capitol and one in the garden of the Governor's mansion.

 OKLAHOMA (OK)
CAPITAL: OKLAHOMA CITY

The high plains of Oklahoma's panhandle suffered during the 1930s windstorms that blew away the topsoil and created the famous dust bowl. Cotton and peanuts grow in the fertile farmland of the Red River but it is beef cattle, in the center and west of the state, and oil—all over the state—that are the main sources of Oklahoma's wealth.

STATEHOOD: November 16, 1907; 46th state

AREA: 69,898 square miles; 20th largest state

STATE FLOWER: Mistletoe

STATE TREE: Redbud

STATE BIRD: Scissor-tailed flycatcher

NORTH DAKOTA

Underground coal or lignite burns in the North Dakota coal fields almost constantly. The heat bakes nearby sediments, creating 50-feet (15-m) thick beds of natural brick called clinker.

 NORTH DAKOTA (ND)
CAPITAL: BISMARCK

Second only to Kansas in wheat production, North Dakota is a state of very large farms whose other main crops are sunflowers, barley, and flax. Far from the ocean, which moderates temperature, and with few hills or trees (only 1 percent of the state is forested) to act as windbreaks or shade, North Dakota has very cold winters and very hot summers.

STATEHOOD: November 2, 1889; 39th state

AREA: 70,700 square miles; 19th largest state

STATE FLOWER: Wild prairie rose

STATE TREE: American elm

STATE BIRD: Western meadowlark

OREGON

The USA's deepest lake is Oregon's 1,932-foot (589 m)- deep Crater Lake. The lake was formed 7,000 years ago in a collapsed volcano.

 **OREGON (OR)**
CAPITAL: SALEM

Once the end of the trail for pioneers heading west, the very fertile Willamette Valley is where half of Oregon's population lives. Electronics and wood processing of forest timbers from the Cascade Range and the Blue Mountains are the main industries in the industrial center, Portland. Cattle ranches are scattered in the semi-arid Great Basin, in the southeast.

STATEHOOD: February 14, 1859; 33rd state

AREA: 93,381 square miles; 9th largest state

STATE FLOWER: Oregon grape

STATE TREE: Douglas fir

STATE BIRD: Western meadowlark

PENNSYLVANIA

PENNSYLVANIA (PA)
CAPITAL: HARRISBURG

Philadelphia is one of the busiest freshwater ports in the country. Steel used to be the main product shipped out but, as the steel industry declined, new industries like the processing of snack foods (including ice cream and chocolate) have grown. Most of Pennsylvania remains rural with most of the farming concentrated in the southeast.

STATEHOOD: December 12, 1787; 2nd state

AREA: 46,055 square miles; 33rd largest state

STATE FLOWER: Mountain laurel

STATE TREE: Hemlock

STATE BIRD: Ruffed grouse

RHODE ISLAND

RHODE ISLAND (RI)
CAPITAL: PROVIDENCE

Because it has so little land, commerce, rather than farming or industry, was the only option for Rhode Island. The state is, in fact, 35 islands in Narragansett Bay with Rhode Island the largest of these. Fashionable resorts, such as Newport, attract wealthy tourists and yachtsmen. The mainland is well known for its silverware and costume jewelry.

STATEHOOD: May 29, 1790; 13th state

AREA: 1,545 square miles; smallest state

STATE FLOWER: Violet

STATE TREE: Red maple

STATE BIRD: Rhode Island Red

SOUTH CAROLINA

SOUTH CAROLINA (SC)
CAPITAL: COLUMBIA

From South Carolina's beautiful beaches, the coastal plain of swamps and marshes stretches 150 miles (242 km) inland. This low land gives way to the Piedmont Plateau west of Columbia, the state capital, then rises to the Blue Ridge Mountains. Textiles and tourism are major industries, while farm produce includes peaches, corn, wheat, and cotton.

STATEHOOD: May 23, 1788; 8th state

AREA: 32,020 square miles; 11th smallest state

STATE FLOWER: Carolina yellow jessamine

STATE TREE: Palmetto

STATE BIRD: Carolina wren

SOUTH DAKOTA

SOUTH DAKOTA (SD)
CAPITAL: PIERRE

More than 90 percent of land in South Dakota is given over to farming. Crops, mainly corn and wheat, grow in the fertile soil east of the Missouri River. Beef cattle and sheep graze in the western grasslands, where there are many Native American reservations. South Dakota also has the USA's most profitable gold mine.

STATEHOOD: November 2, 1889; 40th state

AREA: 77,116 square miles; 17th largest state

STATE FLOWER: American pasqueflower

STATE TREE: Black Hills spruce

STATE BIRD: Ring-necked pheasant

TENNESSEE

Tennessee has borders with eight other states—only Missouri has as many near neighbors.

TENNESSEE (TN)
CAPITAL: NASHVILLE

The eastern part of Tennessee is mountainous and, from the highest point, you can see parts of seven states. Cotton and tobacco farming, cattle ranching, and horse breeding have now been overtaken in importance by industry, mainly around Memphis. Automobiles and chemicals are the major industries.

STATEHOOD: June 1, 1796; 16th state

AREA: 42,143 square miles; 36th largest state

STATE FLOWER: Iris

STATE TREE: Tulip poplar

STATE BIRD: Mockingbird

TEXAS

Around 16 million cattle graze in Texas and the largest ranch, near Corpus Christi, is bigger than the State of Rhode Island.

TEXAS (TX)
CAPITAL: AUSTIN

From 1836 to1845, the Republic of Texas was an independent country with its own army and Texas is still larger than many independent countries. Oil has been the state's major resource with the petroleum industry based in Houston. The area around Houston also has the most fertile farmland while the dry, treeless country in the west is cattle-ranching country.

STATEHOOD: December 29, 1845; 28th state

AREA: 268,581 square miles; 2nd largest state

STATE FLOWER: Bluebonnet

STATE TREE: Pecan

STATE BIRD: Mockingbird

UTAH

The Great Salt Lake, northwest of Salt Lake City in Utah, has such a high evaporation rate that the water in the lake is up to eight times more salty than any ocean.

UTAH (UT)
CAPITAL: SALT LAKE CITY

Mormons, the first settlers, still make up 70 percent of Utah's population. Most of the state is mountain or desert so there is little arable land. The spectacular mountains of the Colorado Plateau attract tourists and are rich in minerals. Most of the population lives in the area around Salt Lake City where hi-tech industries, such as the manufacture of rocket engines and space shuttles, are located.

STATEHOOD: January 4, 1896; 45th state

AREA: 84,899 square miles; 13th largest state

STATE FLOWER: Sego lily

STATE TREE: Blue spruce

STATE BIRD: American or California seagull

VERMONT

Vermont's famous Green Mountains run down the middle of the state like a backbone or spine. The state's name comes from the French words for green mountain vert mont.

VERMONT (VT)
CAPITAL: MONTPELIER

Vermont has no large cities and the smallest capital city in the USA—Montpelier, with 8,000 people. Suitable soil for crops is limited and almost three-quarters of the state is forested. In addition to timber, Vermont quarries provide granite, marble, and slate, some of it used for the US Capitol and US Supreme Court Building.

STATEHOOD: March 4, 1791; 14th state

AREA: 9,614 square miles; 6th smallest state

STATE FLOWER: Red clover

STATE TREE: Sugar maple

STATE BIRD: Hermit thrush

VIRGINIA

Virginia's Natural Bridge is a 215-foot (66 m)-high limestone arch. As a young man, George Washington climbed the Bridge and carved his initials in the rock.

VIRGINIA (VA)
CAPITAL: RICHMOND

Virginia's fertile farmland is in the Shenandoah Valley in the north where there are apple orchards and dairy farms, and Chesapeake Bay in the east, where tobacco, peanuts, and corn grow. Close to Washington D.C., 20 percent of Virginia's population works in federal government offices, agencies, or bases.

STATEHOOD: June 25, 1788; 10th state

AREA: 42,774 square miles; 35th largest state

STATE FLOWER: Dogwood blossom

STATE TREE: Dogwood

STATE BIRD: Cardinal

WASHINGTON

Washington produces 30 percent of the country's hydroelectricity from dams on the Snake and Columbia rivers. One of these dams, the Grand Coulee Dam, is the largest in the USA.

WASHINGTON (WA)
CAPITAL: OLYMPIA

The Cascade Mountains split the state into a wet western half and a dry eastern half. The drier east has cattle and wheat farms, and apple orchards. Most of the population lives in the west, two-thirds of them on the shores of Puget Sound. Fishing, timber, shipbuilding and, more recently, software companies, are the major employers.

STATEHOOD: November 11, 1889; 42nd state

AREA: 71,300 square miles; 18th largest state

STATE FLOWER: Coast rhododendron

STATE TREE: Western hemlock

STATE BIRD: Willow goldfinch

WEST VIRGINIA

West Virginia's northern panhandle is so narrow that one city, Weirton, stretches the whole width of the state.

WEST VIRGINIA (WV)
CAPITAL: CHARLESTON

The hills and mountains that cover almost all of West Virginia are rich in minerals and attract tourists but make farming difficult. Coal is West Virginia's most important resource with half of the state sitting on underground coal beds. Virginia also manufactures chemical and metal products, rubber, and glass, including most of the country's marbles.

STATEHOOD: June 20, 1863; 35th state

AREA: 24,230 square miles; 10th smallest state

STATE FLOWER: Rhododendron

STATE TREE: Sugar maple

STATE BIRD: Cardinal

WISCONSIN

Wisconsin produces more milk, cheese, and butter than any other state. Forty percent of America's cheese comes from Wisconsin.

WISCONSIN (WI)
CAPITAL: MADISON

Wisconsin not only borders two of the Great Lakes but has 15,000 other lakes so the state has many tourists. The northern part of the state is forested while the south is home to 1.4 million dairy cows. The main cities and manufacturing industries, such as paper and beer, are concentrated in the southeast of the state.

STATEHOOD: May 29, 1848; 30th state

AREA: 65,498 square miles; 23rd largest state

STATE FLOWER: Wood violet

STATE TREE: Sugar maple

STATE BIRD: Robin

WYOMING

Wyoming's nickname is "The Equality State". It was the first state to give women the vote (in 1869) and the first to elect a woman governor (in 1925).

WYOMING (WY)
CAPITAL: CHEYENNE

Although Wyoming is in the top ten states in size, it has the smallest population of any state—just over half a million people. Three-quarters of the land is used for grazing cattle and each year 7 million tourists visit Wyoming's huge national parks, but coal mining and oil are the main sources of Wyoming's wealth.

STATEHOOD: July 10, 1890; 44th state

AREA: 97,814 square miles; 10th largest state

STATE FLOWER: Indian paintbrush

STATE TREE: Cottonwood

STATE BIRD: Western meadowlark

Gazetteer

How to use the gazetteer

This gazetteer is a geographical index of places in this atlas. To find the city of Agra in India, for example, look up its name in the gazetteer.

The entry reads: **140   D8   Agra**, India

The number 140 indicates that Agra appears on the map on page 140. The reference D8 tells you that it can be found in square D8. Turn to page 140. Trace down from the letter D at the top of the page (or up from the letter D on the bottom of the page) and then across from the number 8 on the side of the page. You will find Agra within the square where the letter and number intersect.

The symbols below are used to indicate the geographic feature of each entry.

≈ **Bay**
Includes bays and gulfs

Channel
Includes channels, straits and passages

□ **Country**

▣ **Dependent Territory**
Internal administrative region, province or state eg Scotland, Falkland Islands, Manitoba, Queensland

▲ **Desert**
Includes sand dune features

⦂ **Geographic Area**
Includes regions eg Costa Blanca, Tuscany

◗ **Headland**
Includes headlands, points, capes, peninsulas and sand spits

⌘ **Island**
Includes atolls

✶ **Island Group**

⟐ **Lake**
Includes reservoirs

▲ **Mountain**
Includes individual mountains and volcanoes

▲▲ **Mountain Range**

■ **National Capital**

◔ **Ocean**

◇ **Physical Feature**
Includes plains, moors, wetlands, plateaus, peat bogs, mudflats, swamps and marshes

▬ **Polar Base**

⅃ **River**
Includes deltas, rivers, waterfalls, estuaries

◖ **Sea**

★ **Special Feature**

⌂ **State Capital**

▰ **Underwater Feature**
Includes seamounts, reefs, abyssal plains

A name without a symbol indicates a town or city

Abbreviations

UNITED STATES OF AMERICA

Alabama	AL
Alaska	AK
Arizona	AZ
Arkansas	AR
California	CA
Colorado	CO
Connecticut	CT
Delaware	DE
District of Columbia	DC
Florida	FL
Georgia	GA
Guam	GU
Hawaii	HI
Idaho	ID
Illinois	IL
Indiana	IN
Iowa	IA
Kansas	KS
Kentucky	KY
Louisiana	LA
Maine	ME
Maryland	MD
Massachusetts	MA
Michigan	MI
Minnesota	MN
Mississippi	MS
Missouri	MO
Montana	MT
Nebraska	NE
Nevada	NV
New Hampshire	NH
New Jersey	NJ
New Mexico	NM
New York	NY
North Carolina	NC
North Dakota	ND
Ohio	OH
Oklahoma	OK
Oregon	OR
Pennsylvania	PA
Puerto Rico	PR
Rhode Island	RI
South Carolina	SC
South Dakota	SD
Tennessee	TN
Texas	TX
Utah	UT
Vermont	VT
Virginia	VA
Virgin Islands	VI
Washington	WA
West Virginia	WV
Wisconsin	WI
Wyoming	WY

CANADA

Alberta	AB
British Columbia	BC
Manitoba	MB
New Brunswick	NB
Newfoundland and Labrador	NL
Northwest Territories	NT
Nova Scotia	NS
Nunavut	NU
Ontario	ON
Prince Edward Island	PE
Québec	QC
Saskatchewan	SK
Yukon Territory	YT

AUSTRALIA

Australian Capital Territory	ACT
New South Wales	NSW
Northern Territory	NT
Queensland	QLD
South Australia	SA
Tasmania	TAS
Victoria	VIC
Western Australia	WA

A

92	F 1	**A Coruña**, Spain
104	B 8	**Aachen**, Germany
105	E 10	**Aalen**, Germany
101	E 11	**Aalst**, Belgium
101	C 11	**Aalter**, Belgium
101	F 11	**Aarschot**, Belgium
158	H 7	**Aba**, Nigeria
137	K 4	**Ābādān**, Iran
126	H 9	**Abakan**, Russia
80	F 7	**Abancay**, Peru
152	I 2	**Abashiri**, Japan
43	J 5	**Abbeville**, AL, United States
97	I 2	**Abbeville**, France
62	D 10	**Abbotsford**, BC, Canada
133	L 8	**Abbottabad**, Pakistan
159	J 6	**Abéché**, Chad
41	O 2	**Aberdeen**, MD, United States
42	H 2	**Aberdeen**, MS, United States
47	I 5	**Aberdeen**, SD, United States
88	G 7	**Aberdeen**, United Kingdom
56	E 5	**Aberdeen**, WA, United States
66	G 2	**Aberdeen Lake**, NU, Canada ⟐
89	F 12	**Aberystwyth**, United Kingdom
137	I 9	**Abhā**, Saudi Arabia
158	F 7	**Abidjan**, Côte d'Ivoire ■
51	I 5	**Abilene**, TX, United States
41	J 6	**Abingdon**, VA, United States
55	J 6	**Abiquia Reservoir**, NM, United States ⟐
140	C 7	**Abohar**, India
137	M 6	**Abu Dhabi**, United Arab Emirates ■
137	I 3	**Abū Kamāl**, Syria
158	H 6	**Abuja**, Nigeria ■
93	J 5	**Acalá de Henares**, Spain
73	I 7	**Acaponeta**, Mexico
73	K 10	**Acapulco**, Mexico
41	P 4	**Accomac**, VA, United States
158	G 7	**Accra**, Ghana ■
126	H 9	**Achinsk**, Russia
109	H 14	**Acireale**, Italy
50	G 5	**Ackerly**, TX, United States
75	J 3	**Acklins Island**, The Bahamas ⌘
137	J 5	**Ad Dahnā'**, Saudi Arabia ▲
158	E 3	**Ad Dakhla**, Western Sahara
137	K 6	**Ad Dammām**, Saudi Arabia
58	D 10	**Adak**, AK, United States
58	D 10	**Adak Island**, AK, United States ⌘
38	G 5	**Adams**, NY, United States
130	G 9	**Adana**, Turkey
159	M 6	**Addis Ababa**, Ethiopia ■
141	B 16	**Addu Atoll**, Maldives ⌘
43	L 5	**Adel**, GA, United States
169	I 9	**Adelaide**, SA, Australia ⌂
33	I 3	**Adelaide Island**, Antarctica ⌘
33	N 7	**Adélie Land**, Antarctica ⦂
137	J 10	**Aden**, Yemen
57	F 9	**Adin**, CA, United States
38	H 6	**Adirondack Mountains**, NY, United States ▲▲
131	I 9	**Adiyaman**, Turkey
59	O 8	**Admiralty Island**, AK, United States ⌘
169	K 1	**Admiralty Islands**, Papua New Guinea ✶
141	D 12	**Adoni**, India
158	G 3	**Adrar**, Algeria
50	F 2	**Adrian**, TX, United States
108	G 7	**Adriatic Sea**, Europe ◖
113	H 11	**Aegean Sea**, Greece/Turkey ◖
133	K 7	**Afghanistan**, Asia □
159	N 8	**Afgooye**, Somalia
137	I 7	**'Afif**, Saudi Arabia
59	K 8	**Afognak Island**, AK, United States ⌘
30	D 7	**Africana Seamount**, Indian Ocean ▰
100	G 5	**Afsluitdijk**, Netherlands ◇
130	E 8	**Afyon**, Turkey
158	H 5	**Agadez**, Niger
158	F 2	**Agadir**, Morocco
141	I 9	**Agartala**, India
27	I 9	**Agassiz Fracture Zone**, Pacific Ocean ▰
58	B 9	**Agattu Island**, AK, United States ⌘
131	N 7	**Ağdam**, Azerbaijan
97	J 10	**Agde**, France
96	H 9	**Agen**, France
113	G 11	**Agiokampos**, Greece
113	H 11	**Agios Efstratios**, Greece ⌘
113	I 13	**Agios Kirykos**, Greece

56	D 8	**Agness**, OR, United States
140	D 8	**Agra**, India
131	L 7	**Ağri**, Turkey
109	G 15	**Agrigento**, Italy
173	L 3	**Agrihan**, Northern Mariana Islands ⌘
109	H 11	**Agropoli**, Italy
72	G 3	**Agua Prieta**, Mexico
73	J 7	**Aguascalientes**, Mexico
54	F 9	**Aguila**, AZ, United States
93	K 9	**Águilas**, Spain
73	I 9	**Aguililla**, Mexico
30	C 7	**Agulhas Bank**, Indian Ocean ▰
30	D 8	**Agulhas Basin**, Indian Ocean ▰
30	D 7	**Agulhas Plateau**, Indian Ocean ▰
29	I 10	**Agulhas Ridge**, Atlantic Ocean ▰
172	E 1	**Ahipara Bay**, New Zealand ≈
59	I 8	**Ahklun Mountains**, AK, United States ▲▲
141	B 10	**Ahmadabad**, India
141	C 11	**Ahmadnagar**, India
137	K 4	**Ahvāz**, Iran
113	F 12	**Aigio**, Greece
173	M 3	**Ailinginae**, Marshall Islands ⌘
173	N 4	**Ailinglaplap**, Marshall Islands ⌘
173	N 3	**Ailuk**, Marshall Islands ⌘
46	H 8	**Ainsworth**, NE, United States
47	M 4	**Aitkin**, MN, United States
97	L 10	**Aix-en-Provence**, France
141	J 9	**Aizawl**, India
152	H 8	**Aizu-Wakamatsu**, Japan
97	N 11	**Ajaccio**, Corsica
159	J 2	**Ajdābiyā**, Libya
140	C 8	**Ajmer**, India
54	F 10	**Ajo**, AZ, United States
153	E 11	**Akashi**, Japan
131	L 5	**Akhaltsʻikhe**, Georgia
130	C 7	**Akhisar**, Turkey
67	I 7	**Akimiski Island**, NU, Canada ⌘
152	H 7	**Akita**, Japan
158	E 4	**Akjoujt**, Mauritania
64	B 6	**Aklavik**, NT, Canada
141	D 10	**Akola**, India
63	J 6	**Akpatok Island**, NU, Canada ⌘
113	H 11	**Akra Akrathos**, Greece ◗
113	G 11	**Akra Drepano**, Greece ◗
113	G 14	**Akra Maleas**, Greece ◗
113	G 11	**Akra Paliouri**, Greece ◗
113	F 14	**Akra Tainaro**, Greece ◗
45	J 12	**Akron**, OH, United States
130	G 8	**Aksaray**, Turkey
130	E 8	**Akşehir**, Turkey
148	F 4	**Aksu**, China
132	H 5	**Aktau**, Kazakhstan
133	I 3	**Aktyubinsk**, Kazakhstan
158	H 7	**Akure**, Nigeria
120	C 5	**Akureyri**, Iceland
58	G 10	**Akutan Island**, AK, United States ⌘
137	K 4	**Al ʻAmārah**, Iraq
136	G 4	**Al ʻAqabah**, Jordan
137	M 6	**Al ʻAyn**, United Arab Emirates
137	I 8	**Al Bāḥah**, Saudi Arabia
159	J 2	**Al Baydā'**, Libya
137	J 10	**Al Baydā'**, Yemen
137	I 3	**Al Fallujah**, Iraq
137	K 5	**Al Farwānīyah**, Kuwait
137	M 6	**Al Hajar'al Gharbi**, Oman ▲▲
136	H 4	**Al Hamād**, Jordan/Saudi Arabia ▲
137	I 2	**Al Ḥasakah**, Syria
136	G 5	**Al Hijāz**, Saudi Arabia ⦂
137	J 4	**Al Hillah**, Iraq
137	I 10	**Al Ḥudaydah**, Yemen
137	K 6	**Al Hufūf**, Saudi Arabia
137	K 5	**Al Jahrah**, Kuwait
159	J 4	**Al Jawf**, Libya
137	I 4	**Al Jawf**, Saudi Arabia
137	K 5	**Al Jubayl**, Saudi Arabia
137	N 8	**Al Khalif**, Oman
137	M 6	**Al Khasab**, Oman
159	I 2	**Al Khums**, Libya
137	J 4	**Al Kūt**, Iraq
137	I 4	**Al Labbah**, Saudi Arabia ⦂
136	H 2	**Al Lādhiqīyah**, Syria
137	L 9	**Al Mahrah**, Yemen ▲▲
137	J 6	**Al Majmaʻah**, Saudi Arabia
137	L 6	**Al Manāmah**, Bahrain ■
137	K 10	**Al Mukallā**, Yemen
137	K 3	**Al Muqdādīyah**, Iraq
137	I 2	**Al Qāmishlī**, Syria
43	I 3	**Alabama**, AL, United States ★
43	I 4	**Alabama**, AL, United States ⅃
130	G 7	**Alaca**, Turkey

74 G 8 Alajuela, Costa Rica
173 L 4 Alamagan, Northern Mariana Islands
57 J 12 Alamo, NV, United States
54 E 8 Alamo Lake, AZ, United States
55 K 10 Alamogordo, NM, United States
55 K 5 Alamosa, CO, United States
121 G 11 Åland, Finland
121 G 11 Ålands Hav, Finland
130 E 10 Alanya, Turkey
59 K 4 Alaska, AK, United States
59 J 7 Alaska Range, AK, United States
22 B 3 Alaska Range, North America
58 H 10 Alaskan Peninsula, AK, United States
93 K 7 Albacete, Spain
113 E 10 Albania, Europe
43 K 4 Albany, GA, United States
40 G 6 Albany, KY, United States
39 I 7 Albany, NY, United States
66 H 7 Albany, ON, Canada
56 E 6 Albany, OR, United States
168 E 9 Albany, WA, Australia
172 F 4 Albatross Point, New Zealand
41 L 7 Albemarle, NC, United States
41 O 6 Albemarle Sound, NC, United States
97 I 2 Albert, France
47 M 7 Albert Lea, MN, United States
65 F 11 Alberta, AB, Canada
41 N 5 Alberta, VA, United States
97 I 9 Albi, France
38 D 7 Albion, PA, United States
121 C 13 Ålborg, Denmark
55 J 8 Albuquerque, NM, United States
169 K 9 Albury, NSW, Australia
92 F 7 Alcácer do Sal, Portugal
109 F 14 Alcamo, Italy
93 L 4 Alcañiz, Spain
117 O 8 Alchevs'k, Ukraine
30 E 4 Aldabra Islands, Indian Ocean
127 L 8 Aldan, Russia
38 H 6 Alder Creek, NY, United States
89 H 16 Alderney, United Kingdom
158 E 4 Aleg, Mauritania
92 D 10 Alegranza, Spain
96 H 4 Alençon, France
136 H 2 Aleppo, Syria
32 D 7 Alert, Canada
97 K 9 Alès, France
108 B 6 Alessandria, Italy
121 B 9 Ålesund, Norway
26 G 1 Aleutian Basin, Pacific Ocean
58 D 10 Aleutian Islands, AK, United States
26 G 2 Aleutian Trench, Pacific Ocean
59 N 8 Alexander Archipelago, AK, United States
43 J 3 Alexander City, AL, United States
33 J 3 Alexander Island, Antarctica
172 C 10 Alexandra, New Zealand
159 K 2 Alexandria, Egypt
42 E 5 Alexandria, LA, United States
47 K 5 Alexandria, MN, United States
112 H 8 Alexandria, Romania
41 N 3 Alexandria, VA, United States
38 G 5 Alexandria Bay, NY, United States
113 I 10 Alexandroupoli, Greece
92 F 9 Algarve, Portugal
92 H 10 Algeciras, Spain
158 G 2 Algeria, Africa
109 B 11 Alghero, Italy
158 H 1 Algiers, Algeria
93 L 6 Alginet, Spain
47 M 8 Algona, IA, United States
131 O 7 Äli Bayramli, Azerbaijan
93 L 8 Alicante, Spain
168 H 6 Alice Springs, NT, Australia
140 E 8 Aligarh, India
57 J 12 Alkali Flat, NV, United States
100 F 6 Alkmaar, Netherlands
141 E 9 Allahabad, India
41 L 4 Allegheny Mountains, WV, United States
38 F 7 Allegheny Plateau, NY, United States
38 H 9 Allentown, PA, United States
141 D 14 Alleppey, India
46 F 9 Alliance, NE, United States
43 M 4 Alma, GA, United States
47 I 11 Alma, NE, United States
69 I 5 Alma, QC, Canada
93 L 7 Almansa, Spain
92 H 5 Almanzor, Spain
133 M 5 Almaty, Kazakhstan
100 J 7 Almelo, Netherlands
92 G 7 Almendralejo, Spain
100 G 7 Almere, Netherlands
93 K 9 Almería, Spain
173 K 10 Alofi, Niue
145 K 10 Alor, Indonesia
144 F 6 Alor Setar, Malaysia
45 I 8 Alpena, MI, United States
32 D 6 Alpha Ridge, Arctic Ocean
100 F 8 Alphen, Netherlands
23 I 3 Alps, Europe
120 H 4 Alta, Norway
23 K 3 Altai Mountains, Asia
43 M 4 Altamaha, GA, United States
73 K 9 Altamirano, Mexico
109 J 11 Altamura, Italy
41 M 5 Altavista, VA, United States
149 I 3 Altay, Mongolia
22 E 7 Altiplano, South America
80 F 6 Alto Purús, Peru
38 F 9 Altoona, PA, United States
148 G 5 Altun Shan, China
57 G 9 Alturas, CA, United States
73 M 9 Alvarado, Mexico
121 D 11 Alvdalen, Sweden
140 D 8 Alwar, India
117 I 5 Alytus, Lithuania
53 N 6 Alzada, MT, United States
159 J 6 Am Timan, Chad
67 K 2 Amadjuak Lake, NU, Canada
153 A 14 Amakusa-nada, Japan
145 N 9 Amamapare, Indonesia
153 J 14 Amami-Ō-shima, Japan
153 J 15 Amami-shotō, Japan
50 G 2 Amarillo, TX, United States
22 E 6 Amazon, South America
22 E 6 Amazon Basin, South America
28 E 6 Amazon Cone, Atlantic Ocean
80 E 4 Ambato, Ecuador
97 L 7 Ambérieu-en-Bugey, France
68 C 9 Amberley, ON, Canada
145 L 9 Ambon, Indonesia
145 L 9 Ambon, Indonesia
163 M 9 Ambovombe, Madagascar
57 J 14 Amboy, CA, United States
58 C 10 Amchitka Island, AK, United States
58 C 10 Amchitka Islands, AK, United States
100 H 4 Ameland, Netherlands
52 H 9 American Falls, ID, United States
52 H 9 American Falls Reservoir, ID, United States
173 K 9 American Samoa, United States
29 G 11 American-Antarctic Ridge, Atlantic Ocean
43 K 4 Americus, GA, United States
100 G 8 Amersfoort, Netherlands
33 O 3 Amery Ice Shelf, Antarctica
47 M 9 Ames, IA, United States
127 L 8 Amga, Russia
69 M 7 Amherst, NS, Canada
97 I 2 Amiens, France
30 F 5 Amirante Trench, Indian Ocean
58 E 10 Amlia Island, AK, United States
136 H 4 Ammān, Jordan
32 C 9 Ammassalik, Greenland
130 F 11 Ammóchostos, Cyprus
137 L 2 Amol, Iran
113 I 13 Amorgos, Greece
68 E 5 Amos, QC, Canada
93 M 5 Amposta, Spain
69 K 4 Amqui, QC, Canada
141 D 10 Amravati, India
140 C 7 Amritsar, India
100 F 7 Amstelveen, Netherlands
100 G 7 Amsterdam, Netherlands
30 G 8 Amsterdam Fracture Zone, Indian Ocean
30 H 7 Amsterdam Island, France
105 I 11 Amstetten, Austria
133 J 6 Amudar'ya, Asia
65 D 5 Amundsen Gulf, NT, Canada
26 H 11 Amundsen Sea, Pacific Ocean
33 M 4 Amundsen-Scott, United States
127 L 10 Amur, China/Russia
136 H 5 An Nafūd, Saudi Arabia
137 J 4 An Najaf, Iraq
137 J 4 An Nāşiriyah, Iraq
127 O 5 Anadyr', Russia
113 I 14 Anafi, Greece
57 H 15 Anaheim, CA, United States
130 F 10 Anamur, Turkey
141 D 13 Anantapur, India
81 J 7 Anápolis, Brazil
173 L 4 Anatahan, Northern Mariana Islands
130 D 7 Anatolia, Turkey
82 G 8 Añatuya, Argentina
59 K 7 Anchorage, AK, United States
108 G 8 Ancona, Italy
83 E 12 Ancud, Chile
149 N 3 Anda, China
92 H 9 Andalucía, Spain
43 I 5 Andalusia, AL, United States
31 I 3 Andaman Basin, Indian Ocean
141 J 13 Andaman Islands, India
31 J 2 Andaman Sea, Indian Ocean
101 G 13 Andenne, Belgium
59 K 5 Anderson, AK, United States
41 J 8 Anderson, SC, United States
22 E 7 Andes, South America
133 L 6 Andizhan, Uzbekistan
133 K 7 Andkhvoy, Afghanistan
93 N 3 Andorra, Europe
93 N 3 Andorra La Vella, Andorra
58 D 10 Andreanof Islands, AK, United States
50 G 5 Andrews, TX, United States
109 I 10 Andria, Italy
113 H 12 Andros, Greece
75 I 2 Andros Island, The Bahamas
93 I 8 Andújar, Spain
93 M 2 Aneto, Spain
23 L 3 Angara, Asia
127 I 10 Angarsk, Russia
121 E 9 Ånge, Sweden
96 G 5 Angers, France
74 H 2 Angillia Cays, Cuba
144 G 5 Angkor Wat, Cambodia
89 F 11 Anglesey, United Kingdom
51 L 3 Angleton, TX, United States
83 E 11 Angol, Chile
162 G 6 Angola, Africa
28 I 8 Angola Basin, Atlantic Ocean
96 H 7 Angoulême, France
92 B 9 Angra do Heroísmo, Portugal
75 N 4 Anguilla, United Kingdom
59 I 6 Aniak, AK, United States
163 M 6 Anjouan, Comoros
149 L 7 Ankang, China
130 F 7 Ankara, Turkey
44 H 11 Ann Arbor, MI, United States
158 H 1 Annaba, Algeria
144 G 3 Annam Highlands, Laos/Vietnam
41 O 2 Annapolis, MD, United States
140 G 8 Annapurna, Nepal
97 L 7 Annecy, France
43 J 2 Anniston, AL, United States
149 M 8 Anqing, China
149 N 5 Anshan, China
149 K 9 Anshun, China
47 I 10 Ansley, NE, United States
51 I 4 Anson, TX, United States
130 E 9 Antalya, Turkey
130 E 10 Antalya Körfezi, Turkey
163 M 8 Antananarivo, Madagascar
33 I 2 Antarctic Peninsula, Antarctica
93 I 9 Antequera, Spain
55 J 11 Anthony, NM, United States
97 M 10 Antibes, France
44 D 8 Antigo, WI, United States
69 O 7 Antigonish, NS, Canada
75 N 5 Antigua, Antigua and Barbuda
75 N 5 Antigua and Barbuda, North America
113 G 14 Antikythira, Greece
130 H 10 Antioch, Turkey
26 G 9 Antipodes Islands, New Zealand
82 E 7 Antofagasta, Chile
163 M 8 Antsirabe, Madagascar
163 N 6 Antsiranana, Madagascar
101 E 10 Antwerp, Belgium
149 M 6 Anyang, China
109 F 10 Anzio, Italy
153 I 12 Aoga-shima, Japan
152 H 6 Aomori, Japan
43 K 6 Apalachee Bay, FL, United States
100 I 7 Apeldoorn, Netherlands
22 H 3 Apennines, Europe
173 J 9 Apia, Samoa
81 I 3 Apoera, Suriname
44 C 6 Apostle Islands, WI, United States
22 D 4 Appalachian Mountains, North America
44 E 9 Appleton, WI, United States
41 M 5 Appomattox, VA, United States
80 F 2 Apure, Venezuela
80 F 6 Apurímac, Peru
137 I 3 Ar Ramādī, Iraq
136 H 2 Ar Raqqah, Syria
137 N 6 Ar Rustāq, Oman
137 I 3 Ar Ruţbah, Iraq
30 G 2 Arabian Basin, Indian Ocean
23 J 5 Arabian Peninsula, Asia
30 G 2 Arabian Sea, Indian Ocean
81 L 6 Aracaju, Brazil
81 J 8 Araçatuba, Brazil
112 F 6 Arad, Romania
26 D 6 Arafura Sea, Pacific Ocean
93 L 4 Aragón, Spain
81 J 6 Araguaia, Brazil
81 J 5 Araguaína, Brazil
137 K 3 Arāk, Iran
144 E 3 Arakan Yoma, Myanmar
133 I 4 Aral Sea, Kazakhstan/Uzbekistan
133 J 4 Aral'sk, Kazakhstan
93 J 4 Aranda de Duero, Spain
93 J 5 Aranjuez, Spain
81 L 6 Arapiraca, Brazil
131 L 7 Aras, Azerbaijan/Turkey
131 I 9 Aratürk Baraji, Turkey
169 M 2 Arawa, Papua New Guinea
159 M 7 Ārba Minch, Ethiopia
137 J 2 Arbil, Iraq
43 M 9 Arcadia, FL, United States
57 D 9 Arcata, CA, United States
83 D 14 Archipiélago de la Reina Adelaida, Chile
83 D 13 Archipiélago de los Chonos, Chile
74 H 3 Archipiélago de los Jardines de la Reina, Cuba
52 H 8 Arco, ID, United States
32 D 7 Arctic Ocean,
33 I 2 Arctowski, Poland
137 K 1 Ardabīl, Iran
101 F 14 Ardennes, Belgium
121 C 12 Arendal, Norway
113 F 14 Areópoli, Greece
80 F 7 Arequipa, Peru
108 E 8 Arezzo, Italy
113 G 12 Argalasti, Greece
83 F 9 Argentina, South America
29 E 10 Argentine Abyssal Plain, Atlantic Ocean
29 F 9 Argentine Basin, Atlantic Ocean
133 J 9 Arghandab, Afghanistan
23 M 3 Argun', Asia
121 C 14 Århus, Denmark
141 A 14 Ari Atoll, Maldives
82 E 5 Arica, Chile
54 F 8 Arizona, AZ, United States
133 J 3 Arkalyk, Kazakhstan
22 D 4 Arkansas, North America
126 E 5 Arkhangel'sk, Russia
97 K 10 Arles, France
41 N 3 Arlington, VA, United States
158 H 5 Arlit, Niger
101 H 15 Arlon, Belgium
89 D 10 Armagh, United Kingdom
125 B 7 Armavir, Russia
131 M 7 Armenia, Asia
80 E 3 Armenia, Colombia
169 L 3 Armidale, NSW, Australia
53 J 3 Armington, MT, United States
66 H 8 Armstrong, ON, Canada
67 K 4 Arnaud, QC, Canada
100 H 8 Arnhem, Netherlands
168 H 4 Arnhem Land, NT, Australia
108 E 7 Arno, Italy
173 N 4 Arno, Marshall Islands
120 G 4 Arnøya, Norway
89 E 9 Arran, United Kingdom
97 I 2 Arras, France
92 D 10 Arrecife, Spain
73 N 10 Arriaga, Mexico
113 E 11 Arta, Greece
131 M 7 Artashat, Armenia
55 L 10 Artesia, NM, United States
131 K 6 Artvin, Turkey
75 L 7 Aruba, Netherlands
163 K 4 Arusha, Tanzania
66 H 4 Arviat, NU, Canada
120 G 7 Arvidsjaur, Sweden
126 D 6 Arzamas, Russia
137 K 7 As Salamiyah, Saudi Arabia
137 J 4 As Samāwah, Iraq
137 J 2 As Sulaymānīyah, Iraq
137 J 8 As Sulayyil, Saudi Arabia
136 H 3 As Suwaydā', Syria
133 L 7 Asadābād, Afghanistan
152 I 3 Asahi-dake, Japan
152 H 3 Asahikawa, Japan
141 H 9 Asansol, India
22 G 6 Ascension, Atlantic Ocean
105 D 9 Aschaffenburg, Germany
108 G 8 Ascoli Piceno, Italy
159 N 7 Āsela, Ethiopia
54 F 7 Ash Fork, AZ, United States
172 D 9 Ashburton, New Zealand
41 L 7 Asheboro, NC, United States
133 I 6 Ashgabat, Turkmenistan
153 H 9 Ashikaga, Japan
153 D 13 Ashizuri-misaki, Japan
41 I 3 Ashland, KY, United States
39 M 2 Ashland, ME, United States
56 E 8 Ashland, OR, United States
47 I 4 Ashley, ND, United States
53 I 7 Ashton, ID, United States
131 J 7 Aşkale, Turkey
159 M 5 Asmara, Eritrea
55 J 4 Aspen, CO, United States
159 N 5 Assab, Eritrea
100 J 5 Assen, Netherlands
66 E 7 Assiniboine, MB, Canada
133 K 2 Astana, Kazakhstan
108 B 6 Asti, Italy
92 H 3 Astorga, Spain
56 E 5 Astoria, OR, United States
126 C 8 Astrakhan', Russia
29 I 12 Astrid Ridge, Atlantic Ocean
33 N 1 Asuka, Japan
173 L 3 Asuncion, Northern Mariana Islands
82 I 7 Asunción, Paraguay
159 L 3 Aswân, Egypt
159 L 3 Asyût, Egypt
137 I 7 Aţ Ţā'if, Saudi Arabia
136 H 5 Aţ Ţubayq, Jordan/Saudi Arabia
82 F 6 Atacama Desert, Chile
158 E 4 Atâr, Mauritania
159 L 5 Atbara, Sudan
159 M 5 Atbara, Sudan
42 F 7 Atchafalaya Bay, LA, United States
101 D 12 Ath, Belgium
65 G 12 Athabasca, AB, Canada
43 L 2 Athens, GA, United States
113 G 12 Athens, Greece
45 J 13 Athens, OH, United States
51 L 5 Athens, TX, United States
89 C 11 Athlone, Ireland
39 J 7 Athol, MA, United States
159 J 6 Ati, Chad
58 E 10 Atka, AK, United States
58 E 10 Atka Island, AK, United States
43 K 2 Atlanta, GA, United States
47 L 9 Atlantic, IA, United States
41 O 8 Atlantic, NC, United States
28 E 6 Atlantic Ocean,
30 D 10 Atlantic-Indian Ridge, Indian Ocean
30 D 11 Atlantic-Indian-Antarctic Basin, Southern Ocean
28 E 5 Atlantis Fracture Zone, Atlantic Ocean
22 H 4 Atlas Mountains, Africa
43 I 5 Atmore, AL, United States
153 H 10 Atsugi, Japan
67 I 7 Attawapiskat, ON, Canada
44 F 13 Attica, IN, United States
58 B 8 Attu Island, AK, United States
83 F 10 Atuel, Argentina
132 H 4 Atyrau, Kazakhstan
101 H 15 Aubange, Belgium
43 J 4 Auburn, AL, United States
57 F 11 Auburn, CA, United States
39 K 7 Auburn, MA, United States
47 K 11 Auburn, NE, United States
56 F 4 Auburn, WA, United States
96 H 10 Auch, France
172 F 3 Auckland, New Zealand
23 O 9 Auckland Islands, Oceania
105 F 11 Augsburg, Germany
43 M 3 Augusta, GA, United States
39 L 5 Augusta, ME, United States
168 E 9 Augusta, WA, Australia
116 H 5 Augustów, Poland
55 K 2 Ault, CO, United States
173 N 3 Aur, Marshall Islands
141 C 11 Aurangabad, India
97 I 8 Aurillac, France
44 E 11 Aurora, IL, United States
47 M 7 Austin, MN, United States
57 I 11 Austin, NV, United States
51 J 7 Austin, TX, United States
27 J 7 Austral Fracture Zone, Pacific Ocean
173 M 11 Austral Islands, French Polynesia
168 H 6 Australia, Oceania
169 K 9 Australian Capital Territory, Australia
105 I 12 Austria, Europe
97 J 5 Auxerre, France
38 H 11 Avalon, NJ, United States
173 L 10 Avarua, Cook Islands
92 F 5 Aveiro, Portugal
97 K 9 Avignon, France
93 I 5 Ávila, Spain
92 H 1 Avilés, Spain
38 F 6 Avon, NY, United States
89 H 13 Avon, United Kingdom
43 M 8 Avon Park, FL, United States
96 G 4 Avranches, France
153 E 12 Awaji-shima, Japan
172 E 1 Awanui, New Zealand
172 B 9 Awarua Point, New Zealand
159 I 3 Awbārī, Libya
80 F 7 Ayacucho, Peru
92 F 9 Ayamonte, Spain

43 K 5 Blakely, GA, United States
93 O 3 Blanes, Spain
163 K 7 Blantyre, Malawi
172 E 7 Blenheim, New Zealand
68 B 10 Blenheim, ON, Canada
158 H 1 Blida, Algeria
52 F 9 Bliss, ID, United States
39 K 9 Block Island, RI, United States
163 I 10 Bloemfontein, South Africa
89 C 9 Bloody Foreland, Ireland ▶
47 N 10 Bloomfield, IA, United States
44 D 13 Bloomington, IL, United States
44 F 14 Bloomington, IN, United States
55 J 4 Blue Mesa Reservoir, CO, United States
56 H 6 Blue Mountains, OR, United States
38 G 9 Blue Mountains, PA, United States
23 J 5 Blue Nile, Africa
74 G 7 Bluefields, Nicaragua
41 K 4 Bluestone Lake, WV, United States
172 B 11 Bluff, New Zealand
54 H 5 Bluff, UT, United States
46 H 6 Blunt, SD, United States
57 K 15 Blythe, CA, United States
149 M 5 Bo Hai, China
80 H 3 Boa Vista, Brazil
28 B 8 Boa Vista, Cape Verde
74 F 7 Boaco, Nicaragua
158 F 6 Bobo-Dioulasso, Burkina Faso
163 M 8 Boby, Madagascar ▲
74 G 8 Bocas del Toro, Panama
67 K 8 Bochart, QC, Canada
104 C 7 Bochum, Germany
28 G 8 Bode Verde Fracture Zone, Atlantic Ocean
120 H 7 Boden, Sweden
120 E 6 Bodø, Norway
130 C 9 Bodrum, Turkey
42 G 5 Bogalusa, LA, United States
130 G 7 Boğazliyan, Turkey
148 H 4 Bogda Feng, China ▲
148 H 4 Bogda Shan, China
144 H 9 Bogor, Indonesia
80 F 3 Bogotá, Colombia
116 E 8 Bohemia, Czech Republic
116 D 8 Bohemian Forest, Czech Republic/Germany
44 H 8 Bois Blanc Island, MI, United States
52 E 8 Boise, ID, United States
137 M 2 Bojnūrd, Iran
121 A 12 Bokna Fjord, Norway
40 D 7 Bolivar, TN, United States
82 F 5 Bolivia, South America □
97 K 9 Bollene, France
121 F 10 Bollnäs, Sweden
169 K 7 Bollon, QLD, Australia
108 E 7 Bologna, Italy
89 G 11 Bolton, United Kingdom
130 E 6 Bolu, Turkey
108 E 4 Bolzano, Italy
162 F 4 Boma, Democratic Republic of Congo
75 L 7 Bonaire, Netherlands Antilles
168 F 4 Bonaparte Archipelago, WA, Australia
53 J 8 Bondurant, WY United States
140 I 8 Bongaigaon, India
97 N 11 Bonifacio, Corsica
43 J 5 Bonifay, FL, United States
104 C 8 Bonn, Germany
52 F 1 Bonners Ferry, ID, United States
54 F 2 Bonneville Salt Flats, UT, United States
65 H 11 Bonnyville, AB, Canada
41 J 6 Boone, NC, United States
159 O 6 Boosaaso, Somalia
64 H 4 Boothia Peninsula, NU, Canada ▶
73 J 4 Boquillas del Carmen, Mexico
173 M 10 Bora-Bora, French Polynesia
52 G 7 Borah Peak, ID, United States ▲
121 D 13 Borås, Sweden
137 L 5 Borāzjān, Iran
96 G 8 Bordeaux, France
69 M 6 Borden, PE, Canada
100 J 5 Borger, Netherlands
50 G 2 Borger, TX, United States
121 F 13 Borgholm, Sweden
121 E 11 Borlänge, Sweden
145 I 8 Borneo, Asia
121 E 15 Bornholm, Denmark
130 C 8 Bornova, Turkey
144 H 10 Borobudur, Indonesia *
101 I 14 Borscheid, Luxembourg
137 K 3 Borūjerd, Iran
112 C 7 Bosanska Dubica, Bosnia-Herzegovina
112 C 7 Bosanska Gradiška, Bosnia-Herzegovina
112 C 7 Bosnia-Herzegovina, Europe □
130 D 6 Bosporus, Turkey
159 J 7 Bossangoa, Central African Republic
148 G 4 Bosten Hu, China
39 K 7 Boston, MA, United States
38 E 10 Boswell, PA, United States
113 G 9 Botevgrad, Bulgaria
112 I 5 Botoșani, Romania
162 H 8 Botswana, Africa □
104 B 7 Bottrop, Germany
158 E 4 Boû Bleïine, Mauritania
158 F 6 Bouaké, Côte d'Ivoire
159 I 7 Bouar, Central African Republic
69 M 6 Bouctouche, NB, Canada
169 L 2 Bougainville, Papua New Guinea
158 E 6 Bougouni, Mali
55 K 3 Boulder, CO, United States
57 J 13 Boulder City, NV, United States
97 I 1 Boulogne-sur-Mer, France
57 H 12 Boundary Peak, NV, United States ▲
26 G 9 Bounty Islands, New Zealand
26 G 9 Bounty Trough, Pacific Ocean
97 K 7 Bourg-en-Bresse, France
97 I 6 Bourges, France
169 K 8 Bourke, NSW, Australia
89 H 14 Bournemouth, United Kingdom
54 E 9 Bouse, AZ, United States
29 I 11 Bouvetøya, Atlantic Ocean
46 G 1 Bowbells, ND, United States
54 H 10 Bowie, AZ, United States
51 J 4 Bowie, TX, United States
40 F 5 Bowling Green, KY, United States
45 I 12 Bowling Green, OH, United States
41 N 4 Bowling Green, VA, United States
46 F 4 Bowman, ND, United States
33 P 5 Bowman Island, Antarctica
42 E 5 Boyce, LA, United States
53 K 5 Boyd, MT, United States
65 G 11 Boyle, AB, Canada
163 I 3 Boyoma Falls, Democratic Republic of Congo
53 I 5 Bozeman, MT, United States
130 D 7 Bozüyük, Turkey
33 I 2 Brabant Island, Antarctica
112 C 8 Brač, Croatia
89 H 11 Bradford, United Kingdom
92 F 4 Braga, Portugal
92 G 3 Bragança, Portugal
141 I 9 Brahmanbaria, Bangladesh
141 G 11 Brahmapur, India
23 L 5 Brahmaputra, Asia
112 J 7 Brăila, Romania
101 E 12 Braine-l'Alleud, Belgium
47 L 4 Brainerd, MN, United States
80 H 4 Branco, Brazil
162 G 8 Brandberg, Namibia ▲
104 G 6 Brandenburg, Germany
62 G 10 Brandon, MB, Canada
33 I 2 Bransfield Strait, Antarctica
69 O 6 Bras d'Or Lake, NS, Canada
81 J 7 Brasília, Brazil
112 H 6 Brașov, Romania
101 E 10 Brasschaat, Belgium
43 K 1 Brasstown Bald, GA, United States ▲
116 F 9 Bratislava, Slovakia
127 I 9 Bratsk, Russia
127 I 9 Bratskoye Vodokhranilishche, Russia
105 H 11 Braunau am Inn, Austria
104 E 6 Braunschweig, Germany
28 A 8 Brava, Cape Verde
57 J 16 Brawley, CA, United States
80 H 5 Brazil, South America □
29 G 9 Brazil Basin, Atlantic Ocean
22 F 7 Brazilian Highlands, South America
51 K 6 Brazos, TX, United States
162 F 4 Brazzaville, Congo
51 I 4 Breckenridge, TX, United States
101 F 9 Breda, Netherlands
101 H 11 Bree, Belgium
105 E 12 Bregenz, Austria
46 H 4 Breien, ND, United States
104 D 6 Bremen, Germany
104 D 5 Bremerhaven, Germany
56 F 4 Bremerton, WA, United States
104 D 5 Bremervörde, Germany
51 K 7 Brenham, TX, United States
108 D 5 Brescia, Italy
108 E 4 Bressanone, Italy
117 I 6 Brest, Belarus
96 D 4 Brest, France
56 G 4 Brewster, WA, United States
43 I 5 Brewton, AL, United States
97 L 8 Briançon, France
57 G 11 Bridgeport, CA, United States
39 J 9 Bridgeport, CT, United States
46 F 9 Bridgeport, NE, United States
53 K 5 Bridger, MT, United States
75 O 6 Bridgetown, Barbados
69 M 8 Bridgewater, NS, Canada
39 L 5 Bridgton, ME, United States
105 C 13 Brig, Switzerland
54 G 1 Brigham City, UT, United States
44 H 11 Brighton, MI, United States
89 I 14 Brighton, United Kingdom
109 K 11 Brindisi, Italy
169 L 7 Brisbane, QLD, Australia
41 J 6 Bristol, TN, United States
89 G 14 Bristol, United Kingdom
59 I 8 Bristol Bay, AK, United States
89 F 14 Bristol Channel, United Kingdom
57 J 15 Bristol Lake, CA, United States
65 D 11 British Columbia, BC, Canada
75 M 4 British Virgin Islands, United Kingdom □
96 E 4 Brittany, France
43 J 5 Britton Hill, FL, United States ▲
97 I 8 Brive-la-Gaillarde, France
116 F 8 Brno, Czech Republic
53 N 5 Broadus, MT, United States
65 K 12 Broadview, SK, Canada
39 K 7 Brockton, MA, United States
68 F 8 Brockville, ON, Canada
62 H 4 Brodeur Peninsula, NU, Canada ▶
56 I 7 Brogan, OR, United States
169 J 8 Broken Hill, NSW, Australia
31 I 6 Broken Plateau, Indian Ocean
50 H 5 Bronte, TX, United States
56 D 8 Brookings, OR, United States
47 K 6 Brookings, SD, United States
59 I 3 Brooks Range, AK, United States
168 E 9 Brookton, WA, Australia
168 F 5 Broome, WA, Australia
50 G 4 Brownfield, TX, United States
52 H 2 Browning, MT, United States
51 K 11 Brownsville, TX, United States
51 I 5 Brownwood, TX, United States
68 C 8 Bruce Peninsula, ON, Canada ▶
105 J 12 Bruck an der Mur, Austria
101 C 10 Bruges, Belgium
145 I 7 Brunei, Asia □
43 M 5 Brunswick, GA, United States
39 L 5 Brunswick, ME, United States
169 K 11 Bruny Island, TAS, Australia
55 L 2 Brush, CO, United States
101 E 11 Brussels, Belgium
51 K 6 Bryan, TX, United States
126 C 6 Bryansk, Russia
80 F 2 Bucaramanga, Colombia
158 E 7 Buchanan, Liberia
112 I 7 Bucharest, Romania
41 L 3 Buckhannon, WV, United States
41 M 4 Buckingham, VA, United States
116 G 9 Budapest, Hungary
140 E 8 Budaun, India
42 F 5 Bude, MS, United States
80 E 3 Buenaventura, Colombia
83 G 10 Buenos Aires, Argentina
38 E 6 Buffalo, NY, United States
46 F 5 Buffalo, SD, United States
51 K 6 Buffalo, TX, United States
53 M 7 Buffalo, WY, United States
116 H 6 Bug, Poland/Ukraine
92 D 10 Bugio, Portugal
137 J 3 Buḩayrat ar Razāzah, Iraq
137 I 3 Buḩayrat ath Tharthār, Iraq
52 F 9 Buhl, ID, United States
163 J 4 Bujumbura, Burundi
163 I 3 Bukavu, Democratic Republic of Congo
133 J 6 Bukhara, Uzbekistan
163 I 8 Bulawayo, Zimbabwe
113 J 9 Bulgaria, Europe □
172 D 7 Buller, New Zealand
169 K 2 Bulolo, Papua New Guinea
168 E 9 Bunbury, WA, Australia
169 L 7 Bundaberg, QLD, Australia
168 G 5 Bungle Bungles, WA, Australia
153 C 13 Bungo-suidō, Japan
163 J 2 Bunia, Democratic Republic of Congo
93 L 6 Buñol, Spain
130 H 8 Bünyan, Turkey
144 H 5 Buôn Mê Thuôt, Vietnam
137 J 6 Buraydah, Saudi Arabia
57 H 15 Burbank, CA, United States
169 K 5 Burdekin, QLD, Australia
130 D 9 Burdur, Turkey
113 J 9 Burgas, Bulgaria
41 N 8 Burgaw, NC, United States
93 J 3 Burgos, Spain
97 J 6 Burgundy, France
141 D 10 Burhanpur, India
169 I 5 Burketown, QLD, Australia
158 F 6 Burkina Faso, Africa □
52 G 9 Burley, ID, United States
55 M 3 Burlington, CO, United States
47 O 10 Burlington, IA, United States
39 J 4 Burlington, VT, United States
57 F 9 Burney, CA, United States
169 K 11 Burnie, TAS, Australia
56 H 7 Burns, OR, United States
56 H 8 Burns Junction, OR, United States
93 M 6 Burriana, Spain
130 D 6 Bursa, Turkey
145 L 9 Buru, Indonesia
163 J 4 Burundi, Africa □
137 L 5 Būshehr, Iran
168 E 9 Busselton, WA, Australia
163 I 2 Buta, Democratic Republic of Congo
38 D 9 Butler, PA, United States
145 K 9 Buton, Indonesia
52 H 5 Butte, MT, United States
145 L 5 Butuan, Philippines
112 I 7 Buzău, Romania
117 K 6 Byarezina, Belarus
116 F 5 Bydgoszcz, Poland
54 H 10 Bylas, AZ, United States
116 G 7 Bytom, Poland

C

144 G 6 Ca Mau, Vietnam
145 K 4 Cabanatuan, Philippines
69 J 5 Cabano, QC, Canada
162 F 4 Cabinda, Angola
83 F 15 Cabo Buen Tiempo, Argentina ▶
92 E 6 Cabo Carvoeiro, Portugal ▶
80 E 3 Cabo Corrientes, Colombia ▶
74 G 3 Cabo Corrientes, Cuba ▶
72 H 8 Cabo Corrientes, Mexico ▶
75 I 4 Cabo Cruz, Cuba ▶
93 O 3 Cabo de Creus, Spain ▶
93 M 7 Cabo de la Nao, Spain ▶
93 L 8 Cabo de Palos, Spain ▶
92 H 1 Cabo de Penas, Spain ▶
93 M 7 Cabo de San Antonio, Spain ▶
92 F 9 Cabo de Santa Maria, Portugal ▶
92 E 9 Cabo de São Vincente, Portugal ▶
92 E 8 Cabo de Sines, Portugal ▶
83 G 13 Cabo Dos Bahías, Argentina ▶
92 E 7 Cabo Espichel, Portugal ▶
92 E 2 Cabo Fisterra, Spain ▶
93 L 7 Cabo Huertas, Spain ▶
93 J 1 Cabo Machichaco, Spain ▶
81 J 3 Cabo Norte, Brazil ▶
81 J 3 Cabo Orange, Brazil ▶
92 F 1 Cabo Ortegal, Spain ▶
83 E 15 Cabo Pilar, Chile ▶
83 E 12 Cabo Quilán, Chile ▶
73 L 7 Cabo Rojo, Mexico ▶
93 J 10 Cabo Sacratif, Spain ▶
74 G 3 Cabo San Antonio, Cuba ▶
83 G 16 Cabo San Diego, Argentina ▶
72 F 6 Cabo San Lázaro, Mexico ▶
72 G 7 Cabo San Lucas, Mexico
72 G 7 Cabo San Lucas, Mexico ▶
72 E 3 Cabo San Quintín, Mexico ▶
74 F 7 Cabo Santa Elena, Costa Rica ▶
92 E 3 Cabo Silleiro, Spain ▶
92 G 10 Cabo Trafalgar, Spain ▶
83 G 14 Cabo Tres Puntas, Argentina ▶
83 F 15 Cabo Virgenes, Argentina ▶
72 F 3 Caborca, Mexico
67 N 8 Cabot Strait, NS, Canada
93 O 6 Cabrera, Spain
92 G 6 Cáceres, Spain
81 L 8 Cachoeiro do Itapemirim, Brazil
51 M 4 Caddo Lake, TX, United States
44 G 9 Cadillac, MI, United States
145 K 5 Cadiz, Philippines
92 G 10 Cádiz, Spain
57 J 15 Cadiz Lake, CA, United States
96 G 3 Caen, France
82 G 8 Cafayate, Argentina
145 K 6 Cagayan de Oro, Philippines
109 B 12 Cagliari, Italy
75 M 4 Caguas, Puerto Rico
97 I 9 Cahors, France
117 K 11 Cahul, Moldova
75 K 3 Caicos Islands, Turks and Caicos Islands
169 K 4 Cairns, QLD, Australia
159 L 3 Cairo, Egypt
43 K 5 Cairo, GA, United States
44 D 16 Cairo, IL, United States
80 E 5 Cajamarca, Peru
109 J 12 Calabria, Italy
83 E 15 Calafate, Argentina
93 K 3 Calahorra, Spain
97 I 1 Calais, France
39 N 3 Calais, ME, United States
82 F 7 Calama, Chile
93 K 4 Calatayud, Spain
145 K 5 Calbayog, Philippines
141 H 10 Calcutta, India
92 E 6 Caldas da Rainha, Portugal
82 E 8 Caldera, Chile
52 E 7 Caldwell, ID, United States
51 K 7 Caldwell, TX, United States
83 F 13 Caleta Olivia, Argentina
57 J 16 Calexico, CA, United States
65 G 13 Calgary, AB, Canada
80 E 3 Cali, Colombia
141 C 14 Calicut, India
57 K 12 Caliente, NV, United States
57 G 13 California, CA, United States *
57 E 11 Calistoga, CA, United States
80 E 6 Callao, Peru
109 G 14 Caltanissetta, Italy
144 H 5 Cam Ranh, Vietnam
81 L 7 Camaçari, Brazil
75 I 3 Camagüey, Cuba
92 C 9 Câmara de Lobos, Portugal
97 K 10 Camargue, France ◆
144 G 5 Cambodia, Asia □
97 J 2 Cambrai, France
89 F 13 Cambrian Mountains, United Kingdom
52 E 6 Cambridge, ID, United States
47 M 5 Cambridge, MN, United States
172 F 4 Cambridge, New Zealand
45 J 13 Cambridge, OH, United States
89 I 13 Cambridge, United Kingdom
64 G 6 Cambridge Bay, NU, Canada
41 K 9 Camden, SC, United States
40 E 6 Camden, TN, United States
54 G 7 Cameron, AZ, United States
42 D 6 Cameron, LA, United States
44 B 8 Cameron, WI, United States
159 I 8 Cameroon, Africa □
43 K 5 Camilla, GA, United States
82 G 6 Camiri, Bolivia
54 G 8 Camp Verde, AZ, United States
44 I 13 Campbell Hill, OH, United States ▲
23 O 9 Campbell Island, Oceania
26 G 9 Campbell Plateau, Pacific Ocean
40 G 5 Campbellsville, KY, United States
69 L 5 Campbellton, NB, Canada
73 O 8 Campeche, Mexico
81 M 5 Campina Grande, Brazil
81 J 9 Campinas, Brazil
81 I 8 Campo Grande, Brazil
109 H 10 Campobasso, Italy
81 L 8 Campos dos Goytacazes, Brazil
65 H 12 Camrose, AB, Canada
144 G 6 Cân Tho, Vietnam
62 G 7 Canada, North America □
32 C 5 Canada Abyssal Plain, Arctic Ocean
50 H 1 Canadian, TX, United States
32 C 4 Canadian Basin, Arctic Ocean
22 D 2 Canadian Shield, North America
130 B 6 Çanakkale, Turkey
72 G 3 Cananea, Mexico
92 A 10 Canary Islands, Spain
169 L 9 Canberra, ACT, Australia
47 K 6 Canby, MN, United States
73 P 7 Cancún, Mexico
47 I 2 Cando, ND, United States
149 M 5 Cangzhou, China
67 L 5 Caniapiscau, QC, Canada
33 J 5 Canisteo Peninsula, Antarctica ▶
130 F 6 Cankiri, Turkey
97 M 10 Cannes, France
56 E 5 Cannon Beach, OR, United States
46 G 4 Cannonball, ND, United States
81 J 10 Canoas, Brazil
55 K 4 Canon City, CO, United States
89 J 14 Canterbury, United Kingdom
172 D 9 Canterbury Bight, New Zealand
172 D 9 Canterbury Plains, New Zealand
42 G 3 Canton, MS, United States
38 H 4 Canton, NY, United States
45 J 12 Canton, OH, United States
59 K 6 Cantwell, AK, United States
50 G 2 Canyon, TX, United States
53 I 4 Canyon Ferry Lake, MT, United States
158 D 3 Cap Barbas, Western Sahara ▶
93 O 5 Cap de Formentor, Spain ▶
96 F 2 Cap de la Hague, France ▶
93 O 6 Cap de ses Salines, Spain ▶
93 C 6 Cap des Freu, Spain ▶
63 J 6 Cap Hopes Advance, QC, Canada ▶
50 G 4 Cap Rock Escarpment, TX, United States ▲
158 D 5 Cap Vert, Senegal ▶

41 P 7 Cape Hatteras, NC, United States
33 M 7 Cape Adare, Antarctica
23 I 8 Cape Agulhas, Africa
39 L 7 Cape Ann, MA, United States
130 G 10 Cape Apostolos Andreas, Cyprus
169 I 3 Cape Arnhem, NT, Australia
64 E 6 Cape Baring, NT, Canada
29 J 9 Cape Basin, Atlantic Ocean
64 C 6 Cape Bathurst, NT, Canada
67 O 6 Cape Bauld, NL, Canada
56 D 8 Cape Blanco, OR, United States
30 F 11 Cape Boothby, Antarctica
69 O 6 Cape Breton Island, NS, Canada
172 E 1 Cape Brett, New Zealand
145 J 6 Cape Bulíluyan, Philippines
145 J 5 Cape Calavite, Philippines
172 E 7 Cape Campbell, New Zealand
43 N 7 Cape Canaveral, FL, United States
69 O 7 Cape Canso, NS, Canada
68 A 5 Cape Cargantua, ON, Canada
41 P 5 Cape Charles, VA, United States
33 M 7 Cape Cheetham, Antarctica
127 J 4 Cape Chelyuskin, Russia
32 B 8 Cape Chidley, Canada
141 E 12 Cape Chirala, India
66 G 4 Cape Churchill, MB, Canada
39 L 8 Cape Cod, MA, United States
39 L 8 Cape Cod Bay, MA, United States
32 D 7 Cape Columbia, Canada
141 D 15 Cape Comorin, India
64 D 14 Cape Cook, BC, Canada
43 M 9 Cape Coral, FL, United States
169 K 2 Cape Cretin, Papua New Guinea
64 C 6 Cape Dalhousie, NT, Canada
30 G 11 Cape Darnley, Antarctica
56 E 5 Cape Disappointment, WA, United States
67 J 3 Cape Dorset, NU, Canada
67 L 1 Cape Dyer, NU, Canada
39 L 5 Cape Elizabeth, ME, United States
172 D 6 Cape Farewell, New Zealand
41 N 9 Cape Fear, NC, United States
56 E 3 Cape Flattery, WA, United States
168 G 4 Cape Ford, NT, Australia
172 D 7 Cape Foulwind, New Zealand
33 N 7 Cape Freshfield, Antarctica
169 K 1 Cape Girgir, Papua New Guinea
31 L 11 Cape Goodenough, Antarctica
33 O 7 Cape Gray, Antarctica
130 G 11 Cape Greko, Cyprus
169 J 3 Cape Grenville, QLD, Australia
22 F 9 Cape Horn, South America
68 C 8 Cape Hurd, ON, Canada
172 E 1 Cape Karikari, New Zealand
33 O 7 Cape Keltie, Antarctica
172 G 5 Cape Kidnappers, New Zealand
65 B 12 Cape Knox, BC, Canada
67 L 4 Cape Labrador, NL, Canada
31 K 7 Cape Leeuwin, Australia
168 F 5 Cape Leveque, WA, Australia
41 O 8 Cape Lookout, NC, United States
38 H 11 Cape May, NJ, United States
169 J 4 Cape Melville, QLD, Australia
57 D 10 Cape Mendocino, CA, United States
67 L 2 Cape Mercy, NU, Canada
31 L 11 Cape Morse, Antarctica
169 L 3 Cape Nelson, Papua New Guinea
58 H 5 Cape Nome, AK, United States
69 O 5 Cape North, NS, Canada
33 L 1 Cape Norvegia, Antarctica
162 H 11 Cape of Good Hope, South Africa
172 F 7 Cape Palliser, New Zealand
158 E 7 Cape Palmas, Côte d'Ivoire/Liberia
64 D 6 Cape Parry, NT, Canada
31 I 11 Cape Penck, Antarctica
31 K 11 Cape Poinsett, Antarctica
172 A 10 Cape Providence, New Zealand
172 D 1 Cape Reinga, New Zealand
41 M 10 Cape Romain, SC, United States
43 M 10 Cape Romano, FL, United States
172 G 3 Cape Runaway, New Zealand
43 N 11 Cape Sable, FL, United States
69 M 9 Cape Sable Island, NS, Canada
145 L 6 Cape San Agustin, Philippines
65 C 13 Cape Scott, BC, Canada
169 I 4 Cape Shield, NT, Australia
169 M 3 Cape Siri, Papua New Guinea
66 H 5 Cape Tatnam, MB, Canada
162 H 11 Cape Town, South Africa
172 G 6 Cape Turnagain, New Zealand
28 A 7 Cape Verde, Africa
28 G 6 Cape Verde Basin, Atlantic Ocean
28 G 6 Cape Verde Islands, Atlantic Ocean
28 G 5 Cape Verde Plateau, Atlantic Ocean
33 P 6 Cape Waldron, Antarctica
64 K 4 Cape Wilson, NU, Canada
88 E 5 Cape Wrath, United Kingdom
169 J 3 Cape York, QLD, Australia
169 J 4 Cape York Peninsula, QLD, Australia
75 K 4 Cap-Haïtien, Haiti
109 A 11 Capo Caccia, Italy
109 C 13 Capo Carbonara, Italy
109 J 13 Capo Colonna, Italy
109 C 11 Capo Comino, Italy
109 B 10 Capo del Falcone, Italy
109 B 12 Capo della Frasca, Italy
109 H 15 Capo delle Correnti, Italy
109 H 13 Capo di Milazzo, Italy
109 C 11 Capo di Monte Santu, Italy
109 G 14 Capo Gallo, Italy
109 I 12 Capo Palinuro, Italy
109 J 13 Capo Rizzuto, Italy
109 F 14 Capo San Vito, Italy
109 K 12 Capo Santa Maria di Leuca, Italy
109 H 15 Capo Scaramia, Italy
109 B 13 Capo Spartivento, Italy
109 I 13 Capo Vaticano, Italy
130 G 8 Cappadocia, Turkey
109 G 11 Capri, Italy
162 H 7 Caprivi Strip, Namibia
80 E 4 Caquetá, Colombia
141 K 14 Car Nicobar, India
112 G 8 Caracal, Romania
80 G 1 Caracas, Venezuela
44 D 15 Carbondale, IL, United States
97 I 10 Carcassonne, France
89 G 14 Cardiff, United Kingdom
89 F 12 Cardigan Bay, United Kingdom
112 F 5 Carei, Romania
52 G 8 Carey, ID, United States
30 G 5 Cargados Carajos Islands, Mauritius
39 M 1 Caribou, ME, United States
57 J 10 Carlin, NV, United States
38 F 10 Carlisle, PA, United States
89 G 10 Carlisle, United Kingdom
89 D 12 Carlow, Ireland
55 L 10 Carlsbad, NM, United States
30 F 2 Carlsberg Ridge, Indian Ocean
65 K 12 Carlyle, SK, Canada
65 B 9 Carmacks, YT, Canada
54 G 11 Carmen, AZ, United States
92 H 8 Carmona, Spain
168 D 7 Carnarvon, WA, Australia
33 J 6 Carney Island, Antarctica
159 I 7 Carnot, Central African Republic
81 K 5 Carolina, Brazil
173 J 1 Caroline Islands, Federated States of Micronesia
23 I 3 Carpathian Mountains, Europe
108 D 6 Carpi, Italy
43 K 6 Carrabelle, FL, United States
108 D 7 Carrara, Italy
89 A 13 Carrauntuohil, Ireland
47 I 3 Carrington, ND, United States
55 K 9 Carrizozo, NM, United States
47 L 9 Carroll, IA, United States
57 G 11 Carson City, NV, United States
80 E 2 Cartagena, Colombia
93 L 8 Cartagena, Spain
74 G 8 Cartago, Costa Rica
159 I 1 Carthage, Tunisia
67 N 6 Cartwright, NL, Canada
57 I 11 Carvers, NV, United States
54 G 10 Casa Grande, AZ, United States
158 F 1 Casablanca, Morocco
172 B 9 Cascade Point, New Zealand
56 E 8 Cascade Range, OR/WA, United States
52 F 6 Cascade Reservoir, ID, United States
27 J 2 Cascadia Basin, Pacific Ocean
39 L 5 Casco Bay, ME, United States
45 I 9 Caseville, MI, United States
33 P 6 Casey, Australia
53 M 9 Casper, WY, United States
132 G 3 Caspian Depression, Kazakhstan/Russia
23 J 4 Caspian Sea, Asia
81 J 4 Castanhal, Brazil
93 M 6 Castelló de la Plana, Spain
97 I 10 Castelnaudary, France
92 G 6 Castelo Branco, Portugal
54 G 4 Castle Dale, UT, United States
65 G 14 Castlegar, BC, Canada
75 O 6 Castries, St Lucia
83 E 12 Castro, Chile
109 I 12 Castrovillari, Italy
75 J 2 Cat Island, The Bahamas
42 E 5 Catahoula Lake, LA, United States
93 N 3 Cataluña, Spain
82 G 8 Catamarca, Argentina
109 H 14 Catania, Italy
109 J 13 Catanzaro, Italy
39 I 7 Catskill, NY, United States
38 H 7 Catskill Mountains, NY, United States
80 E 2 Cauca, Colombia
23 J 4 Caucasus, Asia/Europe
83 E 10 Cauquenes, Chile
158 E 7 Cavally, Côte d'Ivoire/Libya
41 I 4 Cave Run Lake, KY, United States
81 J 10 Caxias do Sul, Brazil
81 J 3 Cayenne, French Guiana
74 H 4 Cayman Brac, Cayman Islands
74 H 4 Cayman Islands, United Kingdom
74 H 3 Cayo Largo, Cuba
74 G 6 Cayos Miskitos, Nicaragua
28 F 7 Ceara Abyssal Plain, Atlantic Ocean
145 K 6 Cebu, Philippines
47 N 8 Cedar, IA, United States
54 F 5 Cedar City, UT, United States
47 N 8 Cedar Falls, IA, United States
62 G 9 Cedar Lake, MB, Canada
47 O 9 Cedar Rapids, IA, United States
168 H 8 Ceduna, SA, Australia
73 J 8 Celaya, Mexico
26 D 5 Celebes Sea, Pacific Ocean
44 H 12 Celina, OH, United States
112 B 6 Celje, Slovenia
104 E 6 Celle, Germany
89 D 14 Celtic Sea, Ireland/United Kingdom
28 H 3 Celtic Shelf, Atlantic Ocean
40 G 6 Center Hill Lake, TN, United States
159 J 7 Central African Republic, Africa
26 D 4 Central Basin, Pacific Ocean
40 F 5 Central City, KY, United States
173 M 8 Central Line Islands, Kiribati
22 D 4 Central Lowlands, North America
133 J 10 Central Makran Range, Pakistan
26 G 5 Central Pacific Basin, Pacific Ocean
169 J 1 Central Range, Papua New Guinea
23 K 2 Central Siberian Plateau, Asia
56 F 5 Centralia, WA, United States
109 I 10 Cerignola, Italy
130 F 6 Çerkeş, Turkey
83 E 14 Cerro Arenales, Chile
80 A 7 Cerro Azol, Galapagos Islands
74 G 8 Cerro Chirripó Grande, Costa Rica
72 E 2 Cerro de La Encantada, Mexico
80 E 6 Cerro de Pasco, Peru
83 E 14 Cerro Murallón, Argentina/Chile
83 E 15 Cerro Paine, Chile
83 E 13 Cerro San Valentín, Chile
83 F 10 Cerro Tupungato, Argentina/Chile
93 N 3 Cervera, Spain
108 F 7 Cesena, Italy
116 D 8 České Budějovice, Czech Republic
92 H 10 Ceuta, Spain
130 H 9 Ceyhan, Turkey
30 H 3 Ceylon Plain, Indian Ocean
137 N 6 Chābahār, Iran
80 E 5 Chachapoyas, Peru
159 I 5 Chad, Africa
41 M 8 Chadbourn, NC, United States
46 F 8 Chadron, NE, United States
133 J 8 Chaghcharān, Afghanistan
30 G 4 Chagos Archipelago, Indian Ocean
30 H 4 Chagos Trench, Indian Ocean
30 G 4 Chagos-Laccadive Ridge, Indian Ocean
30 F 3 Chain Ridge, Indian Ocean
69 L 5 Chaleur Bay, NB, Canada
113 G 12 Chalkida, Greece
26 E 5 Challenger Deep, Pacific Ocean
27 K 8 Challenger Fracture Zone, Pacific Ocean
26 G 8 Challenger Plateau, Pacific Ocean
52 G 7 Challis, ID, United States
97 K 6 Chalon-sur-Saône, France
97 K 3 Châlons-en-Champagne, France
47 I 7 Chamberlain, SD, United States
39 M 2 Chamberlain Lake, ME, United States
54 H 8 Chambers, AZ, United States
38 F 10 Chambersburg, PA, United States
97 L 7 Chambéry, France
97 M 7 Chamonix-Mont-Blanc, France
44 E 13 Champaign, IL, United States
39 I 4 Champlain, NY, United States
73 O 8 Champotón, Mexico
82 E 8 Chañaral, Chile
42 H 6 Chandeleur Islands, LA, United States
140 D 7 Chandigarh, India
69 M 4 Chandler, QC, Canada
141 E 11 Chandrapur, India
149 N 4 Changchun, China
149 L 8 Changde, China
149 N 9 Changhua, Taiwan
148 G 4 Changji, China
149 L 8 Changsha, China
149 N 7 Changshu, China
149 L 6 Changzhi, China
149 M 7 Changzhou, China
113 G 14 Chania, Greece
57 G 15 Channel Islands, CA, United States
89 G 16 Channel Islands, United Kingdom
89 K 14 Channel Tunnel, United Kingdom/France
50 G 2 Channing, TX, United States
149 M 10 Chaozhou, China
81 J 9 Chapecó, Brazil
68 B 5 Chapleau, ON, Canada
65 J 13 Chaplin, SK, Canada
41 J 4 Chapmanville, WV, United States
33 J 3 Charcot Island, Antarctica
133 J 6 Chardzhev, Turkmenistan
133 K 7 Chārīkār, Afghanistan
101 F 13 Charleroi, Belgium
47 N 7 Charles City, IA, United States
44 C 11 Charles Mound, IL, United States
41 L 10 Charleston, SC, United States
41 J 4 Charleston, WV, United States
169 K 7 Charleville, QLD, Australia
97 K 3 Charleville-Mézières, France
44 G 8 Charlevoix, MI, United States
28 F 3 Charlie-Gibbs Fracture Zone, Atlantic Ocean
41 K 7 Charlotte, NC, United States
75 M 4 Charlotte Amalie, Virgin Islands
43 M 9 Charlotte Harbor, FL, United States
69 N 6 Charlottetown, PE, Canada
97 I 4 Chartres, France
96 G 5 Châteaubriant, France
97 I 5 Châteaudun, France
97 I 6 Châteauroux, France
97 J 3 Château-Thierry, France
96 H 6 Châtellerault, France
69 L 6 Chatham, NB, Canada
68 B 10 Chatham, ON, Canada
26 G 9 Chatham Islands, New Zealand
26 G 9 Chatham Rise, Pacific Ocean
40 G 8 Chattanooga, TN, United States
97 K 4 Chaumont, France
141 E 14 Chavakachcheri, Sri Lanka
43 J 3 Cheaha Mountain, AL, United States
126 D 6 Cheboksary, Russia
44 H 8 Cheboygan, MI, United States
144 E 3 Cheduba, Myanmar
133 I 3 Chelkar, Kazakhstan
116 H 7 Chełm, Poland
89 J 13 Chelmsford, United Kingdom
89 H 13 Cheltenham, United Kingdom
126 E 8 Chelyabinsk, Russia
104 G 8 Chemnitz, Germany
56 F 8 Chemult, OR, United States
59 L 5 Chena Hot Springs, AK, United States
149 M 5 Chengde, China
149 J 8 Chengdu, China
141 E 13 Chennai, India
44 E 12 Chenoa, IL, United States
41 L 8 Cheraw, SC, United States
96 G 3 Cherbourg, France
126 D 5 Cherepovets, Russia
117 L 8 Cherkasy, Ukraine
126 B 8 Cherkessk, Russia
117 L 6 Chernihiv, Ukraine
117 I 9 Chernivtsi, Ukraine
117 K 7 Chernobyl, Ukraine
116 H 4 Chernyakhovsk, Russia
47 L 8 Cherokee, IA, United States
41 I 6 Cherokee Lake, TN, United States
38 H 10 Cherry Hill, NJ, United States
41 O 5 Chesapeake, VA, United States
41 O 4 Chesapeake Bay, VA, United States
57 F 10 Chester, CA, United States
53 J 2 Chester, MT, United States
69 M 8 Chester, NS, Canada
41 K 8 Chester, SC, United States
39 M 2 Chesuncook Lake, ME, United States
73 P 9 Chetumal, Mexico
53 N 11 Cheyenne, WY, United States
46 E 7 Cheyenne, SD/SK, United States
55 M 4 Cheyenne Wells, CO, United States
149 N 10 Chiai, Taiwan
144 F 4 Chiang Mai, Thailand
144 F 3 Chiang Rai, Thailand
131 L 5 Chiat'ura, Georgia
153 I 10 Chiba, Japan
67 K 8 Chibougamau, QC, Canada
44 E 11 Chicago, IL, United States
59 N 8 Chichagof Island, AK, United States
73 O 8 Chichén Itzá, Mexico
40 G 7 Chickamauga Lake, TN, United States
59 L 5 Chicken, AK, United States
80 D 5 Chiclayo, Peru
83 F 13 Chico, Argentina
57 F 10 Chico, CA, United States
63 K 9 Chicoutimi, QC, Canada
109 G 9 Chieti, Italy
149 M 4 Chifeng, China
72 H 4 Chihuahua, Mexico
50 H 3 Childress, TX, United States
83 E 11 Chile, South America
83 E 13 Chile Chico, Chile
27 L 8 Chile Rise, Pacific Ocean
83 E 11 Chillán, Chile
45 I 13 Chillicothe, OH, United States
56 F 8 Chiloquin, OR, United States
73 K 9 Chilpancingo, Mexico
80 E 6 Chimbote, Peru
163 J 7 Chimoio, Mozambique
149 I 6 China, Asia
163 I 6 Chingola, Zambia
163 J 7 Chinhoyi, Zimbabwe
133 L 8 Chiniot, Pakistan
54 H 7 Chinle, AZ, United States
53 K 2 Chinook, MT, United States
26 G 2 Chinook Trough, Pacific Ocean
108 F 6 Chioggia, Italy
113 H 12 Chios, Greece
113 I 12 Chios, Greece
163 J 6 Chipata, Zambia
69 L 6 Chipman, NB, Canada
39 M 3 Chiputneticook Lakes, ME, United States
74 E 6 Chiquimula, Guatemala
133 L 5 Chirchik, Uzbekistan
59 J 9 Chirikof Island, AK, United States
67 J 7 Chisasibi, QC, Canada
117 K 10 Chişinău, Moldova
127 J 10 Chita, Russia
59 L 6 Chitina, AK, United States
141 D 13 Chitradurga, India
141 I 10 Chittagong, Bangladesh
141 E 13 Chittoor, India
163 J 7 Chitungwiza, Zimbabwe
83 G 11 Choele Choel, Argentina
51 J 9 Choke Canyon Lake, TX, United States
96 G 6 Cholet, France
163 I 7 Choma, Zambia
116 D 7 Chomutov, Czech Republic
144 G 5 Chon Buri, Thailand
149 O 4 Ch'ŏngjin, North Korea
149 K 8 Chongqing, China
149 O 6 Chŏnju, South Korea
53 I 3 Choteau, MT, United States
149 L 3 Choybalsan, Mongolia
172 D 8 Christchurch, New Zealand
172 L 7 Christmas Island, Kiribati
26 H 4 Christmas Ridge, Pacific Ocean
83 F 12 Chubut, Argentina
127 O 3 Chuckchi Sea, Russia
153 C 12 Chūgoku-sanchi, Japan
53 N 10 Chugwater, WY, United States
32 D 5 Chukchi Abyssal Plain, Arctic Ocean
32 D 5 Chukchi Plateau, Arctic Ocean
32 D 4 Chukchi Sea, Arctic Ocean
127 O 4 Chukotskiy Peninsula, Russia
57 I 16 Chula Vista, CA, United States
149 O 5 Ch'unch'ŏn, South Korea
149 O 5 Ch'ungju, South Korea
82 E 6 Chuquicamata, Chile
105 D 13 Chur, Switzerland
66 G 4 Churchill, MB, Canada
66 G 5 Churchill, MB, Canada
67 M 6 Churchill, NL, Canada
67 M 6 Churchill Falls, NL, Canada
67 L 8 Chute-des-Passes, QC, Canada
173 L 1 Chuuk Islands, Federated States of Micronesia
117 K 10 Ciadîr Lunga, Moldova
130 F 5 Cide, Turkey
116 H 5 Ciechanów, Poland
75 I 3 Ciego de Ávila, Cuba
74 H 3 Cienfuegos, Cuba
93 K 8 Cieza, Spain
130 F 8 Cihanbeyli, Turkey
144 H 10 Cilacap, Indonesia
44 H 14 Cincinnati, OH, United States
101 G 13 Ciney, Belgium
109 J 12 Cirà Marina, Italy
59 L 4 Circle, AK, United States
53 M 3 Circle, MT, United States
51 I 5 Cisco, TX, United States
108 F 8 Città di Castello, Italy

73 J 4 Ciudad Acuña, Mexico
80 G 2 Ciudad Bolívar, Venezuela
73 I 4 Ciudad Camargo, Mexico
73 K 7 Ciudad de Valles, Mexico
73 N 9 Ciudad del Carmen, Mexico
73 I 4 Ciudad Delicias, Mexico
80 H 2 Ciudad Guayana, Venezuela
73 I 8 Ciudad Guzmán, Mexico
72 H 2 Ciudad Juárez, Mexico
73 L 7 Ciudad Madero, Mexico
73 K 7 Ciudad Mante, Mexico
72 G 4 Ciudad Obregón, Mexico
93 I 7 Ciudad Real, Spain
92 G 5 Ciudad Rodrigo, Spain
73 K 6 Ciudad Victoria, Mexico
93 P 5 Ciudadela, Spain
130 H 6 Civa Burnu, Turkey
108 G 8 Civitanova Marche, Italy
109 E 9 Civitavecchia, Italy
44 H 9 Clare, MI, United States
172 E 7 Clarence, New Zealand
172 E 7 Clarence, New Zealand
75 J 3 Clarence Town, The Bahamas
50 H 2 Clarendon, TX, United States
38 D 8 Clarion, PA, United States
27 I 4 Clarion Fracture Zone, Pacific Ocean
43 L 2 Clark Hill Reservoir, GA, United States
41 K 2 Clarksburg, WV, United States
42 G 2 Clarksdale, MS, United States
56 I 5 Clarkston, WA, United States
40 E 6 Clarksville, TN, United States
51 L 3 Clarksville, TX, United States
41 M 6 Clarksville, VA, United States
41 P 1 Claymont, DE, United States
55 M 6 Clayton, NM, United States
57 E 11 Clear Lake, CA, United States
47 M 7 Clear Lake, IA, United States
38 E 9 Clearfield, PA, United States
65 F 13 Clearwater, BC, Canada
43 L 8 Clearwater, FL, United States
52 F 4 Clearwater, ID, United States
52 F 5 Clearwater Mountains, ID, United States
169 K 6 Clermont, QLD, Australia
97 J 7 Clermont-Ferrand, France
101 I 14 Clervaux, Luxembourg
40 H 7 Cleveland, TN, United States
51 L 7 Cleveland, TX, United States
45 J 11 Cleveland, OH, United States
43 N 9 Clewiston, FL, United States
41 I 7 Clingmans Dome, TN, United States
65 E 13 Clinton, BC, Canada
44 H 11 Clinton, MI, United States
68 C 9 Clinton, ON, Canada
27 I 5 Clipperton Fracture Zone, Pacific Ocean
27 K 5 Clipperton Island, Pacific Ocean
169 J 5 Cloncurry, QLD, Australia
89 C 12 Clonmel, Ireland
47 M 3 Cloquet, MN, United States
57 E 11 Cloverdale, CA, United States
55 M 8 Clovis, NM, United States
112 G 6 Cluj-Napoca, Romania
172 C 10 Clutha, New Zealand
65 G 12 Clyde, AB, Canada
89 F 9 Clyde, United Kingdom
53 J 5 Clyde Park, MT, United States
65 C 10 Coast Mountains, BC, Canada
57 E 9 Coast Ranges, CA/OR/WA, United States
67 I 3 Coats Island, NU, Canada
73 M 9 Coatzacoalcos, Mexico
74 E 5 Cobán, Guatemala
168 H 3 Cobourg Peninsula, NT, Australia
82 F 5 Cochabamba, Bolivia
141 D 14 Cochin, India
83 F 14 Cochrane, Chile
68 C 4 Cochrane, ON, Canada
75 K 3 Cockburn Town, Turks Islands and Caicos
74 F 6 Coco, Honduras/Nicaragua
141 J 13 Coco Channel, India
31 I 4 Cocos Basin, Indian Ocean
31 I 5 Cocos Islands, Australia
27 L 5 Cocos Ridge, Pacific Ocean
172 B 11 Codfish Island, New Zealand
53 K 7 Cody, WY, United States
52 E 3 Coeur d'Alene, ID, United States
100 J 6 Coevorden, Netherlands
42 H 4 Coffeeville, AL, United States
169 L 8 Coffs Harbour, NSW, Australia
96 G 7 Cognac, France
83 E 13 Coihaique, Chile
141 D 14 Coimbatore, India
92 F 5 Coimbra, Portugal
53 J 10 Cokeville, WY, United States
81 L 8 Colatina, Brazil
89 J 13 Colchester, United Kingdom
57 H 11 Cold Spring, NV, United States
44 G 11 Coldwater, MI, United States
39 K 4 Colebrook, NH, United States
56 I 5 Colfax, WA, United States
73 I 9 Colima, Mexico
88 D 7 Coll, United Kingdom
42 G 4 Collins, MS, United States
64 G 5 Collinson Peninsula, NU, Canada
97 M 4 Colmar, France
104 B 8 Cologne, Germany
80 E 3 Colombia, South America
28 C 6 Colombian Basin, Atlantic Ocean
141 E 15 Colombo, Sri Lanka
83 H 10 Colón, Argentina
74 H 8 Colón, Panama
173 J 1 Colonia, Federated States of Micronesia
55 J 3 Colorado, CO, United States
72 E 2 Colorado, Mexico
22 E 8 Colorado, South America
54 E 9 Colorado, United States
50 H 5 Colorado City, TX, United States
57 I 15 Colorado Desert, CA, United States
22 D 4 Colorado Plateau, North America
55 K 4 Colorado Springs, CO, United States
42 E 4 Columbia, LA, United States
41 O 6 Columbia, NC, United States
41 K 9 Columbia, SC, United States
40 F 7 Columbia, TN, United States
56 G 6 Columbia, OR/WA, United States
56 H 5 Columbia Basin, WA, United States
43 K 4 Columbus, GA, United States
44 G 14 Columbus, IN, United States
42 H 3 Columbus, MS, United States
53 K 5 Columbus, MT, United States
41 J 7 Columbus, NC, United States
47 J 10 Columbus, NE, United States
55 J 11 Columbus, NM, United States
51 K 7 Columbus, TX, United States
44 D 10 Columbus, WI, United States
45 I 13 Columbus, OH, United States
59 J 3 Colville, AK, United States
172 F 3 Colville, New Zealand
172 F 2 Colville Channel, New Zealand
108 F 6 Comacchio, Italy
51 J 5 Comanche, TX, United States
74 E 6 Comayagua, Honduras
83 E 9 Combarbalá, Chile
73 N 10 Comitán de Domínguez, Mexico
108 C 5 Como, Italy
83 F 13 Comodoro Rivadavia, Argentina
163 M 6 Comoros, Africa
97 J 3 Compiègne, France
158 D 6 Conakry, Guinea
82 H 5 Concepción, Bolivia
83 E 11 Concepción, Chile
82 I 7 Concepción, Paraguay
83 I 9 Concepción del Uruguay, Argentina
55 L 7 Conchas Lake, NM, United States
72 H 4 Conchos, Mexico
57 E 12 Concord, CA, United States
39 K 6 Concord, NH, United States
83 I 9 Concordia, Argentina
56 G 6 Condon, OR, United States
23 I 6 Congo, Africa
23 I 6 Congo Basin, Africa
28 J 7 Congo Cone, Atlantic Ocean
45 K 11 Conneaut, OH, United States
39 I 8 Connecticut, CT, United States
39 J 8 Connecticut, CT, United States
56 H 5 Connell, WA, United States
53 I 2 Conrad, MT, United States
30 E 9 Conrad Rise, Southern Ocean
112 J 8 Constanța, Romania
158 H 1 Constantine, Algeria
65 I 13 Consul, SK, Canada
64 G 7 Contwoyto Lake, NU, Canada
168 H 7 Coober Pedy, SA, Australia
47 M 2 Cook, MN, United States
59 K 7 Cook Inlet, AK, United States
173 L 9 Cook Islands, New Zealand
172 E 6 Cook Strait, New Zealand
40 G 6 Cookeville, TN, United States
169 K 4 Cooktown, QLD, Australia
168 F 8 Coolgardie, WA, Australia
75 I 1 Cooper's Town, The Bahamas
56 D 7 Coos Bay, OR, United States
121 C 14 Copenhagen, Denmark
82 E 8 Copiapó, Chile
44 E 6 Copper Harbor, MI, United States
83 E 9 Coquimbo, Chile
112 H 8 Corabia, Romania
67 I 3 Coral Harbour, NU, Canada
26 F 7 Coral Sea, Pacific Ocean
26 E 6 Coral Sea Basin, Pacific Ocean
43 L 4 Cordele, GA, United States
92 G 3 Cordillera Cantabrica, Spain
145 K 4 Cordillera Mountains, Philippines
74 G 8 Cordillera Talamanca, Costa Rica/Panama
83 G 9 Córdoba, Argentina
73 L 9 Córdoba, Mexico
93 I 8 Córdoba, Spain
59 L 7 Cordova, AK, United States
113 D 11 Corfu, Greece
40 H 3 Corinth, KY, United States
42 H 1 Corinth, MS, United States
113 G 12 Corinth Canal, Greece
89 B 13 Cork, Ireland
130 C 6 Çorlu, Turkey
67 N 7 Corner Brook, NL, Canada
57 E 10 Corning, CA, United States
38 F 7 Corning, NY, United States
68 G 8 Cornwall, ON, Canada
80 F 1 Coro, Venezuela
172 F 3 Coromandel Peninsula, New Zealand
55 K 8 Corona, NM, United States
74 E 4 Corozal, Belize
51 K 9 Corpus Christi, TX, United States
82 I 8 Corrientes, Argentina
97 N 9 Corsica, France
51 K 5 Corsicana, TX, United States
92 G 8 Cortegana, Spain
55 I 5 Cortez, CO, United States
108 F 4 Cortina d'Ampezzo, Italy
38 G 7 Cortland, NY, United States
131 J 7 Çoruh, Turkey
130 G 7 Çorum, Turkey
81 I 8 Corumbá, Brazil
56 E 7 Corvallis, OR, United States
92 A 8 Corvo, Portugal
97 J 5 Cosne-cours-sur-Loire, France
93 L 8 Costa Blanca, Spain
93 O 4 Costa Brava, Spain
93 I 10 Costa del Sol, Spain
74 G 8 Costa Rica, North America
92 H 1 Costa Verde, Spain
97 L 10 Côte d'Azur, France
158 F 6 Côte d'Ivoire, Africa
104 I 7 Cottbus, Germany
51 I 9 Cotulla, TX, United States
38 F 8 Coudersport, PA, United States
56 H 4 Coulee City, WA, United States
52 E 6 Council, ID, United States
47 K 10 Council Bluffs, IA, United States
101 E 13 Courcelles, Belgium
42 D 4 Coushatta, LA, United States
65 H 13 Coutts, AB, Canada
101 E 14 Couvin, Belgium
89 H 13 Coventry, United Kingdom
54 F 10 Covered Wells, AZ, United States
92 G 5 Covilhã, Portugal
44 D 7 Covington, MI, United States
40 C 7 Covington, TN, United States
73 P 8 Cozumel, Mexico
55 J 2 Craig, CO, United States
112 G 8 Craiova, Romania
56 H 8 Crane, OR, United States
50 G 6 Crane, TX, United States
56 F 8 Crater Lake, OR, United States
169 L 2 Crater Point, Papua New Guinea
44 F 13 Crawfordsville, IN, United States
43 K 6 Crawfordville, FL, United States
89 I 14 Crawley, United Kingdom
108 D 6 Cremona, Italy
112 A 7 Cres, Croatia
57 D 9 Crescent City, CA, United States
43 M 6 Crescent City, FL, United States
43 M 6 Crescent Lake, FL, United States
47 M 10 Creston, IA, United States
53 L 10 Creston, WY, United States
43 J 5 Crestview, FL, United States
113 H 15 Crete, Greece
112 B 7 Crikvenica, Croatia
117 M 11 Crimea, Ukraine
112 D 6 Croatia, Europe
172 C 9 Cromwell, New Zealand
75 J 3 Crooked Island, The Bahamas
47 K 2 Crookston, MN, United States
43 L 6 Cross City, FL, United States
40 G 6 Crossville, TN, United States
109 J 12 Crotone, Italy
53 L 5 Crow Agency, MT, United States
42 E 6 Crowley, LA, United States
55 I 7 Crownpoint, NM, United States
89 I 14 Croydon, United Kingdom
30 G 7 Crozet Basin, Indian Ocean
23 J 9 Crozet Islands, Antarctica
30 E 8 Crozet Plateau, Indian Ocean
44 E 7 Crystal Falls, MI, United States
72 H 4 Cuauhtémoc, Mexico
55 J 7 Cuba, NM, United States
74 H 3 Cuba, North America
23 I 7 Cubango, Africa
80 F 2 Cúcuta, Colombia
141 E 14 Cuddalore, Sri Lanka
141 E 13 Cuddapah, India
80 E 4 Cuenca, Ecuador
93 K 5 Cuenca, Spain
73 K 9 Cuernavaca, Mexico
81 I 7 Cuiabá, Brazil
72 H 6 Culiacán, Mexico
93 L 7 Cullera, Spain
43 J 2 Cullman, AL, United States
41 N 3 Culpeper, VA, United States
80 G 2 Cumaná, Venezuela
41 M 2 Cumberland, MD, United States
40 E 6 Cumberland, TN/KY, United States
63 J 4 Cumberland Peninsula, NU, Canada
40 G 7 Cumberland Plateau, TN, United States
67 L 2 Cumberland Sound, NU, Canada
72 G 3 Cumpas, Mexico
162 F 7 Cunene, Angola
108 A 7 Cuneo, Italy
169 K 7 Cunnamulla, QLD, Australia
75 L 7 Curaçao, Netherlands Antilles
83 E 10 Curicó, Chile
81 J 9 Curitiba, Brazil
57 J 11 Currant, NV, United States
57 J 10 Currie, NV, United States
41 O 6 Currituck, NC, United States
59 K 6 Curry, AK, United States
56 E 7 Curtin, OR, United States
43 K 4 Cusseta, GA, United States
53 L 5 Custer, MT, United States
46 F 7 Custer, SD, United States
43 K 4 Cuthbert, GA, United States
43 N 10 Cutler Ridge, FL, United States
83 F 11 Cutral-Co, Argentina
141 G 11 Cuttack, India
31 J 6 Cuvier Plateau, Indian Ocean
104 D 5 Cuxhaven, Germany
80 F 7 Cuzco, Peru
113 H 13 Cyclades, Greece
130 F 11 Cyprus, Asia
116 E 7 Czech Republic, Europe
116 G 7 Częstochowa, Poland
116 F 5 Człuchów, Poland
112 I 8 Călărași, Romania

D

149 M 3 Da Hinggan Ling, China
144 H 5 Đa Lat, Vietnam
144 H 4 Đa Năng, Vietnam
149 K 7 Daba Shan, China
116 G 7 Dąbrowa Górnicza, Poland
141 I 9 Dacca, Bangladesh
145 J 4 Dagupan, Philippines
137 I 2 Dahūk, Iraq
93 J 7 Daimiel, Spain
153 G 11 Daiō-zaki, Japan
158 D 5 Dakar, Senegal
47 K 8 Dakota City, NE, United States
130 D 9 Dalaman, Turkey
149 K 4 Dalandzadgad, Mongolia
133 J 9 Dalbandin, Pakistan
169 L 7 Dalby, QLD, Australia
40 G 6 Dale Hollow Lake, TN, United States
50 G 1 Dalhart, TX, United States
69 L 5 Dalhousie, NB, Canada
149 J 9 Dali, China
149 N 5 Dalian, China
51 K 4 Dallas, TX, United States
112 A 7 Dalmatia, Croatia
158 E 7 Daloa, Côte d'Ivoire
43 K 1 Dalton, GA, United States
168 H 4 Daly, NT, Australia
168 H 4 Daly Waters, NT, Australia
162 G 8 Damaraland, Namibia
136 H 3 Damascus, Syria
168 E 6 Dampier, WA, Australia
145 I 8 Danau Luar, Indonesia
144 F 7 Danau Toba, Indonesia
145 K 9 Danau Towuti, Indonesia
57 J 15 Danby Lake, CA, United States
149 N 5 Dandong, China
74 E 5 Dangriga, Belize
53 J 9 Daniel, WY, United States
38 F 7 Dansville, NY, United States
23 I 3 Danube, Europe
40 H 4 Danville, KY, United States
41 L 6 Danville, VA, United States
149 N 3 Daqing, China
163 L 5 Dar es Salaam, Tanzania
141 G 9 Darbhanga, India
52 G 5 Darby, MT, United States
130 B 6 Dardanelles, Turkey
159 K 6 Darfur, Sudan
172 E 2 Dargaville, New Zealand
149 K 3 Darhan, Mongolia
43 M 5 Darien, GA, United States
23 N 8 Darling, Australia
89 H 10 Darlington, United Kingdom
105 D 9 Darmstadt, Germany
159 K 2 Darnah, Libya
93 K 4 Daroca, Spain
89 F 15 Dartmoor, United Kingdom
169 J 3 Daru, Papua New Guinea
168 G 3 Darwin, NT, Australia
137 L 4 Daryācheh-ye Bakhtegan, Iran
137 L 3 Daryācheh-ye Namak, Iran
137 N 4 Daryācheh-ye Sīstan, Iran
137 L 4 Daryācheh-ye Tashk, Iran
133 I 5 Dashkhovuz, Turkmenistan
133 I 11 Dasht, Pakistan
137 L 3 Dasht-e Kavir, Iran
137 M 3 Dasht-e Lut, Iran
133 I 9 Dasht-i Margow, Afghanistan
55 I 9 Datil, NM, United States
149 L 5 Datong, China
117 J 3 Daugavpils, Latvia
66 F 7 Dauphin, MB, Canada
141 D 13 Davangere, India
145 L 6 Davao, Philippines
47 O 9 Davenport, IA, United States
74 G 8 David, Panama
65 J 12 Davidson, SK, Canada
30 E 6 Davie Ridge, Indian Ocean
33 P 4 Davis, Australia
50 F 7 Davis Mountains, TX, United States
67 L 2 Davis Strait, NU, Canada
105 E 13 Davos, Switzerland
137 N 8 Dawḩat Şawqirah, Oman
64 A 8 Dawson, YT, Canada
65 F 11 Dawson Creek, BC, Canada
96 G 10 Dax, France
137 I 2 Dayr az Zawr, Syria
40 G 7 Dayton, TN, United States
56 H 5 Dayton, WA, United States
44 H 13 Dayton, OH, United States
43 N 7 Daytona Beach, FL, United States
42 D 5 De Ridder, LA, United States
47 M 9 De Soto, IA, United States
47 P 9 De Witt, IA, United States
136 G 4 Dead Sea, Israel/Jordan
65 C 10 Dease Lake, BC, Canada
57 I 13 Death Valley, CA, United States
57 I 13 Death Valley, CA, United States
116 G 9 Debrecen, Hungary
43 I 2 Decatur, AL, United States
45 D 13 Decatur, IL, United States
45 H 12 Decatur, IN, United States
23 L 5 Deccan Plateau, Asia
47 N 7 Decorah, IA, United States
88 G 7 Dee, United Kingdom
69 L 8 Deer Island, NB, Canada
56 I 4 Deer Park, WA, United States
59 I 4 Deering, AK, United States
133 J 9 Deh Shū, Afghanistan
140 E 7 Dehra Dun, India
101 C 11 Deinze, Belgium
112 G 5 Dej, Romania
30 E 8 Del Cano Rise, Indian Ocean
50 H 8 Del Rio, TX, United States
57 G 14 Delano, CA, United States
41 P 2 Delaware, DE, United States
38 H 8 Delaware, NY, United States
41 P 2 Delaware Bay, DE/NJ, United States
41 N 8 Delco, NC, United States
100 E 8 Delft, Netherlands
100 K 4 Delfzijl, Netherlands
140 D 8 Delhi, India
104 D 6 Delmenhorst, Germany
43 O 9 Delray Beach, FL, United States
55 I 4 Delta, CO, United States
54 F 3 Delta, UT, United States
59 L 5 Delta Junction, AK, United States
43 N 7 Deltona, FL, United States
28 E 6 Demerara Abyssal Plain, Atlantic Ocean
28 E 6 Demerara Plateau, Atlantic Ocean
55 J 10 Deming, NM, United States
162 G 3 Democratic Republic of Congo, Africa
43 I 4 Demopolis, AL, United States
100 F 5 Den Helder, Netherlands
133 K 6 Denau, Uzbekistan
68 E 8 Denbigh, ON, Canada
101 E 11 Dendermonde, Belgium
168 D 7 Denham, WA, Australia
93 M 7 Denia, Spain

56 G 6 **Goldendale**, WA, United States
41 N 7 **Goldsboro**, NC, United States
51 J 6 **Goldthwaite**, TX, United States
159 I 2 **Golfe de Gabès**, Tunisia
96 F 3 **Golfe de St-Malo**, France
97 J 11 **Golfe du Lion**, France
92 G 9 **Golfo de Cádiz**, Spain
74 G 9 **Golfo de Chiriquí**, Panama
74 F 5 **Golfo de Honduras**, Honduras
74 H 8 **Golfo de los Mosquitos**, Panama
83 G 13 **Golfo de San Jorge**, Argentina
93 N 4 **Golfo de Sant Jordi**, Spain
73 M 10 **Golfo de Tehuantepec**, Mexico
93 M 7 **Golfo de Valencia**, Spain
109 G 10 **Golfo di Gaeta**, Italy
74 G 8 **Golfo Dulce**, Costa Rica
29 E 10 **Golfo San Matias**, Argentina
163 J 3 **Goma**, Democratic Republic of Congo
73 I 5 **Gómez Palacio**, Mexico
75 K 4 **Gonaïves**, Haiti
137 M 2 **Gonbad-e Kavus**, Iran
159 M 6 **Gonder**, Ethiopia
141 E 10 **Gondia**, India
100 J 7 **Goor**, Netherlands
57 G 9 **Goose Lake**, CA, United States
126 G 10 **Gora Belukha**, Russia
140 F 8 **Gorakhpur**, India
112 D 8 **Goražde**, Bosnia-Herzegovina
41 M 4 **Gordonsville**, VA, United States
172 C 10 **Gore**, New Zealand
137 M 2 **Gorgān**, Iran
131 L 5 **Gori**, Georgia
131 N 7 **Goris**, Armenia
104 I 8 **Görlitz**, Germany
113 E 8 **Gornji Milanovac**, Serbia
169 K 2 **Goroka**, Papua New Guinea
145 K 8 **Gorontalo**, Indonesia
133 I 4 **Gory Mugodzhary**, Kazakhstan
126 H 6 **Goryna Putorana**, Russia
116 E 5 **Gorzów Wielkopolski**, Poland
104 E 7 **Goslar**, Germany
112 B 7 **Gospić**, Croatia
113 E 9 **Gostivar**, Macedonia
104 E 8 **Gotha**, Germany
46 H 10 **Gothenburg**, NE, United States
121 D 13 **Gothenburg**, Sweden
121 G 13 **Gotland**, Sweden
153 A 14 **Gotō-rettō**, Japan
113 G 10 **Gotse Delchev**, Bulgaria
104 E 7 **Göttingen**, Germany
100 F 8 **Gouda**, Netherlands
29 G 10 **Gough Fracture Zone**, Atlantic Ocean
29 H 10 **Gough Island**, Atlantic Ocean
169 K 9 **Goulburn**, NSW, Australia
168 H 3 **Goulburn Islands**, NT, Australia
81 K 8 **Governador Valadares**, Brazil
149 I 4 **Govi Altayn Nuruu**, Mongolia
141 F 9 **Govind Ballash Pant Sagar**, India
82 H 8 **Goya**, Argentina
109 G 16 **Gozo**, Malta
68 F 7 **Gracefield**, QC, Canada
92 B 9 **Graciosa**, Portugal
92 D 10 **Graciosa**, Spain
112 D 7 **Gradačac**, Bosnia-Herzegovina
47 J 2 **Grafton**, ND, United States
65 B 12 **Graham Island**, BC, Canada
88 F 7 **Grampian Mountains**, United Kingdom
92 B 11 **Gran Canaria**, Spain
82 G 7 **Gran Chaco**, Argentina/Paraguay
55 M 5 **Granada**, CO, United States
74 F 7 **Granada**, Nicaragua
93 J 9 **Granada**, Spain
46 G 5 **Grand**, SD, United States
75 I 1 **Grand Bahama**, The Bahamas
28 E 4 **Grand Banks of Newfoundland**, Atlantic Ocean
54 F 7 **Grand Canyon**, AZ, United States
54 F 7 **Grand Canyon**, AZ, United States
74 H 4 **Grand Cayman**, Cayman Islands
159 I 5 **Grand Erg de Bilma**, Niger
158 G 2 **Grand Erg Occidental**, Algeria/Tunisia
158 H 2 **Grand Erg Oriental**, Algeria/Tunisia
47 J 2 **Grand Forks**, ND, United States
44 F 10 **Grand Haven**, MI, United States
47 J 10 **Grand Island**, NE, United States
55 I 4 **Grand Junction**, CO, United States
69 L 8 **Grand Manan Island**, NB, Canada
47 O 2 **Grand Marais**, MN, United States
47 O 2 **Grand Portage**, MN, United States
66 F 6 **Grand Rapids**, MB, Canada
44 G 10 **Grand Rapids**, MI, United States
47 M 3 **Grand Rapids**, MN, United States
53 J 8 **Grand Teton**, WY, United States
82 G 6 **Grande**, Bolivia
74 F 7 **Grande**, Nicaragua
65 F 12 **Grande Cache**, AB, Canada
163 M 6 **Grande Comore**, Comoros
65 F 12 **Grande Prairie**, AB, Canada
69 O 5 **Grande-Entrée**, QC, Canada
69 L 4 **Grande-Vallée**, QC, Canada
68 H 6 **Grand-Mère**, QC, Canada
68 F 6 **Grand-Remous**, QC, Canada
53 J 10 **Granger**, WY, United States
52 F 5 **Grangeville**, ID, United States
53 J 6 **Granite Peak**, MT, United States
55 I 8 **Grants**, NM, United States
54 F 2 **Grantsville**, UT, United States
96 G 4 **Granville**, France
53 K 4 **Grassrange**, MT, United States
46 F 3 **Grassy Butte**, ND, United States
105 J 12 **Graz**, Austria
75 I 1 **Great Abaco**, The Bahamas
168 G 9 **Great Australian Bight**, SA, Australia
74 H 2 **Great Bahaman Bank**, The Bahamas
172 F 2 **Great Barrier Island**, New Zealand
169 J 3 **Great Barrier Reef**, QLD, Australia
57 J 11 **Great Basin**, NV, United States
64 E 7 **Great Bear Lake**, NT, Canada
141 J 15 **Great Channel**, India
141 J 13 **Great Coco Island**, India
53 L 10 **Great Divide Basin**, WY, United States
23 N 8 **Great Dividing Range**, Australia
172 E 1 **Great Exhibition Bay**, New Zealand
53 I 3 **Great Falls**, MT, United States
75 J 3 **Great Inagua Island**, The Bahamas
28 G 5 **Great Meteor Tablemount**, Atlantic Ocean
141 K 15 **Great Nicobar**, India
89 I 12 **Great Ouse**, United Kingdom
23 M 4 **Great Plain of China**, Asia
22 D 4 **Great Plains**, North America
23 I 6 **Great Rift Valley**, Africa
54 F 2 **Great Salt Lake**, UT, United States
54 F 2 **Great Salt Lake Desert**, UT, United States
159 J 3 **Great Sand Sea**, Egypt/Libya
168 F 6 **Great Sandy Desert**, WA, Australia
65 F 9 **Great Slave Lake**, NT, Canada
168 G 7 **Great Victoria Desert**, SA/WA, Australia
89 K 12 **Great Yarmouth**, United Kingdom
163 J 8 **Great Zimbabwe**, Zimbabwe
75 I 4 **Greater Antilles**, Caribbean Sea
113 G 11 **Greece**, Europe
55 L 2 **Greeley**, CO, United States
53 J 9 **Green**, WY/UT, United States
44 E 9 **Green Bay**, WI, United States
44 F 8 **Green Bay**, MI, United States
65 I 11 **Green Lake**, SK, Canada
39 J 6 **Green Mountains**, VT, United States
54 H 4 **Green River**, UT, United States
53 K 10 **Green River**, WY, United States
40 G 5 **Green River Lake**, KY, United States
44 F 13 **Greencastle**, IN, United States
41 I 6 **Greeneville**, TN, United States
39 J 7 **Greenfield**, MA, United States
32 C 8 **Greenland**, Denmark
32 D 9 **Greenland Plain**, Arctic Ocean
32 D 9 **Greenland Sea**, Arctic Ocean
41 L 6 **Greensboro**, NC, United States
44 G 14 **Greensburg**, IN, United States
42 F 5 **Greensburg**, LA, United States
38 D 9 **Greensburg**, PA, United States
43 I 4 **Greenville**, AL, United States
42 F 3 **Greenville**, MS, United States
44 H 13 **Greenville**, OH, United States
38 D 8 **Greenville**, PA, United States
41 J 8 **Greenville**, SC, United States
51 K 4 **Greenville**, TX, United States
42 G 3 **Greenwood**, MS, United States
41 J 9 **Greenwood**, SC, United States
47 I 8 **Gregory**, SD, United States
169 J 5 **Gregory Range**, QLD, Australia
104 H 4 **Greifswald**, Germany
42 G 2 **Grenada**, MS, United States
75 N 7 **Grenada**, North America
42 G 2 **Grenada Lake**, MS, United States
75 O 7 **Grenadines, The**, St Vincent and the Grenadines
97 L 8 **Grenoble**, France
101 J 15 **Grevenmacher**, Luxembourg
172 D 7 **Grey**, New Zealand
53 L 7 **Greybull**, WY, United States
172 D 7 **Greymouth**, New Zealand
43 K 3 **Griffin**, GA, United States
169 K 9 **Griffith**, NSW, Australia
89 I 11 **Grimsby**, United Kingdom
100 J 4 **Groningen**, Netherlands
169 I 4 **Groote Eylandt**, NT, Australia
108 E 8 **Grosseto**, Italy
105 G 12 **Grossglockner**, Austria
173 O 10 **Groupe Actéon**, French Polynesia
39 K 4 **Groveton**, NH, United States
126 B 8 **Groznyy**, Russia
116 G 5 **Grudziądz**, Poland
73 I 8 **Guadalajara**, Mexico
93 J 5 **Guadalajara**, Spain
172 G 9 **Guadalcanal**, Solomon Islands
93 I 8 **Guadalquivir**, Spain
73 K 5 **Guadalupe**, Mexico
27 J 3 **Guadalupe**, Pacific Ocean
50 E 5 **Guadalupe Peak**, TX, United States
75 O 5 **Guadeloupe**, France
93 I 7 **Guadiana**, Spain
93 J 9 **Guadix**, Spain
27 L 9 **Guafo Fracture Zone**, Pacific Ocean
83 I 9 **Gualeguaychú**, Argentina
173 L 5 **Guam**, United States
72 H 5 **Guamúchil**, Mexico
73 J 8 **Guanajuato**, Mexico
149 K 7 **Guangyuan**, China
149 M 10 **Guangzhou**, China
75 J 4 **Guantánamo**, Cuba
75 J 4 **Guantánamo Bay**, United States
92 G 5 **Guarda**, Portugal
72 G 5 **Guasave**, Mexico
74 D 6 **Guatemala**, Guatemala
74 E 5 **Guatemala**, North America
27 L 5 **Guatemala Basin**, Pacific Ocean
80 F 3 **Guaviare**, Colombia
80 D 4 **Guayaquil**, Ecuador
72 F 4 **Guaymas**, Mexico
137 I 4 **Gudayyidat 'Ar'ar**, Saudi Arabia
141 E 12 **Gudivada**, India
158 E 2 **Guelmine**, Morocco
97 I 7 **Guéret**, France
89 G 16 **Guernsey**, United Kingdom
53 N 9 **Guernsey**, WY, United States
72 E 4 **Guerrero Negro**, Mexico
173 L 4 **Guguan**, Northern Mariana Islands
22 E 6 **Guiana Highlands**, South America
89 I 14 **Guildford**, United Kingdom
149 L 9 **Guilin**, China
158 D 6 **Guinea**, Africa
28 I 7 **Guinea Basin**, Atlantic Ocean
158 D 5 **Guinea-Bissau**, Africa
149 K 9 **Guiyang**, China
133 M 8 **Gujranwala**, Pakistan
133 M 8 **Gujrat**, Pakistan
141 D 12 **Gulbarga**, India
30 E 2 **Gulf of Aden**, Indian Ocean
59 K 8 **Gulf of Alaska**, AK, United States
32 D 3 **Gulf of Anadyr**, Russia
136 G 5 **Gulf of Aqaba**, Asia
65 I 4 **Gulf of Boothia**, NU, Canada
121 G 10 **Gulf of Bothnia**, Finland
72 E 2 **Gulf of California**, Mexico
169 I 4 **Gulf of Carpentaria**, QLD, Australia
113 F 12 **Gulf of Corinth**, Greece
75 I 8 **Gulf of Darién**, Panama/Colombia
126 C 4 **Gulf of Finland**, Europe
116 G 4 **Gulf of Gdańsk**, Poland/Russia
108 C 7 **Gulf of Genoa**, Italy
22 t c **Gulf of Guinea**, Africa
141 A 9 **Gulf of Kachchh**, India
141 B 10 **Gulf of Khambhat**, India
39 L 7 **Gulf of Maine**, ME, United States
141 D 15 **Gulf of Mannar**, India/Sri Lanka
22 D 4 **Gulf of Mexico**, Mexico/United States
109 G 11 **Gulf of Naples**, Italy
137 M 6 **Gulf of Oman**, Iran/Oman
80 D 2 **Gulf of Panama**, Colombia/Panama
169 K 2 **Gulf of Papua**, Papua New Guinea
117 I 2 **Gulf of Riga**, Estonia/Latvia
109 H 11 **Gulf of Salerno**, Italy
159 J 2 **Gulf of Sirte**, Libya
69 N 4 **Gulf of St Lawrence**, QC, Canada
159 L 3 **Gulf of Suez**, Egypt
109 J 12 **Gulf of Taranto**, Italy
144 F 5 **Gulf of Thailand**, Cambodia/Thailand
144 H 4 **Gulf of Tongking**, China/Vietnam
108 F 6 **Gulf of Venice**, Italy/Slovenia
43 I 6 **Gulf Shores**, AL, United States
22 D 4 **Gulf-Atlantic Coastal Plain**, North America
133 K 6 **Gulistan**, Uzbekistan
130 C 9 **Güllük Körfezi**, Turkey
163 J 2 **Gulu**, Uganda
141 D 9 **Guna**, India
32 C 9 **Gunnbjørn Fjeld**, Greenland
55 J 4 **Gunnison**, CO, United States
54 G 4 **Gunnison**, UT, United States
141 D 12 **Guntakal**, India
43 J 2 **Guntersville Lake**, AL, United States
141 E 12 **Guntur**, India
163 K 7 **Gurué**, Mozambique
131 I 8 **Gürün**, Turkey
81 J 6 **Gurupi**, Brazil
158 H 6 **Gusau**, Nigeria
116 H 4 **Gusev**, Russia
153 J 16 **Gushikawa**, Japan
104 D 7 **Gütersloh**, Germany
54 H 10 **Guthrie**, AZ, United States
50 H 4 **Guthrie**, TX, United States
47 O 8 **Guttenberg**, IA, United States
140 I 8 **Guwahati**, India
80 H 2 **Guyana**, South America
133 K 6 **Guzar**, Uzbekistan
133 J 11 **Gwadar**, Pakistan
141 D 9 **Gwalior**, India
163 J 7 **Gweru**, Zimbabwe
149 I 7 **Gyaring Hu**, China
126 H 5 **Gydanskiy Peninsula**, Russia
169 L 7 **Gympie**, QLD, Australia
116 F 9 **Győr**, Hungary
131 L 6 **Gyumri**, Armenia

H

144 H 3 **Ha Long Bay**, Vietnam
100 J 7 **Haaksbergen**, Netherlands
117 I 1 **Haapsalu**, Estonia
100 F 7 **Haarlem**, Netherlands
153 I 12 **Hachijō-jima**, Japan
152 H 6 **Hachinohe**, Japan
141 B 15 **Hadhdhunmathi Atoll**, Maldives
137 K 10 **Ḥaḍramawt**, Yemen
89 G 9 **Hadrian's Wall**, United Kingdom
137 J 5 **Ḥafar al Bāṭin**, Saudi Arabia
173 K 5 **Hagåtña**, Guam
104 C 8 **Hagen**, Germany
100 E 8 **Hague, The**, Netherlands
144 H 3 **Hai Phong**, Vietnam
149 N 5 **Haicheng**, China
136 G 3 **Haifa**, Israel
149 L 11 **Haikou**, China
137 I 5 **Ḥā'il**, Saudi Arabia
149 M 2 **Hailar**, China
120 I 8 **Hailuoto**, Finland
149 L 11 **Hainan**, China
149 L 11 **Hainan Strait**, China
59 N 7 **Haines**, AK, United States
65 A 9 **Haines Junction**, YT, Canada
75 K 4 **Haiti**, North America
137 J 9 **Ḥajjah**, Yemen
152 H 5 **Hakodate**, Japan
159 M 4 **Halaib Triangle**, Egypt/Sudan
121 D 12 **Halden**, Norway
140 E 7 **Haldwani**, India
172 B 11 **Halfmoon Bay**, New Zealand
68 E 7 **Haliburton Highlands**, ON, Canada
69 N 8 **Halifax**, NS, Canada
89 H 11 **Halifax**, United Kingdom
173 L 1 **Hall Islands**, Federated States of Micronesia
67 L 2 **Hall Peninsula**, NU, Canada
101 E 12 **Halle**, Belgium
104 G 7 **Halle**, Germany
105 H 12 **Hallein**, Austria
33 L 2 **Halley**, United Kingdom
46 G 3 **Halliday**, ND, United States
168 G 5 **Halls Creek**, WA, Australia
145 L 8 **Halmahera**, Indonesia
121 D 14 **Halmstad**, Sweden
153 C 12 **Hamada**, Japan
137 K 3 **Hamadān**, Iran
136 H 2 **Ḥamāh**, Syria
153 G 11 **Hamamatsu**, Japan
121 D 11 **Hamar**, Norway
141 F 16 **Hambantota**, Sri Lanka
104 E 5 **Hamburg**, Germany
47 L 10 **Hamburg**, IA, United States
38 E 6 **Hamburg**, NY, United States
121 I 11 **Hämeenlinna**, Finland
104 D 7 **Hameln**, Germany
168 D 6 **Hamersley Range**, WA, Australia
149 O 5 **Hamhŭng**, North Korea
149 I 4 **Hami**, China
42 H 2 **Hamilton**, AL, United States
44 C 12 **Hamilton**, IL, United States
52 G 5 **Hamilton**, MT, United States
172 F 4 **Hamilton**, New Zealand
68 D 10 **Hamilton**, ON, Canada
89 F 9 **Hamilton**, United Kingdom
28 E 3 **Hamilton Bank**, Atlantic Ocean
50 H 4 **Hamlin**, TX, United States
104 C 7 **Hamm**, Germany
42 G 6 **Hammond**, LA, United States
172 D 10 **Hampden**, New Zealand
39 L 6 **Hampton**, NH, United States
56 G 7 **Hampton**, OR, United States
41 O 5 **Hampton**, VA, United States
137 N 4 **Hāmūn Helmand**, Iran
137 N 5 **Hāmūn-e Jaz Mūrīān**, Iran
58 C 5 **Hana**, HI, United States
105 D 9 **Hanau**, Germany
41 M 2 **Hancock**, MD, United States
38 H 8 **Hancock**, NY, United States
149 M 6 **Handan**, China
149 I 3 **Hangayn Nuruu**, Mongolia
149 N 8 **Hangzhou**, China
121 H 11 **Hanko**, Finland
54 G 4 **Hanksville**, UT, United States
65 H 12 **Hanna**, AB, Canada
104 E 6 **Hannover**, Germany
121 E 14 **Hanöbukten**, Sweden
144 H 3 **Hanoi**, Vietnam
149 K 7 **Hanzhong**, China
141 H 10 **Haora**, India
67 M 6 **Happy Valley-Goose Bay**, NL, Canada
149 I 3 **Har Nuur**, Mongolia
149 I 3 **Har Us Nuur**, Mongolia
137 K 6 **Ḥaraḍh**, Saudi Arabia
163 J 7 **Harare**, Zimbabwe
149 N 3 **Harbin**, China
41 K 11 **Hardeeville**, SC, United States
100 J 5 **Haren**, Netherlands
159 N 6 **Hārer**, Ethiopia
159 N 6 **Hargeysa**, Somalia
140 E 7 **Haridwar**, India
116 F 8 **Hařivov**, Czech Republic
41 I 5 **Harlan**, KY, United States
53 K 2 **Harlem**, MT, United States
100 G 5 **Harlingen**, Netherlands
51 J 11 **Harlingen**, TX, United States
53 J 4 **Harlowton**, MT, United States
56 H 8 **Harney Lake**, OR, United States
46 F 7 **Harney Peak**, SD, United States
121 F 9 **Härnösand**, Sweden
137 I 6 **Ḥarrat Rahaṭ**, Saudi Arabia
67 J 8 **Harricanaw**, QC, Canada
40 H 7 **Harriman**, TN, United States
88 D 6 **Harris**, United Kingdom
38 F 10 **Harrisburg**, PA, United States
46 E 8 **Harrison**, NE, United States
41 M 3 **Harrisonburg**, VA, United States
45 I 9 **Harrisville**, MI, United States
89 H 11 **Harrogate**, United Kingdom
120 F 5 **Harstad**, Norway
39 J 8 **Hartford**, CT, United States
40 F 5 **Hartford**, KY, United States
31 J 7 **Hartog Ridge**, Southern Ocean
69 M 2 **Harve-St-Pierre**, QC, Canada
69 L 7 **Harvey**, NB, Canada
46 H 3 **Harvey**, ND, United States
89 J 13 **Harwich**, United Kingdom
101 G 11 **Hasselt**, Belgium
172 G 5 **Hastings**, New Zealand
89 J 14 **Hastings**, United Kingdom
144 F 6 **Hat Yai**, Thailand
55 J 10 **Hatch**, NM, United States
112 G 7 **Haţeg**, Romania
140 D 8 **Hathras**, India
41 P 7 **Hatteras**, NC, United States
41 P 7 **Hatteras Island**, NC, United States
28 D 5 **Hatteras Abyssal Plain**, Atlantic Ocean
42 G 5 **Hattiesburg**, MS, United States
28 G 3 **Hatton Ridge**, Atlantic Ocean
121 A 11 **Haugesund**, Norway
121 B 11 **Haukeligrend**, Norway
121 J 10 **Haukivesi**, Finland
172 F 3 **Hauraki Gulf**, New Zealand
74 G 3 **Havana**, Cuba
44 C 13 **Havana**, IL, United States
53 J 2 **Havre**, MT, United States
69 N 5 **Havre Aubert**, QC, Canada
67 M 7 **Havre-St-Pierre**, QC, Canada
58 A 7 **Hawaii**, HI, United States
58 C 7 **Hawaii**, HI, United States
58 B 4 **Hawaiian Islands**, HI, United States
26 G 4 **Hawaiian Ridge**, Pacific Ocean
172 E 5 **Hawera**, New Zealand
58 D 6 **Hawi**, HI, United States
53 O 10 **Hawk Springs**, WY, United States
172 G 5 **Hawke Bay**, New Zealand
68 G 7 **Hawkesbury**, ON, Canada

47 K 7 Hawkeye Point, IA, United States ▲
57 H 11 Hawthorne, NV, United States
65 F 9 Hay River, NT, Canada
46 F 8 Hay Springs, NE, United States
54 G 10 Hayden, AZ, United States
46 F 6 Hayes, SD, United States
42 E 3 Haynesville, LA, United States
57 E 12 Hayward, CA, United States
44 C 7 Hayward, WI, United States
42 G 4 Hazlehurst, MS, United States
44 D 8 Heafford Junction, WI, United States
30 H 9 Heard Island, Australia ▲
67 I 8 Hearst, ON, Canada
54 G 8 Heber, AZ, United States
53 I 6 Hebgen Lake, MT, United States ≈
47 J 11 Hebron, NE, United States
100 I 5 Heerenveen, Netherlands
100 F 6 Heerhugowaard, Netherlands
101 I 11 Heerlen, Luxembourg
149 M 7 Hefei, China
149 O 2 Hegang, China
104 D 4 Heide, Germany
105 D 10 Heidelberg, Germany
149 N 2 Heihe, China
105 D 10 Heilbronn, Germany
23 M 3 Heilong Jiang, Asia ≈
101 F 11 Heist-op-den-Berg, Belgium
53 I 4 Helena, MT, United States
172 E 3 Helensville, New Zealand
104 C 4 Helgoländer Bay, Germany ≈
93 K 7 Hellín, Spain
56 I 6 Hells Canyon, OR, United States ⠿
52 E 6 Hell's Canyon, ID, United States ⠿
133 I 9 Helmand, Afghanistan/Iran ⤳
101 H 10 Helmond, Netherlands
121 D 14 Helsingborg, Sweden
121 J 11 Helsinki, Finland ⚓
46 F 9 Hemingford, NE, United States
51 L 7 Hempstead, TX, United States
152 G 6 Henashi-zaki, Japan ▶
40 E 4 Henderson, KY, United States
41 M 6 Henderson, NC, United States
40 D 7 Henderson, TN, United States
51 L 5 Henderson, TX, United States
173 P 11 Henderson Island, Pitcairn Islands ▲
41 J 7 Hendersonville, NC, United States
149 I 8 Hengduan Shan, China ▲▲
100 J 7 Hengelo, Netherlands
149 L 9 Hengyang, China
144 E 4 Henzada, Myanmar
56 G 6 Heppner, OR, United States
133 J 8 Herāt, Afghanistan
50 G 2 Hereford, TX, United States
72 G 4 Hermosillo, Mexico
42 G 1 Hernando, MS, United States
104 C 7 Herne, Germany
92 H 6 Herrera del Duque, Spain
43 N 10 Hialeah, FL, United States
41 K 7 Hickory, NC, United States
41 K 4 Hico, WV, United States
73 I 5 Hidalgo del Parral, Mexico
153 F 11 Higashi-ōsaka, Japan
153 A 13 Higashi-suidō, Japan ≋
44 H 8 Higgins Lake, MI, United States ⠿
65 F 10 High Level, AB, Canada
50 G 1 High Plains, TX, United States ⠿
38 H 8 High Point, NJ, United States ▲
43 L 6 High Springs, FL, United States
47 I 6 Highmore, SD, United States
116 H 1 Hiiumaa, Estonia ▲
104 E 7 Hildesheim, Germany
47 M 3 Hill City, MN, United States
39 K 6 Hillsboro, NH, United States
44 H 14 Hillsboro, OH, United States
41 K 5 Hillsville, VA, United States
53 D 6 Hilo, HI, United States
41 K 11 Hilton Head Island, SC, United States ▲
100 G 7 Hilversum, Netherlands
23 K 4 Himalayas, Asia ▲▲
153 E 11 Himeji, Japan
136 H 3 Ḩimṣ, Syria
75 K 4 Hinche, Haiti
169 K 5 Hinchinbrook Island, QLD, Australia ▲
23 K 4 Hindu Kush, Asia ▲▲
141 D 13 Hindupur, India
141 F 10 Hirakud Reservoir, India ≈
152 H 6 Hirosaki, Japan
153 C 12 Hiroshima, Japan
97 J 2 Hirson, France
140 D 7 Hisar, India
75 K 4 Hispaniola, Caribbean Sea ▲
153 I 9 Hitachi, Japan
141 A 16 Hitaddu, Maldives
121 B 5 Hitra, Norway ▲
173 O 9 Hiva Oa, French Polynesia ▲
121 F 12 Hjälmaren, Sweden ≈
121 C 13 Hjørring, Denmark

144 F 1 Hkakabo Razi, Myanmar ▲
144 H 5 Hô Chi Minh, Vietnam
169 K 11 Hobart, TAS, Australia ⌂
55 M 10 Hobbs, NM, United States
43 O 9 Hobe Sound, FL, United States
121 C 13 Hobro, Denmark
40 G 4 Hodgenville, KY, United States
116 G 10 Hódmezővásárhely, Hungary
105 G 9 Hof, Germany
120 C 6 Hofsjökull, Iceland ◇
153 C 12 Hōfu, Japan
22 H 5 Hoggar, Africa ◇
149 L 5 Hohhot, China
172 D 8 Hokitika, New Zealand
152 H 3 Hokkaidō, Japan ▲
54 H 8 Holbrook, AZ, United States
54 F 4 Holden, UT, United States
75 I 3 Holguín, Cuba
44 G 10 Holland, MI, United States
43 O 10 Hollywood, FL, United States
121 B 14 Holstebro, Denmark
47 L 8 Holstein, IA, United States
59 I 6 Holy Cross, AK, United States
89 E 11 Holyhead, United Kingdom
55 M 2 Holyoke, CO, United States
59 K 8 Homer, AK, United States
43 L 5 Homerville, GA, United States
43 N 10 Homestead, FL, United States
117 K 6 Homyel', Belarus
55 K 3 Hondo, NM, United States
74 F 6 Honduras, North America ▶
121 C 11 Hønefoss, Norway
57 G 10 Honey Lake, CA, United States ≈
144 H 3 Hông Gai, Vietnam
149 M 10 Hong Kong, China
149 L 9 Hongshui He, China ⤳
149 N 7 Hongze Hu, China ≈
172 G 9 Honiara, Solomon Islands ⚓
58 C 6 Honokohau, HI, United States
58 B 5 Honolulu, HI, United States ⌂
153 F 10 Honshū, Japan ▲
100 J 6 Hoogeveen, Netherlands
58 F 6 Hooper Bay, AK, United States
100 F 6 Hoorn, Netherlands
44 H 13 Hoosier Hill, IN, United States ▲
131 K 6 Hopa, Turkey
65 F 14 Hope, BC, Canada
42 G 6 Hopedale, LA, United States
40 E 5 Hopkinsville, KY, United States
56 E 4 Hoquiam, WA, United States
117 I 9 Hora Hoverla, Ukraine ▲
26 G 7 Horizon Deep, Pacific Ocean ▤
152 I 4 Horoshiri-dake, Japan ▲
121 C 14 Horsens, Denmark
169 J 10 Horsham, VIC, Australia
101 I 10 Horst, Netherlands
92 B 9 Horta, Portugal
65 D 6 Horton, NT, Canada ⤳
140 D 7 Hoshiarpur, India
101 I 14 Hosingen, Luxembourg
141 D 12 Hospet, India
46 F 7 Hot Springs, SD, United States
148 F 5 Hotan, China
120 F 8 Hoting, Sweden
28 F 8 Hotspur Seamount, Atlantic Ocean ▤
44 E 6 Houghton, MI, United States
44 H 9 Houghton Lake, MI, United States ≈
39 N 2 Houlton, ME, United States
42 F 6 Houma, LA, United States
65 D 12 Houston, BC, Canada
51 L 7 Houston, TX, United States
148 H 3 Hovd, Mongolia
149 J 2 Hövsgöl Nuur, Mongolia ≈
46 G 6 Howes, SD, United States
26 G 5 Howland Island, Pacific Ocean ▲
88 F 5 Hoy, United Kingdom ▲
104 H 7 Hoyerswerda, Germany
121 K 9 Höytiäinen, Finland ≈
116 E 7 Hradec Králové, Czech Republic
131 M 6 Hrazdan, Armenia
117 I 5 Hrodna, Belarus
149 N 9 Hsinchu, Taiwan
80 E 6 Huacho, Peru
149 L 5 Huai'an, China
149 M 7 Huainan, China
149 N 7 Huaiyin, China
73 L 9 Huajuápan de León, Mexico
149 O 9 Hualien, Taiwan
80 E 5 Huallaga, Peru ⤳
162 G 6 Huambo, Angola
80 E 6 Huancayo, Peru
149 M 8 Huangshi, China
82 F 5 Huanuni, Bolivia

72 G 5 Huatabampo, Mexico
51 K 5 Hubbard, TX, United States
51 I 4 Hubbard Creek Lake, TX, United States ≈
141 C 12 Huali, India
89 H 11 Huddersfield, United Kingdom
39 I 7 Hudson, NY, United States ⤳
67 I 4 Hudson Bay, NU, Canada ≈
67 K 3 Hudson Strait, NU, Canada ≈
144 H 4 Huê, Vietnam
50 D 5 Hueco Mountains, TX, United States ▲▲
74 D 5 Huehuetenango, Guatemala
73 L 9 Huejotzingo, Mexico
92 G 9 Huelva, Spain
93 L 3 Huesca, Spain
93 K 8 Huéscar, Spain
169 J 6 Hughenden, QLD, Australia
162 G 7 Huila Plateau, Angola ◇
73 N 11 Huixtla, Mexico
149 M 3 Hulun Nur, China ≈
89 I 11 Humber, United Kingdom ⤳
57 H 10 Humbold, NV, United States
47 M 8 Humboldt, IA, United States
40 D 6 Humboldt, TN, United States
47 J 9 Humphrey, NE, United States
54 G 7 Humphreys Peak, AZ, United States ▲
112 G 6 Hunedoara, Romania
116 F 10 Hungary, Europe ▣
44 G 12 Huntingburg, IN, United States
44 G 12 Huntington, IN, United States
41 J 4 Huntington, WV, United States
57 H 15 Huntington Beach, CA, United States
43 I 1 Huntsville, AL, United States
68 D 8 Huntsville, ON, Canada
51 L 6 Huntsville, TX, United States
159 L 3 Hurghada, Egypt
47 J 6 Huron, SD, United States
149 N 8 Huzhou, China
120 C 6 Hvannadalshnúkur, Iceland ▲
112 C 8 Hvar, Croatia
163 I 7 Hwange, Zimbabwe
46 G 9 Hyannis, NE, United States
149 I 2 Hyargas Nuur, Mongolia ≈
141 E 12 Hyderabad, India
133 K 11 Hyderabad, Pakistan
97 L 10 Hyères, France
149 O 4 Hyesan, North Korea

I

112 I 5 Iaşi, Romania
158 G 7 Ibadan, Nigeria
80 E 3 Ibagué, Colombia
80 E 4 Ibarra, Ecuador
82 H 7 Ibarreta, Argentina
137 J 10 Ibb, Yemen
22 H 4 Iberian Peninsula, Europe ▶
93 N 6 Ibiza, Spain ▲
137 M 7 Ibri, Oman
80 G 4 Içá, Brazil/Columbia ⤳
80 E 7 Ica, Peru
80 G 4 Içana, Brazil ⤳
120 C 5 Iceland, Europe ▣
28 G 3 Iceland Basin, Atlantic Ocean ▤
32 D 9 Icelandic Plateau, Arctic Ocean ⠿
141 C 12 Ichalkaranji, India
153 I 10 Ichihara, Japan
59 I 2 Icy Cape, AK, United States ▶
52 F 7 Idaho, ID, United States ✳
53 I 8 Idaho Falls, ID, United States
159 I 3 Idhān Murzūq, Libya ▲
136 H 2 Idlib, Syria
153 J 16 Ie-jima, Japan ▲
173 K 1 Ifalik, Federated States of Micronesia ▲
109 B 12 Iglesias, Italy
67 I 1 Igloolik, NU, Canada
66 H 3 Igluligaarjuk, NU, Canada
66 G 8 Ignace, ON, Canada
130 C 5 İğneada Burnu, Turkey ▶
113 E 11 Igoumenitsa, Greece
81 I9nF250 Iguaçu Falls, Argentina/Brazil ⤳
73 K 9 Iguala, Mexico
81 L 5 Iguatu, Brazil
141 A 13 Ihavandhippolhu Atoll, Maldives
153 J 15 Iheya-jima, Japan ▲
120 I 7 Iijoki, Finland ⤳
121 J 3 Iisalmi, Finland
100 I 6 IJssel, Netherlands ⤳
100 G 6 IJsselmeer, Netherlands ≈
101 B 10 IJzer, Belgium ⤳
64 D 5 Ikaahuk, NT, Canada
113 I 3 Ikaria, Greece ▲
162 H 3 Ikela, Democratic Republic of Congo

153 A 13 Iki, Japan ▲
153 A 13 Iki-suidō, Japan ≋
133 L 4 Ile, Kazakhstan ⤳
69 O 5 Île Brion, QC, Canada ▲
69 M 3 Île d'Anticosti, QC, Canada ▲
96 F 7 Île de Ré, France ▲
96 G 7 Île d'Oléron, France ▲
96 F 6 Île d'Yeu, France ▲
163 L 8 Île Europa, France ▣
69 M 5 Île Lamèque, NB, Canada ▲
30 F 5 Île Tromelin, France ▲
97 L 10 Îles de Hyères, France ▲
69 N 5 Îles de la Madeleine, QC, Canada ▲
163 M 6 Îles Glorieuses, Seychelles ▣
173 M 9 Iles Sous le Vent, French Polynesia ▲
92 C 9 Ilha da Madeira, Portugal ▲
28 G 8 Ilha da Trindade, Atlantic Ocean ▲
81 J 4 Ilha de Marajó, Brazil ▲
92 D 8 Ilha de Porto Santo, Portugal ▲
92 D 9 Ilhas Desertas, Portugal ▲
28 G 8 Ilhas Martim Vaz, Atlantic Ocean ▲
81 L 7 Ilhéus, Brazil
59 J 8 Iliamna Lake, AK, United States ≈
145 K 6 Iligan, Philippines
131 K 9 Ilisu Baraji, Turkey ⤳
44 D 12 Illinois, IL, United States ✳
44 C 13 Illinois, IL, United States ⤳
145 K 5 Ilcilo, Philippines
158 G 6 Ilorin, Nigeria
32 C 8 Ilulissat, Greenland
121 J 10 Imatra, Finland
43 N 9 Immokalee, FL, United States
108 E 7 Imola, Italy
81 K 5 Imperatriz, Brazil
108 B 7 Imperia, Italy
46 G 11 Imperial, NE, United States
141 J 9 Imphal, India
120 I 5 Inarijärvi, Finland ≈
152 H 3 Inawashiro-ko, Japan ⤳
130 G 5 Ince Burnu, Turkey ▶
130 G 10 İncekum Burnu, Turkey ▶
149 O 5 Inch'ŏn, South Korea
141 C 9 India, Asia ▣
30 H 6 Indian Ocean ⌖
57 J 13 Indian Springs, NV, United States
54 H 7 Indian Wells, AZ, United States
44 F 12 Indiana, IN, United States ✳
38 E 9 Indiana, PA, United States
31 K 10 Indian-Antarctic Basin, Southern Ocean ▤
31 L 9 Indian-Antarctic Ridge, Southern Ocean ▤
44 C 13 Indianapolis, IN, United States ⌂
47 M 9 Indianola, IA, United States
127 L 5 Indigirka, Russia ⤳
57 I 15 Indio, CA, United States
144 G 5 Indonesia, Asia ▣
141 D 10 Indore, India
23 K 4 Indus, Asia ⤳
130 D 5 Inebolu, Turkey
83 F 12 Ingeniero Jacobacci, Argentina
105 F 11 Ingolstadt, Germany
53 L 4 Ingomar, MT, United States
69 O 5 Ingonish, NS, Canada
163 K 9 Inhambane, Mozambique
144 F 3 Inlay Lake, Myanmar ≈
105 G 11 Inn, Germany ⤳
89 D 9 Inner Hebrides, United Kingdom ▲
149 L 4 Inner Mongolia, China ▣
169 K 5 Innisfail, QLD, Australia
105 F 12 Innsbruck, Austria
47 M 1 International Falls, MN, United States
153 I 10 Inubō-zaki, Japan ▶
67 J 5 Inukjuak, QC, Canada
64 B 6 Inuvik, NT, Canada
172 B 11 Invercargill, New Zealand
43 M 7 Inverness, FL, United States
69 O 6 Inverness, NS, Canada
88 F 7 Inverness, United Kingdom
31 J 4 Investigator Ridge, Indian Ocean ▤
163 J 7 Inyangani, Zimbabwe
113 E 11 Ioannina, Greece
113 E 12 Ionian Islands, Greece ▲
113 D 12 Ionian Sea, Greece/Italy ⌀
113 H 13 Ios, Greece ▲
47 L 9 Iowa, IA, United States ✳
47 E 6 Iowa, IA, United States ⤳
47 O 9 Iowa City, IA, United States
47 M 8 Iowa Falls, IA, United States
81 K 8 Ipatinga, Brazil
144 F 7 Ipoh, Malaysia
89 J 13 Ipswich, United Kingdom
67 K 3 Iqaluit, NU, Canada ⌂
82 E 6 Iquique, Chile
80 F 5 Iquitos, Peru
113 H 14 Irakleiou, Greece
137 L 3 Iran, Asia ▣
137 M 4 Iranian Plateau, Iran ▲

137 N 5 Īrānshahr, Iran
73 J 8 Irapuato, Mexico
137 I 3 Iraq, Asia ▣
136 H 3 Irbid, Jordan
89 C 11 Ireland, Europe ▣
145 O 9 Irian Jaya, Indonesia ⠿
163 K 5 Iringa, Tanzania
81 I 5 Iriri, Brazil ⤳
89 E 11 Irish Sea, Ireland/United Kingdom ⌀
127 I 10 Irkutsk, Russia
28 F 3 Irminger Basin, Atlantic Ocean ▤
44 E 7 Iron Mountain, MI, United States
45 I 14 Ironton, OH, United States
44 D 7 Ironwood, MI, United States
144 E 3 Irrawaddy, Myanmar ⤳
23 K 3 Irtysh, Asia ⤳
40 F 4 Irvington, KY, United States
46 G 5 Isabel, SD, United States
153 G 16 Ise, Japan
26 H 11 Iselin Seamount, Pacific Ocean ▤
109 G 10 Isernia, Italy
153 F 11 Ise-wan, Japan ≈
152 G 3 Ishikari-wan, Japan ≈
153 J 16 Ishikawa, Japan
152 I 7 Ishinomaki, Japan
153 D 13 Ishizuchi-san, Japan ▲
163 I 2 Isiro, Democratic Republic of Congo
130 H 10 Iskenderun, Turkey
130 G 10 Iskenderun Körfezi, Turkey ≈
113 G 8 Iskur, Bulgaria ⤳
72 F 3 Isla Ángel de la Guarda, Mexico ▲
72 F 4 Isla Cedros, Mexico ▲
74 G 9 Isla Coiba, Panama ▲
158 H 8 Isla de Bioco, Cameroon ▲
83 F 12 Isla de Chiloé, Chile ▲
74 G 3 Isla de la Juventud, Cuba ▲
74 F 7 Isla de Ometepe, Nicaragua ▲
74 H 8 Isla del Rey, Panama ▲
80 B 8 Isla Española, Galapagos Islands ▲
80 A 7 Isla Fernandina, Galapagos Islands ▲
80 B 6 Isla Genovesa, Galapagos Islands ▲
72 D 3 Isla Guadalupe, Mexico ▲
80 B 7 Isla Isabela, Galapagos Islands ▲
80 B 6 Isla Marchena, Galapagos Islands ▲
80 B 6 Isla Pinta, Galapagos Islands ▲
27 M 7 Isla San Ambrosio, Pacific Ocean ▲
80 C 7 Isla San Cristóbal, Galapagos Islands ▲
27 M 7 Isla San Felix, Pacific Ocean ▲
80 A 6 Isla San Salvador, Galapagos Islands ▲
80 B 7 Isla Santa Cruz, Galapagos Islands ▲
80 B 7 Isla Santa Fé, Galapagos Islands ▲
72 F 6 Isla Santa Margarita, Mexico ▲
80 B 7 Isla Santa Maria, Galapagos Islands ▲
72 F 4 Isla Tiburón, Mexico ▲
133 L 8 Islamabad, Pakistan ⚓
74 F 5 Islas de la Bahía, Honduras ▲
74 G 7 Islas del Maíz, Nicaragua ▲
72 H 7 Islas Marías, Mexico ▲
88 D 8 Islay, United Kingdom ▲
88 D 5 Isle of Lewis, United Kingdom ▲
89 F 10 Isle of Man, United Kingdom ▣
89 H 15 Isle of Wight, United Kingdom ▲
44 E 6 Isle Royale, MI, United States ▲
89 D 15 Isle of Scilly, United Kingdom ▲
159 L 2 Ismā'īliya, Egypt
109 B 10 Isola Asinara, Italy ▲
108 C 8 Isola d'Capraia, Italy ▲
109 D 9 Isola d'Elba, Italy ▲
109 E 15 Isola di Pantelleria, Italy ▲
109 G 13 Isola d'Ischia, Italy ▲
109 H 13 Isola Lipari, Italy ▲
109 H 13 Isola Stromboli, Italy ▲
109 H 13 Isola Vulcano, Italy ▲
109 E 14 Isola Egadi, Italy ▲
109 F 11 Isole Ponziane, Italy ▲
130 E 9 Isparta, Turkey
136 G 3 Israel, Asia ▣
130 D 6 İstanbul, Turkey
144 F 6 Isthmus of Kra, Asia ◇
113 G 12 Istiaia, Greece
73 M 9 Istmo de Tehuantepec, Mexico ◇
112 A 7 Istra, Croatia ▶
81 L 7 Itabuna, Brazil
81 I 5 Itaituba, Brazil
108 E 8 Italy, Europe ▣
38 G 7 Ithaca, NY, United States
113 E 12 Ithaki, Greece ▲
32 D 9 Ittoqqortoormiit, Greenland
120 I 5 Ivalo, Finland
169 I 9 Ivanhoe, NSW, Australia
117 I 8 Ivano-Frankivs'k, Ukraine
67 J 3 Ivujivik, QC, Canada
153 I 9 Iwaki, Japan
153 C 12 Iwakuni, Japan
152 H 6 Iwate-san, Japan ▲

153 J 15 Izena-jima, Japan
126 D 7 Izhevsk, Russia
130 C 8 Izmir, Turkey
130 B 7 Izmir Körfezi, Turkey ≈
26 E 3 Izu Trench, Pacific Ocean
153 I 11 Izu-shotō, Japan

J

136 G 5 Jabal al Lawz, Saudi Arabia ▲
137 L 9 Jabal al Qamar, Oman ▲
137 I 8 Jabal Sawdā', Saudi Arabia ▲
137 J 10 Jabal Taqar, Yemen ▲
137 I 8 Jabal Tuwayq, Saudi Arabia ▲
141 E 10 Jabalpur, India
173 N 4 Jabwat, Marshall Islands
93 L 2 Jaca, Spain
39 L 3 Jackman, ME, United States
57 F 11 Jackson, CA, United States
43 K 3 Jackson, GA, United States
44 H 11 Jackson, MI, United States
42 G 4 Jackson, MS, United States
45 I 14 Jackson, OH, United States
40 D 7 Jackson, TN, United States
53 J 8 Jackson, WY, United States
53 J 7 Jackson Lake, WY, United States
43 M 6 Jacksonville, FL, United States
44 C 13 Jacksonville, IL, United States
41 N 8 Jacksonville, NC, United States
51 L 5 Jacksonville, TX, United States
43 M 6 Jacksonville Beach, FL, United States
93 I 8 Jaén, Spain
141 E 14 Jaffna, India
39 J 7 Jaffrey, NH, United States
137 L 5 Jahrom, Iran
140 D 8 Jaipur, India
112 C 7 Jajce, Bosnia-Herzegovina
144 H 9 Jakarta, Indonesia
121 H 9 Jakobstad, Finland
133 L 3 Jalālābād, Afghanistan
133 L 6 Jalal-Abad, Kyrgyzstan
140 D 7 Jalandhar, India
141 C 10 Jalgaon, India
141 D 11 Jalna, India
173 N 4 Jaluit, Marshall Islands
159 N 8 Jamaame, Somalia
74 I 4 Jamaica, North America
75 J 4 Jamaica Channel, Caribbean Sea
144 G 8 Jambi, Indonesia
47 I 4 James, ND, United States
67 I 6 James Bay, NU, Canada ≈
33 I 2 James Ross Island, Antarctica
47 I 3 Jamestown, ND, United States
38 E 7 Jamestown, NY, United States
140 C 6 Jammu, India
140 D 6 Jammu and Kashmir, Asia
141 B 10 Jamnagar, India
141 G 10 Jamshedpur, India
32 D 9 Jan Mayen, Norway
44 D 10 Janesville, WI, United States
152 G 7 Japan, Asia
26 E 3 Japan Trench, Pacific Ocean
80 G 4 Japurá, Brazil/Columbia
22 E 6 Japurá, South America
81 J 4 Jari, Brazil
26 H 5 Jarvis Island, Pacific Ocean
33 J 2 Jason Peninsula, Antarctica
65 F 12 Jasper, AB, Canada
51 M 6 Jasper, TX, United States
116 F 8 Jastrzębie-Zdrój, Poland
141 F 9 Jaunpur, India
144 G 10 Java, Indonesia
31 J 4 Java Ridge, Indian Ocean
145 I 9 Java Sea, Indonesia
31 K 5 Java Trench, Indian Ocean
159 O 7 Jawhar, Somalia
145 O 8 Jayapura, Indonesia
145 M 8 Jazirah Doberai, Indonesia
136 H 7 Jeddah, Saudi Arabia
47 M 9 Jefferson, IA, United States
53 L 9 Jeffrey City, WY, United States
117 I 13 Jēkabpils, Latvia
116 E 7 Jelenia Góra, Poland
117 I 3 Jelgava, Latvia
145 I 10 Jember, Indonesia
104 F 8 Jena, Germany
41 J 5 Jenkins, KY, United States
75 J 4 Jérémie, Haiti
92 G 9 Jerez de la Frontera, Spain
136 G 4 Jericho, Israel
89 H 16 Jersey, United Kingdom
136 G 4 Jerusalem, Israel
141 H 10 Jessore, Bangladesh
43 M 4 Jesup, GA, United States
141 E 9 Jhansi, India
133 L 8 Jhelum, Pakistan

149 O 3 Jiamusi, China
149 M 9 Ji'an, China
149 M 10 Jiangmen, China
149 L 6 Jiaozuo, China
149 N 7 Jiaxing, China
137 M 8 Jiddat al Ḥarāsis, Oman
116 E 8 Jihlava, Czech Republic
149 O 4 Jilin, China
159 M 7 Jima, Ethiopia
73 I 5 Jiménez, Mexico
149 M 6 Jinan, China
149 J 5 Jinchang, China
149 M 8 Jingdezhen, China
149 M 8 Jingmen, China
149 L 8 Jingsha, China
149 L 8 Jingzhou, China
149 N 8 Jinhua, China
149 L 5 Jining, China
149 M 6 Jining, China
163 K 3 Jinja, Uganda
74 F 7 Jinotepe, Nicaragua
149 N 5 Jinzhou, China
137 N 5 Jīroft, Iran
149 M 8 Jiujiang, China
149 O 3 Jixi, China
137 I 9 Jīzān, Saudi Arabia
81 M 5 João Pessoa, Brazil
140 C 8 Jodhpur, India
121 K 9 Joensuu, Finland
55 M 3 Joes, CO, United States
153 G 9 Jōetsu, Japan
163 I 9 Johannesburg, South Africa
56 H 7 John Day, OR, United States
55 M 5 John Martin Reservoir, CO, United States
88 G 5 John o'Groats, United Kingdom
51 J 7 Johnson City, TX, United States
26 H 4 Johnston Atoll, Pacific Ocean
144 G 7 Johor Bahru, Malaysia
81 J 9 Joinville, Brazil
33 I 2 Joinville Island, Antarctica
120 G 7 Jokkmokk, Sweden
44 E 12 Joliet, IL, United States
68 H 7 Joliette, QC, Canada
145 K 7 Jolo, Philippines
117 I 4 Jonava, Lithuania
41 J 8 Jonesville, SC, United States
121 E 13 Jönköping, Sweden
63 K 9 Jonquière, QC, Canada
136 H 4 Jordan, Asia
53 L 3 Jordan, MT, United States
56 I 8 Jordan Valley, OR, United States
158 H 6 Jos, Nigeria
168 G 4 Joseph Bonaparte Gulf, WA, Australia ≈
100 H 5 Joure, Netherlands
56 E 3 Juan De Fuca Strait, WA, United States
27 M 8 Juan Fernandez Islands, Pacific Ocean
81 L 6 Juàzeiro, Brazil
81 L 5 Juázeiro do Norte, Brazil
159 N 8 Juba, Somalia
159 L 7 Juba, Sudan
93 K 6 Júcar, Spain
73 M 10 Juchitán, Mexico
74 F 7 Juigalpa, Nicaragua
81 K 7 Juiz de Fora, Brazil
120 G 6 Jukkasjärvi, Sweden
80 G 7 Juliaca, Peru
141 B 10 Junagadh, India
51 I 7 Junction, TX, United States
54 F 5 Junction, UT, United States
42 E 3 Junction City, LA, United States
59 N 8 Juneau, AK, United States
83 H 10 Junín, Argentina
56 H 7 Juntura, OR, United States
105 B 12 Jura, France/Switzerland ▲
88 E 8 Jura, United Kingdom
117 I 3 Jūrmala, Latvia
80 E 5 Juruá, Brazil
74 F 6 Juticalpa, Honduras
121 C 14 Jutland, Denmark ►
121 I 10 Jyväskylä, Finland

K

148 E 5 K2, China/Pakistan ▲
120 I 5 Kaamanen, Finland
133 K 8 Kabul, Afghanistan
163 I 6 Kabwe, Zambia
46 C 7 Kadoka, SD, United States
163 J 7 Kadoma, Zimbabwe
158 H 6 Kaduna, Nigeria
158 E 5 Kaédi, Mauritania
159 I 6 Kaélé, Cameroon

149 O 5 Kaesŏng, North Korea
136 H 4 Kāf, Saudi Arabia
163 I 7 Kafue, Zambia
153 B 15 Kagoshima, Japan
58 C 6 Kahoolawe, HI, United States
130 H 9 Kahramanmaraş, Turkey
172 D 8 Kaiapoi, New Zealand
149 M 7 Kaifeng, China
172 E 7 Kaikoura, New Zealand
172 E 7 Kaikoura Peninsula, New Zealand ►
149 K 9 Kaili, China
33 N 4 Kaiser Wilhelm II Land, Antarctica
105 C 10 Kaiserslautern, Germany
172 C 11 Kaitangata, New Zealand
149 J 10 Kaiyuan, China
120 I 8 Kajaani, Finland
168 H 3 Kakadu National Park, NT, Australia
117 M 9 Kakhovs'ke Vodoskhovyshche, Ukraine
141 F 12 Kakinada, India
59 L 2 Kaktovik, AK, United States
68 F 8 Kaladar, ON, Canada
23 I 7 Kalahari Desert, Africa ▲
113 G 10 Kalamaria, Greece
113 F 13 Kalamata, Greece
44 G 11 Kalamazoo, MI, United States
130 F 7 Kalecik, Turkey
168 F 8 Kalgoorlie, WA, Australia
145 I 8 Kalimantan, Indonesia
116 G 4 Kaliningrad, Russia
116 H 4 Kaliningrad, Russia
52 G 2 Kalispell, MT, United States
116 F 6 Kalisz, Poland
121 F 14 Kalmar, Sweden
126 C 6 Kaluga, Russia
113 I 13 Kalymnos, Greece
113 I 13 Kalymnos, Greece
153 H 10 Kamakura, Japan
127 O 8 Kamchatka Peninsula, Russia ►
126 E 7 Kamensk-Ural'skiy, Russia
163 I 5 Kamina, Democratic Republic of Congo
65 F 13 Kamloops, BC, Canada
163 J 3 Kampala, Uganda
100 H 6 Kampen, Netherlands
144 G 5 Kâmpóng Cham, Cambodia
144 G 5 Kâmpóng Saôm, Cambodia
152 G 4 Kamui-misaki, Japan ►
117 J 9 Kam''yanets'-Podil's'kyy, Ukraine
58 D 10 Kanaga Island, AK, United States
162 H 4 Kananga, Democratic Republic of Congo
153 F 10 Kanazawa, Japan
141 E 13 Kanchipuram, India
133 K 9 Kandahār, Afghanistan
126 D 4 Kandalaksha, Russia
141 E 15 Kandy, Sri Lanka
28 E 5 Kane Fracture Zone, Atlantic Ocean
58 B 5 Kaneohe, HI, United States
169 I 9 Kangaroo Island, SA, Australia
67 L 1 Kangeeak Point, NU, Canada ►
149 O 4 Kanggye, North Korea
67 K 4 Kangiqsujuaq, QC, Canada
67 K 4 Kangirsuk, QC, Canada
44 E 12 Kankakee, IL, United States
158 E 6 Kankan, Guinea
158 H 6 Kano, Nigeria
140 E 8 Kanpur, India
126 H 9 Kansk, Russia
173 K 8 Kanton, Kiribati
163 I 9 Kanye, Botswana
149 N 10 Kaohsiung, Taiwan
158 D 5 Kaolack, Senegal
104 H 4 Kap Arkona, Germany ►
32 D 9 Kap Brewster, Greenland ►
32 B 10 Kap Farvel, Greenland ►
131 N 7 Kapan, Armenia
133 M 4 Kapchagayskoye Vodokhranilishche, Kazakhstan
116 F 10 Kaposvár, Hungary
145 I 8 Kapuas, Indonesia
63 J 9 Kapuskasing, ON, Canada
32 F 7 Kara Sea, Arctic Ocean
133 L 5 Kara-Balta, Kyrgyzstan
130 F 6 Karabük, Turkey
133 I 3 Karabutak, Kazakhstan
133 K 11 Karachi, Pakistan
133 L 3 Karaganda, Kazakhstan
137 L 2 Karaj, Iran
133 M 5 Karakol, Kyrgyzstan
140 D 5 Karakoram Range, Asia ▲
23 J 3 Karakum Desert, Asia ▲
130 F 9 Karaman, Turkey
148 G 3 Karamay, China
172 D 7 Karamea Bight, New Zealand ≈
137 J 3 Karbalā', Iraq
113 F 11 Karditsa, Greece

141 B 14 Kardiva Channel, Maldives ≈
113 H 10 Kärdzhali, Bulgaria
120 H 5 Karesuando, Finland
120 I 5 Karigasniemi, Finland
141 E 11 Karimnagar, India
169 K 1 Karkar Island, Papua New Guinea
112 B 6 Karlovac, Croatia
113 H 9 Karlovo, Bulgaria
116 D 7 Karlovy Vary, Czech Republic
121 E 12 Karlskoga, Sweden
121 E 12 Karlskrona, Sweden
105 D 10 Karlsruhe, Germany
47 K 2 Karlstad, MN, United States
121 E 12 Karlstad, Sweden
140 D 7 Karnal, India
113 J 14 Karpathos, Greece
113 J 14 Karpathos, Greece
113 F 12 Karpenisi, Greece
131 L 6 Kars, Turkey
133 J 6 Karshi, Uzbekistan
113 H 12 Karystos, Greece
130 D 10 Kaş, Turkey
23 I 6 Kasai, Africa
163 J 5 Kasama, Zambia
163 J 3 Kasese, Uganda
66 G 8 Kashabowie, ON, Canada
137 L 3 Kāshān, Iran
67 I 7 Kashechewen, ON, Canada
148 E 4 Kashi, China
153 I 9 Kashima-nada, Japan ≈
113 I 14 Kasos, Greece
159 M 5 Kassala, Sudan
104 E 8 Kassel, Germany
130 G 6 Kastamonu, Turkey
113 F 11 Kastoria, Greece
153 G 11 Kasugai, Japan
153 I 9 Kasumiga-ura, Japan ≈
59 L 7 Katalla, AK, United States
113 F 11 Katerini, Greece
168 H 4 Katherine, NT, Australia
141 B 10 Kathiawar Peninsula, India ►
140 G 8 Kathmandu, Nepal
141 H 9 Katihar, India
116 F 7 Katowice, Poland
158 H 6 Katsina, Nigeria
133 K 6 Kattakürgan, Uzbekistan
121 D 13 Kattegat, Denmark ≈
58 B 4 Kauai, HI, United States
58 C 5 Kaunakakai, HI, United States
117 I 4 Kaunas, Lithuania
113 F 10 Kavadarci, Macedonia
113 H 10 Kavala, Greece
169 L 1 Kavieng, Papua New Guinea
153 H 10 Kawasaki, Japan
53 M 8 Kaycee, WY, United States
54 H 6 Kayenta, AZ, United States
158 E 5 Kayes, Mali
130 G 8 Kayseri, Turkey
133 J 3 Kazakhstan, Asia
126 D 7 Kazan', Russia
113 H 9 Kazanluk, Bulgaria
131 L 4 Kazbek, Georgia ▲
120 G 6 Kebnekaise, Sweden ▲
131 J 8 Keban Baraji, Turkey
159 N 7 K'ebri Dehar, Ethiopia
113 H 13 Kea, Greece
58 D 6 Keaau, HI, United States
116 G 9 Kecskemét, Hungary
117 I 4 Kėdainiai, Lithuania
69 K 5 Kedgwick, NB, Canada
162 G 9 Keetmanshoop, Namibia
113 E 12 Kefallonia, Greece
120 B 6 Keflavik, Iceland
65 F 10 Keg River, AB, Canada
121 I 9 Keitele, Finland
169 I 9 Keith, SA, Australia
153 I 14 Kekeroma-jima, Japan
116 G 9 Kékes, Hungary
144 F 7 Kelang, Malaysia
131 I 7 Kelkit, Turkey
65 F 14 Kelowna, BC, Canada
56 F 5 Kelso, WA, United States
131 I 7 Kemah, Turkey
126 H 9 Kemerovo, Russia
120 I 7 Kemi, Finland
120 I 6 Kemijärvi, Finland
120 I 6 Kemijoki, Finland
53 J 10 Kemmerer, WY, United States
33 O 2 Kemp Land, Antarctica
105 E 12 Kempten, Germany
59 K 7 Kenai, AK, United States
59 K 7 Kenai Peninsula, AK, United States
145 K 9 Kendari, Indonesia
133 I 5 Keneurgench, Turkmenistan
46 G 2 Kenmare, ND, United States
56 H 5 Kennewick, WA, United States
66 G 8 Kenora, ON, Canada

44 E 11 Kenosha, WI, United States
50 E 6 Kent, TX, United States
44 F 12 Kentland, IN, United States
40 H 5 Kentucky, KY, United States
40 E 5 Kentucky Lake, KY, United States
144 F 3 Kentung, Myanmar
163 K 2 Kenya, Africa
145 N 9 Kepulauan Aru, Indonesia
145 K 8 Kepulauan Banggai, Indonesia
144 F 8 Kepulauan Batu, Indonesia
145 M 9 Kepulauan Kai, Indonesia
145 I 9 Kepulauan Kangean, Indonesia
144 G 8 Kepulauan Lingga, Indonesia
144 H 7 Kepulauan Natuna, Indonesia
145 L 7 Kepulauan Talaud, Indonesia
145 M 10 Kepulauan Tanimbar, Indonesia
145 K 8 Kepulauan Togian, Indonesia
145 L 9 Kepulauan Tukangbesi, Indonesia
113 G 13 Keratea, Greece
117 N 10 Kerch, Ukraine
130 F 5 Kerempe Burnu, Turkey ►
30 G 8 Kerguelen Islands, France
30 G 8 Kerguelen Plateau, Indian Ocean
163 K 3 Kericho, Kenya
113 E 11 Kerkyra, Greece
26 G 8 Kermadec Trench, Pacific Ocean
137 M 4 Kermān, Iran
137 K 3 Kermanshah, Iran
50 F 5 Kermit, TX, United States
51 I 7 Kerrville, TX, United States
130 F 11 Keryneia, Cyprus
59 P 9 Ketchikan, AK, United States
56 I 3 Kettle Falls, WA, United States
121 I 10 Keuruu, Finland
44 E 6 Keweenaw Point, MI, United States ►
43 N 11 Key Largo, FL, United States
43 O 10 Key Largo, FL, United States
43 M 11 Key West, FL, United States
41 M 2 Keyser, WV, United States
127 M 10 Khabarovsk, Russia
133 K 10 Khairpur, Pakistan
137 M 9 Khalij al Ḥalāniyāt, Oman ≈
137 N 8 Khalij Maşirah, Oman ≈
137 I 8 Khamis, Saudi Arabia
141 D 10 Khandwa, India
141 H 10 Kharagpur, India
117 N 7 Kharkiv, Ukraine
159 L 5 Khartoum, Sudan
131 L 5 Khashuri, Georgia
113 H 9 Khaskovo, Bulgaria
127 I 6 Khatanga, Russia
162 H 11 Khayelitsha, South Africa
117 L 10 Kherson, Ukraine
117 J 8 Khmel'nyts'kyy, Ukraine
137 L 3 Khomeynishahr, Iran
144 G 4 Khon Kaen, Thailand
137 K 3 Khorramābād, Iran
133 L 7 Khorugh, Tajikistan
158 F 2 Khouribga, Morocco
127 L 7 Khrebet Cherskogo, Russia ▲
127 L 9 Khrebet Dzhugdzhur, Russia ▲
127 M 7 Khrebet Kolymskiy, Russia ▲
133 K 6 Khujand, Tajikistan
141 I 10 Khulna, Bangladesh
133 L 8 Khushab, Pakistan
137 J 1 Khvoy, Iran
133 L 7 Khyber Pass, Afghanistan/Pakistan ◇
113 E 10 Kičevo, Macedonia
158 G 4 Kidal, Mali
89 G 13 Kidderminster, United Kingdom
104 E 4 Kiel, Germany
116 G 7 Kielce, Poland
104 E 4 Kieler Bay, Germany ≈
117 K 7 Kiev, Ukraine
163 J 3 Kigali, Rwanda
163 J 4 Kigoma, Tanzania
153 E 12 Kii-suidō, Japan ≈
153 K 14 Kikai, Japan
153 K 14 Kikai-jima, Japan ≈
113 E 6 Kikinda, Serbia
162 G 4 Kikwit, Democratic Republic of Congo
58 A 4 Kilauea, HI, United States
173 N 4 Kili Island, Marshall Islands
163 K 4 Kilimanjaro, Tanzania ▲
89 C 12 Kilkenny, Ireland
89 B 13 Killarney, Ireland
51 I 6 Killeen, TX, United States
67 L 4 Killiniq, QC, Canada
89 F 9 Kilmarnock, United Kingdom
163 K 5 Kilosa, Tanzania
55 M 5 Kim, CO, United States
169 L 2 Kimbe, Papua New Guinea
163 I 10 Kimberley, South Africa
168 F 4 Kimberley Plateau, WA, Australia ◇
149 O 4 Kimch'aek, North Korea

65 I 12 **Kindersley**, SK, Canada
158 D 6 **Kindia**, Guinea
33 I 2 **King George Island**, Antarctica
169 J 10 **King Island**, TAS, Australia
168 F 4 **King Leopold Ranges**, WA, Australia
33 J 5 **King Peninsula**, Antarctica
168 F 4 **King Sound**, WA, Australia
32 C 8 **King Wilhelm Land**, Greenland
64 H 5 **King William Island**, NU, Canada
54 E 7 **Kingman**, AZ, United States
26 H 5 **Kingman Reef**, Pacific Ocean
89 J 12 **King's Lynn**, United Kingdom
54 H 2 **Kings Peak**, UT, United States
43 M 5 **Kingsland**, GA, United States
41 I 6 **Kingsport**, TN, United States
75 I 4 **Kingston**, Jamaica
39 I 7 **Kingston**, NY, United States
89 I 11 **Kingston upon Hull**, United Kingdom
75 O 6 **Kingstown**, St Vincent and the Grenadines
51 J 10 **Kingsville**, TX, United States
152 I 8 **Kinka-san**, Japan
101 H 10 **Kinrooi**, Belgium
162 G 4 **Kinshasa**, Democratic Republic of Congo
41 N 7 **Kinston**, NC, United States
89 E 9 **Kintyre**, United Kingdom
58 H 7 **Kipnuk**, AK, United States
133 L 5 **Kirghiz Range**, Kazakhstan/Kyrgyzstan
173 J 8 **Kiribati**, Pacific Ocean
130 H 10 **Kirikhan**, Turkey
130 G 7 **Kirikkale**, Turkey
120 J 4 **Kirkenes**, Norway
68 D 5 **Kirkland Lake**, ON, Canada
130 C 5 **Kirklareli**, Turkey
137 J 2 **Kirkūk**, Iraq
88 G 5 **Kirkwall**, United Kingdom
126 D 6 **Kirov**, Russia
117 L 9 **Kirovohrad**, Ukraine
120 G 6 **Kiruna**, Sweden
163 I 3 **Kisangani**, Democratic Republic of Congo
153 I 10 **Kisarazu**, Japan
126 G 9 **Kiselevsk**, Russia
153 E 12 **Kishiwada**, Japan
58 C 9 **Kiska Island**, AK, United States
159 N 8 **Kismaayo**, Somalia
153 G 10 **Kiso-sanmyaku**, Japan
43 N 8 **Kissimmee**, FL, United States
163 K 3 **Kisumu**, Kenya
55 M 4 **Kit Carson**, CO, United States
153 B 13 **Kita-Kyūshū**, Japan
163 K 2 **Kitale**, Kenya
152 I 3 **Kitami**, Japan
68 C 9 **Kitchener**, ON, Canada
65 C 12 **Kitimat**, BC, Canada
120 I 6 **Kitinen**, Finland
38 D 9 **Kittanning**, PA, United States
120 I 6 **Kittilä**, Finland
41 P 6 **Kitty Hawk**, NC, United States
163 I 6 **Kitwe**, Zambia
130 G 7 **Kizilirmak**, Turkey
131 J 9 **Kiziltepe**, Turkey
116 E 7 **Kladno**, Czech Republic
105 I 13 **Klagenfurt**, Austria
116 H 4 **Klaipėda**, Lithuania
57 D 9 **Klamath**, CA, United States
56 F 8 **Klamath Falls**, OR, United States
112 C 7 **Ključ**, Bosnia-Herzegovina
105 E 13 **Klosters**, Switzerland
112 B 8 **Knin**, Croatia
105 I 12 **Knittelfeld**, Austria
101 C 10 **Knokke-Heist**, Belgium
173 N 4 **Knox**, Marshall Islands
40 H 6 **Knoxville**, TN, United States
32 C 7 **Knud Rasmussen Land**, Greenland
153 E 11 **Kōbe**, Japan
105 C 9 **Koblenz**, Germany
59 J 4 **Kobuk**, AK, United States
59 J 4 **Kobuk**, AK, United States
153 D 13 **Kōchi**, Japan
59 J 8 **Kodiak**, AK, United States
59 J 9 **Kodiak Island**, AK, United States
153 H 10 **Kōfu**, Japan
117 J 1 **Kohtla-Järve**, Estonia
133 L 6 **Kokand**, Uzbekistan
133 L 7 **Kokcha**, Afghanistan
121 H 9 **Kokkola**, Finland
133 K 2 **Kokshetau**, Kazakhstan
126 E 4 **Kola Peninsula**, Russia
120 H 6 **Kolari**, Finland
158 D 5 **Kolda**, Senegal
141 C 12 **Kolhapur**, India
141 A 15 **Kolhumadulu Atoll**, Maldives
158 E 5 **Kolokani**, Mali
126 C 6 **Kolomna**, Russia
173 M 1 **Kolonia**, Federated States of Micronesia
163 I 5 **Kolwezi**, Democratic Republic of Congo
127 M 6 **Kolyma**, Russia
153 F 11 **Komaki**, Japan
153 F 10 **Komatsu**, Japan
113 H 10 **Komotini**, Greece
127 M 9 **Komsomol'sk-na-Amure**, Russia
133 K 7 **Kondūz**, Afghanistan
32 C 9 **Kong Christian IX Land**, Greenland
32 C 8 **Kong Frederik IX Land**, Greenland
32 D 8 **Kong Frederik VIII Land**, Greenland
121 C 11 **Kongsberg**, Norway
121 D 11 **Kongsvinger**, Norway
148 E 5 **Kongur Shan**, China
116 F 6 **Konin**, Poland
113 E 11 **Konitsa**, Greece
112 D 8 **Konjic**, Bosnia-Herzegovina
120 G 5 **Könkämäeno**, Sweden
117 L 7 **Konotop**, Ukraine
105 D 12 **Konstanz**, Germany
130 F 9 **Konya**, Turkey
112 A 6 **Koper**, Slovenia
137 M 1 **Kopet Dag**, Iran
113 E 10 **Korçë**, Albania
149 N 5 **Korea Bay**, North Korea
149 O 7 **Korea Strait**, South Korea
113 G 13 **Korinthos**, Greece
152 I 8 **Kōriyama**, Japan
148 G 4 **Korla**, China
105 K 10 **Korneuburg**, Austria
163 L 4 **Korogwe**, Tanzania
173 I 1 **Koror**, Palau
117 K 7 **Korosten'**, Ukraine
101 C 11 **Kortrijk**, Belgium
127 O 6 **Koryakskiy Khrebet**, Russia
153 B 14 **Koshiki-kaikyō**, Japan
113 E 9 **Kosovska Mitrovica**, Serbia
173 M 2 **Kosrae**, Federated States of Micronesia
133 J 2 **Kostanay**, Kazakhstan
159 L 6 **Kosti**, Sudan
117 N 8 **Kostyantynivka**, Ukraine
116 F 4 **Koszalin**, Poland
141 D 9 **Kota**, India
144 G 6 **Kota Bharu**, Malaysia
145 J 7 **Kota Kinabalu**, Malaysia
121 J 11 **Kotka**, Finland
113 D 9 **Kotor**, Montenegro
59 I 4 **Kotzebue**, AK, United States
58 H 4 **Kotzebue Sound**, AK, United States
159 I 6 **Koumra**, Chad
81 J 3 **Kourou**, French Guiana
158 F 6 **Koutiala**, Mali
121 J 11 **Kouvola**, Finland
117 I 7 **Kovel**, Ukraine
59 J 5 **Koykuyuk**, AK, United States
59 I 5 **Koyuk**, AK, United States
113 F 11 **Kozani**, Greece
153 H 11 **Kōzu-shima**, Japan
144 F 6 **Krabi**, Thailand
113 E 8 **Kragujevac**, Serbia
116 G 7 **Kraków**, Poland
113 E 8 **Kraljevo**, Serbia
117 N 8 **Kramators'k**, Ukraine
112 A 6 **Kranj**, Slovenia
126 B 7 **Krasnodar**, Russia
126 H 9 **Krasnoyarsk**, Russia
117 O 8 **Krasnyy Luch**, Ukraine
104 B 8 **Krefeld**, Germany
117 M 8 **Kremenchuk**, Ukraine
117 L 8 **Kremenchuts'ka Vodoskhovyshche**, Ukraine
55 K 3 **Kremmling**, CO, United States
105 J 11 **Krems an der Donau**, Austria
141 D 12 **Krishna**, India
141 H 9 **Krishnanagar**, India
141 D 13 **Krishnaraja Sagara**, India
121 B 12 **Kristiansand**, Norway
121 E 14 **Kristianstad**, Sweden
121 C 9 **Kristiansund**, Norway
112 A 7 **Krk**, Croatia
112 B 6 **Krško**, Greece, Slovenia not Greece
113 F 8 **Kruševac**, Serbia
117 M 9 **Kryvyy Rih**, Ukraine
144 G 7 **Kuala Lumpur**, Malaysia
144 G 7 **Kuala Terengganu**, Malaysia
144 G 7 **Kuantan**, Malaysia
144 H 8 **Kuching**, Malaysia
153 B 16 **Kuchino-shima**, Japan
141 A 15 **Kuda Huvadu Channel**, Maldives
64 E 6 **Kugluktuk**, NU, Canada
137 J 2 **Kūh-e Chehel Chashmeh**, Iran
137 J 2 **Kūh-e Ḩājī Ebrāhīm**, Iraq
137 M 4 **Kūh-e Ilazārān**, Iran
120 J 8 **Kuhmo**, Finland
162 G 6 **Kuito**, Angola
113 E 9 **Kukës**, Albania
140 I 8 **Kula Kangri**, Bhutan
130 F 8 **Kulu**, Turkey
153 B 13 **Kumamoto**, Japan
113 F 9 **Kumanovo**, Macedonia
158 F 7 **Kumasi**, Ghana
158 H 7 **Kumba**, Cameroon
141 E 14 **Kumbakonam**, India
153 J 16 **Kume-jima**, Japan
104 G 5 **Kummerower See**, Germany
159 I 6 **Kumo**, Nigeria
145 J 6 **Kundat**, Malaysia
162 F 7 **Kunene**, Namibia
121 D 13 **Kungsbacka**, Sweden
23 K 4 **Kunlun Shan**, Asia
149 J 3 **Kunming**, China
168 G 4 **Kununurra**, WA, Australia
121 J 9 **Kuopio**, Finland
145 L 10 **Kupang**, Indonesia
59 C 8 **Kupreanof Island**, AK, United States
131 M 6 **Kür**, Azerbaijan/Turkey
153 C 12 **Kurashiki**, Japan
131 L 9 **Kurdistan**, Turkey
153 D 12 **Kure**, Japan
126 E 8 **Kurgan**, Russia
127 N 10 **Kuril Islands**, Russia
26 E 2 **Kuril Trench**, Pacific Ocean
141 D 12 **Kurnool**, India
153 B 15 **Kuro-shima**, Japan
126 C 6 **Kursk**, Russia
148 G 4 **Kuruktag**, China
153 B 13 **Kurume**, Japan
132 H 5 **Kuryk**, Kazakhstan
130 B 8 **Kusadasi Körfezi**, Turkey
152 J 3 **Kushiro**, Japan
59 I 7 **Kuskokwim**, AK, United States
58 H 7 **Kuskokwim Bay**, AK, United States
59 J 6 **Kuskokwim Mountains**, AK, United States
152 J 3 **Kussharo-ko**, Japan
130 D 7 **Kütahya**, Turkey
131 K 5 **K'ut'aisi**, Georgia
112 C 7 **Kutina**, Croatia
67 L 5 **Kuujjuaq**, QC, Canada
67 J 6 **Kuujjuaraapik**, QC, Canada
120 J 7 **Kuusamo**, Finland
137 K 4 **Kuwait**, Asia
137 K 5 **Kuwait**, Kuwait
126 C 7 **Kuznetsk**, Russia
120 F 4 **Kvaløya**, Norway
173 M 3 **Kwajalein**, Marshall Islands
149 O 6 **Kwangju**, South Korea
113 H 12 **Kymi**, Greece
153 E 10 **Kyōga-misaki**, Japan
153 F 11 **Kyōto**, Japan
133 L 5 **Kyrgyzstan**, Asia
113 G 14 **Kythira**, Greece
113 H 13 **Kythnos**, Greece
153 B 13 **Kyūshū**, Japan
113 F 9 **Kyustendil**, Bulgaria
117 K 7 **Kyyivs'ke Vodoskhovyshche**, Ukraine
126 H 10 **Kyzyl**, Russia
133 J 5 **Kyzylkum Desert**, Uzbekistan
133 J 4 **Kyzylorda**, Kazakhstan

L

82 G 8 **La Banda**, Argentina
53 J 9 **La Barge**, WY, United States
96 F 5 **La Baule-Escoublac**, France
43 N 9 **La Belle**, FL, United States
93 J 8 **La Carolina**, Spain
74 F 5 **La Ceiba**, Honduras
44 C 9 **La Crosse**, WI, United States
92 B 11 **La Gomera**, Spain
56 H 6 **La Grande**, OR, United States
55 L 5 **La Junta**, CO, United States
83 E 9 **La Ligua**, Chile
65 H 10 **La Loche**, SK, Canada
101 E 12 **La Louvière**, Belgium
109 C 10 **La Maddalena**, Italy
75 I 8 **La Palma**, Panama
92 A 10 **La Palma**, Spain
82 F 5 **La Paz**, Bolivia
72 G 6 **La Paz**, Mexico
152 G 1 **La Pérouse Strait**, Japan
56 F 7 **La Pine**, OR, United States
83 I 10 **La Plata**, Argentina
82 F 8 **La Rioja**, Argentina
96 G 7 **La Rochelle**, France
96 G 6 **La Roche-sur-Yon**, France
93 K 7 **La Roda**, Spain
75 L 4 **La Romana**, Dominican Republic
65 I 11 **La Ronge**, SK, Canada
83 E 9 **La Serena**, Chile
93 N 3 **La Seu**, Spain
93 J 7 **La Solana**, Spain
108 C 7 **La Spezia**, Italy
68 H 6 **La Tuque**, QC, Canada
93 L 8 **La Unión**, Spain
158 E 3 **Laâyoune**, Western Sahara
158 E 5 **Labé**, Guinea
68 G 7 **Labelle**, QC, Canada
67 M 5 **Labrador**, NL, Canada
32 B 9 **Labrador Basin**, Arctic Ocean
67 L 7 **Labrador City**, NL, Canada
32 B 9 **Labrador Sea**, Arctic Ocean
67 L 6 **Lac Caniapiscau**, QC, Canada
158 E 6 **Lac de Buyo**, Côte d'Ivoire
158 F 6 **Lac de Kossou**, Côte d'Ivoire
159 I 7 **Lac de Ladgo**, Cameroon
158 E 5 **Lac de Manantali**, Mali
105 B 13 **Lac de Neuchâtel**, Switzerland
68 E 5 **Lac Decelles**, QC, Canada
68 D 5 **Lac Des Quinze**, QC, Canada
158 F 5 **Lac Faguibine**, Mali
68 G 6 **Lac Kempt**, QC, Canada
68 E 5 **Lac Kipawa**, QC, Canada
47 M 2 **Lac La Croix**, MN, United States
162 G 3 **Lac Mai-Ndombe**, Democratic Republic of Congo
67 K 8 **Lac Mistassini**, QC, Canada
158 F 5 **Lac Niangay**, Mali
162 G 3 **Lac Ntomba**, Democratic Republic of Congo
162 E 3 **Lac Onangue**, Gabon
67 K 4 **Lac Payne**, QC, Canada
69 K 3 **Lac Sainte Anne**, QC, Canada
66 G 7 **Lac Seul**, ON, Canada
68 E 5 **Lac Simàrd**, QC, Canada
68 H 5 **Lac St-Jean**, QC, Canada
163 I 5 **Lac Upemba**, Democratic Republic of Congo/Uganda
30 G 2 **Laccadive Islands**, India
169 J 9 **Lachlan**, NSW, Australia
112 J 7 **Lacul Razim**, Romania
112 J 7 **Lacul Sinoie**, Romania
140 D 6 **Ladakh**, India/Pakistan
173 M 3 **Lae**, Marshall Islands
169 K 2 **Lae**, Papua New Guinea
121 C 13 **Laeso**, Denmark
42 E 6 **Lafayette**, LA, United States
81 J 10 **Lages**, Brazil
83 E 14 **Lago Argentino**, Argentina
83 E 13 **Lago Buenos Aires**, Argentina
163 J 6 **Lago de Cahora Bassa**, Mozambique
74 E 5 **Lago de Izabal**, Guatemala
74 F 7 **Lago de Managua**, Nicaragua
74 F 7 **Lago de Nicaragua**, Nicaragua
82 F 5 **Lago de Poopó**, Bolivia
83 F 16 **Lago Fagnano**, Argentina
74 H 8 **Lago Gatún**, Panama
83 E 13 **Lago General Carrera**, Chile
83 E 12 **Lago Llanquihué**, Chile
83 G 9 **Lago Mar Chiquita**, Argentina
83 F 13 **Lago Musters**, Argentina
83 E 12 **Lago Nahuel Huapi**, Argentina
83 E 14 **Lago San Martin**, Argentina
81 J 10 **Lagoa dos Patos**, Brazil
81 I 11 **Lagoa Mangueira**, Brazil
81 I 11 **Lagoa Mirim**, Brazil/Uruguay
158 G 7 **Lagos**, Nigeria
92 E 9 **Lagos**, Portugal
73 J 7 **Lagos de Moreno**, Mexico
55 J 8 **Laguna**, NM, United States
74 G 6 **Laguna Caratasca**, Honduras
73 J 8 **Laguna de Chapala**, Mexico
74 G 8 **Laguna de Chiriquí**, Panama
74 G 7 **Laguna de Perlas**, Nicaragua
73 N 9 **Laguna de Terminos**, Mexico
73 L 6 **Laguna Madre**, Mexico
51 K 10 **Laguna Madre**, TX, United States
82 F 4 **Laguna Rogaguado**, Bolivia
82 G 4 **Laguna San Luis**, Bolivia
82 E 6 **Lagunas**, Chile
58 C 5 **Lahaina**, HI, United States
133 M 9 **Lahore**, Pakistan
121 I 10 **Lahti**, Finland
159 N 6 **Lake Abbe**, Djibouti/Ethiopia
56 G 8 **Lake Abert**, OR, United States
68 D 4 **Lake Abitibi**, ON, Canada
163 J 2 **Lake Albert**, Democratic Republic of Congo/Uganda
168 G 7 **Lake Amadeus**, NT, Australia
168 G 4 **Lake Argyle**, WA, Australia
65 H 9 **Lake Athabasca**, SK/AB, Canada
168 E 8 **Lake Austin**, WA, Australia
127 I 10 **Lake Baikal**, Russia
133 M 4 **Lake Balkhash**, Kazakhstan
168 F 8 **Lake Ballard**, WA, Australia
163 J 5 **Lake Bangweulu**, Zambia
168 E 8 **Lake Barlee**, WA, Australia
47 K 6 **Lake Benton**, MN, United States
43 K 4 **Lake Blackshear**, GA, United States
169 I 8 **Lake Blanche**, SA, Australia
109 E 9 **Lake Bolseno**, Italy
168 F 8 **Lake Carey**, WA, Australia
168 F 7 **Lake Carnegie**, WA, Australia
22 t c **Lake Chad**, Africa
39 J 4 **Lake Champlain**, NY/VT, United States
42 D 6 **Lake Charles**, LA, United States
56 G 4 **Lake Chelan**, WA, United States
44 C 7 **Lake Chippewa**, WI, United States
43 L 6 **Lake City**, FL, United States
108 C 5 **Lake Como**, Italy
51 L 7 **Lake Conroe**, TX, United States
105 D 12 **Lake Constance**, Europe
168 F 8 **Lake Cowan**, WA, Australia
40 H 5 **Lake Cumberland**, KY, United States
168 F 6 **Lake Disappointment**, WA, Australia
89 G 10 **Lake District**, United Kingdom
163 J 3 **Lake Edward**, Democratic Republic of Congo/Uganda
45 J 11 **Lake Erie**, Canada/United States
169 I 7 **Lake Eyre North**, SA, Australia
169 I 8 **Lake Eyre South**, SA, Australia
169 I 8 **Lake Frome**, SA, Australia
169 I 8 **Lake Gairdner**, SA, Australia
108 D 5 **Lake Garda**, Italy
41 N 6 **Lake Gaston**, VA, United States
105 B 13 **Lake Geneva**, Italy/Switzerland
44 D 7 **Lake Gogebic**, MI, United States
168 G 5 **Lake Gregory**, WA, Australia
172 C 9 **Lake Hawea**, New Zealand
67 I 10 **Lake Huron**, ON, Canada
45 I 8 **Lake Huron**, Canada/United States
163 I 7 **Lake Kariba**, Zambia/Zimbabwe
51 I 3 **Lake Kemp**, TX, United States
41 I 8 **Lake Keowee**, SC, United States
149 P 3 **Lake Khanka**, China/Russia
126 C 4 **Lake Ladoga**, Russia
168 F 8 **Lake Lefroy**, WA, Australia
51 K 4 **Lake Lewisville**, TX, United States
51 K 6 **Lake Limestone**, TX, United States
51 L 6 **Lake Livingston**, TX, United States
65 G 13 **Lake Louise**, AB, Canada
168 G 6 **Lake Mackay**, WA, Australia
168 D 7 **Lake MacLeod**, WA, Australia
108 B 5 **Lake Maggiore**, Italy/Switzerland
172 B 10 **Lake Manapouri**, New Zealand
62 H 9 **Lake Manitoba**, MB, Canada
80 F 2 **Lake Maracaibo**, Venezuela
41 L 10 **Lake Marion**, SC, United States
43 J 3 **Lake Martin**, AL, United States
41 O 7 **Lake Mattamuskeet**, NC, United States
46 G 10 **Lake Mcconaughy**, NE, United States
54 E 7 **Lake Mead**, AZ/NV, United States
50 G 2 **Lake Meredith**, TX, United States
44 F 11 **Lake Michigan**, Canada/United States
168 F 8 **Lake Minigwal**, WA, Australia
168 E 8 **Lake Moore**, WA, Australia
41 L 10 **Lake Moultrie**, SC, United States
169 J 2 **Lake Murray**, Papua New Guinea
41 K 9 **Lake Murray**, SC, United States
68 D 8 **Lake Muskoka**, ON, Canada
163 J 5 **Lake Mweru**, Democratic Republic of Congo/Zambia
159 L 4 **Lake Nasser**, Egypt
168 G 6 **Lake Neale**, NT, Australia
66 H 8 **Lake Nipigon**, ON, Canada
68 D 7 **Lake Nipissing**, ON, Canada
168 E 8 **Lake Noondie**, WA, Australia
41 K 7 **Lake Norman**, NC, United States
159 L 4 **Lake Nuba**, Egypt/Sudan
163 K 6 **Lake Nyasa**, Africa
51 L 4 **Lake O' the Pines**, TX, United States
46 H 6 **Lake Oahe**, SD, United States
43 L 3 **Lake Oconee**, GA, United States
47 L 1 **Lake of the Woods**, Canada/United States
172 C 9 **Lake Ohau**, New Zealand
113 E 10 **Lake Ohrid**, Albania/Macedonia
126 D 5 **Lake Onega**, Russia
68 E 9 **Lake Ontario**, Canada/United States
57 F 10 **Lake Oroville**, CA, United States
56 I 7 **Lake Owyhee**, OR, United States
51 L 5 **Lake Palestine**, TX, United States

M

N

169 K 8 Narrabri, NSW, Australia
41 K 5 Narrows, VA, United States
117 J 1 Narva, Estonia
117 J 1 Narva laht, Estonia
120 F 5 Narvik, Norway
133 M 5 Naryn, Kyrgyzstan
141 C 11 Nashik, India
53 M 2 Nashua, MT, United States
39 K 6 Nashua, NH, United States
40 F 6 Nashville, TN, United States
75 I 2 Nassau, The Bahamas
81 M 5 Natal, Brazil
30 E 7 Natal Basin, Indian Ocean
30 D 7 Natal Valley, Indian Ocean
69 N 2 Natashquan, QC, Canada
42 F 4 Natchez, MS, United States
42 E 4 Natchitoches, LA, United States
158 G 6 Natitingou, Benin
31 J 7 Naturaliste Fracture Zone, Indian Ocean
31 K 7 Naturaliste Plateau, Southern Ocean
172 H 8 Nauru, Pacific Ocean
55 J 6 Navajo Lake, NM, United States
117 J 4 Navapolatsk, Belarus
133 J 6 Navoi, Uzbekistan
72 G 5 Navojoa, Mexico
141 B 10 Navsari, India
133 K 10 Nawabshah, Pakistan
131 M 7 Naxşşivan, Azerbaijan
113 H 13 Naxos, Greece
113 I 13 Naxos, Greece
136 G 3 Nazareth, Israel
27 M 7 Nazca Ridge, Pacific Ocean
153 K 14 Naze, Japan
159 N 6 Nazrēt, Ethiopia
137 N 7 Nazwá, Oman
159 J 7 Ndélé, Central African Republic
159 I 6 Ndjamena, Chad
163 J 6 Ndola, Zambia
58 B 8 Near Islands, AK, United States
132 H 6 Nebitdag, Turkmenistan
46 G 9 Nebraska, NE, United States
47 K 10 Nebraska City, NE, United States
51 L 6 Neches, TX, United States
105 D 10 Neckar, Germany
83 H 11 Necochea, Argentina
57 K 14 Needles, CA, United States
66 F 7 Neepawa, MB, Canada
126 E 7 Neftekamsk, Russia
173 M 2 Negetik Atoll, Federated States of Micronesia
136 G 4 Negev, Israel
141 E 15 Negombo, Sri Lanka
83 G 11 Negro, Argentina
80 G 4 Negro, Bolivia/Brazil
145 K 6 Negros, Philippines
149 K 8 Neijiang, China
80 E 3 Neiva, Colombia
159 L 6 Nek'emtē, Ethiopia
47 J 9 Neligh, NE, United States
141 E 13 Nellore, India
65 G 14 Nelson, BC, Canada
172 E 6 Nelson, New Zealand
158 F 5 Néma, Mauritania
116 H 4 Nemunas, Lithuania
152 J 3 Nemuro, Japan
152 J 2 Nemuro-kaikyō, Japan
47 L 9 Neola, IA, United States
140 F 8 Nepal, Asia
112 C 9 Neretva, Bosnia-Herzegovina
113 H 10 Nestos, Greece
100 F 6 Netherlands, Europe
75 L 6 Netherlands Antilles, Netherlands
67 K 2 Nettilling Lake, NU, Canada
104 H 5 Neubrandenburg, Germany
101 H 14 Neufchâteau, Belgium
33 L 1 Neumayer, Germany
104 E 4 Neumünster, Germany
83 F 11 Neuquén, Argentina
83 F 11 Neuquén, Argentina
105 F 12 Neuschwanstein Castle, Germany
104 B 8 Neuss, Germany
105 C 9 Neuwied, Germany
57 H 11 Nevada, NV, United States
80 F 7 Nevado Coropuna, Peru
82 F 7 Nevado de Cachi, Argentina
80 E 3 Nevado del Huila, Colombia
80 E 6 Nevado Huascarán, Peru
82 F 8 Nevado Ojos del Salado, Argentina/Chile
82 F 5 Nevado Sajama, Bolivia
97 J 6 Nevers, France
126 B 8 Nevinnomyssk, Russia
130 G 8 Nevşehir, Turkey
44 G 14 New Albany, IN, United States
42 H 2 New Albany, MS, United States
81 I 2 New Amsterdam, Guyana
41 O 7 New Bern, NC, United States
169 L 2 New Britain, Papua New Guinea
69 L 6 New Brunswick, NB, Canada
172 G 10 New Caledonia, France
26 F 7 New Caledonia Trough, Pacific Ocean
38 D 9 New Castle, PA, United States
39 I 9 New City, NY, United States
140 D 8 New Delhi, India
39 K 6 New England, United States
28 D 4 New England Seamounts, Atlantic Ocean
69 N 7 New Glasgow, NS, Canada
145 N 9 New Guinea, Asia/Oceania
39 K 5 New Hampshire, NH, United States
65 D 12 New Hazelton, BC, Canada
42 E 6 New Iberia, LA, United States
169 L 1 New Ireland, Papua New Guinea
38 H 10 New Jersey, NJ, United States
55 J 8 New Mexico, NM, United States
42 G 6 New Orleans, LA, United States
57 G 9 New Pine Creek, CA, United States
172 E 5 New Plymouth, New Zealand
69 L 5 New Richmond, QC, Canada
47 I 3 New Rockford, ND, United States
127 K 4 New Siberia Islands, Russia
169 K 8 New South Wales, Australia
38 F 7 New York, NY, United States
39 I 9 New York, NY, United States
172 E 5 New Zealand, Pacific Ocean
41 O 2 Newark, DE, United States
39 I 9 Newark, NJ, United States
57 J 10 Newark Lake, NV, United States
56 E 6 Newberg, OR, United States
41 K 9 Newberry, SC, United States
68 F 8 Newboro, ON, Canada
39 I 8 Newburgh, NY, United States
89 H 14 Newbury, United Kingdom
39 K 6 Newburyport, MA, United States
69 L 6 Newcastle, NB, Canada
169 L 9 Newcastle, NSW, Australia
53 O 7 Newcastle, WY, United States
89 H 9 Newcastle upon Tyne, United Kingdom
38 E 6 Newfane, NY, United States
67 O 8 Newfoundland, NL, Canada
67 N 6 Newfoundland and Labrador, NL, Canada
28 E 4 Newfoundland Ridge, Atlantic Ocean
168 E 6 Newman, WA, Australia
56 E 6 Newport, OR, United States
38 F 9 Newport, PA, United States
39 K 8 Newport, RI, United States
41 I 6 Newport, TN, United States
89 H 14 Newport, United Kingdom
39 J 4 Newport, VT, United States
56 I 4 Newport, WA, United States
41 O 5 Newport News, VA, United States
137 N 2 Neyshābūr, Iran
73 K 8 Nezahualcóyo, Mexico
173 I 1 Ngajangel, Palau
159 I 7 Ngaoundéré, Cameroon
173 J 1 Ngulu, Federated States of Micronesia
144 H 5 Nha Trang, Vietnam
38 E 6 Niagara Falls, NY, United States
38 E 6 Niagara Falls, NY, United States
68 D 10 Niagara Falls, ON, Canada
158 G 5 Niamey, Niger
144 F 8 Nias, Indonesia
74 F 6 Nicaragua, North America
97 M 10 Nice, France
43 J 6 Niceville, FL, United States
141 J 15 Nicobar Islands, India
130 F 11 Nicosia, Cyprus
100 G 8 Nieuwegein, Netherlands
130 G 9 Niğde, Turkey
22 H 5 Niger, Africa
158 H 5 Niger, Africa
158 G 6 Nigeria, Africa
152 G 8 Niigata, Japan
153 D 12 Niihama, Japan
58 A 5 Niihau, HI, United States
153 H 11 Nii-jima, Japan
100 H 8 Nijmegen, Netherlands
117 M 9 Nikopol', Ukraine
113 D 9 Nikšić, Montenegro
141 A 15 Nilandhoo Atoll, Maldives
23 I 4 Nile, Africa
44 G 11 Niles, MI, United States
97 K 9 Nimes, France
31 I 6 Ninetyeast Ridge, Indian Ocean
149 N 8 Ningbo, China
46 H 8 Niobrara, NE, United States
158 E 5 Nioro, Mali
96 G 7 Niort, France
65 J 11 Nipawin, SK, Canada
66 H 8 Nipigon, ON, Canada
113 F 8 Niš, Serbia
173 J 9 Niua Group, Tonga
173 K 10 Niue, New Zealand
141 E 11 Nizamabad, India
126 G 7 Nizhnevartovsk, Russia
126 D 6 Nizhniy Novgorod, Russia
126 E 7 Nizhniy Tagil, Russia
127 I 7 Nizhnyaya Tunguska, Russia
158 H 7 Nkongsamba, Cameroon
153 C 14 Nobeoka, Japan
153 I 10 Noda, Japan
54 G 11 Nogales, AZ, United States
72 G 3 Nogales, Mexico
153 I 10 Nojima-zaki, Japan
121 H 10 Nokia, Finland
58 H 5 Nome, AK, United States
173 L 1 Nomwin, Federated States of Micronesia
144 F 5 Nonthaburi, Thailand
59 I 4 Noorvik, AK, United States
32 E 9 Nord Kapp, Norway
32 E 8 Nordaustlandet, Svalbard
104 F 7 Nordhausen, Germany
104 C 6 Nordhorn, Germany
47 J 9 Norfolk, NE, United States
41 O 5 Norfolk, VA, United States
51 J 10 Norias, TX, United States
126 H 6 Noril'sk, Russia
41 L 6 Norlina, NC, United States
169 J 5 Norman, QLD, Australia
64 D 8 Norman Wells, NT, Canada
96 G 4 Normandy, France
169 J 5 Normanton, QLD, Australia
40 H 6 Norris Lake, TN, United States
121 F 12 Norrköping, Sweden
121 G 11 Norrtälje, Sweden
168 F 9 Norseman, WA, Australia
28 D 5 North American Basin, Atlantic Ocean
141 J 13 North Andaman, India
41 J 10 North Augusta, SC, United States
31 K 5 North Australian Basin, Southern Ocean
65 I 12 North Battleford, SK, Canada
68 D 6 North Bay, ON, Canada
172 E 1 North Cape, New Zealand
120 I 3 North Cape, Norway
41 L 7 North Carolina, NC, United States
46 H 3 North Dakota, ND, United States
22 H 3 North European Plain, Europe
26 G 7 North Fiji Basin, Pacific Ocean
89 K 13 North Foreland, United Kingdom
57 J 9 North Fork, NV, United States
104 D 3 North Frisian Islands, Germany
32 C 7 North Geomagnetic Pole, Arctic Ocean
172 E 2 North Head, New Zealand
141 B 15 North Huvadhu Atoll, Maldives
172 F 4 North Island, New Zealand
149 O 5 North Korea, Asia
141 A 14 North Maalhosmadulu Atoll, Maldives
141 B 13 North Miladunmadulu Atoll, Maldives
46 H 10 North Platte, NE, United States
46 F 10 North Platte, NE, United States
59 L 5 North Pole, AK, United States
32 D 6 North Pole, Arctic Ocean
56 I 6 North Powder, OR, United States
65 H 12 North Saskatchewan, AB/SK, Canada
28 I 3 North Sea, Atlantic Ocean
88 D 6 North Uist, United Kingdom
168 D 6 North West Cape, WA, Australia
88 E 7 North West Highlands, United Kingdom
168 E 9 Northam, WA, Australia
39 J 7 Northampton, MA, United States
89 I 13 Northampton, United Kingdom
27 I 3 Northeast Pacific Basin, Pacific Ocean
173 L 9 Northern Cook Islands, Cook Islands
23 J 2 Northern Dvina, Europe
89 D 10 Northern Ireland, United Kingdom
173 L 7 Northern Line Islands, Kiribati
173 K 3 Northern Mariana Islands, United States
108 D 6 Northern Plain, Italy
168 H 6 Northern Territory, Australia, Australia
69 M 6 Northumberland Strait, PE, Canada
28 D 2 Northwest Atlantic Mid-Ocean Channel, Atlantic Ocean
26 F 2 Northwest Pacific Basin, Pacific Ocean
64 F 8 Northwest Territories, NT, Canada
32 D 4 Northwind Plain, Arctic Ocean
58 H 5 Norton Sound, AK, United States
40 E 5 Nortonville, KY, United States
45 I 12 Norwalk, OH, United States
121 B 11 Norway, Europe
32 D 10 Norwegian Basin, Arctic Ocean
32 E 9 Norwegian Sea, Arctic Ocean
39 J 8 Norwich, CT, United States
89 J 12 Norwich, United Kingdom
113 J 9 Nos Emine, Bulgaria
113 J 8 Nos Kaliakra, Bulgaria
113 J 8 Nos Shabla, Bulgaria
152 K 3 Nosapu-misaki, Japan
163 N 6 Nosy Bé, Madagascar
163 N 7 Nosy Boraha, Madagascar
153 F 9 Noto-hantō, Japan
67 J 8 Nottaway, QC, Canada
89 H 12 Nottingham, United Kingdom
158 D 4 Nouâdhibou, Mauritania
158 D 4 Nouakchott, Mauritania
172 H 11 Noumea, New Caledonia
112 C 7 Nova Gradiška, Croatia
81 K 8 Nova Iguaçu, Brazil
92 B 9 Nova Lajes, Portugal
69 N 7 Nova Scotia, NS, Canada
108 B 6 Novara, Italy
126 F 4 Novaya Zemlya, Russia
113 E 8 Novi Pazar, Serbia
113 E 7 Novi Sad, Serbia
81 J 10 Novo Hamburgo, Brazil
126 G 9 Novokuznetsk, Russia
33 M 1 Novolazarevskaya, Russia
126 C 6 Novomoskovsk, Russia
126 B 7 Novorossiysk, Russia
126 G 9 Novosibirsk, Russia
163 I 8 Ntwetwe Pan, Botswana
159 L 4 Nubian Desert, Sudan
73 J 4 Nueva Rosita, Mexico
74 E 6 Nueva San Salvador, Netherlands Antilles
72 H 3 Nuevo Casas Grandes, Mexico
73 K 5 Nuevo Laredo, Mexico
59 K 2 Nuiqsut, AK, United States
173 O 8 Nuku Hiva, French Polynesia
173 K 10 Nuku'alofa, Tonga
173 L 2 Nukuoro, Federated States of Micronesia
133 I 5 Nukus, Uzbekistan
168 G 8 Nullarbor Plain, WA, Australia
64 H 6 Nunavut, NU, Canada
58 G 7 Nunivak Island, AK, United States
100 H 7 Nunspeet, Netherlands
109 C 11 Nuoro, Italy
105 F 10 Nuremberg, Germany
120 J 8 Nurmes, Finland
131 K 9 Nusaybin, Turkey
32 B 9 Nuuk, Greenland
32 C 8 Nuussuaq, Greenland
148 H 8 Nyainqêntanglha Shan, China
159 K 6 Nyala, Sudan
121 C 15 Nyborg, Denmark
163 K 3 Nyeri, Kenya
116 H 9 Nyíregyháza, Hungary
148 H 8 Nyingchi, China
121 D 15 Nykøbing, Denmark
121 F 12 Nyköping, Sweden
169 K 8 Nyngan, NSW, Australia
117 I 5 Nyoman, Belarus
152 G 6 Nyūdō-zaki, Japan
158 E 6 Nzérékoré, Guinea

O

58 B 5 Oahu, HI, United States
39 L 8 Oak Bluffs, MA, United States
56 F 4 Oak Harbor, WA, United States
57 G 12 Oakhurst, CA, United States
57 E 12 Oakland, CA, United States
41 L 2 Oakland, MD, United States
47 K 9 Oakland, NE, United States
56 E 7 Oakland, OR, United States
56 F 7 Oakridge, OR, United States
172 D 10 Oamaru, New Zealand
57 K 9 Oasis, NV, United States
73 L 10 Oaxaca, Mexico
23 J 2 Ob', Europe
88 E 8 Oban, United Kingdom
145 L 8 Obi, Indonesia
152 I 3 Obihiro, Japan
126 G 6 Obsakaya Guba, Russia
117 N 10 Obytichna Kosa, Ukraine
43 M 7 Ocala, FL, United States
55 K 6 Ocate, NM, United States
41 P 3 Ocean City, MD, United States
28 E 4 Oceanographer Fracture Zone, Atlantic Ocean
57 I 16 Oceanside, CA, United States
43 N 10 Ochopee, FL, United States
43 L 4 Ocmulgeee, GA, United States
41 P 7 Ocracoke Island, NC, United States
153 H 10 Odawara, Japan
130 C 8 Ödemiş, Turkey
121 C 14 Odense, Denmark
116 F 7 Oder, Europe
104 H 5 Oderhaff, Germany/Poland
117 L 10 Odesa, Ukraine
50 G 5 Odessa, TX, United States
46 F 8 Oelrichs, SD, United States
131 J 6 Of, Turkey
105 D 9 Offenbach, Germany
105 C 11 Offenburg, Germany
46 G 10 Ogallala, NE, United States
158 H 7 Ogbomoso, Nigeria
54 G 2 Ogden, UT, United States
43 M 4 Ogeechee, GA, United States
66 H 8 Ogoki, ON, Canada
117 I 3 Ogre, Latvia
22 D 4 Ohio, North America
45 I 12 Ohio, OH, United States
172 F 5 Ohura, New Zealand
67 L 1 Oikiqtarjuaq, NU, Canada
101 G 9 Oirschot, Netherlands
153 C 13 Ōita, Japan
133 L 9 Okara, Pakistan
162 H 7 Okavango Delta, Botswana
153 D 12 Okayama, Japan
153 G 11 Okazaki, Japan
43 N 9 Okeechobee, FL, United States
127 M 8 Okhotsk, Russia
117 M 7 Okhtyrka, Ukraine
153 J 16 Okinawa, Japan
153 K 15 Okinawa, Japan
153 K 15 Okinawa-shotō, Japan
153 J 15 Okinoerabu-jima, Japan
153 D 13 Okino-shima, Japan
153 C 11 Oki-shotō, Japan
126 D 7 Oktyabr'skiy, Russia
153 K 15 Oku, Japan
152 G 5 Okushiri-tō, Japan
57 H 13 Olancha, CA, United States
121 F 14 Öland, Sweden
83 H 11 Olavarría, Argentina
109 C 10 Olbia, Italy
53 J 7 Old Faithful, WY, United States
59 J 9 Old Harbor, AK, United States
104 D 5 Oldenburg, Germany
100 K 7 Oldenzaal, Netherlands
89 H 11 Oldham, United Kingdom
38 E 7 Olean, NY, United States
117 L 8 Oleksandriva, Ukraine
127 J 6 Olenek, Russia
92 F 9 Olhão, Portugal
47 L 6 Olivia, MN, United States
116 F 8 Olomouc, Czech Republic
145 J 4 Olongapo, Philippines
116 G 5 Olsztyn, Poland
112 I 8 Oltenița, Romania
56 F 5 Olympia, WA, United States
47 K 10 Omaha, NE, United States
56 H 4 Omak, WA, United States
137 M 7 Oman, Asia
159 L 5 Omdurman, Sudan
159 M 7 Omo Wenz, Ethiopia
127 N 6 Omolon, Russia
126 F 8 Omsk, Russia
47 M 4 Onamia, MN, United States
149 L 3 Öndörhaan, Mongolia
141 A 15 One and a Half Degree Channel, Maldives
38 H 6 Oneida, NY, United States
38 G 6 Oneida Lake, NY, United States
47 I 8 O'Neill, NE, United States
141 E 12 Ongole, India
131 L 5 Oni, Georgia
158 H 7 Onitsha, Nigeria
168 D 6 Onslow, WA, Australia
41 N 8 Onslow Bay, NC, United States
66 G 7 Ontario, ON, Canada
56 I 7 Ontario, OR, United States
93 L 7 Ontinyent, Spain
44 D 7 Ontonagon, MI, United States
101 B 10 Oostende, Belgium
101 F 9 Oosterhout, Netherlands
101 D 9 Oosterschelde, Netherlands
43 J 3 Opelika, AL, United States
42 E 5 Opelousas, LA, United States
116 F 7 Opole, Poland
172 G 4 Opotiki, New Zealand
54 G 10 Oracle, AZ, United States
112 F 5 Oradea, Romania
54 H 7 Oraibi, AZ, United States

200

55 K 3 Platteville, CO, United States
39 I 4 Plattsburgh, NY, United States
105 G 9 Plauen, Germany
104 G 5 Plauer See, Germany
116 D 8 Plechý, Czech Republic
113 H 8 Pleven, Bulgaria
116 G 6 Płock, Poland
112 I 7 Ploiești, Romania
113 I 12 Plomari, Greece
113 H 9 Plovdiv, Bulgaria
52 E 3 Plummer, ID, United States
44 F 12 Plymouth, IN, United States
39 L 7 Plymouth, MA, United States
75 N 5 Plymouth, Montserrat
89 F 15 Plymouth, United Kingdom
116 D 7 Plzeň, Czech Republic
108 D 6 Po, Italy
108 F 6 Po Delta, Italy
52 H 9 Pocatello, ID, United States
41 P 4 Pocomoke City, MD, United States
81 K 8 Poços de Caldas, Brazil
113 D 9 Podgorica, Montenegro
113 E 10 Pogradec, Albania
149 P 6 P'ohang, South Korea
173 M 1 Pohnpei, Federated States of Micronesia
44 E 6 Point Abbaye, MI, United States
57 D 11 Point Arena, CA, United States
57 D 11 Point Arena, CA, United States
59 J 2 Point Barrow, AK, United States
57 F 14 Point Conception, CA, United States
59 I 2 Point Franklin, AK, United States
58 H 3 Point Hope, AK, United States
141 E 14 Point Pedro, Sri Lanka
39 I 10 Point Pleasant, NJ, United States
57 E 12 Point Reyes, CA, United States
57 E 13 Point Sur, CA, United States
75 N 5 Pointe-à-Pitre, Guadaloupe
162 F 4 Pointe-Noire, Congo
96 H 6 Poitiers, France
116 G 5 Poland, Europe
130 F 7 Polatli, Turkey
117 J 4 Polatsk, Belarus
32 D 7 Pole Plain, Arctic Ocean
145 J 9 Polewali, Indonesia
93 O 6 Pollença, Spain
52 G 3 Polson, MT, United States
117 M 8 Poltava, Ukraine
113 F 10 Polykastro, Greece
45 J 14 Pomeroy, OH, United States
104 H 4 Pommersche Bay, Germany
109 H 11 Pompei, Italy
75 M 5 Ponce, Puerto Rico
141 E 14 Pondicherry, India
92 G 2 Ponferrada, Spain
81 L 8 Ponta da Baleia, Brazil
92 C 9 Ponta Degada, Portugal
81 J 9 Ponta Grossa, Brazil
97 L 6 Pontarlier, France
92 F 3 Ponte da Barca, Portugal
92 F 3 Ponteareas, Spain
92 F 2 Pontevedra, Spain
45 I 10 Pontiac, MI, United States
144 H 8 Pontianak, Indonesia
97 I 3 Pontoise, France
66 F 6 Ponton, MB, Canada
117 J 4 Ponya, Belarus
89 H 14 Poole, United Kingdom
172 F 2 Poor Knights Islands, New Zealand
80 E 3 Popayán, Colombia
53 N 2 Poplar, MT, United States
42 G 5 Poplarville, MS, United States
73 K 9 Popocatépetl, Mexico
169 K 3 Popondetta, Papua New Guinea
108 F 5 Pordenone, Italy
112 A 7 Porec, Croatia
121 H 10 Pori, Finland
172 F 6 Porirua, New Zealand
33 O 7 Porpoise Bay, Antarctica
120 H 4 Porsangen, Norway
121 C 12 Porsgrunn, Norway
65 E 14 Port Alberni, BC, Canada
51 M 7 Port Arthur, TX, United States
169 I 8 Port Augusta, SA, Australia
172 C 10 Port Chalmers, New Zealand
43 M 9 Port Charlotte, FL, United States
45 I 11 Port Clinton, OH, United States
69 M 6 Port Elgin, NB, Canada
68 C 8 Port Elgin, ON, Canada
163 I 11 Port Elizabeth, South Africa
42 F 4 Port Gibson, MS, United States
158 H 7 Port Harcourt, Nigeria
65 D 13 Port Hardy, BC, Canada
69 O 7 Port Hawkesbury, NS, Canada
168 E 6 Port Hedland, WA, Australia
45 I 9 Port Hope, MI, United States
45 I 10 Port Huron, MI, United States
51 K 9 Port Lavaca, TX, United States
169 I 9 Port Lincoln, SA, Australia
163 O 8 Port Louis, Mauritius
169 K 3 Port Moresby, Papua New Guinea
75 O 7 Port of Spain, Trinidad and Tobago
56 D 8 Port Orford, OR, United States
169 I 9 Port Pirie, SA, Australia
41 L 11 Port Royal, SC, United States
41 N 4 Port Royal, VA, United States
159 L 2 Port Said, Egypt
45 I 10 Port Sanilac, MI, United States
159 M 4 Port Sudan, Sudan
172 H 10 Port Vila, Vanuatu
89 D 10 Portadown, United Kingdom
44 D 10 Portage, WI, United States
62 H 10 Portage la Praire, MB, Canada
92 F 6 Portalegre, Portugal
55 M 8 Portales, NM, United States
75 K 4 Port-au-Prince, Haiti
69 K 3 Port-Cartier, QC, Canada
75 K 4 Port-de-Paix, Haiti
162 E 3 Port-Gentil, Gabon
44 G 13 Portland, IN, United States
39 L 5 Portland, ME, United States
56 F 6 Portland, OR, United States
89 G 15 Portland Bill, United Kingdom
69 M 3 Port-Menier, QC, Canada
92 F 4 Porto, Portugal
81 J 10 Porto Alegre, Brazil
28 B 8 Porto Inglês, Cape Verde
28 A 7 Porto Novo, Cape Verde
92 D 9 Porto Santo, Portugal
109 B 11 Porto Torres, Italy
80 G 6 Porto Velho, Brazil
74 H 8 Portobelo, Panama
108 D 8 Portoferraio, Italy
158 G 7 Porto-Novo, Benin
80 D 4 Portoviejo, Ecuador
88 D 7 Portree, United Kingdom
39 L 6 Portsmouth, NH, United States
45 I 14 Portsmouth, OH, United States
89 I 14 Portsmouth, United Kingdom
41 O 5 Portsmouth, VA, United States
92 E 9 Portugal, Europe
121 I 11 Porvoo, Finland
82 I 8 Posadas, Argentina
51 I 4 Possum Kingdom Lake, TX, United States
112 A 6 Postojna, Slovenia
47 N 7 Postville, IA, United States
51 J 8 Poteet, TX, United States
109 I 11 Potenza, Italy
131 K 5 P'ot'i, Georgia
41 O 3 Potomac, United States
82 G 6 Potosí, Bolivia
104 G 6 Potsdam, Germany
38 G 9 Pottsville, PA, United States
172 H 4 Poverty Bay, New Zealand
92 F 4 Póvoa de Varzim, Portugal
53 N 5 Powder, MT, United States
53 M 8 Powder River, WY, United States
44 E 8 Powers, MI, United States
41 N 4 Powhatan, VA, United States
149 M 8 Poyang Hu, China
73 L 8 Poza Rica, Mexico
113 F 7 Požarevac, Serbia
112 C 7 Požega, Croatia
116 F 6 Poznań, Poland
82 I 7 Pozo Colorado, Paraguay
116 E 7 Prague, Czech Republic
28 B 8 Praia, Cape Verde
108 E 7 Prato, Italy
43 I 4 Prattville, AL, United States
51 J 10 Premont, TX, United States
141 J 12 Prepari Island, India
73 N 10 Presa de la Angostura, Mexico
73 J 9 Presa del Infiernillo, Mexico
54 F 8 Prescott, AZ, United States
68 G 8 Prescott, ON, Canada
82 H 8 Presidencia Roque, Argentina
50 E 8 Presidio, TX, United States
53 I 10 Preston, ID, United States
47 N 7 Preston, MN, United States
89 G 11 Preston, United Kingdom
163 I 9 Pretoria, South Africa
113 E 12 Preveza, Greece
58 F 8 Pribilof Islands, AK, United States
54 G 3 Price, UT, United States
113 E 8 Prijepolje, Serbia
113 F 10 Prilep, Macedonia
65 I 11 Prince Albert, SK, Canada
64 E 5 Prince Albert Peninsula, NT, Canada
67 J 1 Prince Charles Island, NU, Canada
33 O 3 Prince Charles Mountains, Antarctica
30 D 9 Prince Edward Fracture Zone, Indian Ocean
69 M 6 Prince Edward Island, PE, Canada
30 E 9 Prince Edward Islands, Southern Ocean
41 O 3 Prince Frederick, MD, United States
65 E 12 Prince George, BC, Canada
59 O 9 Prince of Wales Island, AK, United States
64 G 4 Prince of Wales Island, NU, Canada
169 J 3 Prince of Wales Island, QLD, Australia
65 C 12 Prince Rupert, BC, Canada
33 O 4 Princess Elizabeth Land, Antarctica
44 D 12 Princeton, IL, United States
44 E 14 Princeton, IN, United States
38 H 10 Princeton, NJ, United States
41 K 5 Princeton, WV, United States
162 E 3 Príncipe, São Tomé and Príncipe
56 G 7 Prineville, OR, United States
117 J 6 Pripet, Belarus
117 J 6 Pripet Marshes, Belarus/Ukraine
113 F 9 Priština, Serbia
97 K 8 Privas, France
113 E 9 Prizren, Serbia
145 I 10 Probolinggo, Indonesia
51 J 5 Proctor Lake, TX, United States
81 I 3 Professor Van Blommestein Meer, Suriname
73 O 7 Progreso, Mexico
32 D 4 Proliv Longa, Arctic Ocean
56 F 8 Prospect, OR, United States
97 L 10 Provence, France
39 K 8 Providence, RI, United States
39 L 7 Provincetown, MA, United States
54 G 3 Provo, UT, United States
59 K 2 Prudhoe Bay, AK, United States
116 G 6 Pruszków, Poland
117 L 7 Pryluky, Ukraine
116 H 8 Przemysl, Poland
113 H 12 Psara, Greece
126 C 5 Pskov, Russia
113 F 11 Ptolemaïda, Greece
117 J 5 Ptsich, Belarus
80 E 6 Pucallpa, Peru
73 L 9 Puebla, Mexico
55 L 4 Pueblo, CO, United States
83 E 13 Puerto Aisen, Chile
73 L 10 Puerto Ángel, Mexico
80 G 3 Puerto Ayacucho, Venezuela
80 B 7 Puerto Ayora, Ecuador
80 B 7 Puerto Baquerizo Moreno, Ecuador
74 E 5 Puerto Barrios, Guatemala
74 G 6 Puerto Cabezas, Nicaragua
80 G 2 Puerto Carreño, Colombia
83 E 13 Puerto Cisnes, Chile
74 G 8 Puerto Cortés, Costa Rica
92 C 10 Puerto del Rosario, Spain
73 L 10 Puerto Escondido, Mexico
74 G 6 Puerto Lempira, Honduras
83 G 12 Puerto Madryn, Argentina
80 F 6 Puerto Maldonado, Peru
83 E 12 Puerto Montt, Chile
83 E 15 Puerto Natales, Chile
75 K 4 Puerto Plata, Dominican Republic
145 J 6 Puerto Princesa, Philippines
75 M 5 Puerto Rico, United States
28 D 6 Puerto Rico Trench, Atlantic Ocean
83 F 14 Puerto San Julián, Argentina
82 I 6 Puerto Suárez, Bolivia
73 I 8 Puerto Vallarta, Mexico
80 A 7 Puerto Villamil, Ecuador
93 I 7 Puertollano, Spain
172 F 3 Pukekohe, New Zealand
112 A 7 Pula, Croatia
173 K 1 Pulap, Federated States of Micronesia
38 G 5 Pulaski, NY, United States
40 F 7 Pulaski, TN, United States
41 K 5 Pulaski, VA, United States
145 N 10 Pulau Dolak, Indonesia
173 K 1 Pulawat, Federated States of Micronesia
173 I 2 Pulo Anna, Palau
173 K 1 Pulusuk, Federated States of Micronesia
82 F 7 Puna de Atacama, Argentina
82 G 5 Punata, Bolivia
145 N 9 Puncak Jaya, Indonesia
141 C 11 Pune, India
140 D 7 Punjab, India/Pakistan
80 F 7 Puno, Peru
109 J 12 Punta Alice, Italy
92 H 10 Punta Almina, Spain
83 H 11 Punta Alta, Argentina
83 F 15 Punta Arenas, Chile
83 G 12 Punta Bermeja, Argentina
109 B 10 Punta Caprara, Italy
80 E 3 Punta Chirambirá, Colombia
83 F 15 Punta de Arenas, Argentina
93 J 10 Punta de las Entinas, Spain
72 H 8 Punta de Mita, Mexico
74 G 7 Punta del Mono, Nicaragua
72 E 4 Punta Eugenia, Mexico
83 E 12 Punta Galera, Chile
73 P 8 Punta Herrero, Mexico
82 E 7 Punta Jorjino, Chile
83 E 11 Punta Lavapié, Chile
83 E 9 Punta Lengua de Vaca, Chile
83 F 14 Punta León, Argentina
83 G 14 Punta Medanosa, Argentina
80 D 5 Punta Negro, Peru
83 G 12 Punta Ninfas, Argentina
80 D 5 Punta Pariñas, Peru
83 H 12 Punta Rasa, Argentina
72 G 5 Punta Rosa, Mexico
80 E 7 Punta Santa Maria, Peru
74 F 8 Puntarenas, Costa Rica
141 G 11 Puri, India
100 F 7 Purmerend, Netherlands
80 H 5 Purus, Brazil/Peru
121 K 10 Puruvesi, Finland
144 H 9 Purwakarta, Indonesia
149 P 6 Pusan, South Korea
82 E 5 Putre, Chile
172 A 11 Puysegur Point, New Zealand
126 B 8 Pyatigorsk, Russia
144 E 3 Pyè, Myanmar
120 I 8 Pyhäjoki, Finland
121 K 9 Pyhäselkä, Finland
113 F 13 Pylos, Greece
149 O 5 P'yŏngyang, North Korea
57 G 10 Pyramid Lake, NV, United States
22 H 3 Pyrenees, Europe
113 F 13 Pyrgos, Greece

Q

133 K 8 Qalāt, Afghanistan
137 I 8 Qal'at Bīshah, Saudi Arabia
133 J 7 Qal'eh-ye, Afghanistan
66 H 2 Qamanittuaq, NU, Canada
149 I 8 Qamdo, China
133 L 6 Qarokŭl, Tajikistan
137 L 6 Qatar, Asia
159 K 2 Qattâra Depression, Egypt
137 K 2 Qazvīn, Iran
159 L 3 Qena, Egypt
149 I 5 Qilian Shan, China
149 N 6 Qingdao, China
149 J 6 Qinghai Hu, China
149 M 5 Qinhuangdao, China
149 N 3 Qiqihar, China
137 L 3 Qom, Iran
39 J 7 Quabbin Reservoir, MA, United States
149 N 9 Quanzhou, China
67 K 4 Quaqtaq, QC, Canada
109 C 12 Quartu Sant'Elena, Italy
54 E 9 Quartzsite, AZ, United States
137 M 2 Quchan, Iran
67 K 7 Québec, QC, Canada
67 L 9 Québec, QC, Canada
65 C 12 Queen Charlotte, BC, Canada
65 B 12 Queen Charlotte Islands, BC, Canada
65 C 13 Queen Charlotte Sound, BC, Canada
62 G 3 Queen Elizabeth Islands, NU, Canada
33 C 4 Queen Mary Land, Antarctica
33 L 2 Queen Maud Land, Antarctica
33 L 5 Queen Maud Mountains, Antarctica
169 J 6 Queensland, Australia
172 B 9 Queenstown, New Zealand
169 J 11 Queenstown, TAS, Australia
56 E 4 Queets, WA, United States
163 K 7 Quelimane, Mozambique
55 8 Quemado, NM, United States
73 K 8 Querétaro, Mexico
133 K 9 Quetta, Pakistan
74 D 6 Quezaltenango, Guatemala
145 K 5 Quezon City, Philippines
144 H 5 Qui Nhon, Vietnam
80 E 3 Quibdó, Colombia
141 D 15 Quilon, India
83 E 10 Quilpue, Chile
96 E 4 Quimper, France
96 E 5 Quimperlé, France
56 E 4 Quinault, WA, United States
57 F 10 Quincy, CA, United States
44 B 13 Quincy, IL, United States
42 H 4 Quitman, MS, United States
80 E 4 Quito, Ecuador

R

120 I 8 Raahe, Finland
145 J 10 Raba, Indonesia
158 F 1 Rabat, Morocco
169 L 2 Rabaul, Papua New Guinea
136 H 7 Rābigh, Saudi Arabia
144 G 6 Rach Gia, Vietnam
44 E 10 Racine, WI, United States
67 J 7 Radisson, QC, Canada
116 H 7 Radom, Poland
83 H 9 Rafaela, Argentina
137 J 5 Rafḩā', Saudi Arabia
137 M 4 Rafsanjān, Iran
42 D 5 Ragley, LA, United States
109 H 15 Ragusa, Italy
133 L 10 Rahimyar Khan, Pakistan
173 M 10 Raiatea, French Polynesia
141 D 12 Raichur, India
65 F 10 Rainbow Lake, AB, Canada
141 F 10 Raipur, India
141 F 10 Raj- Nandgaon, India
141 F 12 Rajahmundry, India
141 D 14 Rajapalaiyam, India
140 C 8 Rajasthan, India
141 B 10 Rajkot, India
141 H 9 Rajshahi, Bangladesh
172 D 8 Rakaia, New Zealand
41 M 7 Raleigh, NC, United States
173 M 3 Ralik Chain, Marshall Islands
50 G 4 Ralls, TX, United States
137 J 10 Ramlat as Sab'atayn, Yemen
137 J 9 Ramlat Dahm, Yemen
112 G 7 Râmnicu Vâlcea, Romania
57 I 16 Ramona, CA, United States
140 E 8 Rampur, India
144 E 3 Ramree, Myanmar
89 K 14 Ramsgate, United Kingdom
141 D 9 Rana Pratap Sagar, India
83 E 10 Rancagua, Chile
141 G 10 Ranchi, India
121 C 14 Randers, Denmark
55 I 3 Rangely, CO, United States
68 B 6 Ranger, ON, Canada
172 D 8 Rangiora, New Zealand
144 F 4 Rangoon, Myanmar
141 H 9 Rangpur, Bangladesh
141 A 9 Rann of Kachchh, India
44 E 13 Rantoul, IL, United States
46 F 7 Rapid City, SD, United States
44 F 7 Rapid River, MI, United States
173 L 10 Rarotonga, Cook Islands
136 H 6 Rās Abū Madd, Saudi Arabia
137 N 7 Rās al Ḩadd, Oman
137 K 10 Rās al Kalb, Yemen
137 M 6 Ras al Khaimah, United Arab Emirates
137 N 8 Rās al Madrakah, Oman
137 K 5 Rās az Zawr, Saudi Arabia
136 H 6 Rās Baridī, Saudi Arabia
159 O 5 Rās Caluula, Somalia
159 O 5 Rās Caseyr, Somalia
159 M 5 Rās Dashen, Ethiopia
137 L 9 Rās Fartak, Yemen
137 I 10 Rās 'Īsá, Yemen
136 H 6 Rās Karkūmā, Saudi Arabia
159 M 5 Rās Kasar, Sudan
137 M 9 Rās Naws, Oman
158 D 4 Rās Nouâdhibou, Mauritania
137 M 8 Rās Şawqirah, Oman
137 M 9 Rās Sharbithāt, Oman
137 K 5 Rās Tanāqib, Saudi Arabia
158 D 4 Rās Timirist, Mauritania
159 O 6 Rās Xaafuun, Somalia
137 K 2 Rasht, Iran
58 C 10 Rat Island, AK, United States
58 B 9 Rat Islands, AK, United States
173 M 3 Ratak Chain, Marshall Islands
121 E 9 Rätansbyn, Sweden
141 D 9 Ratlam, India
141 B 12 Ratnagiri, India
55 L 6 Raton, NM, United States
121 H 10 Rauma, Finland
141 G 10 Raurkela, India
52 G 3 Ravalli, MT, United States
57 G 10 Ravendale, CA, United States
108 F 7 Ravenna, Italy
105 E 12 Ravensburg, Germany
168 F 9 Ravensthorpe, WA, Australia
133 L 9 Ravi, India/Pakistan
137 I 3 Rāwah, Iraq
133 L 8 Rawalpindi, Pakistan
53 L 10 Rawlins, WY, United States
83 G 12 Rawson, Argentina

56 F 4 Tacoma, WA, United States
83 I 9 Tacuarembó, Uruguay
69 J 5 Tadoussac, QC, Canada
149 O 6 Taegu, South Korea
149 O 6 Taejŏn, South Korea
28 H 4 Tagus Abyssal Plain, Atlantic Ocean
149 N 1 Tahe, China
173 N 10 Tahiti, French Polynesia
158 G 5 Tahoua, Niger
149 N 9 T'aichung, Taiwan
172 C 10 Taieri, New Zealand
172 F 5 Taihape, New Zealand
169 I 9 Tailem Bend, SA, Australia
149 N 10 T'ainan, Taiwan
149 N 9 Taipei, Taiwan
144 F 7 Taiping, Malaysia
149 O 10 Taiwan, Asia
149 N 10 Taiwan Strait, China/Taiwan
149 L 6 Taiyuan, China
149 N 8 Taizhou, China
137 J 10 Ta'izz, Yemen
133 L 6 Tajikistan, Asia
92 H 6 Tajo, Spain
153 D 12 Takamatsu, Japan
153 F 9 Takaoka, Japan
172 F 3 Takapuna, New Zealand
153 H 9 Takasaki, Japan
153 F 11 Takatsuki, Japan
23 L 4 Taklimakan Desert, Asia
158 F 7 Takoradi, Ghana
133 L 5 Talas, Kyrgyzstan
93 I 5 Talavera de la Reina, Spain
83 E 10 Talca, Chile
83 E 11 Talcahuano, Chile
133 M 4 Taldykorgan, Kazakhstan
145 K 8 Taliabu, Indonesia
43 K 6 Tallahassee, FL, United States
117 I 1 Tallinn, Estonia
42 F 4 Tallulah, LA, United States
82 E 7 Taltal, Chile
158 F 6 Tamale, Ghana
158 H 4 Tamanrasset, Algeria
89 F 14 Tamar, United Kingdom
73 K 8 Tamazunchale, Mexico
158 D 5 Tambacounda, Senegal
126 C 7 Tambov, Russia
43 L 8 Tampa, FL, United States
43 L 8 Tampa Bay, FL, United States
121 I 10 Tampere, Finland
73 L 7 Tampico, Mexico
169 L 8 Tamworth, NSW, Australia
120 I 4 Tana Bru, Norway
58 D 10 Tanaga Island, AK, United States
168 H 5 Tanami Desert, NT, Australia
59 J 5 Tanana, AK, United States
83 H 11 Tandil, Argentina
153 C 15 Tanega-shima, Japan
163 L 4 Tanga, Tanzania
158 F 1 Tangier, Morocco
148 G 7 Tangra Yumco, China
149 M 5 Tangshan, China
145 I 8 Tanjung, Indonesia
144 H 9 Tanjung Bugel, Indonesia
144 G 9 Tanjung Cina, Indonesia
145 N 8 Tanjung d'Urville, Indonesia
144 G 10 Tanjung Guhakolak, Indonesia
144 G 9 Tanjung Lumut, Indonesia
145 L 7 Tanjung Sopi, Indonesia
145 N 10 Tanjung Vals, Indonesia
145 J 7 Tanjungredeb, Indonesia
159 L 2 Tanta, Egypt
58 H 7 Tanunak, AK, United States
163 J 4 Tanzania, Africa
55 K 6 Taos, NM, United States
158 F 4 Taoudenni, Mali
149 N 9 T'aoyüan, Taiwan
73 N 11 Tapachula, Mexico
81 I 5 Tapajós, Brazil
41 O 4 Tappahannock, VA, United States
113 D 8 Tara, Montenegro
145 J 7 Tarakan, Indonesia
93 J 6 Tarancón, Spain
109 J 11 Taranto, Italy
80 E 5 Tarapoto, Peru
97 K 7 Tarare, France
173 I 7 Tarawa, Kiribati
133 L 5 Taraz, Kazakhstan
96 H 10 Tarbes, France
168 H 8 Tarcoola, SA, Australia
169 L 9 Taree, NSW, Australia
112 H 7 Târgovişte, Romania
112 G 7 Târgu Jiu, Romania
112 H 6 Târgu Mureş, Romania
82 G 6 Tarija, Bolivia
148 F 5 Tarim Basin, China
148 F 4 Tarim He, China
145 N 8 Taritatu, Indonesia
145 J 4 Tarlac, Philippines
116 G 8 Tarnów, Poland
93 N 4 Tarragona, Spain
130 G 9 Tarsus, Turkey
117 J 2 Tartu, Estonia
136 H 3 Ţarţūs, Syria
108 C 4 Tarvisio, Italy
133 K 5 Tashkent, Uzbekistan
133 L 5 Tash-Kömür, Kyrgyzstan
144 G 7 Tasik Kenyir, Malaysia
67 K 5 Tasiujaq, QC, Canada
26 F 9 Tasman Basin, Pacific Ocean
172 E 6 Tasman Bay, New Zealand
26 F 8 Tasman Sea, Southern Ocean
169 J 11 Tasmania, Australia
158 H 3 Tassili n'Ajjer, Algeria
116 F 9 Tatabánya, Hungary
127 M 9 Tatarskiy Proliv, Russia
55 M 9 Tatum, NM, United States
131 K 8 Tatvan, Turkey
89 G 14 Taunton, United Kingdom
172 G 4 Taupo, New Zealand
116 H 4 Tauragė, Lithuania
172 F 4 Tauranga, New Zealand
172 E 2 Tauroa Point, New Zealand
23 I 4 Taurus Mountains, Europe
130 D 9 Tavas, Turkey
144 F 5 Tavoy, Myanmar
144 F 5 Tavoy Point, Myanmar
141 D 10 Tawa Reservoir, India
45 I 9 Tawas City, MI, United States
73 K 9 Taxco, Mexico
88 F 8 Tay, United Kingdom
92 F 9 TaÚira, Portugal
47 I 9 Taylor, NE, United States
126 H 6 Taz, Russia
131 M 6 T'bilisi, Georgia
116 G 5 Tczew, Poland
172 F 4 Te Kuiti, New Zealand
73 N 9 Teapa, Mexico
131 M 5 Tebulosmt'a, Georgia/Russia
73 I 9 Tecomán, Mexico
73 K 10 Técpan, Mexico
133 I 7 Tedzhen, Turkmenistan
89 G 10 Tees, United Kingdom
74 F 6 Tegucigalpa, Honduras
57 G 14 Tehachapi, CA, United States
137 L 2 Tehran, Iran
73 L 9 Tehuacán, Mexico
73 M 10 Tehuantepec, Mexico
130 C 6 Tekirdağ, Turkey
136 G 3 Tel Aviv-Jaffa, Israel
89 G 12 Telford, United Kingdom
58 H 5 Teller, AK, United States
55 I 5 Telluride, CO, United States
116 H 3 Telšai, Lithuania
145 K 9 Teluk Bone, Indonesia
144 H 7 Teluk Datu, Malaysia
145 M 9 Teluk Kamrau, Indonesia
145 K 8 Teluk Tomini, Indonesia
57 I 15 Temecula, CA, United States
133 L 3 Temirtau, Kazakhstan
68 D 6 Temiscaming, QC, Canada
51 K 6 Temple, TX, United States
83 E 11 Temuco, Chile
141 J 14 Ten Degree Channel, India
51 M 5 Tenaha, TX, United States
141 E 12 Tenali, India
158 H 4 Ténéré du Tafassâsset, Niger
92 B 11 Tenerife, Spain
168 H 5 Tennant Creek, NT, Australia
40 D 7 Tennessee, TN, United States
40 D 7 Tennessee, TN, United States
120 I 6 Tenniöjoki, Finland
120 I 5 Tenojoki, Finland
81 L 7 Teófilo Otôni, Brazil
73 K 8 Teotiuacan, Mexico
73 I 7 Tepic, Mexico
116 E 7 Teplice, Czech Republic
73 J 8 Tequila, Mexico
109 G 9 Teramo, Italy
92 B 9 Terceira, Portugal
81 K 5 Teresina, Brazil
50 F 8 Terlingua, TX, United States
133 K 7 Termez, Uzbekistan
101 D 10 Terneuzen, Netherlands
109 F 9 Terni, Italy
117 I 8 Ternopil', Ukraine
33 M 7 Terra Nova Bay, Italy
65 C 12 Terrace, BC, Canada
109 F 10 Terracina, Italy
44 E 13 Terre Haute, IN, United States
51 K 4 Terrell, TX, United States
53 N 4 Terry, MT, United States
100 G 4 Terschelling, Netherlands
93 L 5 Teruel, Spain
152 G 2 Teshio, Japan
163 J 7 Tete, Mozambique
65 F 12 Tête Jaune Cache, BC, Canada
117 K 7 Teteriv, Ukraine
53 I 8 Teton Range, WY, United States
113 E 9 Tetovo, Macedonia
51 M 4 Texarkana, TX, United States
51 I 6 Texas, TX, United States
100 F 5 Texel, Netherlands
144 H 3 Thai Nguyên, Vietnam
144 F 4 Thailand, Asia
137 M 9 Thamarit, Oman
172 F 3 Thames, New Zealand
89 H 13 Thames, United Kingdom
141 B 11 Thane, India
144 H 3 Thanh Hoa, Vietnam
141 E 14 Thanjavur, India
23 K 5 Thar Desert, Asia
113 G 10 Thasos, Greece
144 F 4 Thaton, Myanmar
53 I 9 Thayne, WY, United States
66 F 6 The Pas, MB, Canada
46 H 9 Thedford, NE, United States
53 L 8 Thermopolis, WY, United States
113 G 10 Thessaloniki, Greece
42 F 6 Thibodaux, LA, United States
47 K 2 Thief River Falls, MN, United States
97 J 7 Thiers, France
158 D 5 Thiès, Senegal
141 B 13 Thiladhunmathee Atoll, Maldives
140 I 8 Thimphu, Bhutan
97 L 3 Thionville, France
113 H 14 Thira, Greece
113 G 12 Thiva, Greece
41 L 2 Thomas, WV, United States
43 K 3 Thomaston, GA, United States
43 I 4 Thomasville, AL, United States
43 K 5 Thomasville, GA, United States
66 F 5 Thompson, MB, Canada
97 L 6 Thonon-les-Bains, France
33 M 1 Thorshavnheiane Mountains, Antarctica
53 I 5 Three Forks, MT, United States
149 K 8 Three Gorges Dam, China
172 D 1 Three Kings Island, New Zealand
51 I 4 Throckmorton, TX, United States
101 E 13 Thuin, Belgium
32 C 7 Thule, Greenland
105 C 13 Thun, Switzerland
66 H 8 Thunder Bay, ON, Canada
88 F 5 Thurso, United Kingdom
33 J 5 Thurston Island, Antarctica
148 F 4 Tian Shan, China
149 M 5 Tianjin, China
149 K 7 Tianshui, China
53 I 2 Tiber Reservoir, MT, United States
159 I 4 Tibesti, Chad
148 G 6 Tibet, China
73 O 8 Ticul, Mexico
158 E 4 Tidjikja, Mauritania
149 O 3 Tieli, China
149 N 4 Tieling, China
23 K 4 Tien Shan, Asia
101 F 11 Tienen, Belgium
121 F 11 Tierp, Sweden
55 J 6 Tierra Amarilla, NM, United States
83 F 16 Tierra del Fuego, Argentina
81 J 8 Tietê, Brazil
43 L 5 Tifton, GA, United States
56 J 3 Tiger, WA, United States
117 K 10 Tighina, Moldova
69 M 6 Tignish, PE, Canada
80 E 4 Tigre, Peru
23 J 4 Tigris, Asia
72 D 2 Tijuana, Mexico
74 E 5 Tikal, Guatemala
27 J 6 Tiki Basin, Pacific Ocean
137 J 3 Tikrit, Iraq
101 G 9 Tilburg, Netherlands
56 E 6 Tillamook, OR, United States
65 H 13 Tilley, AB, Canada
113 J 14 Tilos, Greece
172 D 9 Timaru, New Zealand
158 F 5 Timbuktu, Mali
112 F 6 Timişoara, Romania
68 C 4 Timmins, ON, Canada
44 D 8 Timms Hill, WI, United States
145 K 10 Timor, Asia
31 L 5 Timor Sea, Indian Ocean
121 F 10 Timrå, Sweden
158 F 3 Tindouf, Algeria
173 L 5 Tinian, Northern Mariana Islands
113 H 13 Tinos, Greece
113 H 13 Tinos, Greece
140 K 8 Tinsukia, India
113 E 10 Tirana, Albania
117 K 10 Tiraspol, Moldova
88 D 8 Tiree, United Kingdom
172 F 4 Tirua Point, New Zealand
141 E 14 Tiruchchirappalli, India
141 D 15 Tirunelveli, India
141 E 13 Tirupati, India
141 D 14 Tiruppur, India
141 E 13 Tiruvannamalai, India
158 H 1 Tizi Ouzou, Algeria
73 P 7 Tizimin, Mexico
73 I 8 Tlaquepaque, Mexico
158 G 1 Tlemcen, Algeria
163 N 7 Toamasina, Madagascar
75 O 7 Tobago, Trinidad and Tobago
133 J 2 Tobol, Kazakhstan
126 F 7 Tobol'sk, Russia
159 K 2 Tobruk, Libya
81 J 6 Tocantins, Brazil
43 J 1 Toccoa, GA, United States
41 I 8 Toccoa, SC, United States
82 E 7 Tocopilla, Chile
173 M 2 Tofol, Federated States of Micronesia
59 I 8 Togiak, AK, United States
158 G 6 Togo, Africa
55 I 7 Tohatchi, NM, United States
59 L 6 Tok, AK, United States
153 G 11 Tōkai, Japan
153 B 15 Tokara-rettō, Japan
153 J 16 Tokasiki-jima, Japan
130 H 7 Tokat, Turkey
173 K 8 Tokelau Islands, New Zealand
152 I 4 Tokkachi, Japan
172 G 4 Tokoroa, New Zealand
153 K 14 Toku-no-shima, Japan
153 K 14 Tokunoshima, Japan
153 E 12 Tokushima, Japan
153 C 12 Tokuyama, Japan
153 H 10 Tokyo, Japan
44 I 11 Toledo, OH, United States
93 I 5 Toledo, Spain
51 M 5 Toledo Bend Reservoir, LA/TX, United States
163 L 8 Toliara, Madagascar
112 A 6 Tolmin, Slovenia
93 K 2 Tolosa, Spain
73 K 9 Toluca, Mexico
126 D 7 Tol'yatti, Russia
44 C 9 Tomah, WI, United States
152 H 4 Tomakomai, Japan
42 H 4 Tombigbee, AL, United States
54 H 11 Tombstone, AZ, United States
39 I 10 Toms River, NJ, United States
126 G 8 Tomsk, Russia
56 H 3 Tonasket, WA, United States
145 K 8 Tondano, Indonesia
173 J 11 Tonga, Pacific Ocean
26 G 7 Tonga Trench, Pacific Ocean
173 K 10 Tongatapu, Tonga
149 K 6 Tongchuan, China
149 O 4 Tonghua, China
149 N 4 Tongliao, China
140 D 8 Tonk, India
144 G 5 Tônlé Sap, Cambodia
57 I 12 Tonopah, NV, United States
121 C 12 Tønsberg, Norway
169 L 7 Toowoomba, QLD, Australia
168 H 4 Top Springs, NT, Australia
57 K 14 Topock, CA, United States
137 N 2 Torbat-e Heydarīyeh, Iran
137 N 2 Torbat-e Jām, Iran
101 C 11 Torhout, Belgium
120 G 5 Torneälven, Sweden
120 H 7 Tornio, Sweden
92 H 4 Toro, Spain
68 D 9 Toronto, ON, Canada
89 F 15 Torquay, United Kingdom
93 I 2 Torrelavega, Spain
73 I 6 Torreon, Mexico
92 F 6 Torres Novas, Portugal
169 J 3 Torres Strait, QLD, Australia
92 E 6 Torres Vedras, Portugal
53 O 9 Torrington, WY, United States
116 G 5 Toruń, Poland
153 D 13 Tosa-wan, Japan
153 H 11 To-shima, Japan
82 H 8 Tostado, Argentina
153 D 11 Tottori, Japan
97 L 4 Toul, France
97 L 10 Toulon, France
97 I 10 Toulouse, France
97 J 1 Tourcoing, France
101 C 12 Tournai, Belgium
96 H 5 Tours, France
152 H 6 Towada-ko, Japan
46 H 2 Towner, ND, United States
53 I 4 Townsend, MT, United States
169 K 5 Townsville, QLD, Australia
152 H 4 Tōya-ko, Japan
153 F 10 Toyama, Japan
153 F 9 Toyama-wan, Japan
153 G 11 Toyohashi, Japan
153 G 11 Toyota, Japan
131 L 5 Tqibuli, Georgia
131 J 6 Trabzon, Turkey
89 B 12 Tralee, Ireland
33 L 4 Transantarctic, Antarctica
23 L 10 Transantarctic Mountains, Antarctica
30 D 7 Transkei Basin, Indian Ocean
112 F 6 Transylvania, Romania
112 F 7 Transylvanian Alps, Romania
109 F 14 Trapani, Italy
105 I 11 Traun, Austria
44 G 8 Traverse City, MI, United States
83 J 10 Treinta y Tres, Uruguay
83 F 12 Trelew, Argentina
54 G 1 Tremonton, UT, United States
89 I 12 Trent, United Kingdom
108 E 5 Trento, Italy
38 H 10 Trenton, NJ, United States
68 E 9 Trenton, ON, Canada
55 K 6 Tres Piedras, NM, United States
108 F 5 Treviso, Italy
105 B 9 Trier, Germany
108 G 5 Trieste, Italy
113 F 11 Trikala, Greece
141 E 15 Trincomalee, Sri Lanka
82 G 4 Trinidad, Bolivia
55 L 6 Trinidad, CO, United States
75 O 7 Trinidad, Trinidad and Tobago
83 I 10 Trinidad, Uruguay
75 O 7 Trinidad and Tobago, North America
51 M 7 Trinity, TX, United States
59 J 9 Trinity Islands, AK, United States
113 F 13 Tripoli, Greece
136 G 3 Tripoli, Lebanon
159 I 2 Tripoli, Libya
29 I 9 Tristan da Cunha, Atlantic Ocean
29 G 9 Tristan da Cunha Fracture Zone, Atlantic Ocean
141 D 15 Trivandrum, India
68 H 7 Trois-Rivières, QC, Canada
121 D 12 Trollhättan, Sweden
120 G 5 Tromsø, Norway
121 D 9 Trondheim, Norway
43 J 4 Troy, AL, United States
52 F 2 Troy, MT, United States
39 I 7 Troy, NY, United States
97 J 4 Troyes, France
57 G 11 Truckee, CA, United States
74 F 5 Trujillo, Honduras
80 E 6 Trujillo, Peru
92 H 6 Trujillo, Spain
69 N 7 Truro, NS, Canada
65 E 11 Trutch, BC, Canada
55 J 9 Truth Or Consequences, NM, United States
113 J 9 Tsarevo, Bulgaria
162 H 4 Tshikapa, Democratic Republic of Congo
64 B 7 Tsiigehtchic, NT, Canada
153 F 11 Tsu, Japan
153 I 10 Tsuchiura, Japan
152 G 5 Tsugaru-kaikyō, Japan
162 G 7 Tsumeb, Namibia
152 H 7 Tsuruoka, Japan
153 A 12 Tsushima, Japan
173 N 9 Tuamotu Archipelago, French Polynesia
27 J 7 Tuamotu Fracture Zone, Pacific Ocean
54 G 7 Tuba City, AZ, United States
105 D 11 Tübingen, Germany
54 G 10 Tucson, AZ, United States
55 L 7 Tucumcari, NM, United States
93 K 3 Tudela, Spain
27 I 2 Tufts Abyssal Plain, Pacific Ocean
145 K 4 Tuguegarao, Philippines
64 C 6 Tuktoyaktuk, NT, Canada
126 C 6 Tula, Russia
73 L 8 Tulancingo, Mexico
112 J 7 Tulcea, Romania
141 D 13 Tumkur, India
113 I 9 Tundzha, Bulgaria
141 D 12 Tungabhadra Reservoir, India
42 G 2 Tunica, MS, United States
159 I 1 Tunis, Tunisia
159 I 1 Tunisia, Africa
80 F 3 Tunja, Colombia
42 H 2 Tupelo, MS, United States
82 G 6 Tupiza, Bolivia
23 K 4 Turan Lowland, Asia
136 H 4 Turayf, Saudi Arabia
133 J 10 Turbat, Pakistan
41 L 9 Turbeville, SC, United States
112 G 6 Turda, Romania
113 I 8 Türgovishte, Bulgaria
93 L 6 Turia, Spain
108 B 6 Turin, Italy
133 K 5 Turkestan, Kazakhstan

- 89 I 12 Wash, The, United Kingdom
- 44 C 7 Washburn, WI, United States
- 41 N 3 Washington, DC, United States
- 41 O 7 Washington, NC, United States
- 45 I 13 Washington, OH, United States
- 38 D 10 Washington, PA, United States
- 41 M 3 Washington, VA, United States
- 56 F 4 Washington, WA, United States
- 44 F 8 Washington Island, WI, United States
- 42 G 2 Water Valley, MS, United States
- 39 J 8 Waterbury, CT, United States
- 41 K 8 Wateree Lake, SC, United States
- 89 D 13 Waterford, Ireland
- 47 N 8 Waterloo, IA, United States
- 44 D 7 Watersmeet, MI, United States
- 47 J 6 Watertown, SD, United States
- 56 G 4 Waterville, WA, United States
- 89 I 13 Watford, United Kingdom
- 46 F 3 Watford City, ND, United States
- 65 J 12 Watson, SK, Canada
- 65 C 10 Watson Lake, YT, Canada
- 57 F 12 Watsonville, CA, United States
- 40 H 7 Watts Bar Lake, TN, United States
- 159 K 7 Wau, Sudan
- 44 E 11 Waukegan, IL, United States
- 38 G 8 Waverly, PA, United States
- 101 F 12 Wavre, Belgium
- 68 A 5 Wawa, ON, Canada
- 43 M 5 Waycross, GA, United States
- 40 E 7 Waynesboro, TN, United States
- 41 I 7 Waynesville, NC, United States
- 57 E 9 Weaverville, CA, United States
- 29 F 12 Weddell Abyssal Plain, Atlantic Ocean
- 83 H 15 Weddell Island, Falkland Islands
- 29 F 13 Weddell Sea, Atlantic Ocean
- 57 E 9 Weed, CA, United States
- 101 H 10 Weert, Netherlands
- 149 M 6 Weifang, China
- 104 F 8 Weimar, Germany
- 41 K 1 Weirton, WV, United States
- 43 J 2 Weiss Lake, AL, United States
- 101 I 14 Weiswampach, Luxembourg
- 172 D 6 Wekakura Point, New Zealand
- 57 H 14 Weldon, CA, United States
- 163 I 9 Welkom, South Africa
- 169 I 4 Wellesley Islands, QLD, Australia
- 172 F 7 Wellington, New Zealand
- 57 J 9 Wells, NV, United States
- 105 H 11 Wels, Austria
- 57 K 10 Wendover, NV, United States
- 173 L 1 Weno, Federated States of Micronesia
- 149 N 8 Wenzhou, China
- 101 H 13 Werbomont, Belgium
- 104 E 8 Werra, Germany
- 104 B 7 Wesel, Germany
- 104 D 6 Weser, Germany
- 39 N 4 Wesley, ME, United States
- 169 I 3 Wessel Islands, NT, Australia
- 33 K 4 West Antarctica, Antarctica
- 42 G 7 West Bay, LA, United States
- 44 E 10 West Bend, WI, United States
- 172 A 10 West Cape, New Zealand
- 26 E 5 West Caroline Basin, Pacific Ocean
- 83 H 15 West Falkland, Falkland Islands
- 173 K 1 West Fayu, Federated States of Micronesia
- 100 F 4 West Frisian Islands, Netherlands
- 52 G 2 West Glacier, MT, United States
- 39 N 3 West Grand Lake, ME, United States
- 44 F 13 West Lafayette, IN, United States
- 43 O 9 West Palm Beach, FL, United States
- 41 O 4 West Point, VA, United States
- 29 D 12 West Scotia Ridge, Atlantic Ocean
- 23 K 3 West Siberian Plain, Asia
- 41 K 3 West Virginia, WV, United States
- 55 K 5 Westcliffe, CO, United States
- 168 F 7 Western Australia, Australia
- 117 J 3 Western Dvina, Belarus/Latvia
- 141 C 11 Western Ghats, India
- 158 E 3 Western Sahara, Morocco
- 101 D 10 Westerschelde, Netherlands
- 38 D 7 Westfield, NY, United States
- 46 G 1 Westhope, ND, United States
- 41 N 2 Westminster, MD, United States
- 41 K 3 Weston, WV, United States
- 89 B 11 Westport, Ireland
- 172 C 7 Westport, New Zealand
- 44 F 12 Westville, IN, United States
- 145 L 10 Wetar, Indonesia
- 58 H 3 Wevok, AK, United States
- 169 J 1 Wewak, Papua New Guinea
- 89 D 13 Wexford, Ireland
- 65 J 13 Weyburn, SK, Canada
- 69 L 8 Weymouth, NS, Canada
- 172 G 4 Whakatane, New Zealand
- 66 H 3 Whale Cove, NU, Canada
- 172 E 2 Whangarei, New Zealand
- 31 I 5 Wharton Basin, Indian Ocean
- 43 I 1 Wheeler Lake, AL, United States
- 55 K 6 Wheeler Peak, NM, United States
- 41 K 1 Wheeling, WV, United States
- 65 E 14 Whistler, BC, Canada
- 57 J 12 White, NV, United States
- 46 G 7 White, SD, United States
- 46 F 4 White Butte, ND, United States
- 69 O 5 White Hill, NS, Canada
- 172 G 3 White Island, New Zealand
- 39 K 5 White Mountains, NH, United States
- 23 I 5 White Nile, Africa
- 126 D 4 White Sea, Russia
- 53 J 4 White Sulphur Springs, MT, United States
- 41 L 4 White Sulphur Springs, WV, United States
- 158 F 6 White Volta, Burkina Faso/Ghana
- 65 G 12 Whitecourt, AB, Canada
- 44 G 7 Whitefish Bay, MI, United States
- 44 G 7 Whitefish Point, MI, United States
- 39 I 6 Whitehall, NY, United States
- 89 F 10 Whitehaven, United Kingdom
- 65 B 9 Whitehorse, YT, Canada
- 41 K 8 Whitmire, SC, United States
- 169 K 5 Whitsunday Group, QLD, Australia
- 59 K 7 Whittier, AK, United States
- 169 I 9 Whyalla, SA, Australia
- 53 O 4 Wibaux, MT, United States
- 51 I 3 Wichita, TX, United States
- 51 J 3 Wichita Falls, TX, United States
- 88 G 5 Wick, United Kingdom
- 54 F 9 Wickenburg, AZ, United States
- 40 D 5 Wickliffe, KY, United States
- 105 K 11 Wiener Neustadt, Austria
- 105 C 9 Wiesbaden, Germany
- 55 L 3 Wiggins, CO, United States
- 56 H 4 Wilbur, WA, United States
- 169 J 8 Wilcannia, NSW, Australia
- 65 G 12 Wildwood, AB, Canada
- 104 C 5 Wilhelmshaven, Germany
- 38 G 8 Wilkes Barre, PA, United States
- 33 O 6 Wilkes Land, Antarctica
- 56 E 6 Willamette, OR, United States
- 55 K 8 Willard, NM, United States
- 54 H 10 Willcox, AZ, United States
- 75 L 7 Willemstad, Netherlands Antilles
- 57 E 11 Williams, CA, United States
- 65 E 13 Williams Lake, BC, Canada
- 41 J 4 Williamson, KY, United States
- 38 F 8 Williamsport, PA, United States
- 41 O 7 Williamston, NC, United States
- 46 F 2 Williston, ND, United States
- 47 L 5 Willmar, MN, United States
- 57 E 9 Willow Creek, CA, United States
- 57 E 10 Willows, CA, United States
- 41 P 2 Wilmington, DE, United States
- 41 N 9 Wilmington, NC, United States
- 44 H 13 Wilmington, OH, United States
- 45 J 12 Wilmott, OH, United States
- 41 N 7 Wilson, NC, United States
- 39 L 4 Wilton, ME, United States
- 46 H 3 Wilton, ND, United States
- 44 F 12 Winamac, IN, United States
- 52 E 4 Winchester, ID, United States
- 40 F 8 Winchester, TN, United States
- 41 M 2 Winchester, VA, United States
- 162 G 8 Windhoek, Namibia
- 47 L 7 Windom, MN, United States
- 41 O 6 Windsor, NC, United States
- 68 B 10 Windsor, ON, Canada
- 75 O 6 Windward Islands, Caribbean Sea
- 75 J 4 Windward Passage, Caribbean Sea
- 66 H 6 Winisk, ON, Canada
- 57 H 9 Winnemucca, NV, United States
- 57 G 10 Winnemucca Lake, NV, United States
- 42 E 4 Winnfield, LA, United States
- 51 M 7 Winnie, TX, United States
- 66 F 7 Winnipeg, MB, Canada
- 47 N 6 Winona, MN, United States
- 42 G 3 Winona, MS, United States
- 41 K 6 Winston- Salem, NC, United States
- 100 J 8 Winterswijk, Netherlands
- 105 D 12 Winterthur, Switzerland
- 41 O 6 Winton, NC, United States
- 172 B 10 Winton, New Zealand
- 169 J 6 Winton, NSW, Australia
- 44 C 9 Wisconsin, WI, United States
- 59 K 4 Wiseman, AK, United States
- 104 F 5 Wismar, Germany
- 44 D 8 Wittenberg, WI, United States
- 104 F 6 Wittenberge, Germany
- 116 G 6 Włocławek, Poland
- 116 F 7 Wodzisław Śląski, Poland
- 173 K 1 Woleai, Federated States of Micronesia
- 53 I 4 Wolf Creek, MT, United States
- 105 I 13 Wolfsberg, Austria
- 104 F 6 Wolfsburg, Germany
- 69 M 7 Wolfville, NS, Canada
- 65 I 9 Wollaston Lake, SK, Canada
- 64 F 6 Wollaston Peninsula, NU, Canada
- 169 K 9 Wollongong, NSW, Australia
- 100 I 5 Wolvega, Netherlands
- 89 G 12 Wolverhampton, United Kingdom
- 149 O 5 Wŏnsan, North Korea
- 42 H 1 Woodall Mountain, MS, United States
- 43 M 5 Woodbine, GA, United States
- 69 K 7 Woodstock, NB, Canada
- 42 F 5 Woodville, MS, United States
- 172 F 6 Woodville, New Zealand
- 51 M 6 Woodville, TX, United States
- 45 J 12 Wooster, OH, United States
- 89 F 10 Workington, United Kingdom
- 53 L 7 Worland, WY, United States
- 105 D 10 Worms, Germany
- 89 I 14 Worthing, United Kingdom
- 47 L 7 Worthington, MN, United States
- 173 M 3 Wotho, Marshall Islands
- 173 N 3 Wotje, Marshall Islands
- 127 N 4 Wrangel Island, Russia
- 32 E 5 Wrangel Sea, Arctic Ocean
- 59 O 8 Wrangell, AK, United States
- 55 M 3 Wray, CO, United States
- 43 L 3 Wrens, GA, United States
- 51 M 4 Wright Patman Lake, TX, United States
- 116 F 7 Wrocław, Poland
- 149 K 5 Wuhai, China
- 149 M 8 Wuhan, China
- 149 N 7 Wuhu, China
- 104 C 8 Wuppertal, Germany
- 105 E 9 Würzburg, Germany
- 149 N 7 Wuxi, China
- 149 K 6 Wuzhong, China
- 149 L 10 Wuzhou, China
- 89 G 13 Wye, United Kingdom
- 168 G 4 Wyndham, WA, Australia
- 53 K 8 Wyoming, WY, United States
- 53 J 8 Wyoming Range, WY, United States
- 41 K 5 Wytheville, VA, United States

X

- 131 O 5 Xaşmaz, Azerbaijan
- 163 K 9 Xai-Xai, Mozambique
- 73 L 8 Xalapa, Mexico
- 144 G 3 Xam Hua, Laos
- 131 N 7 Xankändi, Azerbaijan
- 113 H 10 Xanthi, Greece
- 93 L 7 Xátiva, Spain
- 149 N 9 Xiamen, China
- 149 L 7 Xi'an, China
- 149 L 7 Xiangfan, China
- 149 L 8 Xiangtan, China
- 149 K 7 Xianyang, China
- 149 N 2 Xiao Higgan Ling, China
- 148 G 8 Xigaz, China
- 149 M 4 Xilinhot, China
- 149 M 6 Xingtai, China
- 81 J 5 Xingu, Brazil
- 149 J 6 Xining, China
- 149 M 6 Xintai, China
- 149 L 6 Xinxiang, China
- 149 M 7 Xinyang, China
- 149 M 7 Xuchang, China
- 149 L 11 Xuwen, China
- 149 M 7 Xuzhou, China

Y

- 113 G 8 Yablanitsa, Bulgaria
- 56 E 7 Yachats, OR, United States
- 82 G 6 Yacuiba, Bolivia
- 159 I 2 Yafran, Libya
- 29 D 11 Yaghan Basin, Atlantic Ocean
- 65 G 14 Yahk, BC, Canada
- 149 M 2 Yakeshi, China
- 56 G 5 Yakima, WA, United States
- 153 C 16 Yaku-shima, Japan
- 59 M 7 Yakutat, AK, United States
- 127 L 7 Yakutsk, Russia
- 117 M 11 Yalta, Ukraine
- 152 H 8 Yamagata, Japan
- 153 C 12 Yamaguchi, Japan
- 126 G 5 Yamal Peninsula, Russia
- 113 I 9 Yambol, Bulgaria
- 158 F 7 Yamoussoukro, Côte d'Ivoire
- 55 I 2 Yampa, CO, United States
- 148 H 8 Yamzho Yumco, China
- 127 L 6 Yana, Russia
- 149 L 6 Yan'an, China
- 136 H 6 Yanbu' al Baḩr, Saudi Arabia
- 133 K 6 Yangiyul, Uzbekistan
- 149 L 6 Yangquan, China
- 149 J 9 Yangtze, China
- 149 M 7 Yangzhou, China
- 149 O 4 Yanji, China
- 47 J 8 Yankton, SD, United States
- 149 N 6 Yantai, China
- 159 I 8 Yaoundé, Cameroon
- 173 J 1 Yap, Federated States of Micronesia
- 145 N 8 Yapen, Indonesia
- 72 G 4 Yaqui, Mexico
- 130 D 10 Yardimci Burnu, Turkey
- 89 J 12 Yare, United Kingdom
- 172 H 7 Yaren, Nauru
- 148 F 5 Yarkant He, China
- 69 L 9 Yarmouth, NS, Canada
- 126 D 6 Yaroslavl', Russia
- 131 I 6 Yasun Burnu, Turkey
- 153 B 14 Yatsushiro, Japan
- 141 E 11 Yavatmal, India
- 137 L 4 Yazd, Iran
- 42 G 3 Yazoo City, MS, United States
- 43 N 8 Yeehaw Junction, FL, United States
- 126 E 7 Yekaterinburg, Russia
- 88 H 3 Yell, United Kingdom
- 149 K 5 Yellow, China
- 149 N 6 Yellow Sea, China
- 65 F 9 Yellowknife, NT, Canada
- 53 L 5 Yellowstone, MT, United States
- 53 J 7 Yellowstone Lake, WY, United States
- 133 I 7 Yeloten, Turkmenistan
- 41 K 11 Yemassee, SC, United States
- 137 J 10 Yemen, Asia
- 144 E 3 Yenangyaung, Myanmar
- 126 H 7 Yenisey, Russia
- 126 H 8 Yeniseyskiy Kryazh, Russia
- 89 G 14 Yeovil, United Kingdom
- 131 M 7 Yerevan, Armenia
- 131 N 6 Yevlax, Azerbaijan
- 117 M 11 Yevpatoriya, Ukraine
- 149 K 8 Yibin, China
- 149 L 8 Yichang, China
- 149 O 2 Yichun, China
- 149 K 6 Yinchuan, China
- 149 N 5 Yingkou, China
- 148 G 4 Yining, China
- 149 L 8 Yiyang, China
- 144 H 10 Yogyakarta, Indonesia
- 153 F 11 Yokkaichi, Japan
- 153 H 10 Yokohama, Japan
- 153 I 10 Yokosuka, Japan
- 153 D 11 Yonago, Japan
- 149 N 9 Yong'an, China
- 39 I 9 Yonkers, NY, United States
- 42 H 4 York, AL, United States
- 47 J 10 York, NE, United States
- 38 G 10 York, PA, United States
- 89 I 11 York, United Kingdom
- 169 I 9 Yorke Peninsula, SA, Australia
- 65 J 12 Yorkton, SK, Canada
- 41 O 5 Yorktown, VA, United States
- 153 K 15 Yoron-tō, Japan
- 57 G 12 Yosemite Village, CA, United States
- 126 D 6 Yoshkar-Ola, Russia
- 45 K 12 Youngstown, OH, United States
- 57 E 9 Yreka, CA, United States
- 133 M 5 Ysyk-Köl, Kyrgyzstan
- 149 J 9 Yuan, China
- 57 F 11 Yuba City, CA, United States
- 73 O 7 Yucatan Channel, Mexico
- 73 O 8 Yucatan Peninsula, Mexico
- 149 L 8 Yueyang, China
- 127 N 5 Yukagirskoye Ploskogor'ye, Russia
- 22 C 2 Yukon, North America
- 65 B 9 Yukon Territory, YT, Canada
- 149 L 10 Yulin, China
- 149 L 6 Yulin, China
- 54 E 10 Yuma, AZ, United States
- 149 I 5 Yumen, China
- 58 F 10 Yunaska Island, AK, United States
- 27 L 7 Yupanqui Basin, Pacific Ocean
- 153 J 14 Yuwan-dake, Japan
- 127 N 10 Yuzhno-Sakhalinsk, Russia
- 117 L 9 Yuzhnoukrayinsk, Ukraine

Z

- 100 F 7 Zaandam, Netherlands
- 116 F 7 Zabrze, Poland
- 73 J 7 Zacatecas, Mexico
- 112 B 8 Zadar, Croatia
- 92 G 7 Zafra, Spain
- 112 B 6 Zagreb, Croatia
- 23 J 4 Zagros Mountains, Asia
- 137 N 4 Zāhedān, Iran
- 113 E 13 Zakynthos, Greece
- 113 E 13 Zakynthos, Greece
- 116 E 10 Zalaegerszeg, Hungary
- 149 N 3 Zalantun, China
- 132 H 5 Zaliv Kara-Bogaz-Gol, Turkmenistan
- 127 N 7 Zaliv Shelikhova, Russia
- 112 G 5 Zalău, Romania
- 23 I 7 Zambezi, Africa
- 163 I 6 Zambia, Africa
- 145 K 6 Zamboanga, Philippines
- 92 H 4 Zamora, Spain
- 73 J 8 Zamora de Hidalgo, Mexico
- 116 H 7 Zamość, Poland
- 45 J 13 Zanesville, OH, United States
- 137 K 2 Zanjān, Iran
- 163 L 4 Zanzibar, Tanzania
- 149 M 6 Zaozhuang, China
- 126 G 9 Zapadnyy Sayan, Russia
- 83 F 11 Zapala, Argentina
- 51 I 10 Zapata, TX, United States
- 29 G 9 Zapiola Seamount, Atlantic Ocean
- 117 M 9 Zaporizhzhya, Ukraine
- 131 I 7 Zara, Turkey
- 133 K 6 Zarafshon, Tajikistan
- 93 L 4 Zaragoza, Spain
- 133 J 9 Zaranj, Afghanistan
- 133 K 8 Zarghūn Shahr, Afghanistan
- 158 H 6 Zaria, Nigeria
- 41 M 7 Zebulon, NC, United States
- 100 G 8 Zeist, Netherlands
- 116 G 4 Zelenogradsk, Russia
- 112 D 8 Zenica, Bosnia-Herzegovina
- 127 L 9 Zeyskoye Vodokhranilishche, Russia
- 149 O 4 Zhangguangcai Ling, China
- 149 M 5 Zhangjiakou, China
- 149 N 9 Zhangzhou, China
- 149 L 10 Zhanjiang, China
- 148 G 7 Zhari Namco, China
- 149 L 7 Zhengzhou, China
- 149 N 7 Zhenjiang, China
- 133 K 3 Zhezkazgan, Kazakhstan
- 117 K 5 Zhlobin, Belarus
- 33 P 3 Zhongshan, China
- 149 M 8 Zhuzhou, China
- 132 H 2 Zhympity, Kazakhstan
- 117 K 7 Zhytomyr, Ukraine
- 149 M 6 Zibo, China
- 116 E 6 Zielona Góra, Poland
- 149 K 8 Zigong, China
- 158 D 5 Ziguinchor, Senegal
- 73 J 9 Zihuatanejo, Mexico
- 163 I 7 Zimbabwe, Africa
- 158 H 6 Zinder, Niger
- 137 J 10 Zinjibār, Yemen
- 126 E 7 Zlatoust, Russia
- 116 F 8 Zlín, Czech Republic
- 159 I 2 Zlīţan, Libya
- 100 F 8 Zoetermeer, Netherlands
- 130 E 6 Zonguldak, Turkey
- 158 E 3 Zouérat, Mauritania
- 137 L 9 Ẓufār, Oman
- 105 D 12 Zug, Switzerland
- 105 F 12 Zugspitze, Germany
- 100 I 4 Zuidhorn, Netherlands
- 55 I 7 Zuni Mountains, NM, United States
- 149 K 9 Zunyi, China
- 112 D 7 Županja, Croatia
- 105 D 12 Zürich, Switzerland
- 100 I 7 Zutphen, Netherlands
- 158 E 7 Zwedru, Liberia
- 104 G 8 Zwickau, Germany
- 100 I 7 Zwolle, Netherlands
- 133 N 2 Zyryanovsk, Kazakhstan

Acknowledgments

Conceived and produced by Weldon Owen Pty Ltd
61 Victoria Street, McMahons Point
Sydney, NSW 2060, Australia

Group Chief Executive Officer John Owen
Chief Executive Officer Terry Newell
Publisher Sheena Coupe
Creative Director Sue Burk
Vice President, International Sales Stuart Laurence
Vice President, Sales and New Business Development Amy Kaneko
Administrator International Sales Kristine Ravn

Project Editors Angela Handley, Emma Hutchinson
Text Janine Flew, Lynn Humphries, Limelight Press, Margaret McPhee, Lesley McFadzean
Design Consultant John Bull
Designers Melanie Calabretta, Avril Makula, Heather Menzies, Craig Peterson

Revised and expanded edition:
Project Editor Lesley McFadzean
Designers Suzanne Keating, Amellia O'Brick
Publishing Coordinator Mike Crowton

Maps Map Illustrations
Chief Cartographer Laurie Whiddon
Cartographers Encompass Graphics
Cartographic Consultant Colin Arrowsmith
Information Graphics Andrew Davies
Flags Flag Society of Australia

Color reproduction by Chroma Graphics (Overseas) Pte Ltd
Printed by Tien Wah Press Pte Ltd
Printed in Singapore

A Weldon Owen Production

Key t=top; l=left; r=right; tl=top left; tc=top center; tr=top right; cl=center left; c=center; cr=center right; b=bottom; bl=bottom left; bc=bottom center; br=bottom right

AA = The Art Archive; AAA = The Ancient Art & Architecture Collection Ltd.; AAP = Australian Associated Press; AFP = Agence France-Presse; AMNH = American Museum of Natural History; APL/Corbis = Australian Picture Library/Corbis; AVA = The Advertising Archive Ltd.; BA = Bridgeman Art Library (www.bridgeman.co.uk); GC = The Granger Collection; GI = Getty Images; KC = Kobal Collection; MEPL = Mary Evans Picture Library; APL/MP = Australian Picture Library/Minden Pictures; N_G = NASA/Great Images in NASA; N_J = NASA/Jet Propulsion Laboratory; N_T = NASA/Total Ozone Mapping Spectrometer; NASA = National Aeronautics and Space Administration; PD = Photodisc; PE = PhotoEssentials; SML = The Science Museum, London; TPL = photolibrary.com; TPL/SPL = photolibrary.com/Science Photo Library

8b Craig Mahew/Robert Simmon/NASA/GSFC tc NASA/GSFC/METI/ERSDAC/JAROS & US/Japan Aster Science Team **9**tl NASA/GSFC/METI/ERSDAC/JAROS & US/Japan Aster Science Team tr Restec Japan/TPL/SPL **10**b NASA Goddard Space Flight Center/Reto Stöckli/Robert Simmon/MODIS/USGS/Defense Meteorological Satellite Program tc N_G **11**tl NASA/TPL/SPL tr N_T **12**bl N_J br Adastra/GI cl APL/Corbis cr The Image Bank/GI tc NASA/TPL/SPL **13**br SRTM Team/NASA/JPL/NIMA c NASA/GSFC/MITI/ERSDAC/JAROS & US/Japan Aster Science Team tl NASA/GSFC/METI/ERSDAC/JAROS & US/Japan Aster Science Team tr Jacques Descloitres/MODIS Rapid Response Team/NASA/GSFC **16**c Shin Yoshino/APL/MP c Jim Brandenburg/APL/MP **17**c, cr APL/Corbis cr Mitsuaki Iwogo/APL/MP tr Norbert Wu/APL/MP **18**bc Tom Owen Edmunds/GI bc Connie Coleman/GI cl APL/Corbis **19**cr APL/Corbis **60**c APL/Corbis tr Angela Handley **61**bc, bl, c, tl, tr APL/Corbis br PE **63**tr AMNH **70**bl, c APL/Corbis tr AA/Tate Gallery, London **71**bc, bl, br, c, tr APL/Corbis cr AA/National Trust Quebec House/Eileen Tweedy cr AVA **76**br, cr, tr APL/Corbis **77**bc, c, cl, cr, tc, tr APL/Corbis c Andrew Furlong **84**bl, br Angela Handley cl PD **85**bc, c, cl, cr, t, tl APL/Corbis br AFP br Bibliotheque Nationale, Paris, France/BA cr American Museum of Natural History, New York, USA/BA **90**br, cl, cr, tr APL/Corbis **91**bc Belvoir Castle, Leicestershire, UK/BA bl, br, c, cl, cr APL/Corbis c Paul Maeyaert/BA cl Lambeth Palace Library, London, UK/BA cl Christie's Images/BA tr Ashmolean Museum, Oxford, UK/BA **94**bc AFP bl APL/Corbis **95**bc AA/Museo Picasso Barcelona/Dagli Orti c, cl, cr BA tl Rafael Macia/photolibrary.com **98**cl APL/Corbis tr PD tr TPL/David Barnes **99**bc TPL bl APL/Corbis br AA/Bibliotheque Nationale Paris c Lauros/Giraudon/BA cr GI/BA/Rossetti tr AVA **102**bc, bl APL/Corbis **103**bc, br, c, cl, cr, tr APL/Corbis c, tc AFP tl Graphische Sammlung Albertina, Vienna, Austria/BA **106**c APL/Corbis **107**bl AVA br, cl APL/Corbis cl Germanisches National Museum, Nuremberg, Germany/BA tl Lauros/Giraudon/BA tr Christie's Images/BA **110**bl, br APL/Corbis c Peter Johnson **111**bc, tr APL/Corbis bc Alessi cl Valerie Martin **114**cl APL/Corbis **115**bc, cl, cr APL/Corbis bc AA/Nicolas Sapieha tl GC **118**bc, bl, cl APL/Corbis tr GI/Taxi/Dan Sams **119**bc, bl, br, cr, tr APL/Corbis c Tretyakov Gallery, Moscow, Russia/BA cl BA/Archives Charmet tc Museo Civico di Storia ed Arte, Modena, Italy/Alinari/BA **122**bl, br APL/Corbis **123**bc, cr, tc, tr APL/Corbis br Polar Music/Reg Grundy Prods/KC cl AA/Nasjonal Gallericht, Oslo/Album/Joseph Martin **128**br, c, cl, tc APL/Corbis **129**bc, c, cl, cr, tr APL/Corbis tc Mark Gallery/London, UK/BA tl Museum of Tropinin & His Contemporaries, Moscow, Russia/BA **134**bc APL/Corbis View bl APL/Corbis cl Persian School/British Museum London, UK/BA **135**bc, bl, br, c, tc, tr APL/Corbis cr Topkapi Palace Museum, Istanbul, Turkey/BA **138**bl David W. Hamilton/GI cr APL/Corbis **139**bc MEPL bl, br, cl, cr, tc APL/Corbis **142**cr APL/Corbis **143**bc, br, c, cl, tl APL/Corbis cl AA/Bodleian Library Oxford/The Bodleian Library cr Victoria & Albert Museum, London/BA tr British Library, London, UK/BA **146**c Digital Vision/GI cr APL/Corbis tc MEPL **147**bc, bl, c, cr, tc APL/Corbis tr Bushnell/Soifer/GI **150**br AAP Image/Xinhua Photo/Du Huajau **151**bc, c, tc APL/Corbis bl Bibliotheque Nationale, Paris, France/BA bl SML (Science & Society Picture Library) tr Paul Freeman/BA **154**br, cr Japan National Tourist Organisation c Chris Shorten cl, tr APL/Corbis **155**bc, bl, br, tc, tr APL/Corbis **160**bc, bl, tc APL/Corbis **161**bc, c APL/Corbis br PE c AAA tl APL/Zefa **164**br APL/Corbis **165**bl, br, c, cr, tc, tr APL/Corbis c Pascal Goetgheluck/TPL/SPL **170**bl, c APL/Corbis **171**bc, br, c, tl APL/Corbis c AAP Image cl By permission of the National Library of Australia cr Allport Library and Museum of Fine Arts, State Library of Tasmania tr By permission of the South Australian Museum **174**bl, br, cl APL/Corbis **175**bc, bl, br, c, cr APL/Corbis bl AAP Image/AP c PE tl La Trobe Picture Collection, State Library of Victoria

Illustrators: Susanna Addario; Paul Bachem; Graham Back; Anne Bowman; Gregory Bridges; Danny Burke; Fiammetta Dogi; Simone End; Christer Eriksson; Chris Forsey; John Crawford Fraser; Mark A. Garlick/space-art.co.uk; Jon Gittoes; Mike Gorman; Lorraine Hannay; Robert Hynes; INKLINK; David Kirshner; Frank Knight; Mike Lamble; Iain McKellar; James McKinnon; Marlene McLoughlin; Rob Mancini; Peter Mennim; Moonrunner Design Ltd.; Nicola Oram; Peter Bull Art Studio; Evert Ploeg; Tony Pyrzakowski; Oliver Rennert; John Richards; Edwina Riddell; Barbara Rodanska; Trevor Ruth; Claudia Saraceni; Michael Saunders; Peter Schouten; Marco Sparaciari; Roger Swainston; Steve Trevaskis; Thomas Trojer; Guy Troughton; Glen Vause; Rod Westblade; Ann Winterbotham; Murray Zanoni.

Bernard Thornton Artists UK: Tony Gibbons, Adam Hook, Christa Hook, Richard Hook, Stephen Seymour.

Illustrationweb.com: Andrew Beckett, Steinar Lund, Sharif Tarabay.

The Art Agency: Robin Carter, Tom Connell, Ray Grinaway, David Hardy, Philip Hood, Ian Jackson, Ken Oliver, Michael Langham Rowe, Myke Taylor.

THE ARCTIC
32

GREENLAND
32

ALASKA
58

Iceland
120

CANADA
62

Azores
92

Madeira
92

UNITED STATES
OF AMERICA
36

THE ATLANTIC OCEAN
28

Canary
Islands
92

Hawaii
58

MEXICO
72

CENTRAL AMERICA AND
THE CARIBBEAN
74

Cape
Verde
28

THE PACIFIC OCEAN
26

Galapagos
Islands
80

NORTHERN
SOUTH AMERICA
80

THE PACIFIC ISLANDS
172

SOUTHERN
SOUTH AMERICA
82